POSITIVE PSYCHOLOGY

Steve R. Baumgardner

University of Wisconsin-Eau Claire

Marie K. Crothers

University of Wisconsin-Eau Claire

Prentice Hall

Upper Saddle River, New Jersey 07458

Library of Congress Cataloging-in-Publication Data

Baumgardner, Steve R.
  Positive psychology / Steve R. Baumgardner, Marie K. Crothers.—1st ed.
    p. cm.
ISBN-13: 978-0-13-174441-7 (alk. paper)
ISBN-10: 0-13-174441-0 (alk. paper)
1. Positive psychology. I. Crothers, Marie K. II. Title.
BF204.6.B38 2009
150.19'8—dc22

                                                                    2008032715

EIC, Intro Psychology: Jessica Mosher
Executive Editor, Core Psychology: Jeff Marshall
Editorial Assistant: Aaron Talwar
Managing Supplements Editor: Ginny Livsey
Director of Marketing: Brandy Dawson
Marketing Manager: Kate Mitchell
Marketing Assistant: Jennifer Lang
Production Manager: Kathy Sleys
Creative Director: Jayne Conte
Cover Design: Bruce Kenselaar
Cover Illustration/Photo: ©David Arky/CORBIS All Rights Reserved
Full-Service Project Management/Composition: Shiji Sashi/Integra Software Services
Printer/Binder: Hamilton Printing Company
Cover Printer: Phoenix Color Corp.

Credits and acknowledgments borrowed from other sources and reproduced, with permission, in this textbook appear on appropriate page within text.

Prentice Hall
is an imprint of

www.pearsonhighered.com

10 9 8 7 6 5 4
ISBN-13: 978-0-13-174441-7
ISBN-10:   0-13-174441-0

To the love and joy of my family
Peg, Garrett, Jenny,
Chrissy, Dan, Grace, Paige, Maya, and Elise.
SRB

To Ruth and Erwin Crothers, my Mom and Dad
For giving me true bearings, secure moorings,
and the fairest of winds for sailing. . .
. . .and for being my lifelong lighthouse and my safe harbor.
MKC

CONTENTS

PREFACE

Positive psychology has emerged only within the last 10 years or so. Peterson (2006) has remarked that positive psychology has a long history and a short past. He means that the positive side of human nature has been of long-standing interest to both philosophers and psychologists, but it is only recently that the positive side of human behavior has attracted serious and more widespread empirical study. At present, positive psychology is an evolving mosaic of research and theory from many different areas of psychology, tied together by a common focus on positive aspects of human behavior. Although several undergraduate level positive psychology texts have emerged in recent years, the field is still in an early developmental stage. The literature on positive psychology consists primarily of professional journal articles, graduate and professional level anthologies of research and theory, and books devoted to intensive treatment of specialized topics. This state of affairs is typical for a rapidly developing new area of psychology.

Our first goal for this book is to make positive psychology accessible to undergraduate students by reviewing and summarizing the major empirical findings and theories within the major areas of positive psychology. Specifically, we hope to bridge the gap between an undergraduate audience and the complexity of professional source material. A second goal is to present the core topics of positive psychology in a way that preserves the richness and excitement of findings in this new area of psychology. Positive psychology addresses important questions about how we lead our lives, find happiness and satisfaction in life, and deal with life's challenges. As a result, the subject matter of positive psychology has high intrinsic interest. We hope to engage and maintain this interest by making frequent connections and applications to the everyday lives of our readers.

A third goal is to present positive psychology without compromising the complexities of research and theory. That is, our goal is to present positive psychology as it is—a work in progress. Put another way, this book is a "nuts and bolts" view of positive psychology with a primary emphasis on the results of empirical studies and the theories that help explain them. While Chapter 12 is devoted to ways in which knowledge from positive psychology may be used to increase individual happiness, this is not our overarching purpose. Our major goal is to present positive psychology in its raw form, before it is cooked by desires for self-improvement. This reflects the fact that empirical studies evaluating programs and strategies for increasing happiness are few and far between. Positive psychology has a good deal to say about the meaning of a good life, but far less to say, at this point in time, about the means by which to achieve it.

At the most general level, positive psychology can be considered a dynamic new area with a promising future. At present, no one knows what new understandings that future may include. This book is an invitation to join in positive psychology's journey, explore the questions it addresses, and learn about some of its answers.

INTENDED AUDIENCE

This book is designed to serve as a primary text for an undergraduate college course in positive psychology. Consistent with our "nuts and bolts" presentation of positive psychology, in many places throughout the book we provide detailed coverage of individual research studies, methodological issues, and theoretical controversies. For this reason, some student background in the social sciences is recommended as a course prerequisite. Our guess is that an introductory psychology or sociology course and sophomore standing or above would probably be sufficient. Some instructors may be interested in teaching positive psychology as an upper-level junior or senior seminar and may wish to supplement the text with articles from the primary journal literature. If students are asked to read, review, and critique professional research articles, a research methods course in psychology or sociology is recommended as a course prerequisite.

TOPICAL ORGANIZATION AND THEMES

Twelve chapters cover what we believe to be positive psychology's core subject matter. We chose topics based on the frequency of their coverage in the major professional and graduate-level anthologies that have been published in the last decade. Certain issues, theories, and lines of research appear repeatedly in these books and in the professional literature. There is no official list of topics that define positive psychology. However, we believe most professionals familiar with the field would agree that we have covered the most important areas to introduce positive psychology to an undergraduate audience.

Thematic and integrative themes are few and far between in the young and developing area of positive psychology. However, in the first chapter we provide an overview of positive psychology's history and the issues and concerns that led to its development. The reader is first guided through the logic of how positive psychology emerged as a response to the imbalanced focus of traditional psychology on negative aspects of human experience and behavior. The issues and questions addressed by *positive* psychology have been largely unexamined within the history of psychology. Secondly, areas of research and theory in positive psychology are grounded in the sub-disciplines from which they emerged. Summaries of these sub-disciplinary roots provide descriptions of topics that are covered in subsequent chapters of the book. Finally, the development of positive psychology is connected to the broader culture of which it is a part. Positive psychology's emergence was due, in part, to the recognition of an apparent paradox in our country—at the same time that our material affluence was dramatically rising, measures of our psychological well-being were dramatically declining.

In addition to the broad themes established in the introductory chapter, two additional themes receive detailed discussion in Chapter 2—"The Meaning and Measure of Happiness." In one way or another, nearly all of positive psychology is about well-being, the meaning of a good life, and a life well-lived. What describes a happy and healthy person? Well-being includes all aspects of physical, emotional, psychological, and social functioning. Two traditions of well-being research and theory have emerged in positive psychology. A hedonic tradition has emphasized individuals' own subjective judgments about the quality of their lives. The hedonic view defines well-being and happiness in terms of satisfaction with life, with an abundance of positive emotional experiences and relatively few negative emotions. On the other hand, the eudaimonic tradition (the root *daimon* meaning 'true self') describes well-being in terms of the expression of inner talents, values, strengths, and potentials judged according to criteria of health and optimal functioning. From the eudaimonic perspective, happiness is intimately tied to psychological health that stems from the realization of inner potentials, successful adaptation to life's many challenges, and positive healthy functioning. The eudaimonic view has sought to describe the attributes of a healthy and fully functioning person. Those who ascribe to the eudaimonic perspective suggest that the hedonic view does not answer the question of *why* people are happy or unhappy, satisfied or dissatisfied with their lives.

Much of the research and theory in positive psychology falls within one or the other of these two traditions. Hedonic and eudaimonic views are compared and contrasted in Chapter 2 and presented as complementary rather than conflicting. Students are drawn back to these two overarching themes in subsequent chapters of the book. This occurs when research and theory from the two traditions converge on a particular topic. The two views can then be compared and contrasted to help organize the different lines of research following each tradition.

Hedonic and eudaimonic perspectives are also reflected in the topics covered in different chapters. Each tradition has led to somewhat separate and distinct lines of research. For example, hedonic researchers have dominated the research on happiness and subjective well-being, while eudaimonic researchers have focused on developing descriptions of positive mental health, successful aging, and optimal functioning. These two perspectives help students tie together and differentiate many of the topics, theories, and lines of research within positive psychology. Taken together, the hedonic and eudaimonic perspectives offer a comprehensive and complementary picture of the topics, research, and theory within positive psychology.

WITH STUDENTS IN MIND

This book was written with students foremost in mind. We have worked hard to engage and maintain the reader's intrinsic interest in the subject matter of positive psychology. We employed undergraduate readers to review chapter drafts and took seriously their comments regarding readability and interest as we made revisions. In addition, many concrete examples are provided and readers are asked to reflect on their own life experiences, in order to grasp the meaning and significance of research findings, concepts, and theories. One reason positive psychology is popular with students is the relative ease of applying positive psychology to understand one's own experiences. Reports of our student readers increased our confidence in the clarity and intrinsic interest of our text for an undergraduate audience.

FOCUS SECTIONS

Throughout each chapter, students are given close-up looks at the research, methods, and theories that have shaped the development of positive psychology. Articles were selected because they represented an interesting and engaging finding, a seminal study in the field, or a new research method or theory. Focus sections provide a detailed look at the specifics of positive psychology to complement the more general review of material within each chapter. Focus sections are not separated from the text in boxed inserts—a practice that typically causes students to ignore the separated material. The content of focus sections fits the material under consideration. That is, focus sections do not disrupt the flow of ideas within the chapter, but instead expand upon those ideas. Focus section material flows out of, and back into the chapter, providing a more detailed look at the topic under consideration.

CHAPTER SUMMARY QUESTIONS

Summary questions at the end of each chapter lead students through a review of chapter material. Questions follow chapter subheadings to provide a clear review of material in the sequence in which it was discussed in the text. The purpose of these questions is practical, not inspirational. More creative and conceptual questions that invite critical examination and application of positive psychology are raised within individual chapters. Answers to the chapter summary questions represent what we think an average student should get out of each chapter. The questions require students to learn and understand the main points and supporting details of research and theory in positive psychology. Students can use the study questions to review and test their understanding of text material. We think the summary questions represent a fair answer to student questions about their responsibility for text material. That is, "What do I need to know for the exam?"

KEY TERMS AND CONCEPTS

Positive psychologists have developed their own terminology for the phenomena they study. Terms and concepts are a significant part of an understanding of this new area. Important terms and concepts are boldfaced in the body of the text and are listed at the end of each chapter for review.

WEB RESOURCES

Numerous informative web sites are available for exploring positive psychology on the Internet. At the end of each chapter, brief descriptions of relevant sites are provided. Because web addresses change frequently and new sources are continuously added, we suggest terms for internet searches along with web addresses of established sites.

SUGGESTED READINGS

In this text, a number of "seminal" articles are reviewed in the Focus on Research, Theory, and Methodology sections of each chapter. Focus sections provide informative and detailed reviews that ease the pain of undergraduates' difficulty in comprehending professional journal articles. Many of the individual articles an instructor might want students to review are given detailed coverage in focus sections. For this reason, suggested readings emphasize summary articles and books devoted to reviewing an area of positive psychology and resources likely to have high reader interest because they connect research and theory to everyday life.

CHAPTER-BY-CHAPTER

Chapter 1—What is Positive Psychology?

This chapter describes the historical development of positive psychology in terms of the issues and questions it addresses—questions that have been largely unexamined in the past. Positive psychology is rooted in the sub-disciplines from which it emerged and the broader culture of which it is a part. A major purpose of the chapter is to summarize positive psychology's assumptions, its goals and research agenda, and the current definitions of this new area of psychology.

Chapter 2—The Meaning and Measure of Happiness

This chapter provides detailed discussion of how psychologists have defined and measured well-being and happiness. Readers are invited to consider how they would define happiness and the good life, and then compare their own ideas to conceptions within positive psychology. Research and theory are organized around hedonic and eudaimonic views of psychological well-being. The chapter examines how each perspective defines and measures well-being. Scales and questionnaires are included in the chapter so the reader can see how happiness and well-being are assessed. Readers can also score their own responses. The chapter ends with a comparative discussion of hedonic and eudaimonic views of happiness. These two perspectives are also related to subsequent chapters in the book.

Chapter 3—Positive Emotions and Well-Being

This chapter reviews exciting new research on how emotions affect our physical and psychological health and our success in life endeavors. Psychologists have known for some time that negative emotions compromise our ability to fight disease and cope with stress. What is new, and a specific focus of positive psychology, is how *positive* emotions may *enhance* immune-system functioning and *build* psychological and social resources for coping with stressful life challenges. Positive emotions appear to be just as biologically grounded and influential as negative emotions, which have historically received considerably more research attention. Positive emotions have been shown to contribute to mental health and to more successful performance. The chapter ends with a discussion of ways in which people can actively cultivate positive emotions to increase their well-being and coping skills.

Chapter 4—Resilience

This chapter is a celebration of human strength in the face of adversity. Researchers studying child development, adulthood, aging, clinical disorders, and coping with trauma and loss have all found significant numbers of people who bounce back, and even grow, from adversity. One researcher (Ann Masten) described these resilient responses as "ordinary magic," meaning that everyday people often show amazing strength in the face of major life challenges. The chapter describes the psychological and social sources of resilience and how trauma may lead to personal growth.

Chapter 5—Happiness and the Facts of Life

This chapter reviews the major research findings based on the hedonic view of happiness. Readers are asked to consider why many of the facts of our lives, such as our age, gender, and where we live, do not make much difference when it comes to our level of happiness, despite the fact that so many people think they do. Only marriage seems to make a significant difference. Explanations for people's difficulty in predicting the impact of life events and stages are reviewed. Research on the connection between these facts of life and happiness is coupled with explanations for *why* the objective features of life bear so little relationship to health and happiness.

Chapter 6—Money, Happiness, and Culture

This chapter begins with a discussion of what has been called the "paradox of affluence." Within American and other Western cultures, personal income and ownership of material possessions have risen dramatically over the last 40 years, but levels of happiness as measured in large-scale national surveys have remained unchanged. The major purpose of this chapter is to review research and theory focused on this *lack* of a money–happiness connection. Much of this research involves international comparisons of happiness levels in countries around the world. Differences in the ways specific cultures define the meaning of happiness are covered in the last portion of the chapter.

Chapter 7—Personal Goals as Windows to Well-Being

The rich and evolving research on personal goals offers a revealing look at individual life motivations and their impact on health and happiness. Across the life course, much of our behavior is directed toward the achievement of personally significant goals. Goals organize our efforts and give purpose and direction of life. This chapter reviews the major research findings and theories that help answer the question of *which* goals and motives are most likely to enhance well-being. Both the content of personal goals and the motives that lie behind them are examined. The final section of the chapter explores the effects of materialism on personal well-being. Recent studies examining the origins and negative consequences of excessive materialism are reviewed.

Chapter 8—Self-Regulation and Self-Control

Self-regulation and self-control are critical components in the achievement of personally significant goals. Without self-control, personal goals are simply wishes and desires that have little chance of becoming realities. Self-regulation seems particularly important today when so many people lead hectic lives, have multiple goals, and confront many competing demands on their time. Staying on task in pursuing significant personal goals can be challenging. At a general level, self-regulation research helps clarify these challenges and the ways they might be overcome. This chapter examines (a) the importance of self-control in a successful life, (b) the major models describing the self-regulation process, (c) how and why self-control processes may break down, (d) the types of personal goals that are especially hard to achieve because of the self-regulation difficulties they create, and (e) ways to improve the regulation of behavior so that personal goals can be achieved.

Chapter 9—Positive Traits

Chapter 9 reviews research on personal traits that are considered "positive" because of their connection to health and happiness. Positive traits help explain why some people are happier than others. Research shows that a substantial percentage of individual differences in well-being is related to genetic and biological factors. The chapter begins with a review of research supporting this conclusion, together with a discussion of the physiological and psychological processes that may underlie the genetics–happiness relationship. The second half of the chapter is devoted to personality traits and self-conceptions that have consistently been shown to characterize happy/healthy people. These include comparisons of happy versus unhappy people, differences between people with high versus low self-esteem, and differences between optimists and pessimists. A good deal of the discussion concerns how and why these traits contribute to well-being.

Chapter 10—Virtue and Strengths of Character

This chapter begins with a discussion of the importance of morality and virtue to individual and social well-being. Long avoided by psychologists, the study of virtue has made a come-back in the form of an extensive study called the Values in Action Project, culminating in the publication of *Character strengths and virtues: A handbook of classification* (Peterson & Seligman, 2004). The goal of the project was to describe those human behaviors and aspects of character that have been universally regarded as strengths and virtues in every culture and throughout human history. It offers a comprehensive picture of the qualities and behaviors that have defined virtuous life across time and culture, in the form of 6 human virtues and 24 strengths of character. In addition to an overview of the Values in Action Project, several exemplary virtues are reviewed in more detail. These include wisdom, spirituality/religion, gratitude, and forgiveness. Each topic exemplifies the importance of virtue in people's lives and the role virtue can play in individual well-being. National surveys, for example, show that an extremely large majority of Americans endorse the importance of religion and spirituality in their lives. Psychological investigations affirm the many potential ways in which religious/spiritual convictions and practices may contribute to well-being, especially as resources for coping with adversity.

Chapter 11—Close Relationships and Well-Being

The importance of relationships to health and happiness has been called one of psychology's "deep truths." Of all the aspects of our lives, relations with others have the most significant influence on our happiness and well-being. The irony of relationships is that they contribute powerfully to both joy and well-being, *and* to pain and suffering. This chapter reviews the characteristics that distinguish healthy close relationships from unhealthy ones. Documentation and explanations for the many positive benefits of good relationships are reviewed and set in a cultural context. Societal changes over the past 40 years have had a dramatic impact on the institution of marriage, the importance of being in love, and the ease and prevalence of divorce. The chapter ends by considering what studies of long-term happily married couples can tell us about the ingredients of a successful marriage.

Chapter 12—Life Above Zero

This final chapter has two purposes. The first purpose is to review and summarize what positive psychology has to say about the psychological foundations of a good life. The second purpose is to suggest some of the means by which we may be able to attain a good life. A recent, groundbreaking model of Complete Mental Health (Keyes, 2007) is used to exemplify positive psychology's emphasis on the need for a comprehensive model of positive health that goes beyond traditional views of health as simply the absence of illness. Keyes' research highlights a major premise of positive psychology: The basis of health and happiness is not simply the absence of illness and unhappiness. A good life requires the *presence* of human *strengths*–not just the *absence* of human *weaknesses*. Other prominent models and meanings of health, happiness, and a good life are presented and discussed in terms of the research and theory reviewed in previous chapters of the book.

The remainder of the chapter is focused on means by which to achieve a good life. Despite its early and tentative stage of development, a growing literature has begun to examine how people might increase their psychological health and happiness. Promising, empirically-supported strategies are reviewed. A comprehensive approach to improving well-being is suggested by studies of a state of mental awareness called mindfulness. Both Western psychology and Eastern philosophy have linked mindfulness to improved well-being. A developing literature examining the meaning, effects, and practice of mindfulness supports its value in moving people toward many of the criteria for a "good life," as described by positive psychologists.

CAVEATS

Readers may wonder why our book does not have a chapter or chapters on major cultural institutions such as work, leisure, schools, and the family. Individual behavior is clearly shaped by these institutions and Seligman (2003) argues that one goal of positive psychology is to study and help develop institutions that foster well-being. Our decision to omit separate coverage of these topics reflected several considerations. First, we do discuss the institutional and social context of behavior when it is the primary focus or when it is directly relevant to current positive psychology research and theory. A noteworthy example is the work of Cory Keyes (2005, 2007), who offers a new, empirically-based model of positive health that may revolutionize long-standing assumptions and practices of mental health professionals. Another example would be the straightforward connections between personal goal research and the realms of work and leisure. Research regarding the types of goals likely to be experienced as satisfying and meaningful provide clear recommendations for how to choose satisfying careers and leisure activities.

A second consideration is the limited amount of work in positive psychology (similar to that of Keyes' work) that applies to other institutions. As research progresses, the science of positive psychology may provide a basis for social change in education, in work, and in our thinking about families, communities, and even national policy. However, at present (with few exceptions), the implications of positive psychology for social reform are largely that—implications. Positive psychology provides a positive image of human nature focused on human strengths. One can think of how such an image might inform revisions in education, work, families, and communities. In fact, a recent anthology entitled *Positive psychology in practice* does just that (Linley & Joseph, 2004). This is an excellent book for practitioners. It covers the implications of positive psychology for teaching, work, community-building, and counseling, among other endeavors. We have reviewed many of these implications; however, we did not believe that the current state of theoretical and empirical work supported a separate chapter. Finally, we chose not to review the extensive psychological and sociological literature on institutions (e.g., work, family, leisure) or to pull out studies and models fitting with a positive psychology theme. Our decision was to leave that task to people with expertise in these areas of social and institutional life.

ACKNOWLEDGMENTS

A number of undergraduate students participated in the early development of this book. They gave us helpful and honest evaluations from a student's perspective about the interest-level and readability of early chapter drafts. We are grateful for the feedback and encouragement of Kelly Zidek, Holly Wohlfeil, Molly Fillipek, Mindy Kramer, Kevin Randleman, Michele Stiehl, Ashley Owen, Jessica Dolens, Erica Bodenstab, Ben Stefonik, Ben Nichols, and Rebecca Hix.

We also express our appreciation to the University of Wisconsin-Eau Claire Office of Research and Sponsored Programs for providing several Faculty–Student Collaborative Research Grants to fund student involvement in this project.

We are grateful to all of those reviewers who provided their valuable input: Michael McRae, University of North Carolina at Chapel Hill; Theodore A. Avtgis, West Virginia University; Mona Ibrahim, Concordia College; George Whitman, Tidewater Community College; Holly Schiffrin, University of Mary Washington; Joel Morgovsky, Brookdale Community College; Edward Chang, University of Michigan; Arvind Singhal, Ohio University; Paul Silvia, University of North Carolina at Greensboro; Jamie Kurtz, University of Virginia; Nancy Etcoff, Harvard Medical School; and Rebecca Lafleur Ferrebee, The College of New Rochelle.

Steve Baumgardner thanks his wife for enduring 3 years of his off-and-on–again, "space cadet," self-absorbed mental state. He also thanks Leon Rappoport, Professor Emeritus at Kansas State University, for his "voice of experience" in the emotional ups and downs of writing. Both Steve and Mickey (Marie) thank each other because we thoroughly enjoyed working together.

Jeff Marshall at Pearson Prentice Hall deserves special mention for his unwavering encouragement, faith, and trust over the course of our book's development. We would also like to thank Shiji Sashi of Integra Software Services for her outstanding editorial assistance.

Special thanks to Joel Morgovsky and his students, who tested the pre-publication versions of the book in the trenches of his positive psychology class. Joel and his students provided invaluable feedback and enthusiastic support for our text. Their suggestions guided many significant improvements to early drafts of the book.

1

What Is Positive Psychology?

TRADITIONAL PSYCHOLOGY

My major professor used to say that the surest way to become famous in psychology was to publish a study showing that human nature is even worse than we had imagined. His point was not to impugn the integrity of anyone who conducted such a study, but rather to note people's fascination with the dark side of human nature. A case in point is the one study that nearly every college student in introductory psychology remembers, namely Stanley Milgram's (1974) famous research on obedience to authority. In Milgram's study, ordinary people delivered what they believed to be painful electric shocks to a middle-aged man as he made errors on a simple learning task. At the direction of a white-coated lab technician, people increased the level of "shocks" despite strident protests from the recipient. These protests included refusals to continue the experiment, agonizing screams, demands that he be let out of the study, and complaints that his heart was starting to bother him. The participants were visibly upset by the effects on the victim of what they believed to be genuine electric shocks. However, 66% still obeyed the commands of the experimenter, marched up the shock scale, and pulled the last switch at the highest shock level of 450 volts, despite clear markings on the control panel indicating that the shocks were dangerous. How bad is human nature? Milgram's classic study suggests that ordinary people will go against their own judgment and moral values under minimal pressure from a legitimate authority. Human nature, it appears, cannot be counted upon to insulate society from acts of brutality.

The connections between the Milgram study and real-life cases of people following orders to commit acts of brutality are compelling. Adolph Eichman, tried for crimes against humanity for his part in the Holocaust death camps run by the Nazis in World War II, said repeatedly in his own defense that he was just following orders. Captured in philosopher Hanna Arendt's famous phrase, "the banality of evil" (1963), those who carried out extraordinary acts of brutality in the systematic killing of Jews were utterly ordinary people—not pathological monsters. Like participants in Milgram's study, they were just following orders.

A positive psychologist might ask, why aren't there equally dramatic studies showing the human capacity for goodness? It certainly is not because goodness does not exist in the world. History provides countless examples. People risked their lives to help Jews escape from Nazi Germany during World War II, and priests and ministers aboard the *Titanic* sacrificed their own lives for others by giving their life preservers to fellow passengers. And, who can forget the imagery of heroic firefighters, police officers, and ordinary citizens following the September 11 terrorist attacks? A basic positive psychology premise is that the field of psychology is out of balance, with more focus on the negatives in human behavior than on the positives. Positive psychology does not deny the negative, nor does it suggest that all of psychology focuses on the negative. Rather, the new and emerging perspective of positive psychology embraces a more realistic and balanced view of human nature that includes human strengths and virtues without denying human weakness and capacity for evil. Each of us confronts a share of sadness and trauma in our life; but we also experience our share of joy and happiness. Historically, psychology has had more to say about the downs than about the ups. A large number of college students complete a general psychology course as part of their college education. Studies show that they recall mostly the negatives of human behavior, such as mental illness and the Milgram study (see Fineburg, 2004, for a review). Positive psychology

aims to offset this negative image of human nature with a more balanced view.

Why the Negative Focus?

NEGATIVE ASPECTS PERCEIVED AS MORE AUTHENTIC AND "REAL" Sigmund Freud is perhaps too easy a target for criticism regarding psychology's emphasis on negatives. Yet undoubtedly, Freud *was* influential in promoting the belief that beneath the veneer of everyday politeness and kindness lurked more self-serving motives. Let's say you sacrifice some of your own study time to help your roommate with a difficult homework assignment. Looks positive and altruistic on the surface, but some would argue that in actuality, you are just expressing your need to dominate and feel superior to others. You give blood at a university blood drive, but in actuality you were motivated by sexual attraction to one of the blood drive volunteers. You commit your life to helping others for low pay, but Freud might argue that you are just trying to compensate for feelings of inadequacy and guilt caused by traumatic childhood experiences. Freud believed that human behavior is motivated primarily by self-serving drives that must be controlled and channeled in productive ways for society to function effectively. Freud did not necessarily believe self-serving behaviors were bad. From his perspective they simply express our biologically inherited needs and impulses. The legacy of Freud's views within psychology, however, has been to perpetuate a negative image of human nature. It is difficult to deny that behaviors and traits that are seemingly positive on the surface are sometimes rooted in negative motives. However, positive psychology emphasizes that this is not always the case. From a positive psychology perspective, positive qualities and motives are just as authentic as negative ones and they affirm the positive side of human nature.

In addition to the Freud-inspired suspicion that negative motives lie beneath the surface of positive behaviors, there is also a science-inspired skepticism concerning the scientific legitimacy of topics studied in positive psychology—topics that some perceive as reminiscent of the popular psychology literature. Historically, psychologists have used pop psychology and self-help books as examples of the folly of unscientific and empirically unsupported ideas about human behavior. Many psychologists view the success of the self-help industry as evidence of laypersons' gullibility and the importance of a critical scientific attitude. Telling an empirically-minded psychologist that his or her research smacks of pop psych would be an extremely disparaging criticism.

One of my students gave the following description of positive psychology: "Positive psychology is pop psychology with a scientific basis." The student's description is insightful because it acknowledges the connections between the subject matter of positive psychology and many long-standing mainstays of pop psychology. Current topics in positive-psychology include the study of happiness, love, hope, forgiveness, positive growth after trauma, and the health-promoting benefits of a positive, optimistic attitude. These topics read like a rundown of books in the pop psych section of your local bookstore. In summary, two reasons for psychology's greater focus on negative than positive phenomena are rooted in negative beliefs about the basic nature of humanity, and skepticism about the scientific basis of positive psychology's subject matter.

NEGATIVES AS MORE IMPORTANT Ironically, research suggests that the greater weight and attention given to the negatives in human behavior compared to the positives may reflect a universal tendency (i.e., such a focus may be inherent in human nature). Generally, in human behavior the **"bad is stronger than the good"** (Baumeister, Bratslavsky, Finkenauer, & Vohs, 2001). Studies of impression formation show that information about negative traits and behaviors contributes more to how we think about others than does positive information—a finding dubbed the "trait negativity bias" (Covert & Reeder, 1990; Rozin & Royzman, 2001). Research has also shown that the presence of conflict and negative behavior makes a greater contribution to relationship satisfaction (or lack thereof) than does the amount of positive behavior (Reis & Gable, 2003). Studies strongly suggest that one negative comment can undo many acts of kindness and one bad trait can undermine a person's reputation.

Part of the reason for the power of the negative is that we seem to assume that life is generally going to be good, or at least ok. This assumption may reflect our everyday experience, in which good or neutral events are more frequent than bad ones. As a result, negative events and information stand out in distinct contrast to our general expectations. Research supports this idea that because positive events are more common in our experience, negative ones violate our expectations and are consequently given more attention (Gable & Haidt, 2005).

The fact that we attend more to the "bad" than to the "good" may also reflect an adaptive evolutionary behavior (Reis & Gable, 2003). Aversive events and negative behaviors may represent threats to our survival, therefore justifying, in an evolutionary survival sense, greater attention and impact. Evolution may thus help explain the "attention-grabbing power of negative social information" described by Pratto and John (1991). So, another reason for psychology's focus on the negative may be that psychologists are simply human, studying what attracts the greatest attention and what has the greatest impact on human behavior.

THE DISEASE MODEL Martin Seligman (2002a, 2002b, 2003) argues that the dominance of the disease model within psychology has focused the field on treating illness and away from building strengths. The disease model has produced many successes in treating psychopathology. Based on the disease model, psychology has built an extensive understanding of mental illness and a language to describe the various pathologies that affect millions of people. However, Ryff and Singer (1998) argue that psychology should be more than a "repair shop" for broken lives. The disease model is of limited value when it comes to promoting health and preventing illness. Psychologists know far less about mental health than about mental illness. We lack a comparable understanding or even a language for describing the characteristics of mentally healthy people; yet it is clear that mental health is not simply the absence of mental illness. Eliminating illness does not ensure a healthy, thriving, and competent individual. This fact points out that another contributor to psychology's focus on the negative has been the well-intentioned desire to reduce human misery, guided by the disease model.

POSITIVE PSYCHOLOGY

Martin Seligman may have been the first contemporary psychologist to call this new perspective "positive psychology." In his 1998 presidential address to the American Psychological Association, Seligman made a plea for a major shift in psychology's focus (Seligman, 1998), from studying and trying to undo the worst in human behavior to studying and promoting the best in human behavior. He asked his audience why psychology shouldn't study things like "joy and courage." Seligman supported his call for positive psychology by noting the imbalance in psychology we discussed earlier: too much attention to weaknesses and reducing human misery, and not enough attention to strengths and promoting health. Seligman's hope was that positive psychology would help expand the scope of psychology beyond the disease model to promote the study and understanding of healthy human functioning. The standing ovation at the close of his address indicated an enthusiastic response to Seligman's ideas.

New areas of psychology do not emerge in a vacuum. The concerns and perspectives of positive psychology, given clarifying description by Seligman, have scattered representation throughout psychology's history. Terman's (1939) studies of gifted children and determinants of happiness in marriage (Terman, Buttenwieser, Ferguson, Johnson, & Wilson, 1938) are early examples of research emphasizing positive characteristics and functioning, as noted by Seligman and Csikszentmihalyi (2000). The origins of research on subjective well-being can be found in early research starting in the 1920s and reinforced by the polling techniques of George Gallup and others (Diener, Lucas, & Oishi, 2002). Within psychology's recent history, the humanistic movement may have been one of the stronger voices for a more positive psychology. Humanistic psychology (a popular perspective in the 1960s) also criticized the tendency of traditional psychology to focus on negative aspects of human functioning. Humanistic psychologists Abraham Maslow and Carl Rogers viewed human nature as basically positive, insisting that every individual is born with positive inner potentials, and that the driving force in life is to actualize these potentials. Humanistic psychologists believed that the goal of psychology should be to study and promote conditions that help people achieve productive and healthy lives.

What is new about positive psychology, however, is the amount of research and theory it has generated, and the scientific respectability it has achieved. Psychologists can now study hope, forgiveness, or the physical and emotional benefits of positive emotions without feeling that they are leaving their scientific sensibilities behind, and without being regarded as pop psychologists. One may still receive some good-natured ribbing, however. For example, one of our colleagues refers to your first author's positive psychology class as "the happiness course."

While there is no official or universally accepted definition, positive psychology draws on research and theory from established areas of psychology. Positive psychology is, in part, a mosaic of research and theory from many different areas of psychology tied together by their focus on positive aspects of human behavior. Below is a brief sketch of research and theory from different areas of psychology that have contributed most to positive psychology. Hopefully, an overview of its relationship to more established and familiar areas of psychology will clarify what positive psychology is about.

Health Psychology

Positive psychology and health psychology share much in common (Taylor & Sherman, 2004). Health psychologists have long suspected that negative emotions can make us sick and positive emotions can be beneficial. However, only recently has a scientific and biological foundation been developed for these long-standing assumptions. Our understanding of the relationship between body and mind has advanced dramatically in the last several decades. Research findings affirm the potential health-threatening effects of stress, anger, resentment, anxiety, and worry (Cohen & Rodriguez, 1995; Friedman & Booth-Kewley, 1987; Salovey, Rothman, & Rodin, 1998; Taylor, 1999; Vaillant, 1997, 2000). The pathways and mechanisms involved are complex and are just beginning to be understood. They involve the brain, the nervous system, the endocrine system, and the immune system (Maier, Watkins, & Fleshner, 1994). A variety of research shows that people going through long periods of extreme stress are more vulnerable to illness (Cohen, 2002; Kiecolt-Glaser & Glaser, 1987; Ray, 2004; Vaillant, 1997). One reason that stress and negative emotions are bad for us is that they seem to suppress the functioning of the immune system and reduce our body's ability to fight disease.

Positive psychologists are very interested in the most recent studies suggesting that positive emotions may have effects equal to negative emotions, but in the opposite direction. While negative emotions compromise our health, positive emotions seem to help restore or preserve the health of both our minds and our bodies. Positive emotions appear to set in motion a number of physical, psychological, and social processes that enhance our physical well-being, emotional health, coping skills, and intellectual functioning. Summarized in Fredrickson's (2001) broaden-and-build theory, positive emotions like joy, contentment, interest, love, and pride "all share the ability to broaden people's thought-action repertoires and build their enduring personal resources, ranging from physical and intellectual resources to social and psychological resources" (p. 219).

Our increasing knowledge of the physiological processes underlying emotions provides a biological foundation for positive psychology. It seems reasonable to conclude that positive emotions have every bit as much biological and evolutionary significance as the negative emotions that have attracted so much research attention. Consistent with the goal of restoring balance to the field, positive psychology emphasizes examination of the value of positive emotions in our lives.

Focus on Research: Living Longer Through Positive Emotions—The Nun Study

Do people who experience an abundance of positive emotions in their lives—emotions like cheerfulness, joy, and contentment—live longer than those whose emotional lives are less positive? Sounds reasonable, but how could you untangle all the complex factors that affect people's health to show that emotions made the difference? The "Nun Study," perhaps destined to become a classic in positive psychology, took advantage of the unique features of the religious life of sisters of the Catholic Church. The Nun Study was conducted by Danner, Snowdon, Friesen (2001) from the University of Kentucky. The study's formal title was "Positive emotions in early life and longevity: Findings from the Nun Study." Danner and her colleagues examined the relationship between positive emotions and longevity in a sample of 180 nuns. Why nuns? Nuns were an ideal group of people for such a study because many of the factors affecting physical health were controlled or minimized. Nuns don't smoke or drink excessively; they live in similar life circumstances; they are childless, so they have the same reproductive histories; and they eat the same bland diet. The "sameness" of their lives eliminated many of the variables that might confound an understanding of which specific factors were responsible for a long life.

What led the researchers to believe that a person's emotional life might predict longevity? First of all, prior research (reviewed in the article's introduction) supports the connection between emotions and health. Negative emotions have been shown to suppress the immune system and other aspects of physiological functioning and thereby increase the risk of disease. Positive emotions seem to enhance these same processes and thus reduce the risk of disease. Second, temperament has shown long-term stability over the life span. That is, emotional expressiveness, such as whether we have a positive and cheerful outlook or a negative and more guarded outlook, tends to be fairly consistent over a person's lifetime, from childhood through adulthood. Third, temperament is known to influence how well a person copes with the stress and challenges of life. People with cheerful temperaments and positive outlooks fare better than those with less cheerful and more negative outlooks. Finally, research has shown that writing about significant life events can capture a person's basic emotional outlook. When we write about things that are important to us, we express emotions that reflect aspects of our basic temperament. Taken together, these findings of prior research made it reasonable to assume that autobiographies written early in life would capture basic aspects of emotional expressiveness. Differences in emotional expressiveness might then predict health and longevity.

The nuns in Danner and colleagues' study had been asked to write a brief 2- to 3-page autobiographical sketch as part of their religious vows. These sketches were written in the 1930s and 1940s when the sisters were about 22 years old and just beginning their careers with the church. Researchers were able to retrieve the autobiographies from church archives. Then, they coded each autobiography by counting the number of positive-, negative-, and neutral-emotion words and sentences that it contained. Because few of the autobiographies contained negative emotions, the researchers concentrated on the number of positive-emotion words, positive-emotion sentences, and the number of different positive emotions expressed. Here are two sample portions of autobiographies—one low in positive emotion and the other high in positive emotion. Sister A—coded as low in positive emotion:

> I was born on September 26, 1909, the eldest of seven children, five girls and two boys . . . . My candidate year was spent in

the Motherhouse, teaching chemistry and Second Year at the Notre Dame Institute. With God's grace, I intend to do my best for our order, for the spread of religion and for my personal sanctification."

Sister B—coded as high in positive emotion:

God started my life off well by bestowing on me a grace of inestimable value. The past year, which I spent as a candidate studying at Notre Dame College has been a very happy one. Now I look forward with eager joy to receiving the Holy Habit of Our Lady and to a life of union with Love Divine.

Scores resulting from the coding system provided numeric indices to describe the women's early emotional lives. These scores were then analyzed in relation to mortality and survival data for the same group of women 60 years later. At the time the study was done in 2001, the surviving nuns were between 75 and 94 years of age. Forty-two percent of the sisters had died by the time of the follow-up study.

The results of the study were rather amazing. Researchers found a strong relationship between longevity and the expression of positive emotion early in life. For every 1.0% increase in the number of autobiographical sentences expressing positive emotion, there was a corresponding 1.4% decrease in mortality rate. Comparisons of those nuns expressing many different positive emotions with those expressing only a few, showed a mean difference in age of death of 10.7 years. The most cheerful nuns lived a full decade longer than the least cheerful! By age 80, some 60% of the least cheerful group had died, compared to only 25% for the most cheerful sisters. The probability of survival to an advanced age was strongly related to the early-life expression of positive emotions. Figure 1.1 shows the positive-emotion/survival relationship beginning at age 75. The probability of survival to age 85 was 80% for the most cheerful nuns (Quartile 4 in Figure 1.1) and

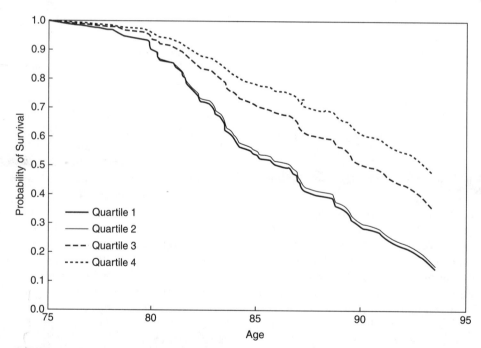

FIGURE 1.1   Positive Emotions and Survival
Probability of survival to different ages after age 75 as a function of positive emotions expressed early in life by 180 participants in the Nun Study. Positive emotional expression arranged in rank order from lowest (Quartile 1) to highest (Quartile 4).   *Source:* Danner, D.D., Snowdon, D.A., & Friesen, W.V. (2001). Positive emotions in early life and longevity: Findings from the Nun study. *Journal of Personality and Social Psychology, 80,* 804–813. Copyright 2001 by the American Psychological Association. Reprinted by permission.

54% for the least cheerful (Quartile 1). The odds of survival to age 90 were 65% for the upbeat sisters, but only 30% for the less upbeat. By age 94, the survival odds were over half (54%) for the most positive sisters and only 15% for the least positive.

According to the results of the Nun Study, the phrase, "don't worry, be happy" is excellent advice. You may live longer! In Chapter 3, "Positive Emotions and Well-Being," we explore research that helps explain why positive emotions may lead to a longer life.

Clinical Psychology

The disillusionment of many clinical psychologists with sole reliance on the disease model has been another factor contributing to the development of positive psychology. Mental health professionals are beginning to view the work of reducing psychological misery as only part of their task. There will always be clients in need of help, and it will continue to be an important mission of psychologists to provide such help. However, many clinicians have begun shifting from the single-minded purpose of treating psychopathology toward a perspective that includes prevention of illness and promotion of positive mental health. Fundamental to this shift is the need to develop models of positive mental health. That is, what personal characteristics and what type of life define the extreme opposite of mental illness—a state Keyes and Haidt (2003) call "flourishing?" In the past, mental health was defined mostly in terms of the absence of disease. One goal of positive psychology is to establish criteria and a language defining the presence of mental health that parallels our current criteria and language for describing and diagnosing mental illness.

Developmental Psychology

A long-standing focus of developmental psychologists has been examination of conditions that threaten healthy development. Following a deficit-focused model, it was assumed that most children growing up under conditions of adversity (e.g., poverty, abuse, parental alcoholism, or mental illness) would be at heightened risk for deficits in social, cognitive, and emotional development compared to children not subjected to such adversities. These assumptions began to change in the 1970s when many psychiatrists and psychologists drew attention to the amazing resilience of certain children and adults subjected to

potentially debilitating life challenges (Masten, 2001). Cases of resilience—meaning "good outcomes in spite of serious threats to adaptation or development" (Masten, p. 228) —are more common than previously supposed. Research documenting the amazing resilience of ordinary people facing difficult life circumstances highlights a major theme of positive psychology, namely human strengths.

Perhaps even more intriguing is the concept of **posttraumatic growth** (PTG) as a counterpoint to posttraumatic stress disorder (PTSD). Researchers have documented that positive growth can occur as a result of traumatic experiences like serious illness, loss of a loved one, or a major accident or disability (Ryff & Singer, 2003a). In the aftermath of such events, many people report a greater appreciation for life and their loved ones, an increased sense of personal strength, and more clarity about what is most important in life. Studies of resilience and posttraumatic growth underscore positive psychology's emphasis on human strengths and positive coping abilities.

Survey Research and Subjective Well-Being

Public opinion polling has been a long-standing research tool for social psychologists and sociologists. Beginning with national surveys of opinions toward issues, groups, and political candidates, survey research subsequently branched out to include quality-of-life measures. Ed Diener (2000) is a prominent contemporary researcher who studies happiness, defined as **subjective well-being** (SWB). Measures of SWB assess a person's level of life satisfaction and the frequency of positive and negative emotional experiences. Studies of happiness have established a reliable pattern of intriguing findings (e.g., Diener, 2000; Diener, Suh, Lucas, & Smith, 1999; Myers, 2000a). The most noteworthy of these is that material success (i.e., money and wealth) bears only a weak relationship to happiness. Increases in income and possession of consumer goods beyond what is necessary to meet basic needs are not reliably related to increases in happiness. You may dream of winning a multimillion dollar lottery, but studies show that winners quickly return to their pre-lottery levels of happiness (see Csikszentmihalyi, 1999 and Diener, 2000 for reviews).

Survey research raises an interesting question. If money doesn't buy happiness, what does? This question is one way to think about positive psychology. Once basic needs are met, objective life circumstances (such as the amount of money you make, or your age, race, or gender) do not have much influence on your level of happiness. So, the difference between happy and unhappy people must involve more psychological and subjective factors. Positive psychology follows the lead of early survey research in examining the traits and states that help explain differences in the level of happiness. Much of the research in positive psychology is focused on *traits*, such as self-esteem, physical attractiveness, optimism, intelligence, and extraversion, and on *states*, such as work situation, involvement in religion, number of friends, marital status, and the quality of relationships. Taken together, these traits and states help explain one of the major questions of positive psychology: "Why are some people happier than others?"

Social/Personality Psychology and the Psychology of Religion

Social psychologists have provided extensive evidence of the critical importance of satisfying social relationships and support from others for our health and happiness (e.g., Baumeister & Leary, 1995; Ryff & Singer, 2000; Taylor, Repetti, & Seeman, 1997; Uchino, Cacioppo, & Kiecolt-Glaser, 1996). A satisfying life is founded on satisfying relationships, such as a happy marriage and good friends. Social psychologists have also sensitized us to the different cultural understandings of well-being and happiness. Concepts of happiness in America and Japan, for example, are quite different. In addition to studies across diverse cultures, social psychologists have investigated a potential dark side of affluence and materialism among advanced consumer cultures such as our own (e.g., Cushman, 1990; Kasser & Kanner, 2004). These latter studies show that materialistic people who sacrifice fulfillment of important psychological needs in their pursuit of fame and fortune may also sacrifice their own happiness and life satisfaction. Related research has contributed to an understanding of the amazing process of human adaptation that helps explain why increases in income, like the sudden wealth of lottery winners, has only short-term effects (Diener & Oishi, 2005). In short, why money does not buy happiness.

Studies by personality psychologists have identified positive traits and personal strengths that form the foundation of health and happiness. These studies include investigations of the genetic basis of a happy temperament (e.g., Lykken, 1999) and personality traits related to individual well-being such as optimism (Peterson, 2000; Seligman, 1990), self-esteem (Baumeister, 1999), extraversion (McCrae & Costa, 1997), a positive life outlook (e.g., Taylor, 1989; Taylor & Brown, 1988), and how the pursuit of personally meaningful goals contributes to happiness (Emmons, 1999b).

Both social and personality psychology researchers have contributed to an understanding of the roles that religion and morality play in people's lives (e.g., Pargament, 1997; Spilka, Hood, Hunsberger, & Gorsuch, 2003). Religion has become an important topic within positive psychology because it is a significant foundation of well-being for most people. The study of virtue also has a prominent position because the meaning of a good life and a life well-lived is strongly connected to human virtues, such as honesty, integrity, compassion, and wisdom (Peterson & Seligman, 2004). And, expressing human virtues contributes to individual well-being and the well-being of others. For example, acts of forgiveness (McCullough, 1999) and gratitude (Emmons & McCullough, 2004) tend to increase life satisfaction for both givers and recipients.

POSITIVE PSYCHOLOGY: ASSUMPTIONS, GOALS, AND DEFINITIONS

Martin Seligman's call for a positive psychology was aimed at refocusing the entire field of psychology. He will likely be disappointed if positive psychology becomes simply one more area of specialized research. It is encouraging, then, to find elements of positive psychology represented in so many different areas of psychology, from physiological to clinical psychology. Positive psychology is both a general perspective on the discipline of psychology and a collection of research topics focused on positive aspects of human behavior.

To sum up our discussion, we may point to several common themes that run through much of the developing literature in positive psychology. A major assumption of positive psychology is that the field of psychology has become unbalanced (Simonton & Baumeister, 2005). A major goal of positive psychology is to restore balance within the discipline. This goal is reflected in two areas of research and theory that need further development.

First, there is a need for improved understanding of positive human behaviors to balance the negative focus of much mainstream research and theory (Sheldon & King, 2001). Related to this is the need for psychologists to overcome their skepticism about the scientific and "authentic" status of positive psychology's subject matter. A second need is to develop an empirically-based conceptual understanding and language for describing healthy human functioning that parallels our classification and understanding of mental illness (Keyes, 2003). It is arguably just as important to understand the sources of health as it is to understand the causes of illness, particularly if we are interested in preventing illness by promoting healthy lifestyles (Ryff & Singer, 1998).

The themes of positive psychology are captured in various attempts to define this new area of psychology. Sheldon and King (2001) define positive psychology as "nothing more than the scientific study of ordinary human strengths and virtues" (p. 216). This definition reflects the emphasis on psychology's lack of attention to people's everyday lives, which are typically quite positive. Gable and Haidt (2005, p. 104) suggest that positive psychology is "the study of the conditions and processes that contribute to the flourishing or optimal functioning of people, groups and institutions." This definition has much in common with Seligman's (2003) description of the three pillars of positive psychology. Positive psychology is built on the study of (1) positive subjective experiences (such as joy, happiness, contentment, optimism, and hope); (2) positive individual characteristics (such as personal strengths and human virtues that promote mental health); and (3) positive social institutions and communities that contribute to individual health and happiness.

In a more specific formulation, Seligman and his colleagues have proposed that happiness as a central focus of positive psychology can be broken down into three components: the pleasant life, the engaged life, and the meaningful life (Seligman, 2003, Seligman, Rashid, & Parks, 2006). These three aspects of happiness capture the two major themes in positive psychology to be reviewed in Chapter 2, namely that positive psychology is the scientific study of optimal mental functioning and happiness. The **pleasant life** reflects the emphasis in positive psychology on understanding the determinants of happiness as a desired state—what some people might call the "good life." Specifically, what life circumstances and personal qualities make people happy, content, and fulfilled?

The **engaged life** is an aspect of happiness focused on active involvement in activities (e.g., work and leisure) and relationships with others that express our talents and strengths and that give meaning and purpose to our lives. Such involvements promote a zestful and healthy life. A **meaningful life** is an aspect of happiness that derives from going beyond our own self-interests and preoccupations. This is a deeper and more enduring aspect of happiness that stems from giving to, and being involved in, something larger than your self—what Seligman and his colleagues (2006) call "positive institutions." Examples might include a religious community, a personal philosophy of life, your family, a charitable community organization, or a political, environmental, or social cause. The point is that a life well-lived means being connected to something "larger than the self" (Seligman et al., 2006, p. 777).

Life Above Zero

In summary, you can think of positive psychology as the study of what we might call life on the positive side of zero, where zero is the line that divides illness from health and unhappiness from happiness. Traditional psychology has told us much about life at and below zero, but less about life above zero. What takes us from just an absence of illness and unhappiness to a life that is meaningful, purposeful, satisfying, and healthy—in short, a life worth living? Positive psychology is all about the personal qualities, life circumstances, individual choices, life activities, relationships with others, transcendent purposes, and sociocultural conditions that foster and define a good life. By combining these factors with the criteria positive psychologists have used to define a good life, we suggest the following definition of positive psychology: *Positive psychology is the scientific study of the personal qualities, life choices, life circumstances, and sociocultural conditions that promote a life well-lived, defined by criteria of happiness, physical and mental health, meaningfulness, and virtue.*

Culture and the Meaning of a Good Life

The particular meanings of a good life and a life well-lived are obviously shaped by one's culture. Conceptions of a good life are part of every culture's ideals, values, and philosophic/religious traditions (Ryff & Singer, 1998). Because positive psychology is largely a Western enterprise, it is appropriate to ask whether its ideas about health and happiness reflect a Western view and, therefore, do not apply to other cultures. For positive psychologists this is largely an empirical issue, but one that has its share of controversy. Certainly, researchers in the emerging field of positive psychology do not want to impose a "one-size-fits-all" definition that suggests there is only one kind of good life. Instead, they want to tease out universal from culture-specific ideas and define a life well-lived according to broad and flexible criteria that allow for individual and cultural differences. Studies comparing people from widely diverse cultural backgrounds find both differences and commonalities in their understanding of the meaning and general defining features of a good life. Through intensive cultural comparisons, researchers have sought not only to respect differences, but also to identify the commonalities across cultures—that is, what all or most cultures share regarding their descriptions of positive human qualities and the meaning of a good life. The details of cultural differences and commonalities are reviewed in Chapters 6 and 7.

Why Now?

Why has positive psychology attracted so much enthusiastic interest from psychologists today? Calls for psychologists to give more attention to positive human behaviors have been made before. Why were they heard only recently? New ideas emerge in part because they fit or capture some essential theme that is prominent at particular point in history. Historians often refer to this as the *zeitgeist*, which means the spirit of the times. Several authors (e.g., Keyes & Haidt, 2003; Seligman & Csikszentmihalyi, 2000) have argued that positive psychology gave expression to concerns and issues widespread in our culture and in psychology that surfaced in the late 1990s and continue into the new millennium.

Foremost among these is the stark contrast between unprecedented levels of affluence in our society and increasing signs of subjective distress. Csikszentmihalyi (1999) captures this concern in the title of his article, "If we are so rich, why aren't we happy?" In short, most indicators of material affluence, from personal income and ownership of computers and DVD players to GNP, have gone up over the last 30 years. The 1990s are perhaps epitomized in the bumper sticker stating, "the one with the most toys wins." However, the **"paradox of affluence,"**

as Myers (2000b) describes it, is that many indicators of distress and unhappiness have also gone up.

The "misery index" includes rates of divorce, child abuse, childhood poverty, and adolescent suicide. Seligman (1998) notes that we are twice as rich as we were 40 years ago, but we are also 10 times more likely to get depressed. According to many clinical psychologists, depression in the United States is currently at the epidemic level. Themes related to the emptiness and dark side of affluence have also found expression in movies and documentaries such as *American Beauty, Bowling for Columbine,* and the PBS investigation titled, *The Lost Children of Rockdale County* (Frontline, 2002). The latter examined a group of affluent teenagers in a suburb of Augusta, Georgia, who grew up in "good homes" with every advantage money could buy. In the absence of adequate parental supervision, these teens lapsed into exploitive and abusive group sexual relationships culminating in an outbreak of sexually transmitted diseases. When their troubled experiences were discovered, these young people told painful stories of inner emptiness and unfulfilled lives.

Perhaps the most fundamental idea in these descriptions of our culture is an old one—namely, that money doesn't buy happiness. Recognition of the limits in the ability of affluence to bring personal satisfaction has raised questions about the sources of a healthy and satisfying life. The fact that psychology has historically offered no ready answers to these questions has contributed, in part, to the surge of interest in positive psychology. In the aftermath of the September 11 terrorist attacks, our own safety and security may have taken center stage. However, the questions addressed by positive psychology are enduring, and much of its subject matter is directly relevant to our current, uncertain times.

TWO FINAL NOTES

Positive Psychology Is Not Opposed to Psychology

Any description of the issues and concerns that led to the development of positive psychology necessarily involves the question of how positive psychology is different from psychology as a whole. For purposes of clarification, positive psychologists frequently contrast this new area with "traditional psychology." Describing what something *is,* inevitably involves describing what it *is not.* We do not want to create the impression that positive psychology is somehow opposed to psychology. Psychologists have developed an extensive understanding of human behavior and the treatment of psychopathology. Psychology's history shows a steady advance in knowledge and in effective treatments. Positive psychologists are not so much concerned about what *has* been studied in psychology, as they are concerned about what has *not* been studied. It is the relatively one-sided focus on the negatives that is of concern. Sheldon and King (2001) describe the fundamental message of positive psychology as follows: "Positive psychology is thus an attempt to urge psychologists to adopt a more open and appreciative perspective regarding human potentials, motives and capacities" (p. 216). Positive psychology aims to expand—not replace—psychology's understanding of human behavior.

Positive Psychology and the Status Quo

Research in positive psychology shows that our attitude toward life makes a significant contribution to our happiness and health. But does this mean that life circumstances are not important? If you are poor, living in a high-crime area, and have no job, is your happiness dependent on your attitude and not your situation? If happiness is more a matter of attitude than money, do we need to worry much about the amount of poverty in our country? In other words, does positive psychology serve the status quo by helping to justify the unequal distribution of resources and power in our society? If our happiness is more a product of subjective personal factors than it is of material factors, why should we be concerned about who gets what?

There are a number of reasons why positive psychology should *not* be seen as justifying the status quo. First, an individual's external situation is clearly important to the quality of his or her life; and

there are limits to people's ability to maintain a positive attitude in the face of challenging life experiences. Poor people are less happy than those who are not poor, and certain traumas, like death of a spouse, do have lasting effects on personal happiness (Diener, 2000).

Second, most of the research on subjective well-being involves people who are, economically speaking, living relatively comfortable lives. For individuals in this group, life satisfaction is more dependent on psychological and social factors because basic needs have been met. The fact that most Americans seem reasonably happy (Myers, 2000a) may reflect the optimism and satisfaction that results from having the freedom to make personal choices and to pursue satisfying endeavors. Both are made possible, in part, by relative economic comfort. However, knowing that someone is economically well-off does not tell us whether he or she is happy or satisfied with his or her life. One important message of positive psychology is this: A shortage of money can make you miserable, but an abundance of money doesn't necessarily make you happy.

Finally, questions concerning what makes us happy and questions about what is just and fair in the distribution of resources and in how people are treated, might best be answered separately. That is, whatever positive psychologists may discover about the sources of happiness, issues of justice and fairness will remain. The primary reasons for promoting equality, equal opportunity, and equal treatment have to do with the foundational values of our country. Policies to remove discriminatory barriers or to improve the equal distribution of resources do not require misery or unhappiness as justification. Discrimination and inequality may create misery, but being treated fairly and having equal opportunity are rights of every citizen regardless of how she or he may feel. No one should have to show that he or she is miserable and unhappy to justify fair treatment or equal opportunity.

Chapter Summary Questions

1. From the perspective of positive psychology, why does the Milgram study present an imbalanced view of human nature?
2. Why are negative aspects of human behavior perceived as more authentic and real than positive aspects?
3. Why are negative behaviors given more weight than positive behaviors?
4. How does the disease model promote a focus on negatives?
5. Why is positive psychology necessary according to Seligman, and how is positive psychology related to humanistic psychology?
6. What does recent evidence from health psychology suggest about the differing effects of positive and negative emotions on our physical health?

7. a. Why did researchers in the Nun Study hypothesize that expressed emotions could predict longevity?
   b. Briefly describe the study's design and major findings.
8. Describe two reasons why clinical psychologists are becoming interested in positive psychology.
9. How do developmental psychologists' studies of resilience and posttraumatic growth contribute to positive psychology?
10. What does survey research suggest about the importance of money to individual happiness?
11. How have social and personality psychology contributed to positive psychology? Describe three examples.

12. What is the major assumption and goal of positive psychology?
13. Describe the components of Seligman's three-part definition of happiness (i.e., pleasant, engaged, and meaningful life).
14. a. How may positive psychology be thought of as the study of life above zero?
    b. How do your textbook authors define positive psychology?
15. What cultural changes and paradoxes have contributed to the development of positive psychology?
16. How does positive psychology complement rather than oppose traditional psychology?
17. Discuss the issue of positive psychology's relationship to the status quo.

Key Terms

bad is stronger than the good *3*

disease model *3*

subjective well-being *7*

posttraumatic growth *7*

pleasant life *9*

engaged life *9*

meaningful life *9*

paradox of affluence *10*

Web Resources

Positive Psychology

www.positivepsychology.org Site for the Positive Psychology Center at the University of Pennsylvania. A wealth of information about positive psychology's goals, research, and theories.

www.apa.org Web page for the American Psychological Association, with links to articles and books about positive psychology.

www.pos-psych.com Site for the *Positive Psychology News Daily*. Web site put together by graduates of the Master's Degree program at the University of

Pennsylvania. Contains recent research and "fun" information.

The Nun Study

www.mc.uky.edu/nunnet/ University of Kentucky web page for research related to the famous Nun Study.

Authentic Happiness

www.authentichappiness.org Martin Seligman's link to his popular 2002 book *Authentic happiness*. Contains research summaries and positive psychology self-assessment tests.

Suggested Readings

Argyle, M. (2001). *The psychology of happiness* (2nd ed.). Great Britain: Routledge.

Aspinwall, L. G., & Staudinger, U. M. (Eds.). (2003). *A psychology of human strengths: Fundamental questions and future directions for a positive psychology*. Washington, DC: American Psychological Association.

Gable, S. L., & Haidt, J. (2005). What (and why) is positive psychology? *Review of General Psychology, 9*, 103–110.

Keyes, C. L. M., & Haidt, J. (Eds.). (2003). *Flourishing: Positive psychology and the life well-lived*. Washington, DC: American Psychological Association.

Linley, P. A., & Joseph, S. (2004). *Positive psychology in practice*. Hoboken, NJ: John Wiley & Sons.

Myers, D. G. (1992). *The pursuit of happiness*. New York: Avon Books.

Seligman, M. E. P., & Csikszentmihalyi, M. (2000). Positive psychology: An Introduction. *American Psychologist, 55*, 5–14.

Sheldon, K. M., & King, L. (2001). Why positive psychology is necessary. *American Psychologist, 56*, 216–217.

Snyder, C. R., & Lopez, S. J. (Eds.). (2002). *Handbook of positive psychology*. New York: Oxford University Press.

2

The Meaning and Measure of Happiness

In this chapter, we begin an exploration of psychology's answer to some ancient questions. What is a good life? What is a life worth living? What is the basis for happiness that endures beyond short-term pleasures? The ancient Greeks contemplated the answers to these questions. Is a good life built on maximizing pleasures and minimizing pain, as the hedonic philosophy of the Epicureans prescribed? Minimizing pain, as the Stoics believed? Or is happiness to be found in the expression of the true self, or *daimon*, as described by Aristotle's eudaimonic view of happiness?

Every day we are asked, "how are you doing?" Few of us consult classical philosophy to address this question. Yet our answers reflect some assessment of our well-being, even if only the temporary and fleeting assessment of our feelings at a given moment. In the larger scheme of things, much depends on how we describe and define happiness and "the good life." The kind of society we wish to have reflects our culture's image of what a good life represents. The efforts of parents, teachers, government, and religion are based on assumptions about the kind of qualities and behaviors that "should" be promoted and encouraged. As individuals, we each have some notion of the life we hope to lead, and the goals and ambitions we want to pursue. No matter how we describe the particulars, most of us hope for a happy and satisfying life. What makes up a happy and satisfying life is the question. Positive psychology has addressed this question from a subjective psychological point of view. This means that primacy is given to people's own judgments of well-being based on their own criteria for evaluating the quality of life. We now consider why a subjective and psychological perspective is important.

WHY A PSYCHOLOGY OF WELL-BEING?

We Americans collect a wealth of information related to the question, "how are we doing as a society?" We count, rate, and measure many aspects of our collective and individual lives. Information collected by federal, state, and local governments, along with numerous private agencies, provides a statistical picture of the "state" of different life domains. Economic indicators assess our collective economic well-being. They include statistics on the rate of unemployment, the number of people defined as poor, average annual income, new jobs created, home mortgage interest rates, and performance of the stock market. A variety of social indicators assess the state of our health, families, and communities (Diener, 1995; Diener & Suh, 1997). A picture of our physical health is suggested by statistics describing such things as how long we live, the number of people suffering from major illnesses (like cancer, heart disease, and AIDS), levels of infant mortality, and the percentage of people who have

health insurance. A picture of mental health is provided by statistics showing the percentage of people suffering from emotional problems like depression, drug abuse, anxiety disorders, and suicide. An aggregate view of community and family well-being may be seen in statistics on such things as divorce, single-parent families, poor families, unwed mothers, abused children, serious crimes, and suicide.

What kind of answer do these statistics offer to the question, "how are we doing?" Taken in total, they describe what we might call our country's "**misery index.**" That is, they give us information about how many people are suffering from significant problems that diminish the quality of their lives. To be poor, depressed, seriously ill without health insurance, unemployed, or coping with the suicide of a family member seems like a recipe for misery and unhappiness. Most of us would agree that decreasing the misery index is an important goal of governmental, social, and economic policy. Within psychology, a good deal of research and professional practice has been devoted to preventing and treating the problems reflected in the misery index. Positive psychologists agree that these problems are significant and applaud efforts to deal with them. However, a positive psychological perspective suggests that national statistics provide an incomplete and somewhat misleading answer to the question, "how are we doing?"

Objective versus Subjective Measures

Researchers discovered early on that many economic and social indicators of a person's "objective" life circumstances (e.g., income, age, and occupation) were only weakly related to people's own judgments of their well-being (Andrews & Withey, 1976; Campbell, Converse, & Rodgers, 1976). In a major review of this research, Diener (1984) argued that subjective well-being (SWB), defined by ratings of life satisfaction and positive emotional experience, was a critical component of well-being that was missing from the equation. Subjective well-being, or happiness, in everyday terms, reflects an individual's own judgment about the quality of his or her life. From a subjective well-being (SWB) perspective, economic and social indicators are incomplete because they do not directly assess how happy or satisfied people are with their lives (Diener & Suh, 1997). Although these indicators describe the "facts" of a person's life, they do not tell us how a person thinks and feels about these facts.

Personal, subjective evaluations are important for several reasons. First, different individuals may react to the same circumstances (as described by economic and social statistics) in very different ways because of differences in their expectations, values, and personal histories. Subjective evaluations help us interpret the "facts" from an individual's point of view. Second, happiness and life satisfaction are important goals in their own right. The "pursuit of happiness" is described in the Declaration of Independence as one of Americans' inalienable rights, and surveys show that people rank happiness high on the list of desirable life goals. For example, a survey of over 7,000 college students in 42 different countries found the pursuit of happiness and life satisfaction to be among students' most important goals (Suh, Diener, Oishi, & Triandis, 1998). Happiness is a central component of people's conception of a good life and a good society (Diener, Oishi, & Lucas, 2003). How happy people are with their lives is therefore an important part of the answer to the question, "how are we doing?"

Economic and social indicators may be misleading if we consider them to be sufficient indices of happiness and satisfaction. Research shows that a person's level of happiness depends on many factors that are not measured by economic and social statistics. For example, the amount of money a person makes is only marginally related to measures of happiness (Csikszentmihalyi, 1999; Diener, Suh, Lucas, & Smith, 1999). Over the last 50 years, average personal income has tripled. Yet, national surveys conducted during the same 50-year period showed that levels of expressed happiness did not go up, but remained unchanged. Clearly, some social statistics do tell us something about who is likely to be *unhappy*. The approximately 20% of Americans who are depressed are, by definition, dissatisfied with their lives (Kessler et al., 1994). However, most national statistics tell us little about who is likely to be happy. If we knew a particular person had a good job and adequate income, was married, owned a home, was in good physical health, and was not suffering from a mental disorder, we would still not know if he or she was also happy and satisfied. Diener and colleagues summarize the importance of happiness by arguing that the measurement of happiness is an essential third ingredient, along with economic and social indicators, for assessing the quality of life within a society (Diener et al., 2003).

Negative versus Positive Functioning

Other researchers have argued that national statistics are also incomplete because they fail to assess human strengths, optimal functioning, and positive mental health (Aspinwall & Staudinger, 2003; Keyes, Shmotkin, & Ryff, 2002; Ryan & Deci, 2001). For example, Ryff and Keyes (1995) described six aspects of positive functioning and actualization of potentials as the basis for what they called "psychological well-being:" autonomy, personal growth, self-acceptance, life purpose, environmental mastery, and positive relations with others. They argue that it is the presence of these strengths and realized potentials that define well-being and a fully functioning person. From this perspective, national statistics (particularly those related to mental illness) are incomplete because they only examine the presence or absence of illness and negative functioning, and fail to take into account the presence of strengths and positive functioning. Mental health statistics are focused on pathological symptoms of mental illness—not on positive markers of mental wellness (Keyes, 2002; Ryff & Singer, 1998). As noted by Keyes (2003), the absence of mental illness does not necessarily indicate the presence of mental health.

The major point of Keyes' analysis is shown in Figure 2.1. About 26% of American adults suffer from a diagnosable mental disorder in a given year. Does this mean that the other 74% are mentally healthy? Keyes' research suggests that the answer is no. Only 17% of Americans were found to enjoy complete mental health or to be flourishing, and 10% were estimated to be languishing. Languishing is a state of distress and despair, but it is not severe enough to meet current mental illness criteria and so is not included in official statistics.

Positive psychologists argue that without measures of SWB and positive functioning, our answer to the question "how are we doing?" is likely to be incomplete. In line with this conclusion, Diener and Seligman (2004) have recently provided a detailed examination of the social policy implications of well-being research. They argue for the development of a national indicator of well-being that would complement economic and social statistics. A national well-being index would highlight important features of our individual and collective lives that are not

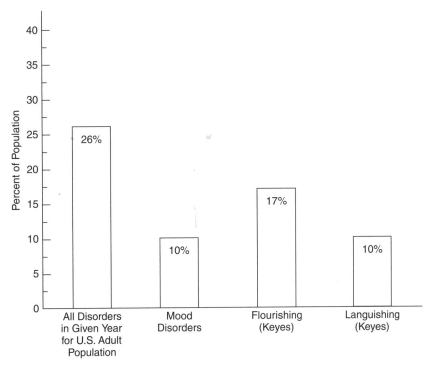

FIGURE 2.1   Mental Illness and Mental Health

Source: Mental disorders data from National Institute of Mental Health. The numbers count: Mental disorders in America, Rev. 2006. Retrieved August 2007 at http://www. nimh.nih.gov/publicat/numbers.cfm. Flourishing/languishing percentages from Keyes, C.L.M. (2007). Promoting and protecting mental health and flourishing: A complementary strategy for improving national mental health. *American Psychologist, 62,* 95–108.

currently measured in any systematic way. Such an index could have important and positive effects on social policies, and on how we think about the quality of our lives. Several countries in Europe have already begun to address this issue. For example, the German Socioeconomic Panel in Germany and the Eurobarometer in European Union nations are two examples of government-sponsored programs that regularly collect information about life satisfaction and well-being.

WHAT IS HAPPINESS? TWO TRADITIONS

From your own individual point of view, how would you answer the questions raised at the beginning of this chapter? What is a good life? What is happiness? What defines a satisfying life or a life well-lived? What kind of life do you wish to lead? And in the end, how do you hope people will remember you?

Hedonic Happiness

Probably most of us would hope first for a long life—one that does not end prematurely. Suicide, however, is a reminder that the quality of life is more important to many people than the quantity of life. As for quality of life, happiness might be number one on our list. Most people would likely hope for a happy and satisfying life, in which good things and pleasant experiences outnumber bad ones. Particularly in American culture, as we noted earlier, happiness seems to be an important part of how people define a good life. Defining the good life in terms of personal happiness is the general thrust of the hedonic view of well-being (Kahneman, Diener, & Schwarz, 1999; Ryan & Deci, 2001; Waterman, 1993). Hedonic psychology parallels aspects of the philosophy of hedonism. While there are many varieties of philosophical hedonism dating back to the ancient Greeks, a general version of hedonism holds that the chief goal of life is the pursuit of happiness and pleasure. Within psychology, this view of well-being is expressed in the study of SWB (Diener, 1984; Diener et al., 1999). Subjective well-being takes a broad view of happiness, beyond the pursuit of short-term or physical pleasures defining a narrow hedonism. **Subjective well-being** is defined as life satisfaction, the presence of positive affect, and a relative absence of negative affect. Together, the three components are often referred to as happiness. Research based on the SWB model has burgeoned in the last 5 years (Ryan & Deci, 2001). Studies have delineated a variety of personality characteristics and life experiences that help answer questions about who is happy and what makes people happy. A major portion of this book is devoted to reviewing the research and theory on SWB.

Eudaimonic Happiness

Is happiness enough for a good life? Would you be content and satisfied if you were happy and nothing else? Consider a hypothetical example suggested by Seligman (2002a). What if you could be hooked to an "experience machine" that would keep you in a constant state of cheerful happiness, or whatever positive emotion you desired, no matter what happened in your life. Fitting the hedonic view, you would experience an abundance of happiness all the time. Would you choose to be hooked up? We might like it for awhile, but to experience only one of our many emotions, and to have the same cheerful reaction to the diversity of life events and challenges might actually impoverish the experience of life. And some of what we would lose might be extremely valuable. For example, negative emotions like fear help us make choices that avoid threats to our well-being. Without fear and other negative emotions we might make very bad choices. We'd be happy, but we might not live very long. Seligman (2002a) argues that we would likely also reject the experience machine because we want to feel we are entitled to our positive emotions, and to believe they reflect our "real" positive qualities and behaviors. Pleasure, disconnected from reality, does not affirm or express our identity as individuals.

Above all, most of us would probably reject the experience machine because we believe that there is more to life than happiness and subjective pleasure. Or as Seligman (2002a) describes it, there is a deeper and more "authentic happiness." Much

of classical Greek philosophy was concerned with these deeper meanings of happiness and the good life. Waterman (1990, 1993) describes two psychological views of happiness distilled from classical philosophy. Hedonic conceptions of happiness, discussed above, define happiness as the enjoyment of life and its pleasures. The hedonic view captures a major element of what we mean by happiness in everyday terms: We enjoy life; we are satisfied with how our lives are going; and good events outnumber bad events.

In contrast, eudaimonic conceptions of happiness, given fullest expression in the writings of Aristotle, define happiness as self-realization, meaning the expression and fulfillment of inner potentials. From this perspective, the good life results from living in accordance with your *daimon* (in other words, your true self). That is, happiness results from striving toward self-actualization—a process in which our talents, needs, and deeply held values direct the way we conduct our lives. "Eudaimonia" (or happiness) results from realization of our potentials. We are happiest when we follow and achieve our goals and develop our unique potentials. Eudaimonic happiness has much in common with humanistic psychology's emphases on the concepts of self-actualization (Maslow, 1968) and the fully functioning person (Rogers, 1961) as criteria for healthy development and optimal functioning.

What kinds of experiences lead to eudaimonic happiness? Waterman (1993) argued that eudaimonic happiness results from experiences of personal expressiveness. Such experiences occur when we are fully engaged in life activities that fit and express our deeply held values and our sense of who we are. Under these circumstances we experience a feeling of fulfillment, of meaningfulness, of being intensely alive—a feeling that this is who we really are and who we were meant to be.

At this point, you might ask whether hedonic and eudaimonic views of happiness are very different. Aren't activities that bring us pleasure also generally the ones that are meaningful because they express our talents and values? Waterman believes that there are many more activities that produce hedonic enjoyment than activities that provide eudaimonic happiness based on personal expression. Everything from alcohol consumption and eating chocolate, to a warm bath can bring us pleasure, but there are fewer activities that engage significant aspects of our identity and give a deeper meaning to our lives.

To evaluate the similarities and differences between hedonic enjoyment and personal expressiveness (eudaimonic enjoyment), Waterman (1993) asked a sample of college students to list five activities that addressed the following question: "If you wanted another person to know about who you are and what you are like as a person, what five activities of importance to you would you describe?" (p. 681). This question was meant to evoke activities that define and express a person's personality, talents, and values. Each activity listed was then rated on scales describing personal expressiveness and hedonic enjoyment of the activity. Expressive items included questions about whether the activity gave strong feelings of authenticity (who I really am), fulfillment and completion, intense involvement, and self-activity-fit. Hedonic questions focused on whether the activity produced good feelings such as a warm glow, happiness, pleasure, or enjoyment. Waterman found substantial overlap in expressive and hedonic ratings. Half to two-thirds of the time, personally expressive activities also generated a comparable level of hedonic enjoyment. However, the two forms of happiness also diverged for some activities. Hedonic enjoyment was associated with activities that made people feel relaxed, excited, content or happy, and that led to losing track of time and forgetting personal problems. Feelings of personal expressiveness (eudaimonic happiness) were more strongly related to activities that created feelings of challenge, competence, and effort, and that offered the opportunity for personal growth and skill development.

Focus on Research: Positive Affect and a Meaningful Life

Until recently, Waterman was one of the few researchers who examined the similarities and differences between hedonic and eudaimonic conceptions of happiness. However, in a recent study, Laura King and her colleagues have revisited this issue by examining the relationship between positive affect and meaningfulness (King, Hicks, Krull, & Del Gaiso, 2006). Positive affect is a summary term for pleasurable emotions such as joy, contentment, laughter, and love. Meaningfulness refers to more personally expressive and engaging activities that may connect us to a broader and even transcendent view of life.

King and her colleagues note that historically, positive affect has been thought of as more central to hedonic than to eudaimonic conceptions of well-being. In fact, "the good life," from a eudaimonic perspective, suggests that the pursuit of pleasure may detract from a personally expressive and meaningful life. Pleasure is seen as a shallow and unsatisfying substitute for deeper purposes in life. The potential opposition between pleasure and meaning is one reason for the scant research examining their potential interrelation. However, King and colleagues' study suggests that the line between positive affect and meaning in life is not as clear as previously imagined. Positive affect may enhance people's ability to find meaning and purpose in their lives.

As a basis for their study, King and her colleagues note the considerable research linking meaning with positive psychological functioning. Experiencing life as meaningful consistently predicts health and happiness across the life span. Finding meaning in life's difficulties contributes to positive coping and adaptation. Meaning in life may stem from a person's goals, intrinsically satisfying activities, interpersonal relationships, self-improvement efforts, or a transcendent philosophy or religion that provides a larger sense of understanding and coherence to the journey through life. Whatever the basis of their understanding, people are clearly capable of making global judgments about the meaning and purpose of life. Researchers do not typically define "meaning in life" for study participants, but let each person use his or her own understanding. People's self-described perceptions of meaning and purpose are highly related to well-being outcomes.

How might positive affect contribute to meaning in life? King and her colleagues believe that positive emotions open up people's thinking to more imaginative and creative possibilities by placing current concerns in a broader context. These effects of positive emotions may enhance meaning if they also cause people to think of their lives in terms of a larger system of meaning. For example, an enjoyable walk in the mountains on a beautiful day or a fun evening with friends may lead you to think of your place in nature's scheme of things or the importance of relationships in a satisfying life.

Positive emotions may also be markers of meaningful events and activities. Progressing toward important goals makes us feel good. Judgments of global life satisfaction are enhanced by a current or recent positive mood. Meaningful and expressive activities are typically accompanied by enjoyment. It is likely that these connections between positive affect and meaning are represented in our memories as well-learned linkages. In the same way that the sights, sounds, and smells of Christmas may bring back fond childhood memories, positive affect may give rise to a sense of meaning in life. Positive emotions may be intimately bound to the meaning of meaning.

In a series of six studies, King and her colleagues found positive affect to be consistently related to meaning in life. Whether people were asked to make global life judgments or daily assessments, meaning and positive emotion were highly correlated. Taking a long-term view, people who characteristically experience many positive emotions (i.e., trait positive affectivity) report greater meaningfulness in their lives than people who typically experience more frequent negative emotions (i.e., trait negative affectivity). In day-to-day life, the same relationship was found. A day judged as meaningful included more positive than negative emotional events. People's ratings of statements such as, "Today, my personal existence was very purposeful and meaningful" or, "Today, I had a sense that I see a reason for being here" were significantly related to their daily diary entries describing positive emotional experiences occurring during the day. And the effect of positive emotion was above and beyond that of goal progress assessments. Goal pursuits are a significant source of purpose in life. When King and her fellow investigators factored out the effects of individual goal assessments, positive affect was still significantly related to enhanced life meaning. Experimental manipulations of positive and negative mood also supported the role of positive affect. People who were primed to think about, or induced to feel positive emotions rated life as more meaningful and made clearer discriminations between meaningful and meaningless tasks, compared to participants in neutral emotional conditions.

Overall, King and her colleagues' work suggests that meaning and positive emotion may share a two-way street. In other words, meaningful activities and accomplishment bring enjoyment and satisfaction to life, and positive emotions may bring an enhanced sense of meaning and purpose. As King and her associates conclude, "the lines between hedonic pleasure and more 'meaningful pursuits' should not be drawn too rigidly." " . . . pleasure has a place in the meaningful life" (King et al., p. 191).

Despite their apparent overlap, hedonic and eudaimonic conceptions of happiness are the bases for two distinct lines of research on well-being (Ryan & Deci, 2001). Studies of SWB have explored the hedonic basis of happiness; and studies of optimal functioning, positive mental health, and flourishing have examined the underpinnings of well-being fitting the eudaimonic view. The definitions and measures of well-being developed within each of these empirical traditions will be reviewed separately. A comparative analysis will then examine the overlapping and the distinctive features of the hedonic and eudaimonic views.

SUBJECTIVE WELL-BEING: THE HEDONIC BASIS OF HAPPINESS

Subjective well-being shares a common core of meaning with the more everyday term *happiness*. The term "subjective" means, from the point of view of the individual. That is, it refers to a person's own assessment of his or her life, rather than assessment by an external observer or evaluator, or as might be inferred from more objective measures of factors such as physical health, job status, or income. As Myers and Diener (1995) put it, the final judge of happiness is "whoever lives inside the person's skin" (p. 11). Diener (2000) describes SWB as follows: "SWB refers to people's evaluations of their lives—evaluations that are both affective and cognitive. People experience an abundance of SWB when they feel many pleasant and few unpleasant emotions, when they are engaged in interesting activities, when they experience many pleasures and few pains, when they are satisfied with their lives" (p. 34). In short, a person with high SWB has a pervasive sense that life is "good." In our review, we will use the terms *subjective well-being* and *happiness* interchangeably.

Measuring Subjective Well-Being

Early survey researchers assessed people's sense of well-being directly. In national surveys, tens of thousands of people responded to questions that asked for an overall global judgment about happiness, life satisfaction, and feelings (see Andrews & Withey, 1976; Campbell et al., 1976, for reviews). Survey researchers asked questions like the following: "Taking all things together, how would you say things are these days—would you say you are very happy, pretty happy or not too happy?" "How satisfied are you with your life as a whole? Are you very satisfied? Satisfied? Not very satisfied? Not at all satisfied?" Other researchers asked people to choose from a series of faces to indicate their degree of

FIGURE 2.2   Face Measure of Happiness

happiness (Andrew & Withey, 1976). Participants are simply asked to indicate which face comes closest to expressing how they feel about their life as a whole. An example of such a series of faces is shown in Figure 2.2

In current research, SWB is widely considered to have three primary components that are assessed by multi-item scales and inventories (Andrews & Robinson, 1992; Argyle, 2001; Diener, 2000; Diener et al., 1999). These three components are *life satisfaction, positive affect,* and *negative affect.* Life satisfaction is a cognitive judgment concerning how satisfied a person is with his or her life. The emotional components—positive and negative affect—refer to peoples' feelings about their lives. Positive affect refers to the frequency and intensity of pleasant emotions such as happiness and joy. Negative affect refers to the frequency and intensity of unpleasant emotions such as sadness and worry.

This three-part structure of SWB has been widely confirmed in research using large samples of people who completed a variety of measures of happiness, satisfaction, and emotions (e.g., Bryant & Verhoff, 1982; Compton, Smith, Cornish, & Qualls, 1996; Lucas, Diener, & Suh, 1996). Responses were then examined using a statistical technique called factor analysis to assess the relationships among the various measures. The results have generally revealed two prominent findings. First, statistical analyses reveal a single factor that underlies all the different measures. That is, despite the diversity of SWB measures, they all seem to tap a common dimension. Second, studies also reveal three components of SWB: a "life situation factor," a "positive affect factor," and a "negative affect factor." These three components (life satisfaction, positive affect, and negative affect) correlate strongly with the common dimension, but only moderately with one another. That is, each makes a relatively independent and distinct contribution. This finding (that measures of SWB reliably parcel themselves out into three related, but somewhat independent parts) serves as the basis for the three-component view of SWB.

The interrelationship of the three components is noteworthy because most researchers do not assess all three components (Diener et al., 2003). Researchers assess SWB in a variety of ways. The fact that different measures share a common underlying dimension permits a comparative and cumulative evaluation of research results, despite differences in how SWB is assessed. However, Diener (2000) notes that this situation is less than ideal. It would be better, from a scientific measurement point of view, if studies assessed all three components. Developing more detailed and widely shared measures of SWB is an important task for the development of positive psychology.

Many of the measures to be described can be taken online at Martin Seligman's Authentic Happiness web site described at the end of this chapter. You can obtain a profile of your scores on a variety of measures developed by positive psychologists.

Life Satisfaction

Single-item measures of life satisfaction have given way to multi-item scales with greater reliability and validity. One of the more widely used measures of life satisfaction is the Satisfaction with Life Scale (Diener, Emmons, Larsen, & Griffen, 1985). This five-item scale asks the participant to make a global evaluation of his or her life (adapted from Diener, Lucas, & Oishi, 2002, p. 70). You may be interested in completing the items yourself. To fill out the scale, simply indicate your degree of agreement or disagreement with each of the five statements using the 1–7 ratings described below:

7	*Strongly agree*
6	*Agree*
5	*Slightly agree*
4	*Neither agree nor disagree*
3	*Slightly disagree*
2	*Disagree*
1	*Strongly disagree*

_____ *In most ways my life is close to my ideal.*

_____ *The conditions of my life are excellent.*

_____ *I am satisfied with my life.*

_____ *So far I have gotten the important things in life.*

_____ *If I could live my life over, I would change almost nothing.*

To score your responses, add up your ratings across all five items.

Diener et al. (2002) suggests the following interpretations. Scores below 20 indicate a degree of dissatisfaction with one's life, which can range from extremely dissatisfied (scores of 5 through 9), through very dissatisfied (10 through 14), to slightly dissatisfied (15 through 19). A score of 20 is the neutral point (i.e., not particularly satisfied or dissatisfied). Levels of satisfaction can vary from somewhat satisfied (21 through 25), through very satisfied (26 through 30), to extremely satisfied (31 through 35). Data from large-scale surveys show that most Americans are somewhat satisfied with their lives (scoring between 21 and 25) (Diener et al., 1985).

Life satisfaction can also be assessed by examining the levels of satisfaction in different life domains. A researcher might ask people how satisfied they are with their jobs, families, health, leisure activities, and social relationships. Overall life satisfaction would be expressed in terms of the average or sum of satisfaction ratings for these different aspects of life. This is the approach taken by "quality of life" researchers who ask about everything from satisfaction with physical health and the environment one lives in, to satisfaction with body appearance and sex life (see Power, 2003, for a review). To obtain a more detailed picture of the basis for people's overall life satisfaction, a recent model of SWB suggests that domain satisfaction be included as a fourth component of SWB (Diener, Scollon, & Lucas, 2004). Measures of domain satisfaction provide information on what specific aspects of a person's life make the largest contribution to her or his overall satisfaction. This is particularly important if a researcher is interested in how different life domains (e.g., work, family, or health) affect life satisfaction as a whole.

Positive Affect, Negative Affect, and Happiness

A variety of scales are used to measure people's emotional experiences (see Argyle, 2001; Larsen & Fredrickson, 1999; Lucas, Diener, & Larsen, 2003, for reviews). Some scales ask only about positive emotions, like happiness or joy, while others assess both positive and negative feelings. For example, Bradburn (1969) asked people to indicate the percentage of time they had experienced different positive and negative feelings, using questions like the following:

Within the last few weeks have you ever felt . . .

> . . . *particularly excited about something?*
>
> . . . *pleased about having accomplished something?*
>
> . . . *proud because someone complimented you on something you did?*
>
> . . . *that things were going your way?*
>
> . . . *on top of the world?*
>
> . . . *very lonely or remote from people?*
>
> . . . *so restless you couldn't sit long in a chair?*
>
> . . . *very depressed or very unhappy?*

A more common method of assessing feelings is to ask people to rate the frequency and intensity of different emotions they experienced during a given time period. For example, Diener and Emmons (1984) used nine descriptors to assess affect valence. The descriptors for positive affect were happy, pleased, joyful, and enjoyment/fun. The adjectives for negative or unpleasant affect were worried/anxious; frustrated; angry/hostile; unhappy; and depressed/blue.

Another example of a scale that is widely used to measure positive and negative affect is the Positive Affectivity and Negative Affectivity Schedule (PANAS) (Watson, Clark, & Tellegen, 1988). It may be interesting to see how you score. To complete this measure, use the 1–5 rating scale to indicate how you feel right now.

1	2	3	4	5
very slightly or not at all	*a little*	*moderately*	*quite a bit*	*extremely*

____ *interested (PA)*	____ *irritable (NA)*
____ *distressed (NA)*	____ *alert (PA)*
____ *excited (PA)*	____ *ashamed (NA)*
____ *upset (NA)*	____ *inspired (PA)*
____ *strong (PA)*	____ *nervous (NA)*
____ *guilty (NA)*	____ *determined (PA)*
____ *scared (NA)*	____ *attentive (PA)*
____ *hostile (NA)*	____ *jittery (NA)*
____ *enthusiastic (PA)*	____ *active (PA)*
____ *proud (PA)*	____ *afraid (NA)*

To score your responses, add up separately your ratings for the 10 positive affect items (PA) and your ratings for the 10 negative affect items (NA). Each score can range from 10 to 50, indicating the degree of positive and negative affect. You can also see from this scale which emotions had the greatest impact on your current mood.

Using scales like the PANAS, researchers can ask people to rate the intensity and/or the frequency of their emotional experiences. Researchers can also vary the time period for which the ratings are made. To measure short-term or immediate emotional experience, people are asked to rate how they feel right now, or during the past day. To measure longer-term emotions, a researcher might ask people how frequently they experienced positive and negative emotions during the past week, the past month, or past few months. Other scales used to measure positive and negative feelings employ longer lists of adjectives that can be grouped into subscales of related emotions (see Lucas et al., 2003, for a review). Positive and negative affect can also be measured by facial and physiological expressions of emotions. The human face is highly expressive of emotion. For example, Ekman and Friesen (1976, 1978) developed the Facial Action Coding System that allows trained observers to interpret emotional expression by a particular constellation of muscle movements in the face.

Focus on Research: Is Your Future Revealed in Your Smile?

An intriguing study by Harker and Keltner (2001) examined life outcomes for women showing one of two kinds of smiles in their college yearbook photographs. When asked to smile for the camera, some of us break into spontaneous, genuine, and authentic smiles that make us look as if we are happy or have just been told a good joke. Others look like we are going through the motions of smiling, but it doesn't look like the real thing. It looks more like we have been told a joke that we didn't find funny, and are faking a smile as a social obligation to the joke teller. Trained coders can easily distinguish a genuine, authentic smile (called a "Duchenne smile") from one that looks inauthentic and forced (non-Duchenne). The 141 women in the study had graduated from Mills College in 1958 and 1960 when they were either 21 or 22 years old. Their college senior yearbook photos were coded according to the Duchenne or non-Duchenne classification. Only a handful of the women did not smile in their photos and about half showed the Duchenne or "natural" smile. All the women in the study were contacted again when they were age 27, 43, and 52. The follow-up study at age 52 occurred 30 years after graduation from college. The researchers were interested in whether or not the expression of positive emotionality, shown among the women graduates with the Duchenne smile, would be related to personality and outcomes later in life.

During each of the follow-up periods, study participants provided information about their personalities, the quality of their relationships, their marital histories, and their personal well-being. Compared to the non-Duchenne group, women showing the Duchenne smile in their college yearbook photos showed lower negative emotionality and higher competence and affiliation with others across all three follow-up periods. Competence was expressed in higher levels of mental focus, organization, and achievement orientation. Affiliation was expressed in stronger and more stable bonds with others. The Duchenne women also showed consistently higher levels of personal well-being and life satisfaction, and lower levels of physical and psychological problems than the non-Duchenne group. Most interestingly, the Duchenne group of women were more likely to be married at age 27 and more likely to have stable and satisfying marriages throughout the 30 years since graduating from college. A number of researchers have noted the important role of positive emotions in avoiding and solving conflict and in maintaining the vitality of a relationship. The positive emotionality of the Duchenne group may have contributed to the development of more social and psychological resources for more creative solutions to life challenges, and may also have contributed to more stable and satisfying relationships and a happier life.

Issues in the Study of Affect

Before considering more global measures of happiness, we should note two issues concerning the relationship between positive and negative affect. The first issue concerns the controversy among researchers regarding the independence of positive and negative affect. The question is, are positive and negative feelings opposite ends of a single dimension (i.e., are they negatively correlated)? If so, this would mean that the presence of positive emotion indicates the absence of negative emotion and *vice versa*. Or, are negative and positive emotions two separate dimensions with different causes and effects (moderate negative correlations)? If so, this would mean that people could experience both positive and negative emotions at the same time. There are arguments and research findings that support both the unidimensional and the bidimensional view (see Argyle, 2001; Diener & Emmons, 1984; Keyes & Magyar-Moe, 2003; Lucas et al., 2003; Watson & Tellegen, 1985). Several recent theories have attempted to resolve this issue (e.g., Keyes & Ryff, 2000; Zautra, Potter, & Reich, 1997). Moderate negative correlations found in research ($r = -0.4$ to -0.5) suggest that positive and negative emotions are somewhat independent, but the issue is still being debated (Lucas et al., 2003).

Lucas and his colleagues note that part of the issue has to do with how emotions are measured, and in particular, the time frame that is used (Lucas et al., 2003). To illustrate, let's say you are asked how you are feeling right now, and you say, "happy and relaxed." The odds would be low that you would also say you are feeling "depressed and uptight." In the short term, positive and negative emotions are likely to show a strong inverse relationship, supporting a unidimensional view (Diener & Larsen, 1984). On the other hand, if you were asked to report on your emotions over the past month, odds are that you would have experienced both positive and negative emotions. A longer-term assessment would likely show more independence in the experience of positive and negative feelings, supporting a more bidimensional view. Until the controversy is resolved, Diener (2000) recommends that both positive and negative affect be measured so that the contribution of each emotion to SWB can be evaluated.

A second and related issue concerns how much the intensity, and how much the frequency of emotional experiences contribute to SWB. Diener and his colleagues (Diener, Sandvik, & Pavot, 1991; Schimmack & Diener, 1997) have found that the frequency of emotions is more important than their intensity. Happiness is not built so much on intense feelings of happiness or joy, but rather on milder positive emotions that are experienced most of the time. That is, happy people are those who experience positive emotions relatively frequently and negative emotions relatively infrequently. This is true even if the positive emotions are mild rather than intense. Diener and colleagues (1991) found that intense positive emotions are very rare, even for the happiest people. People with high SWB report frequent experiences of mild to moderate positive emotions and infrequent negative emotions.

Global Measures of Happiness

Some researchers use more global "life-as-a-whole" measures that assess a person's overall happiness–unhappiness instead of separate measures for positive and negative affect. For example, the Subjective Happiness Scale (SHS) measures the extent to which an individual sees himself or herself as a happy or unhappy person (Lyubomirsky & Lepper, 1999). If you wish to complete this measure, circle the number on the 7-point scale above each of the four questions, that you feel best describes you.

---

1. In general, I consider myself:

1	2	3	4	5	6	7

not a very   *a very*
happy person   *happy person*

2. Compared to most of my peers, I consider myself:

1	2	3	4	5	6	7

less   *more*
happy   *happy*

3. Some people are generally very happy. They enjoy life regardless of what is going on, getting the most out of everything. To what extent does this characterization describe you?

1	2	3	4	5	6	7

not at   *a great*
all   *deal*

4. Some people are generally not very happy. Although they are not depressed, they never seem as happy as they might be. To what extent does this characterization describe you?

1	2	3	4	5	6	7

not at   *a great*
all   *deal*

To evaluate your ratings, you first need to reverse code your response to question number four. In other words, if your rating for question four was a 1, replace the 1 with a 7. If your rating was a 2, replace it with a 6. A rating of 3 is replaced with a 5; a rating of 4 remains a 4; a rating of 5 is replaced with a 2; and a rating of 1 is replaced with a 7. Now, add up your ratings for all four questions and divide by 4. Your composite score can range from 1 to 7. A rating of less than 4 indicates some degree of unhappiness, ranging from very unhappy (scores of 1 and 2) to somewhat unhappy (scores of 3 and 4). A rating of 4 or greater indicates some degree of happiness, ranging from somewhat happy (scores of 4 and 5) to very happy (scores of 6 and 7). The SHS measures people's global assessment of how happy or unhappy they are. Despite the global nature of the SHS, individuals' responses to the scale are strongly related to their scores on more complex and detailed measures of positive and negative affect (Lyubomirsky, 2001). An individual's judgment about whether he or she is a happy or unhappy person would seem to be a good summary and a useful, brief measure of positive and negative affect.

Reliability and Validity of SWB Measures

A substantial amount of research shows that self-report measures of the various components of SWB have good psychometric properties (see Argyle, 2001; Diener & Lucas, 1999; Diener et al., 2004; Lucas et al., 1996, 2003, for reviews). Measures of SWB are internally reliable and coherent, stable over time, and validated by behavioral measures and the reports of others. Internal reliability assesses the coherence and consistency of responses to a particular measure. If responses to items on the scale are highly correlated with one another it suggests that the scale is measuring a coherent, single variable. The internal reliabilities of life satisfaction scales and measures of positive and negative affect are quite high (correlation coefficients [rs] of 0.84 or so) (Argyle, 2001; Diener, 1993; Pavot & Diener, 1993).

Measures of SWB also show reasonably high stability over time. Reviews of research show life satisfaction scores to be moderately stable over time periods of 4 years (rs at approximately 0.58) and still somewhat stable at 10 and 15 years (rs near 0.3) (Argyle, 2001; Diener et al., 2004). Measures of positive and negative affect also show moderate stability (rs of 0.3 to 0.5) over periods of 6 to 7 years (Costa & McCrae, 1988; Watson & Walker, 1996). Further

evidence for stability can be seen in studies that examined SWB across different life situations. Diener and Larsen (1984) asked participants to record measures of SWB at multiple times during the day for a number of days. They found high correlations between life satisfaction and positive/negative affect across such diverse situations as work and recreation, being alone or in a social setting, and being in a familiar or new environment. Taken together, these studies suggest that people's overall evaluations of their lives are fairly stable and enduring across time and situations.

We should note that SWB measures are also sensitive to significant life events and changes. That is, within a general pattern of stability, life changes can increase or decrease SWB, at least in the short term. Research has shown that positive or negative changes in our lives can affect our level of happiness (e.g., Headey & Wearing, 1991). A good day at work, an enjoyable activity with friends, a new romance, or praise from others for our accomplishments can all increase our feelings of happiness and satisfaction, just as a bad day at work, conflict with friends, a failed romance, or criticism from others can make us unhappy and dissatisfied. However, research shows that most of these effects are short-lived (e.g., Brickman, Coates, & Janoff-Bulman, 1978; Eid & Diener, 1999). Within a day, a week, or a month we are back to our more typical level of happiness. Even the effects of major life events, like being fired from your job, have been found to decrease SWB for only a period of several months (Suh, Diener, & Fujita, 1996). Exceptions to these short-term effects include loss of a spouse and marriage. Widowhood produces longer-term decreases in SWB, while marriage produces longer-term increases in SWB (Winter, Lawton, Casten, & Sando, 1999).

If people say they are happy on measures of SWB, do they also behave in ways that confirm their self-reported happiness, and do others see them as happy? This question addresses the validity of a test. Is it measuring what it claims to be measuring? A number of studies support the validity of SWB measures. Individual self-reported happiness has been confirmed via assessments by peers (Watson & Clark, 1991), family members and friends (Sandvik, Diener, & Seidlitz, 1993), and spouses (Costa & McCrae, 1988). When asked to recall positive and negative life events, happy people recall more positive events than unhappy people (Seidlitz, Wyer, & Diener, 1997). A review of differences between happy and unhappy people also supports the validity of SWB measures (Lyubomirsky, 2001). People with high SWB are more likely to perceive life in positive ways, expect a positive future, and express confidence in their abilities and skills. People with lower SWB are more focused on negative life events and show more self-absorbed rumination about themselves and their problems.

Experience Sampling Method

Despite evidence supporting their reliability and validity, global self-report measures of SWB are not free of potential biases. The most important sources of bias are those that may be introduced by distortions in memory and the effects of temporary mood. Suppose you were asked the following question: "Taking all things together how happy are you these days?" What would be the basis for your answer? Ideally, you would recall and reflect on the many significant events in your life (both positive and negative), and then make a reasoned judgment about what they all add up to in terms of your overall level of happiness. But what if you recalled only good experiences, or only bad experiences, or only your most recent experiences? What if your current mood affected your judgment of overall happiness? Using only one kind of remembered experience, or just your current mood as the basis for your judgment, might bias and distort your rated level of happiness. Studies show that this sort of bias can, in fact, occur. Schwarz and Strack (1999) have shown that such things as finding a small amount of money, hearing that your country's soccer team won the championship, being in a pleasant room, or being interviewed on a sunny day can increase people's self-reports of general life satisfaction. Conversely, hearing that your team lost, spending time in a noisy, overheated, and dirty laboratory, or being interviewed on a rainy day can decrease reports of satisfaction.

Work by Kahneman and his colleagues suggests that people may summarize and remember emotional experiences in complex and counterintuitive ways (see Kahneman, 1999, for a review). Common sense would indicate that the longer an emotional episode lasts, the more effect it should have on how we evaluate it. People who endure a long and uncomfortable medical procedure, for example, should rate it as more negative than people who go through the same procedure, but of

shorter duration. However, research with people undergoing a colonoscopy revealed that retrospective evaluations of pain and discomfort were not related to the duration of the procedure and were not a simple function of moment-to-moment ratings of pain during the procedure (Redelmeir & Kahneman, 1996). When people evaluated the experience as a whole, their responses followed what Kahneman calls the "**peak-end rule.**" Global judgments were predicted by the peak of emotional intensity during the experience (in this case, pain), and by the ending emotional intensity. The duration of the experience did not affect overall - evaluations. The peak-end rule has been confirmed with a variety of emotional episodes (Fredrickson & Kahneman, 1993; Kahneman, Fredrickson, Schreiber, & Redelmeir, 1993). The peak-end rule accurately predicted the basis of evaluations of an unpleasant film showing an amputation, immersing one hand in ice water, and exposure to aversive sounds of varying intensity and duration. In each of these studies, participants gave moment-to-moment intensity ratings for the emotions they were feeling, and an overall global judgment after the experience. Consistent with the peak-end rule, global ratings are strongly related to the average between the peak of the moment-to-moment intensity ratings and the ending intensity ratings. Global ratings are much less related to a simple average of all the moment-to-moment ratings of intensity.

The peak-end rule suggests that people's evaluations of emotionally significant events are heavily influenced by intensity and how the experience ends, and less influenced by how long the experience lasts. People selectively focus on certain features of an emotional episode to represent and judge the entire experience. Kahneman believes that only by examining moment-to-moment feelings can we come to understand the basis of people's summary evaluations. Global summary measures do not tell us what aspects of the experience are most important or how these aspects are combined.

The potential for biases in self-report measures has led some researchers to argue that moment-to-moment measures of experience are both more accurate and more revealing of the factors and processes that underlie SWB. **Experience sampling methods** (ESM) encompass a variety of measures that provide a "day-in-the-life" view of emotions and events in people's lives (Larsen &

Fredrickson, 1999; Stone, Shiffman, & DeVries, 1999). Measures of what people are doing and how they are feeling may be taken in real time as they occur, or they may be taken retrospectively, shortly after events occur within the sampled time frame (e.g., keeping a daily diary). Real-time measures provide a picture of the specific events and emotions that people experience in their daily lives. Because responses are taken while or shortly after events actually happen, real-time measures are less susceptible to the distortions that may occur in delayed evaluations that rely on memory of the events.

Real-time studies might use a watch alarm, pager, or palm computer to signal people at random or predetermined times during the day. At the signal, participants take a few moments to fill out various measures of what they are doing and how they are feeling. For example, research reviewed by Stone and colleagues (1999) examined the relationship of momentary measures of mood taken throughout the day, to participants' end-of-day mood summaries. The review indicated that people's overall judgment of how their day has gone is primarily determined by how the day ends. Events occurring earlier in the day seem to be ignored in people's daily summaries. One problem with real-time measures is that they can be burdensome for research participants because they require people to stop what they are doing and fill out scales and inventories. Such disruption and investment of time might be particularly bothersome in the work setting.

Retrospective ESM measures ask people to reconstruct and review their activities and feelings related to life events after they have occurred. While a variety of methods have been developed (see Larson & Fredrickson, 1999, for a review), daily diary methods are most common because they are easiest to use. In these studies, people fill out a variety of measures at the end of each day for a number of days. These measures ask about significant events and emotional reactions that occurred during each day. Results can be summarized according to time period (e.g., days of the week) or significant events (e.g., personal relationships). Studies show, for example, that people's moods tend to fluctuate predictably over days of the week (e.g., Egloff, Tausch, Kohlmann, & Krohne, 1995; Larsen & Kasimatis, 1990). As you might expect, moods are generally more positive on the weekends than during weekdays—perhaps because on weekends people have greater freedom in choosing what they want to do and they participate in more enjoyable activities and pleasant social interactions than on weekdays (Reis, Sheldon, Gable, Roscoe, & Ryan, 2000).

Focus on Method: How Do We Spend Our Time?

THE DAY RECONSTRUCTION METHOD   Kahneman and colleagues (Kahneman, Krueger, Schkade, Schwarz, & Stone, 2004) have recently tested a new measure called the **day reconstruction method** (DRM), which promises to combine the accuracy of real-time measures with the efficiency of daily diaries. In the DRM, people first construct a diary of the *previous* day's events. Participants are asked to think of their day as a sequence of episodes or scenes in a film. Separate recording pages are provided for morning, afternoon, and evening episodes. To help them remember the day's events, people are encouraged to give each episode a short name, such as driving to work, shopping, or relaxing. After identifying daily episodes, study participants then respond to a set of structured questions. For each episode, participants are asked to indicate what they were doing (e.g., commuting, working, watching TV, or socializing), where they were (e.g., at home, at work), and for episodes involving other people, with whom they interacted (e.g., boss, friend, children, or spouse). Participants then rate a number of positive and negative emotions to indicate how they felt during each episode. These include emotions such as feeling relaxed, happy, tired, frustrated, anxious, impatient, and competent. The researchers also ask for demographic and work-or health-related information and for more global ratings of life satisfaction and mood.

To test this new method, Kahneman and his colleagues studied a group of 909 employed women living in Texas. Their average age was 38 years and their average household income was $54,700. The women represented a mix of 49% white, 24% African American, and 22% Hispanic. Most were married and had young children. Following the day reconstruction method, all participants completed the questionnaire describing their experiences and feelings for the previous day. Most of the episodes that people identified lasted from 15 minutes to 2 hours, with an average episode length of 61 minutes. The average number of episodes per day was 14. Each episode was rank-ordered according to the degree of positive and negative affect. Positive affect was based on the average ratings for feelings of happiness, relaxation, and enjoyment. Negative affect was reflected by average ratings for feelings such as: frustrated, annoyed, depressed, hassled, put down, angry, and worried. Overall, the intensity and frequency of positive affect was much higher than the intensity and frequency of negative affect. Negative affect was quite rare and of low intensity, while some positive affect was present in nearly every episode during the day.

When the day's activities were ranked according to the degree of positive affect, both some predictable and some surprising patterns emerged. As you might expect, people felt most positive when they were involved in intimate relationships with their spouses, family members, and friends. Socializing was high on the "enjoying myself" list, as were relaxing, eating, prayer, and meditation activities. Somewhat surprisingly, watching TV was rated more positively than shopping or taking a nap. Even more surprising, of 16 activities rated for positive and negative affect, "taking care of my children" was fifth from the bottom. Watching TV, preparing a meal, shopping, and exercising were all rated as more positive than childcare. Only housework, working, commuting, and responding to e-mail on the computer were rated lower than childcare. The lower enjoyment related to taking care of kids highlights the difference between global-belief-based measures of well-being and the "in-the-trenches" view captured by the DRM. Surveys reviewed by Kahneman and colleagues show that people typically *say* that they enjoy their children and find deep satisfaction in raising them. Such expressions of satisfaction are undoubtedly true in the general sense and also reflect the socially desirable thing to say. However, on any given day, kids can be a pain. Our overall judgment of taking care of children does not necessarily reflect our specific day-to-day experiences.

In addition to providing an interesting picture of a "day-in-the-life" of working women, the results of this study showed a high degree of similarity to findings from studies using moment-to-moment experience sampling methods. The DRM seems to produce accurate recall of daily events, as evidenced by the fact that the results parallel findings from ESM studies, in which events are evaluated as they occur. The DRM also reduces the burdens of disruption and time commitment imposed on research participants with the ESM approach.

Experience Sampling versus Global Measures of Subjective Well-Being

We noted earlier that global self-report measures of SWB have good psychometric properties. The three components of SWB (life satisfaction, positive affect, and negative affect) are interrelated, but make independent contributions to overall well-being. Measures of each component are internally coherent, show consistency over time, and are appropriately sensitive to life changes. However, global measures that require people to recall and integrate information may be susceptible to memory errors and the influence of current mood. Experience sampling and day reconstruction methods both provide "as it happens" pictures of well-being that are less influenced by memory. What is the relationship between the two kinds of measures? Is one better than the other, or do they represent complementary pictures of SWB?

We do not have definitive answers to these questions because experience sampling methods are so new to well-being research. Initially, researchers saw the relationship between ESM and global self-reports as an issue of validation. In other words, they wondered whether measures of well-being based on ESM would correlate with global measures. If so, this would increase our confidence that global measures are valid summaries of people's actual experiences and that they are not distorted by errors or lapses in memory. The results here are mixed. Some studies show moderate relationships between global and ESM measures (e.g., Kahneman, et al., 2004; Sandvik et al., 1993), while others show much weaker relationships (e.g., Stone et al., 1999; Thomas & Diener, 1990). At this point, it seems appropriate to think of ESM and global measures as related, but not identical, ways to assess SWB. Each measure may tap somewhat different phenomena and different aspects of a person's life and psychological makeup. Part of the difference involves how sensitive each measure is to the effects of traits and states on SWB.

Experience sampling methods are particularly sensitive to momentary alterations in mood resulting from events that occur during the time period studied (e.g., during a day). Experience sampling effectively captures how life events affect our emotional state at a particular moment and across a particular period of time. However, we would also expect that personal qualities (traits) would affect a person's emotional reactions to daily events. For example, happy people interpret life events (including negative ones) in more positive ways than unhappy people (Lyubomirsky, 2001). Experience sampling methods, while maximally sensitive to the effects of events (states) on SWB, would also show the effects of an individual's personality (traits) in between-person comparisons.

A similar, but opposite argument can be made for global self-report measures of SWB. **Global measures** are heavily influenced by genetic temperament and personality traits like extraversion, neuroticism, self-esteem, and optimism (see Diener & Lucas, 1999; Diener et al., 1999; Myers, 1992; Myers & Diener, 1995, for reviews). One reason global measures show long-term stability is that they reflect stable and enduring personality characteristics. Research has shown adult personality to be very stable over time (Costa & McCrae, 1988). Global measures that ask people to make overall summary judgments of well-being are likely to be highly sensitive to the makeup of a person's personality (traits), and somewhat less sensitive to their current situation (state). Our current mood, particularly if intense, can certainly affect our assessment of overall well-being. However, if our current emotional state were the primary determinant of SWB, then studies would not consistently find that a person's level of well-being is quite stable over time.

One of the tasks for future research is to explore the relationship between, and the differing information that may be provided by, global and ESM measures. These and other measurement issues are central concerns within positive psychology. Based on a literature search of psychology journals, Diener and Seligman (2004) found that most researchers measure only one aspect of SWB and too often rely on single-item measures. One researcher may measure only life satisfaction, while another may measure only positive affect, but both discuss their findings in terms of SWB and happiness. We noted in an earlier discussion that the three components of SWB are interrelated, thus providing a degree of comparability among studies that measured different SWB components. However, Diener and Seligman urge researchers to pursue more comprehensive measures

and models of SWB in order to advance and expand our understanding of the complexities and multiple aspects of human happiness.

SELF-REALIZATION: THE EUDAIMONIC BASIS OF HAPPINESS

Conceptions of SWB, like positive psychology as a whole, are works in progress. Though widely confirmed in research, the three-component view of SWB has been expanded by some psychologists to include personal qualities and life activities believed to be the psychological underpinnings of happiness. Seligman (2002a, 2002b) and Diener and Seligman (2004) have argued for a broader conception of well-being that would include measures of active engagement in absorbing activities or "flow experiences" (Csikszentmihalyi, 1997) and measures of meaning in life that concern purposes that transcend the self, such as religion. These expanded conceptions express the eudaimonic view by defining happiness in terms of striving for self-realization. As explained earlier, happiness, from the eudaimonic perspective, results from the development and expression of our inner potentials (daimon) that include our talents, personalities, and values. Following the hedonic view, measures of SWB ask people *if* they are happy and satisfied with their lives. Eudaimonic measures of happiness also ask *why* people are happy.

Psychological Well-Being and Positive Functioning

In an article titled, "Happiness is everything, or is it? Explorations on the meaning of psychological well-being," Carol Ryff (1989) argued that the three-component model of SWB fails to describe the features of a person's life that provide the basis and meaning of well-being. Well-being, in Ryff's view, is more than happiness with life. Well-being should be a source of resilience in the face of adversity and should reflect positive functioning, personal strengths, and mental health. Consider the following question: Are happy people also mentally healthy people? At first glance the answer would seem to be yes. It is hard to imagine people suffering from depression or anxiety disorders also being happy. However, people with delusional belief systems or people who derive pleasure from hurting others might be happy and, at the same time, mentally ill; and in the latter case, considered so partly *because* of the pleasure they receive from hurting others. Eudaimonic conceptions of happiness include consideration of the difference between healthy and unhealthy happiness. What is missing from the three-part model of SWB is a conceptualization and assessment of positive functioning. Ryff (1989) argues that well-being and happiness are based on human strengths, personal striving, and growth.

Drawing on theories of positive mental health within personality and clinical psychology, Ryff and her colleagues have developed a model they call "**psychological well-being**" (PWB), based on descriptions of positive psychological and social functioning (Keyes, 1998; Keyes et al., 2002; Ryff & Keyes, 1995; Ryff & Singer, 1998). Originally used to describe positive functioning across the life span, this conceptualization has been extended to describe positive mental health (Keyes, 1998, 2003; Keyes & Lopez, 2002; Keyes & Magyar-Moe, 2003). The goal of these researchers was to formulate and validate a description of SWB that would delineate positive aspects of mental health. That is, just as mental illness is defined in terms of symptoms that express underlying pathology, these researchers asked, "What markers express underlying mental *health* and *well-being?*" As expanded by Keyes and colleagues, this model incorporates both hedonic and eudaimonic views of happiness.

At a general level, well-being is conceived, from this perspective, as involving the two broad dimensions of emotional well-being and positive functioning (Keyes & Magyar-Moe, 2003). Emotional well-being is defined by the three-component view of SWB. It includes life satisfaction and positive and negative affect. A psychological dimension and a social dimension define positive functioning. All together, well-being is described as a global combination of emotional well-being, psychological well-being, and social well-being. This comprehensive model is meant to serve as a more complete description of SWB. The major elements of the model are described below (adapted from Keyes, 2003, Table 13.1, p. 299, and Keyes & Magyar-Moe, 2003, Table 26.2, pp. 417–418). Each element is described as a marker of positive mental health and well-being. Example items from assessment scales developed to measure each symptom are also given. A minus sign after an item indicates it is reversed scored.

EMOTIONAL WELL-BEING

Positive Affect—experience of positive emotions like joy and happiness.

> *During the last 30 days, how much of the time did you feel cheerful; in good spirits; extremely happy; calm and peaceful; satisfied and full of life?*

Negative Affect—absence of emotions suggesting life is unpleasant.

> *During the last 30 days, how much of the time did you feel so sad nothing could cheer you up; nervous; restless or fidgety; hopeless; that everything was an effort; worthless?*

Life Satisfaction—sense of contentment and satisfaction with life.

> *During the last 30 days, how much of the time did you feel satisfied; full of life? Over all these days, how satisfied are you with your life?*

Happiness—having a general feeling and experience of contentment and joy.

> *Overall these days, how happy are you with your life?*

> *How frequently have you felt (joy, pleasure, or happiness) in the past week, month, or year?*

PSYCHOLOGICAL WELL-BEING

Self-Acceptance—positive attitude toward oneself; accepting of varied aspects of self; feel positive about past life.

> *In many ways I feel disappointed about my achievements in life. (-)*

Personal Growth—feelings of continued development and effectiveness; open to new experiences and challenges.

> *I think it is important to have new experiences that challenge how I think about myself and the world.*

Purpose in Life—possessing goals and beliefs that give direction to life; feeling life has meaning and purpose.

> *I live life one day at a time and don't really think about the future. (-)*

Environmental Mastery—feel competent and able to manage complex environment; able to create personally suitable living situation.

> *The demands of everyday life often get me down. (-)*

Autonomy—feel comfortable with self-direction; possess internal standards; resist negative social pressures from others.

> *I have confidence in my own opinions, even if they are different from the way most other people think.*

Positive Relations with Others—warm, satisfying, and trusting relationships with others; capable of empathy and intimacy.

> *Maintaining close relationships has been difficult and frustrating for me. (-)*

SOCIAL WELL-BEING

Social Acceptance—holds positive attitudes toward others, while understanding their complexities.

> *People who do a favor expect nothing in return.*

Social Actualization—cares about and believes that people have potential; society can evolve in a positive direction.

> *The world is becoming a better place for everyone.*

Social Contribution—feeling that one's life is useful to society and valued by others.

> *I have something valuable to give to the world.*

Social Coherence—has interest in society and believes it is intelligible and somewhat logical, predictable, and meaningful.

> *I cannot make sense of what's going on in the world. (-)*

Social Integration—feels sense of belonging to a community; feels comfort and support from community.

> *I don't feel I belong to anything I'd call a community. (-)*

Despite the complexity of this model (15 total aspects of well-being) and the difficult task of developing assessment tools for each of the various elements, a number of large-scale studies provide validation (see Keyes, 2002, 2003; Keyes & Lopez, 2002; Keyes & Magyar-Moe, 2003; Keyes et al., 2002; Ryff & Keyes, 1995, for reviews). Measures of emotional well-being, psychological well-being, and social well-being show good internal reliability and validity. Research shows that all three of the components are related, but each makes a separate contribution to SWB. Studies also show that these measures of well-being are negatively correlated with symptoms of mental illness. For example, measures of depression correlated in the -0.4 range with emotional well-being, around -0.5 with psychological well-being, and -0.3 with social well-being. These correlations suggest that this expanded mode of SWB is particularly relevant for examining the relationship between well-being and mental health.

Need Fulfillment and Self-Determination Theory

Self-determination theory offers another conception of well-being that embraces a eudaimonic view of happiness (Ryan & Deci, 2000, 2001). **Self-determination theory** (SDT) states that well-being and happiness result from the fulfillment of three basic psychological needs: autonomy, competence, and relatedness. Autonomy needs are fulfilled when activities are freely chosen rather than imposed by others, and are consistent with the individual's self-concept. Competence needs are satisfied when our efforts bring about desired outcomes that make us more confident in our abilities. Needs for relatedness are fulfilled by close and positive connections to others. Social interactions that produce feelings of closeness and support contribute to satisfaction of this need. Research by Ryan, Deci, and their colleagues has confirmed the relationship between need satisfaction and well-being (see Ryan & Deci, 2000, 2001, for reviews).

Focus on Research: What Makes a "Good" Day?

What makes a "good" day and what makes for a "bad" day? A day we enjoy versus a day we don't? As Reis and his colleagues note, the ingredients of a bad day are fairly well established (Reis et al., 2000). Negative life events (both big and small) that produce stress and conflict have consistently been shown to diminish our feelings of well-being, happiness, and enjoyment. The list of negative events would include failure at work or school, arguments and conflicts with others, financial problems, illness, and accidents—experiences that frustrate, disappoint, or cause anger and sadness. But what about a good day? Is a good day just the absence of negative events—no failure, disappointment, or conflict? If you get the flu you may be miserable, but if you are healthy, does that make you happy? Research discussed earlier in this chapter has shown that positive and negative emotions are somewhat independent, with each emotion making a separate contribution to happiness and well-being. This independence may result from the fact that the causes of negative and positive emotions are different. That is, a "good" day may involve different activities and experiences than those that make for a bad day. A study by Reis and colleagues titled, "Daily Well-Being: The Role of Autonomy, Competence, and Relatedness," addressed the question of the psychological meaning of a "good" day. The researchers asked three questions: What kinds of activities and events make our day enjoyable? What makes an activity enjoyable? And third, how much of our enjoyment during the day depends on our personal characteristics, and how much depends on the events we encounter?

The answers to these questions were examined in terms of the three needs described by self-determination theory (SDT). The theory states that needs for autonomy, competence, and relatedness are shared by all humans. These needs are described as the "essential nutrients" from which people grow (Ryan & Deci, 2000). The need for autonomy involves our need for freely chosen actions that express our values, talents, and personalities. Autonomous people follow their inner goals and interests. Inner goals guide and direct their lives, and choices are made in terms of this inner direction rather than outer rewards. For example, an autonomous person would not choose a career or job based primarily on how much money she could make. The intrinsic satisfaction and meaningfulness provided by the work would be more important. Competence is the need for effective action in meeting life's

challenges. A sense of competence involves feelings of confidence that we can solve problems, achieve our goals, master the demands of life, and be successful in new endeavors. The third need, for relatedness, involves feelings of intimacy and connection to other people. People who are skilled in the development and maintenance of close relationships are most likely to have this need fulfilled.

According to SDT, these three needs together form the foundation of well-being and happiness. Each need can be thought of both as a trait and as a state. A trait refers to an enduring personal disposition. Some people characteristically show autonomy in their actions and choices, feel confident in their abilities and pursuit of new challenges, and have rewarding and intimate relationships with others. For these individuals, high levels of well-being and happiness result from qualities they possess that result in fulfillment of the three needs. A state, in contrast, refers to the particular situation we are in at the moment. The fulfillment of the three needs can vary from day to day and from situation to situation. Activities that meet the need for autonomy are those that are freely chosen, personally rewarding, and expressive of our interests and talents. Competence needs are fulfilled by successfully completing a challenging task, solving a difficult problem, or expressing our talents and abilities. When competence needs are met, we feel confident about our abilities and take pride in our personal accomplishments. Relatedness needs are fulfilled and expressed when we feel close to others, have meaningful conversations, and enjoy the company of our romantic partner, our family members, and our friends.

In a study of 76 college students, Reis, Sheldon, and colleagues (2000) measured autonomy, competence, and relatedness both as states and as traits. Self-determination theory predicted that both trait and state measures would be related to a person's daily level of well-being and happiness. That is, traits (in the form of personal qualities indicating high levels of autonomy, competence, and relatedness) and states (in the form of need-fulfilling daily activities) would both be related to higher degrees of well-being on a given day. Reis and colleagues' research first assessed the three needs as traits by asking their college student participants how often they engaged in freely chosen and personally meaningful activities (autonomy), how confident they typically felt when facing new tasks and challenges (competence), and about the quality of their attachments to others (relatedness). In a version of the ESM, state measures were based on a daily diary that was kept for 14 days. At the end of each day, before going to bed, students completed measures of well-being for that day. These included the extent of positive and negative emotion they experienced during the day, their level of energy, and physical symptoms of illness (e.g., symptoms of a cold). Then they were asked to list the three activities (excluding sleep) that took up the most time during the day. Each activity was rated according to why it was done. Reasons suggesting autonomous actions were those for which the activity was freely chosen, intrinsically interesting, and involved expression of personal identity and values. Non-autonomous activities resulted from the demands of an external situation or were based on the desire to avoid guilt and anxiety. Participants also rated each of the three activities to indicate to how competent it made them feel.

Daily relatedness needs were assessed in a similar way. The three social interactions that took up the most time during the day were listed. Each of the three social interactions was rated according to how close and connected it made the student feel toward others and the extent to which the interaction fulfilled or did not fulfill relatedness needs. Having fun with others, and feeling understood and appreciated indicated need fulfillment. Non-fulfillment or need frustration was suggested by social interactions that caused feelings of insecurity, self-consciousness, hostility, or anger.

Consistent with self-determination theory, Reis and colleagues found that a "good day" was related to the fulfillment of needs for autonomy, competence, and relatedness. Trait measures of need fulfillment were positively correlated with well-being and positive mood during the day. On average, students who scored higher in autonomy, competence, and relatedness also showed higher levels of well-being and happiness across the 14 days of the study. People who have personal qualities that contribute to need fulfillment tend to enjoy more well-being and more positive moods on a day-to-day basis.

Figure 2.3 shows the pattern of daily ratings for positive and negative emotional experiences, competence, relatedness, and autonomy across the 7 days of the week. For any given day, well-being was higher and students enjoyed themselves more when the day's activities contributed to feeling autonomous, competent, and connected to others. The more these three needs were positively engaged by activities during the day, the higher their ratings of well-being and positive mood. Of the three needs, relatedness had the most significant impact on daily well-being. Some of the "best" days occurred when social interactions involved discussion of meaningful matters and led to feelings of being understood and appreciated.

Interestingly, the degree to which needs were fulfilled was also significantly related to the days of the week. As you might guess, Monday produced the lowest ratings of positive emotion. Interestingly, negative emotion and feelings of competence were fairly stable across the seven days of the week. Bad moods and feelings of confidence were dependent on activities that did not vary systematically with day of the week. As you might also have guessed, Friday, Saturday, and Sunday were rated the highest with regard to positive emotion, relatedness, and autonomy. Our moods tend to be more positive during weekends because we can more readily enjoy desirable activities. However, this research suggests that a good day, even on the weekend, involves more than just having fun. Needs for autonomy and relatedness are more likely to be satisfied on the weekends. Monday through Friday we often have to follow the expectations, assignments, and demands of others. On the weekends we are more free to choose what we want to do, resulting in a greater sense of self-direction and expression that satisfies our need for autonomy. In addition, weekends often involve getting together with friends and family members. These interactions are enjoyable, but they also fulfill our desire for intimacy and meaningful connections with others. From the perspective of SDT, more "good days" occur during weekends because we are more likely to fulfill needs that increase our sense of well-being and happiness. Part of the nature of a "fun" activity is its ability to fulfill important psychological needs.

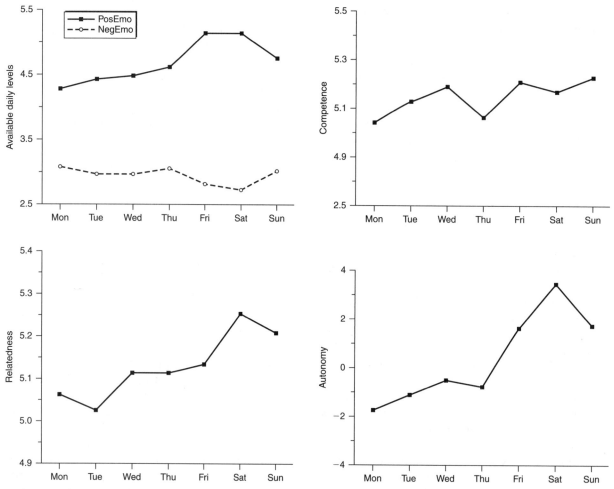

FIGURE 2.3 Positive and Negative Emotions, Competence, Relatedness, and Autonomy Ratings Across Days of the Week
Source: Reis, H. T., Sheldon, K. M., Gable, S. L., Roscoe, J., & Ryan, R. M. (2000). Daily well-being: The role of autonomy, competence, and relatedness. *Personality and Social Psychology Bulletin, 26,* 419–435. Copyright American Psychological Association. Reprinted with permission.

COMPARING HEDONIC AND EUDAIMONIC VIEWS OF HAPPINESS

We have examined a number of measures and two major models of happiness. At this early point in the development of positive psychology, it is too soon to tell which measures and models are the most useful, accurate, or revealing of processes and factors that underlie happiness. All would agree that the refinement of measures and the formulation of more comprehensive theories are essential to the growth and development of positive psychology. Here, we will note similarities and differences between the hedonic and eudaimonic views of happiness. Most of the research within positive psychology can be organized around one, or some combination, of these two conceptions of well-being and happiness.

Definition and Causes of Happiness and Well-Being

The hedonic view, expressed in the model and measures of SWB, defines happiness as an individual's global assessment of positive/negative emotion and satisfaction with life. People who experience an abundance of positive emotions and few negative emotions, and who also feel satisfied with their lives are defined as happy, or high in SWB. Subjective well-being does *not* specify or measure *why* a person is happy or unhappy. Proponents of the hedonic view regard the bases for happiness as an empirical question to be answered by research. That is, they hold that, by comparing the traits and behaviors of people high in SWB to those low in SWB, the psychological meanings and foundations of happiness will emerge through continued investigation. For example, if we find that happy people are optimistic, have good relationships, and are engaged in meaningful work, this will tell us some of the reasons why people are happy. Subjective well-being investigators have adopted a "research-driven" approach to happiness and well-being. Get the research facts first; then theory can be created later. Diener and his colleagues (Diener, Sapyta, & Suh, 1998) argue that this approach has the advantage of not imposing on people a definition of well-being developed by psychologists. Subjective well-being allows people to judge for themselves whether they are happy and satisfied, on the basis of their *own* criteria. The nature of these criteria is the focus of many SWB studies and will hopefully lead to a theory that explains the psychological underpinnings of happiness and well-being.

The eudaimonic view, expressed in models and measures of self-realization and positive mental health, defines well-being as positive or optimal functioning and the fulfillment of basic needs and inner potentials. A happy person is one who has actualized, or is striving to actualize his or her human potential to be a fully functioning, competent, and psychologically healthy person. In contrast to the hedonic conception, eudaimonic models *do* describe the psychological and social traits, behaviors, and needs that are the bases of happiness and psychological health. Proponents of the eudaimonic view believe well-being and happiness involve more than emotional happiness and life satisfaction. Models of well-being and happiness should tell us about psychological *health* and *effective* functioning. Researchers taking the eudaimonic view are particularly interested in developing models of well-being that will describe positive functioning and positive mental health. Achieving this goal requires a delineation of characteristics that define a healthy, happy person—that is, we need a theory of well-being. Therefore, a good deal

of eudaimonic research is "theory-driven." Models and theories of well-being are developed and then evaluated empirically. The theory comes first and then it is checked to see if it holds up to the tests of research.

Complementarity and Interrelationship

Overall, we would emphasize a complementary rather than a conflicting relationship between the hedonic and eudaimonic views. Both perspectives seem to be reflected in what people regard as essential elements of a good life. King and Napa (1998) asked people to rate the importance of factors that might define the meaning of a good life. They found that factors related to both hedonic happiness and eudaimonic expressiveness were important. Research examining the relationships among various measures of well-being find these measures to be organized around broad aspects of both hedonic and eudaimonic well-being, such as happiness and personal growth (Compton et al., 1996), or happiness and personal expressiveness (Waterman, 1993), or happiness and meaningfulness (McGregor & Little, 1998).

Although conceptually distinct and separable in research, measures of hedonic and eudaimonic well-being show substantial correlations. This would seem to result from the fact that people who are happy and satisfied with their lives in a hedonic sense tend also to see their lives as meaningful in the eudaimonic sense of expressing their talents, strengths, deeply held values, and inner potentials. So, whether researchers assess hedonic happiness or eudaimonic happiness, both forms of happiness are reflected in the results. Taken together, the two perspectives provide a more complete picture of well-being and happiness than either one provides alone. For the future, we can anticipate an eventual rapprochement between the research-driven approach of those working from a hedonic view, and the theory-driven approach of those working from a eudaimonic orientation, such that the two will combine into a comprehensive picture of human happiness. Hedonic and eudaimonic views of well-being express two broad themes within positive psychology—one focused on personal happiness and life satisfaction and the other focused on personal meaning, growth, and positive functioning. These same two perspectives will emerge again in subsequent chapters of this text.

Chapter Summary Questions

1. From the perspective of positive psychology, what are the two major limitations in national statistics that answer the question, "How are we doing?"

2. a. Compare and contrast the hedonic and eudaimonic conceptions of happiness and describe an activity from your own experience that leads to hedonic happiness, and an activity that leads to eudaimonic happiness.

   b. Describe the major measures, findings, and conclusions of the study by Laura King and her colleagues concerning the relationship between positive affect and meaning.

3. What three components define SWB?

4. Harker and Keltner studied whether specific types of smiles shown in college yearbook photos were predictive of later life outcomes. What outcomes did they find were associated with the "Duchenne smile," and what might explain these results?

5. How does the time period studied help resolve the issue of the independence of positive and negative affect?

6. What pattern of intensity and frequency of positive and negative emotions describes a happy person?

7. How may memory and temporary mood distort or bias responses to self-report SWB measures?

8. Define and give an example of the peak-end rule.

9. What is the experience sampling method (ESM) and how does it reduce the distortions of memory and mood that may affect global SWB measures?

10. Briefly describe the day reconstruction method and three findings from the study conducted by Kahneman and his colleagues.

11. What are the relationships between global and ESM measures, and between trait and state influences on SWB?

12. What is missing from the three-component hedonic model of SWB, according to Carol Ryff?

13. Briefly describe the three major components of the eudaimonic model of well-being.

14. What three needs are essential for well-being according to self-determination theory? Describe each and give an example of an activity or an experience that would relate to fulfillment of each need.

15. What makes for a "good day" among college students, according to the study by Reis, Gable, and their colleagues?

16. How can the three needs described by self-determination theory be thought of as both traits and as states?

17. How do the hedonic and eudaimonic views of happiness differ as to their definitions and causes of happiness?

18. How are the hedonic and eudaimonic conceptions complementary and interrelated?

Key Terms

misery index *15*
hedonic happiness *17*
eudaimonic happiness *18*
subjective well-being *18*

global measures *29*
experience sampling
  method *26*
peak-end rule *26*

day reconstruction method *27*
psychological well-being *30*
self-determination theory *31*

Web Resources

Authentic Happiness

www.authentichappiness.sas.upenn.edu This is Martin Seligman's site at the University of Pennsylvania. This site offers the most complete set of positive psychology measures available online. You must log in, create a password, and provide demographic information to take the tests and have them scored for you. A profile of scores on all tests is computed and can be accessed at anytime. Measures include several positive–negative emotional inventories, life satisfaction and happiness questionnaires, and personality tests.

Diener, Subjective Well-being, and Happiness

www.psych.uiuc.edu/~ediener Web page for the happiness researcher Ed Diener, with links to articles and descriptions of subjective well-being studies.

Psychological Well-being

www.psychologymatters.org/wellbeing.html American Psychological Association site for information about psychological well-being.

Self-Determination Theory

psych.rochester.edu/SDT/publications/pub_well. html Web page covering research of Deci and Ryan at the University of Rochester focused on self-determination theory. This site highlights a prominent eudaimonic view of well-being.

Suggested Readings

Kahneman, D., Diener, E., & Schwarz, N. (Eds.). (1999). *Well-being: The foundations of hedonic psychology.* New York: Russell Sage Foundation.

Kahneman, D., Krueger, A. B., Schkade, D. A., Schwarz, N., & Stone, A. A. (2004). A survey method for characterizing daily life experience: The day reconstruction method. *Science, 306,* 1776–1780.

Keyes, C. L. M. (2007). Promoting and protecting mental health and flourishing: A complementary strategy for improving national mental health. *American Psychologist, 62,* 95–108.

Lopez, S. J., & Snyder, C. R. (Eds.). (2003). *Positive psychological assessment: A handbook of models and measures.* Washington, DC: American Psychological Association.

Myers, D. G. (1992). *The pursuit of happiness.* New York: Avon Books.

Ryan, R. M., & Deci, E. L. (2000). Self-determination theory and the facilitation of intrinsic motivation, social development, and well-being. *American Psychologist, 55,* 68–78.

Ryan, R. M., & Deci, E. L. (2001). On happiness and human potentials: A review of research on hedonic and eudaimonic well-being. *Annual Review of Psychology, 52,* 141–166.

Ryff, C. D. (1989). Happiness is everything, or is it? Explorations on the meaning of psychological well-being. *Journal of Personality and Social Psychology, 57,* 1069–1081.

Ryff, C. D., & Keyes, C. L. M. (1995). The structure of psychological well-being revisited. *Journal of Personality and Social Psychology, 57,* 1069–1081.

Ryff, C. D., & Singer, B. (1998). The contours of positive human health. *Psychological Inquiry, 9,* 1–28.

3

Positive Emotions and Well-Being

CHAPTER OUTLINE

Consistent with the idea that "the bad is stronger than the good" people pay more attention to negative emotional states such as anxiety, stress, and boredom than they do to positive states such as joy and contentment (Baumeister, Bratslavsky, Finkenauer, & Vohs, 2001). The differential attention given to bad feelings is reinforced by our awareness of conventional medical wisdom that informs us of the damaging effects of prolonged stress. The chronic experience of stress is not good for the mind or the body. Most hospitals have stress-reduction programs and most people have developed ways of reducing stress and other negative emotions. We exercise, read, spend time with friends, take in a movie, go shopping, pursue an enjoyable hobby, or take a vacation. Certainly we may do these things simply for their intrinsic enjoyment, but we are likely to consider their value primarily in terms of offsetting negative emotions—that is, as a kind of self-directed therapy. After a stressful week at work, it is easy to think of an enjoyable evening with friends over a few drinks as a stress-reliever that clears out the accumulated tension of the week. But if we had a great week at work, would we consider the same kind of evening as beneficial to our well-being or just enjoyable and fun?

Considerable research suggests that positive emotions are good for us all the time, and not just when we are distressed (Salovey, Rothman, Detweiler, & Steward, 2000). This is not meant to change the meaning of enjoyable activities by reducing them to their instrumental health value. It simply reflects what appears to be true. Positive emotions have physical and mental health-promoting effects beyond their ability to offset the potentially toxic effects of negative emotions. Many researchers studying the effects of social support on health have reached a similar conclusion. Most of us know that support from others is extremely helpful in times of crisis and tragedy, such as the death of a loved one. But it also seems true that quality relationships with friends and family enhance our overall well-being on an ongoing basis, and again, not just when we are distressed.

In this chapter, we will explore the many connections between positive emotions and well-being. As we saw in Chapter 2, positive emotions are a cornerstone of the hedonic, or subjective well-being (SWB) conception of happiness. Positive emotions also contribute to physical health, successful performance, and the psychological well-being described by the eudaimonic perspective. We end the chapter by considering several ways in which positive emotions may be actively cultivated.

WHAT ARE POSITIVE EMOTIONS?

Our evolutionary heritage and life learning have given us the capacity to experience a rich array of emotions. We can feel sad, happy, anxious, surprised, bored, exhilarated, scared, disgusted, disappointed, frustrated, and feel the bittersweet combination of both sadness and joy, when we move on to new ventures, but have to leave old friends behind. As we saw in Chapter 2, positive psychologists typically measure people's emotional experience in terms of both the positive and the negative affective dimensions. This two-dimensional summary and assessment follows from research suggesting that despite

their diversity, if we evaluate emotions by their psychological and physiological effects, then emotions come in two basic forms, namely positive and negative affect. **Positive affect** refers to emotions such as cheerfulness, joy, contentment, and happiness. **Negative affect** refers to emotions such as anger, fear, sadness, guilt, contempt, and disgust. Evidence for this conclusion comes from two primary sources.

First, analyses of people's self-reported emotional experiences show that positive and negative affect form a basic, underlying structure for people's emotional lives (e.g., Watson, 2002; Watson & Tellegen, 1985; Watson, Wiese, Vaidya, & Tellegen, 1999). Studies also show that differences in people's characteristic levels of positive and negative affective experiences are significantly related to measures of personality and well-being (details reviewed in Chapter 9). Secondly, physiological studies have found a discernable pattern of nervous system arousal, brain activity, hormonal, and neurotransmitter output that distinguishes positive from negative emotions, but no clear distinction between discrete positive or negative emotions (Barrett, 2006; Cacioppo, Berntson, Larsen, Poehlmann, & Ito, 2000; Larsen, Hemenover, Norris, & Cacioppo, 2003). That is, our bodies seem to be doing something different when we are in a positive emotional state versus when we are in a negative state; but physiologically speaking, it is hard to tell whether we are angry, scared, or anxious, or to tell whether someone is happy, joyful, or contented. For our purposes, the major benefit of these studies is their potential to identify the physiological mechanisms and the psychological functions of positive emotions. We begin our discussion of the potential value of positive emotions with Barbara Fredrickson's (2001) broaden-and-build-theory of positive emotions.

Focus on Theory: The Broaden-and-Build Theory of Positive Emotions

Barbara Fredrickson's (2001) broaden-and-build theory of positive emotions provides an overview of how positive emotions help build physical, psychological, and social resources. Her theory has received considerable attention from positive psychologists. This is because Fredrickson has provided one of the first theories describing the potential value of positive emotions. An understanding of negative emotions (such as fear and anger) has been worked out in relation to evolution and survival. The purpose and influence of negative emotions seems reasonably clear. However, up until Fredrickson's theory, positive emotions not only received little attention, but were not regarded as having much importance, aside from making us feel good. The **broaden-and-build theory** describes how positive emotions open up our thinking and actions to new possibilities, and how this expansion can help build physical, psychological, and social resources that promote well-being.

Two distinctions are important to the focus of Fredrickson's theory. The first is between mood and emotion. According to Fredrickson, mood is a more general concept than emotion because it refers to our overall feelings, usually over a long period of time (perhaps a week or month). When we say, "I've been in a bad mood all week," we are making a statement about our general emotional state. Emotions, in contrast, are more temporary states that are tied to personally meaningful events. Feeling proud because you got an "A" on your term paper would express a particular emotion. Unlike mood, which we experience as either a pleasant or unpleasant feeling (e.g., a good mood or a bad mood), emotions often fall into discrete, highly specific categories like anger, fear, joy, disgust, or surprise. Fredrickson's theory is focused on discrete positive emotions like joy, love, interest, pride, and contentment. Her theory describes the effects of positive emotions as essentially opposite to the effects of negative emotions.

Secondly, Fredrickson (2002) believes that positive emotions should not be confused with simple sensory pleasures such as sexual gratification or eating when you are hungry. These experiences are certainly associated with positive feelings, but she considers sensory pleasures as relatively automatic responses to physiological needs. In contrast, positive emotions are more psychological in nature and depend on the appraisal and meaning of events in people's lives rather than just physical stimulation of the body. In other words, Fredrickson's theory is not about the hedonic pleasures of the body, even though these may have their benefits.

Her description of the value of positive emotions begins with a contrast to negative emotions. The purpose of negative emotions, like anger and fear, is often described in terms of specific action tendencies. This means that a particular negative emotion (such as fear) is associated with a tendency to engage in specific kinds of actions. Fear is associated with a desire to escape, while anger is associated with a desire to attack or fight. The concept of specific action tendencies does not mean that people always act in a specific way as a result of a particular negative emotion. The effect of negative emotions is to narrow the focus of our thoughts and possible actions. Think of the last time you were very angry with someone because he or she hurt your feelings. Probably most of your thoughts were focused on the person and your anger. Why did she say that? How could she say that? You probably also thought about actions you might take. How can I get even? How shall I go about letting her know how I feel or explaining why her actions were unfair and hurtful? Whether or not you actually carried out these actions is not the point of the specific action-tendency concept. The point is that negative emotions tend to narrow our thinking and our range of possible actions. From a biological and evolutionary perspective, this narrowing of thoughts and actions contributes to our survival. To focus our thoughts on how to deal with threatening events that produce emotions like fear and anger, increases the immediacy and potential effectiveness of our actions. In life-threatening situations, quick action focused on dealing with a significant threat may increase our chances for survival.

Positive emotions, however, do not fit very well with the notion of specific action tendencies. Research reviewed by Fredrickson shows that emotions like joy are related to more diffuse, rather than specific behaviors and thoughts. Her broaden-and-build theory of positive emotions states that ". . . positive emotions—including joy, interest, contentment, pride and love—although phenomenologically distinct, all share the ability to broaden people's momentary thought-action repertoires and build their enduring personal resources, ranging from physical and intellectual resources to social and psychological resources" (Fredrickson, 2001, p. 219). The benefits of positive emotions are more general and long-term than the more specific, short-term effects of negative emotions. Joy, for example, creates a desire to play, to explore new possibilities, and to express our creative talents. Play is an important activity in the development of children. Physical play helps build strength and stamina. Play involving fun and laughter helps build positive relationships and attachments to others. Play involving puzzle-solving, artistic expression (in the form of drawing or make-believe play) contributes to the development of intellectual and creative talents.

Each of these possible effects of play can be seen as building physical resources, psychological resources for solving problems and coping with life challenges and social resources in the form of help and support from others.

Fredrickson describes four ways that positive emotions can broaden our thought-action repertoires and build our personal resources to increase well-being (see Figure 3.1). Because increased well-being may produce increases in the experience of positive emotions, an upward spiral of health and happiness may be possible.

POSITIVE EMOTIONS BROADEN OUR THOUGHT-ACTION REPERTOIRES Negative emotions tend to narrow our thoughts to a limited set of possible actions that might be taken in response to an emotion-evoking situation. When we are angry or fearful, we become self-focused and absorbed in the emotion. This may result in a kind of tunnel vision and an unduly limited consideration of all the possible options. It is harder to think in a free and creative way when we are angry or fearful. In contrast, positive emotions seem to open up people's thinking to a wider array of possible actions. Perhaps because we are not so self-focused, more options and ways of thinking about a situation come to mind when we are content or happy than when we are upset. In one demonstration of this "opening up"

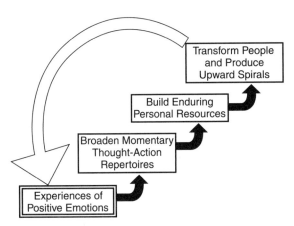

FIGURE 3.1 The Broaden-and-Build Theory of Positive Emotion

Source: Fredrickson, B.L. (2002). Positive emotions. In C. R. Snyder, & S. J. Lopez (Eds.), *Handbook of positive psychology* (pp. 120–134). New York: Oxford University Press. Copyright Oxford University Press. Reprinted with permission.

of possibilities as a result of positive emotions, Fredrickson and her colleagues asked research participants to watch emotionally charged film clips (see Fredrickson, 2001). The clips were selected for the purpose of inducing one of four emotions: joy, contentment, anger, or fear. A neutral, non-emotional clip served as a control condition. After watching the film clip, participants were asked to think of a situation that created feelings similar to those aroused by the film clip. Given the feelings created by the imagined situation, they were asked to list all the things they would like to do right then. That is, they were asked what came to mind as actions they would like to take. The results of this study supported the broaden-and-build theory. People in the joy and contentment conditions described more things they would like to do right then, than people in the anger or fear conditions. Further, people experiencing anger or fear identified fewer desirable actions than people in the neutral, non-emotional control condition. The broadening of thought-action possibilities, resulting from positive emotions, helps build intellectual resources for solving important life problems, because the more options we consider, the more likely we are to find an effective solution.

POSITIVE EMOTIONS UNDO NEGATIVE EMOTIONS Positive emotions and negative emotions seem to produce opposite effects. Our thinking and possible actions are narrowed by negative emotions and broadened by positive emotions. Positive emotions and negative emotions also seem incompatible with each other, in the sense that it is hard to imagine experiencing both at the same time. Have you ever been very happy and very angry at the same time? Joyfully sad? Fearfully relaxed? Combinations of emotional feelings are certainly possible, but the simultaneous experience of both intense positive and intense negative emotions seems unlikely.

Given this incompatibility, is it possible that positive emotions might undo the effects of negative emotions? To answer this question, Fredrickson and her colleagues examined the cardiovascular consequences of negative and positive emotions (see Fredrickson, 2001). Specifically, they designed a study to determine whether positive emotions would speed up recovery from the increased cardiovascular activity engendered by negative emotions. Negative emotions, like fear, increase cardiovascular activity such that more blood flows to the appropriate skeletal muscles necessary for a possible "fight-or-flight" response.

Imagine yourself in one of Fredrickson's studies. You show up to participate in a study and are told that you have one minute to prepare a speech that describes why you are a good friend. Your speech will be given in front of a live audience of other students and your talk will also be videotaped. As you would expect, giving a speech with little time to prepare made students very anxious and nervous. This was verified using measures of heart rate and blood pressure. After preparing for their speech, students were then assigned to one of four film conditions. One group of students watched a short film that was emotionally neutral; a second group saw a film selected to induce mild joy; a third group watched a film selected to produce mild contentment; and a fourth group saw a film selected to evoke sadness. The researchers measured how much time it took students to return to baseline levels of cardiovascular activity. As predicted, students in the joy and contentment film conditions returned to baseline significantly faster than those in the neutral or sad conditions. The sad film was associated with the longest recovery time. The experience of joy and contentment apparently helped undo the cardiovascular effects of the anxiety caused by the speech-preparation task.

POSITIVE EMOTIONS ENHANCE RESILIENCE Resilience is the ability to bounce back from stressful events and regain composure and a sense of well-being. Positive emotions may increase our resilience and ability to cope by offsetting the effects of negative emotions caused by stressful experiences. To examine the relationship between resilience and positive emotions, Fredrickson and her colleagues (Fredrickson, 2001) measured students' self-reported resilience using a scale that assesses how strong and confident people feel when facing challenge and stress. Fredrickson's research team used the same time-pressured speech preparation task to create anxiety and stress in participants. Students showing high levels of resilience on the self-report resilience measure tended to report more positive emotions during the preparation of their speeches and they showed faster return to baseline cardiovascular functioning after the speech task was completed. Resilient individuals seem (knowingly or unknowingly) to use positive emotions to offset negative emotions. Their tendency to cultivate positive

emotions in times of stress may be one source of their resilience and effective coping.

POSITIVE EMOTIONS BUILD ENDURING RESOURCES AND IMPROVE WELL-BEING Depression can produce a downward spiral of increasing negative mood and pessimistic thinking. Negative mood causes more pessimism, and more pessimism causes intensified negative mood. Conversely, Fredrickson proposes that positive emotions may create a comparable upward spiral of well-being. As summarized above, research has shown that positive emotions broaden our outlook, offset negative emotions, enhance our resilience, and improve our emotional well-being. A broadened outlook and increased resilience may, in turn, increase the experience of positive emotions, and so on. In short, positive emotions may help build our physical resources for fighting disease, our individual psychological resources for coping with stress, and our social resources (in the form of support from others) that are important in dealing with nearly all life challenges. We now turn to some of the specific research that has examined the importance of these three resources in physical health and how positive emotions may contribute to them.

POSITIVE EMOTIONS AND HEALTH RESOURCES

Most of us have seen first hand or have heard of the importance of a positive outlook in the face of serious illness and the idea that losing hope may foretell losing a battle against disease. As a poignant example of hope found and lost, consider the following story. A young boy named Jim suffered a form of abdominal cancer called Burkitt's lymphoma. By age 10, Jim had endured a painful year of chemotherapy and radiation, but the cancer was still progressing. Despite the failing hope of his doctors, Jim was upbeat and optimistic about the future. He said he intended to grow up, become a doctor, and find a cure for the disease that threatened his life and the lives of other children. Jim pinned his immediate hopes on the upcoming visit of a well-known specialist, who had taken an interest in his case and had promised to stop in Salt Lake City to visit Jim on his way to a professional conference. Jim had kept a diary of his symptoms and hoped it would give the specialist ideas about how to cure his disease. On the day the specialist was scheduled to visit Jim, the Salt Lake City airport was fogged in, so the specialist had to continue directly to his conference destination without stopping. Jim cried quietly when he heard the news. Listlessness replaced his earlier excitement and optimism. The next morning he developed a high fever and pneumonia. He was in a coma by evening and died the following afternoon (Visintainer & Seligman, 1983). It is hard not to see Jim's initial resilience in the face of his disease as resulting from his optimism and hope for the future. And it is equally hard not to believe that his rapid decline and death may have been due, at least in part, to his loss of hope.

In his widely read *Anatomy of an Illness* (1979), Norman Cousins describes how he used laughter to deal with the pain of ankylosing spondylitis—a disease that causes inflammation of connective tissue in joints and vertebrae. It is excruciatingly painful and potentially life threatening. Fed up with lying in a hospital bed, Cousins checked himself out of the hospital and into a motel where he watched his favorite Marx Brothers movies. He attributes his rather amazing recovery to the healing power of laughter. By his account, 10 minutes of laughter allowed him 2 hours of pain-free sleep and also reduced inflammation in areas of his body affected by the disease.

For many years, stories like these were just stories—anecdotal accounts that were intriguing, but not supported or understood scientifically. Today, compelling evidence shows that our emotions do affect our health. Research is beginning to clarify the multiple pathways and mechanisms that link emotions to well-being. Salovey and colleagues (2000) provide what may be regarded as a working hypothesis for the burgeoning research on health and emotions: "In general, negative emotional states are thought to be associated with unhealthy patterns of physiological functioning, whereas positive emotional states are thought to be associated with healthier patterns of responding in both cardiovascular activity and the immune system, although the data regarding negative states is more plentiful" (Salovey et al., 2000, p. 111). These authors also note that the mechanisms responsible for the associations between emotional states and health are complex and are only beginning to be understood. They involve multiple interacting systems and variables that make specifying cause–effect relationships difficult. However, evidence from many studies (e.g., Koenig & Cohen, 2002), new theories

concerning the different effects of negative and positive emotions (e.g., Fredrickson, 2001), and the opinions of numerous researchers (e.g., Folkman & Tedlie Moskowitz, 2000; Isen, 2002; Ray, 2004; Ryff & Singer, 2002; Taylor, Dickerson, & Cousino Klein, 2002) converge in support of Salovey and colleagues' general statement. Negative and positive emotions have the potential to set in motion a variety of physical, psychological, and social changes that can either compromise or enhance our health.

Research has described a number of pathways whereby emotions may affect health. Following Fredrickson's theory, we may classify these pathways as involving physical resources, psychological resources, and social resources. Physical resources involve the health and integrity of the body and the strength of the body's defenses against disease. Psychological resources refer to the effectiveness of people's responses in dealing with stressful experiences and the personal qualities they possess that provide strength and resilience in facing life's challenges. Social resources refer to the number and quality of relationships with others that provide support in times of need. The strength of each of these resources has been shown to influence our health. The basic premise underlying our discussion is that positive emotions contribute to the enhancement of our health resources and negative emotions contribute to their depletion. There is an extensive literature in the field of health psychology that focuses on the adverse influences of negative emotions on health (Taylor & Sherman, 2004). In contrast, research in positive psychology is just beginning to support the value of positive emotions in building health-promoting resources and in explaining why certain resources are more effective than others. Positive emotions may contribute to our physical resources by enhancing immune-system functioning. They may contribute to psychological resources by buffering or offsetting the detrimental effects of stress. Positive emotions may also help explain why certain personal traits and beliefs that appear to promote positive emotions (like optimism and self-esteem) are associated with better health. Finally, positive emotions may enhance people's social resources by facilitating the development and maintenance of supportive social relationships.

Physical Resources

Physical or biological resources important to our health involve four interacting systems studied within the field of psychoneuroimmunology. These systems involve the brain, the nervous system as a whole, the endocrine system, and the immune system (Maier, Watkins, & Fleshner, 1994). Because these systems are interconnected, mind and body are in a mutually influential relationship. The physical experience of sweaty palms and dry mouth caused by your psychological state of anxiety while giving a speech in front of an audience provides an everyday example of mind influencing body. And if you remember how you felt emotionally the last time you had the flu, you know how the body can influence the mind. In a recent article titled, "How the mind hurts and heals the body," Ray (2004) argues that research investigating the physiological and biochemical processes within these four systems allows us to conclude that "it is literally true that as experience changes our brains and thoughts, that is, changes our minds, we are changing our biology" (p. 32).

Many researchers have targeted the immune system as a major pathway for the effects of emotions on health. The primary purpose of the immune system is to destroy or neutralize pathogens that might make us sick. A number of specialized biochemical, hormonal and cellular processes are involved. For example, T-cells recognize pathogens, and respond by multiplying rapidly and killing the invaders. Natural killer cells (NK cells) attack anything foreign within the body. Researchers can evaluate the relative state of the immune system by measuring levels of T cells, NK cells, stress hormones, production of antibodies to different viruses, and a variety of other aspects of immune-system functioning (see Koenig & Cohen, 2002, for a review). Negative emotions *suppress* these measurable outputs of the immune system, and positive emotions appear to *enhance* their output, providing evidence of one pathway by which emotions influence our health.

A significant body of research has shown how stress can suppress immune-system functioning (e.g., Cohen, 2002; Friedman & Booth-Kewley, 1987; Rabin, 2002). Some of the clearest evidence comes from studies that measure an individual's level of stress, monitor immune-system functioning, and track health outcomes over time. One exemplary study investigated the immune-system consequences of medical school exams among first-year medical students (Kiecolt-Glaser & Glaser, 1987). Students' baseline levels of stress and immune-system functioning

were assessed immediately after a vacation, before any exams occurred. These same measures were taken again later, during important exam periods. The researchers found that as students' stress levels increased during exam periods, the effectiveness of their immune-system functioning decreased (as evidenced by a decrease in the number of NK cells). Students also reported more illnesses, such as upper respiratory infections, during this same exam period.

In addition to the numerous studies on stress, research has also found that negative moods can decrease immune-system activity. There are strong associations among clinical depression, depressed mood and reduced immune-system responses (e.g., Cohen & Rodriguez, 1995; Herbert & Cohen, 1993). Depressed people may be more vulnerable to illnesses because of reduced body defenses caused by their chronic depressed mood. Controlled laboratory studies also provide evidence of the harmful impact of negative emotional states. For example, people exposed to a respiratory virus while they were in a negative mood developed more severe respiratory symptoms than those who were in a more positive mood at the time of exposure (Cohen et al., 1995).

There are far fewer studies of how positive emotions may influence the immune system, and the results are not entirely consistent. However, results to date strongly suggest that the effects of positive emotion are more or less opposite the effects of stress and negative moods. For example, Stone and his colleagues examined the relationship between antibody production and daily mood (Stone et al., 1994). Forty-eight adult men maintained daily diaries for 12 weeks. The men recorded their moods and experiences at work, at home, and in leisure activities, and in their relationships with spouses, friends, and children. Each man also took a harmless protein antigen pill every day during the 12-week period. (An antigen is a substance capable of generating an immune response. Specifically, the body responds to an antigen by producing antibodies that help defend against invading pathogens.) Participants gave daily saliva samples that were used to measure the levels of antibody produced. A clear association was found between the participants' moods and their responses to the antigen (as measured by their production of antibodies). The more positive events the men experienced during a given day, the more antibodies they produced. The more negative events they experienced, the less antibodies they produced. Although this study assessed only one aspect of immune-system functioning and used a non-disease-causing antigen, the results suggest the potential for positive and negative emotions to have opposing influences on the immune system.

Laughter, one of the more expressive positive emotions, is also associated with positive changes in the immune system, and with better recovery from illness. Studies reviewed by Lefcourt (2002) show that humor and laughter increase the body's production of antibodies and NK cells, and that humor helps people cope with serious illness such as cancer. Laughter induced by a humorous videotape was found to produce significant increases in salivary immunoglobulin A (S-IgA) (Dillon, Minchoff, & Baker, 1985). S-IgA is an antibody that is widely regarded as the body's first line of defense against the common cold. In another study, people who watched a Bill Cosby comedy routine exhibited similar positive immune-system effects (Lefcourt, Davidson, & Kueneman, 1990).

Much more research is needed to confirm and clarify the beneficial effects of positive emotions. The issues here, both psychological and physiological, are very complex. A recent review concluded that evidence for the general value of positive affect is "provocative but not definitive" (Pressman & Cohen, 2005, p. 963). These reviewers note that there is considerable evidence connecting positive emotions to self-reported reductions in illness symptoms, decreased levels of pain, and better health. There is also suggestive evidence linking positive affect to enhanced immune-system functioning and longevity. However, there are also studies suggesting that for diseases with high and rapid mortality rates (e.g. certain forms of cancer), positive emotions may actually be harmful. An optimistic outlook may cause people to ignore symptoms or have unrealistic expectations, causing them to avoid getting the medical attention they need (Salovey et al., 2000).

Positive emotions are obviously not a magic bullet cure-all. The final word on positive emotions awaits future and well-controlled research. So, we must conclude with a bit of caution. The evidence, at the very least, seems to be strongly suggestive that people who are generally happy and cheerful (whether it's a result of enjoyable experiences, their sense of humor, their temperament, or their active cultivation of a positive attitude) are likely to reap health benefits compared to those who are generally sad, unhappy, pessimistic, and humorless (Lyubomirsky, King, & Diener, 2005). The increased longevity of the more cheerful sisters in the "Nun Study" (Danner, Snowdon, & Friesen, 2001, reviewed in Chapter 2) is undoubtedly the result of a complex interaction of multiple factors. Yet many of these factors are probably related to the nuns' cheerful, positive dispositions. In addition to its potential effects on the immune system, a cheerful attitude may have helped the nuns cope with stressful experiences, led them to take better care of their health, and/or enabled them to establish more supportive relationships with others. The next section considers positive emotion as a psychological resource for coping with stress, and describes how positive emotions may help explain the importance of individual traits associated with beneficial health outcomes.

Psychological Resources

POSITIVE EMOTIONS AND COPING WITH STRESS
Knowledge of the health-threatening effects of stress has inspired extensive research regarding coping behaviors that might help people reduce stress and thereby improve their health (Somerfield & McCrae, 2000). Psychological resources for managing stress involve the strength and effectiveness of our intellectual, behavioral, and emotional efforts to reduce and offset stressful experiences. Many factors affect how people cope with stress. Coping behaviors are often grouped into two general categories: problem-focused coping and emotion-focused coping (Lazarus & Folkman, 1984). **Problem-focused coping** involves behaviors directed at altering, reducing, or eliminating the source of stress, such as seeking concrete help from others, taking action to change a stressful life situation, or gathering and evaluating information to assess one's alternatives. **Emotion-focused coping** involves an attempt to change or reduce one's own response to a stressful experience. Examples of emotion-focused coping would include avoiding the problem, denying the problem exists, seeking emotional support from others, venting one's emotions to relieve stress, and positive self-talk (e.g., "counting your blessings") (see Tamres, Janicki, & Helgeson, 2002, for a recent meta-analytic review of coping behaviors).

Aspinwall and Taylor (1997) have suggested a third category of coping called **proactive coping,** which involves efforts to prevent stress from happening in the first place. An example of a proactive approach would be going to the doctor when you first notice symptoms that might indicate a serious illness, rather than worrying about your symptoms, hoping they will go away, or waiting until you *do* have a serious illness. Another example would be finishing your term paper ahead of the deadline to avoid the stressful feeling that, "it's due tomorrow!"

Positive emotion has only recently received systematic attention as a coping resource. Research on coping has focused primarily on ways to reduce or eliminate emotional distress caused by stressful experiences. Much less attention has been given to the possible role of positive emotions in coping with stress and in strengthening psychological resources. This situation has begun to change as several prominent coping researchers have considered the value of positive emotions in coping (e.g., Aspinwall, 1998; Hobfoll, 1989; Lazarus, 2000; Somerfield & McCrae, 2000; Vaillant, 2000). Folkman and Tedlie Moskowitz (2000) argue that positive emotions play an important role in coping with stress and life traumas. They review research showing that positive emotions can co-occur with distress, even in highly stressful life situations such as a loved one being diagnosed with cancer. Despite adverse circumstances, people find ways to laugh together, enjoy shared memories, and learn positive life lessons. Positive emotional experiences in the midst of distress may benefit people by buffering or helping to offset the negative effects of stress. Positive emotions may bolster depleted psychological resources by promoting optimism, hope, and confidence, and may contribute to physical resources that enhance immune-system functioning. Research investigating the role of positive affect (i.e., positive emotion) as a coping resource supports many of these possibilities.

Research has identified several ways that positive affect may help people cope with stressful, threatening, or problematic situations (see Aspinwall, 1998; Hobfoll, 1989; Isen, 2002, 2003, for reviews). In general, people experiencing positive affect tend to show more proactive coping styles and skills (Aspinwall & Taylor, 1997). Positive affect leads people to think about how to prevent stressful situations rather than just how to cope with them after the fact. Individuals experiencing positive affect also show more flexibility and creativity in solving problems. For example, positive affect in medical students was associated with improved ability to make medical diagnoses, and with more accepting and flexible consideration of alternatives (Estrada, Isen, & Young, 1997). Positive affective states may make people less defensive in response to criticism or information that

threatens their self-image (Trope & Pomerantz, 1998). Further, individuals experiencing positive affect may be less likely to deny or distort information that does not agree with their beliefs and preconceptions (Estrada et al., 1997). These findings affirm the contribution of positive emotions to our psychological resources for coping with life's challenges.

Focus on Application: Finding the Positive in the Negative

As we noted, people facing serious illness report surprisingly frequent experiences of positive emotions. How do people find the positive in the negative? Can we actively cultivate positive emotions to improve our well-being and ability to deal with challenging life events? Based on a longitudinal study of AIDS caregivers, Folkman and Tedlie Moskowitz (2000) describe three kinds of coping that generate positive affect: positive reappraisal, goal-directed problem-focused coping, and infusing ordinary events with positive meaning. Each of these three coping styles will be explored below.

POSITIVE REAPPRAISAL Positive reappraisal refers to a cognitive strategy that reframes the problem in a more positive light. Whatever situation you are in, it could be worse. Even when confronting the death of a loved one from AIDS there are things to appreciate and value. Despite the emotional pain and stress of caring for someone dying of AIDS, many caregivers in Folkman and Tedlie Moskowitz's (2000) study reported positive feelings associated with their efforts. They saw their devotion to caregiving as an expression of the depth of their love for their partners and believed their efforts had preserved their partners' dignity. They believed their efforts were both valued and worthwhile. These positive reappraisals were associated with increases in positive mood for the caregivers in the study. In the next chapter on resilience, we will review additional studies showing how people facing traumatic and painful situations are able to cultivate positive experiences, find personal meaning, and discover benefits.

PROBLEM-FOCUSED COPING Problem-focused coping refers to actions taken to reduce the distress of a painful situation. In the case of terminal illness, it may seem that the situation is uncontrollable and therefore no action can be taken. This is why terminal illness is so distressing. However, in their study of AIDS caregivers, Folkman and Tedlie Moskowitz (2000) found that, even though people could not control the final outcome, they did not adopt a helpless or passive stance. Instead, caregivers focused on smaller problems that they *could* solve, such as changing aspects of living arrangements to make their partner more comfortable; arranging planned outings; managing medications; preparing food; or planning entertainment activities. These activities, like positive reappraisal, were related to higher levels of positive affect. Further, solving problems encountered in the daily activities of caregiving contributed to a sense of personal effectiveness, mastery and control.

INFUSING ORDINARY ACTIVITIES WITH POSITIVE MEANING Folkman and Tedlie Moskowitz (2000) asked AIDS caregivers in their study about things they had done that made them feel good, were personally meaningful, and helped them get through the day. Somewhat amazingly, in over 1,700 interviews in which this question was asked, 99.5% of the participants recalled and reported positive events. Many of these events appear quite ordinary, such as planning a special meal for their partner or a getting together with friends. However, the active planning that went into these events and the comfort they were able to provide for their partners led to both positive feelings and a sense of purpose and personal meaning. Caregivers also reported unplanned events and experiences, such as receiving a compliment for a small task or encountering something like a beautiful flower. These events added a bit of cheer and good feeling to the daily routine of caregiving. Each of these ordinary activities, infused with positive meaning, produced positive feelings and helped caregivers make it through the day.

POSITIVE TRAITS AND HEALTH The contribution of positive emotions to our psychological resources suggests that any personal quality, experience, or activity that generates positive emotion, particularly when we are faced with a stressful experience, may have health benefits. Positive emotions, whether they arise from an enduring personal quality (a trait) like a cheerful temperament, a routinely practiced activity (a state) like an enjoyable hobby, or a coping strategy such as looking for the bright side of a bad situation, all share the potential to improve our health. Research has identified a number of traits that are associated with improved health. For

example, optimism, self-esteem, resilience, and emotional expression have all been linked to positive health outcomes (Chapter 9 gives a full discussion of positive traits). At this point, psychologists do not have direct evidence linking the positive health benefits of these traits to the role of positive emotions. However, the potential contribution of positive emotion is increasingly recognized (e.g., Aspinwall, 1998; Fredrickson, 2001; Hobfoll, 1989; Salovey et al., 2000).

People with high self-esteem typically feel good about themselves and have a positive sense of self-worth. Myers (1992) argues that self-esteem is one of the best predictors of personal happiness. If you feel good about yourself you are also likely to be reasonably happy with your life. One prominent theory of self-esteem called self-affirmation theory (Steele, 1988) views self-esteem as a psychological resource that people can draw upon in challenging situations. When life deals a blow to our self-image, high self-esteem allows us to bounce back, stay on course, and affirm continuation of a positive self-image. Self-esteem is like "money in the bank." If you have ample savings, a $500 car repair bill may not cause much upset; but if your bank account is at zero, that same bill will pose a big problem. People with high self-esteem are generally happier, fare better in stressful situations, are less prone to depression, and lead healthier lives overall than people with low self-esteem (e.g., Antonucci & Jackson, 1983; Crocker & Luthanen, 2003; Crocker & Park, 2004; Hobfoll & Lieberman, 1987; Kernis, 2003a, 2003b; Myers, 1992). There are many reasons why self-esteem and positive emotions are valuable psychological resources, such as the strong association between self-esteem and personal happiness, and the beneficial role of positive emotions in coping with stress.

Positive emotions may also play a role in the relationship between optimism and health. Optimism and pessimism are general expectations about the future. Optimists expect that more good things will happen to them than bad, while pessimists expect the opposite (Carver & Scheier, 2002a). A person's answer to the question, "Is the glass half empty or is it half full?" captures one fundamental difference between an optimistic and a pessimistic outlook.

Numerous studies have shown that optimists enjoy generally better health than pessimists (e.g., Affleck, Tennen, & Apter, 2002; Peterson & Bosio, 1991; Scheier & Carver, 1992; Scheier, Carver, & Bridges, 2001; Seligman, 1990). For example, compared to their more pessimistic classmates, optimistic college students suffered from fewer colds, sore throats, and bouts with the flu over the course of a year. Larger-scale studies over long time periods provide strong support for the influence of optimism and pessimism on health. A 10-year study of 1,300 men living in Boston found optimists to be 50% less likely to suffer from coronary disease than their more pessimistic counterparts (Kubzansky, Sparrow, Volkonas, & Kwachi, 2001). A prospective study by Peterson and his colleagues (Peterson, Seligman, & Vaillant 1988) followed up with a group of men 35 years after they had graduated from Harvard, and found optimists to be significantly healthier than their pessimistic fellow alumni.

What explains these relationships between optimism and better health? Like self-esteem, a variety of factors may be involved. Optimists may be more likely to engage in protective health behaviors such as scheduling regular visits to the doctor, and by gathering and responding to information about their health.

Recent research suggests that optimists may also exhibit stronger positive immune responses when under stress than pessimists (e.g., Segerstrom, Taylor, Kemeny, & Fahey, 1998). The link between optimism and positive emotion is suggested by the fact that an optimist expects good outcomes. This attitude may contribute to a positive state of mind, which may be a useful resource in times of stress or illness. Studies show that optimists cope more effectively with stress than pessimists (Scheier & Carver, 1992); positive emotion may be part of the reason for this finding. Optimism is also strongly correlated with happiness and life satisfaction (Myers, 1992; Scheier & Carver, 1992). Optimistic people tend to be upbeat, happy, and satisfied with their lives. If optimism leads to more frequent experiencing of positive emotional states, this may also help explain the health benefits of an optimistic attitude.

A number of other traits and states have shown similar relationships to health and to positive emotion. For example, all of the following have been found to be positively associated with health and/or happiness: sense of humor, hope, extraversion, belief in personal control over life outcomes, and forgiving others (see Lopez & Snyder, 2003; Myers, 1992; Snyder & Lopez, 2002, for reviews). Even though our understanding is at a beginning stage, it seems reasonable to suggest that positive emotions play a role in these relationships, just as they appear to help explain the benefits of

self-esteem and optimism. Positive emotions are obviously not the whole story, given the complex factors that affect our health. A central aim of positive psychology is to develop a research-based understanding of the role positive emotions *do* play.

Social Resources

Of all the diverse aspects of our lives, if we had to pick one that had the most powerful influence on overall happiness and health, it would have to be our relationships with others. Countless studies find that people involved in a network of close, supportive relationships enjoy better health and more personal happiness than those who lack such a network (Baumeister & Leary, 1995; Ryff & Singer, 2000). Confirming evidence is so overwhelming that Myers (1992) described the connection between relationships and well-being as a "deep truth" (p. 154). The fact that Myers' observation has been repeated by several authors reviewing the relationship literature (e.g., Berscheid & Reis, 1998; Reis & Gable, 2003) is also testimony to the weight of supporting evidence.

The most impressive evidence for the importance of relationships comes from large-scale epidemiological studies involving thousands of people. These studies have found that people involved in a wide variety of social relationships (e.g., with spouses, friends, family members, neighbors, communities, and social or religious groups) get sick less often and live longer than people with few social involvements (see Cohen, Underwood, & Gottlieb, 2000; House Landis, & Umberson, 1988, for reviews). A 9-year follow-up study of mortality rates of 7,000 California residents found that the more social contacts a person had, the longer she or he lived (Berkman & Syme, 1979). This finding was true across the board: for rich and poor, for women and for men, for young and old, and for people of differing ethnic and racial backgrounds. Through interviews with over 2,500 adults during visits to their doctors, House and colleagues (1988) found that the most socially active men were 2 to 3 times more likely to survive over the next decade than their socially isolated counterparts. The same researchers also examined the association between relationship status and a set of widely recognized risk factors. Statistically, the health risks associated with a lack of social ties exceeded the risks of cigarette smoking and obesity (House et al., 1988).

On the negative side, we know that a lack of social ties, involvement in conflictual relationships, or loss of a significant relationship can contribute to loneliness, depression, personal distress, and unhappiness (e.g., Berscheid, 2003; Berscheid & Reis, 1998; Reis & Gable, 2003). For example, death of a spouse can have dramatic effects on both physical and emotional well-being (Stroebe & Stroebe, 1993). Studies show that the mortality risk for surviving partners doubles in the week following the loss of their spouse (Kaprio, Koskenvuo, & Rita, 1987). Psychotherapists report that troubled relationships are one of the most common problems among their patients (Berscheid & Reis, 1998). Interpersonal relationships are a frequent source of stress and upset. When national survey participants were asked to describe "the last bad thing that happened to [them]," they most often mentioned conflict or disruption in their important relationships (e.g., with family members, friends, co-workers, or spouses) (Veroff, Douvan, & Kulka, 1981).

The irony of relationships is that they contribute most to our enduring happiness and joy, but also to our distress and misery. Our relationships have the potential both to enhance and to compromise our health. What explains the role of relationships in health? One long-standing explanation is built on the value of social support as a resource for coping with stress. The **buffering hypothesis** states that social support from others reduces (i.e., buffers) the potential debilitating effects of stress (Berscheid & Reis, 1998). By sharing our burden with others, our own burden becomes lighter, stress levels are reduced, and stress-induced suppression of the immune system may decrease (Cohen, 2002). Support for the buffering hypothesis comes from studies showing the health benefits of disclosing traumatic events to others. For example, Pennebaker and O'Heeron (1984) compared the health outcomes of spouses whose partners had committed suicide or died in automobile accidents. Surviving spouses who had shouldered the burden of their loss alone had more health problems than those who talked openly and shared their feelings with others. Disclosure of emotions about past traumas seems helpful, even if we simply write them down. Pennebaker, Kiecolt-Glaser, and Glaser (1988) asked 50 undergraduates to engage in "disclosure writing" either about personal and traumatic events in their lives or about trivial topics. Students wrote for 20 minutes each day for 4 days. The personal traumas described by students included divorce of their parents, death of a loved one, sexual and physical abuse, failed relationships, loneliness, and fears about the future. Immune system measures were collected at the beginning of the study, at the end, and at 6-week and 4-month follow-ups. Students who wrote about traumatic events showed healthier immune responses than those who wrote about trivial events.

Other studies confirm the value of emotional disclosure of personally painful events. Cancer patients who discussed their feelings with other patients in a support group setting showed better health outcomes than cancer patients who were not involved in support groups (see Spiegel & Fawzy, 2002, for a review). Recent experimental studies have directly manipulated participants' stress levels and the availability of social support, and then examined the intensity of stress-related physiological responses within the sympathetic and endocrine systems (see Taylor et al., 2002, for a review). In these studies, participants were alone, or with one of their own friends, or with a supportive stranger assigned by the experimenter. Stress response measures were taken during and after participants' performance of a stressful task, such as giving a public speech. Results showed that the presence of a friend or supportive stranger reduced the intensity of stress responses and led to faster recovery of from the physiological effects of acute stress.

The buffering hypothesis suggests that people benefit from social support only in times of stress. However, proponents of the **direct effects hypothesis** argue that social support contributes to an individual's health independent of his or her level of stress (Stroebe & Stroebe, 1996). People involved in close, caring relationships are generally happier and healthier because of their supportive relationships, whether or not they are dealing with stressful life experiences (Berscheid & Reis, 1998). The health benefits of social support may stem from the positive emotions associated with close relationships and the feelings of security that come from the knowledge that people care about you and will be there when you need them (Salovey et al., 2000). These positive feelings may, in turn, enhance immune-system functioning.

The Limits of Positive Emotions

This chapter has reviewed some of the factors that contribute to the physical, psychological, and social resources that help fight disease and counteract the negative effects of stress. Positive emotions are increasingly recognized as contributing to these resources. To keep the role of positive emotions in proper perspective, a few words of caution are in order. First, as mentioned earlier in this section, we know considerably more about the health-threatening effects of negative emotions and stress than we know about the health-enhancing effects of positive emotions. At present, research findings strongly suggest a link between positive emotions and health. The value of positive emotions is becoming increasingly recognized and researched. Possible explanations have been offered regarding specific mechanisms by which positive emotions may contribute to better health. However, research confirming these explanations is at a preliminary stage. It seems fair to say that positive emotions do make a significant difference in people's health. Understanding the specific pathways that explain *how* they make a difference is one goal of research in positive psychology.

Secondly, there are limits to the power of positive emotions. No serious scientist views positive emotion, an optimistic outlook, or social support as a miracle cure for serious illness, or as providing any guarantee of a long and happy life. Traumatic experiences, like death of a spouse, can overwhelm our coping resources. Prolonged and severe trauma, such as the stress associated with war, is damaging. No amount of good humor, cheerfulness, or optimism in the face of major life challenges ensures a happy or healthy ending. The critical standard for evaluating the effects of positive emotions is a relative one. That is, other things being equal, people who experience and cultivate positive emotions may have an edge in terms of the strength of their physical, psychological, and social resources for coping with illness and stress, compared to people with less frequent positive emotional experiences. The health benefits of positive emotions are relative—not absolute. Positive emotions don't cure in an absolute sense: you were sick and now you are not. Positive emotions help, and we know this because of empirical comparisons with the effects of negative emotions. The bottom line here is this: Research suggests that positive emotions contribute to faring better. Better than what? Better than you would fare without them, and better than you might fare with negative emotions.

POSITIVE EMOTIONS AND WELL-BEING
Happiness and Positive Behavior

Chapter 2 described positive emotions as a central component of the SWB definition of happiness. People who enjoy frequent positive emotions and experience few negative emotions, along with a judgment that their life is satisfying, are considered happy. A number of studies show that people in a positive mood act quite differently than when they are in a bad mood or experiencing a distressing emotion. This is hardly news, but it is interesting that many of the behaviors we consider to be positive are enhanced by positive affect. Happy people, whether by temperament or recent experiences, are more tolerant and less prejudicial, more compassionate, more focused on others rather than self-focused, more helpful to others, and more enjoyable to be with (Isen, 2003; Myers, 1992). Evidence supporting the broaden-and-build theory suggests that positive emotions contribute to more flexible, creative and resilient responses in the face of challenge (Fredrickson, 2001, 2002). These findings led Myers (1992) to suggest that happiness might be viewed as a desirable state in and of itself because it is linked to so many positive behaviors. As Myers noted, it is negative emotions and unhappiness—not happiness—that causes us to be self-absorbed, self-centered, and focused on our own preoccupations. Happiness seems to produce a more expansive view of the world around us.

Positive Emotions and Success

In American culture, it is widely believed that success makes people happy. This makes sense and subsequent chapters will review evidence documenting its validity. A recent extensive research review examined whether the causal arrow might also point the other way (Lyubomirsky et al., 2005). Might positive affect and happiness promote success? More specifically, these researchers asked, are chronically happy people, defined as those who have frequent experiences of positive emotions, more successful in multiple domains of life? The answer is yes. In their analysis of hundreds of cross-sectional, longitudinal, and experimental studies, happy people were consistently found to enjoy greater success in marriage, friendship, income, work, and mental and physical health. Compared to their less happy peers, happy people have more satisfying marriages, are more likeable and extraverted and have a richer network of friends, receive more favorable evaluations from their employers, take better care of their physical health, cope more effectively with challenge, and have higher incomes. Moreover, longitudinal studies show that happiness precedes as well as follows success and many of the effects of positive emotions were paralleled by experimental research that induced positive affect in well-controlled studies.

The sources of an individual's happiness might stem from an enduring trait, current life circumstances, or the satisfaction derived from intentionally chosen activities, such as satisfying work or investment in one's family. Whatever its source, the evidence seems clear that happy people fare better in many areas of life. Lyubomirsky and her colleagues believe that their empirical review provides strong support for Fredrickson's broaden-and-build theory of positive emotions. Positive emotions do seem to build people's intellectual, psychological, and social resources that contribute to success and positive well-being, and success seems to contribute to enhanced happiness, as well. The two-way street of happiness and success, with each contributing reciprocally to the other, supports Fredrickson's idea of a potential upward spiral of well-being.

Positive Emotions and Flourishing

The strong connections between positive emotions and individual success and health raise the possibility that positive emotions might signify optimal functioning. That is, if positive emotions were not somehow a central aspect of positive functioning, why would researchers find so many aspects of health related to them? In an intriguing article, Fredrickson and Losada (2005) describe a quantitative relationship between people's emotional experience and their level of optimal functioning. These researchers drew on the work of Corey Keyes (2002, 2007) and his model of complete mental health as flourishing (reviewed in Chapter 2). **Flourishing** is a state of optimal human functioning that is at the opposite end of the continuum from mental illness. In other words, flourishing is complete mental *health*. **Languishing** is a state that divides mental health from mental illness and is characterized by a feeling of emptiness, hollowness, or what people used to call melancholy. Languishing individuals have few symptoms of

mental illness, but they also have few symptoms of mental health. In other words, there is no serious pathology, but there is little purpose, meaning, or zest for life either.

Drawing on Fredrickson's broaden-and-build theory of positive emotions and the substantial research connecting positive emotions to enhanced well-being and performance, Fredrickson and Losada (2005) hypothesized that the ratio of positive-to-negative emotions and behaviors that people experience during a given time period might be an index of the flourishing–languishing dimension. That is, might there be some critical ratio of positive-to-negative that divides optimal functioning (flourishing) from poor functioning (languishing)? Fredrickson and Losada reviewed evidence from studies of effective business management teams, intensive observational research with married couples, and investigations of depressed patients before and after treatment. In each of these studies, positive and negative behaviors and emotions were measured and their ratio calculated in relationship to quality-of-outcome measures. The evidence from these studies converged on a "**critical positivity ratio**" of 2.9. That is, within a given time period, a ratio at or above roughly three times the positive affect to negative affect signifies flourishing, and ratios below that signify languishing. In everyday life, this would suggest that if during a week you experienced 12 significant positive events and only 4 negative events, you probably had a good week with a ratio of 12/4 = 3.

To investigate the discriminative validity of this ratio in relation to mental criteria for flourishing and languishing, Fredrickson and Losada had two samples of college students complete Keyes' (2002) mental health measures and keep a daily log of their emotional experiences over a 1-month period. Measures of flourishing were drawn from the work of Corey Keyes (2002, 2007). Flourishing is defined by scores on questionnaire items measuring high SWB (frequent positive affect and high life satisfaction), self-acceptance, personal growth, purpose in life, environmental mastery, autonomy, positive relations with others, and positive social functioning, including social acceptance, actualization, contribution, coherence, and integration (see Chapter 4 for detailed description of each attribute and sample measurement items). The presence of a majority of these characteristics (six), together with the absence of mental illness symptoms, define flourishing in Keyes' conceptualization.

The primary results for this study were based on dividing the monthly total of positive emotional experiences by the total for negative emotional experiences, and examining the relation of the resulting ratio to the criteria for flourishing. Consistent with predictions, flourishing students had ratios at or above 2.9 (average was 3.2) and non-flourishing students were below the 2.9 threshold.

A GENERAL THEORY OF POSITIVITY? A general theory of positivity is an intriguing and potentially integrative addition to positive psychology's growing arsenal of informative theories, and fertile ground for future research. The robustness of the evidence for the 2.9 ratio is supported by the fact that it was found in such diverse samples and life domains (i.e., business, marriage, depressed patients, college students) and also when different measures of positivity, negativity, and outcome assessments were used. As described by Fredrickson and Losada, a **general theory of positivity** predicts that the line dividing human flourishing from languishing among individuals and groups is strongly associated with positivity ratios of 2.9.

You may wonder if there is an upper limit to this ratio. Is there such a thing as too much positivity? Fredrickson and Losada provide evidence suggesting that the answer is yes. While not empirically assessed, mathematical models suggest that at very high ratios (11.6) the relationship of positive emotion to flourishing begins to break down. As these authors note, a certain amount of negativity seems to be necessary for healthy functioning. Conflict, pain, and distress all represent opportunities for personal growth, and for growth in relationship to others. Negativity contributes to flourishing by helping to build psychological growth and resilience. In any case, a life with no negative experiences is impossible. It is probably unhealthy as well.

CULTIVATING POSITIVE EMOTIONS

Life is full of simple pleasures that we simply enjoy for themselves and/or use to reduce stress and bad feelings. Examples would include fixing a delicious meal for family or friends, taking a hot bath, going for a casual stroll, reading a good book with a glass of wine in the evening, a cup of coffee with the morning paper, and a host of more elaborate activities such as gardening, painting, photography, woodworking, and other hobbies. A major message of this chapter is that these activities are good for us, not only because they offset negative emotions, but also because positive emotions, independent of their detoxifying effects, are good for us. We end this chapter by considering two examples of positive emotion-promoting activities that are probably familiar to you. They are simple, free, and enjoyable.

Flow Experiences

Think of an activity or experience in which you become totally absorbed and lose yourself in the moment. At the same time, you are highly effective in expressing your skill and don't have to think about what you are doing. In fact, once you start to think and analyze, the whole experience ends and you are back to your everyday state of mind. As a mini-example of this kind of experience (which Csikszentmihalyi calls "flow") (Csikszentmihalyi, 1990, 1997; Nakamura & Csikszentmihalyi, 2002, 2003), consider what happened to your textbook's first author. I golf. Not well, but I've had my moments. One of these moments occurred on a round at my favorite course while golfing with a friend. I was just thoroughly enjoying the game and being outdoors and I seemed to be in a groove, playing well. On the next-to-the-last hole my partner pointed out that I was two over par which, for me, was the round of my life. I started wondering why I was doing so well. I started thinking about my grip, stance, address to the ball, swing, etc. Of course, this was the kiss of death for my good round. The 17th hole was along a lakefront. I put my drive in the lake. The final hole had a small pond and a sand trap. I managed to get into both. I ended the round 8 over par! Thinking too much ruined my game.

I am convinced that one of the reasons that Michael Jordan of the Chicago Bulls was such an attraction when he played was not only because he was consistently a good player, but on many occasions he had phenomenal games of 40 to 50 or more points. Everything he did worked. He played "unconsciously," was "in the zone," and could make baskets even when he was off-balance and had multiple defenders in his face. But you don't have to be a star to experience flow. In Csikszentmihalyi's (1990) interview studies, ordinary people described this same kind of experience that many referred to as "flow." Rock climbers, dancers, chess players, basketball players, musicians and painters described how they often got lost in the moment of creativity or performance—doing their best, but feeling "outside themselves," as if they were watching it all happen from an external perspective. They engaged in flow-producing activities for the intrinsic enjoyment those activities yielded. The simple *doing* of the activity was its own reward. They also described the exhilaration they felt during or after such flow experiences.

The experience of flow can be contrasted with our more typical state of mind that we will call our "8-to-5 mind." Our 8-to-5 mind is the one that goes to work, balances the checkbook, and analyzes what, when, and how we are going to solve problems and tackle various daily tasks. This is not to say that people cannot experience flow at work. In fact, Csikszentmihalyi and his colleagues have found that the most satisfying and productive work involves a level of challenge appropriate to our skill that actively engages our talents, is deeply meaningful, and produces a sense of "vital engagement" and flow (see Nakamura & Csikszentmihalyi, 2002, 2003). So, our contrast of flow with an 8-to-5 mind-set is not meant to be a work-versus-play distinction, since some people have the good fortune to combine the two. Rather, it points to the fact that flow is less common than our "normal" state of consciousness. In this regard, we might consider flow as a naturally occurring altered state of consciousness when compared to the more frequently experienced 8-to-5 mindset. In flow, we are "out of our minds" in the sense of breaking through the dominance of normal consciousness. Consistent with this idea and our golf example, when "normal mind" intrudes, flow is lost. Table 3.1 shows the differences between normal mind and flow (out of your mind).

Duality means to be aware of yourself and the environment as two separate objects. Self-control refers to consciously directing our actions. That is, "I am doing this now, and next I will do that." We consciously monitor our actions related to a task or activity. In flow, there is a merging of action, awareness, and the sense of self, such that we lose the feeling of consciously controlling our actions (loss of self). This does not mean that we literally lose ourselves. It means we don't have to think in a self-reflective way about what we are doing. It just flows—seems to happen by itself. If you play a musical instrument, you know the difference between having to think consciously about each

TABLE 3.1 Flow versus the 8-to-5 Mind

Normal Mind 8 to 5	Out of Your Mind – (Flow)
1. Duality	1. Oneness
2. Self-control	2. Loss of self
3. Attention wanders	3. Total absorption
4. Time conscious	4. Time flies–frozen
5. Internal talk	5. Talk destroys it
6. Confusion	6. Clarity of action
7. Negative emotions	7. Exhilaration
8. Stress accumulates	8. Discharges stress

note, and having the music just flow effortlessly because it's so well-learned.

Attention and time-consciousness are frequent problems in our 8-to-5 minds. We daydream at work and in class; we have trouble focusing on the task at hand; we watch the clock and can't believe how time drags. Of course, this assumes that one's job or class is not overwhelmingly interesting or challenging. In flow, attention is never a problem because we are totally absorbed in the activity. Neither is time an issue, because it seems to fly or stand still. An hour can go by in what feels like a moment.

In our 8-to-5 minds, we are often confused and concerned about our performance and what other people think of us. We also carry on conversations with ourselves (in a kind of internal talk) in which we analyze, ruminate about the future or past, and consider what is going on around us. In flow, there is utter clarity of action. We know exactly what we are doing and we get ongoing and immediate feedback from the environment. In sports, music, and writing, you see and hear the results of your efforts as they occur. As we discussed earlier, internal talk, self-reflection, and conscious thinking leads to kind of "paralysis-by-analysis" of flow.

Finally, although not specifically evaluated, many of Csikszentmihalyi's research participants commented on the discharge of stress and the feeling of leaving your troubles behind that resulted from flow experiences. This stands in contrast to the 8-to-5 mind; by the end of a week at school or work, most of us feel at least a bit stressed, worn down, and ready for the weekend. Because flow is associated with enjoyment and an ending feeling of "Whew, that was great!" it would seem to follow that reduced stress would be one of the benefits of flow. In addition, our review of the beneficial physiological effects of positive emotions suggests that people who regularly participate in flow activities might enjoy some enhancement of physical and mental health.

Savoring

Most of us have experienced the difference between hurriedly eating a hamburger at a fast-food restaurant and a relaxed candlelight dinner where each bite of food and each sip of wine is consumed slowly in order to appreciate, prolong, and enjoy the sensual pleasure it offers. Based on their studies, Bryant and Verhoff (2007) argue that savoring a good meal offers a more general model for savoring good moments in life and increasing the intensity and frequency of our positive experiences.

The basic assumption of **savoring** is that "people have capacities *to attend to, appreciate, and enhance the positive experiences in their lives*" (Bryant & Verhoff, 2007, p. 2, italics in original). Savoring may occur spontaneously. We may find ourselves captivated by a striking sunset. Appreciation and enjoyment arise from immersing ourselves in the beauty of the colors and patterns of light. Bryant and Verhoff believe that whether planned or spontaneous, three preconditions must be met for savoring to occur. First, we must have a sense of immediacy of what is happening in the moment—here and now. That is focused attention, and it's easiest to think of in terms of a specific object or activity (e.g., a sunset or a hot bath), but it also applies to internal thoughts and feelings. A person might savor a memory, such as a great time with good friends or a treasured childhood experience. One might also savor the anticipation of a future positive event, like getting married or graduating from college. Whatever the focus, it needs to fully absorb your attention in order for savoring to occur.

Secondly, to experience savoring, social and self-esteem needs must be set aside. If you are worried or thinking about how others view you, or preoccupied with getting ahead in your career, with family issues, or all your life responsibilities, there is little room for savoring the moment. Given the hectic lives most of us lead today, Bryant and Verhoff believe that people may have to intentionally set aside time for relaxation and disengagement from the endless stream of thoughts, worries, and concerns that dominate our everyday consciousness. Savoring requires an attentive, but a quiet and relaxed state of mind.

Thirdly, savoring requires a mindful focus on the pleasurable features of a current experience—fully appreciating one particular thing and all it has to offer, rather than thinking of several things at once that may divert attention away from the present moment and what is in front of us. This means we need to take a break from analytical thinking and just take in the experience, allowing ourselves, to some extent, to "get lost" in it. This aspect of savoring is somewhat similar to the "total absorption" that characterizes the flow experience. However, flow (as we have seen) gets disrupted by too much self-awareness. Savoring is a more self-aware activity, in which thinking still occurs, but is focused on enhancing the experience. Bryant and Verhoff believe that attending to, thinking about, and identifying the emotions associated with savoring can heighten its positive effects. That is, asking ourselves, "What emotion am I feeling?" Is the savoring emotion a feeling of awe, warmth, comfort, joy, inspiration, happiness, pleasure, gratefulness, mellowness, contentment, or connectedness to others? By focusing on the specifics and subtleties of savoring emotions, we may become more aware of the rich complexity of our emotions and the kinds of savoring experiences that can create them.

Savoring is a relatively simple and straightforward way to enhance our positive experiences. It is not difficult to think of how we might punctuate each day with savoring moments and unplug for a time from our hectic lives. With practice over time, one might also find that savoring becomes a more general mindset applied to more and more aspects of life, and that it may begin to occur spontaneously when we encounter moments worth appreciating.

The evidence reviewed in this chapter strongly suggests that increasing our experience of positive emotions, whether through savoring, flow, socializing with friends, or other enjoyable activities, pays dividends in the form of enhanced well-being. Consistent with Fredrickson's broaden-and-build-theory, positive emotions enhance our physical, psychological, and social coping resources. However, positive emotions are also "good" for us whether or not we are in distress. Positive emotions contribute to a happy and satisfying life.

Chapter Summary Questions

1. What evidence suggests that positive and negative affect underlie our emotional experience?
2. a. How do negative emotions fit the concept of specific action tendencies?
   b. Why don't positive emotions fit the specific action-tendencies concept?
3. Describe four ways in which positive emotions broaden thought-action repertoires and build personal resources, according to Fredrickson's theory. Give an example of each.
4. a. What are the effects of stress and negative emotions on immune-system functioning? Describe and give a research example.
   b. What are the effects of positive emotions on immune-system functioning? Describe and give a research example.
5. Describe problem-focused, emotion-focused, and pro-active coping.
6. Describe three ways in which positive emotions might influence successful coping.
7. Describe and give examples of the following three coping strategies that help generate positive emotions (described by Folkman and Tedlie Moskowitz):
   • positive reappraisal
   • problem-focused coping based on positive emotions
   • infusing ordinary activities with positive meaning
8. a. What does research show about the relationships among self-esteem, optimism, and health?
   b. What role may positive emotions play in explaining these relationships?
9. Describe a study showing the relationship between social contacts and health.
10. a. How does the buffering hypothesis explain the effects of social relationship?
    b. Describe a study that supports the buffering hypothesis.
11. What is the direct effects hypothesis?
12. What are the limits of positive emotions? What comparisons are involved?
13. What kinds of positive behaviors and life successes are related to happiness and positive affect? Give four examples.
14. a. How is the "critical positivity" ratio of 2.9 measured in research?
15. What are the limits and qualifications to a general theory of positivity?
16. What are four differences between a flow experience and the "8-to-5" mind?
17. What three preconditions are necessary for savoring to occur?

Key Terms

positive affect *39*
negative affect *39*
broaden-and-build theory *40*
problem-focused coping *45*
emotion-focused coping *45*

proactive coping *45*
positive reappraisal *46*
buffering hypothesis *49*
direct effects hypothesis *49*
flourishing *51*

languishing *51*
critical positivity ratio *51*
general theory of positivity *52*
flow experience *53*
savoring *54*

Web Resources

Positive Emotions

www.unc.edu/peplab/barb_fredrickson_page.html
Web site for the research of Barbara Fredrickson and the broaden-and-build theory of positive emotions.

APA Online: Positive Emotions, Affect, and Health

www.apa.org American Psychological Association site. Search for articles and recent research on positive emotions and affect.

Creating Flow Experiences

www.positivepsychology.org Web site for Positive Psychology Center at the University of Pennsylvania. Search for links to flow experiences.

Suggested Readings

Bryant, F. B., & Verhoff, J. (2007). *Savoring: A new model of positive experience*. Mahwah, NJ: Lawrence Erlbaum.

Cousins, N. (1979). *Anatomy of an illness*. New York: Norton.

Csikszentmihalyi, M. (1997). *Finding flow*. New York: Basic Books.

Fredrickson, B. L. (2001). The role of positive emotions in positive psychology: The broaden-and-build theory of positive emotions. *American Psychologist, 56*, 218–226.

Fredrickson, B. L., & Losada, M. F. (2005). Positive affect and the complex dynamic of human flourishing. *American Psychologist, 60*, 678–686.

Koenig, H. G., & Cohen, H. J. (Eds.). (2002). *The link between religion and health: Psychoneuroimmunology and the faith factor*. New York: Oxford University Press.

Lyubomirsky, S., King, L., & Diener, E. (2005). The benefits of frequent positive affect. *Psychological Bulletin, 131*, 803–855.

Pressman, S. D., & Cohen, S. (2005). Does positive affect influence health? *Psychological Bulletin, 131*, 925–971.

Salovey, P., Rothman, A. J., Detweiler, J. B., & Steward, W. T. (2000). Emotional states and health. *American Psychologist, 55*, 110–121.

4

Resilience

CHAPTER OUTLINE

A major tenet of positive psychology is that our capacity to experience and actively cultivate positive emotions is one foundation of health and happiness. In this chapter, we examine human resilience as another foundation of well-being. Resilience refers to humans' amazing ability to bounce back and even thrive in the face of serious life challenges. Research suggests that resilience is a widely shared human capacity that many people may not know they possess until confronted with trauma or crisis. Consider the following example of human resilience among children who spent the first years of life in some of the worst conditions imaginable.

In 1989, the people of Romania overthrew the brutal dictatorship of Nicolae Ceasescu. In the months that followed, Western nations learned of the bizarre family policies that resulted in over 150,000 children living under appalling conditions in state-run Romanian orphanages (Center for Family Development, 2004; Witness, 2004). Ceasescu took power in 1965 and wanted to double Romania's population in a generation. His regime required women to have 5 children by age 45, before they were allowed access to birth control and abortions. Economic conditions in Romania were harsh. Ceasescu was exporting grain to pay off a large national debt and he siphoned off money to fund grandiose projects, including his own life of luxury. Basic food necessities like meat and potatoes were rationed for Romanian citizens. The stark reality for many poor Romanian families was that they simply could not afford to feed and clothe the number of children required by the government. As a consequence, thousands of children were turned over to state-run orphanages. Ceasescu regarded children of poor families as "undesirables"—nothing more than a source of cheap labor for the future.

News reports and documentaries provided dramatic images of the horrific conditions in Romania's orphanages. Children were malnourished and slept in dirty cribs, or four children to a cot. Blankets were soaked in urine and infected with lice. Few children had shoes or pants, even during winter. Orphanage buildings were often unheated and had broken windows. Many children suffered from severe diarrhea and infectious diseases. Observers reported seeing children rocking themselves to sleep in their cribs. Many children at 2 and 3 years of age still hadn't learned to walk and were not yet potty trained. Because of the absence of adult supervision, older children often bullied and intimidated younger children on the playground. Nearly every ingredient for healthy physical and psychological development was missing from these children's lives.

The heart-rending images of Romanian orphanages led people from all over the world to pursue adoption of these neglected children. Two psychologists tracked the progress of some of these adopted children. Elinor Ames (1997) compared three groups of children. The first group consisted of 46 children who had spent between 8 months and 4½ years in Romanian orphanages and were adopted by Canadian parents. The average age at adoption was 18.5 months. The second group consisted of 46 non-adopted Canadian-born children growing up in their birth families. These children were matched in age and gender to the sample of orphanage children. The third group of children had been adopted from Romanian maternity hospitals before 4 months of age. Michael Rutter and the English and Romanian Adoptees Study Team (1998) evaluated 111 Romanian orphanage children adopted to English families before the age of 2, and compared them to 52 children of similar ages adopted within England.

As would be expected, many adopted children did suffer a continuation of significant problems caused by harsh orphanage conditions. Ames (1997) reported serious problems in four specific areas: IQs below 85; behavior problems severe enough to require professional help; insecure attachment to adopting parents; and persistence of stereotyped behavior from the orphanage environment (e.g., rocking). She found that 30% of orphanage children, 3 years after adoption, had either three or all four of these problems. The longer the children had been in the orphanage, the more severe and long-lasting their difficulties were.

However, both Ames and Rutter found dramatic improvements in physical and cognitive development among adopted orphanage children. Two years after adoption, Rutter described the gains in cognitive abilities among children in his study as "spectacular" (Rutter et al., 1998). In the Ames study, 35% had none of the four serious problems studied and 35% had only one or two of the problems. Both studies found that children who were adopted before 6 months of age were indistinguishable from comparison samples. These results are all the more powerful, given that the majority of children in each study showed significant delays in development before adoption. The ability of so many children to recover from truly horrific conditions is a testament to human strength and resilience in the face of severe adversity.

WHAT IS RESILIENCE?

Developmental Perspectives

Definitions of resilience share a common core of meaning, focusing on good outcomes following significant life challenges. Such challenges have the potential to derail normal development and undercut healthy functioning. Ann Masten (2001, p. 228) defines **resilience** as "a class of phenomenon characterized by *good outcomes in spite of serious threats to adaptation or development*" (author's italics). Ryff and Singer (2003a, p. 20), define resilience as "*maintenance, recovery, or improvement in mental or physical health following challenge*" (italics in original).

It is important to recognize that descriptions of resilient responses or resilient individuals are judgment calls. As Masten (2001) notes, two factors are involved. For a judgment of resilience to be made, a person must first face a "significant" threat or risk that has the potential to produce negative outcomes. Research has investigated a variety of factors that may threaten normal development. Studies show that children who grow up in physically abusive homes, who have parents suffering from mental illness or alcoholism, or who are raised in poverty are at significant risk for a variety of problems (Masten, 2001; Masten & Reed, 2002; Ryff & Singer, 2003a). Compared to children raised by healthy parents, for example, children raised by parents with mental illnesses are at greater risk for developing mental illnesses themselves (Rutter, 1985). A judgment of resilience, then, requires that the person has faced a significant risk or threat to well-being. Without a demonstrated risk, there is no resilience.

The second part of resilience requires judgment of a favorable or good outcome. The standards for judging outcomes may be defined by the normative expectations of society for the age and situation of the individual (Masten, 2001). For example, if a test of reading ability shows that 90% of third graders across the U.S. achieve a certain average score, this information could be used to define a "third grade reading standard." A third grade child who scores significantly below the standard is not reading up to expectations for his or her grade level. A child scoring well above average exceeds the standard. A similar logic has led to the development of standards for judging intelligence, social behavior, and mental health. Researchers may also use comparison groups like those in the Romanian orphanage studies. Orphanage children were compared to "normal" adopted and non-adopted children for purposes of evaluating deficits and delays in development. Finally, Masten (2001) notes that some researchers have also defined resilience as an absence of problem behaviors or psychopathology following adversity. Children of alcoholic, mentally ill, or abusive parents may be judged resilient if they *don't* develop substance abuse problems, suffer mental illness, become abusive parents themselves, or show symptoms of poor adjustment.

Resilient responses to adversity are common across the life span. We all encounter a variety of challenges as we journey through life. Raising kids, divorce, relocation, job loss, illness, loss of a significant other, and physical declines late in life are all common parts of the human experience. Researchers studying adult development and the aging process have focused on how people maintain their health and well-being and continue to grow as individuals despite the inevitable challenges of life. As in childhood, resilient responses to challenge are quite common across the life span—a phenomenon Ann Masten (2001) calls **"ordinary magic."** Consistent with Masten's concept of "ordinary magic," researchers have emphasized the normal and everyday bases of resilience (see Ryff & Singer, 2003a, 2003b, for reviews). The foundations of resilience include psychological resources such as a flexible self-concept that permits people to change key features of their self-definition in response to changing circumstances, a sense of autonomy and self-direction, and environmental mastery and competence. Social resources are also important to resilience. Included here are quality relationships with others who provide intimacy and social support.

Clinical Perspectives

As we have seen, developmental researchers have examined children who faced adversity during some part of their growing up years. Resilient responses were documented by the fact that some children showed healthy outcomes despite facing serious threats to normal development. Within the clinical psychology literature, studies of resilience have a somewhat different focus. Compared to developmental research, clinical investigations have examined how people cope with more specific life challenges occurring within a shorter frame of time. Developmental studies of resilience often involve long-term, longitudinal studies of children facing multiple risks. In contrast, research in clinical psychology has investigated shorter-term reactions to specific events, such as loss (e.g., death of a loved one) and trauma (i.e., violent or life-threatening situations). Bonanno (2004) describes a resilient response to a specific loss or trauma as "the ability of adults in otherwise normal circumstances who are exposed to an isolated and potentially disruptive event, such as a death of a close relation or a violent or life-threatening situation, to maintain relatively stable, healthy levels of psychological and physical functioning" (p. 20). Within the clinical research literature, the concept of resilience has been described in contrast to the more long-standing concept of recovery (Bonanno, 2004).

Recent studies evaluating people's emotional reactions to loss and trauma suggest that recovery and resilience represent two distinct patterns of response (see Figure 4.1). Bonanno (2004) argues that **recovery,** judged by mental health criteria, involves a period of clinically significant symptoms (e.g., of posttraumatic stress or depression) lasting at least 6 months. This period is followed by a much longer time frame of several years, during which the individual gradually returns to the level of mental health that existed before the trauma or loss. Resilience, on the other hand, involves short-term disturbances in a person's normal functioning lasting only for a period of weeks. This disturbance is followed by a return to relatively stable and generally healthy functioning. Resilience is characterized by "bouncing back" from negative experiences

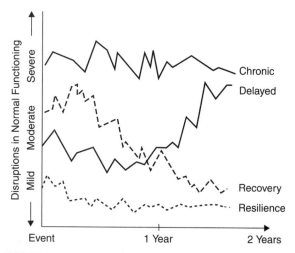

FIGURE 4.1 **Patterns of Disruptions in Normal Functioning Across Time Following Loss and Trauma**

Source: Bonanno, G. A. (2004). Loss, trauma and human resilience: Have we underestimated the human capacity to thrive after extremely aversive events? *American Psychologist, 59,* 20–28. Copyright American Psychological Association. Reprinted by permission.

within a relatively short period of time. The concept of resilience highlights the strength of the individual and his or her coping resources. Recovery begins with more severe reactions and takes considerably more time before the person returns pre-event levels of functioning. The concept of recovery highlights individual vulnerability and coping resources that have been overwhelmed. Chronic and delayed patterns of response to trauma are characterized by enduring or delayed disruptions, respectively.

Clinical psychologists have begun to explore the implications of resilience for the diagnosis and treatment of trauma-related psychopathology. For example, Bonanno (2004) argues that clinical psychologists may have underestimated the prevalence of resilient responses to trauma and loss. This underestimation may occur because clinicians tend to see only those people who suffer persistent reactions and therefore seek out professional help. As a consequence, clinicians may tend to believe that severe reactions to trauma and loss are relatively common, and resilient responses relatively rare. Furthermore, resilient responses may be misinterpreted as signs of poor adjustment or inadequate coping—in short, symptomatic of pathology. That is, people who did not go through a prolonged grieving process were thought to be avoiding or denying the reality of their distress. Avoidance and denial signified maladaptive

coping that could potentially result in a delayed grief reaction at some later time. Bonanno notes that these assumptions have been challenged by recent research showing that many people experience relatively short-term disturbances after loss, rather than prolonged periods of distress, grieving, or depression. There is little evidence that the absence of distress is pathological, and virtually no evidence supporting a delayed grief reaction. In addition, people showing low levels of grief and distress following loss of a loved one have *not* been found to be cold, callous, or insensitive individuals. To avoid pathologizing normal reactions, Bonanno argues for a greater awareness that resilience is both a common and a healthy response to loss and trauma.

RESILIENCE RESEARCH

Studies of resilience are most prominent in developmental psychology. Interest in resilience grew out of a shared awareness among developmental researchers studying at-risk children (Masten, 2001). In the 1970s, scientists began to take notice of the significant number of children in their studies who showed healthy development despite having faced serious adversity. Adverse conditions examined in research include war, poverty, parental alcoholism and mental illness, family violence, natural disasters, divorce, and single parenthood (Cicchetti & Garmezy, 1993; Garmezy, 1991; Hetherington, Bridges, & Insabella, 1998; Luthar & Zigler, 1991; Masten, Best, & Garmezy, 1990; Masten & Coatsworth, 1998; Masten & Reed, 2002; Ryff & Singer, 2003a; Werner & Smith, 1992). Despite these difficult life circumstances, researchers consistently found resilient children who somehow managed to prevail and become competent, healthy adults. One of the most famous studies of resilience is a longitudinal study of children born in Kauai, Hawaii (Werner & Smith, 1982, 1992). Beginning in 1955, a large sample of children was followed for over three decades. Because of naturally-occurring life circumstances, one-third of the children were exposed to multiple risks for developmental problems. The following risks were present before 2 years of age: poverty, parental mental illness, family conflict, and poor environmental conditions for raising children. Werner and Smith found that one-third of these high-risk children grew up to be well-adjusted, caring, and competent adults.

At the other end of the age spectrum, studies of the aging process also show people's resilience in response to life challenges. Contrary to popular belief, most people over the age of 65 are not in ill-health, are not lonely, and are not suffering from depression (Williamson, 2002). In fact, ratings of life satisfaction and self-esteem are, on average, as high in old age as in any other period of adulthood (Charles, Reynolds, & Gatz, 2001; Diener & Suh, 1998). Research has examined how people respond to a variety of challenges and changes associated with the later years (e.g., Carstensen & Freund, 1994; Carstensen, Isaacowitz, & Charles, 1999; Rowe & Kahn, 1987; Rowe & Kahn, 1998; Ryff & Singer, 2003a). These include chronic illness, death of spouse, retirement, change in place of residence, declining abilities, prolonged stress as a caregiver, and declining economic resources. The extensive literature on aging provides strong support for resilient responses in the face of adversity. In reference to this literature, Ryff and Singer (2003a) conclude that "empirical findings have documented that, indeed, many individuals are able to maintain, or even enhance, their well-being as they encounter various life challenges" (p. 22). Recognition of resilience in the later years is also expressed in recent conceptions of *successful aging* (Rowe & Kahn, 1998) and *optimal aging* (Baltes & Baltes, 1990) that describe aging in terms of the potential for positive and enhanced outcomes.

Sources of Resilience

Who prevails over adversity? Is it only a select few with extraordinary emotional strength and toughness? Ann Masten (2001) would answer an emphatic no. Her review of relevant research suggests that resilience is best characterized as ordinary magic. She concludes that resilience in the face of challenge is quite common and does not arise from superhuman effort or abilities. Perhaps you can affirm Masten's observation. Do you know someone—a parent, grandparent, elementary school, high school, or college classmate—who faced a tough situation, trauma, or loss and bounced back in a relatively short period of time? Did you admire that person's strength, or wonder how she or he did it?

Most of us have witnessed people confronting the loss of a loved one, a serious accident or health condition, the divorce of parents, or the end of a close relationship. We have probably also seen both ends of the resilience continuum in different individuals' responses. On one hand, some people become overwhelmed by life's challenges and tragedies.

They suffer significant symptoms of emotional and physical distress and need help and support during a long period of recovery. Adverse life events can undermine people's confidence in themselves, and make them bitter, angry, depressed, or anxious about life. On the other hand, other people seem remarkably able to maintain their bearings in the face of adversity. After a brief period of disturbance, some people quickly return to competent and healthy functioning. Similar to a rubber band that is stretched, but does not break, resilient individuals are able to regain their composure and confidence, and move forward with their lives. Before considering the question of what might explain the difference between these two extreme patterns of response, it is important to clarify a potential source of misunderstanding concerning resilience.

The Dangers of Blaming the Victim

An important caveat is in order here. Studies of resilience must not be taken to mean that people are personally responsible for the level of distress they experience following an adverse life event. Discussion of resilience necessarily involves comparisons of people who experience significant and prolonged distress after trauma with those who show resilient responses. On the surface, these comparisons may seem to imply that certain people are "weaker" and others "stronger" in the face of adversity. Indeed, some of the protective factors involved in resilience are within the person—in his or her abilities, personality, and coping skills. However, it is critical that we avoid the potential dangers of assuming that people who suffer more severe reactions to adversity and need help to recover are somehow *responsible* for their difficulties. To tell a grieving husband that he needs to "get over" the death of his wife, "snap out of it," and "get on with life" would not only be extremely insensitive; it would also imply that the individual is partially responsible for his own distress and that a stronger person, or one who worked harder at recovery, would be doing better. This would be both unfair and unhelpful. Blaming a victim for her or his own distress can impede recovery by adding an additional source of stress, and by reducing the social support a person needs to recover. If individuals feel at fault for their own distress, this implies that they, and they alone, have to solve the problem. A major reason for studying resilient individuals is to learn about the protective factors that contribute to resilience in order to help people cope more effectively with life challenges. The focus is on increasing our understanding and the availability of these protective factors. Blaming people for the absence of protective factors is unwarranted, counter-productive, and contradictory to the purpose of resilience research.

Keeping this important caveat in mind, what are the protective factors involved in resilience? It is certainly true that some people are more resilient than others in the face of adversity. What explains the difference between resilient and less resilient people? Trait explanations of resilience have attempted to profile the characteristics of the "resilient personality." Such concepts as ego-resilience (Block & Block, 1980), hardiness (Kobasa, Maddi, & Kahn, 1982), toughness (Dienstbier & Pytlik Zillig, 2002), self-enhancement (Taylor & Brown, 1988), and optimism (e.g., Carver & Scheier, 2002b; Tennen & Affleck, 2002) have all been related to more effective coping with stressful life events. It is important to note that the traits and abilities associated with resilience are part of most people's psychological makeup. They are not highly unusual or rare. It is also important to recognize that whatever traits contribute to resilience, together they comprise only one component. To regard resilience as primarily dependent on the inner strength of the individual would be both misleading and incomplete. It might lead to the problem of blaming the victim, as discussed above.

For Masten, resilience expresses the operation of basic human adaptational and protective systems—not a rare or exceptional set of talents. Resilience is quite common because human protective systems are part of nearly everyone's life. Research points again and again to the same list of factors that serve protective functions. Based on studies of children and youths, Masten and Reed (2002) have described three general categories of protective factors: those within the child, within the family, and within the community. (The description below is adapted from Masten & Reed, 2002, p. 83, Table 6.2.)

Sources of Resilience in Children

Protective factors *within the child* include:

- Good intellectual and problem-solving abilities
- An easy-going temperament and a personality that can adapt to change

- A positive self-image and personal effectiveness
- An optimistic outlook
- Ability to regulate and control emotions and impulses
- Individual talents that are valued by the individual and by his or her culture
- A healthy sense of humor

Protective factors *within the family* include:

- Close relationships with parents or other primary caregivers
- Warm and supportive parenting that provides clear expectations and rules
- An emotionally positive family with minimal conflict between parents
- A structured and organized home environment
- Parents who are involved in their child's education
- Parents who have adequate financial resources

Protective factors *within the community* include:

- Going to a good school
- Involvement in social organizations within the school and community
- Living in a neighborhood of involved and caring people who address problems and promote community spirit
- Living in a safe neighborhood
- Easy availability of competent and responsive emergency, public health, and social services

Resilience, according to Masten, has more to do with the health of these protective systems than with the specific nature of the adversity faced. That is, an individual with few protective resources may suffer significant negative outcomes in the face of even a low level of adversity. An individual who has most or all of these protective resources may be able to deal with significant adversity with a minimum of disturbance.

Masten's concept of ordinary magic summarizes two aspects of resilience research. First, it points to the finding that *many* people show resilient responses to significant life challenges. In other words, resilience is not rare—it is common. Second, it points to a lack of extraordinariness in the sources of resilience. Resilience arises from everyday features of people's lives–not from superhuman abilities. The media often celebrate people who have beaten cancer or overcome a disability as exceptional individuals, who triumphed over tragic circumstances. Resilience research affirms and celebrates people's ability to triumph over tragedy, but would suggest that such cases are not as exceptional as media coverage implies. Odds are that each of us already knows a few individuals who are examples of ordinary magic.

Focus on Research: Resilience Among Disadvantaged Youth

Twenty percent of all children in the United States live in poverty; that's 1 out of every 5, representing 13.5 million children and youths under the age of 18 (U.S. Census Bureau, 1999). A substantial amount of research shows that children living in poverty are at risk for a variety of problems, ranging from emotional disorders and drug use to school failure and juvenile delinquency (see McLoyd, 1998, Myers, 2000b; Steinberg, Dornbusch, & Brown, 1992). These and other potential problems reflect the stressful and disadvantaged nature of impoverishment. Poor children are more likely to have parents who suffer from emotional disturbances or drug addictions, and are more likely than middle-class children to witness violence and engage in criminal behavior such as vandalism and illegal drug use. In addition, poor children have fewer resources in the form of supportive community agencies, high-quality schools, and health care (McLoyd, 1998). Despite these risks, the *majority* of poor children do *not* engage in criminal behavior, drop out of school, or suffer debilitating emotional problems. A probable reason for this is that many poor children benefit from the protective factors described by Masten (2001) and thus show resilience in the face of adversity. A stable and caring family, for example, has been strongly linked to successful development in the face of economic disadvantage (Myers, 2000b).

What particular constellation of life circumstances and individual characteristics differentiates resilient from less resilient children living in poverty?

Buckner, Mezzacappa, and Beardslee (2003) recently addressed this question in a study of 155 young people (ages 8 to 17) and their mothers. The sample was nearly balanced between males and females, and a variety of racial and ethnic groups were represented (35% Caucasian, 21% African American, 36% Puerto Rican Latino, and 8% other Latino). The mothers and children were extremely poor and a substantial percentage had been homeless in the recent past. Mothers were interviewed extensively about their own and their children's lives. The researchers gathered detailed information about mental health, exposure to abuse and violence, social support, and about the children's developmental histories and current behavior patterns. A number of standardized measures of children's emotional and behavior problems, mental health symptoms, level of functioning, and competence were also taken. Based on responses to these measures, Buckner and his colleagues identified a resilient group and non-resilient group of children. Resilient children (45 youths, or 29% of the sample) had no clinically significant mental health symptoms and showed generally positive functioning. These resilient children were doing well across multiple measures of health and competence, despite the challenges presented by their impoverishment. In contrast, non-resilient children (70 youths, or 45% of the sample) evidenced significant mental health problems and at least some deficits in functioning. Forty youths in the study did not fit into either the resilient or non-resilient pattern (ie., they were in the middle).

The researchers explored the specific factors that differentiated the resilient from the non-resilient youths. Specifically, they examined the number of negative life events experienced, the level of chronic stress, cognitive abilities, self-esteem, self-regulation skills, social support, and parental monitoring and supervision. Buckner and colleagues (2003) found that resilience was clearly linked to the number of negative life events and to chronic stress. Non-resilient children had suffered significantly more negative life events such as physical and sexual abuse, death of a friend, parental arrests, serious family illness, and more chronic stress. Chronic stress was related to such concerns as not having enough to eat, not feeling safe, and other daily difficulties associated with poverty. Resilient children faced serious threats and stress, but at lower levels of frequency and intensity.

Paralleling the findings of other research, the resilient youths in Buckner and colleagues' study showed higher levels of intellectual competence and self-esteem than the non-resilient group. Intellectual skills contribute to academic success and to solving and coping with the many problems associated with poverty. Self-esteem helps maintain a positive self-image in the face of the challenges to self-concept that result from being poor.

Another characteristic that differentiated resilient from non-resilient youths was related to self-regulation skills. In fact, self-regulation was the most powerful predictor of resilience in this study. Self-regulation refers to a person's ability to guide and direct behavior toward desirable goals over time and across varying situations. It involves the ability to control and modulate thinking, emotions, attention, and behavior. Self-regulation is particularly important in coping with stressful life situations. People with good self-regulation skills are more likely to anticipate and proactively prevent stressful situations from occurring, find ways to redirect and offset negative emotions, and engage in effective problem solving as a coping strategy. Self-regulation skills function like an internal gyroscope to keep us centered and directed as we encounter events that challenge our stability and our achievement of important life goals.

Cognitive and Emotional Self-Regulation Skills

Buckner and his colleagues (2003) found that resilient youths, compared to non-resilient youths, scored significantly higher on measures of cognitive and emotional self-regulation. Cognitive self-regulation serves an executive function in directing action and solving problems. Youths with good cognitive self-regulation skills are well-organized, self-disciplined, and able to carry out plans from beginning to end. They can focus their attention on the important features of a task by concentrating and channeling their efforts toward successful completion. Their thinking shows flexibility in considering alternative solutions, and tasks are considered abstractly rather than concretely. In other words, cognitive self-regulation involves the ability to see the big picture—the forest rather than just the trees.

Emotional self-regulation is equally important to resilient living. Emotional self-regulation refers to the ability to keep your cool in tough situations. Youths with this skill are able to suppress their anger rather than lashing out. That is, they are adept at controlling how intensely they express their emotions and find ways of showing emotion that do not alienate or cause negative reactions in others. Emotional regulation is an important part of social competence that contributes to the development and maintenance of effective and supportive relationships with others. The absence of emotional regulation skills, as noted

by Buckner and his colleagues, has been strongly linked to mood disorders and behavioral disorders. Poor emotional regulation can lead to considerable trouble for children and adolescents.

Taken together, you can imagine the value of cognitive and emotional self-regulation skills for youths living in poverty. Being able to stay on task, accomplish goals, deal effectively with daily hassles and challenges, control negative emotions, channel energies toward appropriate goals, and deal effectively with others are important skills for youths in any environment. But in an environment that presents a constant array of challenges and stressful events, these skills may make the difference between a healthy and successful life, and a life plagued by emotional disorder, academic failure, and crime.

Developing Self-Regulation Abilities

One final finding from Buckner and colleagues' study of poor youths merits particular attention. The degree of parental monitoring also differentiated resilient from non-resilient youth. Mothers who scored high on parental monitoring reported that they always knew where their children were, and who was with their children. This was especially important when the mother was away from home. Parental monitoring is an important aspect of the child's environment, given that there are real threats to children's safety and some of these are heightened in low-income neighborhoods. Monitoring probably also contributed to children's awareness that they were cared for and valued, thereby perhaps contributing to their own sense of worth and their development of self-regulation skills. Mothers who actively monitored their children's whereabouts may have provided a positive role model to help children develop self-monitoring of their own behavior.

Sources of Resilience in Adulthood and Later Life

Many of the factors that contribute to resilient responses in childhood also contribute to adult resilience. Carol Ryff and her colleagues have provided one of the more extensive and empirically-supported models of well-being (see Keyes, 2002; Keyes & Lopez, 2002; Keyes, Shmotkin, & Ryff, 2002; Ryff & Keyes, 1995; Ryff & Singer, 2003b). The six dimensions presented below describe psychological well-being (see Chapter 2 for a detailed discussion of this topic). Although not originally focused on resilience, research has shown that these factors are predictive of resilient responses in the face of adversity, and in successful aging and the maintenance of good mental health (see Keyes & Lopez, 2002; Ryff & Singer, 2003a, 2003b). In short, the six dimensions describe aspects of an individual's personality, self-concept, competence, and social relationships that represent resources for effective living. The six dimensions are described below.

Self-Acceptance. Self-acceptance defines a person who has a positive attitude toward himself or herself and accepts all the varied aspects of self, including both strengths and weaknesses. Such a person feels positive about his or her life so far. Self-acceptance means you embrace and like who you are.

Personal Growth. Personal growth refers to a person's feelings of continued development and effectiveness, and an openness to new experiences and challenges. Personal growth is exhibited by a person who is still excited about life and learning new things.

Purpose in Life. Purpose in life means that you have goals and beliefs that give direction to your life. Your life has meaning and purpose, perhaps because of satisfying work, religious beliefs, or devotion to a cause or to the needs of others. To have purpose means that you feel you are making a positive difference in the world and that your life is personally meaningful.

Environmental Mastery. Mastery refers to a feeling of competence and the ability to manage the complex environment of today's fast-paced life. Mastery is reflected in a person's ability to create a personally suitable living situation, including successful management of work, finances, family, housing, health, and all the conditions necessary for a successful life.

Autonomy. Autonomous people are comfortable with self-direction, taking initiative, and working independently. Such people possess internal standards that guide their actions and allow them to resist negative social pressures from others. Being your own person and following your own values and interests would express a sense of autonomy.

Positive Relations with Others. People who have positive relations have warm, satisfying, and trusting interactions with others and are capable of empathy and intimacy. Positive relations refer to the quality, rather than the quantity of our relationships. Having good friends, a satisfying marriage, and supportive relations with co-workers all express this dimension.

Successful Aging

Recent studies focusing on the process of aging support the operation of basic adaptive and protective systems that provide strength and resilience as people enter the final stages of life. We noted earlier that older people are, on average, as happy as people in other periods of adulthood. Large-scale epidemiological studies show low rates of nearly all psychological disorders among older adults, with the exception of dementia (Regier et al., 1988). However, at some point, most elderly persons do suffer the loss of loved ones and reductions in their own cognitive and physical abilities. These changes raise the issue of personal mortality. How do elderly people maintain their emotional stability and continue to enjoy life when they are faced with the challenges of aging? One recent theory called socioemotional selectivity theory helps explain how age-related changes can be the basis for a more satisfying, pleasurable, and hassle-free life, and for stronger social support (Carstensen, 1992; Carstensen et al., 1999).

Carstensen argues that people's perception of how much time they have left in life exerts a powerful influence over the goals they choose to pursue. Young people have an expansive perception of time because most of their lives lie ahead of them. Aged individuals tend to perceive time as limited because most of their lives lie behind them. Time may be viewed, quite literally, as running out. Perception of personal time available as either expansive or limited has a determining effect on the goals people choose to pursue. Goals, in turn, have a determining effect on behavior and the dominant activities in a person's life. Goals energize and direct behavior toward their realization. For example, a college student is typically focused on activities related to the goals of getting a college degree, exploring careers, and establishing relationships in preparation for the future.

According to **socioemotional selectivity theory,** as people realize they have fewer years remaining in their lives, they begin to shift their energy and attention away from activities and goals related to the future and come to focus more on the present. This transition involves a shift in emphasis, from knowledge-related social goals that prepare a person for the future, to emotion-related social goals that maintain and enhance one's present life situation. The predicted pattern of importance for knowledge-related and emotion-related goals is shown in Figure 4.2. When we are young and our futures stretch out in front of us, we are naturally oriented toward exploring new experiences, meeting new people, and gaining knowledge and skills that may help us in the future. When we are older and time is limited, we are less likely to change or give up our enjoyable activities, everyday routines, or significant relationships for the possibility of future gains. We are more focused on emotional satisfaction in the present. This may seem like a recipe for stagnation, but research suggests quite the contrary.

Numerous studies by Carstensen and her colleagues (see Carstensen et al., 1999; Carstensen & Charles, 2003, for reviews) support the potential for such a refocusing of goals by elderly individuals to produce heightened life satisfaction and peace of mind. Being relieved of the burden of preparing for the future, and recognizing the fragility of life and its

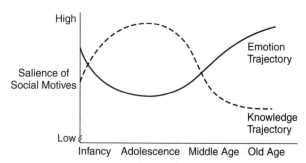

FIGURE 4.2 Socioemotional Selectivity Theory's Conception of the Importance of Knowledge and Emotional Satisfaction Across the Life Span

Note: Both knowledge and emotions are considered "social motives" relating to social understanding and emotionally satisfying relations with others.

Source: Carstensen, L. L., Isaacowitz, D. M., & Charles, S. T. (1999). Taking time seriously: A theory of socioemotional selectivity. *American Psychologist, 54,* 165–181. Copyright American Psychological Association. Reprinted with permission.

approaching end seems to bring out the best in people. For example, compared to middle-aged couples, older couples showed better regulation of emotions while dealing with conflicts involving such issues as finances, children, and in-laws. In other words, discussions of these issues by older couples were characterized by less severe conflict; lower levels of anger, belligerence, and complaining; and more expressions of affection than similar discussions by middle-aged couples. Older couples also expressed more pleasure in their marriages and in activities such as talking about their children and grandchildren, and doing things together (e.g., vacations). Long-term married couples have also been shown to grow closer in their later years. They become more concerned with enjoying each other's company and less concerned with trying to change, impress, or dominate their partners (Levenson, Carstensen, & Gottman, 1993, 1994).

Carstensen argues that these changes occur because a time-limited perspective shifts attention toward the value of a smaller, but higher-quality social network in which one is most likely to be validated and loved. Elderly people often choose to refine their social relationships in order to maximize the quality and satisfaction of their most important social partners. Research supports these predictions (Carstensen et al., 1999). Older people devote less time and energy to casual acquaintances and meeting new people, and more to long-standing relationships with their spouses, best friends, children, and grandchildren. The frequency of interactions with acquaintances was found to decline with age, while interactions with spouses and immediate family members remained constant or increased in frequency. People in their later years seem to develop an "inner circle" of close relationships that are optimally equipped to fulfill supportive and emotional needs. The age-related changes described by the socioemotional selectivity theory can be seen as adaptive responses that create resources for resilience as one faces the inevitable challenges of aging.

GROWTH THROUGH TRAUMA

A growing body of empirical literature reveals that many people find meaningful life lessons, a renewed appreciation for life, and increased feelings of personal strength as a result of traumatic experiences (see Affleck & Tennen, 1996; Nolen-Hoeksema & Davis, 2002; Tedeschi & Calhoun, 1995; Tennen & Affleck,

2002, for reviews). In contrast to the negative outcomes that characterize posttraumatic stress disorder (PTSD), positive outcomes arising from traumatic experiences have been referred to as **posttraumatic growth** (PTG) (Tedeschi, Park, & Calhoun, 1998). Posttraumatic growth captures the main theme of research showing the potential for growth and enhancement that may result from personal suffering. The posttraumatic growth literature is closely related to the literature on resilience because both focus on human strengths in the face of challenging life events. One difference is that resilience research has emphasized how people can bounce back to pre-trauma levels of functioning following adversity (in other words, return to their previous level of adjustment). In contrast, PTG research has explored *positive* changes and *enhanced* functioning following trauma (in other words, a person might grow *beyond* his or her pre-trauma level of adjustment). Our discussion of positive growth through trauma will first examine early research focused on why life traumas can be so disruptive and distressing. We will then review recent research describing how positive growth can emerge in the aftermath of adverse life events.

Negative Effects of Trauma

Research has examined how people cope with a wide variety of traumas including catastrophic fires; loss of a loved one; caring for a seriously ill infant; surviving a heart attack or natural disaster; dealing with HIV infection, rheumatoid arthritis or cancer; coping with disabilities; and being victimized in a sexual assault. The life-changing effects of such traumas cannot be underestimated. In addition to the physical pain and bodily harm often involved in life-threatening events, there is also a distressing and painful psychological aftermath. Janoff-Bulman and Frieze (1983) note that "common emotional reactions to victimization include shock, confusion, helplessness, anxiety, fear and depression" (p. 2). Some percentage of people experiencing trauma develop symptoms fitting the American Psychiatric Association's (2000) definition of posttraumatic stress disorder (PTSD). PTSD symptoms include repeated reliving of the traumatic event in memory, and intrusive thoughts and feelings associated with the event (*Diagnostic and Statistical Manual of Mental Disorders*, American Psychiatric Association, 2000). Other symptoms of PTSD include reduced responsiveness, shown in detachment from others, constriction of feelings and emotional expression, and decreased interest in previously significant activities.

Janoff-Bulman argues that the psychological toll of trauma occurs, in large part, because traumatic events shatter people's basic assumptions about themselves and the world they live in (Janoff-Bulman, 1992; Janoff-Bulman & Frieze, 1983). She describes three basic assumptions that are challenged by trauma: "(1) the belief in personal invulnerability; (2) the perception of the world as meaningful and comprehensible; and (3) the view of ourselves in a positive light" (Janoff-Bulman & Frieze, p. 3). The first assumption refers to the belief that "it can't happen to me." Research consistently shows that people underestimate the likelihood of serious negative events happening to them. People believe that bad things always happen to "the other guy" (e.g., Perloff, 1983). After victimization occurs, people know something bad *can* happen to them and they spend considerable time and energy worrying that trauma may occur again. Their belief in a safe, secure world has been challenged by increased awareness of a more uncertain and dangerous world, in which they feel more vulnerable to bad events. A traumatic experience opens the door to the possibility of thinking that "if *this* can happen, *anything* can happen." A person's former belief in his or her invulnerability to traumatic events now seems like an illusion.

The second assumption, that life is meaningful and comprehensible, may also be contradicted by a traumatic experience. After trauma, a person's life may seem chaotic and confusing. Victims frequently ask themselves, "why me?" or "what did I do to deserve this?" Lerner (1980) argues that many people operate on the assumption of a just world. In other words, they believe people get what they deserve. To a victim of a violent mugging who was simply at the wrong place at the wrong time, the world may now look like a very unjust place. People may come to believe that they have far less control over negative events than they previously thought. The third assumption, concerning positive self-image, may undergo a similar transformation. Research shows that people's sense of personal worth and self-esteem is often deflated and undermined by trauma. People may feel helpless, weak, out of control, powerless, or needy following victimization (Janoff-Bulman & Frieze, 1983).

Positive Effects of Trauma

Surprisingly, Park (1998) reports that after a traumatic experience a significant number of people actually say that "it was the best thing that ever happened" to them. Given the negative effects just reviewed, how can positive benefits emerge from adversity? The general explanation for PTG is that challenged beliefs and assumptions about life can provide a basis and an opportunity for personal growth. Initially, traumatic experiences are disorienting and frightening. Over time, however, people may learn deeper lessons about themselves and about life. These lessons have the potential to enhance individuals' understanding of themselves, their relationships, and what is most important in life. These lessons may also contribute to more effective coping and adjustment. Table 4.1 shows are some of the positive changes reported in the PTG literature (Ryff & Singer, 2003a; Tedeschi et al., 1998).

Are these positive changes real, or just convenient rationalizations and distortions of the actual effects of trauma? Early research tended to view reports of positive change following trauma as defensive responses that might help a person cope temporarily, by artificially softening the effects of the trauma. Positive changes were not viewed as real and enduring (Tennen & Affleck, 2002). Researchers today, while acknowledging the difficulty in distinguishing between self-reported and objectively documented change, are more likely to believe that trauma can, in fact, produce genuine positive change in people's lives.

Explanations for Growth Through Trauma

Explanations for positive growth through trauma have drawn on the work of existential psychiatrist Viktor Frankl (1976/1959). Frankl argued that a "*will to meaning*" was a basic motivating force in people's lives. He thought that people need an overarching sense of purpose, meaning, and direction to sustain them through life's journey. A meaningful life is expressed in people's goals and ambitions that, in turn, direct their energy toward the future. When traumatic experiences shatter or disrupt these goals and purposes, life may be perceived as meaningless. Under such conditions, people are highly motivated to restore a sense of meaning and purpose to their lives. Such circumstances present opportunities for personal growth as people develop and commit themselves to new goals, ambitions, and purposes that re-establish their sense of meaning and direction. These goals involve fundamental assumptions about life. They involve the "big" questions concerning what makes life meaningful and the nature of a person's life purposes. They are bound up with an individual's identity and self-definition. To the extent that

---

TABLE 4.1 Positive changes reported in the PTG literature

Changes in Perception

An increased feeling of personal strength, confidence, and self-reliance

Greater appreciation of the fragility of life, including one's own

Perceptions of self as a survivor rather than a victim

Changes in Relationships

Closer ties to family

Greater emotional disclosure and feelings of closeness to others

More compassion for others and more willingness to give to others

Changes in Life Priorities

Increased clarity about what is most important in life

A deeper and often spiritual sense of the meaning in life

A new commitment to take life easier

Less concern with acquiring material possessions, money, and social status

trauma causes a redefinition of basic life assumptions, the result may be a major redefinition of one's identity. The same negative experiences that shatter basic assumptions may also provide opportunities for positive growth as people find life-renewing purpose.

How do people create growth and find meaning out of trauma and suffering? **Meaning-making** refers to an active process of reappraisal and revision of how an event might be interpreted or what it might signify (Baumeister & Vohs, 2002). Researchers have focused on two forms of meaning-making following tragedy: making sense of the event, and finding benefits or positive outcomes (Nolen-Hoeksema & Davis, 2002). **Sense-making** refers to making the event comprehensible in terms of beliefs about how the world operates. In Western cultures, for example, we tend to assume that there is some order and predictability to events. Negative events do not occur randomly or unpredictably. This is the idea behind Lerner's work (1980) on the tendency to believe in a just world. Many people believe that the world operates (not in every case, but in general) on the principle that you get what you deserve. How, then, can we make sense of a person who dies "too early," as in the case of a young adult with a terminal illness? Research suggests that this is, indeed, a difficult task because it contradicts our sense of the natural order of things and our notions of a just world. Davis and Nolen-Hoeksema and their colleagues interviewed people who had lost loved ones to terminal illness (see Nolen-Hoeksema & Davis, 2002, for a review). They asked people directly whether they could make sense of their loss. When the lost loved one was 72 years of age or older, 87% of those interviewed reported that they were able to make sense of the death. However, when the loss involved someone much younger, far fewer people reported being able to make sense of it.

How a person makes sense of trauma or loss may be highly individualized. Each person's life story is somewhat different. The sense an individual makes of an adverse event will, in part, reflect how it fits within the broader framework of that individual's life story. Some may see the event in religious terms, as part of God's plan for them or for the person they lost. A belief that a loved one has been "called home," or is now with God,

provides comfort and gives meaning to a painful loss. Others may see death as an inevitable and natural part of the cycle of life—dying is a part of living. Work by McAdams (1996) and Pennebaker (1993) suggests that writing about traumatic events helps create structure, coherence, and meaning. For example, McAdams asked people to view their lives as a book, complete with title, chapters (significant events), and an underlying plot or theme. This endeavor provided an opportunity to put their lives in perspective and reflect on purposes, important goals, and ambitions. Pennebaker and his colleagues suggest that writing may help people make sense of trauma (Esterling, L'Abate, Murray, & Pennebaker, 1999). In their studies, writing about emotional upheaval was associated with improved physical and mental health (e.g., Pennebaker & Beall, 1986; Pennebaker, Colder, & Sharp, 1990).

The second form of meaning-making is called **benefit-finding.** This involves finding benefits or positive outcomes in trauma and loss. Research consistently finds that people report positive benefits from adversity. For example, Davis, Nolen-Hoeksema, and Larson (1998) found that 6 months after losing a loved one to a terminal illness, 73% of bereaved people reported positive outcomes (Nolen-Hoeksema & Davis, 2002). Eighteen months later, 77% reported some benefit from their loss. Studies of people dealing with a seriously ill infant, property damage by tornado or fire, or a serious medical emergency, have found a similar percentage of people who report some growth and benefit as a result of negative life events (see Tennen & Affleck, 2002, for a review). Reported benefits typically fall within the three categories described earlier: perceptions of the self as stronger, closer relationships, and greater clarity concerning what is truly important in life.

These changes make sense if we consider that, up until a crisis occurs, our resilience and strength may not have been tested; the importance of our relationships may have been taken for granted; and what is *most important* in life may have been overlooked in the *busyness* of everyday life. One reason people may say after an adverse life event that "it was the best thing that ever happened" to them, is that they have developed a new awareness regarding themselves and previously taken-for-granted assumptions about life.

Consider a hypothetical example: A 60-year-old woman's husband suffers a severe heart attack that puts him in the hospital for an extended period of time. The wife has been a homemaker all her life. Her husband was a good provider, but very controlling when it came to finances. He was something of a workaholic and also had a drinking problem.

In the aftermath of her husband's heart attack, the woman assumes the role of "head of the household" and essentially switches roles with her husband. She now makes the financial decisions. She oversees her husband's care in the hospital and negotiates with their health insurance company to make sure all of his treatment is covered. When her husband comes home, she makes sure he follows his diet and home therapy routine and gets to all his doctor appointments. Her husband, partly as a result of discussion with his doctor, now sees that his hard-driving lifestyle and drinking were major reasons why he suffered the heart attack. He commits himself to taking it easy and is surprised to see his wife handling all the financial and health-care decisions so competently. Sounds like a TV soap opera! For our purposes, the main point here is that the woman and her husband might very well say the heart attack was the "best thing that ever happened" to them, and this would make sense—not as a rationalization of a bad situation, but because it was true. And if the woman reported that she was more self-confident, had a closer relationship with her husband, and appreciated life more, that would also be an accurate assessment of real changes and positive outcomes. Studies of resilience and growth through trauma provide consistent evidence for the human ability to overcome adversity and to prosper and grow in its aftermath. Clearly, not every tragedy has a happy ending. However, research findings suggest that resilience and PTG are more common features of human experience than previously supposed—expressing, in Masten's words, *ordinary magic.*

Focus on Research: In Their Own Words—Making Sense of Loss

As we have discussed, benefit-finding and sense-making are two ways of making tragedy and loss comprehensible. Loss of a loved one often unsettles our view of ourselves and the world we live in.

Finding something positive in the loss experience and being able to make sense of it are widely believed to help people cope and may also provide opportunities for personal growth. Davis, Nolen-Hoeksema, and Larson (1998) examined these two meaning-making processes in a prospective interview study with 200 people in a San Francisco hospice program. These individuals would soon lose a family member to a terminal illness. Participants were interviewed before their loss, and again at 6, 13, and 18 months after their loss. As part of the interview, family members were asked whether they could make sense of their loved one's death and whether they had found anything positive in their loss. For sense-making, the question was, "Do you feel you have been able to make sense of the death?" For benefit-finding the question was, "Sometimes people who lose a loved one find some positive aspect in the experience. For example, some people feel they learn something about themselves or others. Have you found anything positive in the experience?" (Davis et al., 1998 p. 565). Nearly 70% of those interviewed reported being able to make sense of their loss and 80% reported finding positive benefits. Examples of interview results, in the words of individual family members, are presented in Tables 4.2 and 4.3 (adapted from Davis et al., 1998, Table 1, p. 566). Interview responses were classified according to the different types of sense-making and benefits described by the 200 family members in the study.

Davis and his colleagues also found that family members who were able to make sense of their loss and find something positive in the experience suffered less post-loss distress, as measured by levels of anxiety and symptoms of depression and posttraumatic stress. Interestingly, however, making sense of loss contributed to less distress only if it occurred during the first year after the loss. Those who were able to make sense of the loss only *after* the first year did not experience significantly reduced distress. Exactly why this relationship occurred is unclear. Finding positive benefits was associated with lower distress in the 13- and 18-month follow-up interviews. That is, benefit-finding was associated with longer-term adjustment to loss.

These researchers also found that an optimistic attitude predicted finding benefits in the loss, and a religious or spiritual orientation

TABLE 4.2 Making sense of loss

Predictability

"It always made sense to me. I mean, he smoked for years. It's perfectly sensible to me."

Acceptance as a Natural Part of the Life Cycle

"My basic attitude to life was that there's a beginning and an end, and it's going to happen to one or the other of us sooner or later, and you have to cope with it. That's all. There's nothing you can do to prevent these things from happening. They're part of life."

God's Plan

"I think that my father's illness was meant to be, and that was God's plan. He lived a really long life, and everybody has their way to go from this world, and that was his way . . . "

Lost Loved One Accepted Death

"He was very much at peace with his dying. I think that helped me become more at peace. And he could talk very freely about dying . . . "

Preparation/Expectation

"I accepted that I was going to lose him before he even passed away, and I really was prepared for his death."

Life Lessons

"It's a very meaningful experience. My goodness, everyone should go through that. (One learns) so much about life and about themselves, about the person dying—a very important process to understand, because they're going to go through it too . . . "

predicted making sense of the loss, and both optimism and religious beliefs were associated with lower levels of distress. Optimism and religious beliefs may have lowered distress levels directly or may have been mediated by the two forms of meaning-making. That is, optimists may have found more positive benefits in their loss which, in turn, led to lowered distress. Religious beliefs may have made it easier to make sense of the loss, thereby reducing distress.

TABLE 4.3 Finding positive benefits

Personal Growth

"Yes, (I found) a growth and a freedom to give fuller expression to my feelings, or to assert myself, to do things I want to do."

Perspective on Life

"In that having your health and living life to its fullest is a real blessing. I appreciate my family, friends, nature and life in general. I see goodness in people. . . . It makes me more mature."

Family Togetherness

"We definitely learned a lot about ourselves and about each other within the family circle. There was a rallying of support, and camaraderie that I think only shows itself . . . when something like this happens."

Support From Others

"I have learned and seen a lot of positive things in people—they just glowed. It was nice to get that blessing in disguise. The people who rallied around were wonderful."

Learning and Benefiting Others

"It caused me to desire to be more knowledgeable and aware of AIDS. I've become more active with the gay community in support of healthier lifestyles and safer sex."

Chapter Summary Questions

1. How do studies of Romanian orphanage adoptees show evidence of surprising resilience?
2. a. How is resilience defined from a developmental perspective?
   b. According to Ann Masten, what two factors are involved in a judgment of resilience?
3. How do the clinical and developmental views of resilience differ?
4. According to Bonanno, what is the significance of resilience research for clinical psychology's understanding of reactions to trauma and loss?
5. Describe three findings from developmental research on resilience.
6. What does Ann Masten mean by "ordinary magic?"
7. How might misunderstanding of resilience research lead to victim-blaming?
8. Research has identified protective factors that operate within the child, within the family, and within the community. List three from each category.
9. a. What factors differentiated resilient from non-resilient youths living in poverty?
   b. What are cognitive and emotional self-regulation skills and why are they important bases for a resilient response to poverty?
10. What factors are associated with resilient responses in adulthood?
11. a. What changes in social relationships typically occur for elderly individuals?
    b. Describe socioemotional selectivity theory. How does socioemotional selectivity theory describe these changes as adaptive, and as sources of resilience for aging individuals?
12. What is posttraumatic growth and how does it differ from resilience?
13. What three basic life assumptions are challenged by trauma, according to Janoff-Bulman?
14. Research shows that trauma can result in changes in perception, relationships, and life priorities. List two examples of each of these three types of change.
15. What are two ways in which people find meaning through trauma? Describe and give an example of each.

Key Terms

resilience *58*
ordinary magic *59*
recovery *59*
blaming the victim *61*

socioemotional selectivity theory *66*
posttraumatic growth (PTG) *67*

meaning-making *69*
sense-making *69*
benefit-finding *69*

Web Resources

Resilience

The Mayo Clinic, the American Psychological Association and *Psychology Today* magazine have information and self-tests for resilience as featured topics. These sites are among the first listed by a Google search with "resilience" as the key term.

Posttraumatic Growth

www.ptgi.uncc.edu This web site is by posttraumatic growth researchers at the University of North Carolina–Charlotte, including Lawrence Calhoun and Richard Tedeschi. This site provides current information about their ongoing PTG research.

MIDUS Study—Successful Aging

www.midus.wisc.edu/midus2 This web site reviews the large-scale study of aging supported by the Federal Government's Department of Aging. Many studies of psychological well-being across the life span are based on the MIDUS study data.

Suggested Readings

Baumeister, R. F. (1991). *Meanings of life.* New York: Guilford.

Bonanno, G. A. (2004). Loss, trauma and human resilience: Have we underestimated the human capacity to thrive after extremely aversive events? *American Psychologist, 59,* 20–28.

Carstensen, L. L., & Freund, A. (1994). The resilience of the aging self. *Developmental Review, 14,* 81–92.

Masten, A. S. (2001). Ordinary magic: Resilience processes in development. *American Psychologist, 56,* 227–238.

Reivich, K., & Shatte, A. (2002). *The resilience factor.* New York: Broadway Books.

Tedeschi, R. G., Park, C. L., & Calhoun, L. G. (Eds.). (1998). *Posttraumatic growth: Positive changes in the aftermath of crisis.* Mahwah, NJ: Erlbaum.

5

Happiness and the Facts of Life

No, this chapter isn't about sex! It is about how the circumstances of our lives influence our level of happiness. If you are a student reading this book for a college class, consider the following question: Unless you are dealing with significant personal problems or events, can you think of one good reason why this period in your life shouldn't be the happiest you have experienced and probably will ever experience? Sure, childhood was good, but you were closely supervised by adults. In your teen years, you had less responsibility, but parents and teachers were still looking over your shoulder and you did not have the freedom you enjoy now. Adulthood may look appealing, but working, paying your mortgage, and raising a family are pretty serious business—satisfying, but not really fun. College certainly can be stressful with exams to take and term papers to write; but stressful compared to what? Is a big paper for your professor in the same league as a big report for your boss? One might cost you a lower grade, but the other might cost you your job. So here you are, freedom to explore everything from ideas to romance, with lots of parties thrown in for good measure. Lots of time, probably enough money, and not many big-time responsibilities. You should be happy as a pig in mud. Well . . . come up with an answer yet? Probably you have a number of responses including a measure of resentment at the implication that if you're not happy there must be something wrong with you.

The point here is not whether college is or should be the happiest time of life, or whether the portrait of college life painted here is simply an envy-driven stereotype held by adults who wish they had more fun and less responsibility in their lives. The point is that, from the outside looking in, lots of stages and life events may look good or bad. But from the inside looking out, our experience is often very different, not quite as good or quite as bad as we had imagined. In this chapter and the next, we explore why many of the things we *think* matter, don't, and why we frequently exaggerate the emotional impact of life stages and life events.

We noted in Chapter 1 that early studies of happiness grew out of national survey research examining the relationships between well-being and demographic variables (e.g., Campbell, Converse, & Rodgers, 1976; Wilson, 1967). Survey researchers followed the hedonic model of subjective well-being (SWB) by defining happiness in terms of life satisfaction and the balance of positive and negative emotions. Demographic information describes prominent "facts" of a person's "objective" life circumstances. This is the kind of information you are usually asked to supply when you fill out a credit application (e.g., your age, sex, marital status, education, job, income, and place of residence). Demographic information is considered "objective" because it can be described independent of personal judgment. For instance, I can know how much money you make per year without having to consider whether you feel your income is fair or equitable compensation for the work you do.

Researchers have asked two questions about demographics and happiness. First, to what extent is an individual's level of happiness (i.e., SWB) related to his or her life circumstances and demographic profile? In other words, do the objective facts of people's lives predict their levels of happiness? Second, do differences in life circumstances account for differences in people's levels of reported happiness? Because many demographic variables represent important goals and advantages that most of us strive to achieve (e.g., a job that pays well), common sense suggests that the answer to both questions should be "yes." Suppose you had information about a particular person's income, gender, age, race, attractiveness, employment status, religion, level of education, social class, marital status, and physical health. Wouldn't you also have a guess about that person's level of happiness? If these things are not related to happiness, why do we spend so much of our lives going to school, finding a good job, saving for a nice house, going to church, worrying about our appearance, and hoping for a successful marriage? Common sense would also suggest that certain combinations of life circumstances should predict an individual's level of happiness. Wouldn't you expect that a young, attractive college graduate who lands a high-paying job would be happier than an elderly, retired person living on Social Security, whose health and youthful appearance are fading?

Surprisingly, life circumstances and demographic variables have generally been found to have a much weaker relationship to happiness than most people would suspect. This counterintuitive finding has been called the "paradox of well-being" (Mroczek & Kolarz, 1998). Research shows that people whose demographic profiles show many apparent advantages (e.g., young people with higher incomes) are not significantly happier than those with fewer apparent advantages (e.g., elderly individuals with lower incomes). It is not that circumstances are *unimportant*. Certainly, poverty is stressful. Loneliness is painful. Major illness is distressing. However, for most of us, whose basic health and daily living needs are met, life circumstances do not offer much explanation for why some are happier than others. In fact, factoring out the contribution of demographic variables to differences in happiness leaves most of the variance unexplained. Estimates of how much of the difference in people's reported levels of happiness are explained by all the objective features of life taken together, range from a low of 8% to a high of 20% (Andrews & Withey, 1976; Argyle, 1999; Campbell et al., 1976; Diener, Sandvik, Seidlitz, & Diener, 1993). This means that objective factors *do* relate to happiness, but the relationship is actually quite small. Knowing a person's income, age, gender, and marital status won't tell you much about how happy the person is. One major purpose of the current chapter is to review the research findings that have led to this conclusion.

Our second purpose in this chapter is to explore the question of *why* life circumstances are such weak predictors of happiness. The answers are intriguing. Part of the answer has to do with the fact that the major sources of SWB lie in the psychological realm. Happiness is a subjective psychological state that depends more on the quality, rather than the quantity, of our lives. Research investigating the connection between demographic variables and happiness may tell us more about what *does not*, rather than what *does* make us happy. Knowing what is not related to happiness is important, in part because it raises the interesting possibility that people may look for happiness in the wrong places. The specific ways in which this may happen—particularly regarding the pursuit of money and material possessions—will be explored in Chapter 7.

Another part of the explanation for the surprisingly small demographics–happiness relationship has to do with how the objective facts of our lives may mask important underlying psychological differences. Two people who differ on some objective feature of life may show similar levels of happiness. However, the similarity in their subjective happiness may be rooted in very different processes and factors. Take gender, for example. Several large-scale studies have found that men and women have roughly the same overall levels of self-reported happiness (e.g., Diener & Suh, 1998; Inglehart, 1990). However, research also suggests that women's emotional lives are typically quite different than men's. How it is that men and women come to report approximately the same average levels of happiness, despite these differences, is a very interesting story.

A final piece of the happiness demographics puzzle involves the issue of cause and effect. Though the correlations are small, certain life circumstances do relate to happiness. The question is, "Which came first, the circumstance or the happiness?" For example, married people, on average, are happier than single people (Myers, 2000a). Historically, this finding has been taken to mean that marriage makes us happier. However, several studies suggest that the causal arrow may also point in the opposite direction (Lucas, Clark, Georgellis, &

Diener, 2003; Mastekaasa, 1992). Marriage may make people happier, but it also seems true that happy people are more likely to get married in the first place. The beneficial effects of marriage may actually be smaller than previously thought, because those who marry are, on average, happier before they get married than people who remain single. We will begin our exploration of the demographics of happiness by considering happiness across the life span.

HAPPINESS ACROSS THE LIFE SPAN

If you were asked to pick the period in your life when you would probably be happiest, and the period when you would probably be least happy, what might you guess? If you are a college student, would you guess that right now is the happiest time of your life? Or might it be after you graduate and start earning a living in your chosen career? What about the least happy period? Would you guess the turbulent teenage years when you were dealing with puberty and trying to fit in with your peers? Or old age, when everything from your income to your health might be waning?

If you are a college student guessing that graduating and entering the world of work will make you happier, you may have to guess again. Most college alumni have fond memories of their college days (Baumgardner, 1989, 2001) because, compared to the world of work, college is recalled as a time of less responsibility, more freedom, and more fun. Full-time work certainly brings its share of satisfaction, but few alumni describe work as "fun!" In hindsight, many alumni regard college as one of the happier times in their lives.

If you guessed adolescence or old age as the least happy period of life, you are in good company. Surveys show that most people assume these two stages are the most unhappy and least rewarding times in life (Freedman, 1978). The teen years are widely viewed as a period of "storm and stress," and people tend to associate old age with declining incomes, social disengagement, and failing health. However, research actually shows that these long-standing beliefs are both mistaken. Adolescence has not been found to be an unhappy period of life compared to other ages (Diener & Suh, 1998; Inglehart, 1990). Regarding happiness (or the lack thereof) in old age, one study confirmed that we tend to hold negative expectations about aging, but the same study debunked such expectations. Borges and Dutton (1976) asked young adults to rate their anticipated life satisfaction in old age, and then compared these ratings to the real-time ratings of life satisfaction given by people who had actually reached old age. The findings showed that the young respondents' ratings of their anticipated happiness in old age were significantly lower than the ratings given by older adults (Borges & Dutton, 1976).

Predicting how life changes will affect our happiness is tricky business. In general, people are not very good at anticipating the actual impact of life events. The study of people's predictions about the emotional effects of future life events is called **affective forecasting** (Wilson & Gilbert, 2003). Research shows that people consistently overestimate the impact of both positive and negative events. To evaluate the accuracy of an affective forecast, an individual's *predictions* about the emotional impact of specific events are compared to the *real-life reactions* of people who actually experience those events. Predicted impact typically exaggerates both the intensity and duration of people's actual emotional reactions. For example, one of Wilson and Gilbert's studies (2003) found that non-tenured college professors anticipated a significant increase in happiness that would last several years once they received tenure; but tenured faculty members were not found to be happier 2 years after receiving tenure, than their non-tenured junior colleagues. In a second example, people predicted that they would experience more regret if they missed a subway train by just a few minutes than if they missed the train by a wider margin of time. However, in real life, subway riders were no more upset if they missed the train by a minute than if they missed it by a wider margin (Gilbert, Morewedge, Risen, & Wilson, 2004; Wilson & Gilbert, 2003). This exaggeration in the strength and duration of anticipated emotional reactions is called the **impact bias** (Gilbert, Driver-Linn, & Wilson, 2002).

One reason for the impact bias seems to be that when we contemplate the emotional effect of an event, we narrow our attention to that one single event. Wilson, Meyers, and Gilbert (2001) coined the term **focalism** to describe our tendency to restrict our attention to the event in question and ignore the consequences and context of the event. As a result of focalism, we neglect to think about how other aspects of our lives might offset or reduce the emotional impact of an event. So, we may eagerly anticipate a new job in a new city, but might not think about the hassle of finding a new place to live, how much we may miss our friends, or the potential stress involved in learning a new job. In a similar vein, we might think the break-up of a romantic relationship would be the "end of the world." But if a break-up actually occurred, we might actually find that support from family members and friends, enjoyable activities, or satisfying work helped offset our emotional pain.

Another reason for the impact bias is known as **immune neglect** (Gilbert, Pinel, Wilson, Blumberg, & Wheatley, 1998; Wilson & Gilbert, 2003). As we noted in Chapter 4, people can be amazingly resilient in the face of trauma and loss. Each of us has a psychological, as well as a physiological, "immune system" that helps us bounce back from negative life events. Immune neglect occurs when people do not consider their own resilience when anticipating how they will react to future emotionally charged experiences. Particularly in the case of negative events, we seem to forget the power of our own psychological immune system and our ability to cope, adapt, and perhaps even benefit from bad situations. In foresight, a future event may seem ominous and threatening, but in hindsight we often recognize that we recovered more easily and readily than we had imagined. How many times have you felt certain that it would be just awful if a particular event happened, but then when that event actually occurred, it wasn't nearly as bad as you had expected?

Focus on Research: Happiness and Where We Live

Would you guess that people living in sunny California would be happier than those living in the cold, snowy Midwest? Do you think that college students assigned to their preferred dormitory would be happier than those assigned to a less-preferred dorm? Most of us would probably answer yes to both questions. However, studies of affective forecasting show that our beliefs about the emotional impact of where we live may not measure up to the facts.

Are Californians happier than Midwesterners? To find out, Schkade and Kahneman (1998) posed this question to a sample of nearly 2,000 college students. About half of the students lived in the

Midwest and were attending the University of Michigan or Ohio State University, and about half lived in Southern California and were attending the University of California at either Los Angeles or Irvine. The sample was nearly equally balanced between males and females and among freshmen, sophomores, juniors, and seniors. To compare students' predictions about life satisfaction and living in the Midwest or California to the actual satisfaction of people living in these two areas of the country, Schkade and Kahneman randomly assigned students to one of two conditions. In the *self condition*, students rated how satisfied they were with their lives overall, their level of satisfaction in different domains of life (such as job prospects, financial situation, academic opportunities, personal safety, social life, and the climate for each season of the year). Participants also rated the importance of each of these domains to their own personal well-being. Students in the *self condition* assessed their own, actual personal life satisfaction. Students in the *other condition* were asked to rate the same life domains, but instead of rating the personal importance of each domain to themselves, they were asked to respond in the way they predicted another person would respond. Specifically, they were asked to try to predict the ratings that would be made by a hypothetical student attending one of the other universities, either in the same region where the respondent lived, or in a different region of the country. In other words, students were asked to imagine how a student from their own area or from the other area of the country would fill out the life satisfaction survey. All students in this *other condition* were instructed to assume that their hypothetical counterpart had values and interests similar to their own. The *other condition* assessed students' beliefs about the personal life satisfaction of a student, similar to themselves, going to a university in the same region or a different region of the country. These two conditions permitted a comparison of the actual level of satisfaction among students in California and the Midwest, to the level of satisfaction *predicted* for each area. So, is the happiness of Californians a fact or an illusion?

Midwesterners take heart! Stay put! You won't be happier in California just because of the sunny weather, even though everyone seems to believe this to be the case. Schkade and Kahneman (1998) found that students in both California and the Midwest predicted higher life

satisfaction ratings for those living in California. But surprisingly, the results of the study did not agree with students' predictions with respect to *overall* life satisfaction. Californians *were* happier with their sunny winter climate than Midwesterners were with their snow and cold, but there was *no* statistical difference between the ratings of overall life satisfaction of the two groups. Both groups were, in fact, equally happy.

What explains the difference between students' predicted and actual happiness ratings? Why did the weather have such a large impact on judgments of overall happiness? Schkade and Kahneman (1998) suggest that the answer has to do with a specific kind of focalism that the researchers call the **focusing illusion.** The focusing illusion occurs when we make a summary judgment about an entire object or issue, but have only attended to a few features of the object or issue in question. This restricted focus is likely to produce errors in judgment because we give too much weight to too few aspects of the situation. That appears to be what happened when students in the *other condition* thought about the happiness of Californians. They failed to appreciate the fact that weather does not have much bearing on *overall* life satisfaction. Neither the Midwestern nor the Californian students rated weather as a major contributor to their own personal happiness. In the *self condition*, job opportunities, financial factors, personal safety, and social relationships were rated as much more important than the weather. The focusing illusion did not occur when students rated their own personal life satisfaction. When we think about ourselves we seem to take a broader perspective that is sensitive to the many important aspects of our lives. However, in our judgments of others we seem to focus only on the most distinctive features. Students in the study focused primarily on differences in the weather between California and the Midwest. This exemplifies the focusing illusion that led to the erroneous belief that good weather makes people happier. California does enjoy nice weather, but it does not make its residents happy, despite the fact that Midwesterners and even Californians seem to think it does!

Another example of how people may focus on a few distinctive features of a situation rather than the whole picture comes from a study of students' satisfaction with their dormitory assignments (Dunn, Wilson, & Gilbert, 2003). For most college students, dorm-room assignments are a critical aspect of college life. Stories or experiences with a "roommate from hell" or the "the most run-down dorm on campus" suggest how the social and physical aspects of student housing may affect students' happiness with campus life. Dunn and her colleagues took advantage of a unique dormitory assignment system at a major university to see how much *predicted* impact, and how much *actual* impact dorm assignments had on student satisfaction levels.

At the university where the study was conducted, freshmen students are randomly assigned to one of 12 dorms. All students are required to live in dormitories throughout their first 3 years of college. A unique feature of the assignment policy is that near the end of the freshman year, each student has the opportunity, in collaboration with peers, to choose his or her own roommate and a group of up to 15 friends who will all be assigned to the same dorm for the following 2 years. Groups of students apply together, so before the time of the spring lottery drawing for housing assignments, students already know and like many of the people they will be living with the following year. The lottery settles only the question of which specific dorm they will be living in. Under these conditions would you worry very much about the particular dorm you were assigned to? Regardless of the assigned dorm, you know you will have all your friends and your preferred roommate. What more do you want? However, the results of the study were surprising. Students were actually very concerned about where they would live. First-year students often stayed up all night waiting for their dorm assignments and were elated if they got their preferred choice and extremely disappointed if assigned to a non-preferred choice. Dunn and her colleagues posed three questions. First, how did students decide which dorms were desirable and which were undesirable? Second, did the happiness or misery they felt when they first heard their dorm assignments continue as they began actually living in the dorms? Third, what was the best predictor of actual dorm-life satisfaction?

To answer these questions, Dunn and her colleagues compared students' predicted happiness before moving into their assigned dorms, to their actual happiness later on. Students were surveyed shortly before they learned of their assignments. They rated their predicted happiness for each of the 12 dorms to which they might be assigned. Students also provided information regarding the basis for their judgments by rating the expected quality of life for each dorm in terms of its physical features (such as location, attractiveness, and room size) and its social features (such as relationships with roommates and the sense of community within the dorm as a whole). To provide a comparison between predicted happiness and actual happiness, these same ratings were taken again after 1 year of living in the assigned dorm (sophomore year), and again after 2 years (junior year).

First question: How did students decide which dorms were good and which were bad? The answer to this question is part of the title for Dunn, Wilson, and Gilbert's article "Location, location, location!" Students' judgments of a good or bad assignment were based primarily on the dorm's location on campus and its physical characteristics (e.g., room size and dining facilities).

Second question: Were students actually as happy or miserable with their dorm assignments as they believed they would be? Answer: No. Analysis of predicted and actual happiness ratings revealed strong evidence of an impact bias. Students significantly overestimated how happy they would be with their preferred dorm assignment, as well as how unhappy they would be with an undesirable assignment. Students assigned to their desired dorms were less happy than they had predicted and students assigned to a less-desired dorm turned out to be happier than they had predicted. Overall, the vast majority of students were satisfied with life in their dorms.

Third question: What predicted actual dorm-life satisfaction? Answer: Social relationships. Dunn and her colleagues found the quality of students' social lives was the most powerful predictor of actual happiness. By their sophomore and junior years, the location and physical features of a dorm (that students *thought* was so important) bore no significant relationship to student happiness. Ironically, students in this study began their dorm lives with the most important contributor to their satisfaction already established. Because all students chose their own roommate and many of their dorm mates, they were virtually guaranteed to feel at home and have good friends in the dorm, regardless of the specific dorm to which they were assigned. So why did freshmen students base their predictions of anticipated happiness on the location and physical features of the dorms?

Dunn and her colleagues (2003) suggest that an **isolation effect** helps explain why students focused on dorm location rather than social relationships. The isolation effect may be considered a more specific case of the focusing illusion. A focusing illusion may result when our attention is drawn to a few features as we try to arrive at a judgment between differing options, because these features stand out and command too much of our attention (like the weather differences in the Schkade & Kahneman study). The isolation effect occurs when people try to simplify the amount of information they need to consider when making choices. If we disregard or cancel out the many features that alternatives have in common, this permits an "isolation" of the differences (which are typically fewer in number). This can be an efficient way to reduce the complexity of choosing among potential options. However, in thinking about how happy we will be with a particular choice, the isolation effect can cause an impact bias if we focus only on the differences and forget about the contribution of the shared features. An isolation effect was shown, in that social-life variables were constant among the 12 dorm alternatives; students disregarded social life and focused on differences in physical features in making their judgments. As a result, students exaggerated the anticipated satisfaction or dissatisfaction with their dorm assignment.

Dunn and colleagues' study (2003) provides especially compelling evidence for the impact bias because of its longitudinal design (i.e., surveying the same students at three different times) and the random assignment of participants to significant life outcomes (i.e., importance of dorm assignment to students). Their study highlights the potential of affective forecasting and impact bias research to help explain our difficulty in predicting the effects of age-related changes and life events. Still, it may seem that age *should* make a difference in people's level of happiness. Many events and achievements bear some correlation to age (e.g., first job, marriage, buying a home, or retirement); and with advancing age, our income and health often decline and we may suffer the loss of friends or a spouse. For these reasons, you would think that age would be closely related to happiness. Surprisingly, many studies have found that age shows little relationship to a person's reported level of happiness (e.g., Diener & Lucas, 2000; Diener & Suh, 1998; Inglehart, 1990). Subjective

well-being is extremely stable over the life span. Based on interviews with nearly 170,000 people from 16 different nations, Inglehart (1990) found that every age group, from 15 years to 65 and beyond, expressed almost identical levels of happiness and life satisfaction. Nearly 80% of people at all ages reported that they were satisfied with their lives, overall. Figure 5.1 summarizes Inglehart's study of age and life satisfaction.

Many other studies affirm the stability of well-being across the life span (e.g., Kunzmann, Little, & Smith, 2000; Lawton, 2001; Lucas & Gohm, 2000). Some studies have found age-related declines in well-being, but the decreases were very small and occurred only among the very old. For example, a recent study of the life satisfaction component of SWB found a curvilinear relationship between age and satisfaction (Mroczek & Avron, 2005). The life satisfaction ratings of nearly 2,000 men were found to increase slightly to a peak at age 65, and then to show a small decline to age 85. Such findings do not negate the overall conclusion about happiness and age. Researchers consistently find that advancing age does not necessarily bring unhappiness or declining well-being. On average, SWB and self-esteem are as high in old age as at any other time of life (e.g., Charles, Reynolds, & Gatz, 2001; Diener & Suh, 1998). Some studies have even found an increase in well-being among the elderly (e.g., Carstensen, 1998; Mroczek & Kolarz, 1998).

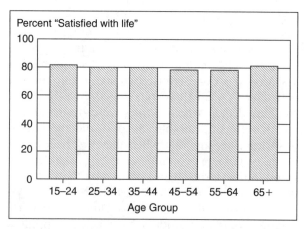

FIGURE 5.1 Relationship of Age and Well-Being in 16 Nations

Data from Inglehart, R. (1990). Figure from Myers, D. G., & Diener, E. (1995). Who is happy? *Psychological Science, 6,* 10–19. Copyright American Psychological Society. Reprinted by permission.

Research has also failed to support beliefs about the emotional effects of what are often regarded as turning points in life. For example, women going through menopause or "change of life" are often thought to be vulnerable to depression and increases in negative emotions. However, studies of women experiencing menopause (reviewed by Myers, 1992) have not shown an increase in depression compared to non-menopausal women. The critical determinant of the effects of menopause seems to be a woman's attitude toward this change of life, rather than the change itself. Women who view menopause as a liberation from concerns about pregnancy and menstrual periods report high levels of emotional stability and happiness. Further, in Myers' review, he found little evidence for another turning point thought to affect women's life happiness: the "empty nest syndrome" (Myers & Diener, 1995). The supposed decrease in happiness caused by loneliness when children grow up and leave home, and the confusion in purpose as the role of mother fades, have not been borne out by research. Most mothers are happy to see their children begin their careers, marry, and start their own families. Raising a family can be deeply satisfying, but going through it once is probably enough. Parents enjoy the freedom to pursue new interests and activities in their "life-after-kids."

Researchers have also failed to find evidence supporting the "mid-life crisis" assumed to hit men during their 40s. This crisis was thought to occur as men contemplated their position in life and what lay ahead. The mid-life crisis has generally been considered a period of soul-searching as men realize their career dreams may not be fulfilled, the mirror reveals an aging body, marriage has become routine, and men look for ways to re-invigorate their lives. A long-standing belief has been that the turmoil created by these despairing realizations might lead to dramatic career changes, affairs with younger women, or pursuit of "daring" activities that prove men are still young. However, research has failed to support mid-life crisis as a widespread stage in men's lives (McCrae & Costa, 1990; Wethington, Cooper, & Holmes, 1997). Most men seem to go sedately through middle age without the need for dramatic new adventures. Research suggests that older adults often enjoy greater well-being, more contentment, and less anxiety than young adults (e.g., Lawton, Kleban, & Dean, 1993).

Stability in Well-Being Despite Life Changes

Subjective well-being, then, is amazingly stable across the life span, despite the events, stages, and turning points that we think should influence happiness. What is not so clear is why this would be true. Why does overall happiness *not* change much with age, when we know that the life challenges, life concerns, and life activities *do* change with age? Teens are concerned with being popular among their friends, young adults with starting their careers and families, and older adults with finding meaningful activities after they retire from work. We will examine four lines of research that address the stability question: (1) research showing strong genetic influences on SWB; (2) age-related changes in the intensity, frequency, and balance of positive and negative emotions; (3) issues concerning the measurement and definition of positive emotions; and (4) lifespan changes in the psychological and social foundations of well-being.

TEMPERAMENT AND SUBJECTIVE WELL-BEING Many researchers have concluded that people's emotional lives are heavily influenced by genetic temperament factors (DeNeve, 1999; DeNeve & Cooper, 1998; Lykken, 1999; Lykken & Tellegen, 1996; Tellegen et al., 1988). The "Nun Study" (reviewed in Chapter 1) provides one kind of evidence for the long-term stability of people's characteristic emotional response to the world. Studies of identical twins, separated at birth and raised in different environments, provide even more powerful evidence for the role of genetics in determining an individual's long-term level of emotional well-being. About 40% of the differences in people's experience of positive emotions, 55% of negative emotions, and as much as 80% of long-term SWB appear to be inherited (Lykken, 1999; Lykken & Tellegen, 1996). People appear to inherit a happiness or emotional "set point" that determines their general level of cheerfulness (Headey & Wearing, 1992). **A set point** is like an internal gyroscope that stabilizes our response to events that push us off balance. Research investigating the effects of life changes on long-term well-being supports the idea of a return to set point. For example, being divorced, getting a new job, or moving to a new place to live does not significantly alter most people's long-term level of well-being (Costa, McCrae, & Zonderman, 1987). Studies of genetic influences on temperament provide a straightforward answer to the stability question: "It's in your genes!" If you were a happy and cheerful child, odds are that you will be a happy and cheerful adult and senior citizen. If you were moody, cautious, and reserved in childhood, you are likely to carry that same disposition throughout the course of your life.

FREQUENCY, INTENSITY, AND BALANCE OF POSITIVE AND NEGATIVE EMOTIONS Because many studies use global and summary measures of SWB, researchers have wondered whether a more complex story of aging and happiness might be revealed in the specific components of SWB. That is, global measures of SWB (i.e., life satisfaction and affect balance) might not be sensitive to subtle, age-related changes. To get a clearer picture of what may and may not change with age, researchers have examined the emotional aspects of SWB separately. Studies have compared the frequency, intensity, and balance of positive and negative emotions among people of widely differing ages.

Frequency and Intensity of Emotions. One way that overall SWB could stay the same despite differences in emotional experiences has to do with the frequency of intense emotions. This is a matter of simple averages. One person who has extreme emotional highs and lows may have the same average, overall affect balance as someone who has less extreme, more consistent emotional experiences. Several studies suggest that intense emotions are fairly typical among teens and young adults, but decline with age. Using the experience sampling method, Csikszentmihalyi and Larsen (1984) asked teenagers to record their moods and activities whenever they received a beeper signal at various times during the day. The researchers found that moods among teens can go down from extreme highs, and up from extreme lows in less than an hour. Both elation and despair can come and go within an amazingly short period of time. The emotional lives of older adults tend to be more even-keeled and stable (Costa et al., 1987; Diener, Sandvik, & Larsen, 1985). Consistent with this idea, a recent review (Charles et al., 2001) found that as people age, they show a dramatic decline in high-arousal emotions. Items asking about "feeling on top of the world" or "being excited about something" show the largest age-related declines (Charles et al., 2001). Figure 5.2

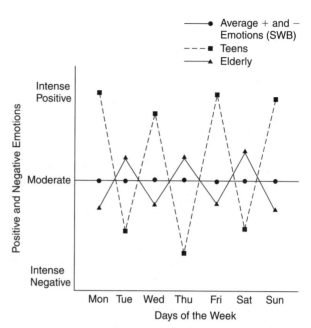

FIGURE 5.2 How Different Emotional Experiences Can Represent the Same Average Level of SWB

shows a hypothetical example of how the same *average* SWB may result, despite differences in the emotional experiences of teens and the elderly. All this suggests that the effects of everyday life events soften with age. Younger people's happiness reflects an averaging-out of more extreme emotions, while for older adults happiness reflects a steady and less fluctuating emotional life with a lower frequency of extreme emotions. It's not that older adults don't enjoy life, but accumulated life experience teaches them not to get too excited or too upset about the many daily events, the effects of which are often temporary. Older adults come to focus on longer-term satisfactions such as developing supportive, high-quality relationships or personally meaningful activities. So, despite changes in the frequency of intense emotions, overall happiness remains stable across the life span. Our overall emotional experiences appear to shift from an averaging-out of strong reactions to life events, to less extreme and more steady emotional experiences.

Balance of Positive and Negative Emotions. Another way that differences in emotional experience might result in similar overall SWB has to do with the balance between positive and negative emotions. The emotional component of well-being is typically assessed by subtracting rating totals on the negative affect scale from totals on the positive affect scale.

This combined scoring method may mask important and independent changes in positive and negative affect. You may recall from Chapter 2 that measures of positive and negative affect show only small correlations with one another. Each type of affect makes a relatively independent contribution to SWB. If positive and negative affect are examined separately, rather than combined into a single score, researchers can determine whether the overall score obscures important changes. For example, if both positive affect and negative affect each increased to the same degree as people got older, then affect balance would remain the same. Or, if both positive and negative affect declined to the same degree, the result would also be a stable overall affect balance across the life span. Studies examining age-related changes in positive and negative affect have found independent changes in the two types of emotions. Perhaps more intriguing, some studies have found that emotional well-being may actually increase with age.

The pattern for age-related changes in negative emotions seems fairly clear. Both cross-sectional and longitudinal studies show that negative affect tends to decline with age (e.g., Charles et al., 2001; Mroczek & Almeida, 2004; Mroczek & Kohlarz, 1998; Pinquart, 2001). Negative emotions are less frequently reported among older adults and less frequently observed by researchers, with most studies supporting this general trend. A leveling-off or slight increase in negative affect has been found only among the very old. Carstensen and her colleagues found that negative affect decreased from age 18 to about age 60, and then did not change appreciably from age 60 to age 94 (Carstensen, Pasupathi, Mayr, & Nesselroade, 2000). In a study of approximately 6,000 people from 43 different nations, Diener and Suh (1997) found that negative affect decreased between ages 20 and 60, and then increased slightly among the oldest people in the study. In general, negative affect tends to decline with age.

Studies of positive affect across the life span have revealed a more mixed pattern of results. Some studies have shown an increase in positive affect among older adults as compared to younger adults (Gross et al., 1997), whereas some studies have shown a decrease in positive affect (Diener & Suh, 1998; Lucas & Gohm, 2000), and still other studies have revealed no change (e.g., Vaux & Meddin, 1987). Compared to cross-sectional research, longitudinal studies show somewhat more stability in positive affect, with slight declines only for the oldest adults (Costa et al., 1987; Stacey & Gatz, 1991).

Despite the mixed pattern of results for positive affect, when taken in total studies of positive and negative affect affirm, rather than contradict, the stability of well-being across the life span. This tendency is most clearly seen in terms of the small overall relationship between age and affect. A meta-analysis by Pinquart (2001) found that the average correlation between age and positive affect (across many studies) was $r = -0.03$, and for negative affect $r = -0.01$. These are extremely small relationships. Because they are based on large samples of people, such small correlations achieve "statistical" significance. However, converted to a measure of association or shared variance, these correlations mean that less than 1% of the variability in affect is associated with differences in age. Ninety-nine percent of the variability is due to other factors.

MEASUREMENT AND DEFINITIONAL ISSUES

Measurement. Several researchers have noted that the decline in positive affect found in some studies may result from the use of scales that measure only high-arousal emotions (e.g., Charles et al., 2001; Diener & Suh, 1998). Studies that assess only high-intensity emotions may present a misleading picture because they suggest a decline in positive emotion, when in actuality it may be only the most intense positive emotions that fade with age. Positive emotions seem to be just as frequent, but not as intense. Charles and colleagues (2001) used Bradburn's (1969) Affect Balance Scale in a study of 2,800 people representing four generations of families. The positive affect component of the scale asks people to answer "yes" or "no" to the following five statements:

> *"During the past few weeks, did you feel...*
>
> *particularly excited or interested in something?*
>
> *proud because someone complimented you on something you had done?*
>
> *pleased about having accomplished something?*
>
> *on top of the world?*
>
> *that things were really going your way?"*

The findings suggested that the largest age-related declines in positive affect occurred on items concerning intense emotions. Specifically, the greatest declines were for the questions concerning feeling "particularly excited about something," "on top of the world," and feeling that "things are really going my way."

Definitions. A second issue involves how positive affect is defined. Positive affect appears to be made up of at least two distinct types of positive emotion that have been shown to be relatively independent (e.g., Watson & Tellegen, 1985; Watson, Wiese, Vaidya, & Tellegen, 1999), and that may have different influences on people's thinking and behavior (e.g., Fredrickson, 2001). The independence of the two types of positive affect opens the possibility that each type may show a different trajectory across the life span. A recent study by Kunzmann, Stange, and Jordan (2005) examined just this possibility. These researchers described the two types of positive affect as **pleasant affect** and **positive involvement.** Pleasant affect is defined as a positive emotional state involving relatively low arousal. Examples would include feeling satisfied, content, and happy. On the other hand, positive involvement refers to higher-arousal states such as feeling inspired, alert, or active. Pleasant affect seems to require comparatively low effort, is frequently self-centered in focus, and is more likely to result from having achieved, rather than being in active pursuit of, a goal. Positive involvement, in contrast, requires more effort, is often other-oriented, and is more focused on the activity involved in achieving a goal rather than the goal itself.

According to Kunzmann and colleagues, each type of affect may also be involved in two different lifestyles and value orientations. A hedonic lifestyle would seem to emphasize pleasant affect through the pursuit of personal enjoyment, pleasure, and consumption. Seeking the approval of others and developing close relationships may also fit a hedonic value orientation if the motivation is primarily for benefits received by the individual. A more eudaimonic lifestyle (which the authors called growth-related) is consistent with positive involvement. People expressing a growth-related lifestyle are concerned with personal development, and with contributing to the welfare of others and to the environment in which they live. They are concerned with finding purpose in life and helping family and community members, and are more actively involved in organizations and groups that contribute to the betterment of society.

The Kunzmann research studied pleasant affect, positive involvement, and the hedonic and growth-related lifestyles in a sample of young (15 to 20 years old), middle-aged (30 to 40 years old), and older adults (ages 60 to 70). For our purposes, two of their findings are particularly noteworthy. First, these researchers found that measures of pleasant affect and positive involvement showed only small correlations with one another. This finding reinforces a conception of positive affect as involving several relatively independent dimensions. Second, their results suggest that the mixed findings in previous studies investigating the relation of age and positive affect (i.e., studies showing declines, no change, or increases) may be due to differences in the approach to measuring positive affect. This possibility arises because these researchers found a different age-related pattern for pleasant affect than for positive involvement. The positive emotions of younger adults were more likely to involve experiences of pleasant affect, fitting a more hedonic lifestyle. Older adults were more likely to experience feelings of positive involvement, expressing a more growth-related lifestyle.

In this investigation, the answer to the question of whether positive affect increases or decreases with age is both yes and no, depending on which aspect of positive affect we focus on. Positive affect, when defined and measured as pleasant affect, declined with age ($r = -0.38$). However, positive affect, when defined and measured in terms of positive involvement, increased with age ($r = 0.42$). Positive emotions, then, were typical for all ages. However, the basis for personal enjoyment shifted from a hedonically-oriented lifestyle focused on pleasant affect among the young, to a more eudaimonic lifestyle focused on positive involvement among older adults. The findings of this study suggest that future research on the age-affect question may benefit from the development of multi-dimensional models of affect.

In summary, research consistently shows that negative emotions decline with age. Taking into consideration measurement biases and definitional issues, findings to date suggest that positive emotions either do not change very much, or may actually increase with age. A decrease in negative affect and a stable or slight increase in positive affect indicate that overall emotional well-being and happiness might actually increase with age. This possibility is consistent with eudaimonic theories of well-being, to be considered next.

THE SHIFTING BASIS OF LIFE SATISFACTION

Researchers taking a eudaimonic perspective have addressed the stability question by examining changes in the basis of life satisfaction as people age. We would not expect that the sources of happiness for teens and young adults would be the same as for the middle-aged and elderly. Studies following the eudaimonic perspective suggest that people at different ages may be equally happy, but for very different reasons. For example, Carstensen's **socioemotional selectivity theory** (Carstensen, 1992; Carstensen & Charles, 2003; Carstensen, Isaacowitz, & Charles, 1999) predicts no general age-related declines in well-being. In fact, Carstensen's theory provides a number of reasons for believing that emotional well-being may increase with age. Her theory is generally consistent with the research on emotions over the life span, as just reviewed.

Socioemotional selectivity theory was reviewed in Chapter 4 as one explanation for resiliency in old age. The theory describes how older people shift their priorities from the future to their present life circumstances and activities. This shift occurs as a consequence of their increased awareness of the diminished time remaining in their lives. Unlike young people who are oriented toward the future, older adults focus on increasing life satisfaction in the present. They tend to express this changed focus by investing in the people and things that matter most, and unplugging from the "rat race" and constant worry about impressing others and getting ahead. Workers who have been at the same job for many years report greater satisfaction with their work after middle age than before (Rhodes, 1983; Warr, 1992). The major reason for the increase in satisfaction seems to be a change in attitude toward work. In accord with socioemotional selectivity theory, older workers focus more on the day-to-day aspects of their jobs and on enjoyable social relationships with co-workers, and less on advancing their careers and competing with others (Levinson, 1978; Rybash, Roodin, & Hoyer, 1995).

As a consequence of their bounded view of the future, older people give priority to maximizing positive emotional experiences and minimizing negative ones. That is, they tend to avoid situations that result in negative emotions and gravitate to those that they enjoy. You may have a grandparent who seems to have a peculiar quirk, such as refusing to go out to eat in a crowded restaurant or to travel long distances in a car to visit relatives. You may think your grandparent is being stubborn or insensitive to what others want to do, but it may be that he or she simply doesn't like those activities. When you get older, with most of your life behind you, it makes little sense to continue to do things that you don't enjoy—including social interactions. Research shows that older individuals often structure their environments to avoid negative interactions with others (Carstensen, Gross, & Fung, 1998) and become more adept at regulating their emotions. Studies of married couples show that older adults express fewer negative emotions when discussing areas of conflict (Carstensen, Graff, Levenson, & Gottman, 1996) and display fewer negative emotions like disgust or anger, compared to middle-aged spouses (Levenson, Carstensen, & Gottman, 1994). These changes are part of a general shift toward establishing stronger relationships within a smaller social support network. Your spouse, children, grandchildren, and close friends become more important than expanding social relationships by meeting new people. Older adults are more concerned with cultivating enjoyable relationships, and less concerned than younger adults with changing, dominating, or impressing others. Consistent with this greater investment in valued relationships, marital satisfaction typically increases in long-term married couples (Levenson, Carstensen, & Gottman, 1993).

To summarize, despite changes in our emotional lives, personal goals, and sources of happiness across the life span, happiness is not related to age. This is shown in the general stability of SWB across the life span and the fact that a person's level of personal happiness does *not* reliably covary with his or her age. In short, every age is potentially as happy as any other, even though each period of life presents new challenges and a continuing need for adaptation to change. The lack of connection between age and happiness suggests that we should take each stage of life as it comes. Embrace and enjoy what each new phase of life offers for happiness and well-being. Personal happiness is not "out there" in the future at some later age, and neither is it in the "good old days" of the past. *Carpe Diem!*

GENDER AND HAPPINESS

Who is happier—men or women? The overall answer seems to be neither. Large-scale surveys find that women and men report approximately the same levels of happiness (e.g., Inglehart, 1990). Figure 5.3 shows results from life satisfaction and gender surveys of nearly 170,000 people in 16 nations.

Other national surveys affirm the general conclusion that there are few (if any) significant gender differences in overall happiness (Diener, Suh, Lucas, & Smith, 1999; Manstead, 1992). Men and women are, on average, equally likely to report feeling happy and satisfied with their lives as a whole. For example, one study of 18,000 college students representing 39 different countries found no significant gender differences (Michalos, 1991). Even studies that *do* report gender differences also report that the differences are small in magnitude. In their meta-analytic review of research, Haring, Stock, and Okun (1984) concluded that men showed a slight tendency to report higher levels of well-being than women. On the other hand, a meta-analysis by Wood, Rhodes, and Whelan (1989) reported a similar, slight tendency toward more happiness, but for women rather than men. The emphasis here is on the word "slight." Two other reviews show that gender accounts for less than 1% of the difference in people's reported levels of well-being (Fujita, Diener, & Sandvik, 1991; Haring et al., 1984). In other words, knowing a person's gender won't tell you much about his or her happiness.

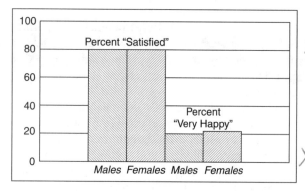

FIGURE 5.3   Gender and Life Satisfaction Surveys in 16 Nations

Data from Inglehart, R. (1990). Figure from Myers, D. G., & Diener, E. (1995). Who is happy? *Psychological Science, 6,* 10–19. Copyright American Psychological Society. Reprinted by permission.

Yet there are significant differences in the emotional lives of men and women, as affirmed by everyday experience and the research to be reviewed next. The fact of overall similarity in happiness and the differences in emotional experiences creates an apparent paradox of gender, similar to the paradox of aging. How does overall well-being remain the same amidst abundant differences? Delineating and explaining this paradox is a major purpose of our discussion of gender and happiness.

Gender Differences in Emotional Experience

NEGATIVE EMOTIONS   Women are much more likely to experience negative emotions and internalizing disorders such as depression and anxiety than men (Kessler et al., 1994; Nolen-Hoeksema, 1995; Nolen-Hoeksema & Rusting, 1999). **Internalizing disorders** involve intense negative emotions. Research reviewed by Nolen-Hoeksema and Rusting (1999) also shows that gender differences in depression and anxiety disorders appear early in life. Among girls, mood disorders typically appear between the ages of 11 and 15. No such early developmental onset is found for boys.

Lucas and Gohm (2000) question whether the different rates of mood disorders between men and women tell us anything about the emotional lives of people *not* suffering distress. We can say that differences in emotional disorders do share interesting parallels with differences in men's and women's everyday experiences. Several reviews (Brody & Hall, 1993; Feingold, 1994; Hall, 1984) conclude that women report experiencing more sadness, fear, anxiety, shame, and guilt than men. Women not only *experience*, but also *express* these negative emotions more than men. For example, Nolen-Hoeksema and Rusting (1999) review studies showing that women express more sadness and fear when presented with negative emotional material.

In contrast to internalizing disorders, **externalizing disorders** and behaviors involve the acting out of emotions. These emotions are directed toward objects, situations, and people. Clinical studies consistently find that men have significantly higher rates of externalizing disorders than women (Nolen-Hoeksema & Rusting, 1999). These disorders include drug abuse, antisocial personality disorder, and problems associated with uncontrolled anger and aggression.

Within non-clinical populations, studies of gender differences in externalizing emotions and behaviors have focused primarily on anger and aggression. Differences in physical aggression are the clearest and most universal. Everywhere in the world it seems males are more physically aggressive than females. A recent meta-analysis of studies conducted in 20 countries found that men showed consistently higher levels of physical aggression (Archer, 2005). Parallel to the early emergence of mood disorders in girls, boys' tendencies toward aggressive behavior also emerge early, becoming evident as early as preschool. However, this seemingly obvious general conclusion needs to be tempered by studies showing that circumstances and social norms may affect when and how each gender expresses anger and aggression (e.g., Bettencourt & Miller, 1996; Eagly & Steffen, 1986; Frodi, Macaulay, & Thomas, 1977; Geen, 1998; Nolen-Hoeksema & Rusting, 1999). For example, Bettencourt and Miller (1996) found men to be more aggressive in unprovoked or neutral conditions, but men and women were equally aggressive when provoked. That is, when individuals feel frustrated, insulted, or threatened, gender differences are diminished. In more neutral everyday situations, men are quicker to aggress because they are more likely to "see" provocation in ambiguous situations.

Another complication involves the type of aggression measured by researchers. Men may engage in more physical aggression, but studies reviewed by Geen (1998) and more recently by Archer and Coyne (2005) show that women use more verbal and relational aggression. Relational aggression means harming another individual's relationships and status with their peers. This might involve spreading damaging negative information about the person. Finally, most research reviews (e.g., Geen, 1998; Nolen-Hoeksema & Rusting, 1999) note that social norms and expectations may play an important role in the mixed findings concerning gender, anger, and aggression. Women have been found to be more conflicted than men about the expression of physical aggression, and women are less aggressive when they may cause harm to another person, feel guilty about what they've done, or fear retaliation. Men and women appear to have different beliefs and are influenced by different social norms that determine the specific circumstances that evoke anger and influence the expression of aggression (Eagly & Steffen, 1986).

POSITIVE MOODS AND BEHAVIORS Self-report studies of positive moods such as happiness, joy, and love also reveal somewhat inconsistent gender patterns. A number of researchers have found that women report experiencing more happiness and more intense positive emotions than men (e.g., Diener et al., 1985; Fujita et al., 1991), while several others have found no differences or somewhat more happiness among men than women (e.g., Diener, 1984; Haring et al., 1984). One consistent finding is that women express more positive emotions than men (Nolen-Hoeksema & Rusting, 1999). More women than men report expressing joy, happiness, and love to others. Observational studies of women's nonverbal behaviors affirm the greater expressiveness of women. For example, hundreds of studies show that women smile more frequently than men (LeFrance, Hecht, & Paluck, 2003). Studies of smiling in magazine and newspaper photos, together with observations of smiling among people in shopping malls and parks, and on city streets all show that women smile more than men (Halberstadt & Saitta, 1987). Women also appear more skillful than men at "reading" nonverbal cues and correctly assessing the emotional states of others (Hall, 1984).

Explaining the Paradox of Gender

Despite complications and controversies about the exact nature of gender differences, it seems clear that on average men and women have rather different emotional lives. Yet, as previously noted, research also shows that the overall level of happiness among men and women is essentially the same. The apparent contradiction of these two sets of findings is the basis for the paradox of gender. The paradox of gender has no clear resolution. However, several possible answers have been offered.

One possible answer comes from studies suggesting that women have more intense emotional experiences than men. For example, some researchers have found that women report higher levels of both pleasant and unpleasant emotions than men (Fujita et al., 1991); that women are more likely than men to report being very happy (Lee, Seccombe, & Shehan, 1991); and that women's greater emotional intensity occurs across many different ages (Diener et al., 1985). These findings suggest to some authors that women are "more emotional" than men, in that women have more intense and extreme emotional lives (e.g., Brody & Hall, 1993; Fujita et al., 1991). Differences in emotional intensity may contribute to the paradox of gender. Diener and his colleagues (1999) have suggested that women's more intense positive emotions may be balanced by their more intense negative emotions. This averaging-out of extremes could result in an overall level of happiness similar to men's. That is, within a large sample of women reporting on their level of happiness, the highs of some may be offset by the lows of others.

Another explanation for the gender paradox suggests that some of the "emotionality" of women may be more apparent than real. Gender stereotypes, and the expectations that follow from them, may influence women's responses on measures of SWB. Several authors have argued that, despite the many gender role changes in our society, stereotypes still strongly affect how people think about the differences between men and women (Brody & Hall, 1993; Nolen-Hoeksema & Rusting, 1999; Woods, Rhodes, & Whelan, 1989). When people are asked to describe a "typical man" or "typical woman," they tend to do so in a way that affirms traditional gender stereotypes. Women are believed to experience more intense emotions than men and to express more love, sadness, and fear (Fabes & Martin, 1991; Grossman & Wood, 1993). Men are seen as less emotional and less expressive, with the notable exceptions of anger and aggression.

What do these stereotypes have to do with the paradox? Brody and Hall (1993) suggest that gender stereotypes may become a kind of self-fulfilling prophecy or normative expectation that influences women's expression of emotion. Gender stereotypes may affect women's outward expression of emotion more than their actual inner emotional experience (Nolen-Hoeksema & Rusting, 1999). This possibility is in line with studies comparing men's and women's actual levels of emotion, as measured in real time by experience sampling methods (ESM), to levels based on retrospective recall (Robinson & Johnson, 1997; Robinson, Johnson, & Shields, 1998). Men and women showed similar levels of emotion on the ESM, but women reported higher levels of emotion than men on the recall measures, and this difference increased with longer recall time delays. The differences found for the retrospective measure may

have resulted from men and women recalling their emotions in ways that were consistent with gender stereotypes. Other researchers have also reported that moment-to-moment measures do not reveal the gender differences found on more global measures (e.g., Feldman Barrett, Robin, Pietromonaco, & Eyssel, 1998).

Finally, the eudaimonic perspective (which defines well-being in terms of healthy functioning rather than happiness) suggests that the paradox of gender may result, in part, from how well-being is defined. Most of the research on gender and happiness has followed the hedonic model, in which the balance of positive and negative emotions is a major defining component of SWB. As a result, the higher rates of depression and more frequent experiencing of negative emotions among women seem to contradict the finding of overall gender similarity in SWB. That is, women's greater vulnerability to negative emotions and mood disorders "should" result in somewhat lower levels of SWB for women than for men.

The eudaimonic view defines well-being in terms of the attributes associated with psychological health—not happiness. According to this view, well-being involves a more complex array of factors than the SWB conception. Ryff, Singer, and their colleagues define well-being and healthy functioning in terms of six dimensions: self-acceptance, positive relations with others, autonomy, environmental mastery, purpose in life, and personal growth (see Ryff & Singer, 2002 and Chapter 2 of this book). Profiles of healthy functioning based on these dimensions parallel the findings of SWB research. Results from many studies have shown men and women to have very similar levels of overall well-being, but some specific dimensions of well-being show clear gender differences. For example, in several studies, women scored higher than men on positive relations with others and personal growth.

Because of their differing conceptions of well-being, hedonic and eudaimonic researchers part company somewhat when it comes to the meaning of these findings. Gender similarity in overall happiness (despite gender differences in emotional experience) raises a paradox within the hedonic view of well-being. Well-being defined eudaimonically as healthy functioning does not raise a similar paradox. Ryff and Singer note that their findings on the well-being and strengths of women do not contradict gender differences in negative moods and depression. Instead, they " . . . enrich the picture by pointing out that psychological vulnerabilities may exist, side by side with notable psychological strengths" (Ryff & Singer, 2002, p. 545). In other words, the co-occurrence of strengths and vulnerabilities is not particularly paradoxical when well-being is defined in terms of healthy psychological functioning. All of us have our strengths and weaknesses, and unless the weaknesses are extreme, they do not necessarily compromise our overall health and well-being. One reason is that strengths can compensate for weaknesses. For example, women's greater emotional vulnerability may be offset by their strengths in developing positive relations with others. We know that positive relationships exert a powerful influence on our health and personal happiness—an effect clearly shown by the influences of marriage on well-being, to be considered next.

There is one last bit of complexity in the relationship between strengths and vulnerabilities. In addition to the co-existence of strengths and vulnerabilities and the possibility of offsetting effects, strengths may have a downside, and weaknesses an upside. It may be, for example, that women's strengths in developing and maintaining positive relationships also contribute to their more frequent experience of negative affect and intense emotions. Empathy and sensitivity to others are important in relationships. Women have been shown to have more of these abilities than men, which may cause women to be more influenced by the negative emotions of others (Nolen-Hoeksema & Rusting, 1999; Woods et al., 1989). Women's higher susceptibility to the emotions of others may be responsible for some of the differences in emotional experience between men and women. On the other hand, men (who show lower scores on the "positive relations with others" dimension) (Ryff & Singer, 2000, 2002) may have diminished social well-being compared to women, but may also have more stable emotions. If men's lower level of empathy and social sensitivity makes them less susceptible to the emotions of others, the result may be a less extreme emotional life for men than for women (with the exception of anger).

So, who is happier, men or women? Answer: Neither. Each gender appears, on average, to share a unique combination of strengths and vulnerabilities. In overall comparisons, these gender-related strengths and vulnerabilities may offset each other, producing no overall differences in average level of happiness. These same differences in strengths and vulnerabilities

also help explain why the emotional lives of men and women are, on average, quite different.

MARRIAGE AND HAPPINESS

Most demographic variables show only small relationships to happiness. One major exception to this general pattern involves the effects of marriage on SWB. About 90% of us eventually marry and the vast majority of us will be happier as a result (Myers, 2000a). An extensive literature documents the relationship between marriage and higher levels of SWB (see Berscheid & Reis, 1998; Diener & Seligman; 2004, Myers, 1999 & 2000a; Myers & Diener, 1995; Woods et al., 1989, for reviews). Higher than what? Higher than people who never married or who are divorced, separated, or widowed. The marriage–happiness relationship has consistently been demonstrated in large-scale surveys of Americans and Europeans (see Diener et al., 1999). A meta-analytic review of nearly 100 studies found marriage to be a strong predictor of life satisfaction, happiness, and overall well-being (Woods et al., 1989). The positive effects of marriage are large. One national survey of 35,000 people in the United States (reviewed by Myers, 2000a) found that the percentage of married adults who said they were "very happy" (40%) was nearly double that of those who never married (26%). Even when researchers control for the possible confounding effects of other variables such as income and age, there is still a significant relationship between marriage and well-being (e.g., Gove, Hughes, & Style, 1983; Haring-Hidore, Stock, Okun, & Witter, 1985). Compared to other domains of life (such as job status and health), being married and having a family repeatedly show the strongest connection to life satisfaction and happiness (Campbell et al., 1976; Inglehart, 1990).

Benefits of Marriage

What is responsible for the marriage–happiness relationship? Is it the beneficial effects of marriage? Or are people who get married simply happier to begin with? Arguments for the benefits of marriage may begin with Baumeister and Leary's (1995) argument. They argue that human beings have a basic "need to belong." Countless studies reviewed by these and other authors (e.g., Berscheid, 2003; Deci & Ryan, 1991) show the importance of close, supportive, and stable relationships to people's physical and emotional well-being. People consistently rank close relationships among their top life goals (Emmons, 1999b). Given that marriage is one major vehicle for fulfillment of this basic need, it would follow that married people would report higher levels of well-being and happiness. Marriage has the potential to provide companionship, intimacy, love, affection, and social support in times of crisis. The roles of spouse and parent may also provide opportunities for personal growth and the development of new competencies that increase self-esteem and satisfaction.

A "general benefits" view is supported by the fact that the marriage–happiness relationship is found across widely diverse cultures, independent of whether researchers ask about marriage quality. The significant drop in well-being when marriages end due to death, divorce, or separation provides further evidence for the benefits of marriage. The end of marriage may mean the loss of intimacy, companionship, and emotional support, and decreased financial resources. The benefits of marriage are further revealed in terms of the higher levels of emotional distress and mental illness found among people who are unmarried and living alone with few friends or confidants (see Diener & Seligman, 2004; Myers, 2000a; Waite & Gallagher, 2000, for reviews). In contrast, married people have a lower risk for experiencing depression, loneliness, or physical and mental health problems, and live longer than individuals who are widowed, separated, or divorced. Overall, married people generally enjoy better physical and mental health than unmarried people. Marriage may also help people overcome problems in their lives. A 7-year study of over 800 men and women found decreases in rates of depression and alcoholism among those who got married compared to those who remained single (Horwitz, White, & Howell-White, 1996a). Myers (2000a) argues that most of the available research supports the beneficial effects of marriage as the major reason for the greater well-being of married people. A high percentage of married people appear to be content with their marriages. A majority of married couples say that their spouse is their best friend and that they would marry the same person again (Glenn, 1996; Greeley, 1991).

Clearly, the quality of a marriage is critical to its well-being benefits. As Myers (1992) put it, "In terms of individual happiness, a bad marriage is worse than no marriage at all" (p. 158). An extensive literature documents the negative effects of bad relationships on well-being (Argyle, 2001; Berscheid & Reis, 1998; Diener & Seligman, 2004; Reis & Gable, 2003). The list of destructive marital elements is long, including physical/emotional abuse, alcoholism, conflict, hostility, jealousy, infidelity, and dominance. The adverse effects of a bad marriage on well-being are also numerous (Argyle, 2001; Berscheid & Reis, 1998; Gottman, 1994; Reis & Gable, 2003), highlighted by the fact that problem relationships are among the most common reasons that people seek professional help from counselors and psychotherapists. Questions concerning the distinguishing features of good and bad relationships and how people develop and maintain successful long-term marriages will be addressed in Chapter 11—"Relationships and Well-being."

Selection Effects

The effects of marriage quality and the benefits of marriage offer straightforward explanations for the higher levels of reported happiness among married people. Well-being researchers have examined two other factors that may attenuate the marriage–happiness relationship: selection and adaptation. The term **selection effect** refers to the possibility that people who marry are simply happier, before they get married, than those who don't marry. If this is true, then the effects of marriage on well-being are inflated by who gets married in the first place. These so-called selection effects are based on the assumption that happy people are more desirable marriage partners than unhappy people and are therefore more likely to marry, and to do so sooner (Veenhoven, 1988). This certainly makes some sense, given that most of us prefer the company of people who are upbeat and cheerful rather than moody and irritable. However, studies of selection effects reveal mixed results. A large-scale study in Norway found selection effects in the marriage–happiness relationship among 9,000 people (Mastekaasa, 1992). However, a 12-year longitudinal study found that selection effects made only a small contribution to the higher well-being of married individuals (Johnson & Wu, 2002). Myers (2000a) raises another problem with explanations based on selection effects: If happy people are more likely to marry, and to do so earlier in their lives, then as people age, the happiness of married people as a group would go down, as older and less happy people begin to marry. In other words, the addition of less happy people to the married group would pull down the overall average. A similar change would occur among the never-married group. As less-happy people eventually get married, the most-unhappy people are increasingly left in the never-married group, reducing the average level of happiness. As Myers notes, data on well-being and marital status do not support these predictions based on selection effects. On the contrary, differences in happiness among married and never-married individuals are consistent across age groups.

Focus on Research: Are We Still Happy After the Honeymoon?

Adaptation refers to a return to set point and a longer-term level of happiness, as people adjust to an event's emotional impact. The process of adaptation raises the question of whether the increase in happiness after marriage is a long-term increase, or whether people eventually return to their pre-marriage levels of happiness. A longitudinal study of over 24,000 people living in Germany *not only* found evidence for an overall pattern of adaptation to the emotional impact of marriage, but also found considerable individual variability in how marriage affected pre-marriage levels of happiness (Lucas et al., 2003). Participants were interviewed annually over a 15-year period. Among the measures taken in the study was a rating of overall life satisfaction, on which responses could range from 0 (totally unhappy) to 10 (totally happy). Two marital transitions were studied: getting married and becoming widowed. The effects of these events were evaluated by comparing pre-marriage and pre-widowhood happiness to the levels of happiness shortly after the event and in subsequent years of the study. To better isolate the effects of these marital transitions, only those persons who stayed married for the duration of the study were used to examine the effects of marriage (1,012 participants), and only those who remained widowed (did not remarry) were used to evaluate the effects of losing one's spouse (500 participants).

In Lucas and colleagues' study, marriage produced a small short-term boost in happiness (about one-tenth of a point on an 11-point scale) and this increase faded during subsequent years of marriage. Averages across all of the participants showed people

to be no happier after marriage than they were before. These findings provide strong evidence for the process of adaptation to the emotional consequences of getting married. Results also suggest that selection effects play a role in the marriage–happiness relationship. Participants who got married during the study had higher average levels of happiness (compared to other participants) *before* marriage. How much this selection effect contributed to the increase in satisfaction after marriage is unclear. The magnitude of the selection effect was not assessed. The results for widowed individuals showed much longer-term effects and much slower adaptation. Eight years after losing their spouse, participants' average happiness ratings approached pre-widowhood levels, but did not recover completely. Many widowed individuals showed stable and long-term declines in life satisfaction and therefore did not show complete adaptation to the loss of their spouses.

Lucas and his colleagues (2003) note that the overall pattern of adaptation to marriage must be tempered by the fact of wide variability in individual responses. Based on their data, Lucas and his colleagues plotted the marital trajectory for three hypothetical individuals shown in Figure 5.4. The figure shows that the return to pre-marriage levels

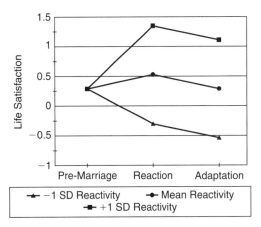

FIGURE 5.4   Three Reactions to Marriage

−1 SD represents someone who reacts negatively to marriage (one standard deviation below the average response), +1 SD represents a positive reaction to marriage (one standard deviation above the average response), and mean reactivity is the average response.   *Source:* Lucas, R. E., Clark, A. E., Georgellis, Y., & Diener, E. (2003). Reexamining adaptation and the set point model of happiness: Reactions to changes in marital status. *Journal of Personality and Social Psychology, 84,* 527–539. Copyright American Psychological Association. Reprinted by permission.

of happiness for participants as a group (Mean Reactivity) masked some quite significant individual variations. The longitudinal design of the study allowed researchers to track changes in happiness for individual participants. These data revealed that many people were much happier after marriage (+1 SD), and this increase in happiness continued across the time span of the study. Interestingly, about an equal number of people reported far *less* happiness after marriage, and this reduction in happiness was maintained across time (−1 SD). These two groups show that many people do not adapt to the effects of marriage, but show long-term increases or decreases in their baseline levels of happiness. Results for these groups also help explain the overall finding of adaptation to marriage. Those whose happiness increased were cancelled out by those whose happiness decreased, resulting in no apparent pre- and post-marriage differences in happiness.

Whether happiness increased or declined was significantly related to people's initial reaction to getting married. Those who reacted positively to marriage increased their long-term levels of happiness. Those who had negative, or less positive initial reactions either showed no long-term changes or became even less happy than they were prior to marriage. Lucas and his colleagues believe a process they call **hedonic leveling** explains some of these differences. Consider this finding from their study: The most satisfied people had the least positive reactions to getting married, but they had the strongest negative reactions to divorce and widowhood. Why would this be? Hedonic leveling involves the effect of a person's existing level of life satisfaction and happiness on the emotional impact of a life event. Happy individuals (who may have many supportive friends) may have less to gain from marriage because their needs for companionship and intimacy are already relatively fulfilled in other relationships. An unhappy or lonely person (who may have fewer friends) may have much to gain from marriage in terms of securing intimacy and companionship. These gains would likely result in higher levels of happiness and life satisfaction. To put it bluntly, if you are quite happy, how much happier can you get? And if you're miserable, it may not take much to cheer you up.

Hedonic leveling may be responsible for the varied individual reactions to marriage that were averaged out in the overall finding. That is, if marriage has little effect on happy people, but a big effect on unhappy people, the differences between the two groups are reduced or leveled out. The same process may affect the impact of widowhood on particular individuals. People who are happy with life because they have satisfying marriages have much to lose if their spouse dies, while loss of a partner in a very unhappy marriage may have much less effect.

Does the overall adaptation to marriage shown in Lucas and colleagues' study contradict research that has consistently shown the benefits of marriage? No single study is ever definitive. Because the participants were all German citizens, additional research will need to address questions concerning the cross-cultural validity of results. However, the power of this study lies in its longitudinal design, which allowed a teasing-out, rather than an averaging-out, of individual reactions to marital transitions. At the very least, the research by Lucas and colleagues indicates the strength of longitudinal methods and the weakness of cross-sectional studies in determining the individualized effects of life events on SWB.

Gender Differences in the Benefits of Marriage

Two final issues in the marriage–happiness relationship involve the question of whether men or women benefit the most from marriage, and whether the benefits of marriage have declined over time. Findings for both issues are mixed. Some studies suggest that men experience more emotional benefits in terms of increases in positive emotions and protection against depression (Diener et al., 1999; Nolen-Hoeksema & Rusting, 1999). However, other research finds no gender differences in life satisfaction, but does suggest that the effects of divorce or separation fall along gender lines, with women experiencing more depression, and men more alcohol abuse (Horwitz, White, & Howell-White, 1996b). Myers (2000a) argues that these mixed results do not alter the basic fact shown in many studies that the gap in happiness between married and unmarried people is about the same for men and for women.

Whether there has been a decline in the strength of the marriage–happiness relationship is also unclear. Several studies in America have shown an apparent decline since the 1970s (e.g., Glenn

& Weaver, 1988; Lee et al., 1991), as well as increased conflict in younger compared to older couples. However, other researchers have found no such decline (Mastekaasa, 1993) and evidence for decline may have resulted from the historical increase in the number of divorced and cohabitating couples in the last 30 years (Kurdek, 1991). Divorced individuals have higher rates of divorce in subsequent marriages, perhaps because they are less able to make a marriage work and may therefore be less happy as a result of marriage. Cohabitating couples undoubtedly benefit from their relationships even though they aren't counted as married. Together, these two facts would decrease the difference between the married and never-married populations, but not the actual benefits of marriage.

In summary, marriage appears to have many potential benefits for individual health and well-being. It is not clear how much of these benefits result from selection effects (the tendency for happy people to marry). Whether marriage enhances or reduces well-being for a given individual depends on many variables, but research has identified the quality of a couple's relationship and hedonic leveling as two important factors. In evaluating the effects of marriage it is important to return to the difference between the hedonic and eudaimonic views of well-being. The emphasis on healthy functioning within the eudaimonic perspective reminds us that there is more to well-being than happiness.

Whether marriage makes us happier may be less important than whether it makes us healthier. A good deal of research shows the health benefits of marriage. Differences between hedonic and eudaimonic definitions of well-being are evidenced by the fact that some factors that promote health may also mortgage happiness, at least in the short run. For example, Ryff and Singer (2000) point out that conflict in marriage (which is bad for happiness) may promote future well-being. Conflict is often the basis for personal growth and increased competence in dealing with life. Resolving differences and reconciling conflicting interests enhances a relationship. Ryff and Singer's review shows that over time, couples typically improve in their ability to manage negative emotions and conflict, and therefore derive more satisfaction from their marriages. In other words, unhappiness at one point in a marriage may be the basis for greater happiness in the future. In short, health and happiness, though related, are not the same thing. A couple not brimming with happiness may still have a healthy relationship that promotes and maintains their individual well-being. If we focus on well-being only through the lens of happiness we may miss the many other factors that contribute to healthy functioning. A more detailed discussion of the ingredients of healthy relationships will be taken up in a subsequent chapter.

OTHER FACTS OF LIFE

A variety of other demographic variables have been examined for their potential contribution to individual health and happiness. Our review of each of these demographics will be brief because some variables have been covered in earlier chapters, others will be discussed in subsequent chapters, and for several demographics, extensive research is lacking. Our discussion will rely heavily on several recent reviews of demographics and happiness (Argyle, 1999, 2001; Diener et al., 1999; Diener, Lucas, & Oishi, 2002; Diener & Seligman, 2004; Myers, 1992; Ryan & Deci, 2001). Readers interested in a more detailed discussion of any particular demographic factor may consult these reviews.

Physical and Mental Health

As discussed in Chapter 3, the connection between SWB and physical/emotional health is a two-way street: Happiness contributes to our health and health contributes to our happiness. The impact of SWB on physical health is shown in the associations between happiness and longer life, lower susceptibility to disease, and better recovery from illnesses such as cardiovascular disease (Diener & Seligman, 2004). These relationships are essentially reversed for people with a history of depression or low SWB. The influence of positive and negative emotions on immune-system functioning undoubtedly plays a role in these relationships (see Chapter 3, "Positive Emotions and Health"). The state of our physical health also affects our level of happiness. Illness and injury involve pain and distress, and may limit our opportunities to engage in pleasurable activities. Negative emotions may increase and positive emotions may decrease as a result of illness. For these reasons, one might expect a straightforward relationship between physical health and SWB, but that does not seem to be the case.

One meta-analytic review found a significant correlation ($r = 0.32$) between *self-reported* health and well-being (Okun, Stock, Haring, & Witter, 1984). However, when researchers obtained *objective measures* of physical health such as doctor reports, the correlations between health and well-being declined substantially. In Okun and colleagues' study, the correlation dropped from 0.32 to 0.16. Other studies affirm these findings (e.g., Brief, Butcher, George, & Link, 1993). The lower correlation highlights the subjective nature of health assessments. People with poor health, as defined by medical professionals, may have high SWB, and people with few objective health problems may have low SWB. How people interpret the meaning and significance of their physical health status has much to do with the influence of health on happiness. Adaptation also contributes to the difference between objective and subjective health evaluations. People may adapt to illness and return to their long-term set point level of happiness. In other words, objective health conditions may remain the same, but subjective evaluations may become more positive as people adjust to their illness and move back toward set point levels of SWB. However, people do not adapt to all aspects of illness. When illness is severe and prolonged, happiness and life satisfaction may show significant and long-term declines. Diener and Seligman (2004) note studies showing that people with congestive heart failure, AIDS, cancer, and rheumatoid arthritis often experience higher levels of anxiety and depression, and lower life satisfaction than individuals in non-ill control groups. These differences were maintained a year after diagnosis.

The lower well-being associated with poor physical health finds an even stronger counterpart in the realm of mental health. In reviewing the impact of mental health, Diener and Seligman (2004, p. 16) conclude that "Not only is mental disorder common, but it almost always causes poor well-being. . . ." For example, these authors' compilation of mental health statistics reveals a dramatic increase in the number of people—particularly young people—suffering from depression. In the past, depression was uncommon among adolescents. The average age of onset was not until 30 years of age. Today, studies find that a significant percentage of teens as young as 14 experience depression. The heightened levels of distress, negative emotions, and anxiety associated with most mental disorders cause low life satisfaction and a lack of personal happiness. An individual's emotional problems may also cause distress among family caregivers and supportive friends. Mental illness within a family can have a negative impact on the entire family's well-being.

The mental health–happiness relationship goes both ways—from mental illness to unhappiness and from happiness to mental wellness. Studies show that happy people report low levels of mental illness symptoms (see Diener & Seligman, 2004, and Chapter 2 of this book). Even more direct evidence for the inverse relationship between well-being and emotional illness comes from research within the eudaimonic tradition. Many studies have found that measures of well-being, defined by aspects of healthy functioning, show negative correlations with symptoms of mental illness (e.g., Keyes, 2003).

Work and Unemployment

The importance of work for personal health and happiness can be seen in the dramatic effects of job loss. Unemployment has relatively immediate and negative affects on well-being, including increased risk for depression, physical illness, lowered self-esteem, and unhappiness (see Argyle, 2001; Diener & Seligman, 2004; Layard, 2005, for reviews). Studies of the aftermath of factory closings have shown the immediacy of unemployment's effects. Longitudinal studies comparing levels of well-being before and after unemployment reveal that unhappiness is caused by job loss and not by a greater likelihood of unhappy people becoming unemployed (e.g., Lucas, Clark, Georgellis, & Diener, 2004). Job loss also has the potential to produce long-term decreases in life satisfaction.

Work, on the other hand, is associated with a number of benefits that promote well-being. A critical factor in the relationship between work and happiness is job satisfaction, and job satisfaction is strongly correlated with life satisfaction. Researchers believe the causal direction of the relationship goes both ways. Happy people find satisfaction in their work, and a satisfying job contributes to individual happiness (Argyle, 2001). In a similar vein, stress, boredom, and interpersonal conflict at work are sources of dissatisfaction and unhappiness in general. Spillover effects have been shown in many studies. For example, a good day at work can contribute to less conflict at home and the opposite can be true of a bad workday (Diener & Seligman, 2004).

Intelligence and Education

Are smart people happier? Does going to college increase individual happiness? A case could easily be made that the answers to these questions should be yes. Highly intelligent people might be more skillful in dealing with life challenges and fulfilling their personal life goals. A college degree opens up more opportunities for personally satisfying and financially rewarding work. Surprisingly, though, a research review by Diener and his colleagues (Diener et al., 1999) concludes that there is no significant correlation between intelligence (as defined by standardized intelligence test scores) and happiness when other demographic variables are taken into account. The lack of connection between intelligence and happiness may reflect the fact that there are different types of intelligence. For example, the concept of emotional intelligence, defined as the ability to use emotional information effectively, has shown connections to behaviors relevant to health and happiness (Salovey, Mayer, & Caruso, 2002). This work is in a preliminary stage, but may offer a future understanding of the type of intelligence that enhances well-being.

College students will be pleased to know that educational level, defined by years of schooling, does show a small positive relationship to happiness (see Argyle's 2001 review). The tendency for people with more education to be slightly happier than those with less, seems to stem from education's influence on occupation and job satisfaction. Advanced education may open greater opportunities and freedom to choose jobs that are more personally satisfying and financially rewarding. One study reviewed by Argyle (2001) found that more education was associated with higher SWB, better mental/physical health, increased personal control, and greater social support from others. Education appears to influence well-being primarily through increased job satisfaction rather than increased income.

Religion

The role of religion and spirituality in people's lives is a complex and challenging issue that will be addressed in Chapter 10. Here, we note two important findings. First, religious beliefs and involvements are widespread among Americans. Over the past 50 years, national surveys by Gallup and others have consistently found that 90 to 95% of Americans express a belief in God or a higher power (Miller & Thoresen, 2003; Myers, 2000a). Two-thirds of Americans belong to a church or synagogue, and 40% attend regularly. Secondly, researchers have found small positive correlations between happiness and religious involvement, and moderate to strong connections between religion and physical health (Argyle, 2001; George, Ellison, & Larson, 2002; Hill & Pargament, 2003; Myers, 2000a; Seeman, Dubin, & Seeman, 2003). Among the health benefits of religion are a longer life and a lower likelihood of cardiovascular disease (Powell, Shahabi, & Thoresen, 2003). Explanations for the connections among health, religion, and spirituality are a current focus of research. Various possibilities have been suggested, from the role of religion in promoting positive emotions, optimism, and transcendent views of purpose and meaning in life, to the social support provided by church members and the healthy lifestyle encouraged by many religious and spiritual traditions.

Race, Ethnicity, and Stigma

Discrimination and negative stereotypes are part of the past and present experience of many minority groups (e.g., African Americans, Hispanics, Asians, and women). Many other groups, including gay and disabled individuals, confront differential treatment and negative beliefs about their personal qualities that result from membership in a stigmatized group. Do these experiences, along with the anger and despair they may produce, have a negative impact on SWB, perhaps by lowering self-esteem and feelings of self-worth? Studies comparing African Americans to Western-European Americans have found somewhat lower levels of self-reported happiness among African Americans (see Argyle, 2001; Crocker, Major, & Steele, 1998, for reviews), but these levels are still in the positive range (Diener, 1984). Some evidence suggests that differences among races have declined over the last several decades, and when income, occupation, and employment status are controlled, these differences become smaller yet. In other words, race *per se* has little effect on SWB; however, economic inequality (which is correlated with race) does have an effect. Evidence suggests that other stigmatized and disadvantaged individuals also show positive levels of well-being (Diener & Diener, 1996). People with disabilities such as blindness and quadriplegia have levels of SWB in the positive range, only slightly lower than averages within the non-disabled population (Diener & Diener, 1996; Frederick & Lowenstein, 1999).

Surprisingly, self-esteem is not necessarily mortgaged by membership in a stigmatized group. For example, the assaults to self-worth that African Americans may experience do not appear to lower self-esteem. Several extensive reviews covering hundreds of studies and involving a half-million participants reported that the self-esteem scores of African Americans are actually somewhat higher than those of whites (Gray-Little & Hafdahl, 2000; Twenge & Crocker, 2002). This finding was consistent across comparisons of children, adolescents, and adults. Twenge and Crocker did find that the self-esteem scores of Hispanic, Asian, and Native American individuals were lower in comparison to whites. It is unclear how the differences in self-esteem among these groups might be interpreted. For stigmatized groups in general, researchers have suggested several ways that self-esteem may be maintained despite prejudicial experiences (Crocker et al., 1998). Stigmatized individuals may attribute negative life outcomes to external discrimination rather than personal failings; they may build a sense of group pride in the face of adversity shared with other group members; and they may increase the likelihood of more favorable and self-esteem-enhancing self-evaluations by restricting comparisons to members of their own group. Whether the higher self-esteem of African Americans compared to other ethnic minorities results from more extensive or more effective use of these self-esteem protective processes remains an open question.

Chapter Summary Questions

1. Explain the paradox of well-being and discuss why it is counterintuitive. Support your explanation with examples of specific studies.

2. a. What is the impact bias?
   b. Discuss two reasons why the impact bias occurs.

3. a. In Schkade and Kahneman's (1998) study, what did students believe, and what did the data actually show regarding the difference between living in the Midwest and living in California?
   b. How does the focusing illusion explain these findings?

4. How does the isolation effect explain the importance of dorm location in Dunn, Wilson, and Gilbert's study?

5. What does research suggest about the emotional impact of commonly assumed life turning points such as menopause, the empty nest syndrome, and mid-life crisis?

6. What does a genetically determined temperament have to do with the stability of SWB across the life span?

7. a. How do changes in the frequency and intensity of emotion help explain the stability of SWB over the life span?
   b. What do studies show regarding age-related changes in negative and positive affect?

8. Explain how the measurement and definitions of affect clarify the meaning of age-related changes in SWB.

9. Describe four age-related changes that support socioemotional selectivity theory's prediction that emotional well-being may increase with age.

10. What is the paradox of gender, and how is this paradox revealed in the different emotional lives of men and women?

11. a. How do differences in the intensity of emotional experiences and gender stereotypes explain the paradox of gender?
    b. From the eudaimonic perspective, why is the paradox of gender not really a paradox?

12. What are the major benefits of marriage, according to research?

13. What were the major findings of the Lucas, Clark, Georgellis, & Diener and his colleagues' (2003) study, and how does hedonic leveling explain individual reactions to becoming married, divorced, or widowed?

14. What is the difference between a hedonic and a eudaimonic view of the benefits of marriage?

15. How does adaptation explain the differences between self-reported and objective measures of physical health?

16. What roles do intelligence, education, and religion play in individual happiness?

17. Why doesn't membership in a stigmatized group necessarily mortgage self-esteem?

Key Terms

affective forecasting *77*
impact bias *77*
focalism *77*
immune neglect *77*
focusing illusions *78*
isolation effect *80*

happiness set point *81*
pleasant affect versus positive
   involvement *84*
socioemotional selectivity
   theory *85*
internalizing disorders *86*

externalizing disorders *86*
selection effects *90*
hedonic leveling *92*

Web Resources

Happiness and Subjective Well-Being

www.psych.uiuc.edu/~ediener Web page for happiness researcher Ed Diener, who has conducted extensive research on the relation of happiness to objective features of life.

www.davidmyers.org/Brix?pageID=20 Web site for David Myers that contains information about his work in positive psychology, including his popular book, *The pursuit of happiness.*

Suggested Readings

Carstensen, L. L., Isaacowitz, D. M., & Charles, S. T. (1999). Taking time seriously: A theory of socioemotional selectivity. *American Psychologist, 54,* 165–181.

Diener, E., Suh, E. M., Lucas, R. E., & Smith, H. L. (1999). Subjective well-being: Three decades of progress. *Psychological Bulletin, 125,* 276–302.

Kahneman, D., Diener, E., & Schwarz, N. (Eds.). (1999). *Well-being: The foundations of hedonic psychology.* New York: Russell Sage Foundation.

Kunzmann, U., Stange, A., & Jordan, J. (2005). Positive affectivity and lifestyle in adulthood: Do you do what you feel? *Personality and Social Psychology Bulletin, 31,* 574–588.

Myers, D. G. (1992). *The pursuit of happiness.* New York: Avon Books.

Myers, D. G. (2000a). The funds, friends, and faith of happy people. *American Psychologist, 55,* 56–67.

Myers, D. G., & Diener, E. (1995). Who is happy? *Psychological Science, 6,* 10–19.

Ryff, C. D., & Singer, B. (2000). Interpersonal flourishing: A positive health agenda for the new millennium. *Personality and Social Psychology Review, 4,* 30–44.

6

Money, Happiness, and Culture

CHAPTER OUTLINE

People appear to be of two minds regarding the relationship between money and happiness. On one hand, few of us would say that money buys happiness; that would be a crass and shallow view of life. Survey research affirms a widespread belief that there is more to life than money. People rank money near the bottom of important sources of life satisfaction. In their classic work on quality of life, Campbell and his colleagues (1976) found that money ranked 11th out of 12 listed sources of a satisfying life. Money and wealth were shown to be largely irrelevant to people's judgments of the "good" life in a study by

King and Nappa (1998). Both college students and adult community members judged happiness and meaningfulness—not wealth—to be the essential features of a life well-lived. A recent *Time* magazine poll asked 1,000 adults, "What one thing in your life has brought you the greatest happiness?" Neither money, wealth, or material possessions were included in the top eight answers (Special Mind & Body Issue: "The Science of Happiness," January 17, 2005, p. A5). Taking a broad view, most of us don't believe that money has much to do with a happy and satisfying life.

On the other hand, when we focus on our own lives, most of us seem to believe that more money would make us happier. National opinion polls have asked people about the role money plays in their personal happiness and life satisfaction (see Myers, 1992, 2000a, 2000b, for reviews). In answer to questions about what would improve quality of life, more money was the most common answer. In response to questions about what aspect of life interferes with achieving the "good life," not having enough money was the most frequent answer. When they were asked what part of life (e.g., job, home, friends, education, etc.) was least satisfying, most people said it was the amount of money they had to live on. The idea expressed in these surveys (that more money will make people happier) makes sense when applied to the poor. The frustrations, stress, and unmet basic needs associated with poverty cause distress, unhappiness, and lower levels of subjective well-being (SWB) (Diener & Seligman, 2004; Diener, Suh, Lucas, & Smith, 1999). But for those with average and above-average incomes, the logic connecting money and happiness through the fulfillment of basic needs makes far less sense. This is clearly evident in a *Chicago Tribune* survey reported by Csikszentmihalyi (1999). The survey showed that regardless of their current income, people believed that more money would make them happier. People making $30,000 per year said that a $50,000 yearly income would allow them to fulfill their dreams. Those at $100,000 said it would take $250,000 to make them satisfied. All of this suggest that people share a general belief that money increases happiness. There seems to be little consideration of the possibility that at some point, more money might not have an appreciable effect.

Surveys of college students taken over the last 30 years indicate that the importance of money in people's lives may be increasing. A 1998 survey of over 200,000 students found that being financially well-off was endorsed as a major life objective by a majority of students (74%), whereas in 1970 only 39% had rated money as a very important objective (see Myers, 2000b, pp. 126–128). The apparent pervasiveness of the belief in a money–happiness connection led Myers to suggest that "the American dream seems to have become life, liberty and the purchase of happiness" (Myers, 2000b, p. 58). Myers' conclusion becomes even more persuasive if we consider people's actual behavior regarding money and material possessions. An emerging body of research within psychology suggests that the accumulation of wealth and material possessions are central features of many people's lives (see Kasser, 2002; Kasser & Kanner, 2004).

A big-picture view of life seems to lead to the conclusion that money and happiness are unrelated, while a smaller-picture view of one's own life, in the here-and-now, seems to lead to an opposite conclusion. In short, people seem to "know" that money doesn't buy happiness, but still act as if it does. This two-sided view raises a number of questions that will be addressed in this chapter. First and foremost are questions concerning whether money *is* related to happiness, and to what extent. Does increased income translate into increased happiness? Are rich people happier than the rest of us? Are people who live in wealthy countries happier than those in poorer countries? As our country has become more affluent, has the level of our happiness increased as well? In addition to these questions, we will also examine whether happiness has the same meaning in different cultures. For example, do Chinese and Japanese individuals place the same value on individual happiness as Americans do? Do the things that make Americans happy also make people happy in other cultures? We begin our discussion by putting the money–happiness issue in a cultural and historical context.

"THE PARADOX OF AFFLUENCE"

The term **"paradox of affluence"** is drawn from the title of David Myers' book *The Paradox of Affluence: Spiritual Hunger in an Age of Plenty* (Myers, 2000b). This book offers a detailed description of the disparity that has developed over the last 40 to 50 years in America between material well-being and psychosocial well-being. A recent review by Diener and

Seligman (2004) also provides extensive statistical evidence that indices of material affluence and of well-being have gone in opposite directions since the 1950s. The disparities are startling. Both reviews note that since the 1950s per capita real income has tripled. Consumer statistics reveal a complementary pattern. Americans have doubled and tripled their ownership of cars, big-screen TVs, dishwashers, clothes dryers, and computers, and go out to eat twice as often as in the past (Myers, 2000a, 2000b). Statistics complied by Easterbrook (2003) provide striking evidence of our increased affluence:

- Nearly 23% of households (63 million people) in the United States make at least $75,000 per year.
- In 2001, Americans spent 25 billion dollars on recreational watercraft. This is more than the entire gross domestic product of North Korea.
- At a pace of 750,000 per year, Americans have purchased more than 3 million all-terrain vehicles since 1995.
- The typical new home averages 2,250 square feet, about double the size of the average home in the 1950s.
- Counting fast-food restaurants, Americans eat out four times a week. Counting only "sit-down" restaurants, the figure is once per week.

During this same period of increased income and consumption, large-scale national surveys reveal that the American level of life satisfaction has remained "virtually flat" (Diener & Seligman, 2004). Figure 6.1 shows the lack of relationship between life satisfaction and rising GNP in the United States. On a 10-point life satisfaction rating scale, with 1 indicating very dissatisfied and 10 indicating very satisfied, the mean life satisfaction of Americans was 7.2, with little variation during the entire period from 1947 to 1998. The percentage of Americans reporting that they are very happy has remained relatively fixed at about 30% from the 1950s through the 1990s (Myers, 2000a). Most Americans are richer, but not happier than in the past.

One might think economic gains would at least have a positive impact on mental health. It seems reasonable to assume that increased material resources might enhance personal happiness by creating more mental health services and preventative programs that would help reduce the number of people suffering from emotional problems. With this assumption in mind, it is all the more surprising that mental health statistics reveal a discouraging picture of increased, rather than decreased, distress correlating with increased material wealth. Mental health statistics are based on incidence rates reported to community, state, and federal agencies, on national surveys that ask about mental illness symptoms, and on diagnostic interviews and intensive study of selected populations. Reviews of the mental health literature conclude that there are more people suffering from mental disorders and emotional distress today than in the past (Diener & Seligman, 2004; Kessler et al., 1994; Keyes, 2003; Keyes & Lopez, 2002). A comparison of national adult surveys taken in 1957, 1976, and 1996 found a steady increase in the percentage of people feeling an "impending nervous breakdown" (an everyday term for extreme subjective distress). In 1957, 18.9% of those surveyed had experienced an impending breakdown. In 1976, the figure was 20.9%, and by 1996 the percentage had risen to 26.4% (Swindle, Heller, Pescosolido, & Kikuzawa, 2000). Diagnostic interviews with samples of adult Americans show that nearly 50% have experienced at least one mental disorder in their lifetime; 30% have had a mental health episode within the last year and nearly 18% within the last month (Kessler & Frank, 1997; Kessler et al., 1994).

Of all mental disorders, depression has shown the most dramatic increase in incidence. Diener and Seligman (2004) estimate a 10-fold increase in incidence rates over the last 50 years and note studies reporting that the average age of onset has fallen from 30 years into the teenage years. These authors review several lines of evidence revealing a substantial rise in the number of people suffering from depression and suggest a link between increased depression and increased affluence. Rates of depression seem to have increased across generations, with younger people suffering much higher rates than older people. Individuals born in the first decade of the twentieth century showed very low rates of depression, and each successive generation has experienced higher rates than the generation before.

Diener and Seligman (2004) reviewed two studies supporting a general connection between depression and affluence. First, a large-scale international study (Cross National Collaborative Group, 1992) found that the depression–affluence relationship,

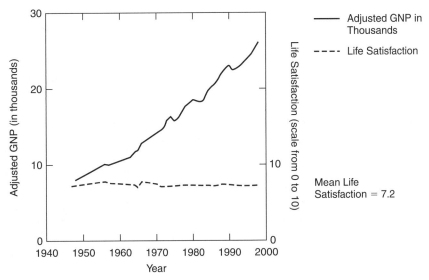

FIGURE 6.1   U.S. Gross National Product and Mean Life Satisfaction from 1947 to 1998
Source: Diener, E., & Seligman, M. (2004). Beyond money: Toward an economy of well-being. *Psychology in the Public Interest, 5,* 1–31. Copyright American Psychological Society. Reprinted with permission.

so strongly evident in the United States, also occurs in a number of other countries. Second, a study of the Amish culture in Pennsylvania (Egeland & Hostetter, 1983) suggests that modern life may be implicated in the rising rates of depression. The Amish live in relative isolation from the modern world. Their communities are close-knit, bound together by a religious faith that rejects most aspects of the modern consumer-oriented society (e.g., electricity, cars, TVs, and computers). Few Americans would describe the Amish lifestyle as affluent, yet measures of SWB show the Amish to be quite satisfied with their lives. Based on rates of depression among the Amish described by Egeland and Hostetter (1983), Diener and Seligman estimate that Amish individuals have only 1/5 to 1/10 the risk of developing depression of those who live in our modern, affluent society.

At this point, it's anybody's guess whether there is a causal association between increasing depression and increasing affluence. The idea that materialism and consumption may produce social and individual malaise has a long history within philosophy. In the next chapter, we will review studies focused on how an individual's excessive materialism may compromise his or her well-being. Here, we note three arguments about social and historical changes that may be responsible for the "darker side" of our affluent culture. In an article titled, "Why the self is empty," Phillip Cushman (1990)

argues that our consumer culture has displaced the deeper meanings and purposes that were traditionally found within family life, social relationships, and religion. He believes that over time, advertising has convinced people that happiness is to be found in the marketplace. The family has become a site of consumption rather than a source of nurturance and close relationships. Holidays have become commercialized; the frantic rush for the perfect Christmas gift has replaced religious and traditional family celebrations. More and more people pursue a consumption-based "life-style solution" to the problem of finding meaning in life. But because material consumption cannot provide deep, sustaining life meanings, Cushman argues that people experience an "inner emptiness." He believes that rising rates of drug abuse, eating disorders, compulsive buying, and depression are manifestations of the **empty self.**

Robert Putnam (2000) agrees that aspects of modern society have damaging effects on social and individual life. Putnam regards people's involvement in community, neighborhood, school, church, and social organizations as "social capital." This social capital contributes to the well-being of individuals and communities by promoting shared trust and mutual help.

Membership in community organizations across the country has been declining. People appear to be more focused on the pursuit of their individual life agendas and less on contributing to the good of their communities. Putnam believes this retreat from public involvement represents a loss of the social capital necessary for a healthy and prosperous life for both communities and individuals. The decline in social capital may play some role in the emotional difficulties so many people seem to be facing today.

In his book, *The Paradox of Choice: Why More Is Less* (2004), Schwartz provides a third view of the paradox of affluence. Schwartz argues that people in modern consumer cultures have unprecedented freedom to choose among a myriad of alternatives in consumer products and individual lifestyles. Compared to the past, a typical American has considerably more freedom in choosing how to dress, what and where to eat, what car to drive, who to marry, and what career to pursue. However, the abundance of choice in nearly all matters of our lives contains a paradox that may undermine its benefits. The more choice we have, the more we may be dissatisfied with the results. Schwartz argues that high levels of choice within a society encourage a **"maximizing"** philosophy that increases the pressure to choose the "best possible" option, rather than be content with a "good enough" choice by following what he calls a **"satisficing"** policy.

The problem with maximizing is that finding the best possible choice among a myriad of alternatives can be stressful and even paralyzing; ask college students trying to choose a college major and future career. More importantly, maximizing increases the intensity of self-blame and regret if our choices do not work out as planned. Freedom of choice and individual responsibility for those choices are strongly linked. Because *we* make the choices, it is easy to blame ourselves for poor ones. Because there are so many choices, it is also easy to second-guess ourselves. In the aftermath of a decision, we may experience some agony of regret over what we did not choose. Second-guessing may cause us to feel that initially rejected options are really lost opportunities.

In support of these arguments, studies have shown that people with a maximizing orientation are more likely to experience regret, self-blame, and second-guessing than those following a "satisficing" or "good enough" philosophy (Schwartz & Ward, 2004). Because self-blame,

second-guessing, and regret all detract from the potential well-being benefits of choice, they help explain Schwartz's notion of a **paradox of choice,** in which more choice may reduce rather than increase well-being. Affirming this conclusion, researchers have found that compared to satisficers, maximizers are less happy, less optimistic, have lower self-esteem and higher levels of neuroticism, and greater risk of mild depression (see Schwartz & Ward, 2004, for a review). If Schwartz is right, then people might enjoy greater well-being if they relinquished their stressful pursuit of perfectionistic and "best possible choice" ideals and adopted a less problematic and more satisfying principle of "good enough."

WELL-BEING ACROSS NATIONS

Americans' increased income over the last 50 years has *not* led to a corresponding rise in SWB. Is this because money is simply unrelated to a person's level of happiness? Or might it result from the fact that most Americans are, and have been, fairly satisfied with life, so more money has had little effect on happiness? Comparisons of the wealth and well-being relationship across a broad array of countries help answer these questions. Much of the data for national comparisons comes from the World Values Survey—one of the largest ongoing international surveys. Over a 25-year period, surveys conducted by a consortium of social scientists from all over the world have been completed by hundreds of thousands of people in over 80 countries. Robert Inglehart at the University of Michigan's Institute for Social Research has coordinated the compilation of findings. Information about these surveys can be found at the World Values Survey web site: http://www.worldvalues-survey.org/ or http://wvs.isr.umich.edu/. Ruut Veenhoven and his colleagues at Erasmus University Rotterdam-Netherlands have created the World Database of Happiness. Its web site is http://worlddatabaseofhappiness.eur.nl/index.html. Together with studies by independent researchers, these international databases provide a wealth of information concerning the relationship of well-being to a variety of social, economic, and political variables within different countries. The major findings of international studies are summarized in a number of excellent review articles and books (e.g., Diener & Biswas-Diener, 2002; Diener & Suh, 2000a, 2000b; Easterbrook, 2003; Inglehart, 1990, 1997).

Between-Nations Comparisons

Between-nations comparisons have found substantial correlations (in the range of 0.50 to 0.70) between average per capita income and average level of SWB (see Diener & Biswas-Diener, 2002; Diener & Diener, 1995; Diener & Oishi, 2000). For example, in a study of 65 different nations, Inglehart and Klingemann (2000) reported a correlation of 0.70 between a combined measure of life satisfaction and happiness and a measure of purchasing power. Table 6.1 (following page) shows a sample of life satisfaction ratings and income rankings for 29 different nations, reported by Diener (2000). Life satisfaction ratings were made on a 10-point scale and were based on the World Values Survey, which sampled about 1,000 people in each country (World Values Survey Study Group, 1994). Income figures were based on estimates of purchasing power parity (PPP). This measure provides a common metric for comparing income levels among countries. The purchasing power measure may range from 0 to 100 (see World Bank, 1992).

Examining the table you can see the general pattern of relationship between national income and life satisfaction. On average, people living in wealthy nations are happier than those living in less wealthy nations. However, you can also see some surprises. For example, the Irish have relatively high SWB but only moderate income, while the Japanese enjoy high income but only moderate SWB. The United States is at the top of the income measure, but 6th in self-reported life satisfaction. India and China both rank near the bottom in income, but show satisfaction ratings higher than Japan. Even countries in fairly close geographic proximity show large differences in life satisfaction. For example, among Western European countries, Denmark has consistently ranked higher in satisfaction ratings than Germany, France, or Italy. Based on percentage responses rather than the 10-point rating scale, some 50 to 65% of Danes have reported that they are very satisfied with their lives, over the last 25 years (Inglehart & Klingemann, 2000). Over the same period, the percentage of French and Italians reporting that they were very satisfied was never over 15% and the percentage of very satisfied Germans has been roughly half that of Danes. The

relative rankings of countries in terms of SWB and income, with a few exceptions, have been quite stable over the 25-year history of international surveys (see Inglehart & Klingemann, 2000). That is, national measures of well-being do not seem to be the product of short-term events that might inflate or depress the average level of life satisfaction within a society.

Within-Nation Comparisons

Within-nation comparisons tell us about the difference in happiness between rich and poor people who live in the same country. In contrast to the moderately strong correlations found in between-nation comparisons, within-nation correlations between income and happiness are quite small. Diener and Oishi (2000) report an average within-nation correlation of only 0.13 (with 40 different nations studied). Within the United States, the correlation was 0.15. However, these low overall correlations mask two general patterns in the income–happiness relationship. Specifically, income and well-being show moderate correlations within poor countries and very small or non-significant correlations within wealthy countries. In the Diener and Oishi study, the highest correlations were found in the poorest countries (e.g., in South Africa the correlation was 0.38 and in Slovenia, 0.29). This is consistent with a study of extremely poor people living in Calcutta slums that found a happiness–income correlation of 0.45 (Biswas-Diener & Diener, 2001). Studies showing that financial satisfaction correlates more strongly with life satisfaction in poor than in rich countries also support the importance of money for those who have little (Oishi, Diener, Lucas, & Suh, 1999).

However, within more affluent counties, the income–happiness connection essentially disappears. At a gross domestic product per capita of $10,000 per year, there is only a very small correlation ($r = 0.08$) between income and life satisfaction (Diener & Seligman, 2004). A *Time* magazine survey conducted in the United States found that happiness and income increased in tandem until people reached an annual income of about $50,000 (Special Mind & Body Issue: "The Science of Happiness," January 17, 2005, p. A33). After that, increased income had no appreciable effect on happiness.

One explanation for the apparent contribution of income to happiness among poor countries and its lack of significant contribution among wealthy countries has to do with fulfillment of basic needs

TABLE 6.1 Life satisfaction and income rankings across nations

Nation	Life Satisfaction	Income Rank (PPP)
Switzerland	8.36	96
Denmark	8.16	81
Canada	7.89	85
Ireland	7.88	52
Netherlands	7.77	76
United States	7.73	100
Finland	7.68	69
Norway	7.68	78
Chile	7.55	35
Brazil	7.38	23
Italy	7.30	77
China (PRC)	7.29	9
Argentina	7.25	25
Germany	7.22	89
Spain	7.15	57
Portugal	7.07	44
India	6.70	5
South Korea	6.69	39
Nigeria	6.59	6
Japan	6.53	87
Turkey	6.41	22
Hungary	6.03	25
Lithuania	6.01	16
Estonia	6.00	27
Romania	5.88	12
Latvia	5.70	20
Belarus	5.52	30
Russia	5.37	27
Bulgaria	5.03	22

Source: Diener, E. (2000). Subjective well-being: The science of happiness and a proposal for a national index. *American Psychologist, 55*, 34–43. Copyright American Psychological Association. Reprinted by permission.

Note: Rankings of countries are presented in reverse order (i.e., most satisfied to least satisfied) from that of the original article.

(see Veenhoven, 1995). It is not difficult to conclude that a level of income insufficient to provide for basic needs such as nutrition, health care, sanitation, and housing would be frustrating and distressing, and would contribute to low levels of SWB. On the other hand, once basic needs are fulfilled and one enjoys a level of income that is shared by many others in one's society, the source of happiness might shift away from income to other aspects of life. This explanation is consistent with Maslow's classic model of the hierarchy of human needs (Maslow, 1954). Maslow argued that motivation to achieve higher-order needs for personal fulfillment, self-expression, and actualization of individual potentials was put on hold until lower-order needs relating to physiology (e.g., food, safety, and security) were met. Some research suggests that basic needs are not the whole story in the income–well-being relationship. One study reported that income beyond what is necessary to fulfill basic needs still added a measure of additional happiness (Diener, Diener, & Diener, 1995). Once basic needs are satisfied, increased income offers diminishing returns in happiness, but some returns, nonetheless.

INTERPRETING NATIONAL COMPARISONS

You may be wondering why the between-country income–happiness relationship is so strong ($r = 0.50$ to 0.70), while the within-country relationship is so weak ($r =$ about 0.13). The difference is, in part, an artifact of the information that goes into each correlation (Argyle, 2001; Diener & Oishi, 2000). Between-nation comparisons reflect the pattern of relationship among different countries for two numbers: the average level of well-being and average income. National averages aggregate *across individuals* in the country surveyed. This aggregation causes individual variability in the income–happiness relationship to be effectively factored out of the comparison. In contrast, within-country correlations are based on individual variability and are affected by many factors other than income. For example, we know that, independent of their income, extraverted people report higher levels of well-being than introverts. A very outgoing person at a low-income level may have a higher level of happiness than an introverted person making a lot of money. In other words, the connection of extraversion to well-being weakens the correlation between money and happiness. Because within-country correlations will be affected by the contribution of personality to well-being, they are lower than between-country correlations, which are not affected by personality differences.

A further complication in interpreting national differences involves the many factors that co-vary with income. Money is certainly not the only difference between a rich nation and a poor one. For example, compared to poorer countries, affluent nations tend to have more democratic forms of government, offer more freedom and individual rights to citizens, and provide better health care, sanitation, and consumer goods. Studies show that freedom, individual rights, and trust in government are related to higher levels of satisfaction and happiness, and well-being is generally higher in democratic than in communist countries (see Diener & Seligman, 2004; Inglehart & Klingemann, 2000; Veenhoven, 2000, for reviews). Diener and Seligman note that when these variables are taken into consideration, the correlations between nations' wealth and the happiness of their citizens become non significant. Much more research is needed to disentangle all the variables related to the income–happiness relationship across nations. Researchers acknowledge that money is only a rough index of all the complex and interrelated variables associated with happiness. The contribution of cultural variables to differences in happiness will be examined in a later section of this chapter.

UNDERSTANDING MONEY AND HAPPINESS

What can we conclude about the contribution of money to individual happiness? So far, our discussion suggests the following. People living in rich nations are, on average, happier than those living in poor nations; however, this conclusion must be tempered by all the factors that co-vary with wealth that may be responsible for the relationship. Among individuals within a particular country, the money–happiness correlation is quite small and primarily evident among the very poor. The role of income in fulfilling basic needs helps explain the importance of money for people living in poverty. Among economically and technologically advanced nations, increased economic growth over the last several decades has had little appreciable effect on SWB. In affluent nations the money–happiness association appears to be curvilinear, with money making a greater difference at lower income levels, but much less so at moderate or higher levels, so that the curve levels out after a certain income is reached. Within wealthy nations, beyond a certain point, increasing income does not yield continued increases in happiness. Even the richest Americans are only slightly happier than those with more moderate incomes. A study of people listed by *Forbes* magazine as the wealthiest Americans found about a one-point difference in life satisfaction (on a 7-point scale) between the super-rich and the average American (Diener, Horwitz, & Emmons, 1985). Overall, money makes a substantial contribution to the well-being of those who are poor, but contributes little to the happiness of those who have achieved some "average" level of income relative to others in their society. Two other lines of research reinforce this conclusion.

At the individual level, the most relevant evidence for evaluating the importance of money comes from longitudinal studies that track the impact of increased or decreased income. Longitudinal studies follow the same individual over time. If money has a consistent relationship to happiness, then as a person's income goes up or down, so should his or her level of happiness. Interestingly, Diener and Biswas-Diener's review (2002) concluded that longitudinal studies do not show such a consistent relationship. Several studies report no effect of increased income on well-being and some have even found increased happiness associated with decreased income. Studies of pay raises also show mixed results (see Argyle, 2001). Pay increases produce only short-term gains in satisfaction and pay reductions seem to have little or no effect. Some of the most powerful evidence for the lack of direct connection between money and happiness comes from a study of lottery winners who reported no long-term increase in SWB despite their dramatic increases in income (Brickman, Coates, & Janoff-Bulman, 1978).

Because the amount of money a person earns co-varies with many other factors such as education, employment status, and age, we may also ask whether income still affects SWB when these variables are controlled. A number of studies suggest that income has a small correlation with happiness and life satisfaction that is independent of many individual and social variables (Argyle 2001; Diener & Biswas-Diener, 2002; Diener et al., 1995). Income appears to have a direct, but relatively small correlation with well-being. In comparison, being married, being employed, and having supportive relationships are variables that make much more substantial contributions to happiness.

Focus on Research: Do Happy People Make More Money?

Even the small effect of money on happiness may have to be tempered by the bidirectional nature of the relationship. More money may make us somewhat happier, but happy people also seem to make more money. This is the finding of a longitudinal study by Diener, Nickerson, Lucas, and Sandvik (2002). These researchers took advantage of two large data sets made available by the Andrew W. Mellon Foundation. Both the Mellon Foundation ("College and Beyond" survey) and the University of California at Los Angeles ("The American Freshmen" survey) conduct annual surveys of thousands of college students at hundreds of universities across the United States. Surveys include both small private colleges and large public universities, as well as several historically black universities and colleges. These surveys ask about the attitudes, values, aspirations, abilities, personalities, and career plans of each entering freshmen class. The Mellon Foundation also conducts periodic follow-up surveys of students after graduation, collecting information regarding income, job history, life satisfaction, civic involvement, and evaluations of college experience.

Diener and his colleagues studied survey data for 13,676 freshmen, who began their college careers in 1976 and were surveyed again about 19 years later between 1995 and 1997. Their index of happiness was a self-rated measure of cheerfulness included in the freshmen surveys. Students were asked to rate their level of cheerfulness in comparison to the average student of the same age on a five-point scale (1 = the lowest 10% of cheerfulness relative to the average student; 2 = below average; 3 = average, 4 = above average; and 5 = the upper 10%). Three variables were examined from the follow-up survey: income, job satisfaction, and unemployment history. Unemployment was defined as a period of 6 months or longer when the person was not working for pay. The overall pattern of results showed that those students who were the most cheerful at college entry went on to make more money, enjoyed higher job satisfaction, and suffered substantially less unemployment compared to their less cheerful classmates.

The relationship of cheerfulness to income increased steeply at first, then leveled off. That is, increased cheerfulness had a larger effect at lower levels of cheerfulness and less effect at higher levels. As shown in Figure 6.2, for example, students whose parents had substantial annual incomes showed the following relationship between self-rated cheerfulness and current income, reported 19 years after graduation. Students rating themselves in the lowest 10% of cheerfulness (1) when they entered college were making about $50,000 per year. Students rating themselves below average (2) were making a little over $58,000. Those average in cheerfulness (3) were at $63,500. Students above average in cheerfulness (4) reported incomes of nearly $66,000, and those who considered themselves in the highest 10% of cheerfulness (5) were making a little over $65,000. Moving from the lowest cheerfulness category (1) to the next (2) was associated with an income increase of $8,000; the difference between (2) and (3) was associated with a $5,500 increase; the difference between cheerfulness ratings of (3) and (4) was associated with an

income gain of $2,500; and the difference in income between those rating cheerfulness as (4) and (5) was associated with a decrease of $1,000. In other words, if you are an unhappy college student, cheer-up, even if only a little bit—you'll make a lot more money if you do! And if you're already above average in cheerfulness, don't try to make it to the top 10%—it might cost you $1,000 per year!

Findings also showed that parental income moderated the effects of cheerfulness. Cheerfulness had a stronger association with current income for individuals whose parents had high incomes. As parents' income increased, the effect of cheerfulness also increased. For example, at the lowest parental income level, students with the lowest cheerfulness ratings were making $39,232, while those with the highest cheerfulness made $44,691—a difference of $5,459. At the highest parental income level, students lowest in cheerfulness averaged $60,585 per year, while those with the highest cheerfulness were making $85,891—a difference of $25,306. For students with poor parents, increased cheerfulness had a relatively small effect on current income. For students with affluent parents, being more cheerful had quite large effects on income.

Why do cheerful college students make more money than their less cheerful classmates? Assuming that a cheerful disposition remains relatively stable across time, Diener and his colleagues offer three possible explanations. First, a cheerful outlook may create a "can do" attitude that motivates students to meet new challenges and to suffer less from setbacks. This may result in more persistence and hard work that is valued by employers and therefore translates into higher incomes. Second, cheerfulness is a positive quality that others admire and it may also be related to better social skills. A cheerful disposition may make a person more approachable and easier to work with. Cheerful people may be better at persuading others concerning their ideas and may be skillful in increasing people's willingness to provide assistance and support. Less cheerful people may not have these advantages. Finally, to the extent that cheerful people are simply more likeable because of their upbeat, positive attitude, employers may give them higher performance evaluations. Cheerfulness may create a halo effect. That is, even if a cheerful and less cheerful employee performed at the same level, employers might give

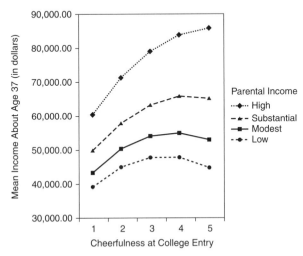

FIGURE 6.2   Mean after College Income as a Function of Cheerfulness and Parental Income at College Entry

Source: Diener, E., & Seligman, M. (2004). Beyond money: Toward an economy of well-being. *Psychology in the Public Interest, 5,* 1–31. Copyright American Psychological Society. Reprinted with permission.

the cheerful worker the edge because they are easier to like and work with.

Diener and his colleagues were disappointed to find that parental income was so strongly related to students' later earnings. Why should a cheerful student from a rich family go on to make considerably more money than an equally cheerful student from an economically disadvantaged family? As these researchers note, children from affluent families enjoy many advantages, from the quality of their pre-college education to enhanced extracurricular activities that allow for the development of personal and social talents. Perhaps for these and other reasons, students from advantaged backgrounds are more likely to get high-status professional jobs than students from disadvantaged backgrounds. Whatever the reasons, Diener and his colleagues conclude that "It is surprising and disturbing that the superb educations and opportunities offered by the collegiate institutions in this study are apparently not sufficient in many cases to overcome the disadvantages of having grown up in a less affluent family" (2002, p. 250).

Why Doesn't Money Matter More?

Why do income and wealth show such a small relationship to happiness when money is so clearly related to many positive outcomes and advantages? In the United States, everything from the size of your house and the amount of crime in your neighborhood to the quality of health care and education for your kids is tied, in one way or another, to the amount of money you make. The small effect of income on happiness seems puzzling given the apparent advantages money can bring. Several explanations have been developed to address why money does not have a larger impact on SWB. Several of these explanations were discussed briefly in Chapter 5 to account for the small or short-term effects of life events and demographic variables on happiness.

GENETICS, PERSONALITY, AND RELATIONSHIPS
In Chapter 5, we discussed the role of genetically determined temperament and personality in producing long-term stability in people's levels of happiness. Simply put, each of us seems to inherit or develop, early in life, a characteristic outlook that remains relatively consistent across the life span.

This outlook plays a major role in how we react to life events, make decisions, and live our lives in general. Research shows that a variety of personality traits such as cheerfulness, optimism, extraversion, self-esteem, and a sense of personal control are strongly related to SWB (see Argyle, 2001; Diener & Lucas, 1999; Diener, Oishi, & Lucas, 2003; Diener et al., 1999; Lykken, 1999; Lyubomirsky, 2001; Myers, 1992; Ryan & Deci, 2001, for reviews). People at the positive end of these trait dimensions are considerably happier than those at the negative end (e.g., those with neurotic, pessimistic characteristics, and low self-esteem). How these traits contribute to the development and maintenance of happiness will be taken up in a subsequent chapter. Here, we note that if SWB is substantially rooted in internal traits and dispositions, it makes sense that external circumstances and changes would have less impact on a person's happiness. For example, heritability studies discussed in Chapter 5 suggest that 40 to 55% of a person's current level of happiness reflects a genetically determined temperament. Based on her studies comparing differences between happy and unhappy people, Lyubomirsky (2001, p. 244) concludes that happy and unhappy people ". . . appear to experience—indeed, to reside in—different subjective worlds." Faced with the same situation, event, or task, happy individuals think and act in ways that sustain their happiness, and unhappy individuals think and act in ways that sustain their unhappiness. That is, it is people's subjective interpretation of the world, rather than the world itself, that makes the biggest difference. Because money can't buy you a cheerful personality, money isn't a major contributor to individual happiness.

The same kind of argument can be made regarding the importance of relationships. We have noted in several previous discussions that there is overwhelming evidence for the contribution of supportive and caring relationships to personal happiness (e.g., Diener & Seligman, 2004; Ryff & Singer, 2000). Just as money won't buy you a happy temperament, it is also hard to imagine that money will buy you good relationships. Poverty and tight finances can certainly contribute to stress and conflict within marriages and families, but in most marriages conflict over money is symptomatic of problems in the relationship, rather than being the problem itself. The ability to buy expensive consumer goods for your family doesn't make you a good parent or spouse. One only has to look at the sordid family and marital lives of the "rich and famous" to see that money and stable relationships are largely unrelated. The bottom line on personality, relationships, and money is this: some of the most significant sources of happiness are not much affected by how much money you make.

ADAPTATION AND THE HEDONIC TREADMILL
Sensory adaptation is a familiar part of everyday experience. When you walk out of a building into the bright sunlight you have trouble seeing clearly until your eyes adapt to the bright light. If you go into a dark room the same thing happens until you adjust to the dim light. Similarly, if you enter someone's house that has a strong and unpleasant odor you may wonder how the occupants live with it, but after a few minutes you no longer notice the odor. If you go outside and then come back in, the smell is strong again. In general, our senses respond more to changing stimulation than to constant stimulation. We become largely oblivious to an unchanging or repeated stimulation. When people who wear glasses put them on in the morning they can feel the pressure against their nose and ears, but shortly, and for the rest of the day, they are unaware of these sensations and "forget" that they wear glasses.

The idea of a *hedonic adaptation*, meaning adaptation to stimuli that arouse emotions, was drawn by analogy with sensory adaptation and the adaptation-level theory developed by Helson (1964). In a classic and much-cited article on adaptation, Brickman and Campbell (1971) argued that people are doomed to a **hedonic treadmill** that results in stable and relatively neutral levels of long-term happiness. Like a treadmill, where you walk and walk but don't get anywhere, our emotional experiences fluctuate, but our overall level of long-term happiness does not change. The new car, the bigger house, and the pay raise all make us happier for awhile, but then the good feelings fade. This occurs because people quickly adapt to both negative and positive life changes and return to pre-event levels of happiness. Just as bright sunlight produces fading sensations of brightness overtime, the effects of emotionally-charged events quickly fade. And just as we can only re-experience brightness by closing our eyes or going into a darkened building, we only re-experience emotions by generating or encountering new emotional events (e.g.,

another new and more expensive car or an even bigger house). Emotions, like many sensory experiences, do not last.

Hedonic adaptation most likely evolved in humans to serve various protective and survival-enhancing functions (Frederick & Lowenstein, 1999; Frijda, 1999; Zajonc, 1998). Our sensitivity to change makes us alert to things that might threaten or enhance our well-being. The fading of emotional responses over time reduces the potential negative effects of long-term emotional arousal.

We noted in Chapter 4 that chronic stress and fear have destructive effects on the immune system. You can imagine how disruptive it would be if the fear you experienced the last time you narrowly missed having a car accident, or if the intense anger you felt when treated unfairly, or if the pain of a failed romantic relationship lasted for years. And we all might have very small families if all our sexual desires were fulfilled the first time we had sex. Emotions, such as fear, appear to serve short-term purposes (e.g., the fight or flight response) and are not made to last. As Myers argues (1992, p. 53, italics in original), "*Every* desirable experience—passionate love, a spiritual high, the pleasure of a new possession, the exhilaration of success—is transitory."

Focus on Research: Adaptation to Extreme Events—Lottery Winners and Accident Victims

Dramatic evidence for adaptation comes from a classic study by Brickman and his colleagues (1978). Their research participants were two very different types of people: major lottery winners and individuals who had become paralyzed as the result of accidental injury. Based on adaptation-level theory, Brickman and his colleagues predicted that in the long run, lottery winners would be no happier, and victims of catastrophic injury would be no worse off emotionally than the rest of us. Adaptation-level theory offers two reasons for this prediction: **contrast** and **habituation.** The contrast explanation suggests that a major positive event like winning the lottery may cause more mundane and everyday pleasures to pale by comparison. Spending time with friends or watching TV in the evening may bring less pleasure because they contrast so sharply with the excitement of having won a lot of money. As a result, lottery winners may not experience any overall net gain in happiness because the thrill of winning is offset by a decline in everyday pleasures. Habituation means growing accustomed to new events so that their emotional impact is reduced. As lottery winners get used to the pleasures made possible by their dramatic increase in wealth, these pleasures will contribute less and less to their happiness. Contrast and habituation were predicted to have essentially the opposite effects for the adaptation of accident victims who suffered paraplegia or quadriplegia. Everyday activities—the simple pleasures of life—may bring increased enjoyment because they are contrasted with an extreme negative and life-threatening event. Habituation may occur as accident victims adjust and become more accustomed to the effects of paralysis.

To test their hypothesis, the researchers interviewed three groups of people. The first group consisted of 22 individuals, who had won at least $5,000 (in 1978 dollars) in the Illinois State Lottery in the preceding 18 months. The second group was comprised of 11 paraplegic and 18 quadriplegic individuals who were patients at a rehabilitation institute as a result of injuries sustained within the past year. Using the phone book, the researchers identified 88 control participants who lived in close geographic proximity to the lottery winners, and were able to interview 22 of these individuals.

The participants were asked questions about changes in their lifestyle, whether they thought they deserved what had happened to them, and to rate their winning of the lottery or their paralysis on a six-point scale ranging from (0) "the worst thing that could happen . . ." to (5) "the best thing that could happen. . . ." Happiness was rated regarding three time frames: (1) how happy they were at present; (2) how happy they were

either before they won the lottery or before they became paralyzed, depending on their situation; and (3) how happy they expected to be in a couple of years. Participants also rated the pleasure obtained from seven mundane everyday activities (e.g., hearing a joke, talking with a friend, watching TV, etc.). The control group answered similar questions. Mean ratings for each group are shown in Table 6.2

As you might expect, paralyzed individuals rated their accident as an extremely negative event, and lottery winners described their winning as a very positive event. Consistent with adaptation-level theory, however, lottery winners gave the seven ordinary life activities lower pleasure ratings than the control subjects. Also consistent with the theory, the lottery winners did not differ significantly from control subjects in their ratings of present, past, or anticipated happiness. In short, people who had won a major lottery were delighted to have won, but found less enjoyment in ordinary activities than control subjects, and did not report higher overall happiness levels than control subjects. In the short run, winning a large amount of money seems to make everyday activities less enjoyable by comparison, and over time, people habituate to having lots of money. The net result is no increase in overall happiness. Results for lottery winners provide strong evidence for the power of adaptation.

Less support for the effects of contrast and habituation was shown among accident victims. Accident victims rated their past happiness as much higher and their present happiness significantly lower than the control group. Surprisingly, though, the accident victims' happiness ratings were above the midpoint of the rating scale, suggesting they were not as unhappy as we might expect. However,

TABLE 6.2 Mean general happiness and mundane pleasure ratings

Condition	General Happiness			Mundane Pleasures
	Past	Present	Future	
Winners	3.77	4.00	4.20	3.33
Controls	3.32	3.82	4.14	3.82
Victims	4.41	2.96	4.32	3.48

Source: Brickman, P. D., Coates, D., & Janoff-Bulman, R. (1978). Lottery winners and accident victims: Is happiness relative? *Journal of Personality and Social Psychology, 36,* 917–927. Copyright American Psychological Association. Reprinted with permission.

contrary to predictions, enjoyment of everyday activities did not increase. This seemed to have occurred because the contrast for accident victims was between the pleasure obtained from ordinary activities in their past, and the present, in which those activities were no longer possible because of their paralysis. Paralyzed individuals experienced strong nostalgia for the way their lives were before the accident. The contrast between an unrecoverable past life and a forever-changed present life seemed to be the basis for the lower enjoyment of everyday events and overall happiness. Unlike the case for lottery winners, contrast and habituation effects did not return accident victims to their pre-accident levels of happiness.

One limitation of this study is the small sample size (22 lottery winners and 29 accident victims). Other studies of lottery winners and people who inherited large sums of money have found evidence for an increase in happiness resulting from newfound wealth (see Diener & Biswas-Diener, 2002; Diener & Seligman, 2004, for reviews). However, studies also suggest that for many people the effects of dramatic increases in wealth or income may bring personal costs in the form of stress and damaged relationships. Lottery winners may quit their jobs and move to new neighborhoods and thus lose long-time friends. Friends and relatives may expect to share in the winnings and be angered or disappointed by what they receive. Having lots of money can create a variety of interpersonal problems and conflicts, including an increased risk of divorce, that may eventually mortgage short-term gains in happiness.

Another limitation of Brickman and colleagues' study is that it was not longitudinal. The amount of time that had passed since winning the lottery or suffering an accident varied considerably among study participants. Brickman and his colleagues did not find a significant relationship between time and present happiness. However, they acknowledge that studying the same individuals over longer periods of time would more accurately assess the extent and course of adaptation. Subsequent longitudinal studies generally support the concept of adaptation to life events, but have modified the idea of a hedonic treadmill and suggested that adaptation has its limits. For example, Silver (1982) studied spinal cord injury victims over an 8-week period following the accident that caused the paralysis. She found that the strong negative emotions immediately following

the accident decreased over time while positive emotions increased, and by the 8th week positive emotions were stronger than negative emotions. Headey and Wearing (1989) studied 649 people over an 8-year period and tracked their reactions to a variety of good and bad life events (e.g., making new friends, conflicts with children, increases or decreases in financial situation). These researchers found that people initially had strong reactions, but then returned to their baseline levels of happiness. Personality was also found to moderate both the effects and the occurrence of life changes.

Based on their research, Headey and Wearing (1989, 1992) made several modifications to the hedonic treadmill conception, in which people were thought to adapt quickly to new events and return to relatively neutral levels of happiness. Their **dynamic equilibrium model** suggests that people have positive rather than neutral happiness baselines, and that people return to differing baselines depending on their personalities. In addition, people's level of happiness affects the likelihood of experiencing positive or negative events. In their study, happy people were found to experience more positive events and unhappy people more negative events. Adaptation processes are thus individualized—not uniform as suggested by the hedonic treadmill theory. Further evidence of the limitations of the hedonic treadmill hypothesis is revealed by studies finding that people do not adapt completely to all life events. Adaptation to increased income and material possessions is well-supported. However, people who have lost a child or a spouse, who have cared for a family member with Alzheimer's disease, or who have a progressive disease such as multiple sclerosis, do not adapt to these conditions and return to baseline levels of happiness (see Diener et al., 1999; Frederick & Lowenstein, 1999, for reviews). Instead, well-being appears to be significantly and rather permanently lowered.

RISING EXPECTATIONS AND THE "TYRANNY OF THE UNNECESSARY" Suppose your income increased by $10,000 per year—let's say from $50,000 to $60,000. Ten-thousand dollars per year may seem like a lot, but a newer car, a house remodeling project, a few more vacations, more expensive Christmas gifts for your family, and a higher speed internet connection might leave your end-of-the-month checkbook balance no larger than it was when you were making $50,000. And odds are that you would begin thinking about what you could do when you hit $70,000. Both of your textbook authors experienced the "poverty" of graduate school and the "riches" of a full-time faculty position, and were amazed by how quickly their increased income disappeared. Spending habits quickly catch up to income.

Easterbrook (2003) argues that rising incomes in the United States have brought rising expectations, made wants seem like needs, and produced a "tyranny of the unnecessary." As he notes, most of us would probably agree that every home should have a television set. However, evidence shows that the average home has 3 televisions, that 5 sets in a single household is fairly common, and 65% of those under 18 years of age have a TV in their bedrooms (Easterbrook, 2003). A similar pattern of buying more of what you already have is true for CD and DVD players, cars, phones, and a variety of other consumer products. Easterbrook notes that the square footage of new homes has doubled over the last generation, while the average number of occupants has fallen. The storage shed business is booming! Homebuilders report that a frequent complaint of buyers is the lack of adequate storage space for all their possessions. This is part of the tyranny of the unnecessary—what to do with all our stuff—much of which sits idle most of the time. The other part of the tyranny is the tendency for yesterday's wants to become today's needs in an unending cycle of greater income and greater consumption.

Diener and Biswas-Diener (2002) argue that rising expectations create a perpetual gap between material aspirations (things we would like to have) and current material possessions (things we already have), and a "chronic salience of desires." Put simply, most people want more than they have, regardless of how much they have at any point in time. Some of the evidence Diener and Biswas-Diener cite in support of this conclusion includes the following: (1) Studies show that the amount of income needed to fulfill people's consumer aspirations has doubled in recent years. (2) Surveys show that 84% of people now think the "good life" includes a vacation home. (3) A majority of people say they always have something in mind that they want to buy and, on average, people have six things on their "wish list," with nearly half wanting a bigger house. Because each level of increased income seems to establish a higher level of expectation, we are always looking forward to what we want, rather than backward to what we have. Rising expectations are one major reason more money doesn't bring more happiness. Our material expectations, wants, and desires always stay ahead of our incomes.

SOCIAL COMPARISONS "Keeping up with the Joneses" is a familiar phrase describing the important role that others may play in individual judgments of material well-being. While we can and do judge ourselves by our own standards, we often rely on social comparisons as well. Social comparison effects are clearly demonstrated by a study that asked college students to keep track of their mental comparisons with others (Wheeler & Miyake, 1992). For 2 weeks, students made diary entries about comparisons of grades, social skills, physical attractiveness, opinions, personality, and money or possessions. Upward comparisons to those who were better off consistently caused negative feelings, while downward comparisons to those who were worse off resulted in positive feelings. Social comparisons not only affect our feelings, but also affect our "needs." Many of our wants and needs are socially created, and social influence begins early. Probably every parent has had their child come home from school announcing that he or she "has to have" some new fashion or electronic device because "everyone has one except me." An effective way to short-circuit this budding consumerism is to call the parents of your child's friends. Not only will you gain support for resisting your child's demands, but you will probably also find that the more accurate version of the statement, "everyone has one" is actually, "only one child has one." Social comparison seems to be a pervasive basis for consumer choices and "needs" (Easterbrook, 2003). For example, it is hard to imagine that millions of people independently concluded or discovered that they needed SUV's and cell phones. In the case of SUV's, the standard joke is that the vast majority of owners only go "off-road" when they miss their driveways at 3:00 in the morning and end up on their lawns.

Social comparison and the idea of *relative deprivation* offer a straightforward explanation for why objective life circumstances generally, and income in particular, do not have more consistent effects on happiness (Tyler & Smith, 1998). How satisfied people are with their incomes is relative to points of comparison. An affluent person may feel dissatisfied or "deprived" relative to the super-rich, and a low-income individual may feel relatively well-off compared to the poor, so that both have similar levels of happiness. Social comparison may also help explain the small effect of increased income on happiness. If we consistently compare ourselves to similar others, and if each rise in income raises our point of comparison, then increased money would have little net effect on happiness. A bigger house may not seem so big because it is in a neighborhood of comparably sized homes. Csikszentmihalyi (1999) argues that we Americans may all feel some relative deprivation because of the phenomenally high standards of affluence available as reference points. The increasingly large disparity in incomes within the United States may cause even the very affluent to feel deprived. In comparison to the Bill Gates and Donald Trumps of the world, most of us are "poor." Feelings of relative deprivation might also contribute to the lower sense of well-being in less affluent countries. Increasing access and exposure to Western media (e.g., television and movies) that focus so much on affluent lifestyles may create a strong contrast for people living in less developed nations. Whether social comparisons have these effects is dependent on one critical question: How are social comparisons selected? Are comparisons imposed by the external environment in which we live? Do we simply observe others around us and feel satisfied or not, depending on how we stack up? Do we look to the media? Does each individual decide for himself or herself which comparisons to make, and with whom?

Research suggests that social comparison processes do affect people's evaluation of specific aspects of life, but the effects are often temporary and may not play a major role in long-term and overall happiness. Social comparisons do not have consistent effects largely because each individual seems to select her or his own reference points. People are not necessarily influenced by standards imposed by the external environment in which they live. For example, studies have found that people with moderate incomes report about the same level of happiness, whether they live in a wealthier or poorer region of the country (Diener, Sandvik, Seidlitz, & Diener, 1993). International studies have found a positive correlation between the average SWB within countries and the affluence of neighboring countries, rather than the negative correlation suggested by social comparison theory (Diener et al., 1995).

The comparisons we make seem to involve people similar to ourselves, and are focused on specific domains of life. For example, the effect of income on job satisfaction seems to depend on one's relative, rather than absolute level of pay (e.g., Clark & Oswald, 1996). The relevant question seems to be, do I earn more, less, or the same income as someone in the same occupation with a similar level of education and skill? If you make less than your co-workers, you may feel dissatisfied because your compensation may seem "unfair." Making more than your co-workers may increase your job satisfaction, but the critical factor seems to be an evaluation of "fair" compensation, in which the pay of similar others is a relevant point of comparison. Our focus seems to be on local and personal comparisons, rather than on remote and impersonal points of reference. We may believe that professional baseball players make outrageously high salaries or that the neighbors up the street make more than they deserve, but these kinds of judgments don't have much effect on our happiness or satisfaction. However, to find out that a co-worker with a similar job and work history makes considerably more than you do may cause resentment and unhappiness.

Self-relevance is one important factor influencing the effects of social comparisons. Suppose a good friend, spouse, or family member has more success than you. How would you react? Would you take pride in that person's accomplishments, or would you be envious because you were overshadowed? Tesser (1988) argues that the critical variable is the extent to which the success of others is relevant to our self-conception. If we take pride in a particular ability, personal trait, or accomplishment, the greater success of significant others in these self-relevant areas may diminish our own satisfaction. For example, your job satisfaction may be diminished if your spouse makes more money than you do (see Argyle, 2001; Diener & Seligman, 2004). But a man who thinks of himself as primary breadwinner in the family will likely feel pride rather than envy if his wife wins an award for her work in a charitable organization. Her success does not threaten or compete with his self-image (i.e., it is not self-relevant).

The small money–happiness relationship does not seem to be the result of social comparison processes. We are not passive "victims" of everyone we encounter in life or in the media who makes more money than we do. Instead, we actively select social comparisons to help us cope and prosper in life.

So, for example, we might use an upward comparison to help motivate ourselves to develop particular talents and personal qualities by modeling ourselves after someone we admire. On the other hand, making a downward comparison might help offset the effects of negative life events. This possibility is clearly shown in studies of people facing personal threats such as breast cancer. Bogart and Helgeson (2000) asked 300 women diagnosed with early stage breast cancer to record, over a period of 7 weeks, their thoughts regarding the plight of other breast cancer patients they had encountered or heard about. A majority of the women made downward comparisons to patients who were worse off, which conceivably helped them feel better about their own condition. Stories of breast cancer patients provide specific examples of these comparisons (Taylor, 1989). Women who had a lump removed considered how awful it would be if they had needed a full mastectomy. Older mastectomy patients imagined how much worse it must be for young women to lose a breast.

EXCESSIVE MATERIALISM Recent research has begun to detail the potential negative side of materialism (Kasser & Kanner, 2004). The "dark" side of materialism will be taken up in the next chapter. Here, we note that an additional reason why more money may not increase happiness is that rising affluence may actually compromise well-being. People who place a high value on money and material possessions have been found to have lower levels of well-being compared to less materialistic individuals. The relationship between materialism and happiness seems to be a two-way street. On one hand, excessive materialism may interfere with fulfillment of those psychological and social needs that contribute the most to personal happiness (e.g., quality relationships). On the other hand, insecure and unhappy people may be attracted to materialism as a way to compensate for unmet needs. In either case, less rather than more happiness is the result.

THE MEANING OF HAPPINESS: RELATIVE OR UNIVERSAL?

One final issue in the money–happiness relationship concerns the varying interpretations and meanings of happiness in different cultures. The influence of culture is suggested by the different relationship between income and SWB across countries. While a positive relationship between well-being and income is most evident for very poor nations, not all poor nations have significantly lowered well-being (see Table 6.1). As Argyle (2001) has noted, a number of South American countries (like Brazil, Peru, and Chile) have levels of satisfaction "higher than they should be" given their average per capita income levels. These countries also have quite high positive affect scores. Do Latin American countries have different social norms governing the expression of happiness? Do Latin American cultures cultivate or emphasize positive emotion more than other cultures? These questions point up the potential importance of cultural differences in the meaning of well-being and happiness. At the most specific level, we may ask whether a survey question about happiness and life satisfaction has the same meaning in different cultures. Does happiness have the same meaning in Japan, India, and Latin America as it does in the United States, Canada, or Western Europe? If the meaning of happiness is relative to specific cultures, rather than universal across cultures, how can we compare or rank nations according to their levels of SWB?

Given the fact that the definition and measurement of SWB were developed by researchers from Western cultures, do cross-cultural comparisons contain a cultural bias against non-Western cultures? Does the lower level of life satisfaction in Japan mean that the Japanese are less satisfied than other affluent countries? Or do the Japanese have a different conception of satisfaction that is not captured by Western SWB measures? Ryan and Deci (2001) point out that SWB researchers have received their share of criticism for inadequate attention to cultural biases. The magnitude of cultural influences on SWB findings is still an open question. There is considerable evidence that aspects of SWB have culturally influenced meanings and causes. These influences will be discussed in the next section on Culture and Well-Being. Here, we consider evidence and arguments supporting some degree of universality in the understanding and importance of SWB.

Diener and his colleagues (Diener et al., 2003) argue that SWB is important because it gives voice to people's own personal appraisals of their lives. These authors believe life evaluations are important to the quality of life in all societies because it is hard to imagine either a good life or a good society without a positive sense of SWB. They doubt that a country with high levels of dissatisfaction and unhappiness (i.e., low SWB) would fit anybody's idea of a good society. Happiness is not the only measure of a society, but it seems reasonable to argue that it is an important one.

Diener and Suh (2000b) acknowledge that the basis of happiness may be quite different in different cultures. However, they argue that every culture sets goals and values that are used to some extent by individuals in their own life evaluations. If we assume that people are likely to have higher SWB if they fulfill their goals than if they do not, then SWB may have some measure of cross-cultural validity and universality. Despite the varied goals that may be pursued in different cultures, if SWB reflects the satisfaction that comes from achieving goals, then it has some measure of validity across different cultures.

The importance of SWB across cultures is supported by the findings of a survey of over 7,000 college students in 42 countries (Diener, 2000). Although the individual country sample sizes were somewhat small for purposes of representing an entire country (100–300 in most cases), the general pattern of results was quite consistent. In all countries, students rated life satisfaction and happiness as important goals. A majority rated happiness (69%) and life satisfaction (62%) as very important. There was a slight tendency for SWB to be rated as more important in Western cultures, but overall, happiness and satisfaction were valued goals across cultures.

The universality of SWB measures depends, in part, on a shared understanding of the meaning of satisfaction and happiness. When these terms are translated into different languages, do they have the same or similar meanings? Veenhoven (2000) argues that, for the most part, they do. For example, the Swiss report much higher well-being than the French, Germans, or Italians even though each of these three languages is spoken in Switzerland. According to the Embassy of Switzerland web site, recent census reports show 63.9% of Swiss people speaking German, 19.5% speaking French, and 6.6% speaking Italian (www.eda.admin.ch/washington_emb/c/home/culedu/cultur//langua.html, retrieved October 14, 2005). If ratings of life satisfaction depended on the particular meaning of the word "satisfaction" as translated into different languages, then the Swiss might have SWB levels similar to German, French, and Italian individuals living in their respective countries. The fact that this does not occur suggests to

Veenhoven that well-being primarily reflects a shared historical experience and not language differences in the meaning of satisfaction. Diener and Suh (2000b) note a study showing similar results for translation between Chinese and English.

It is important to note that cross-cultural researchers typically employ bilingual individuals and experts to conduct back-translations of survey questionnaires. For example, Oishi (2000) used Ed Diener's Satisfaction with Life Scale (discussed at length in Chapter 4) in a study of college students from 39 countries in North America, South America, Asia, and Europe. The life satisfaction scale was translated into Spanish, Japanese, Korean, and Chinese by one group of bilingual individuals. Then the non-English versions of the questionnaire were translated back into English by a different group of bilingual individuals. Finally, the back-translated questionnaires were rated for "goodness of fit" to Diener's original scale. In Oishi's study, the fit was rated as excellent. These procedures help ensure consistency of meaning from one language to another. They obviously don't ensure identical meanings.

Further support for the cross-cultural validity of well-being measures comes from studies showing that different ways of asking for an overall evaluation of life have little effect on SWB scores. Ratings of life satisfaction, ratings of happiness, or ratings of worst to best possible life show nearly the same identical rank (Veenhoven, 2000). Different measures of SWB, such as experience sampling, ratings of positive and negative affect, and behavioral observations, produce similar results in terms of the well-being rankings of various cultures (see Diener et al., 2003, for review). Veenhoven also argues that, if happiness is a uniquely Western concept that is poorly understood in other parts of the world, then uncertainty in understanding might show up in survey responses. In non-Western countries, one might expect people to pick the "don't know," or "no answer" rating-scale option as a way of dealing with their uncertainty. However, non-Western countries do not show a higher frequency of responses in these two rating categories. In summary, Veenhoven and other major SWB researchers (e.g., Argyle, 2001, Diener et al., 2003), would certainly agree that we need more evidence supporting the cross-cultural validity of SWB. However, they would also agree that it is highly unlikely that the national differences in SWB, and the pattern of correlations with income and other variables are primarily the products of measurement artifacts and cultural differences in the understanding of happiness.

Eudaimonic theories of well-being support a universal basis for SWB by positing basic needs believed to be shared by all human beings (e.g., Ryan & Deci, 2000; Ryff, 1989; Ryff & Keyes, 1995). According to self-determination theory, for example, needs for autonomy, competence, and relatedness are inherent in all humans (Ryan & Deci 2000). Fulfillment of these needs leads to higher levels of health and SWB. Support for the cross-cultural validity of self-determination theory comes from studies in the Untied States, Bulgaria, Russia, and Japan (see Ryan & Deci, 2001). Scores reflecting the degree of fulfillment of the three needs were related to SWB in each of these diverse cultures. Greater need satisfaction was associated with higher SWB, and lesser satisfaction was associated with lower SWB. The measures of need satisfaction also passed tests assessing the equivalence of meaning in different cultures. At this point, it is too early to tell whether the needs described by eudaimonic theories are valid in all or most cultures. Because different theories involve different needs, it is also unclear which needs might be most universal. Answers to these questions can only come from more extensive cross-cultural research. It is important to note that evidence for the universality of well-being does not contradict the importance of culture-specific meanings and causes. Diener and his colleagues (Diener et al., 2003) argue that it is reasonable to assume that there are both universal and culture-specific aspects of SWB. In addition, cultural differences help explain why societies differ in levels of well-being and happiness.

CULTURE AND WELL-BEING

Because societies are complex and multi-dimensional, it is difficult to give an unambiguous definition of the term "culture." However, culture generally refers to the social roles, norms, values, and practices that are shared by a social group or society and are transmitted across generations (see Betancourt & Lopez, 1993; Diener & Suh, 2000a; Segall, Lonner, & Berry, 1998; Triandis, 2000). Cultural differences can be found in groups, both large and small. Commonalities in national heritage, language, religion, ethnicity, race, age, gender, geographic location, and historical events are among

the many factors that contribute to cultural differences among nations. Within a nation, these same factors may contribute to local and regional variations in culture, producing cultures within cultures (e.g., African–American culture). The "standard view," as Kitayama and Markus (2000) refer to it, is that growing up in a particular culture leads to the internalization of shared ways of understanding the world. Parents, schools, peers, and the media instruct children in the ways of their culture. Shared attitudes, norms, and values then come to influence the way people think, act, and feel. Culture influences our goals and values, contributes to how we think about desirable and undesirable individual characteristics and behaviors, and sets normative expectations concerning the meaning and achievement of a successful life. For positive psychology, these influences are most relevant to understanding how culture shapes people's ideas about the meaning of happiness and how to achieve it.

It is important to point out that culture does not form people's lives like a cookie cutter, where everyone turns out the same. Increasing attention is being paid to the large differences among people living in the same culture (e.g., Hong, Morris, Chiu, & Benet-Martinez, 2000). Culture may have less pervasive and consistent effects on people than was previously supposed. This may occur because people internalize more than one cultural tradition (e.g., national and local) and therefore come to reflect a combination of cultural influences. People are increasingly exposed to many potential sources of cultural influence. Hermans and Kempen (1998) argue that there is more mixing of cultures today because of exposure to global media, increased world travel, immigration across different cultures, and the growth of international corporations. People may also adopt values and lifestyles different than the societal majority because they disagree with the dominant beliefs and practices in their cultures. The lack of uniformity in the individual-culture connection is supported by research finding that some traits and behaviors show more variation among individuals within the same culture than between individuals living in different cultures (e.g., Oyserman, Coon, & Kemmelmeier, 2002). Despite these complexities, most researchers believe that culture does have pervasive and predictable influences that permit a meaningful description of general relationships between culture and individual life (Diener et al., 2003; Fiske,

Kitayama, Markus, & Nisbett, 1998; Kitayama & Marcus, 2000; Markus & Kitayama, 1991). Supporting this conclusion, Diener et al. (2003) report that 15% of the variation in life satisfaction was associated with between-nation differences (i.e., culture) in the World Values Survey of 43 nations.

Much of the cross-cultural research relevant to well-being has centered on the self. In essence, self-concept is our theory about who we are. Self refers to each individual's own subjective answer to the question, "Who am I?" (see Baumeister, 1998, for a review). Self-concept includes beliefs about our abilities, weaknesses, desires, goals, and values. The self is at the center of our lives because it filters and evaluates our experiences and has a determining effect on how we respond to people and events. Our self-conception is certainly shaped by our unique life experiences, but it is also heavily influenced by culture.

The Self in Individualistic and Collectivist Cultures

Many cultures can be characterized according to the relative value they place on individualism or collectivism (see Fiske et al., 1998; Kitayama & Markus, 2000; Triandis, 1989, 2000, for reviews). These two orientations represent two contrasting cultural models of the self. **Individualistic cultures** include the industrialized countries of North America (e.g., United States & Canada), Western Europe (e.g., England, France, Denmark, Netherlands), and countries reflecting Western cultural traditions (e.g., Australia & New Zealand). These cultures share an emphasis on individual rights, responsibilities, and freedom. Individualistic cultures value self-reliance, independence, self-direction, individual choice, and assertiveness. Western culture reflects a view of the self as *independent* and distinct from others and defined by a unique combination of qualities and abilities (Markus & Kitayama, 1991; Triandis, 1989). **Collectivist cultures** include countries of East Asia (e.g., China, Japan, Korea), the Middle East (e.g., Pakistan), Africa, and Latin America (e.g., Venezuela, Columbia, Mexico). These societies emphasize an *interdependent* view of self, in which personal identity is defined relationally, according to connections with others (e.g., family, country, peers, employer, religion), and to the immediate social context. Collectivist cultures place a premium on social responsibility, fulfillment of social roles, cooperation

with others, and maintaining social harmony. The individual is defined as part of a larger social network rather than as a unique and separate entity.

One way to think about the individualist–collectivist difference is in terms of the relative emphasis each type of culture places on a personal or social identity (Tajfel, 1982). Personal identity refers to those self-descriptions that distinguish us from others and make us unique. Social identity refers to aspects of self that are defined by our membership in, and connection to groups and social categories. When we make statements about our individual characteristics (e.g., "I am athletic, friendly, and outgoing"), we describe our personal identity, while references to groups to which we belong and with which we identify (e.g., "I am a liberal, Catholic, political science major") define our social identity. The relative importance of personal and social identity within different cultures is shown by studies using the "twenty statements test" (e.g., Bond & Cheung, 1983; Shweder & Bourne, 1984; Trafimow, Triandis, & Gotto, 1991). This measure allows people to describe the most salient aspects of their self-conceptions in their own words. People complete 20 sentences beginning with "I am . . . ." Americans are more likely to complete the sentences with internal psychological trait descriptions ("I am shy" or "I am intelligent"), whereas Asians are more likely to describe social roles, group affiliations, and social relationships ("I am a daughter" or "I am respectful with my parents").

For Americans, the self is viewed in abstract terms and relatively independent of others and situations. We Americans take the same self wherever we go. If the people we are with and the situation we are in had a consistent and major impact on the personal qualities we expressed, it would be hard to maintain a belief in an **independent self.** For Asians, on the other hand, the self is **interdependent** because it is much more intertwined with relationships and social contexts. The meaning and expression of personal attributes is tied to people and situations. When asked to describe themselves in specific contexts such as school, work, and home, Japanese individuals gave *more* abstract internal traits answers than did Americans (Cousins, 1989). Americans, in contrast, tended to qualify their descriptions with "sometimes" or "more-or-less." These qualifications seemed to be motivated by a need to avoid confusing the description of self in a given context with the "real" self that is independent of contexts. To say that "I am sometimes lazy at home" also seems to imply that "I'm not lazy everywhere." Americans seem quite comfortable describing themselves in terms of internal traits when *no* context is specified because this fits their independent view of self (Rhee, Uleman, Lee, & Roman, 1995). Americans appear to have a greater need for self-consistency across situations. Asians appear quite comfortable with internal trait self-descriptions when the context *is* specified because this fits their interdependent view of self. Asians have a more flexible and context-dependent self and are less concerned about being consistent across situations (see Suh, 2000).

The differences here are relative. The individualist-versus-collectivist views of self paint cultural differences in broad, sweeping strokes. Americans also mention group affiliations in their self-descriptions and Asians mention personal attributes. We noted that significant variations can exist within a single culture. For example, people living in the southern United States have somewhat more collectivist views than those living in the western states (Vandello & Cohen, 1999), and American women have more relationally defined selves than American men (Gabriel & Gardner, 1999; Gilligan, Lyons, & Hammer, 1999). However, researchers find that the patterns of relationship among numerous psychological variables clearly differ in the two types of cultures. The two models of self appear to capture important differences in the individual and social lives of people living in individualistic and collectivist cultures.

Culture and the Meaning of Happiness

The individualistic and collectivist (I–C) conceptions of self provide differing bases for well-being and the meaning of happiness. Considerable research has compared European Americans to East Asians, so we will focus our discussion on these two cultural areas. Subjective well-being researchers note that Japan is particularly puzzling because the Japanese have relatively high incomes, but relatively low SWB when compared to Americans using established measures. Early clues that culture contributed to the American–Japanese difference in SWB were revealed when many "established" social psychology findings about the self could not be replicated in Asian cultures. Research comparing the two cultures then expanded to more fully describe the two

cultural models of self (see Baumeister, 1998; Fiske et al., 1998; Gilbert, 1998; Kitayama & Markus, 2000; Suh, 2000, for reviews).

The above reviews suggest that Americans are encouraged to identify and express the unique internal attributes that distinguish them from others, to develop a positive view of self that enhances self-esteem, and to make personal and social judgments primarily on the basis of internal traits and motives. In contrast, Asians are encouraged to identify and express attributes that contribute to harmonious relations and fitting in with others, to develop a self-critical and self-disciplined attitude that enhances self-improvement, and to make personal and social judgments based on sensitivity to the social context and social norms. A number of these differences have specific relevance for understanding the cultural basis of happiness.

The American-Individualistic Style of Happiness

Being happy, having a positive attitude, and feeling good about the self are central values in American culture. The pursuit of happiness is described in the Declaration of Independence as an inalienable right. In a society that offers abundant opportunities and considerable individual freedom, people are encouraged to make life choices based on what makes them happy and satisfied. What makes Americans happy is heavily influenced by their culture's individualistic model of self. Consistent with the SWB conception, happiness in America is an individual's subjective judgment about his or her own life. Happiness is both subjective and individualized, in that the basis of judgment reflects the person's unique personal makeup and his or her own idiosyncratic criteria. As an American, I take it for granted that what makes me happy may not make you happy, because happiness is highly individualized. Extensive research reviews permit a general characterization of the American style of happiness (see Fiske et al., 1998; Kitayama & Markus, 2000; Markus & Katayama, 1991; Matsumoto, 1997; Suh, 2000; Triandis, 2000). From an early age American children seem to be taught two culturally-defined lessons. First, happiness and feeling good about your self are important goals and valid criteria for making choices. That is, people "should" be happy, and when making a decision it is important to consider its effects on one's happiness and satisfaction.

Second, happiness results from finding out who you are, in terms of your individual identity (your abilities and personality traits), and then pursuing those activities that express these self-defining characteristics. Children are encouraged to develop a distinctive sense of self they can feel good about, and then to follow this self largely independent of the influence of others. Happiness results from being "true to yourself."

Considerable research affirms the effects of these cultural lessons among North Americans. The vast majority of North Americans report being happy (Diener & Diener, 1995; Diener et al., 1995; Myers, 2000a). For example, national surveys by Diener and Diener (1995) showed 83% of American men, 82% of American women, 78% of Canadian men, and 79% of Canadian women reporting levels of life satisfaction above neutral (i.e., somewhat to very satisfied). These results can be compared to Asian countries such as Japan, where less than 40% of men and women report above neutral levels of satisfaction, and Korea, where less than 50% expressed positive levels of satisfaction. Diener and his colleagues (Diener & Diener 1995; Deiner et al., 1995) also found that self-esteem was more strongly related to SWB in individualistic than in collectivist cultures, and that North Americans experience positive emotions much more frequently than do East Asians. These findings are consistent with the individualistic cultural views that happiness is important and that it stems from individual self-satisfaction.

Social psychologists have documented a number of self-enhancing tendencies among North Americans that are also consistent with the individualistic model's emphasis on developing and maintaining a positive self-image (see Baumeister, 1998, 1999; Fiske et al., 1998; Fiske & Taylor, 1991; Gilbert, 1998, for reviews). North Americans show a pervasive tendency to perceive themselves as "better than average" in comparisons to others, to exaggerate the amount of control they have over life events, to see only a rosy future ahead that mostly excludes the occurrence of negative events, and to engage in self-serving explanations for behavior. Self-serving explanations involve taking credit for success by attributing them to individual internal characteristics ("I got an "A" on the test because I'm smart and I studied hard"), while defending self-esteem by attributing failure to external circumstances ("I failed the test because the questions were so ambiguous that I couldn't understand what the instructor was asking").

All of these tendencies are self-enhancing in the sense that they promote, maintain, and protect a positive self-image. Dramatic support for the positive self-image of Americans can be seen in a study reported by Kitayama and Markus (2000). The most frequently mentioned self-descriptions, given by a sample of 1,500 adults living in the United States, were "happy," "outgoing," "active," and "independent." Less than 2% of the self-descriptions were negative. These self-enhancing tendencies are much less pronounced in Asian collectivist cultures (Fiske et al., 1998). Overall, North Americans score significantly higher on measures of self-esteem than do the Japanese. This is clearly shown in national surveys. Compare the average level of self-esteem in a sample of North Americans, shown in Figure 6.3 to that of a comparable Japanese sample, shown in Figure 6.4.

The Asian-Collectivist Style of Happiness

In America's individualistic culture, individual happiness is an important cultural value and ideal. Children are encouraged to be emotionally expressive, to take pride in their achievements, stand out from others, and to take a positive and self-enhancing view of themselves. This can be contrasted with Asian cultures, in which happiness has less importance as a cultural ideal and children are encouraged to moderate their emotions, fit in with others, take pride in the achievement of their groups, and to adopt a self-critical and self-effacing attitude toward themselves.

CULTURAL IDEALS Within East Asian societies, happiness appears less important as a culturally prescribed goal, and life satisfaction is based more on external and normative expectations than on individualized criteria. A large-scale international survey with over 62,000 respondents representing 61 nations supported the greater importance of cultural norms in the judgments of life satisfaction among collectivists compared to individualistic cultures (Suh, Diener, Oishi, & Triandis, 1998). Suh (2000) points out that in contrast to North American cultures, East Asian cultural traditions do not emphasize happiness, life satisfaction, or the experience of positive emotions as central life concerns. Several studies support the general conclusion concerning the differential importance of SWB in American and Asian cultures. For example, Diener

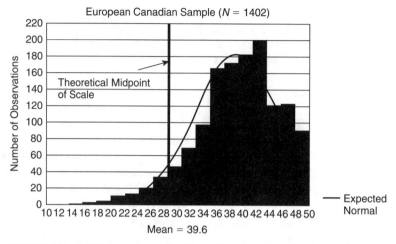

FIGURE 6.3   Self-Esteem Scores for North American Sample of Canadian Europeans

Source: Heine, S. J., Lehman, D. R., Markus, H. R., & Kitayama, S. (1999). Is there a universal need for positive regard? *Psychological Review, 106,* 766–794. Copyright American Psychological Association. Reprinted by permission.

(2000) reported that compared to Americans, East Asians rate happiness and life satisfaction as less important and think less frequently about whether their lives are happy or satisfying. Another study asked Americans and Koreans to make life satisfaction ratings for a culturally ideal person (Diener, Suh, Smith, & Shao, 1995). The level of satisfaction, based on a cultural ideal, was significantly lower for Koreans than for Americans.

Rather than pursuing and cultivating the experience of happiness, Asian cultures tend to regard happiness and other emotions as temporary states that come and go. Emotions are like the weather—sunny today and rainy tomorrow. "Unhappiness is believed to arrive on the heels of happiness, and vice versa" (Suh, 2000, p. 74). That is, an excessive attachment to happiness or great despair about unhappiness would fail to appreciate the fleeting

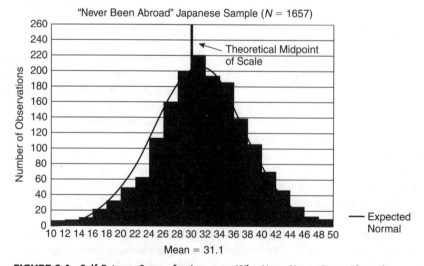

FIGURE 6.4   Self-Esteem Scores for Japanese Who Have Never Been Abroad

Source: Heine, S. J., Lehman, D. R., Markus, H. R., & Kitayama, S. (1999). Is there a universal need for positive regard? *Psychological Review, 106,* 766–794. Copyright American Psychological Association. Reprinted by permission.

nature of emotional experiences. The Asian cultural lesson here is that keeping one's composure by living with "what is," knowing that it will change, makes more sense than constantly striving to be happy or to avoid unhappiness.

EMOTIONAL EXPRESSIVENESS Within Asian culture, excessive exuberance may be regarded as indicating a lack of maturity or refinement. Asians certainly do experience and enjoy happiness, but these emotions do not function as central life goals or prominent criteria for life decisions, as they do for North Americans. The Asian cultural emphasis on moderation and balance in emotional expression led Kitayama and Markus (2000) to conclude that the well-being of East Asians, as measured by SWB criteria, ". . . may be moderate by its very nature" (p. 140). Subjective well-being scales that ask how happy or satisfied people are with their lives may elicit moderate responses within Asian cultures because moderation in emotional expression is a culturally prescribed, normative expectation.

GROUP PRIDE AND SENSITIVITY In Asian cultures, emotional experience and assessments of well-being are intimately connected to relationships. How you are viewed by others is critical to how you view your self. North Americans care about how they are regarded by others, but they are also encouraged to stand on their own two feet and stick to their convictions. An independent self may have to endure the negative regard of others in the service of remaining true to the self. In contrast, East Asian children are taught to develop what Kitayama and Markus (2000) describe as "sympathetic relationships" with others. Sympathy here refers to an interdependent relationship in which individuals are expected to attune themselves empathically to the feelings and thoughts of others. Attunement means taking the perspective of others and acting in manner that both anticipates and serves their needs and desires. Children are expected to learn how to adjust themselves to others so as to enhance and maintain harmonious social relationships. Studies have shown that the emphasis on being independent in American culture, and being connected to others in Asian cultures, influences the types of experiences and goals that lead to positive feelings and high levels of SWB (Kitayama & Markus, 2000; Kitayama, Markus, & Kurokawa, 2000; Oishi & Diener, 2001).

For Americans, positive feelings are more strongly related to individual achievements that produce feelings of pride in individual accomplishment (like getting the highest score on an exam in a college class). Achievement of goals that enhance independence is an important basis of happiness in individualistic cultures. Good feelings for Asians more often result from social relationships, in which pleasing others and fulfilling social expectations lead to feelings of friendliness, closeness, and mutual respect. Achievement of goals that enhance interdependence is important to happiness in collectivist cultures. Interestingly, Oishi and Diener (2001) found that the motive behind pursuit of goals was quite similar for Asian and American college students. When asked whether they pursued their goals for their own satisfaction or to make family and friends happy, both cultural groups identified personal satisfaction much more frequently than a desire to please others.

However, among Asians, only the pursuit of goals related to others was associated with increases in SWB. This finding may result from the fact that Western ideas of independence and self-determination are becoming more popular among Japanese youths, and are expressed as *reasons* for the pursuit of goals. But *satisfaction* with goal achievement may be more dependent on the intimate connection between self and others in Japanese culture. That is, only goals that would also please one's family and friends lead to increased satisfaction.

SELF-CRITICAL ATTITUDES Another significant feature of East Asian relationships is the important role of a self-critical attitude in promoting mutual trust and support. In individualistic cultures, a shared belief in the importance of feeling good about oneself promotes self-enhancement and social exchanges characterized by mutual approval and praise. Receiving social approval requires presenting desirable features of the self to others to invite positive affirmation. This contributes to a positive view of *oneself*. In contrast, within Asian collectivist cultures, social approval requires the expression of a self-critical attitude that invites sympathetic and supporting responses. This contributes to a positive view *from others*. An old American adage advises that "if you can't say something positive, don't say anything at all." In Japan, the adage might be, "if you can't admit your shortcomings, don't expect sympathy from others."

Several studies suggest that modesty, humility, and a self-critical attitude may be central features of Asian self-concept.

In one study, following a period of social interaction in small groups, Chinese and Canadian college students rated their own personal qualities and those of fellow group members (Yik, Bond, & Paulhus, 1998). Chinese students showed a self-critical tendency by rating their own personal qualities less positively than the qualities of others, while Canadian students showed a self-enhancing tendency by rating themselves higher than they rated other group members. A similar pattern was found when Japanese and Canadian college students were asked to judge their performance relative to other students on a test of "Integrative Cognitive Capacity" (Heine, Takata, & Lehman, 2000). The test was purposely made challenging and ambiguous so students would find it very difficult to determine their actual performance. Researchers manipulated performance feedback, leading some students to believe they had done better than the "average student" and others to believe they had done worse. Even with feedback indicating they had performed *worse* than average, Canadian students still expressed a belief that they had done better than average. Perceiving oneself as better than average is one of several self-enhancing tendencies that are consistent with an individualistic conception of self. When Japanese students received feedback that they scored *higher* than the average of fellow students, they were still reluctant to believe they were better than average. A self-critical attitude that merges the self with others (rather than distinguishing the self from others) is consistent with the collectivist self-conception.

FALSE HUMILITY OR SOCIAL SENSITIVITY? Americans may regard self-critical and self-effacing attitudes as manifestations of excessive politeness or self-deprecation. But the Asian view (according to Kityama & Markus, 2000) is that these characteristics reflect sensitivity to personal shortcomings that might jeopardize favorable regard from others. That is, modesty and humility both invite sympathetic treatment and guard against giving offense to others. When self-definition is intimately connected to relationships, the positive regard of others is critical to personal satisfaction and happiness. Self-promotion or considering oneself special and unique (so common in America) is frowned upon in many Asian societies because self-enhancing behaviors separate, rather than blend the individual with the group. In America it is said that "the squeaky wheel gets the grease." Standing out and calling attention to oneself are virtues. In Japan it is said that "the nail that stands out is pounded down." Fitting in and sensitivity to others are viewed as virtues.

Certainly, Americans appreciate modesty and provide support to those who are self-critical and express personal deficiencies. However, self-criticism is not the typical basis for relationships in individualistic cultures. In America someone who is continually self-effacing might be regarded as shy, suffering from low self-esteem, lacking in confidence, or "too" dependent on others. Among East Asians, however, a self-critical attitude is the basis for a social sensitivity that helps ensure close, supportive, and mutually affirming relationships.

Chapter Summary Questions

1. What research findings suggest that people are of "two minds" concerning the money–happiness relationship?
2. a. What is the paradox of affluence? Define and describe four facts that support the idea of this paradox.
   b. How do Phillip Cushman, Robert Putnam, and Barry Schwartz each explain the paradox?
3. Compare and contrast the between-country and the within-country relationship of money and

happiness. What do these relationships mean and why are they so different?
4. Within wealthy nations, what research supports a "diminishing returns" effect of money on individual happiness?
5. a. In the Diener et al. (2002) study, what relationship was found among the cheerfulness of college freshmen, parental income, and students' later earnings?
   b. Give three possible explanations for the effects of cheerfulness on earnings.

6. a. How do the concepts of hedonic adaptation and a hedonic treadmill explain why increasing income does not increase happiness?

  b. How does the study of lottery winners and paralysis victims support the effects of contrast and habituation in the process of adaptation?

7. a. How do rising expectations, social comparisons, and relative deprivation explain why increased income does not bring increased happiness?

  b. People can choose among many different social comparison standards. What do studies suggest about the least and the most important standards that people use in their social comparisons?

8. What arguments and research findings support the cross-cultural validity and universality of SWB measures? Describe four.

9. What are the differences between the individualistic/independent and the collectivist/interdependent cultural conceptions of self-concept?

How are these differences shown in the "I am" self-reports of Americans and Asians?

10. a. What is the role of happiness in the self-concept, life goals, and judgments of Americans?

  b. What research findings support the importance of happiness and a positive self-image in North American culture?

11. a. What role does happiness play in the self-concept, life goals, and judgments of Asians?

  b. Why is there more moderation in emotional expression within Asian cultures? How does this moderation help explain the lower SWB scores of Asians compared to Americans?

12. What different roles do social norms and independence play in the SWB judgments of Asians and Americans?

13. Compare and contrast the role of sympathetic relationships and independence in the emotional lives of Asians and Americans.

14. Compare and contrast the effects of self-criticism and self-enhancement on self-evaluations of Asians and Americans.

Key Terms

paradox of affluence *99*
empty self *101*
maximizing versus satisficing *102*
paradox of choice *102*
sensory adaptation *109*

hedonic treadmill *109*
contrast *109*
habituation *109*
dynamic equilibrium model *111*
social comparison *112*

self-relevance *113*
individualistic versus collectivist cultures *117*
independent versus interdependent self *117*

Web Resources

Diener—Happiness

www.psych.uiuc.edu/~ediener Web page for happiness researcher Ed Diener, who has conducted extensive research on national and cultural differences in happiness.

World Data Base of Happiness

worlddatabaseofhappiness.eur.nl This site is directed by Ruut Veenhoven of the Netherlands. It

reviews thousands of studies related to national differences in happiness based on large-scale world surveys.

American Paradox

www.davidmyers.org/Brix?pageID=21 Informative web site for David Myers, author of *American paradox: Spiritual hunger in an age of plenty.*

Suggested Readings

Brickman, P. D., Coates, D., & Janoff-Bulman, R. (1978). Lottery winners and accident victims: Is happiness relative? *Journal of Personality and Social Psychology, 36,* 917–927.

Diener, E. (2000). Subjective well-being: The science of happiness and a proposal for a national index. *American Psychologist, 55,* 34–43.

Diener, E., Diener, M., & Diener, C. (1995). Factors predicting the subjective well-being of nations. *Journal of Personality and Social Psychology, 69,* 851–864.

Diener, E., Nickerson, C., Lucas, R. E., & Sandvik, E. (2002). Dispositional affect and job outcomes. *Social Indicators Research, 59,* 229–259.

Diener, E., & Seligman, M. (2004). Beyond money: Toward an economy of well-being. *Psychology in the Public Interest, 5,* 1–31.

Diener, E., & Suh, E. M. (Eds.). (2000). *Culture and subjective well-being.* Cambridge: MIT Press.

Easterbrook, G. (2003). *The progress paradox: How life gets better while people feel worse.* New York: Random House.

Kitayama, S., Markus, H. R., & Kurokawa, M. (2000). Culture, emotion, and well-being: Good feelings in Japan and the United States. *Cognition and Emotion, 14,* 93–124.

Markus, H. R., & Kitayama, S. (1991). Culture and the self: Implications for cognition, emotion and motivation. *Psychological Review, 98,* 224–253.

Myers, D. G. (2000). *The American paradox: Spiritual hunger in an age of plenty.* New Haven: Yale University Press.

7

Personal Goals as Windows to Well-Being

oals are central to an understanding of human behavior because they energize action and provide meaning, direction, and purpose to life activities. Goals help explain the "whys" of action—that is, what people are trying to accomplish. Nearly all behavior has a purpose, whether it's washing dishes, having fun with friends, looking for a job, or planning a vacation. Goals explain and make sense of our actions by providing reasons for their occurrence. Whatever our behavior, if someone asks, "What are you doing?" we typically respond by describing the purpose of our actions in terms of a desired outcome (i.e., achieving a goal). Goals also make our lives coherent by establishing connections between specific short-term and more general long-term purposes and desires. For example, if you are a college student reading this book for a class on positive psychology, your specific purpose is to understand the material in this chapter. This specific goal is probably part of a larger goal of doing well in the class; which is a sub-goal of meeting the requirements to graduate from college; which relates to the more general goal of getting a good job; which may relate to an even more encompassing goal of having a satisfying life. In short, our behavior during a day, a week, a year, or a lifetime would not make much sense without an understanding of the goals we are striving to achieve.

Robert Emmons (2003) describes personal goals as "the well-springs of a positive life" (p. 105). In other words, the goals we pursue are intimately connected to our happiness and well-being. The importance of goals is clearly evident in cases where people *do not* have reasonably clear, personally meaningful, and attainable goals. Both goal conflict and unrealistic goals have consistently been linked to lower well-being and higher distress (Austin & Vancouver, 1996; Cantor & Sanderson, 1999; Emmons, 1999b; Karolyi, 1999; Lent, 2004). For example, Emmons and King (1988) found that conflict and ambivalence about personal goals were related to higher levels of negative affect, depressed mood, neuroticism, and physical illness. Even though people spent a good deal of time ruminating about their conflicting goals, this did not lead to action aimed at resolution. Instead, conflict tended to immobilize action and was associated with decreased subjective well-being (SWB).

A further example of the relation between goals and personal distress is shown in the link between unrealistic standards for self-evaluation and clinical depression. Perfectionists, for example, are at higher risk for both depression and suicide because of the self-blame, low self-worth, and chronic sense of failure that result from their inability to meet unrealistic expectations (Baumeister, 1990; Blatt, 1995; Karolyi, 1999). These expectations may be self-imposed through a belief that one must be flawless, or socially imposed through a belief that significant others have expectations and demands that are difficult or impossible to achieve. The chronic inability to satisfy individual standards for self-approval and to meet the perceived expectations of others to gain social approval can cause severe distress. Prolonged distress may lead to what Baumeister (1990) called the "escape from self"—namely, suicide.

On the positive side, attaining personally significant goals, pursuing meaningful aspirations, and involving oneself in valued activities all contribute to enhanced happiness and well-being (Cantor & Sanderson, 1999; Diener, Suh, Lucas, & Smith, 1999; Emmons, 1999b; Emmons & King, 1988; Lent, 2004). Personal goals play a pivotal role in individual well-being because they are the basis for activities that bring happiness and meaning to life. Engagement in meaningful life tasks makes a significant and independent contribution to well-being. For example, in a study of over 600 older adults, involvement in social and community activities was related to higher levels of life satisfaction, even after controlling for personal resources such as health, social support, congeniality, and prior levels of satisfaction (Harlow & Cantor, 1996). In other words, participation in social activities increased well-being above and beyond the effects of personal resources.

GOALS CONNECT "HAVING" AND "DOING"

In addition to their independent contribution, goals may also determine the extent to which personal resources influence well-being. Cantor and Sanderson (1999) note that goals help connect the "having" side to the "doing" side of life (see also Cantor, 1990). This traditional distinction (first made by personality theorist Gordon Allport in 1937) captures the importance of "having" personal resources such as social skills, an optimistic attitude, and supportive friends, as well as the importance of "doing," in the form of developing meaningful goals and pursuing personally significant life activities. That is, both resources (material and personal) and commitment to goals have an important connection to well-being. This connection is exemplified in a study of resources and personal strivings among college students (Diener & Fujita, 1995).

These researchers found that the effect of resources on well-being depended on their congruence with personal goals. Resources measured in the study included skills and abilities (like intelligence and social skills), personal traits (being energetic and outgoing), social support (close ties with family members and friends), and material resources (money and possessions). Goals were assessed through students' descriptions of 15 personal strivings (defined as "the things they were typically trying to do in their everyday behavior") (Diener & Fujita, p. 929). Students rated the relevance of each resource to each personal striving, and also provided ratings on measures of global SWB and experience-sampling measures of daily mood. The critical factor determining the effects of resources on SWB was the degree of congruence between resources and personal strivings. Having resources that facilitated achieving personal goals was related to higher SWB, while a lack of goal-related resources was associated with relatively lower levels of well-being. That is, it did not matter how many resources a student had. What mattered was whether those resources supported the goals they were trying to accomplish.

Diener and Fujita describe two case studies to make this goal–resource relationship concrete. One young woman in the study had strong personal resources in the area of intelligence and self-discipline for work. However, she rated these resources as largely unrelated to her goals. She perceived self-confidence and support from family members and friends as much more relevant. Unfortunately, she was not strong in these areas. In short, her personal resources did not match and support her personal goals. Her level of well-being was extremely low—three standard deviations below the mean for students in the study. A second woman in the study had strong resources in the area of support from friends and family members, and rated these resources as highly relevant to her goals. She was low in athleticism and money, but perceived these resources as unrelated to her goals. The good alignment of resources and goals for this young woman was associated with a very high level of well-being. Her level of SWB was one standard deviation above the sample mean.

The recent surge of interest in goal-related concepts within psychology is, in large measure, a result of their potential to explain how "having" and "doing" co-determine life outcomes and therefore well-being. As soon as we ask why "having" a particular personal resource or life advantage leads to certain behaviors or outcomes, we move from the "having" to the "doing." Because goals are intimately involved in the "doing," they help clarify the effects of "having." For example, an optimistic attitude toward life has consistently been documented to be related to higher levels of well-being. If we ask why optimists are happier than pessimists, the answer might seem obvious. An optimist sees the proverbial glass as being half full, while the pessimist sees the glass as being half empty. What else do we need to know? Yet, if you consider that optimists have happier marriages, are better workers, and enjoy better health, then you begin to think about what optimists *do* that pessimists do *not* do (Chang, 2002a). Much of the answer concerns differences in goals, planning, and perseverance in the face of difficulties.

In this chapter, we address a number of questions concerning why personal goals are important to well-being, happiness, and a meaningful life. What are goals and how are they measured? What needs and purposes do goals fulfill? How are people's multiple goals organized and structured? In terms of their impact on well-being and happiness, does it matter what goals people strive to achieve or why they strive to achieve them? For positive psychologists, finding answers to these questions provides a revealing look at what people are trying to accomplish in their lives, and that, in turn, can be evaluated in terms its impact on well-being. For a student of positive psychology, goal research and theory offer a way to think about your own personal goals in terms of their potential contribution to your individual happiness.

WHAT ARE PERSONAL GOALS?

Defining Personal Goals

In their review of goal constructs in psychology, Austin and Vancouver (1996, p. 338) define goals as ". . . internal representations of desired states, where states are broadly construed as outcomes, events or processes." Graduating from college, meeting new friends, or losing weight would exemplify goals as outcomes, while planning a wedding or having the family over for Thanksgiving would be examples of goals as events. Goals as processes might include activities that are enjoyable in their own right, like reading, nature walks, spending time with friends, or working over time to develop particular skills or interests, such as woodworking, musical talents, or athletic abilities. Desired states may range from fulfillment of biological needs such as hunger, to more complex and long-term desires involved in developing a successful career, to "ultimate concerns" (Emmons, 1999b) with transcendent life meanings expressed through religious and spiritual pursuits.

Karolyi's (1999) review of the goal literature notes that goals may be internally represented in a variety of ways. People may have a specific image of a desired state. For example, many people who live in the upper Midwest, like your textbook authors, start imagining a warm Florida beach in mid-February, after the cold and snow begin to get old. These and other images energize travel plans for many Midwestern university students, who head for Florida during spring break. Personal memories, stories, and if/then scenarios that people use to think about the past, present, and future may also represent goals. A pleasurable or painful memory of a past event may create plans to repeat (or avoid repeating) certain actions and outcomes. Goals in the form of achievements, aspirations, and fulfilled and unfulfilled dreams are a significant part of an individual's life story and personal identity (McAdams, 1996). Many of our feelings about the past are related to our success or lack of success in accomplishing personally important goals, and our future can be actively imagined through the use of if/then and action/outcome possibilities. For example: "If I get good grades, then I can get into graduate school." "If I just accept who I am instead of always trying to please others, then I will be happier."

In summary, goals may be defined as desired outcomes that people expend energy trying to achieve. Goals contain both a cognitive and an emotion-motivational component. Goals are cognitive in the sense that they are mental representations of desired future states. These representations include beliefs, expectations, memories, and images. The emotion-motivational components of goals include the positive and negative feelings associated with thinking about achieving or failing to achieve important goals, evaluations of goal progress, and the

emotions following successful or unsuccessful goal attainment. It is this emotion-motivational component that energizes action in goal pursuits.

Goals and Related Motivational Concepts

Goals are part of a larger motivational framework in which human behavior is energized and directed toward the achievement of personally relevant outcomes. The diverse array of motivational concepts within psychology includes needs, motives, values, traits, incentives, tasks, projects, concerns, desires, wishes, fantasies, and dreams. These sources of motivation run the gamut from "trivial pursuits" to "magnificent obsessions" (Little, 1989), and from consciously developed plans of action, to behaviors expressing motives that lie outside conscious awareness. In recent years, goals have emerged as a kind of middle ground that helps to organize a variety of motivational concepts. Echoing this sentiment, Karolyi (1999) argued that goals make an independent contribution to human behavior that cannot be subsumed or explained away by other motivational constructs. There is considerable controversy concerning this point, especially regarding whether goals are subsumed by, or distinct from personality (see for example McAdams, 1995; Miller & Read, 1987; Read & Miller, 1998, 2002; Winter, John, Stewart, Klohnen, & Duncan, 1998). Most goal researchers, however, would agree that goals are connected to other sources of motivation, but they are also distinct and separate psychological entities.

A case for the unique and distinct status of goals, among other motivational concepts, does not mean that needs, values, traits, and other motives are less important than goals, or that goals are more fundamental explanations for people's actions. In fact, an important topic for this chapter is to examine how goals may express needs, values, and self-concept. As Karolyi (1999) argues, the increased interest in goal-based perspectives within psychology reflects the value of goals as an intermediate level of analysis that connects, mediates, and translates these more general sources of motivation into conscious awareness and intentional action. Goals help make sense of the diverse sources of human motivation by focusing their effects on the more particular reasons and purposes for action over time. Personal goals offer more specific, "here-and-now" insights into people's ongoing journey through life, than do many of the more general and encompassing motivational perspectives. As Karolyi puts it, "goals . . . provide a glimpse into each person's on-line 'command center' " (1999, p. 269).

This online command center involves the individualized translations of general needs and motives into specific expressive forms that characterize unique individuals. For example, the need for belongingness, while clearly an important and fundamental human motive, is expressed in a limitless variety of behaviors and goals that vary widely among individuals. People might fulfill this need by having many casual friends, having a few close friends, maintaining close ties to their parents and siblings, or by committing themselves to their marriages and their own children. These multiple forms of potential expression are part of the reason that belongingness is considered fundamental and universal (Baumeister & Leary, 1995). Self-defined personal goals capture how a need shared by all humans is translated or expressed in a particular individual's life. Personal goals help connect the general to the particular.

The online command center also involves the critical role of goals in self-regulating action over time. (Self-regulated behavior is the topic for Chapter 8.) Goals function as standards and reference points for the evaluation of personal growth and achievement. People's ongoing evaluation of how they are doing, what new actions need to be taken, and how satisfied they are with life are, in large measure, determined by comparisons of their current status in relation to progress toward and achievement of personally meaningful goals. Goals help tie together feelings about our past, evaluations of our present, and hopes for the future.

Measuring Personal Goals

Researchers differ in how they define and measure personal goals; however, all conceptions attempt to capture what people are trying to accomplish in their lives in terms of personally desirable outcomes. Goals have been described as personal concerns (Klinger, 1977, 1998), personal projects (Little, 1989, 1993; Little, Salmela-Aro, & Phillips, 2007; McGregor & Little, 1998; Palys & Little, 1983), personal strivings (Emmons, 1986, 1999b, 2003), and life tasks (Cantor, 1990; Cantor & Sanderson, 1999; Cantor & Zirkel, 1990). Researchers typically give a brief description and orienting example of the goal concept and then ask people to describe their most important current goals. For example, in personal project research, participants are told, "We are interested in studying the kinds of activities and concerns that people have in their lives. We call these **personal projects.** All of us have a number of personal projects at any given time that we think about, plan for, carry out, and sometimes (though not always) complete" (McGregor & Little, 1998, p. 497). Examples of projects might include "completing my English essay" and "getting more outdoor exercise" (Little, 1989).

In his study of goals conceived as personal strivings, Emmons (1999b) instructed research participants to consider **personal strivings** as "the things you are typically or characteristically trying to do in your everyday behavior." Participants were told that these might be either positive objectives they sought, or negative events or things they wanted to avoid. They were also instructed to describe recurring goals rather than one-time goals. Examples of personal strivings include: "trying to persuade others one is right" and "trying to help others in need of help."

In Cantor's research (Cantor, 1990; Cantor & Sanderson, 1999), **life tasks** were introduced to participants with the following instructions. "One way to think about goals is to think about 'current life tasks.' For example, imagine a retired person. The following three life tasks may emerge for the individual as he or she faces this difficult time: (1) being productive without a job; (2) shaping a satisfying role with grown children and their families; and (3) enjoying leisure time and activities. These specific tasks constitute important goals since the individual's energies will be directed toward solving them" (Zirkel & Cantor, 1990, p. 175). Participants in the study were then asked to describe all their current life tasks.

Once a list of self-generated goals is obtained, researchers can ask participants to make a number of additional ratings that get at goal importance, goal conflict, commitment, and perceived attainability. Goals can also be grouped into categories to allow for comparisons among individuals. Depending on the researchers' interests and definition of the term "goal," goal categories might be focused on a particular life stage, circumstance, or time-span, or on more general goals that endure over time. For example, Zirkel and Cantor (1990) asked college students to sort their self-described tasks into six categories: academic success, establishing future goals and plans, making new friends, learning to be on their own without their families, developing their own unique personal identities, and balancing their time between academics and socializing. In contrast, Emmons' (1999b) research on personal strivings asked people to describe goals at a higher and more general level. His research showed that personal goals can be coded into general categories such as achievement, power, affiliation or relationships, personal growth and health, independence, intimacy, and spirituality. To sum up, personal goals open up a rich assortment of interrelated factors for well-being researchers. Goals capture the guiding purposes in people's lives that are central to happiness and satisfaction. As we noted earlier, goals may be considered windows for viewing major determinants of well-being.

Goal Organization

Most goal researchers agree that goals can be arranged in a hierarchy with general, more abstract, and "higher-order" goals at the top and more concrete, specific, and "lower-order" goals at the bottom (Austin & Vancouver, 1996). Goals higher in the hierarchy are considered more important because they control and give meaning to many lower-order goals. Higher-order goals can easily be broken down into the lower-order subgoals they control. For example, the goal of earning a college degree requires successful achievement of numerous subgoals (e.g., meeting college entrance requirements, signing up for classes, studying, fulfilling graduation requirements, and paying tuition). In this example, getting a degree is a higher-order and more important goal because it organizes and gives purpose to many specific subgoals. Higher-order goals may also be more important because of the personal consequences that may occur if they are not achieved. The consequences of failing to obtain a college degree are more significant than failing one class. Clearly, if all or most subgoals are not achieved, higher-order goals will be lost as well.

A variety of models have provided different foundations for ranking goal-related motivations in terms of their personal or universal importance (see Austin & Vancouver, 1996; Carver & Scheier, 1998; and Peterson & Seligman, 2004, for reviews). Nomothetic models have sought to describe relatively universal needs, values, and goals shared by most people, while idiographic models have focused on the unique ordering of goals by particular individuals. While certain need-related and value-related goals appear to have widespread support as being fundamental or universal, there is much less agreement concerning how many goals are necessary to describe the range of human motivations and how they should be arranged in a hierarchic order. Research relating to the universal and individualized views of goal motivations will be the next topics of discussion.

THE SEARCH FOR UNIVERSAL HUMAN MOTIVES

In Chapter 6, we considered the issue of whether happiness has a universal meaning or varies widely across cultures. This section examines the same issue focused on sources of goal-related motivations. If we examined the goals and motives of people from many different cultures, what might we find? Would there be some consensus in the needs and goals considered important around the world? Or, would we end up with an extensive list of motivations too long to be useful? Following in the footsteps of Maslow's famous early work, recent studies have revisited these questions and found some intriguing answers.

Goals and the Fulfillment of Basic Human Needs

Abraham Maslow's classic conception of a hierarchy of human needs (1943, 1954) was one of the earliest examples of a motivational hierarchy that attempted to specify universal sources of human motivation. Originally describing five needs, the model later expanded to eight needs regarded as universal among humans. The expansion occurred as the result of subdividing aspects of self-actualization into separate needs. Each need can be thought of as motivating a particular class of behaviors, the goal of which is need fulfillment.

At the bottom of Maslow's hierarchy are basic *physiological needs* necessary for survival (e.g., needs for food and water). At the second level are needs for *safety and security*—specifically needs for a safe, stable, and comforting environment in which to live, and a coherent understanding of the world. *Belongingness needs,* occupying the third rung of the hierarchy, include people's desires for love, intimacy, and attachment to others through family, friendship, and community relationships. *Esteem needs* are fourth in the hierarchy. These include the need for positive self-regard and for approval, respect, and positive regard from others. Next in line are *cognitive needs*, including needs for knowledge, self-understanding, and novelty. *Aesthetic needs* seek fulfillment in an appreciation of beauty, nature, form, and order. Second-to-the-top-of the hierarchy are *self-actualization needs* for personal growth and fulfillment. Self-actualizing individuals fully express and realize their emotional and intellectual potentials to become healthy and fully functioning. At the very top of the hierarchy is the *need for transcendence*, including religious and spiritual needs to find an overarching purpose for life (Maslow, 1968).

Maslow argued that lower-order needs take precedence over higher-order needs. Higher-order needs are not important, of interest or motivating unless lower-order needs are first satisfied. Maslow viewed human development as the process of progressing up the hierarchy. However, shifting life circumstances can dictate which need commands our attention at any given point in time. Depending on circumstances, a person who was previously motivated by higher-order needs may regress to a lower-order need. For example, many college students have experienced difficulty in finding the motivation to study (cognitive need) after a failed romantic relationship or the death of a loved one (belongingness need).

Maslow's legacy is still visible in positive psychology. For example, common assumptions among positive psychologists are that the more needs a person has fulfilled, the healthier and happier that person will be, and that unmet needs decrease well-being (Veenhoven, 1995). The eudaimonic conception of a healthy and fully functioning person shares much common ground with Maslow's description of a self-actualized individual (Ryan & Deci, 2000; Ryff & Keyes, 1995). However, Maslow's hierarchy has not received extensive research attention, and both its universality and particular ordering of needs have been challenged (Austin & Vancouver, 1996; Peterson & Seligman, 2004). It is also easy to think of examples to counter the idea that higher-order needs are not motivating when lower-order needs are unfulfilled. People die for causes they believe in, and find solace in the love of others and in religion when facing terminal illness. People also sacrifice their own needs for the benefit of others, as any parent can tell you. Yet the basic idea that some needs are more compelling than others finds support in the well-being literature. Recall that in very poor

nations, financial concerns *are* important to well-being, in all likelihood because money is essential to the fulfillment of basic survival needs (e.g., Biswas-Diener & Diener, 2001). In wealthy countries where basic needs are fulfilled, financial factors are *not* strongly predictive of happiness. This finding is in line with the idea that higher-order needs (e.g., esteem and cognitive needs) become important only after lower-order needs are met.

Focus on Research: An Empirical Method for Assessing Universal Needs

Despite difficulties with Maslow's theory, the possibility of establishing a list of universal needs remains appealing. Such a list would help sort and organize the diverse theories postulating widely different needs, values, and goals. A recent study addressed this issue by testing 10 psychological needs as candidates for "universal need" status (Sheldon, Elliot, Kim, & Kasser, 2001). Sheldon and his colleagues identified 10 needs that, based on their similarity, frequency of use, and empirical support within the motivational literature, might be considered universal (Sheldon et al., 2001, adapted from Table 1, p. 328 and Appendix p. 339):

1. *Self-esteem:* The need to have a positive self-image, a sense of worth, and self-respect, rather than a low self-opinion or feeling that one is not as good as others.
2. *Relatedness:* The need to feel intimate and mutually caring connections with others, and to have frequent interactions with others as opposed to feeling lonely and estranged.
3. *Autonomy:* The need to feel that choices are freely made and reflect true interests and values. Expressing a "true self" rather than being forced to act because of external environmental or social pressures.
4. *Competence:* The need to feel successful, capable, and masterful in meeting difficult challenges rather than feeling like a failure, or feeling ineffective or incompetent.
5. *Pleasure/stimulation:* The need for novelty, change, and stimulating, enjoyable experiences rather than feeling bored or feeling that life is routine.
6. *Physical thriving:* The need to be in good health and to have a sense of physical well-being rather than feeling unhealthy and out-of-shape.

7. *Self-actualization/meaning:* The need for personal growth and development of potentials that define who one really is. Finding deeper purpose and meaning in life as opposed to feeling stagnant or feeling that life has little meaning.

8. *Security:* The need to feel safe rather than threatened or uncertain in your present life circumstances; a sense of coherence, control, and predictability in life.

9. *Popularity/influence:* The need to feel admired and respected by other people and to feel that your advice is useful and important, resulting in an ability to influence others' beliefs and behaviors (as opposed to feeling that you have little influence over others and that no one is interested in your advice or opinions).

10. *Money/luxury:* The need for enough money to buy what you want and to have nice possessions (as opposed to feeling poor and unable to own desirable material possessions).

Sheldon and colleagues (2001) set out to evaluate each of these needs to determine its "universality" based on two criteria. The first criterion stems from the assumption that people's most satisfying life experiences are related to fulfillment of important needs. This criterion was tested by first having participants (American and South Korean college students) describe their single most satisfying life event. Participants were then asked to rate the degree of relationship between each of the 10 candidate needs and the "most satisfying" event they had described. The second criterion assumes that the experience of positive and negative emotions is related to need fulfillment. This criterion was tested by asking participants to rate the extent to which they felt 20 different positive and negative moods associated with satisfying and dissatisfying events. Among the most satisfying events mentioned by students were going on a church retreat with friends to clean up a summer camp for a service project, and getting a dream summer job. Their most negative events included breaking up with a romantic partner and being a victim of a violent assault.

Overall findings provided support for the usefulness of these two criteria. Needs were significantly related to satisfying and dissatisfying events, and positive and negative emotions were largely consistent between the U.S. and South Korean samples. Sheldon and colleagues make no claim that their method permits an exact ranking of human needs. However, based on their study, a general and speculative ordering is indicated for the list of needs described above. The numbers 1–10 reflect each need's rank order in the U.S. sample, based on the first criterion (each need's importance and relevance to the participants' most satisfying events). The same rank-ordering of the top four needs emerged using the second criterion (that needs should predict event-related affect): (1) self-esteem, (2) relatedness, (3) autonomy, and (4) competence. The same four needs ranked at the top for the South Korean sample, but their relative positions were slightly different. Specifically, relations with others emerged as more important than self-esteem for South Koreans. This may reflect the difference between the collectivist Asian culture and the individualistic American culture. In both samples, security, physical thriving, and self-actualization occupied middle positions, while popularity-influence and money-luxury appeared to be relatively less important. A slightly different pattern also emerged when students related the candidate needs to their most dissatisfying life event (e.g., failure of a romantic relationship). For unsatisfying events, the strongest predictors were lack of self-esteem, lack of competence, and lack of security, with the absence of security being the most powerful of all. Taken in total, this study suggests that self-esteem, relatedness, autonomy, and competence are strong candidates for consideration as universal human needs.

Goals Expressing Fundamental Values

Fundamental values offer another way to think about universality and hierarchies of human motivation. Most value theories view **values** as desirable states that function as general guides or principles of living (see Rohan, 2000, for a review). Values describe broad and general goals that may motivate a wide range of behaviors. In a hierarchy of human goals, ranging from concrete (e.g., cleaning your house) to abstract (having a satisfying life), values would occupy a position near the top. A recent theory of values addresses both the hierarchy issue and universality issue. Building on the work of Rokeach (1973), Schwartz and his colleagues developed a comprehensive description of 10 human values whose validity and shared meaning have been demonstrated in 65 nations around the world (Sagiv & Schwartz, 1995; Schwartz, 1992, 1994; Schwartz & Bilsky, 1987, 1990; Schwartz & Sagiv, 1995).

In Schwartz's theory, values are conceived as cognitive representations of three universal requirements for human existence: biological needs of the individual, needs for coordinated social interactions, and needs related to the welfare of groups and social institutions. Because of their assumed connection to important requirements of life, the 10 values are regarded as universal across cultures. People and cultures may differ in how they prioritize their values. That is, how people rank order values in terms of their importance will vary from person to person and from culture to culture. A value may be important to one person and less important or even unimportant to another. In Schwartz's theory, the specific hierarchic arrangement of values depends on the individual, group, and culture.

However, despite differences in *priorities*, Schwartz has provided evidence showing that the *content* of 10 human values is widely shared.

Schwartz describes values as "motivational types" because what distinguishes one value from another is the type of motivating goal that each value expresses. Values are regarded as relatively enduring sources of motivation that are stable across adulthood (Rokeach, 1973; Schwartz, 1992). The 10 motivational types of values and relevant goals are summarized in Table 7.1 (adapted from information in Rohan, 2000; Schwartz, 1992).

When you read through Schwartz's descriptions of human values, your own value priorities may become clearer. If you rank each value in terms of its personal importance, you will undoubtedly embrace

TABLE 7.1 Values and related goals

Motivational Type	Description	Goals
Power	Social status and prestige, control, dominance over people and resources	Social power, authority, wealth
Achievement	Personal success demonstrating competence according to social standards	Being successful, capable, influential, hard-working, efficient, achieving goals
Hedonism	Pleasures and sensual gratification of oneself	Pleasure, enjoyment of food, sex, leisure, etc.
Stimulation	Excitement, novelty, challenge in life	Adventure, risk-taking, need for change, new experiences, exciting experiences
Self-direction	Independent thought, action and choice; creating and exploring	Creativity, freedom, independence, curiosity, choosing one's own goals
Universalism	Understanding, appreciation, tolerance and protection of the welfare of all people and of nature	Being broadminded, seeking wisdom, social justice, fairness, a world of peace, beauty, unity with nature and safe-guarding the environment
Benevolence	Preservation and enhancement of the welfare of people with whom you are in frequent contact (e.g., family, friends, co-workers)	Helpfulness, honesty, sincerity, genuineness, forgiveness, loyalty to others, responsibility, dependability, reliability
Tradition	Respect, commitment and acceptance of customs and ideas that traditional culture and religion provide about the self	Humility, modesty, moderation, acceptance of life circumstances, devout adherence to religious faith and beliefs, respect for time-honored traditions
Conformity	Restraint of actions and impulses likely to harm others and violate social norms and expectations	Politeness, courtesy, obedience in meeting obligations, self-discipline, honoring parents and elders
Safety	Safety, harmony and stability of society, relationships and self	Security of loved ones, national security, social order, cleanliness, neatness, reciprocation of favors, avoidance of indebtedness

some values more than others. You can probably also think of differences among people you know in terms of value priorities. Some people value *stimulation* and are always looking for excitement, like to take risks, and get bored easily. Conservative and religious-minded people may place high importance on *tradition* in Schwartz's value scheme.

The connection between goals and values is explicit in Schwartz's theory because values are defined as broad goals that apply to many situations and remain stable across time. Some of your most personally important goals are probably related to one of the 10 values. A helping professional's career goals, for example, may express the importance of a *benevolence* value. Because values help define our personal identities and serve as general principles of living, they represent some of our most important, and therefore, higher-order goals. The fact that the values described by Schwartz are shared across cultures argues for their universal importance.

Personal Goals Across Cultures

Attempts to delineate universal needs and values find a counterpart in a recent study of the content of human goals across 15 cultures (Grouzet et al., 2005). This study provides evidence that the content and organization of personal goals and their connection to fundamental needs and values are shared across cultures.

Nearly 2,000 college students participated in the study representing Western and Eastern Europe, Australia, East Asia, South America, the United States, and Canada. Based on previous studies, Grouzet and colleagues developed a questionnaire to assess the individual importance of 11 different goals. A description of each goal is given in Table 7.2 (adapted from Grouzet et al., 2005, Table 1, p. 802).

Multiple questionnaire items were used to assess each of the 11 goals. Participants rated each item according to its importance as a future life goal, on a scale of 1 (not at all important) to 9 (extremely important). Overall, the content of the 11 goals appears to be widely shared across cultures. Goal measures showed acceptable levels of internal reliability and cross-culture equivalence. More importantly, analysis of participant ratings showed a consistent, coherent, and similar pattern for each of the 15 cultures. Based on the statistical pattern of responses, the content of personal goals showed a clear two-dimensional structure across different cultures, as shown in Figure 7.1.

People in each culture organized the 11 personal goals in similar ways. The two goal dimensions were intrinsic-oriented versus extrinsic-oriented goals, and physical versus self-transcendence goals. Each component of the two dimensions was shown

TABLE 7.2 Personal goals across cultures

Goal	Description
Affiliation	Having satisfying relationships with family and friends
Community feeling	Making the world a better place through giving and activism
Conformity	Fitting in and being accepted by others
Financial success	Being financially successful
Hedonism	Having many sensually pleasurable experiences
Image	Having an appealing appearance that others find attractive
Physical health	Being physically healthy and free of sickness
Popularity	Being admired by others, well-known or famous
Safety	Able to live without threats to personal safety and security
Self-acceptance	Feeling competent, self-aware, self-directed and autonomous
Spirituality	Developing a spiritual/religious understanding of the world

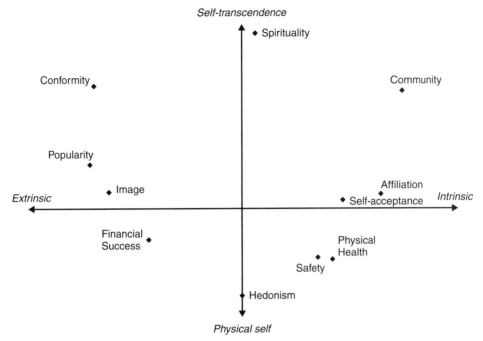

FIGURE 7.1 **Two-Dimensional Representation of 11 Goals Across Cultures**
Source: Grouzet, F. M. E., Kasser, T., Ahuvia, A., Dols, J. M. F., Kim, Y., Lau, S., et al. (2005). The structure of goal contents across 15 cultures. *Journal of Personality and Social Psychology, 89,* 800–816. Copyright American Psychological Association. Reprinted by permission.

to be internally consistent and in opposition to its counterpart. That is, people who rated intrinsic goals as important in their lives also rated extrinsic goals as less important. Those giving high ratings to goals related to physical pleasure and survival gave lower ratings to self-transcendent goals.

INTRINSIC VERSUS EXTRINSIC GOALS **Intrinsic goals** are defined by their connection to important psychological needs that are assumed to make their pursuit and fulfillment inherently satisfying. Of the 11 goals measured in this study, intrinsic goals included self-acceptance, affiliation, community feeling, physical health, and safety. **Extrinsic goals** express desires for external rewards or praise and admiration from others and are assumed to be less inherently or deeply satisfying when pursued or attained. Extrinsic goals included financial success, image, popularity, and conformity. Goals on this dimension showed high internal consistency.

PHYSICAL VERSUS SELF-TRANSCENDENT GOALS
Goals associated with the physical versus self-transcendence dimension showed less internal

consistency and some overlap with intrinsic and extrinsic goals. Some pleasure/survival and self-transcendence goals may also have intrinsic and extrinsic components. Physical goals were defined by hedonism (seeking pleasure and avoiding pain) and needs for safety, security, and good health. Financial success, interpreted as the means to achieve physical goals, was also associated with this dimension. Self-transcendence goals encompassed needs for a spiritual/religious understanding of life, community feeling promoted by benefiting others and improving the world, and conformity needs reflecting desires to fulfill social obligations and be accepted by others.

Taken as a template for the content of human goals, this study suggests that personal goals can be classified according to how much importance people assign to intrinsic psychological needs as opposed to extrinsic rewards on one hand, and how much value is given to physical pleasures and survival rather than self-transcendent spiritual understandings on the other. The authors conclude, ". . . as they approach their goals in life, people apparently take into consideration their psychological needs (intrinsic), their physical survival and pleasure (physical), their desires for rewards and praise (extrinsic), and their quest to have a meaningful place in the broader world (self-transcendence)" (Grouzet et al., 2005, p. 813).

Needs, values, and goals that are endorsed by many cultures necessarily have general rather than specific content. Their universality stems from shared human experience and their basis in the biological, psychological, and social requirements of life. The particular *expression* of goal-related motivations obviously *does* vary among cultures and between individuals. For example, opportunities to develop individualized career goals and fulfill financial aspirations are clearly more limited in poor countries than in rich ones. Just as clearly, people within the same culture, given the opportunity and sufficient resources, pursue a wide array of careers based on their unique talents, desires, and self-conceptions. In other words, the general content and prioritization of personal goals is clearly influenced by culture, but the specifics of a person's goals and his or her manner of expression are highly individualized. Recent theories give personal goals a prominent role in people's self-understanding and self-initiated goal strivings, and they help explain how general goals and motivations become personalized within each person's unique self-conception.

THE PERSONALIZATION OF GOALS IN SELF-CONCEPT

Suppose you were given the task of writing a relatively complete personal history that covered significant life experiences from your past, who you are in the present, and where you're headed in the future. What would such a description include? Certainly you would write about important life experiences, significant relationships, and the personal qualities and traits that define who you are as a unique individual. Odds are that you would also describe personally relevant goals that you have achieved in the past, goals that you are working to accomplish in the present, and goals that you hope to achieve in the future. In short, our self-concept is partly defined by goals that extend across time from past, through present, to future—who I've been, who I am now, and who I might become.

The aspect of self-concept defined by future goals is captured in the idea of "possible selves" as described by Markus and Nurius (1986). **Possible selves** encompass all the potential futures we can imagine for ourselves. Future selves may be positive, in the form of ideal selves that we want to become, or negative, in the form of selves that we are afraid of becoming. Possible selves we hope to become might include a physically fit self, a wealthy self, a popular self, a loved self, a respected self, or a successful, "A-student" self. Selves we fear becoming might be an overweight self, an unemployed self, a depressed or anxious self, a lonely self, a lazy self, or an academically failing self.

A person's self-concept plays an important role in processing information, regulating emotion, and motivating behavior (see Baumeister, 1998; Markus & Wurf, 1987; Pittman, 1998, for reviews). Possible selves are most relevant to the third function of self—the motivational view (see Markus & Nurius, 1986; Markus & Wurf, 1987). This is because possible selves provide a connection between the past, present, and desired future self and therefore provide motivation for self-change. As Markus and Nurius note, past, present, and future possible selves are distinct and separable, but are also intimately connected. Consider a young college woman working toward her degree who, as a child, experienced the divorce of her parents and the resulting financial hardship suffered by her mother and siblings. This hardship was partly due to her mother's lack of education and inability to get a good job. It is not hard to imagine how this life event might influence this student's thinking about her present and future self. Her present, college-student self may be derived and motivated, in part, by a desire to avoid the past self represented by her mother's experience, and her possible selves would likely include images of a successful career and financial independence.

The idea of possible selves makes an explicit connection between the self and motivation. "An individual's repertoire of possible selves can be viewed as the cognitive manifestations of enduring goals, aspirations, motives, fears and threats. Possible selves provide the specific self-relevant form, meaning, organization, and direction to these dynamics. As such, they provide the essential link between the self-concept and motivation" (Markus & Nurius, 1986, p. 954). In other words, possible selves personalize the form and content of more general needs, values, and goals. In the example above, the young woman's motivation for college *could* be thought of as expressing a general need for achievement, or the value of security achieved through a successful career. However, such explanations, while perhaps revealing at a general level, would miss the unique basis and specific content of the young woman's motivation for college. That is, goals are not typically thought of or pursued in the abstract. We may all have achievement needs, and we may all value security, but for a particular individual, it is "my" achievement of "my" goals that is most important, meaningful, and motivating. As Markus and Nurius describe it, "there is a piece of self" in each of our personal goals (1986, p. 961).

The self is increasingly recognized as an important basis for understanding the what, why, and how of goal-directed behavior, and the relation of goals to happiness and well-being (e.g., Brunstein, Schultheiss, & Grassman, 1998; Deci & Ryan, 2000; Lyubomirsky, Sheldon, & Schkade, 2005; Sheldon & Elliot, 1999). Our self-conception helps answer questions concerning *what* goals we choose to pursue and *why* they are important. The self can be viewed as translating broader sources of motivation into their unique individual expression, assigning importance to particular goal-directed actions (Markus & Nurius, 1986; Markus & Wurf, 1987; Vallacher & Wegner, 1987), and serving an executive function in the control and regulation of behavior toward goal achievement (e.g., Austin & Vancouver, 1996; Baumeister, 1998; Carver & Scheier, 1998; Higgins, 1996; Karolyi, 1999). Many researchers would give self-defining goals a top position in a hierarchy of goal-related motivations. Among our many goals, aspirations, needs, and values, those most central to our sense of self are likely to be most important in organizing and directing our lives.

WHAT GOALS CONTRIBUTE MOST TO WELL-BEING?

Goal Progress, Achievement, and Importance

Research supports the general notion that progressing toward and achieving personally important goals increases people's satisfaction with their lives and themselves (e.g., Brunstein, 1993; Cantor & Sanderson, 1999; Emmons, 1996; Emmons & Kaiser, 1996; McGregor & Little, 1998). For example, a semester-long study found that students' perceived progress toward achieving their personal goals was significantly correlated with increases in positive emotion and life satisfaction (Brunstein, 1993). Student goals included such things as improving a relationship with a romantic partner, learning enough Spanish to study in Spain, becoming more independent from parents, and learning to be more assertive and confident with others.

Research also supports a general relationship between goal importance and personal satisfaction. Goals that express fundamental and self-defining aspects of personal identity are likely to be the most deeply satisfying when pursued and achieved. Although mundane activities such as fixing a meal, cleaning your house, and paying bills can bring some satisfaction, these goals are relatively less important to our self-conception and therefore tend to produce smaller and more temporary effects on well-being.

Do these conclusions mean that, as long as they are important to us, it doesn't matter much which goals we pursue or why we choose to pursue them? At first thought, the answer may seem to be yes. After all, why would a person expend energy trying to achieve a goal if it didn't have some importance, and if it is important, shouldn't progress or attainment increase feelings of well-being? But several important qualifications temper this general conclusion. Not all personally important goals and not all progress toward goal achievement lead to increased satisfaction. Both the content of a goal and the reasons for pursuing it have been found to affect well-being. Our review of goal research for this chapter focuses on both the "what" of goal content and the "why" of goal motivations, and how each affects well-being. That is, what types of goals and underlying goal motives are related to enhanced happiness and well-being?

Goals whose effects on well-being depend primarily on self-regulation issues will be discussed in Chapter 8. The well-being outcomes for some goals are largely determined by the ease or difficulty people experience in regulating their actions and staying on course toward goal achievement. For example, the pursuit of avoidance or abstract goals creates a host of self-regulation problems.

The Matching Hypothesis

A number of studies support a **matching hypothesis** as a way of sorting out which goals lead to increased well-being and which do not (see Harackiewicz & Sansone, 1991; Lyubomirsky et al., 2005). The matching hypothesis suggests that the degree of person-goal fit determines the effect of goal progress and goal achievement on well-being. Pursuit of goals that express or fulfill (i.e., "match") an individual's needs, values, motives, or self-conception is more likely to increase well-being than pursuit of goals that do not fit or match with the person. In other words, if you want to increase your happiness and well-being, the "right" goals to pursue are those that fit and express your most important needs, desires, and sense of self. The "wrong" goals are those that are unrelated to these deeper, enduring personal characteristics. The personal characteristics that underlie goals may be unique to the individual or shared by all people. For example, goals related to belongingness needs may make successful relationships and social interactions universally important to well-being.

To test the matching hypothesis, researchers obtain measures of underlying motivations (such as needs, values, or aspects of self) and ask participants to generate a list of important personal goals. Participants' goal-related activities and efforts, and their perceived progress toward achieving goals are also assessed. These measures are then related to assessments of well-being across some time period. The matching hypothesis is supported if goal-directed activities and progress that are related to the underlying motive show higher positive correlations with well-being than goals that are unrelated to such a motive.

A number of studies have found support for this underlying motive-goal-well-being relationship. For example, one study investigated the relationship between goals and two fundamental motives, defined as agency and communion (Brunstein et al., 1998). Agency refers to needs for achievement, power, mastery, independence, and self-assertion. Communion refers to needs for affiliation and intimacy, as expressed in a desire to form close relationships with others. People vary in the relative importance of these two general motivations. Some of us are primarily oriented toward agency and others toward communion. Brunstein and his colleagues examined whether goal-motive congruence (or incongruence) predicted well-being.

In two studies, one spanning 2 weeks and the other a semester, college students were classified as either agency-motivated or communion-motivated based on established measures assessing the relative dominance of each motive.

The relationship between personal goals and agency–communion motives was assessed by asking students to describe specific, current and future goals related to each motive. Goals related to agency were defined as "striving for achievement and mastery experiences," and "striving for independence, social influence, and self reliance." Personal goals relating to communion were defined as "striving for intimacy and interpersonal closeness," and "striving for affiliation and friendly social contacts." Examples of goals reflecting an agency motive included improving understanding of a particular subject, becoming a more independent person, winning an athletic competition, and convincing parents that "my college major is the right thing for me." Communion-related goals included such things as improving a romantic relationship, being more helpful to a sick mother, spending more time with friends, and developing new friendships with fellow dorm mates. Students also made various ratings of progress, commitment, attainability, effort, and success in relation to their personal goals and recorded daily well-being at selected intervals.

Results provide strong support for the matching hypothesis. Students who were achieving personal goals congruent with their underlying motive-orientation showed increased well-being over the course of the study. This was true for students who focused either on achievement (agency) or on relationships (communion). Conversely, students progressing toward motive-incongruent goals, or who were not achieving motive-congruent goals, showed lower levels (or even declines) in well-being. The important point of the matching hypothesis is that the happiness we obtain from fulfilling our goals depends on their fit with our primary motives in life. You can easily imagine a college student who excels academically, but is unhappy because he wants, but does not have, many close friends. Similarly, an outgoing student enjoying an active social life may be unhappy because she has a strong need to succeed in college, but is struggling academically. In short, not all our goal achievements make us happier.

In a similar vein, our fundamental values also help determine what goals and activities bring us the most satisfaction. A recent study examined college students' value-orientation in moderating the degree of satisfaction gained from different types of activities (Oishi, Diener, Suh, & Lucas, 1999). The

10 values in Schwartz's value theory (discussed earlier in this chapter) were used to ascertain participants' value priorities. The 10 values were paired in all possible combinations, and participants were asked to identify which value in each pair held the higher priority for them. This process yielded a prioritized list of each person's values. Participants also rated their daily well-being across 23 days, gave satisfaction ratings for value-related activities, rated global life satisfaction, and rated satisfaction in the specific life domains of romantic relationships, finances, grades, family, and social life. Consistent with the matching hypothesis, success in value-congruent life domains and activities correlated significantly with both global and daily well-being. For example, the global life satisfaction ratings of students who placed high importance on the value of Achievement were heavily influenced by their degree of satisfaction with their most important achievement domain of life—namely, college grades. The global satisfaction ratings of those who prioritized Benevolence were most affected by their success in the domain of social life; for those prioritizing Conformity (honoring parents and elders), the greatest impact came from their degree of satisfaction with family life. Daily well-being was also significantly related to activities that engaged students' most important values. Whether students had a "good" day had much to do with whether they had engaged in activities that expressed their most important values. Students prioritizing Universalism (justice, peace, preserving the environment) reported that recycling efforts and involvement in civic affairs were very satisfying, while activities like shopping and buying expensive clothes were more satisfying to students who placed a premium on Power (prestige and wealth). Overall, a student's value priorities had a determining effect on what areas of life and what activities were the most satisfying.

What Explains the Matching Hypothesis?

The matching hypothesis suggests a simple answer to the question of which goals do or do not enhance well-being. Goals that fit a person's needs, values, and sense of self are likely to increase well-being, while goals that are mismatched with the person will likely lead to no change, or perhaps even to diminished well-being. What explains the importance of person-goal fit for the satisfaction we obtain from the pursuit and achievement of our goals?

PERSONAL GOALS AND SELF-REALIZATION   Waterman (1990, 1993) suggests that goals fitting with core aspects of the self (such as deeply held values) produce intense feelings of involvement, meaningfulness, and satisfaction because they express our "true selves" and our inner potentials. Personally expressive goal activities provide a strong sense of life purpose: "This is who I am and this is what I was meant to do." In short, to the extent that our goals match and express our core sense of self, they become avenues for self-realization and self-fulfillment. Such goals acquire particular value and a deeper meaning because their achievement affirms and completes our sense of self (Vallacher & Wegner, 1987; Wicklund & Gollwitzer, 1982).

Personally expressive goals are particularly important to eudaimonic well-being (i.e., to well-being related to meaning, vitality, and healthy functioning), as opposed to hedonic well-being (which is defined by positive emotions and life satisfaction) (see Chapter 2). From a eudaimonic perspective, it is possible for some goals to increase our happiness, but not contribute to increased meaning or vitality. For example, a college student may be happy with his part-time job because it is easy and provides enjoyable relations with co-workers (in other words, the job has high hedonic value). However, the work required by the job may not be personally meaningful if it does not engage significant aspects of his identity and talents (low eudaimonic value). The reverse can also be true. A goal may be unpleasant to carry out (low hedonic value), but personally meaningful (high eudaimonic value). Being a good parent, for example, requires many unpleasant tasks, such as changing dirty diapers, saying "no" to some of your children's requests, and taking care of sick children. Yet, people regard raising kids as one of life's most deeply satisfying experiences (Kahneman, Krueger, Schkade, Schwarz, & Stone, 2004).

Research supports these distinctions. A variety of goal achievements may increase our hedonic enjoyment. However, achieving goals that express our authentic or true selves seems to contribute most to an enhanced sense of meaning and purpose in life, and to greater psychological health and vitality (e.g., McGregor & Little, 1998; Ryan & Deci, 2000; Sanderson & Cantor, 1995; Sheldon & Elliot, 1999; Sheldon & Kasser, 1995; Sheldon, Ryan, Rawsthorne,

& Ilardi, 1997). McGregor and Little (1998) found that success in accomplishing non-expressive goals was more strongly related to increased happiness than to increased meaning. Just the opposite was found for goals expressing core aspects of self. Self-defining goals were associated with an increased sense of purpose and meaningfulness in life, but less with increased happiness. One explanation for the well-being effects of person-goal matching may involve the satisfaction derived from personally expressive goals. Such goals seem particularly related to enhanced eudaimonic well-being.

INTRINSIC VERSUS EXTRINSIC GOALS Earlier in this chapter, in the section on "Personal Goals Across Cultures," the general differences between intrinsic and extrinsic goals were described. The basis for the distinction has to do with whether the purpose of an activity is defined primarily by internal or external rewards (Pittman, 1998; Waterman et al., 2003). Intrinsic goals have much in common with personally expressive goals, as discussed above. Intrinsic motivation refers to reasons for engaging in an activity that are focused on the activity itself. The reward, value, and goal of the activity are intrinsic to the "doing." That is, the activity acts as its own reward because it is enjoyable, highly interesting, or personally expressive, or creates feelings of intense involvement and mastery. In contrast, the reasons that define extrinsic motivation are focused on outcomes. The activity is a means to an end, where the end is a desirable outcome. The value or purpose of the activity is defined, not by the "doing," but by the end result.

Intrinsic and extrinsic motivation and goals are not inherently incompatible. Most would agree that an ideal job is one that is personally satisfying in terms of permitting the expression of our interests and talents (intrinsic), and also provides an income that supports a comfortable material life (extrinsic). However, research has shown that problems and dissatisfaction may result if the pursuit of extrinsic goals interferes with fulfillment of the intrinsically satisfying goals that determine happiness and well-being. Kasser and Ryan (1993) suggest that extrinsic goals can lead to negative consequences when they become a person's dominant motivation. The intrinsic–extrinsic distinction offers a second explanation for the matching hypothesis. Goals that match with the person are more likely to be intrinsically satisfying. Goals that

do not match may have extrinsic value, but do not necessarily increase well-being.

AUTONOMOUS VERSUS CONTROLLED MOTIVATION
A third explanation for the positive relation between person-goal matching and well-being concerns one's reasons for pursuing a goal. Self-concordance theory is a recent line of thinking that describes how the reasons behind goal pursuit are critical to well-being outcomes (Sheldon & Elliot, 1999). Research supporting the theory suggests that pursuing goals for the "right" reasons leads to better goal achievement and personal adjustment. According to self-concordance theory, the "right reasons" have to do with ". . . the feelings of ownership that people have (or do not have) regarding their self-initiated goals" (Sheldon & Houser-Marko, 2001, p. 152). Sheldon and his colleagues have found that "not all personal goals are personal" in terms of how people experience them (Sheldon & Elliot, 1998, p. 546). Self-concordant goals reflect **autonomous motives** and freely chosen reasons for goal pursuit that generate feelings of ownership and personal expressiveness and lead to increased well-being. In contrast, **controlled motivation** refers to cases in which people pursue goals that they have not freely chosen, or that are not personally expressive. For example, let's say one student is given the opportunity to write a research paper on a topic of great personal interest and relevance to him, while another student is assigned by her professor to write a paper on a topic that has nothing to do with her inherent interests. Concordance theory would predict greater enjoyment, fulfillment, and well-being for the student who experiences personal ownership of his task because he freely chose it, and whose task provides him with an opportunity for personal expressiveness. In the case of the assigned writing project, the writer may not internalize or feel a strong sense of ownership of the goal. This may reduce both the effort expended to achieve the goal and the emotional benefits of goal attainment.

The autonomous motives that define self-concordance may contribute to the well-being effects of person-goal matching. It seems likely that goals which match an individual's needs, values, and personal identity would also be freely chosen and experienced with the sense of ownership described by self-concordant theory. In other words, matched goals may also be self-concordant goals. Some amount of the increased well-being associated with matching may be due to this connection with self-concordance.

The distinction between autonomous and controlled motivations also suggests an important qualification to the matching hypothesis. Even a goal that fits the person may not increase well-being if that goal is not also freely chosen. Many careers might fit our interests, talents, and values, but it is the career we, ourselves select that will likely produce the strongest commitment and lead to the greatest satisfaction. Matching, by itself, may not be sufficient to ensure increased well-being from working toward and achieving our goals. Both the "right goals" and the "right reasons" seem to be necessary.

Focus on Research: Happiness and Success in College

Do students' reasons for attending college make a difference in terms of academic success and satisfaction with college life? This was the general question Sheldon and Houser-Marko (2001) addressed when they conducted a study to test self-concordance theory. They examined the relationships between self-concordant goals and measures of success, well-being, and adjustment during freshmen students' first year of college. They were interested in two specific questions. First, do students coming to college with self-concordant goals fare better than students with non-concordant goals? Second, can the increased happiness derived from goal progress and achievement be maintained and provide the basis for further enhanced well-being, or do people slip back to their original levels of happiness?

Following earlier work on **self-determination theory** (Deci & Ryan, 1991; see Chapter 2), the extent of self-concordance was defined according to four degrees of internalization and ownership: external, introjected, identified, and intrinsic. Each term refers to different reasons for pursuing a particular goal, with these reasons varying along a continuum from controlled/imposed to autonomous/freely-chosen (Sheldon & Houser-Marko, 2001). The following descriptions and example items (arranged from least- to most-autonomous) summarize concepts presented by Sheldon and Houser-Marko (2001, p. 155).

External motives refer to the rewards, approval, praise, or situational demands that explain why we strive for a goal. These motives are the most controlled and least self-concordant. Example item: "You strive for this goal because somebody else wants you to, or because the situation seems to compel it."

Introjected motives involve negative emotions we may experience if we don't try to attain certain goals. These motives are also considered to reflect controlled motives and therefore are not self-concordant. Example item: "You strive for this goal because you would feel ashamed, guilty, or anxious if you didn't."

Identified motives involve valuing a goal because of its personal importance, though people may sometimes come to value a goal because of the influence of others. For example, a teacher might foster respect for the environment among her students. In this case, the original source of the goal is external. However, "identified" means that others (in this case, the students) have internalized the goal and made it their own. Example item: "You strive for this goal because you really believe it's an important goal to have."

Intrinsic motives involve emotional pleasure and enjoyment derived from pursuing a goal. Intrinsic motives are the most autonomous and self-concordant goal motives. Example item: "You strive for this goal because of the enjoyment or stimulation which that goal provides you."

Nearly 200 freshmen at the University of Missouri–Columbia were asked to list their eight most important personal goals as they entered their first semester of college. Getting good grades, getting involved in campus organizations, making friends, not gaining weight, and maintaining weekly contact with parents were among the goals students described. Students categorized their reasons for pursuing each goal according to the four motives described above. Twice each semester students also rated how well they were progressing toward each of their eight goals. At the beginning of the spring semester, students could revise their list of eight goals or retain the ones they had listed in the fall.

Students' reasons for college attendance were measured and classified according to the four levels along the autonomous-to-controlled continuum of motivation. For example, did students feel they "had to" attend college because of parental pressure, because all their friends were going, or because they believed that college was the only way to get a rewarding career (external motives)? Would they feel guilty or anxious if they didn't go, perhaps because they worried they would disappoint their parents, or be unable to get a good job (introjected motives)? Was college attendance motivated by the personal importance and value of a college education that they may have been taught by parents or high school teachers (identified motives)? Or was the primary motivation for college based on the anticipated enjoyment and stimulation that result from encountering intellectual challenge, meeting new friends, learning about new ideas and people with different lifestyles, and being on their own, away from family (intrinsic motives)?

Well-being measures were taken several times during each semester. Students completed measures of social/emotional/academic adjustment to college and measures of their progress toward establishing healthy personal, social, and occupational identities. Academic performance was assessed by students' fall and spring semester grades. Parents and peers also rated each student in the study on several of the well-being and motivation measures to provide a validity check of student responses.

Results support the importance of pursuing self-concordant goals. Students with self-concordant goals did better than those with less concordant goals. In the first-semester phase of the study, students who had expressed identified and intrinsic reasons for college attendance and specific semester goals were more likely to earn grades higher than predicted by their scores on a college placement test called the ACT, and were more likely to attain their personal goals. In turn, goal attainment was predictive of better social, emotional, and academic adjustment to college, clearer personal identity development, and an increased likelihood of adopting even more self-concordant goals in the second-semester phase of the study. The second-semester phase examined whether the benefits of self-concordant goal attainment would be maintained and provide a basis for further increases in well-being. Many students lost some of the well-being they had gained during the first semester, and such losses were related to poor progress toward personal goals in the second semester. However, those students who continued to make progress toward their personal goals in the second semester were able to maintain and, in some cases, even increase beyond previous gains in well-being. This latter finding suggests the possibility of an upward increase in well-being similar to the one described by Fredrickson's broaden-and-build theory of positive emotions (see Chapter 3).

According to Fredrickson's theory, positive emotions help build personal resources that con-

tribute to greater effectiveness and health, thereby producing an upward spiral of well-being. In a similar fashion, self-concordant goals expressing intrinsic and identified motivations appear to contribute to greater goal success which, in turn, increases well-being. Enhanced well-being may then increase the likelihood of pursuing additional self-concordant goals in the future, thus contributing to greater well-being and continuing the upward spiral of increased happiness and well-being. Sheldon and Houser-Marko (2001) note that keeping this cycle going is hard work because, as their data show, the upward spiral of well-being seems to require continued success in attaining personal goals. Given the uncertainties of life and setbacks in achieving our goals, the risk of backsliding to baseline levels of well-being is difficult to avoid (see Chapter 5 for a discussion of adaptation processes). However, Sheldon and Houser-Marko speculate that if increased well-being can be sustained long enough, perhaps an individual may permanently alter her level of expected happiness and adopt a new sense of self as a happy person. This, in turn, might create a self-fulfilling prophecy in which the person thinks, feels, and acts in ways that sustain the new self-definition.

We began this section with the question, "Which goals contribute most to well-being?" Research provides the following answers: Goals that (1) fit or match a person's needs, values, and motives; (2) are deeply expressive of personal identity; (3) are oriented toward intrinsically satisfying activities; and (4) have been autonomously chosen. By implication, goals that are less likely to increase well-being have the opposite characteristics (i.e., goals that are mismatched, disconnected from identity, extrinsic, and arise from controlled origins). Our discussion of goals that are related and unrelated to increased life satisfaction provides a basis for understanding a well-documented finding in positive psychology concerning materialistic goals. People who give high goal priority to the pursuit of money, possessions, social recognition, and physical appearance are likely to be unhappy. Studies reviewed in Chapter 6 concluded that, beyond the point necessary to satisfy basic needs, more money does not have any appreciable positive effect on personal happiness. Research on materialistic life goals not only affirms this conclusion, but also suggests that the single-minded pursuit of money can cause unhappiness.

MATERIALISM AND ITS DISCONTENTS

Psychologists will hopefully excuse our play on Freud's classic work, *Civilization and Its Discontents* (Freud, 1961, initially published in 1930), for the title of this section. The thematic parallels between the discontents of civilization and the discontents of materialism are strong. Freud described the frustrations, sufferings, and dilemmas that result from the inevitable conflict between the self-centered needs of individuals and the co-operative and self-sacrificing requirements of civilized society. Studies of materialism seem to describe a similar dilemma between what Ryan (2002, p. ix) referred to as the "religions of consumerism and materialism" in affluent societies and the unhappiness that befalls their faithful followers.

Materialism and consumption can be blamed for any number of macro-level social and environmental ills, from the great divide between the "haves" and the "have-nots" to global warming and environmental degradation. Psychological studies offer a more micro-level view of the individual consequences of materialistic life aspirations. The research literature documents many personal problems that are both causes and consequences of materialism. Recent theories help explain how materialistic aspirations undermine well-being and why people may come to embrace materialistic life values. We begin with a review of one of the first studies to show the discontents of materialism.

In an article titled, "A dark side of the American dream: Correlates of financial success as a central life aspiration," Kasser and Ryan (1993) examined the relationship between college students' life priorities and measures of well-being. The relative importance of four goals was used to assess students' central life aspirations. Life aspirations were assessed in two ways: a measure of guiding principles and an aspiration index. The guiding principles measure asked students to rank-order the importance of five values: money, family security, global welfare, spirituality, and hedonic enjoyment. The life aspirations index involved rating the importance and likelihood of attaining four goals. Several specific statements represented each goal. *Self-acceptance* refers to people's desire for personal autonomy, psychological growth, and self-esteem. Examples of statements that students rated for this goal were: "At the end of your life you will look back on your life as meaningful and complete." "You will be in charge of your life." "You will know

and accept who you really are." *Affiliation* goals were defined by the importance of family and good friends. Specific statements included: "You will have good friends that you can count on." "You will share your life with someone you love." "You will have people who care about you and who are supportive." *Community feeling* reflects a desire to make the world a better place by contributing to the common good. Statements in this category included: "You will help others improve their lives." "You will donate time or money to charity." "You will work for the betterment of society." *Financial success* is related to the importance placed on attaining wealth and material success. Statements in this goal category included: "You will be financially successful." "You will have a high-status job." "You will buy things just because you want them."

Assessment of health and well-being included measures of self-actualization, vitality, control orientation, and several measures of physical and emotional health. The self-actualization measure assessed accurate perceptions of reality, sense of social interest, personal autonomy, and engagement in relationships. The vitality measure assessed the degree to which people feel energetic, vigorous, and "alive" in their physical and mental activities. Control orientation refers to the relative importance of external factors and rewards in shaping a person's motives and goals.

In three separate studies involving nearly 500 young adults, Kasser and Ryan (1996) found a consistent inverse relationship between financial aspirations and well-being. In other words, placing high priority on financial success was related to lower well-being. Specifically, those people who rated the extrinsic goals of wealth and material success as more important than the intrinsic goals (such as self-acceptance, affiliation, and contributions to the community) showed lower levels of self-actualization, life vitality, and social adjustment, and greater depression and anxiety. It is important to note that the key variable here is the dominance of financial aspirations over other life goals. It was not financial aspirations *per se* that were related to lower well-being. Diminished health and well-being were found only for those people who consistently rated finances as *more* important than the other three goals. Other studies found that, in addition to financial success, emphases on social recognition, social status, and physical appearance were also related to lower well-being (Kasser, 2002; Kasser & Ryan, 1996).

Since the publication of Ryan and Kasser's study, research has documented a number of negative life outcomes associated with materialistic aspirations (see Kasser, 2002, 2004; Kasser & Kanner, 2004, for detailed reviews).

People who are highly committed to extrinsic materialistic goals score lower on a variety of self-reported and independent assessments of quality of life, compared to those who either do not assign high value to materialistic goals, or who show a balance between their financial and intrinsic motivations. Materialistic individuals suffer more physical illness and anxiety symptoms, experience fewer positive emotions, watch more television, use more drugs and alcohol, are at higher risk for personality disorders and depression, and report less satisfying relationships with others. In addition, the general relationship between goal progress and increased well-being that is true for most goals does not hold true in the case of materialistic goals. For example, Sheldon and Elliot (1998) found that making progress toward materialistic aspirations was not related to increases in short- or longer-term well-being. These conclusions have been documented among people within many different age groups, social and economic backgrounds, and cultures. That is, the connections between materialistic values and lower well-being are not confined to American culture. Kasser and Kanner (2004) note studies in Australia, England, Germany, South Korea, Romania, and Russia replicate findings within the U.S. samples.

In short, no matter who or where you are, materialism appears to undercut happiness.

Figure 7.2 shows results from a study by Diener and Oishi (2000) of 7,000 college students in 41 different countries. The importance students assigned to money and love are plotted against their self-reported ratings of life satisfaction. As you can see, the more importance students gave to money, the less they were satisfied with their lives. Love showed an opposite relationship to life satisfaction.

Why Are Materialists Unhappy?

THE CONTENT OF MATERIALISTIC GOALS Why would placing more importance on financial success than on self-acceptance, affiliation, and community contribute to personal unhappiness? A "goal contents" explanation suggests that extrinsic goals (such as financial success or social status) are less satisfying

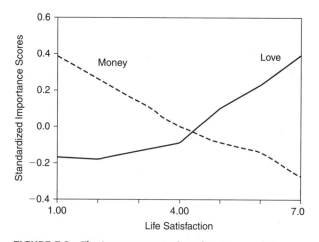

FIGURE 7.2 The Importance Assigned to Love and Money in Relationship to Self-Reported Life Satisfaction
Source: Diener, E., & Biswas-Diener, R. (2002). Will money increase subjective well-being? A literature review and guide to needed research. *Social Indicators Research, 57,* 119–169. Copyright Kluwer Academic Publishing. Reprinted by permission.

than intrinsic goals (such as personal growth or emotional intimacy with others), because intrinsic goals reflect basic psychological needs, satisfaction of which is required for health and happiness (Sheldon, Ryan, Deci, & Kasser, 2004). Intrinsic goals are inherently rewarding because of their connection to fundamental human needs. Extrinsic goals, on the other hand, may not fulfill our most important needs and therefore pursuing them, perhaps at the expense of intrinsically satisfying goals, may lead to lower well-being.

The dominance of extrinsic financial goals may also interfere with the pursuit of intrinsic goals and divert people from the more important and deeper satisfactions in life. For example, people who value self-acceptance are interested in developing the self-understanding necessary to direct their own lives in a manner that is consistent with their talents, inner potentials, and sense of self. As we have seen, goals that are consistent with the self tend to enhance well-being. In contrast, people with strong financial aspirations may deflect their attention away from self-examination and self-expression and make choices that diminish personal satisfaction. Choosing a particular career only because you can make a lot of money, without regard for the kind of work you find meaningful or satisfying, is probably one example of a recipe for later unhappiness.

A high level of concern with finances may also cause people to ignore or fail to invest in developing the close, supportive relationships that are such an important source of well-being. In line with this possibility, a recent series of studies by Vohs and her colleagues (Vohs, Mead, & Goode, 2006) showed that simply *thinking* about money seems to shift people's thoughts toward self-sufficiency and independence from others. Money seems to make us feel self-sufficient and able to make it on our own, but at some cost to our interpersonal relationships. Compared to control groups, people primed to think about money were consistently found to be less helpful and sensitive to others and more desirous of being on their own and completing tasks independently. These findings reinforce the general conclusion that those human needs most important for well-being and personal happiness may be frustrated, ignored, or inadequately fulfilled among people who devote most of their time and energy to pursuing materialistic goals.

THE WHAT AND WHY OF MATERIALISTIC GOALS A second explanation emerged from a controversy concerning the relative importance of goal content and goal motive. Does the materialism–unhappiness association result from the *content* of materialistic goals (in other words, *what* is pursued) or from the *motive* that underlies them (in other words, *why* they are pursued)? As we have seen, the goal contents explanation is focused on how commitment to materialistic aspirations may divert attention away from fulfilling needs that would contribute more to happiness and well-being. On the other hand, the motive explanation focuses on the reason behind goal pursuit—specifically whether the reason is autonomous or controlled (Carver & Baird, 1998; Srivastava, Locke, & Bartol, 2001). As described in our earlier discussion of the self-concordance model, external rewards and introjected motives are controlled motives, while identified and intrinsic motives are autonomous or freely-chosen motives for goal striving.

Critics of the goal contents explanation argue that financial goals are likely to involve controlled sources of motivation, which have been linked to poor well-being outcomes. Desires for money, fame, social recognition, and popularity seem to fit especially well with the concept of controlled motives based on external rewards. Introjected motives stemming from unpleasant feelings of anxiety, guilt,

and insecurity might also lie behind materialistic strivings. In either case, it is the motive—not just goal content—that makes financial aspirations damaging to well-being. Financial goals may not necessarily reduce happiness if people have the "right" motives (i.e., autonomous ones). Carver and Baird (1998) argue that it is quite possible for a person to value a high-income career because of the excitement and enjoyment it brings (intrinsic motives), and/or because she truly believes it is valuable or important (identified motives). In these cases, well-being would likely increase rather than decrease. In Carver and Baird's view, two people with strong desires for wealth, fame, and fortune will have different well-being outcomes depending on whether their motives reflect external/introjected or identified/intrinsic motivations. In short, it's the motive—not goal content—that is important.

A recent study helps sort out explanations for the effects of "what" and "why" in people's goal strivings. Sheldon and his colleagues conducted three studies to evaluate the relative importance of goal content and goal motive (2004). The *content* of personal goals was evaluated by having participants rate the extent to which each of their specific self-identified goals contributed to achievement of six "possible futures." Three of these possible futures represented intrinsic values (achieving meaningful, close, and caring relationships; personal growth resulting in a fulfilled and a meaningful life; and contributing to society by making the world a better place). The other three possible futures were oriented toward extrinsic values (achieving financial success by getting a high-income job and having many material possessions; attaining popularity/fame, as measured by being known and admired by lots of people; and presenting an attractive physical image in terms of looking good and being attractive to others). Goal *motives* were assessed according to participants' ratings of the external, introjected, identified, and intrinsic motives for pursuing a goal. Well-being was assessed using standard measures of the balance of positive and negative emotions and life satisfaction.

Overall, the results of the three studies showed that *both* goal content *and* goal motive made independent contributions to well-being. The participants who expressed the highest levels of well-being were those who were pursuing intrinsic goals for autonomous reasons (i.e., identified or intrinsic motives). Lower well-being was reported by those who were pursuing extrinsic goals for which motivation was controlled (i.e., external or introjected motives). Some of the strongest evidence for the detrimental effects of extrinsic goals and controlled motivation on well-being was shown in one of Sheldon and colleagues' studies that assessed personal goals and well-being among college students over a 1-year period following graduation. Graduates with a controlled motivational orientation who were pursuing extrinsic goals (e.g., money and fame) reported lower levels of well-being than graduates who were striving toward intrinsic goals with autonomous motivations.

COMPENSATION FOR INSECURITY A third explanation for the link between an over-emphasis on financial goals and lower well-being focuses on psychological insecurities and unmet needs (Kasser, 2002, 2004; Kasser & Kanner, 2004; Solberg, Diener, & Robinson, 2004). Some theorists suggest that materialists may be unhappy people to begin with. People who are emotionally and socially insecure may view financial success as a means of enhancing their self-image and social image, thereby reducing their feelings of insecurity. Having lots of money may be seen as a way to "prove" oneself, gain the admiration of others, and compensate for unmet needs. This may seem like a vain and shallow illusion, but what parent wouldn't point with pride to their rich, successful son or daughter? And who hasn't had wishful fantasies of being rich and famous? Many social observers argue that American culture encourages the idea that "being somebody" means making lots of money and having expensive possessions (e.g., Cushman, 1999; Easterbrook, 2003; Paterson, 2006; Storey, 1999).

Why Do People Adopt Materialistic Values?

Three factors appear to exert important influence on the development of materialistic values: (1) growing up in a consumer culture; (2) psychological insecurity; and (3) the connection between materialism and death. Each of these will be explored below.

CONSUMER CULTURE Self, culture, and personal goals are interlinked. All cultures shape children's developing sense of who they are and who they should strive to become. The love of parents, acceptance by peers, and success in life tasks are, at least in part, contingent on embracing your culture's values and practices. In contributing to the general shape of self, culture also influences personal goals. As we saw in Chapter 6, beliefs about the meaning of the good life and how to achieve it differ between Western and Eastern cultures. While the specific meaning and expression vary by individual, culture sets many of the foundational assumptions and dominant values that define success and happiness.

Within consumer societies, the influence of culture on goals provides one avenue for the adoption of materialistic aspirations and values. Even a casual observer can note children's exposure to countless socializing messages and models promoting the individual and social benefits of money and material possessions. Some 12 billion dollars are spent annually on the marketing of products to kids in what Levin and Linn call the "commercialization of childhood" (Levin & Linn, 2004). Toy sales related to blockbuster children's movies like Star Wars and Harry Potter, now rival ticket revenues. Concern over the possible damaging effects of this commercialization led the governments of Norway and Sweden to prohibit ads from targeting children under age 12.

In the adult realm, we are all familiar with advertisements suggesting (either explicitly or implicitly) that our personal problems can be solved and our happiness ensured if we buy the "right" product or service. Some ads are pitched to people's vulnerabilities, such as feelings of inadequacy, social anxiety, boredom, loneliness, and concerns over poor appearance. Others offer the purchase of increased happiness, fun, fame, fortune, adventure, sex, romance, and the envy of friends.

The bottom line of these messages, as Kasser (2004) so aptly put it, is that the good life is the "goods" life. Such ads promote a materialistic value orientation described by Kasser and his colleagues as ". . . the belief that it's important to pursue the culturally sanctioned goals of attaining financial success, having nice possessions, having the right image (produced, in large part, through consumer goods), and having a high status (defined mostly by the size of one's pocketbook and the scope of one's possessions)" (Kasser, Ryan, Couchman, & Sheldon, 2004, p. 13). The key question is, as we buy the products and celebrate models of fame and fortune, do we also buy the assumption that a life centered around materialistic goals is the route to personal happiness?

For some social observers, the answer is clearly yes. Classic sociologists from Marx to Veblen have described the false needs and shallow, materialistic lives promoted by capitalistic societies (see Paterson, 2006; Storey, 1999, for reviews). From this view, consumption as a dominant cultural practice diverts attention from deeper life satisfactions and masks the power and control held by the few over the many. Taking a psychological perspective, Cushman (1990) argues that consumer economies have created an "empty self" by stripping away deeper and more enduring meanings and social connections associated with close family ties, community connections, and satisfying work. An empty self makes people particularly vulnerable to the "make-you-happy" messages of advertisements. However, Cushman believes that the marketplace only offers a "lifestyle solution" to problems of finding purpose and meaning in life. Having the "right" look and the right "stuff" is a poor and unsatisfying substitute for the deeper purposes and caring connections to others that promote healthy well-being.

On the other side of the debate are arguments that consumer societies offer unprecedented opportunities for freedom of choice in how people express their talents, interests, values, and personalities. From this perspective, consumer goods enhance, rather than constrain lifestyle alternatives. The diversity and easy availability of products and services supports highly individualized meanings of a good life. Positive psychology does not settle long-standing debates concerning the virtues and vices of consumerism. However, research does offer some clarification about who is most likely to embrace the materialistic messages of consumer cultures and, consequently, suffer their ill effects.

PSYCHOLOGICAL INSECURITY A growing body of evidence suggests that materialism may find its strongest support among insecure people. Doubts about self-worth and acceptance by others, frustrated needs, and economic hardship all appear to increase the odds of adopting materialistic life goals (see Kasser, 2002; Kasser & Kanner, 2004; Solberg et al., 2004, for reviews). The compensation explanation, discussed earlier, suggests that people may adopt materialistic goals to compensate for negative feelings related to insecurity and unmet needs. Expensive possessions and a big salary may serve as vehicles for obtaining social approval and a sense of self-worth among people whose social and self-competence needs have been frustrated or unfulfilled. This conclusion is supported by research, which has found a consistent relationship between unfulfilled basic needs and materialistic values. Unmet needs are assumed to create a sense of insecurity that may then lead to material goals as compensation. Parenting practices that do a poor job of meeting children's needs have been linked to a materialistic value orientation among children. Parents who are overly controlling, punitive, lacking in warmth, and unsupportive of their children's needs for independence and autonomy increase the odds of materialistic aspirations in their children. Increased materialism in children is also associated with parental divorce. Specifically, research findings suggest that this association results more from the fact that divorce disrupts the fulfillment of children's basic needs for emotional support, love and affection, than from reduced financial resources. Research reviewed by Kasser and Kanner (2004) also shows that people growing up in poor families, in poor countries, and during hard economic times tend to be more materialistic. It is not hard to imagine that poverty and economic stress would make people feel insecure and vulnerable, and that materialistic life goals might become a compensating solution.

MATERIALISM AND DEATH In his Pulitzer Prize winning book, *The Denial of Death*, cultural anthropologist Ernest Becker (1973) argued that fear of death is the ultimate and universal source of human insecurity. Freud focused on the conflicts and repressed feelings surrounding sexuality and death as the underpinnings of human behavior. In contrast, Becker argued that many of humans' individual and collective actions are motivated by a need to deny and blunt the fear caused by awareness of death as an inevitable fact of life. The after-life of religions, monuments from the Egyptian pyramids to modern skyscrapers, and the celebration of cultural heroes who triumph over threats to their destruction, all serve to deny the reality of death by creating symbols and icons suggesting that death can be transcended. The symbolic message of such icons is that we don't really die. Because death is intimately connected to nature, Becker viewed human efforts to control and subdue the natural environment as also expressing a death-defying motivation. Control over nature gives the illusion of control over death.

Within contemporary psychology, **terror management theory** has drawn on Becker's insights in describing how fear of death motivates attempts to restore a sense of safety and security (Greenberg, Solomon, & Pyszczynski, 1999; Solomon, Greenberg, & Pyszczynski, 1991). Terror management theory places fear of death in the context of evolution and the unique ways that each species strives to ensure its own self-preservation. Human survival depends primarily on intelligence and sociability, because our physical defenses are relatively weak compared to other animals. The evolutionary perspective goes on to suggest that, as intelligent social animals, our ancestors developed tools, weapons, and housing, and formed cooperative groups that promoted proliferation and prosperous survival of the species.

Human intelligence, however, comes with a price tag. Intelligence brings with it self-awareness of being alive and the ability to contemplate our past, present, and future. Awareness of our future includes the certainty of our own death and the fact, as Becker so bluntly put it, that we will all end up underground as "food for worms" (1973, p. 26). Thinking of ourselves as worm-food is certainly unpleasant, if not repulsive. We are not likely to focus on this thought for long before we shift our attention to something a bit less gruesome. This mini-version of avoiding thoughts of death exemplifies the assumptions and logic of terror management theory. Humans share with all living things a fundamental biological drive for self-preservation, but humans are unique in their awareness of eventual death. This awareness has the potential to cause overwhelming and incapacitating terror that must be "managed" to reduce and avoid its potentially debilitating effects. Following Becker, terror management theory states that all cultures develop belief systems that serve as defenses against the terror of death. These beliefs give meaning and purpose to life and provide a basis for individual feelings of self-esteem and enduring value. Terror management theory predicts that confronting thoughts or images of death creates feelings of insecurity that motivate a defensive strengthening of worldviews and self-esteem, in order to restore a sense of security. Numerous studies provide support for these predictions (see Greenberg et al., 1999; Solomon, Greenberg, & Pyszczynski, 2004).

What does anxiety about death have to do with materialism? Since research has established a general link between insecurity and materialism, insecurities rooted in thoughts of death may also increase materialistic aspirations. Money, status, and possessions may provide a sense of safety and secu-

rity. To test this idea, Kasser and Sheldon (2000) assessed the preexisting materialistic value-orientation of college students by examining the relative importance they placed on intrinsic goals (self-acceptance, affiliation, community feeling) versus extrinsic goals (financial success, attractive appearance, social recognition). Students were then assigned to one of two conditions. In the *mortality salience* condition, students wrote about the prospect of their own death in terms of the feelings it aroused and what they believed would happen to their physical bodies after death. In the *control* condition, students wrote about listening to music. Next, students in both groups were asked to estimate their financial situation 15 years in the future. Financial expectations included their overall financial worth (salary, investments), pleasure spending (travel, clothes, entertainment), and the value of possessions (car, household possessions, etc.).

Consistent with predictions, students in the *mortality salience* condition gave estimates of future income and wealth that were considerably higher than the estimates given by students in the *control* group. In fact, in some cases, the estimates of students who had written about death were nearly twice as high as those who had written about listening to music. This result seems to stem from the effect of mortality salience, rather than from students' preexisting values. In other words, the financial expectations expressed at the end of the study were unrelated to students' preexisting values, as measured at the beginning of the study.

Further evidence for the effect of mortality salience was shown in a second study by the same authors. In this study, students were instructed to play the role of company owners who were making bids on timber harvest in a national forest. Students were told that if their bids were too small their company might not survive, but if all companies consistently made large bids, the forest resource might be lost. The researchers set up the same *mortality salience* and *control* conditions, and used the same writing assignments as they used in the study described above. Again, the process of thinking about their own death affected students' responses. Students in the *mortality salience* condition gave significantly higher timber bids, suggesting increased feelings of greed and a need to acquire more than others.

Solomon and his colleagues (2004), (the developers of terror management theory) provide a speculative, yet intriguing historical analysis of how death and materialism have become connected. They argue that the appeal of conspicuous consumption (buying well beyond one's needs) may lie in an unacknowledged, and perhaps unconscious, connection of money and material possessions with religion, spirituality, and the transcendence of death. Drawing on the work of Ernest Becker and others, their analysis suggests that the accumulation of money and possessions has a consistent historical link to prestige, symbolic meanings, and spirituality. The concept of money as simply a vehicle for the exchange of goods and services is actually quite recent. In ancient Egypt, for example, gold was largely ignored until it was used to replicate a shell that symbolized life-sustaining powers that would ward off death and prolong the existence of the souls of the already dead. The word *money*, itself, may have originated from the temple of Juno Moneta in Rome, where priests set up the first mints to produce coins. Coins were imprinted with images of gods, kings, and other religious symbols.

If all this seems a bit far-fetched, Solomon and his colleagues might ask you to examine the back of a dollar bill. What are the phrase, "*In God We Trust*" and a picture of pyramid with an eye at the top doing on a dollar bill? One interpretation is that these words and symbols connect money to spirituality and immortality. The pyramid may represent the path to immortality with the eye representing the world of God that is open to those who reach the top. Ernest Becker was convinced that money and the ability to pass on accumulated wealth to posterity were intimately bound up with the denial of death and with attempts to achieve a measure of immortality. You die, but your wealth and possessions live on. Money undoubtedly does contribute to a sense of security and control over life. A fat bank account probably does bring some comfort and a sense of security. The bottom line for both Becker and terror management theory is that, at some unconscious and symbolic level, money increases our sense of personal significance in the face of inevitable death.

Affluence and Materialism

The relationship between psychological insecurity and materialism appears to be a two-way street. As described above, insecurity is both a cause and a consequence of materialistic aspirations. Insecurity contributes to the adoption of materialistic goals

when people try to compensate for unmet needs through financial strivings. Insecurity and unhappiness are also consequences, because material aspirations reduce the likelihood that important needs will be fulfilled. The painful irony here is that materialism seems to frustrate the satisfaction of the very needs from which it originated. Recent studies by developmental psychologists suggest an additional irony to the materialism story. Not only is striving for financial success associated with unhappiness, but achieving it is also a potential source of problems for affluent families. Children growing up in affluent families may be at increased risk for a variety of emotional and behavioral problems caused by the beliefs and practices of their financially successful parents. Whatever beliefs and motivations led to parents' financial success, and whatever affluent parents may teach about material values, affluent lifestyles may not be healthy for children.

In Chapter 6, we reviewed national statistics showing that the nation's increased affluence over the last 50 years has not brought increased happiness. In fact, affluence was associated with some amount of increased misery in the form of higher rates of depression and other personal problems, particularly among young people. Recent investigations of affluent families provide a more specific and revealing look at how affluence may be connected to the problems of children and youths. Despite the widespread assumption that kids of well-to-do parents enjoy a "privileged status," Luthar (1999, 2003) reviews evidence showing that many affluent children suffer more problems than children of low-income families. One of these studies (Luthar & D'Advanzo, 1999) compared lower socioeconomic status (SES) inner-city teens to upper SES youths living in the suburbs. Surprisingly, affluent teens showed greater levels of maladjustment than their low-income, inner-city counterparts. Specifically, they reported higher rates of drug use (e.g., alcohol, marijuana), higher levels of anxiety, and more depressive symptoms. The findings regarding depression among high-SES teens were particularly striking because their depression levels were not only higher than the inner-city group, but were also three times higher than the national average. One in five (20%) of the 10th-grade suburban girls in this study reported clinically significant symptoms of depression. Levels of anxiety among boys and girls in the affluent group were also significantly above national averages. A well-known study by Csikszentmihalyi and Schneider (2000) also found lower levels of well-being among high- compared to low-income teenagers. Based on experience sampling of moods and feelings of over 800 teens, these researchers found that the most affluent teens reported the lowest levels of happiness and those in the low-income group showed the highest levels of happiness.

Why would affluent teens be unhappy? Two preliminary explanations suggest that it is not affluence *per se*, but the behaviors and expectations of parents that are critical to youths' adjustment. Luthar argues that available research and observations of family experts and clinical psychologists point to achievement pressures and isolation from adult supervision as probable causes of distress among high-SES children. Some children face strong pressures to excel in everything they do and much of what they do is arranged by parents. The number of private and public programs devoted to enhancing children's athletic, musical, learning, and growth potentials has increased dramatically. Affluent parents who make sure their kids are enrolled in as many of these programs as possible may blur the distinction between childhood and adulthood, making children's lives more like those of adults. Stress, responsibility, pressures to succeed, and a day filled with activities from morning until night may destroy the idle play and innocence of childhood. Luthar cites evidence suggesting that children faced with these pressures suffer more stress-related illness, from stomachaches and headaches to insomnia. Children may even exaggerate these physical symptoms in order to have an acceptable excuse for taking time out from their hectic lives.

Children in other affluent families may experience an opposite pattern. Two parents who work long hours and come home late and tired may simply not be optimally available to physically and emotionally nurture and supervise their children. Such parents may provide ample money, beautiful homes, cell phones, computers, big-screen TVs, and cars to their children, but may fail to supply the deep involvement and careful supervision that kids need. The PBS documentary examining *The Lost Children of Rockdale County* (see Chapter 1) found that some affluent children seem to lead empty lives. Their homes are devoid of supervision; they lack sufficient contact with their parents and their lives are empty of purpose and direction, aside from whatever short-term pleasures and diversions they may find with their friends. Such teens desire connection, attention, and a sense of direction from others. When parents do not fulfill these needs, peers fill the void, much like Cushman's argument about consumption filling up the empty self. Unfortunately, Rockdale County teens filled up their lives with drug abuse, delinquency, and sexual promiscuity.

Luthar cautions that the investigation of affluent families is still in its very beginning stages. So far, it is mostly people living in the northeastern United States that have been studied. It is too early to tell whether these findings reveal a general pattern or one that applies only to a narrow range of affluent families. Both longitudinal studies and more detailed examinations of specific elements of family life are needed to clarify the causal variables involved. And certainly, there are affluent families in which parents *do* manage to provide effectively for the emotional needs of their children. However, early indications are that the lives of some affluent families may be a troubling example of materialism and its discontents.

Are We All Materialists?

Several important qualifications must be made to avoid overgeneralizing the negative effects of materialism. Most people may be materialists in the sense that they aspire to earn a good income and own a nice house, car, and other possessions. However, these aspirations, in and of themselves, are not problematic. Recall that the negative effects of materialistic values occur *only* for those individuals who place financial aspirations, social recognition, and appearances ahead of other important psychological needs. It is this imbalance, rather than material goals themselves, that seems to cause unhappiness. It is also worth noting that national surveys show a majority of Americans to be reasonably happy and satisfied with their lives (Diener & Diener, 1996). Over the last 50 years, increased affluence and consumer goods have not made us happier, but neither have they made us less happy. Average Americans, on the whole, do not appear to be suffering from unhappiness caused by the type of excessive materialism documented in research. This is not to deny evidence for rising rates of depression, drug use, and other personal problems among well-to-do young people that may document the potential dark side of increasing affluence. However, most of us would probably agree that our everyday experience suggests that the lives of most people we encounter are not dominated by excessive consumption. Instead, there seems to be a balance between the material side of life and involvements in meaningful activities, close relationships, and intrinsically enjoyable experiences. Recent studies also suggest that certain forms of consumption may enrich, rather than detract from the quality of people's lives. "Experiential purchases," as VanBoven and Gilovich call them, involve spending money on activities that provide new experiences and knowledge, such as vacations, or taking a class to learn a new skill or sport (Van Boven, 2005; Van Boven & Gilovich, 2003). Compared to "material purchases," motivated by a desire just to own a particular desirable object, experiential purchases were associated with more intrinsic enjoyment and positive social interactions with others. Going out to dinner with friends, touring a museum with your children, and meeting new people by joining a club are all examples of spending money on activities that are enjoyable and that also contribute to important social relationships. Experiential purchases may also have more lasting effects than material purchases because they are a source of good stories and fond memories, even if they were not pleasant at the time (e.g., a "camping trip from hell").

Chapter Summary Questions

1. a. How do goals connect the "having" and "doing" sides of life?
   b. How did Diener and Fujita's study of college students' goals and resources show this connection?
2. How are personal goals both cognitive and emotional-motivational?
3. How do personal goals capture the individualized expressions of more general motives and needs? Give an example.
4. How do researchers define and measure personal goals? Give two examples.
5. According to Maslow and his hierarchy of human needs, why is it difficult to study for an exam if you have just broken up with your romantic partner?
6. According to the cross-cultural research by Sheldon and his colleagues, what four needs are candidates for universal status?
7. Which of the 10 universal values described by Schwartz are most important in your orientation toward life? Describe and give examples.
8. a. What is the difference between intrinsic and extrinsic goals, and between physical and self-transcendent goals?
   b. How may these dimensions represent a template describing the content of human goals?
9. What are possible selves and how do they represent the "personalization of goal" in self-concept? Explain and give an example.
10. Explain the matching hypothesis and give a supporting research example.
11. How does each of the following explain the matching hypothesis? Self-realization, intrinsic goals, and autonomous motivation.
12. Describe examples of external, introjected, identified, and intrinsic motives/reasons for attending college and their relation to performance and well-being outcomes.
13. a. What four life aspirations were assessed in Kasser and Ryan's classic study of the dark side of the American dream?
    b. What specific pattern of aspirations was related to lower well-being?
14. How do the following help explain why materialists are unhappy? The content of materialistic goals (what); the motives for their pursuit (why); and psychological insecurity.
15. How are consumer culture and psychological insecurity related to the adoption of materialistic life goals?
16. How do humans defend themselves against the potentially incapacitating fear of death.
    a. According to Ernest Becker?
    b. According to terror management theory?
17. What historical examples and psychological arguments connect money, gold, and materialism to immortality, feelings of security, and the denial of death?
18. Why might teens from affluent families have more drug and emotional problems than their inner-city counterparts? Describe two preliminary explanations for these recent findings.

Key Terms

goals *126*
personal projects *129*
personal strivings *129*
life tasks *129*
values *132*
intrinsic goals *135*

extrinsic goals *135*
possible selves *136*
matching hypothesis *137*
autonomous versus controlled
   motivation *140*
self-determination theory *141*

external motives *141*
introjected motives *141*
identified motives *141*
intrinsic motives *141*
terror managment
   theory *147*

Web Resources

Personal Projects—Brian Little

www.brianrlittle.com Site for personal projects and goal researcher Brian Little. Contains research articles and downloadable measures of personal projects.

Self-Determination Theory

psych.rochester.edu/SDT/publications/pub_well.html Web page covering research of Deci and Ryan at the University of Rochester, focused on goals and motives in relation to self-determination theory.

World Values Survey

www.worldvaluessurvey.org This site reviews the findings of the on-going studies of the World Values Surveys, a network of social scientists who conduct large-scale national value surveys around the world. Recent survey results, national comparisons, and historical changes are described.

Suggested Readings

Becker, E. (1973). *The denial of death*. New York: Free Press.

Emmons, R. A. (1999b). *The psychology of ultimate concerns: Motivation and spirituality in personality*. New York: Guilford Press.

Grouzet, F. M. E., Kasser, T., Ahuvia, A., Dols, J. M. F., Kim, Y., Lau, S. et al. (2005). The structure of goal contents across 15 cultures. *Journal of Personality and Social Psychology, 89*, 800–816.

Kasser, T., & Kanner, A. D. (Eds.). (2004). *Psychology and consumer culture: The struggle for a good life in a materialistic world*. Washington DC: American Psychological Association.

Kasser, T., & Ryan, R.M. (1993). A dark side of the American dream: Correlates of financial success as a central life aspiration. *Journal of Personality and Social Psychology, 65*, 410–422.

Little, B. R., Salmela-Aro, K., & Phillips, S. D. (2007). *Personal project pursuit: Goal action and human flourishing*. Mahway, NJ: Lawrence Erlbaum.

Luthar, S. S. (2003). The culture of affluence: Psychological costs of material wealth. *Child Development, 74*, 1581–1593.

Markus, H., & Nurius, P. S. (1986). Possible selves. *American Psychologist, 41*, 954–969.

Sheldon, K. M., & Houser-Marko, L. (2001). Self-concordance, goal attainment, and the pursuit of happiness: Can there be an upward spiral? *Journal of Personality and Social Psychology, 80*, 152–165.

8

Self-Regulation and Self-Control

Both of your textbook authors are college professors who have taught for many years (first author for 34 years). We have dealt with many students who have failed or gotten Ds in our classes, and academic advisees who were placed on academic warning and probation or suspended from the university for poor performance in their classes. Our experience has been that, with few exceptions, students do not fail because of lack of ability. Instead, they fail because of poor planning, poor time-management skills, failure to monitor their class performance, excessive procrastination, competing or conflicting activities, confusion about their college and career goals, or a lack of self-discipline. In short, failure primarily results from students' inability to monitor and adjust their behavior to the demands of college.

Chapter 7 highlighted the relationship between having (the *resources* we have) and doing (the *goals* we adopt), as well as the importance of choosing the "right" goals (personally expressive, need fulfilling, autonomously chosen). Self-control and self-regulation can be thought of as adding a final critical step that facilitates goal achievement and the well-being benefits of success. Having the necessary resources, the right goals and the right motives are all important, but not enough. The ability to regulate our behavior over time, make adjustments, overcome challenges, control side-tracking temptations, and stay on task are essential for goal achievement. Without self-regulation and control, our goals are simply wishes or desires that exist in our minds, but have little chance of becoming realities.

In this chapter, we consider the *how* of goal achievement by examining self-directed, intentional action as a major vehicle for self-change. Our most general goal is to become the kind of people we want to become by directing our lives according to the needs, values, and personal qualities that define who we are as unique individuals, and that are expressed in our personal goals. To be in control of your life or to change your life means regulating and directing actions according to self-defined goals. That is, the ability of the self to change itself by controlling and regulating feelings, thoughts, and actions to achieve personally significant goals is a major vehicle for personal growth and therefore, for well-being. Self-change may be focused either on the self or on the environment (Rothbaum, Weisz, & Snyder, 1982). *Primary control* refers to attempts to change and mold the external environment to fit the needs and goals of the self. For example, a high school graduate going off to college to enhance her career potential, or a movie buff creating an entertainment center in his home are both altering their environments to bring them in line with their goals and desires. In *secondary control*, the emphasis is on changing the self to fit the external environment. For example, college graduates beginning their first career-relevant jobs are likely to be more concerned with "learning the ropes" and fitting in to their work environment rather than trying to change it. Whether we change our world or change our selves, the capacity for self-control prevents us from being passive victims of life events. It allows the possibility of active intervention and some measure of control over the direction of our lives.

However, self-change is not easy. If it were, we would all be happy and fulfilled. The literature on self-control and regulation may strike you as "negative" and perhaps out-of-place in a positive psychology text. Self-control research focuses on why people fail, as much as on why they succeed, and it shows that self-control is often unpleasant (ask any dieter). Two things are worth keeping in mind. First, why we fail has much to tell us about how to succeed. Every life has disappointments. Success depends heavily on what we learn and do in the aftermath of failure. Secondly, if you think about your most satisfying achievements, it is doubtful that any of them came easily, without self-discipline, hard work, and sustained commitment. The challenges of self-control are reminders that positive psychology isn't just about the good things in life. It is also about the interrelation, mutual dependence, and importance of the positive and the negative. Think of it this way: If you took away everything you have learned from the bad events in your life, how happy or successful would you be?

The specific question addressed by self-regulation research is this: Once people have selected a goal, how do they stay on task to ensure its achievement? In everyday terms, attaining important goals is often regarded as requiring discipline, hard work, persistence in the face of obstacles, and the ability to resist and overcome short-term impulses in order to gain longer-term satisfactions. Many of these everyday understandings are reflected in a growing psychological literature describing self-control and the process of self-regulation. Research has identified many differences among the types of goals and processes that lead to progress and achievement, and those that lead to failure and frustration. Describing these differences is a major purpose of this chapter.

THE VALUE OF SELF-CONTROL

Self-control and self-regulation refer to people's ability to initiate and guide their actions toward the achievement of a desired future goal (Karolyi, 1999). Self-regulation may involve organizing actions over long periods of time, such as the 4 years required to obtain a college degree, or over very short periods, such as a dieter resisting a momentary impulse to eat the ice cream he knows is sitting in his freezer. The importance of people's ability to control and direct the course of their lives has been documented extensively by research. Self-control has consistently been linked to positive outcomes, and lack of self-control to negative outcomes (Baumeister, 1998; Peterson & Seligman, 2004; Shapiro, Schwartz, & Astin, 1996).

In a series of classic studies, Walter Mischel and his colleagues studied young children's ability to **delay gratification** (e.g., Mischel, 1974; Mischel, Ebbesen, & Zeiss, 1972). Using a research paradigm often referred to as the "marshmallow test" (Goleman, 1995), children were given a choice between having one marshmallow right now, or getting two marshmallows after the researcher returned from running an errand. Most children chose the two-marshmallow option. During their wait, children could ring a bell at any time and the experimenter would return, but with only one marshmallow. Significant differences were shown in individual children's ability to delay gratification during the 15 minutes that the researcher was gone. Subsequent research found that this simple test of children's ability to delay gratification was related to future outcomes (see Goleman, 1995, 1998; Mischel & Mendoza-Denton, 2003). Compared to the more impulsive children, those children who resisted immediate temptations went on to become more socially and academically competent adolescents, coped more effectively with stress, and achieved significantly higher college placement scores.

Self-control and self-regulation abilities are critical components of health, happiness, and competence. High self-control has been related to better personal adjustment, less psychopathology, healthier relationships, enhanced social skills, and fewer problems with addictive behaviors such as smoking and drug abuse (see Baumeister, Heatherton, & Tice, 1994; Peterson & Seligman, 2004). Self-control has also been identified as one of the most significant predictors of college grades.

A study of 200 college students examined the predictive power of high school grades, SAT scores, and 32 different personality variables, including several measures of self-control (Wolfe & Johnson, 1995). High school grades were the top predictor of college grades. However, self-control was the second-best predictor, followed by SAT scores. Particularly interesting is the fact that, of 32 personality traits assessed in the study, only self-control was related to college grades. Students with good self-control abilities performed significantly better in college. Because of its relation to college success, Wolfe and Johnson suggest that assessment of self-control might be a valuable addition to college admission procedures.

In a similar vein, low self-control and self-regulatory failure appear to underlie a variety of personal and social problems, such as overspending, drug addictions, obesity, gambling, school failure, and criminal behavior (Baumeister et al., 1994; Carver, 2005). In their book titled, *A General Theory of Crime*, Gottfredson and Hirschi (1990) argue that deficiencies in self-control may be a fundamental cause of criminal behavior. Some evidence suggests that parental supervision plays a key role in the development of self-control among children and their subsequent likelihood of engaging in delinquent behavior (e.g., Buckner, Mezzacappa, & Beardslee, 2003; Luthar, 1999; McLoyd, 1998). Parents who closely monitor their children's behavior and whereabouts may assist their children in developing an internalized self-monitoring and self-control system. Conversely, a lack of parental supervision may lead to poor self-control and inability to delay gratification.

PERSONAL GOALS AND SELF-REGULATION

The ability to forgo short-term rewards in preference for longer-term benefits is clearly important in achieving our personal goals. However, working toward distant goals is a complex process that involves more than resisting immediate temptations. People must monitor and adjust their behavior over time, stay focused on the long-term goal, and complete the tasks and develop the skills necessary for goal attainment. Two major theories have been proposed to describe the self-regulation process: control theory and self-discrepancy theory. Each theory postulates a similar set of variables that affect goal-directed behavior, but they differ in their predictions about the emotional outcomes and motivational bases of self-regulation.

Control Theory

Control theory provides a somewhat idealized model of self-regulation based on "feedback loops" that are used to control some process relative to a given reference point (Austin & Vancouver, 1996; Carver & Scheier, 1982, 1998). The feedback loop is often referred to as "TOTE," which stands for *test, operate, test,* and *exit.* The thermostat on your home furnace/air conditioner provides an example (see Figure 8.1). You set the thermostat at 72 degrees (thermostat value setting) and the thermostat compares the room temperature to this standard (comparator test). If the test result is below or above the 72-degree standard (sensed temperature) the furnace/air conditioner is turned on (operate, turn on heater/air conditioner). When the room temperature reaches the thermostat setting, the furnace/air conditioner is shut-off (exit). The TOTE feedback loop requires a reference value or standard, a monitoring/testing system, and an operating system strong enough to reduce the discrepancy between the current state and the standard. Control theory highlights how people use goals as references for directing and regulating action over time.

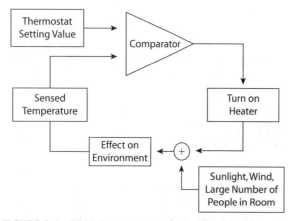

FIGURE 8.1   TOTE Components of a Feedback Loop
The comparator "tests" the room temperature, the heater/air conditioner "operates," changing the room temperature (effect on environment) and "exits" (shuts-off) when thermostat setting is achieved. A variety of factors (e.g., sunlight & wind) effect when and how much the operate function cycle is required.   *Source:* Carver, C. S., & Scheier, M. F. (1998). *On the self-regulation of behavior.* New York: Cambridge University Press. Copyright Cambridge University Press. Reprinted with permission.

According to **control theory,** when people pursue positive goals (e.g., getting a good job after college), their self-regulation efforts are focused on reducing the discrepancy between the current state and a future goal. By successfully completing requirements in their program of study, students move closer to graduation and the opportunity to find a desirable job. Control theory predicts that the emotions experienced during goal-directed actions depend on the person's *rate of progress* toward future goals. Positive emotions result when people make greater-than-expected progress in achieving their goals. Negative emotions result from less-than-expected progress. A student who takes a higher-than-normal credit load and sees that she might graduate in 3½ years is likely to be happier than a student who has dropped or had to repeat courses and is consequently looking at a 4½-year college career. These emotional consequences are independent of the amount of actual discrepancy between where we are now and where we want to go. A college freshman is not necessarily less happy than a college junior, just because he or she has 4 years to go and the junior only has 2 years left. According to control theory, it is one's rate of progress toward the goal that is critical.

Self-Discrepancy Theory

According to **self-discrepancy theory,** self-regulation is directed by "self-guides," which involve comparisons between the actual self, the ideal self, and "ought self" (Higgins, 1987, 1996, 1997, 1998). The actual self represents a person's beliefs about the qualities he or she actually possesses in the present. The ideal self defines our ultimate goals in terms of the abilities and qualities we would ideally like to possess. The "ought self" refers to social obligations, responsibilities, moral convictions, and duties that define who we think we ought to be (e.g., a good parent or employee). In contrast to control theory, self-discrepancy theory views the *magnitude of the discrepancies* between our actual self, ideal self, and ought self as the bases for positive and negative emotions. When there is no discrepancy between the current actual self and the ought or ideal self, people experience positive emotions and are motivated to maintain this congruence. However, when people fall short of their ideals and "oughts" (their moral convictions or obligations), they experience negative emotions. Ideal–actual self-discrepancies are associated with disappointment, dissatisfaction, and sadness. Ought–actual discrepancies seem to produce feelings of unease, threat, and fear. These negative emotions motivate attempts to reduce the discrepancy through self-guided, goal-directed behavior.

Both control theory and self-discrepancy theory assume that discrepancies are central to self-regulation, but make different predictions about their emotional consequences. What might explain the different emotional effects of discrepancies postulated by the two theories? Preliminary evidence for one possibility has been suggested by Boldero and Francis (2002), who argue that the reference values people use in self-regulated behavior may serve two separate evaluative functions. Reference values may be used as *standards* to assess the self in the *present*, and they can also serve as *future goals* to be achieved over time. Self-discrepancy theory is focused on how the current self stacks up against the standards of an ideal and ought self. When reference values are used as standards to assess a desired state for the self in the present, discrepancies signify that we have fallen short of where we want to be and therefore, negative emotional consequences may result. In contrast, within control theory, reference values function as future goals for the self. Proponents of control theory note that, by definition, people are always falling short of their future goals in the sense that they have not yet achieved them (see Carver & Scheier, 1998). However, the discrepancy between our current state and a future goal does not necessarily cause negative feelings. Setting a desirable future goal is a positive event that gives us a sense of purpose and direction. When we are oriented toward future desirable outcomes, what matters is how fast we are moving toward these outcomes. That is, the *rate of discrepancy reduction*—not the *size* of the discrepancy—determines the emotions we are likely to experience. In summary, the emotional effects of self-evaluation relative to future goals seem to depend on our rate of progress in attaining them. However, when self-evaluations are made relative to standards that describe desired states of the self in the present, then positive and negative emotions may be more influenced by the size of the discrepancy. Because our focus here is on how people make progress toward their personal goals over time, we will emphasize the control theory view of self-regulation.

Applied to the pursuit of personal goals, control theory describes self-regulation in terms of three components: **standards, monitoring,** and **strength.** Successful self-regulation requires clear **standards** indicating when a goal has been achieved, effective **monitoring** of progress toward a goal, and the personal **strength** to overcome the temptations, diversions, and procrastinations that might take us off-course. Failures in self-regulation can involve any of these three components. Without clear goals and standards, it is difficult to gauge both progress and attainment. An abstract, non-specific goal, such as a desire to "be a better person," is impossible to achieve without specifying the behavioral standards that will be used to define and evaluate "better." Lack of effective monitoring may also short-circuit successful self-regulation. People who want to cut down on their smoking or alcohol consumption are doomed to fail from the beginning if they do not keep track of how many cigarettes or drinks they have each day. The strength and self-discipline to stick to your goals and conform to the standards you have set for yourself are also essential. Any dieter can tell you that food temptations abound during a diet. These would include all the foods you "can't" eat, but that look so good on a restaurant menu, countless television and magazine ads for scrumptious-looking foods, and the cookie and dessert section of the grocery store.

Unfortunately, research does not fall neatly into the three boxes of standards, monitoring, and strengths. Further, the three aspects of the self-regulation processes are interconnected. For example, certain types of goal standards create problems in self-control strength and monitoring. Our discussion will focus on the differences between effective and ineffective self-regulation. Factors related to standards, monitoring, and strength help explain the "when, why, and how" of successful and failed regulation of goal-directed behavior.

PLANNING FOR SELF-REGULATION SUCCESS

Research shows that much of our success or failure in self-regulation is determined before the fact. That is, the plans we make before actively pursuing a goal have much to do with our success. Gollwitzer (1999) makes an important distinction between goal intentions and implementation intentions. **Goal intentions** refer to our desire to achieve a certain outcome. **Implementation intentions** define our plan of action by specifying the exact steps necessary to achieve the goal. An implementation intention is a plan that says, "When situation *x* arises, I will perform response *y*." (Gollwitzer, p. 494). So, for example, wanting to exercise more is a goal intention, whereas planning to ride an exercise bike for 30 minutes every day while watching the evening news describes an implementation intention. Specifying implementation intentions is a key element in getting started on your goals and has been consistently linked to better goal attainment. A goal intention without an implementation plan is not an effective basis for goal-directed self-regulation, particularly for more difficult and challenging goals. This was clearly shown in studies conducted by Gollwitzer and Brandstatter (1997).

Focus on Research: Planning Makes a Difference

In their first study, university students were asked to describe a difficult and an easy project that they intended to complete during the winter break. Projects included such things as writing a class paper, working on resolving family conflicts, and participating in athletic activities. Students were also asked if they had specific plans about when, where, and how to get started on each project. Project completion was checked after students returned to school. For difficult projects, implementation intentions were clearly related to successful completion. Two-thirds of the students who had made implementation plans finished their projects. Only one-fourth of the students who had not made implementation plans finished their winter break projects. In other words, without specific plans for implementing their goals, most students failed to achieve them. For easier projects, implementation plans were unrelated to completion rates. Whether they had made plans or not, 80% of the students finished their less difficult projects.

In Gollwitzer and Brandstatter's second study, students were asked to write a report on how they spent Christmas Eve. This report was supposedly going to be used for a study of how people celebrate holidays in modern times. Students were instructed to write their reports no later than 48 hours after December 24 and send the report to the experimenter. Half of the students in the study were asked to form implementation intentions by describing exactly when and where they would write the report. The other half were not instructed to make implementation plans. The value of thinking ahead was again shown, with 75% of students who made implementation plans returning their reports within the 48-hour

period, and only 33% of the non-implementation group completing their reports on time.

In addition to their value in achieving difficult goals, implementation intentions are particularly useful for people with poor self-regulation skills. Studies have shown that creating implementation plans increases the effectiveness of self-regulating behaviors among samples of people with schizophrenia, drug-addicted individuals going through withdrawal, and people with injuries to the frontal lobes of the brain (Brandstatter, Lengfelder, & Gollwitzer, 2001). Health-promoting goals such as screening for breast cancer, exercising for cardiovascular wellness, and taking medications on schedule are also enhanced by having people form implementation intentions in advance (see Gollwitzer, 1999 for a review).

Why Planning Helps

Developing clear and specific implementation intentions seems to enhance goal achievement by creating mental and environmental markers that make self-regulation more efficient, more automatic, and less susceptible to distractions and procrastination. Most of us lead busy lives. We have multiple goals we want to achieve and many demands on our time. Without imposing some structure on our lives, we can easily get caught up in the bustle of daily events and feel like we haven't accomplished anything. Connecting personal goals to specifics plans concerning how, when, and where we will work on them makes our goals easier to remember and access. By specifying a time and place for a goal activity, we create environmental cues that may lead to a relatively automatic activation of goal-directed behavior. For example, consider a student who decides to study for a difficult economics class after lunch every Tuesday and Thursday from 1 to 3 PM in her dorm room, while her roommate is at work. Over time, this behavior may not require much conscious effort or self-control to activate. That is, studying economics at a specific time and place may become a routine, like taking a shower every morning. Few of us make plans for taking showers. We just automatically do it because it's part of our daily ritual. Gollwitzer (1999) believes implementation intentions contribute to effective self-regulation by "passing the control of one's behavior to the environment" (p. 495) and thereby bypassing some of the distractions and temptations that affect more conscious, effortful self-control.

AUTOMATIC ACTIVATION OF GOAL BEHAVIORS
Gollwitzer's (1999) conclusions are supported by studies of automaticity in behavior control. Research by Bargh and his colleagues provides extensive support for the value of environmentally activated and relatively automatic goal-directed behavior (Bargh, 1996; Bargh & Chartrand, 1999; Wegner & Bargh, 1998). With enough repetition and consistent pairing of internal and external events, many behaviors can "run off" with little or no conscious control. Driving a car serves as an example. A beginning driver has to pay close, conscious attention to steering, signaling, monitoring surrounding traffic, braking, and checking mirrors. Experienced drivers do all these things automatically. Our ability to listen to the radio or converse with fellow passengers while driving, are possible because the adjustments necessary to respond to changes in the driving environment (e.g., stop signs, changes in the speed of the car in front of you, etc.) can be made without requiring consciously controlled actions. The value of such "automatic guidance systems" (Bargh & Chartrand, 1999, p. 476) is that they efficiently and effectively control behavior without imposing a penalty in energy expenditure. In contrast, conscious self-control comes with an energy price tag. When we are forced to drive on icy roads or during a rainstorm, the concentration required often leaves us exhausted at the end of the trip.

CONSERVING SELF-CONTROL RESOURCES Self-regulation often requires both mental and physical exertion and appears to be a limited resource that can be depleted (Baumeister, 1998). Much like a muscle that tires with exercise, the strength of people's self-control ability appears to weaken with repeated use. Research by Baumeister and his colleague has shown that self-control in one activity reduces self-control in subsequent activities (Baumeister, Bratslavsky, Muraven, & Tice, 1998; Baumeister et al., 1994; Muraven & Baumeister, 2000). In a variety of studies involving two consecutive self-control tasks, people consistently performed more poorly on the second task. Even relatively minor acts of self-control seem to deplete the strength of our self-control abilities. People who exercised self-control by eating vegetables instead of available chocolates, or who suppressed their emotional responses to a movie had greater difficulty and were less persistent in solving a subsequent

puzzle task, compared to those without the prior self-control demands. A recent study suggests that the energy necessary for self-control may be tied to blood glucose levels (Gailliot et al., 2007). The brain relies heavily on glucose for the energy to carry out its many functions, especially those effortful executive function such as self-control. Gailliot and his colleagues found that blood glucose levels were in fact reduced by self-control tasks and that, after this glucose reduction, poor performance followed. For our discussion, the idea of self-control as a limited resource suggests that planning ahead facilitates goal achievement by increasing automaticity, which helps preserve our limited supply of self-control energies.

Commitment and Confidence

Commitment and confidence are two other important factors that contribute to successful goal striving. People who are both committed to their goals and confident in their ability to achieve them are much more likely to be successful (e.g., Brunstein, 1993). Commitment refers to our degree of determination, responsibility, and willingness to persevere over time in the face of obstacles that may threaten goal achievement (Austin & Vancouver, 1996; Brickman, 1987). Commitment means making a decision and then following through on it (Fehr, 1988).

Confidence is related to people's beliefs about their ability to accomplish what they want to accomplish. Self-efficacy, a widely studied measure of confidence, has been consistently shown to enhance goal achievement (Maddux, 2002). Self-efficacy is defined as a belief in one's competence to produce desirable outcomes through one's own efforts (Bandura, 1977, 1997). Albert Bandura emphasized the task-specific nature of people's perceived competence. While some people may possess general confidence, most people's confidence varies in relation to the situation and the specific task. So you may have high self-efficacy about social relationships and meeting new people, but lower self-efficacy concerning your ability to increase your gradepoint average. Or, you may feel confident about your math abilities, but much less confident about writing extensive term papers.

Commitment and confidence work together to increase our persistence and perseverance when we confront obstacles in the pursuit of our goals

(Carver & Scheier, 2003). They provide a source of resilience and determination in the face of the inevitable setbacks and difficulties we encounter when striving toward important and challenging goals. For example, commitment plays a prominent role in several theories of marital satisfaction and stability (see Berscheid & Reis, 1998, for a review). Because every marriage involves periods of conflict and unhappiness, a strong commitment to marriage, spouse, and family helps people get through the hard times. In a similar vein, self-efficacy has been related to greater effort, persistence in the face of failure, and successful goal attainment. In the area of health behaviors, for example, individuals with high self-efficacy are more likely to succeed at efforts to quit smoking, abstain from drinking alcohol, maintain physical fitness, and endure the pain of arthritis and migraine headaches (Bandura, 1999; Maddux, 1995, 2002; Salovey, Rothman, & Rodin, 1998).

The dual importance of commitment and confidence for goal achievement and well-being was specifically assessed in a study by Brunstein (1993). At the beginning of the fall semester, college students were asked to describe their most important personal goals for the next several months. Students described a variety of goals including learning enough Spanish to be able to study in Spain, learning to better manage their finances, improving a relationship with a romantic partner, learning to be more assertive, and becoming more independent from parents. Students rated each goal according to how committed they were to achieving it, and their confidence in its attainability. Subjective well-being (SWB) measures were taken at four separate intervals during the semester. To assess the stability of the commitment and confidence variables, these constructs were also measured during four follow-up testing periods.

Consistent with control theory's predictions, results showed that *progress* toward goal achievement had a positive influence on well-being. Brunstein's results also provide clear evidence for the interaction between commitment and perceived attainability in determining both progress toward goals and positive changes in well-being. Students who expressed high commitment and described favorable conditions for goal attainment showed increased well-being over the span of the study. On the other hand, students with high goal commitment, but low appraisals of attainability experienced decreases in well-being. As Brunstein notes, high

commitment to a goal (perhaps indicating a goal's importance to the individual) sets the stage for the well-being effects of goal pursuit. Some commitment seems to be a necessary condition for success. However, whether goal striving will result in goal progress and increased or decreased well-being depends on a person's confidence and assessment of goal attainability. High commitment by itself is not enough.

GOALS THAT CREATE SELF-REGULATION PROBLEMS

Approach versus Avoidance Goals

A substantial amount of research shows that the process of self-regulation is quite different when people think of a goal in terms of approaching a desirable outcome, rather than avoiding an undesirable one. Any sports fan knows that the strategy and play of a team can be very different depending on whether the team is focused on winning the game or on protecting a lead. Playing "not to lose" can be effective, but it can also backfire. For our important personal goals, an avoidant strategy would not generally be recommended. Many studies suggest that people who focus on avoiding certain outcomes (e.g., failing a college class) generally perform worse than those who think of their goals as striving toward positive outcomes (e.g., getting a good grade). This is true, in part, because of the inherent self-regulation problems involved in avoidance goals that seem to undermine people's sense of competence.

Approach goals are positive outcomes that people hope to move toward, or maintain (e.g., get along better with a roommate, stay physically fit). The approach goal functions as a positive standard and self-regulation is oriented toward *reducing* the discrepancy between this standard and the current state. A college student wanting to earn an "A" in a particular class is likely to monitor his understanding of class material, keep track of his scores on assignments and exams, and adjust his study habits according to the progress he is making toward getting the "A." The larger the discrepancy between his current grade and his "A" standard, the harder he will need to work. The focus of self-regulation is discrepancy *reduction*. **Avoidance goals,** on the other hand, are negative outcomes that people hope to avoid, or prevent (e.g., stop arguing with a roommate, avoid gaining weight). The avoidance goal functions as a negative standard and self-regulation is oriented toward *increasing* the discrepancy with the current state. In other words, the farther away we are from things we want to avoid, the better.

Research comparisons of approach and avoidance goals typically begin by having people list their important personal goals. An individual's number of approach goals versus his or her number of avoidance goals is used to establish an index of the relative dominance of an approach or avoidance orientation. These goal orientations are then related to measures of well-being and goal progress and achievement. For example, Emmons and Kaiser (1996) found that people with a large number of avoidance goals reported higher levels of emotional distress (particularly anxiety) and more physical symptoms than those with approach goals. Both global and daily report measures of emotions showed that negative moods were associated with pursuing avoidance goals. In a similar vein, studies by Elliot and colleagues found that college students with many avoidance goals experienced more problems in making progress toward their goals, and decreased physical and emotional well-being over a 4-month semester (Elliot & Sheldon, 1998; Elliot, Sheldon, & Church, 1997). Other researchers have connected avoidance goals to poorer marital satisfaction (e.g., King & Emmons, 1991), less satisfying friendships (e.g., Elliot, Gable, & Mapes, 2006), less positive psychotherapy outcomes (e.g., Elliot & Church, 2002), poorer physical health (e.g., Elliot & Sheldon, 1998), and less perceived progress toward and satisfaction with goal achievement (e.g., Elliot & Sheldon, 1997).

Both approach and avoidance motivations are implied in any goal. A desire to do well at something, for example, implies a desire not to do poorly. Similarly, a goal to avoid failure implies some motivation to succeed. Given their underlying connection, why should thinking about goals in terms of avoiding a negative outcome rather than approaching a positive outcome make such a difference? In our social relationships, why should a desire to avoid disagreements and conflicts with others, or to avoid being hurt or rejected by friends undermine relationships, while a desire to be more complimentary toward others, or to share more enjoyable activities with friends promote good relationships? In a therapy context, why should a goal of not being so shy or moody, or not letting little things create so much upset be less helpful than

goals of achieving a better understanding of personal feelings, being more accepting of oneself, or becoming more confident in social situations? A number of cognitive, emotional, and behavioral mechanisms appear to be responsible for the debilitating effects of avoidance goals.

WHY AVOIDANCE GOALS ARE DIFFICULT TO REGULATE

First, it is easier to regulate and monitor approach goals than avoidance goals. For approach goals, people only need to identify one effective path to be successful (Schwarz, 1990). For avoidance goals, people have to identify and block all possible paths to the undesirable outcome. This requires constant monitoring and vigilance. If your goal is to do something nice for a good friend, you only have to find one thing. If your goal is not to offend others, you must be alert in all your social interactions to any signs of negative reactions and make adjustments to your behavior if you find them. As our earlier discussion suggested, the energy required for self-regulation appears to be a limited resource. The constant monitoring required for avoidance goals may break down the self-regulation process if this energy is depleted over time.

Secondly, avoidance goals, by their very nature, seem to evoke anxiety, threat, and self-defensiveness (e.g., Elliot & Church, 1997; Elliot & Sheldon, 1997, 1998). Dieters know that avoiding sweets and fatty foods is no fun. Dieters may worry about their ability to resist temptation and feel guilt from the occasional failure. Dieters also face constant reminders of threats to their diets in the form of appealing, but forbidden foods seen in stores, on television, and in magazines. All these factors contribute to high rates of dieting failure and the unpleasant experience of dieting. The anxiety and stress caused by heightened sensitivity to negative information decreases self-regulatory effectiveness and may therefore undermine goal progress and achievement (Baumeister et al., 1994; Higgins, 1996; Wegner, 1994).

Third, avoidance goals have been associated with decreased feelings of competence, self-esteem, intrinsic enjoyment, and self-determination (e.g., Elliot & Church, 2002; Elliot & Sheldon, 1998; Elliot et al., 2006). These factors may mediate and help explain why the negative emotions and self-regulation problems involved in avoidance goals are so often related to negative outcomes, dissatisfaction with progress, and lower emotional/physical well-being. Simply put, regulatory difficulties and frustrations may undermine our feelings of competence and self-esteem by constantly raising the possibility that we will fail.

Fourth, avoidance goals are less likely to be experienced as freely chosen and intrinsically enjoyable (two factors found to enhance well-being and goal achievement) (see Chapter 7 for a thorough discussion). It is easy to think of negative goals (such as "not being such a perfectionist" or "cutting down on alcohol consumption") as self-imposed pressures that make people feel compelled to overcome a habitual or pleasurable behavior. Avoiding long-standing habits and activities we like because we feel we "have to" is unlikely to be fun or pleasant. In view of the connections among avoidance goals, regulatory problems, and reduced feelings of competence, esteem, enjoyment, and general well-being, the pursuit of avoidance goals is generally regarded as a significant source of personal vulnerability (e.g., Elliot & Sheldon, 1997, 1998). That is, people whose personal goals are oriented primarily toward avoiding negative outcomes appear to be at risk for a variety of negative experiences that undermine their well-being.

Finally, some of the problems associated with avoidance goals may be related to the motives that underlie them. Life experiences can dictate whether we are oriented toward approach or avoidance goals in specific areas of our lives. For example, a heart attack caused by clogged arteries is likely to lead a person to avoid fatty foods. However, people also vary in their general goal orientation, with some people having what Higgins (1996, 1998) describes as a *promotion focus* and some a *prevention focus*. In Higgins' self-discrepancy theory, discussed earlier in this chapter, the self plays a prominent role in the selection and general focus of personal goals and as a guide for self-regulated behaviors. Higgins describes an ideal self-guide as the basis for a promotion focus, whereas an ought self-guide underlies a prevention focus. The relative strength of a promotion or prevention focus may originate with different parenting styles. Parents who are primarily focused on *nurturing* their children want to encourage positive experiences, reward independence, and help their children develop the ability to overcome challenges. Their fundamental message is, "this is what I ideally would like you to do." Parents with a prevention focus are more concerned with avoiding negative outcomes concerning their child's *safety* and meeting *social obligations* such as following rules of good conduct. Their message is "this is not what I believe you should do."

The two different parenting styles are assumed to lead children to adopt different orientations toward their own personal goals. Parents concerned with nurturing goals may contribute to the development of an *ideal* self-regulatory system with a promotion focus on approach goals, aspirations, and attempts to fulfill a positive self-image. On the other hand, primary parental concern over what children should *not* do may lead to the adoption of an ought self-regulatory system with a prevention focus on avoidance goals related to security and meeting social obligations and duties. In line with Higgins' analysis, recent studies find that people do differ in their general approach and avoidance motivations, and these differences are related to well-being. Updegraff, Gable, and Taylor (2004) found that people oriented toward approaching rewards and positive experiences selectively used positive experiences as the basis for their daily well-being judgments. Avoidance-oriented individuals did not show this selectivity, and showed much stronger negative emotional reactions to everyday negative events that, in turn, contributed to their lowered life satisfaction ratings.

Researchers have also investigated specific motives that underlie approach and avoidance orientations for achievement and relationship goals. People who focus on avoiding failure may have a fear of failure as a basic achievement motive (e.g., Elliot & Sheldon, 1997). In a similar vein, people who worry about preventing negative relationship experiences may be motivated by an underlying fear of rejection (e.g., Elliot et al., 2006). Elliot and colleagues found that hope for affiliation with others, as a general social motive, was highly predictive of approach friendship goals, positive relationship experiences, less loneliness, and increased well-being over time. In contrast, a fear-of-rejection motive was associated with negative friendship goals, such as avoiding conflicts, embarrassment, betrayal, or being hurt by friends. Individuals with an avoidance orientation experienced more negative relationship events, more loneliness, and more physical symptoms (such as headache, upset stomach, dizziness, and sore muscles).

Goal Conflict

People typically have multiple goals that occupy their efforts and attention in a given time frame. The interrelationship of our many goals has important implications for our ability to direct and regulate efforts toward their achievement. We noted earlier (in Chapter 7) that conflict among personal goals can be a significant source of distress and unhappiness (e.g., Emmons & King, 1998; Palys & Little, 1983). Studies have linked such conflict to a wide variety of emotional and physical problems such as obesity, heart disease, and depression (see Emmons, 1999b, for a review). Goal conflict occurs when the pursuit of one goal interferes with the achievement of one or more other goals that a person also wants to attain. Goal conflict may involve competition for limited resources such as time, money, and energy. Activity aimed at accomplishing one goal reduces the resources available for the pursuit of others. For example, a desire to develop a successful professional career may take both time and energy away from an equally important desire to spend time with one's spouse and children. Conflict may also arise because two goals are inherently incompatible. In Emmons and King's (1988) study, people were asked to rate the degree of interference between all possible pairings of their personal goals. One participant described the following two goals that appear to be highly incompatible: "to appear more intelligent than I am," and "to always present myself in an honest light" (Emmons & King, 1988, p. 1042). How can a person fulfill a desire to create a somewhat dishonest appearance of their actual intelligence and be honest with others at the same time?

Carver and Scheier (1998) suggest that many goal conflicts boil down to scheduling problems. That is, people have multiple goals, but limited time and energy. Gollwitzer's (1999) emphasis on the importance of implementation intentions, in the form of conscious plans about how goals are to be achieved, might be one solution to many goal conflicts. Specifying a time and place for working on each important goal may reduce feelings of conflict and enhance success in achieving multiple goals. Success may also involve establishing priorities and making trade-offs among various important goals. Both of your textbook authors, for example, have women in their classes who are starting their college careers in the aftermath of divorces. Many of these women have young children, jobs, and full-time college course loads. How do they do it? One woman described how every hour of her day from 6 o'clock in the morning until 11 o'clock at night was scheduled with specific activities, including taking her kids to daycare, going to class, working, spending family time, and studying. As long as she or her children didn't get sick or her employer didn't demand extra hours at work, she could fit everything into this hectic schedule. When her schedule did break down (usually because of sick kids), her priorities were with her family; school came second. As a result, she typically ended up with B's in her classes because her exam grades were often either A's or C's, depending on the time her schedule allowed for schoolwork. Consistent with the research on goal conflict, she described her life as very stressful and was looking forward to a more "normal" life after graduation.

A recent study suggests that people who find ways to make their multiple goals work together can increase their level of engagement and persistence in goal-directed actions. Riediger and Freund (2004) assessed both intergoal interference and intergoal facilitation among people's personal goals. **Intergoal facilitation** refers to cases where the pursuit of one goal at the same time enhances the odds of success in achieving another goal. This may occur because of mutual facilitation or because work on one goal overlaps with the other, thereby helping to achieve both. Consider a college student who has the following personal goals: getting good grades, learning about careers in his or her chosen field of study, and making new friends. If each of these goals is pursued independently, there is some potential for conflict in the time and energy required for each. However, joining a campus organization or club devoted to the student's major might contribute to enhanced success toward all three goals. Such organizations often serve social, career, and academic functions by providing opportunities for students with the same career interests to get to know each other, and by offering information on degree requirements, career options, and graduate school. Relationships with other students in your major are also likely to provide "insider" information about course requirements, research interests, and personalities of professors in your department. In short, getting involved in your major by joining a student group may serve multiple goals and pay a variety to dividends. Riediger and Freund found that mutually facilitating goals were associated with higher levels of involvement in goal pursuit. This effect may be due to the greater efficiency in the use of resources. Being able to "kill two birds with one stone," as the saying goes, saves time and energy, and avoids the stress associated with conflicting goals.

"Trivial Pursuits" and "Magnificent Obsessions"

People's goals may vary from the concrete and specific, such as keeping a neat and tidy house and presenting a well-groomed personal appearance, to the abstract and general, such as a desire to become a better person or develop a closer relationship with God. From the perspective of control theory (Carver & Scheier, 1998), our personal goals contain both higher-level and lower-level strivings that are interrelated in a hierarchy. More abstract goals that express our important life purposes are at the top of the hierarchy (e.g., getting a college education). More concrete goals reflecting how to achieve these purposes are lower in the hierarchy (e.g., spend the next 2 hours studying for my economics quiz). This general relationship between abstract and concrete goals is complicated by the fact that people can think of any particular goal or action at different levels of abstraction. This is made clear in action identification theory, to be described next.

Focus on Theory: Thinking About the Meaning of Our Actions

According to **action identification theory,** any action can be identified at more than one level (Vallacher & Wegner, 1987). Lower-order levels refer to how something is done in terms of the concrete and specific behaviors involved. Higher-order levels refer to why an action is carried out in terms of more abstract and general reasons. For instance, a father helping his young son with his math homework could identify or explain what he is doing in terms specific actions, such as answering his son's questions and checking the accuracy of his work. The father might also identify what he is doing at a higher level, such as being a helpful parent or, higher yet, as being a good parent.

The theory suggests that people prefer and gravitate toward higher-level identifications of their actions and maintain them as long as they are effective. That is, we generally choose to put our actions in the context of larger purposes and meanings that explain *why* we are doing something, rather than put them in the smaller context of the specific concrete behaviors that describe *how* we are doing something. However, if higher-level identifications prove unworkable, the theory suggests that people shift down to lower levels. Maintaining actions that

are identified at a high level requires that the "how to" (lower-level) basis for action must be relatively well-learned, automatic, and easy to carry out. The father who defines his actions as "being a helpful parent" may have to shift down to specifics if he doesn't already understand the math required by his son's homework. That is, if he discovers he can't be helpful, he may end up identifying what he's doing as listening to his son explain the math he has to learn, or reading his son's math book to figure out how to be helpful.

Vallacher and Wegner (1987) argue that the different levels of action identification correspond to varying degrees of importance to the self. Low-level identifications, such as the father trying to understand his son's math book, have less importance to the self than higher-level identifications, such as being a good parent. Action-level identification theory supports the general idea that higher-order goals and reasons for actions are more important because they are more related to our self-concept. We care about goals closely identified with the self because such goals are self-defining and self-expressive. The achievement of higher-level goals and the maintenance of high-level action identifications represent self-affirmation or self-completion (Wicklund & Gollwitzer, 1982) by providing evidence of a desired personal identity. A father's success in helping his son with his math affirms the self-image of a good and helpful parent, while reading a math book does not. In short, maintaining our self-conception depends, in part, on the self-affirming evidence provided by our actions and goal achievements.

INDIVIDUAL DIFFERENCES IN GOAL LEVEL IDENTIFICATION In addition to the general relationship between higher- and lower-level goals described by action identification theory, people also differ in the ways they characteristically think about their goals. Little (1989) put this difference dramatically, describing how some people may devote their lives to "magnificent obsessions," while others are content with "trivial pursuits." A similar theme is echoed in Waterman's (1993) comparison of people who appear to be looking primarily for *something to do* versus those focused on finding *someone to be.* You might think that someone who pursues more abstract and self-defining goals would be happier and more satisfied with her life than someone focused only on very narrow and concrete goals. However, Little (1989) suggests that there may be a trade-off between "manageable" and "meaningful." For example, Emmons (1992) classified people as high- or low-level strivers based on measures along the abstract/concrete, specific/general, and self-reflective/non-reflective dimensions of personal goals. High-level strivers had goals that were more abstract, general, and based on self-reflection, while low-level strivers were at the opposite ends of these goal dimensions. High-level strivings were associated with more psychological distress and depression, while low-level strivings were related to less negative emotion, but more physical illness. Why would either a very abstract or a very concrete goal orientation be associated with problems?

In line with Little's idea of a manageable/meaningful trade-off, Emmons suggests that each orientation may trade one set of problems for another. On the one hand, abstract goals may be more meaningful and personally expressive, but are harder to regulate and achieve. In Emmons' study, high-level strivers listed goals such as "appearing knowledgeable on any and all subjects to others," "looking at matters realistically," and "keeping positive thoughts in my mind" (Emmons, 1999b, pp. 53–54). Emmons notes that these goals are admirable, but "fuzzy." What specific actions would you take to appear more knowledgeable? How is a person to know when he is appearing more knowledgeable to others, or whether he has become more realistic? Both the actions necessary to pursue the goals and the standards for measuring goal progress and achievement are unclear. In addition, abstract goals are likely to be long-term affairs. You don't come to appear more knowledgeable on all subjects overnight. All these factors make accomplishing abstract goals more difficult. As a result, people pursuing abstract goals are likely to experience more frustration, distress, and negative emotion associated with the conflict between the personal importance and meaningfulness of the goal and the difficulties encountered in pursuing and achieving it.

On the other hand, concrete goals are more manageable in the sense that they are clearer and easier to accomplish, but they may be less meaningful. Low-level strivers in Emmons' study (1999b, p. 53) described goals such as "Cutting down on frozen dinners," "Looking well-groomed and clean cut," "Keeping good posture/walking straight," and "Drinking more water." So why would a concrete goal orientation be associated with increased physical illness? Emmons (1992) notes a possible link between

a repressive personality type and very concrete and narrowly defined personal goals. Repressive individuals, deny their emotional distress and use distractions to prevent themselves from thinking about their negative emotional states. Despite their denial, repressors have higher physiological arousal and may be more susceptible to psychosomatic illnesses. Low-level striving may reflect a repressive personality and a desire to avoid confronting emotionally-charged issues related to what is important in life. That is, concrete goals may function as distractions from negative feelings and distress. People who "think small" may fill up their lives with many concrete and specific goals to avoid the distress that may result from "thinking big."

Emmons (1999b) suggests that one solution to the manageability–meaningfulness trade-off is to "select concrete, manageable goals that are linked to personally meaningful, higher-order representations" (p. 54). In his view, the problem with either an exclusively abstract or an exclusively concrete goal orientation is the disconnection between meaning and concrete attainability of goals. The matching hypothesis and Gollwitzer's research on the benefits of planning reviewed earlier in this chapter support Emmons' suggestion about the dual importance of meaning and concreteness of personal goals.

Goal Difficulty

The importance of both higher- and lower-level goals also receives indirect support from studies of goal-setting and performance in organizations (see Locke & Latham, 1990, 2002). This research has examined the effects of goal difficulty and specificity on workers' performance, rather than the concrete/abstract goal dimension, but the results show interesting parallels. Considerable research indicates that encouraging workers to simply "do their best" seldom has the desired effect on performance. Like abstract goals, "doing your best" does not have a clear external reference by which to evaluate performance. Workers are left on their own to decide whether their performance is acceptable or not, and this results in lower levels of effort and performance. Specific, easy goals are also ineffective in producing high performance. Similar to concrete goals, they do not engage people's talents or deeper motivations and this results in less effort. What *does* work is providing people with both *specific and difficult goals*. This combination has consistently been found to produce higher levels of effort and performance. A general conclusion following from the performance and personal goal literature would be this: effective work performance and success in fulfillment of personal goals both seem to require meaningful and challenging goals coupled with clear and concrete strategies for achieving them.

The Ironic Effects of Mental Control

Some of the most significant and difficult personal goals are aimed at self-improvement, such as efforts to control personal habits like smoking, or eating and drinking too much. Controling behaviors that have become habitual is challenging because people are typically plagued with thoughts and urges that threaten to break their resolve. Controlling these unwanted thoughts would make it much easier to stay on a diet or quit smoking. What dieter wouldn't like to stop thinking about food? And what smoker trying to quit wouldn't wish that thoughts of cigarettes could just disappear from his mind? Along with various addictions and bad habits, we could add a host of negative emotions such as sadness, guilt, anxiety, and worry to the list of things we would like to get out of our minds. Ironically, some attempts at self-control have a way of backfiring by producing the opposite of the intended effect. The effect is similar to the paradoxical effects of trying to fall sleep when you're having trouble doing so. You can't "make" yourself go to sleep. The harder you try and the more you think about it, the more wide-awake you may become. Wegner's ideas and research on **ironic effects of mental control** offer one explanation for these kinds of paradoxes of self control—when the more we try, the worse it gets (Wegner, 1994).

Wegner's initial research made a simple request of study participants, namely to try not to think of a white bear, but to ring a bell if they did (Wegner, 1989; Wegner, Schneider, Carter, & White, 1987). Suppressing this simple thought was more difficult than you might imagine and people were only partly successful. Most interesting was that efforts to suppress the thought produced an unexpected and ironic side effect. When the thought-suppression task was over, many participants experienced a strong **rebound effect** of thoughts about a white bear. In other words, attempts at suppression *increased*, rather than decreased the occurrence of the thought. You can imagine the painful irony of this rebound effect for a dieter who has

been successful in losing a desired amount of weight by using various distractions to avoid thinking about food while dieting. If active efforts at suppression stop because of dieting success, Wegner's studies would predict a rebound of intrusive thoughts and images of food. The person may have to cope with more thoughts of food than before going on the diet.

Wegner and his colleagues conclude that ". . . the portrayal of suppression as the parent of obsession may contain a degree of truth" (Wegner et al., 1987, p. 11). Trying not to think about something may increase the odds that we can't stop thinking about it. Studies support this possibility. The ironic effects of thought suppression are not limited to white bears. For example, comparisons between people instructed *not* to think about sex and those instructed *to* think about sex found little difference in arousal (Wegner, Shortt, Blake, & Paige, 1990). Trying to suppress thoughts about sex generated as much excitement as thinking actively about sex. Another study suggests that depressed individuals may suffer deficits in their ability to control the occurrence of negative thoughts (Wenzlaff, Wegner, & Roper, 1988). Depressed and non-depressed individuals were asked to imagine themselves in an extremely negative situation described by a story. In the story, the protagonist (the main character) has an important interview for a highly desirable job, but forgets to set the alarm clock and drives over the speed limit, trying to make it to the interview on time. Running through a yellow light results in a car crash in which a young infant is killed. After imagining themselves as the protagonist in this story, participants were asked to record, in writing and moment by moment, whatever thoughts came to mind. Half of the participants were given the additional instruction *not* to think about the story and to make a check in their report every time the story came to mind. As you might imagine, the most common way to suppress a thought is to use distraction, by thinking about something else. Depressed individuals were not only less able to suppress unwanted thoughts of the story, but they also used negative thoughts as distracters. That is, their mental control ability was impaired compared to the non-depressed participants, and they also used negative rather than positive thoughts as distracters. Depressed individuals seem to suffer from a chronic and automatic over-accessibility of negative thoughts that feeds a cycle of negative thinking and feelings.

MENTAL LOAD AND THE PARADOXES OF CONTROL

How can these paradoxical, boomerang effects of attempts at mental control be explained? According to ironic process theory (Wegner, 1994, 1997), the explanation lies in the interactions of two systems involved in mental control. One aspect of this system is an intentional *operating process* that requires conscious effort and can be disrupted by an increased *mental load* (e.g., stress, distractions, time pressures, fatigue, or alcohol consumption). A smoker trying to quit uses this process to suppress or divert attention away from the desire to smoke. For example, if smoking had regularly occurred after a morning cup of coffee, the person might instead go for a walk, get busy on a task, or think about the benefits of quitting to control the urge to smoke. However, a second, *ironic monitoring process* is also at work in mental control. This process is largely unconscious, requires little effort, and is difficult to disrupt or stop. The monitoring process scans the environment, memories, and current thoughts for any signs of the now forbidden object. When thoughts or urges to smoke are detected, they are brought into conscious awareness and the operating system is activated to suppress the thought or urge to smoke. The irony is that long-term smokers have accumulated a large number of environmental and mood associations to smoking. Morning coffee, the end of a meal, taking a break at work, feelings of stress, going out to a bar, and a desire to relax have all likely been paired with smoking. So the monitoring process has many "forbidden" situations, thoughts, and feelings to detect and, therefore, conscious awareness of smoking is increased. If the operating system is unimpaired, the two systems work together to reduce and counteract the urge to smoke.

However, when the efficiency of the operation process is reduced due to increased mental load, the monitoring process may overwhelm mental control efforts and make it extremely difficult to avoid smoking. Mental control may fail because the monitoring process continues unconsciously, without effort and without being affected by the mental or emotional load state of the person. The monitoring process increases the conscious accessibility of smoking desires, whether the person has the capability of suppressing them or not. The irony here is that the monitoring process that is necessary for effective mental control contains the seeds of mental control failure under conditions of heavy mental load. By increasing the person's awareness of the very unwanted thoughts that are the object of the control effort, the ironic monitoring process contributes to the defeat of the mental control process.

In a clever demonstration of how ironic processes operate under conditions of heavy mental load, Wegner and colleagues (Wegner, Ansfield, & Pilloff, 1998) had people try to hold a pendulum steady over a target. The pendulum was a pointed crystal weight attached to a nylon line and the target was an x and y-axis that formed a "+" on a glass plate. A video camera pointed upward underneath the plate recorded any movement of the pendulum. If you have ever tried to keep a camera from moving when shooting a close-up picture without a tripod, or thread a very small needle, you know how difficult stopping muscle movement can be. And ironically (especially if we are stressed, in a hurry or distracted), the more we want to prevent any movement, the more we seem to jiggle and shake. This is exactly what was observed in the pendulum study. Some participants were simply told to hold the pendulum steady, while others were specifically instructed to prevent any sideways movement along the x-axis. In the mental load condition, while trying to hold the pendulum steady, participants were also required to either count backward by 3s from 1,000 or to hold a heavy brick in their opposite hand. Consistent with the ironic effect of mental control, people made more movements in the x-axis direction when they were specifically instructed not to do so. These effects were magnified in the mental load condition. The mental distraction of counting or holding a brick increased the movements in the "forbidden" direction. Following a similar method, Wegner and colleagues also found that when people were distracted, they were more likely to overshoot a golf putt that they were trying hard not to overshoot.

Consistent with Wegner's theory, research reviews find that any number of mental distractions can impair the self-regulation process, leading to failure of self-control efforts (e.g., Carver & Scheier, 1998; Muraven & Baumeister, 2000). Dieters, smokers, and individuals with drug addictions often experience failed self-control when they suffer emotional distress, negative moods, or environmental stressors such as excessive noise or overcrowding. These results generally fit the idea that self-control is a limited resource that can be used up, resulting in self-control failure. Automatic, habitual, and largely unconscious processes take over when conscious and effortful control falls short. From this perspective, negative states (such as stress and bad moods) use up self-control resources because people exert mental and emotional energy trying to cope with them. As a result, control resources are diminished, often causing failure in another area of control. After coping with a highly stressful day at work, a dieter may not have enough control strength remaining to resist tempting foods. Wegner's ironic process theory suggests that the person might even fall victim to a reactive episode of binge eating.

Recent studies suggest that depletion of control resources may be moderated by several factors. First, people may compensate for depleted resources if they are highly motivated by either internal or external incentives to do so. Studies have found that people whose control resources were reduced by their efforts on a self-control exertion task performed well on a subsequent self-control test, when they were given a substantial monetary reward or were led to believe that their self-control efforts would help others (Muraven & Slessareva, 2003). In our dieting example, these findings would suggest that if a dieter was keenly aware that a spouse or a friend was very concerned about the health risks of his/her excess weight, or if his or her employer offered a reduction in health-care premiums for weight loss, the person might well succeed in resisting food temptations despite having a stressful day.

Secondly, proponents of self-determination theory have recently argued that autonomy is a critical variable determining whether self-control depletes energy resources (Moller, Deci, & Ryan, 2006). Autonomy refers to an individual's sense that his or her actions and decisions are freely chosen and expressive of his or her true self (Deci & Ryan, 2000). A person might choose to walk 3 miles each morning because she enjoys walking and because she experiences positive feelings from engaging in regular exercise. Such autonomous actions can be contrasted with behaviors and choices undertaken because of internal (self-imposed) or external pressures (other-imposed). A person might start walking because he feels the need to lose weight, because his doctor recommended more exercise, or because friends have asked him to join their walking group. The critical difference here is between the feeling of freely choosing the activity and the feeling of being controlled or pressured. Moller and colleagues (2006) believe that ego-depletion research has failed to consider this important distinction.

The importance of autonomy in mitigating the depletion of self-control resources has been supported by research findings. Studies have shown that engagement in autonomous, self-regulated actions *increases*, rather than decreases, people's experience of energy and vitality (see Moller et al., 2006). Behavior that occurs in the service of freely chosen and personally expressive goals does not seem to use up self-control energy. From this perspective, acts of self-control do not invariably deplete self-control resources. They do so only when the actions in question are not freely chosen and people feel controlled or pressured. Walking each morning because we enjoy it does not feel like a burden that taxes self-discipline. On the other hand, walking only because we believe we "should" is more likely to test our resolve and self-control strength over time because we feel the tension between walking and the desire to do something else. Support for the moderating role of autonomy was provided by three studies (Moller et al., 2006). Consistent with predictions, individuals in autonomous choice conditions showed greater energy (in the form of longer task persistence) than participants in controlled choice conditions. Only the controlled choice conditions showed evidence of self-control resource depletion.

EVERYDAY EXPLANATIONS FOR SELF-CONTROL FAILURE

We have examined a number of factors that can disrupt people's ability to successfully regulate goal-directed action and obtain the benefits of goal achievement: lack of a clear plan, lack of commitment or confidence, an avoidance goal orientation, goal conflict, personal goals that are overly focused on either abstract or concrete outcomes, and ironic effects of mental control when self-control resources are reduced or depleted. We now consider some of the "everyday" reasons people give for failed self-regulation. Research provides some guidance in sorting out these reasons according to their actual effects on self-control. That is, whether they refer to real difficulties or are simply self-serving rationalizations.

Excuses

When stated plans are not completed, goals not achieved, or self-control fails, people may look bad in their own eyes and in the eyes of others. Laziness, self-indulgence, impulsiveness, lack of discipline, disorganization, procrastination, and untrustworthiness all come to mind as possible explanations for failure. To avoid these negative inferences, people often offer explanations for why they did not keep their commitments, follow through with plans, or meet personal goals: "I had too much else to do;" "I had a personal emergency;" "I wasn't clear on what I was supposed to do;" "I got distracted;" "I just couldn't resist a smoke, a tempting dessert, going out with friends;" etc. Do these explanations reflect real, unforeseen difficulties, or are they just excuses we use in attempts to salvage our self-image and our relationships with others? The answer to this question is obviously a judgment call. On the one hand, we all know people who are prone to giving excuses for their failure to deliver on their plans and stated intentions. On the other hand, unanticipated events over which people have no control can, in fact, interfere with the best of plans.

A recent review by Barry Schlenker and colleagues provides an intriguing look at research and theory concerning how people judge the legitimacy of excuses in social and individual life (Schlenker, Pontari, & Christopher, 2001). Their article builds on an earlier, extensive review by Snyder and Higgins (1998). Excuses are defined as ". . . self-serving explanations or accounts, that aim to reduce personal responsibility for questionable events, thereby disengaging core components of the self from the incident . . ." (Schlenker et al., 2001, p. 15). This definition leaves open the question of whether an excuse is true or false. It focuses on motivation and purpose. The purpose of giving an excuse is to reduce personal responsibility and fault for a negative event by providing reasons that attribute the cause of the event to something or someone else, or to less central and more peripheral features of the self. A peripheral aspect of self might be simple carelessness or forgetfulness. Examples of more central self-features would be untrustworthiness, unreliability, and irresponsibility.

WHAT MAKES A GOOD EXCUSE? Schlenker and his colleagues use a triangle model of responsibility to describe how we evaluate the legitimacy of excuses. The model focuses on our judgments of responsibility. Because excuses deny or soften responsibility, how we assign personal responsibility for negative events is critical to evaluating excuses. The three components of the model are: prescriptive clarity, personal obligation,

and personal control. These components are shown in Figure 8.2. The higher the prescriptive clarity, personal obligation, and personal control, the more personal responsibility for the event is assigned to the individual (identity).

Prescriptive clarity refers to the rules, goals, procedures, and standards that are relevant to the event, which describe what should be done, and how. **Personal obligation** describes the extent to which a person is required, expected, or duty-bound to follow the prescriptions or rules of conduct. For example, a father has a strong obligation to take good care of his kids. **Personal control** is the final component, and refers to the amount of control a person has over the outcome of the event in question.

In this model, excuses are aimed at diminishing one or more of the three components of personal responsibility. Claiming that the rules, goals, or expectations were unclear or ambiguous can reduce responsibility based on prescriptive clarity. Every college professor has heard such claims from students unhappy with their grades on tests or papers: "You didn't make it clear what would be covered on the test." "I didn't know how you wanted the paper organized or how many references I was supposed to have."

Responsibility based on personal obligation can be diminished by claiming that the prescriptions, rules, and standards do not apply to oneself: "That's not my job." "I had a family emergency and couldn't

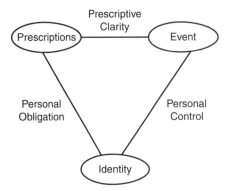

FIGURE 8.2 Triangular Model of Personal Responsibility
Source: Schlenker, B. R., Pontari, B. A., & Christoper, A. N. (2001). Excuses and character: Personal and social implications of excuses. *Personality and Social Psychology Review, 5*, 15–32. Copyright American Psychological Association. Reprinted by permission.

complete the work on time." Finally, responsibility can be diminished by excuses involving personal control. These excuses focus on factors that reduce the ability and capacity to carry out an action. Many college instructors hear stories of computer viruses, failed printers, and lost files as reasons why papers are not turned in. Other familiar reasons for poor performance or missed assignments include, "I overslept because I stayed up all night studying for your exam;" "I'm having personal problems;" and "I just don't do well on this kind of test."

ADVANTAGES OF EXCUSES Excuse-making can have positive benefits by protecting self esteem, motivating enhanced performance, and helping to preserve harmony in relationships. Providing ourselves with a reasonable excuse for failure helps maintain our esteem and confidence (Schlenker et al., 2001). Taking full responsibility for negative events, while necessary and appropriate in some cases, can also overwhelm people with incapacitating guilt and self-blame. Lifting some of the responsibility, by pointing to extenuating circumstances or the actions of others, helps us distance ourselves from the event and reduce the potentially debilitating effects of negative emotions such as depression and anxiety. Research suggests that excuses can help invigorate performance and efforts at self-improvement (Schlenker et al., 2001; Snyder & Higgins, 1988).

Excuses may have similar positive effects in our relationships with others. Brutal honesty is a recipe for disaster. We don't say, "I'm not coming to your dinner party because I find you and your wife uninteresting." Instead we say, "Sorry I can't make it; I'd love to be there, but I have a previous commitment." Demands of social civility require us to consider the feelings of others and avoid damaging our relationships. Schlenker and colleagues' review notes many studies showing how excuses contribute to social harmony by smoothing over potential disruptions in relationships.

DISADVANTAGES OF EXCUSES As you might guess, excuses can come with a price tag, especially if they are used excessively or are transparently false. Any excuse may lead to speculation concerning its truth or falsity and raise questions about the motives that lie behind it and the character of the person who provides it. Further, excuses may undermine the excuse-giver's self-regulation abilities, confidence,

and effectiveness. To see how this might happen, imagine having a co-worker who is always giving excuses for why he is unable to complete his assigned work on time, why he doesn't volunteer to take on new tasks or tackle emergent problems, and why he seldom keeps promises and commitments. How are you likely to view such a person? Unreliable, lacking in integrity, self-centered, ineffectual? Schlenker and colleagues argue that these are just the sorts of judgments that chronic excuse-givers are likely to receive. The effects of habitual excuse-making are potentially quite damaging to the reputation and performance of the excuse-giver.

Continual use of excuses may also reduce an individual's self-control and performance. An important component of self-control and self-discipline involves our responsibility to others. Knowing that we will be accountable to others provides an important source of motivation that encourages us to stay on task and fulfill our obligations. When people fail to meet their obligations, they may offer excuses to disengage and distance themselves from responsibility for their actions. If this distancing includes decreased feelings of responsibility to others, or if excuses lead to strong perceptions of unreliability so that others no longer give much responsibility to the excuse-giver, then an important mechanism of self-regulation is also diminished.

Overall, the most general and detrimental effect of excuses may be the disengagement of the self from tasks. Following Wegner's work, perhaps we should call this the "ironic effect of excuses." To be effective, excuses need to reduce our sense of responsibility for failure, but in the process they may also cause us to second-guess our ability, determination, and motivation to succeed. Schlenker and colleagues (2001) argue that excuses ". . . may rob the excuse-maker of a sense of purposefulness and control" (p. 25). Rather than protecting the self against threats to self-esteem and negative regard by others, chronic excuse-giving may come to produce the very effects they were meant to avoid.

Irresistible Impulses

Another everyday explanation for failed control is the inability to resist temptations and strong emotions. What do people mean when they say that they couldn't resist a strong temptation, or were driven by an overwhelming emotion like anger, jealousy, remorse, frustration, or stress? Are they passive victims of impulses too strong to resist? Taken over by something they could not control? Or was it a decision to give in and cooperate, so to speak, with the impulse, by consciously directing its expression? Is it perhaps more accurate to say they *could* resist, but decided not to?

BELIEFS ABOUT SELF-CONTROL In his book, *The Diseasing of America* (1989), Peele provides many counter-examples to the power of irresistible impulses. During the Vietnam War, many soldiers used heroin. Once back in the United States most recovered quickly from their addictions without treatment. Some even used heroin occasionally without succumbing to addiction. Individual and cultural beliefs about control are also highlighted in Peele's analysis. Alcoholics' binge-drinking may have more to do with their beliefs about a lack of control than with a disease or physical dependency. Within some cultures and societies (American Jews and the French, for example), people drink regularly, but have very low rates of alcoholism. Apparently, strong cultural sanctions against irresponsible behavior and excessive drinking strengthen self-control. These examples suggest that irresistible impulses may be more a matter of belief than of fact. How much control people exert over a behavior or emotion may have less to do with the power of the impulse, and more to do with culturally internalized beliefs about whether they should, or can, exercise self-control.

ACTIVATION OF IMPULSIVE AND REFLECTIVE CONTROL SYSTEMS Research examining the issue of impulse versus restraint is typically based on dual processing models of behavior control similar to Wegner's ironic processing theory (see Carver, 2005; Carver & Scheier, 1998, 2002c; Smith & DeCoster, 2000; Strack & Deutsch, 2004, for recent reviews). Despite differences in details and names for the two processes, most models describe an *impulsive*, emotional, relatively automatic, and quick-acting system, and a more *reflective*, deliberate, less emotional, and slower-acting system. For example, Mischel and his colleagues describe a "hot system" and a "cool system" (Metcalfe & Mischel, 1999; Mischel & Mendoza-Denton, 2003). The **hot** or "go" **system** is activated by emotionally arousing events in the environment that may require fast action, such as those necessary to defend against a threat or take advantage of an opportunity for immediate pleasure. The **cool** or

"know" **system** is slow, unemotional, flexible, rational, and often leads to strategies and plans for long-term actions. According to Mischel's model, whether people follow or control their impulses is determined by which system is in control. The hot system leads to impulsive actions, while the cool system produces controlled actions.

In his classic marshmallow studies discussed earlier, Mischel was able to increase or decrease children's ability to delay gratification by activating the cool or hot system (1974). To engage the hot impulsive system, Mischel instructed some children to think of how chewy and sweet the marshmallow would feel in their mouths. Children in the cool condition were asked to think about marshmallows in more abstract and unemotional terms, as "puffy clouds." Children in the cool condition were able to wait much longer for their larger marshmallow reward than those in the hot condition. In other words, instructions in the hot condition effectively undermined children's ability to delay gratification. These results suggest that people's ability to regulate the activation of the **hot and cool systems** would be one mechanism of self-control. The ability to think "cool" when faced with a "hot" situation may be one explanation for differences in people's self-control capacity.

INDIVIDUAL DIFFERENCES IN SELF-CONTROL It is clear that impulse control is, in part, an individual trait. That is, people respond more or less automatically, in line with their characteristic level of impulse control and restraint. Some people have more self-control and self-discipline than others. Some of us are impulsive and highly sensitive to short-term incentives and rewards, while others are more disciplined. Concepts of ego-control, ego-resilience, hardiness, and conscientiousness all capture elements of a person's ability to regulate actions, control internal and external threats, delay gratification, and follow through on plans and commitments (see Carver, 2005, for a recent review and Gramzow, Sedikides, Panter, & Insko, 2000, for an exemplary study). Differences among individuals in the strength of these qualities have been linked to various forms of restraint involving alcohol, sexual gratification, and foregoing a short-term reward for a larger, long-term reward. For example, Mischel found stable differences in children's ability to wait for a larger reward rather than taking a smaller, more immediate one.

RESISTING TEMPTATIONS Evidence for trait differences does not exclude people's capacity to learn ways to improve their self-control. Many heart attack victims learn to control their drinking, smoking, diet, and exercise. Even young children can show increased self-control. Mischel found that the *same* children who were unable to delay gratification when given *no* instructions about what to do during the delay period were able to tolerate very long delays when instructed to think in cooler terms. That is, left to their own devices, many children showed poor control, but when given helpful suggestions they dramatically improved their self-control abilities.

Researchers have also been able to increase people's self-control by shifting their thinking from a lower level to a higher level; that is, from immersion in the emotions of the immediate situation to a big-picture view (Fujita, Trope, Liberman, & Levin-Sagi, 2006). Fujita and colleagues argue that a key variable leading to higher-level thinking and increased self-control is **psychological distance.** Distance here refers to a psychological separation between the self and the situation, event, or object. Distance may be increased by time, physical and social separation, and by mentally shifting to a consideration of alternatives and looking at the bigger picture. People often reverse their decisions and reconsider a course of action when they take time to think, when they are physically separated from the situation or the people involved, or when they take a broader perspective rather than a narrow one. Creating psychological distance rather than acting in the moment often pays big dividends in the form of better decisions and improved self-control.

The bottom line on irresistible impulses may be this: If we would all just follow the advice we so easily give to others, we might have more self-control. "Take time to think it over." "Don't make an impulsive decision." "Don't let your emotions override your judgment." We have all offered this advice to friends and loved ones, but often find it difficult to follow ourselves. Baumeister and colleagues believe that one reason for this is that self-control is unpleasant, difficult, and emotionally draining (Baumeister et al., 1994). These researchers argue that loss of self-control in the face of supposedly irresistible impulses is more appropriately viewed as giving in than being overwhelmed.

Focus on Research: The Costs and Benefits of Procrastination

Procrastination is probably one of the most frequent reasons that people do not fulfill their obligations, deliver on their promises, or fulfill personal goals. Tice and Baumeister (1997) provide a revealing look at the reasons for, and consequences of doing later, what we know we should do now. As they note, procrastination is widely condemned as evidence of laziness and self-indulgence. Yet surveys reveal that most of us plead guilty to procrastinating at least sometimes. Procrastination is not without its defenses, however. If you finish a project and devote the same amount of time to it, does it matter if you do it later rather than sooner? And some people claim that they do their best work under the pressure of an impending deadline. Time pressures add emotional energy to behavior, perhaps leading to better performance.

In two longitudinal studies, Tice and Baumeister investigated the possible costs and benefits of procrastination. To evaluate the effects of procrastination, these researchers compared the emotional/physical health consequences and the performance of procrastinating and non-procrastinating college students taking a health psychology class. Each of their two studies took place over the course of a semester. Students were classified as procrastinators or non-procrastinators by their score on a standardized scale assessing people's tendency to procrastinate. Health problems were measured in terms of self-reported visits to health-care professionals, and a daily checklist was used to record stress levels and illness symptoms. Data on academic performance included the quality of term papers; whether the term paper was handed in early, on time, or late; exam performance; and final course grade.

Overall, Baumeister and Tice found that procrastination produced short-term benefits, but long-term costs. Early in the semester, procrastinating students enjoyed a period of reduced stress and few health problems, while non-procrastinating students who got to work on their papers and projects right away suffered higher levels of stress and health problems during that time period. However, as end-of-semester deadlines approached, this pattern reversed, with procrastinating students experiencing more stress and health symptoms than non-procrastinators. Further, procrastinations' early advantages were more than offset by later costs. Over the entire semester, the toll in terms of increased stress and negative effects on health was greater for procrastinating students than for non-procrastinators. Further, the performance measures showed that procrastination was consistently associated with lower-quality work. Grades on terms papers and exams were significantly lower for procrastinators than for non-procrastinators. The belief held by some individuals that they do their best work under stress found no support in this study. Instead, the results suggest that postponing work results in lower-quality work, and increases stress and illness. Baumeister and Tice conclude that more often than not, procrastination is self-defeating.

GOAL DISENGAGEMENT

Americans love winners and view "quitters" as "losers." Accounts of people overcoming seemingly insurmountable obstacles are frequent topics for television shows, magazine articles, books, and movies. Such stories celebrate the strength of the human spirit and inspire a "can-do," "never-give-up" attitude toward life's challenges and hardships. The psychological literature also affirms the virtues of sustained individual effort and often portrays those who give up as helpless and hapless (Carver & Scheier, 1998, 2003). Despite these widely held sentiments, Carver and Scheier (2003) contend that giving up is an important and under-appreciated human strength. They point out that an individual's journey through life inevitably involves *disengagement* or letting go of unattainable goals, and that such abandonment is often beneficial. Giving up something that is unattainable prevents us from wasting time following blind alleys and dead ends, and helps avoid the distress that may result from hanging onto goals that cannot be achieved. Carver and Scheier conclude that knowing when to give up versus when to persevere should be regarded as a highly adaptive coping skill. This skill was captured in the Don Schlitz song, *The Gambler*, the lyrics of which say, "You got to know when to hold 'em, know when to fold 'em."

Many everyday life situations present us with this seemingly simple hold-'em-or-fold-'em question. Should we give up, or keep trying? Should we keep shopping for the "perfect gift" for someone, study another hour for a big exam, continue in a relationship that is going poorly, or should we give it up? The difficulty and emotional consequences of giving up depend heavily on the importance of the goal we

are pursuing (Carver & Scheier, 1998). Abandoning a lower level, concrete goal (such as finding the perfect gift) may cause some short-term frustration, but is unlikely to cause major life disruption—at least for most people. However, the decision about whether to give up or keep trying assumes much greater personal significance when goals are self-defining or reflect basic human needs (e.g., trying to preserve an important relationship). Ending a romantic relationship, moving on with life after the death of a loved one, or letting go of a career dream are challenging and highly distressing decisions. Such choices may be fraught with guilt, anxiety, feelings of failure, and despair. The critical question here is, how do we know when disengaging from an important goal is the right thing to do?

Carver and Scheier (1998) argue that the answer to this question is far from clear and involves a difficult dilemma. Both hanging on too long and giving up too soon come with potential price tags. On one hand, the inability to mentally disengage from unattained goals, failures, or losses has been linked to depression and poor adjustment. Research shows that "hanging on" is associated with emotional distress (see Carver & Scheier, 1998, Chapter 12). A person who is unable to get over a lost love, for example, may be both tormented and paralyzed by mental and emotional absorption in the failed relationship. This absorption may prevent the person from getting on with life and developing new relationships. On the other hand, disengaging from goals every time things get difficult or go poorly will certainly undermine success. Important goals are typically challenging and require us to overcome obstacles. Giving up too soon, when a goal is, in fact, attainable with sustained effort, compromises our potential achievements and our sense of competence. Chronic giving up across a variety of life goals is one way of defining "helplessness" (c.f. Seligman, 1975).

As you may imagine, given the differences in people's personalities and life circumstances, knowing whether or not a goal is attainable for a particular individual is a judgment call. College faculty members confront this issue when they advise students regarding career plans. As psychologists, your textbook authors frequently encounter students who want to become clinical psychologists. Getting accepted to a reputable clinical psychology doctoral program requires (among other things) outstanding undergraduate grades. What should we say to a student with a 2.5 grade point average? "Hang in there and you might make it," or "You need to consider another career option"? As advisers and mentors, we are committed to encouraging our students to pursue their goals and dreams, but we also feel obligated to provide them with realistic feedback and counsel. The trouble is, some students with average grades have strong abilities and do go on to productive clinical careers, while some with outstanding grades fail because they lack the personal qualities to become effective clinical psychologists.

Whatever the basis of people's judgments concerning their ability to achieve important goals, one thing seems clear. Unanticipated events, together with limits in time and resources, require all of us to make choices about which goals to pursue and which to abandon. A recent study suggests these decisions have important emotional consequences. Wrosch, Scheier, Miller, Schulz, and Carver (2003) were interested in three questions. First, are there differences among individuals in the ease or difficulty with which they are able to disengage from unattainable goals? Second, are these differences related to subjective well-being? Specifically, do people who find it relatively easy to abandon unattainable goals report higher subjective well-being than those who have a more difficult time letting go? Third, does the ability to redirect efforts toward alternative goals offset the negative consequences of abandoning goals that are perceived to be unattainable? In other words, is goal

reengagement an adaptive self-regulation strategy when confronted with unattainable goals?

Results from three studies that included college students and adult community members provided affirmative answers to each of these research questions. Measures used in the study included assessment of participants' general stances toward their difficulty-ease in disengaging from unattainable goals, their difficulty-ease in reengaging themselves in alternative goals, and measures of SWB. Summary findings showed that, regardless of age or specific life circumstances, people who found it easier to disengage from unattainable goals reported higher SWB than those who had difficulty letting go of goals. People who disengaged more easily also reported a greater sense of self-mastery and lower levels of stress and intrusive thoughts about life problems. Goal reengagement (investing in new alternatives) was also found to be significantly related to all measures of SWB.

Overall, these results provide testimony to the beneficial effects of giving up unattainable goals—particularly when people can at the same time reengage themselves in meaningful goals that provide alternative direction and purpose to life. Despite widespread beliefs to the contrary, giving up has an important place in adaptive self-regulation. At the very least, it seems to be a healthier alternative than hanging onto goals that have little or no likelihood of being achieved.

Chapter Summary Questions

1. How do the classic studies by Walter Mischel and more recent studies of college students show the value of self-control for a successful life?
2. Compare and contrast control theory and self-discrepancy theory as models of goal-directed and self-regulated action.
3. Why does planning help us achieve our goals? How may implementation intentions make goal pursuit "automatic" and help conserve self-control resources?
4. How does the study by Brunstein show the dual importance of commitment and confidence for goal progress?
5. From the perspective of control theory, what is the difference between approach goals and avoidance goals?

6. Why are avoidance goals associated with less success and diminished well-being? Discuss the role of monitoring, self-control resources, negative emotions, feelings of competence, and self-imposed goals.
7. What is the difference between the parenting styles associated with the development of approach (promotion) or avoidance (prevention) goal orientations, according to Higgins?
8. How may intergoal facilitation help solve goal-conflict problems? Explain and give an example.
9. According to action identification theory, what is the difference between higher- and lower-order identifications of action and how do these relate to an individual's self-image?
10. a. What is the "manageable" and "meaningful" trade-off?

b. How might a repressive personality type help explain the association between concrete goals and distress, according to Emmons?

11. How does the rebound effect demonstrate the ironic effect of mental control?

12. How does the interrelationship between the operating process, monitoring process, and mental load explain the ironic effects of mental control?

13. How may autonomously chosen actions help reduce the depletion of self-control resources and the ironic effects of efforts at mental control?

14. What are the major advantages and disadvantages of excuses according to research by Schlenker and his colleagues?

15. What is the difference between thinking "hot" and thinking "cool?"

16. How may "psychological distance" increase our self-control ability?

17. According to research by Tice and Baumeister, what are the short-term advantages but longer-term costs of procrastination?

18. a. What are the two sides of the hanging on versus giving up dilemma regarding personal goals?

b. What are the well-being benefits of goal disengagement and reengagement?

Key Terms

self-control *155*
delay gratification *155*
control theory *156*
self-discrepancy theory *156*
goal intentions *157*
standards, monitoring and strength *157*

implementation intentions *157*
approach goals *160*
avoidance goals *160*
intergoal facilitation *163*
action identification theory *164*
ironic effects of mental control *166*
rebound effect *166*

prescriptive clarity *169*
personal obligation *169*
personal control *169*
hot and cool systems *171*
psychological distance *172*

Web Resources

Self-Regulation and Self-Determination Theory

www.psych.rochester.edu/SDT/measures/selfreg.html This is a link from the self-determination theory site at the University of Rochester. It reviews self-regulation from a self-determination theory perspective, provides examples of self-regulation questionnaires, and offers PDF files for self-regulation research articles.

Ironic Effects of Mental Control

www.wjh.harvard.edu/~wegner/ip.htm This is Daniel Wegner's Harvard University web site. It contains listings of his past and recent studies on the ironic effects of mental control, including the well-known white bear study.

Suggested Readings

Baumeister, R. F., Heatherton, T. F., & Tice, D. M. (1994). *Losing control: How and why people fail at self-regulation.* San Diego, CA: Academic Press.

Carver, C. S., & Scheier, M. F. (1998). *On the self-regulation of behavior.* New York: Cambridge University Press.

Elliot, A. J., & Church, M. A. (2002). Client-articulated avoidance goals in the therapy context. *Journal of Counseling Psychology, 49,* 243–254.

Elliot, A. J., Gable, S. L., & Mapes, R. R. (2006). Approach and avoidance motivation in the social domain. *Personality and Social Psychology Bulletin, 32,* 376–391.

Gollwitzer, P. M. (1999). Implementation intentions: Strong effects of simple plans. *American Psychologist, 54,* 493–503.

Vallacher, R. R., & Wegner, D. M. (1987). What do people think they're doing? Action identification and human behavior. *Psychological Review, 94,* 3–15.

Wegner, D. M. (1989). *White bears and other unwanted thoughts.* New York: Vintage.

9

Positive Traits

CHAPTER OUTLINE

Positive psychologists have examined a wide array of individual differences that help explain why some people are healthier and happier than others. A major reason for the prominence of trait explanations is that the objective features of people's lives account for a relatively smaller percentage of the variability in individual well-being. As we saw in Chapters 5 and 6, life events, income, age, gender, and education do not tell us much about a person's level of happiness and life satisfaction. Differences in personal qualities, on the other hand, are strongly related to differences in well-being. A recent article suggests that 50% of people's long-term level of happiness may be associated with genetically-influenced aspects of temperament and personality (Lyubomirsky, Sheldon, & Schkade, 2005).

Positive traits include an assortment of individual characteristics related to personality, emotions, beliefs, and self-conceptions. Each of these terms refers to a relatively enduring individual disposition that describes a person's characteristic way of thinking, feeling, and acting across a variety of situations. Most traits that influence well-being show significant stability over time, which is the primary basis for their designation as traits. Many personality traits, for example, are very stable across the life span, especially after age 30 (McCrae & Costa, 1990; Roberts & DelVecchio, 2000; Terracciano, Costa, & McCrae, 2006).

Traits are internal dispositions that color how we see and interpret the world. Traits influence the meanings we give to life events, the choices we make, the goals we select, and the actions we take. They represent what Diener (1984) called "top-down" influences on well-being. That is, our inner dispositions (top) exert stable and pervasive influences on many aspects of our lives (down) that affect our health and happiness. Although conceptual distinctions can be drawn among them, many individual characteristics are interconnected and share overlapping meanings. For example, personality traits have been viewed as intimately connected with emotions (e.g., McCrae & Costa, 1991; Watson, 2002) and with generalized beliefs about the self (Robinson & Clore, 2002). We will use the generic term "traits" to refer to all the diverse individual characteristics found to influence well-being.

WHAT MAKES A TRAIT POSITIVE?

The complexities of human behavior and the diversity of evaluative standards make it difficult to distinguish between positive and negative characteristics. Positive psychologists would be the first to admit to these difficulties (see Aspinwall & Staudinger, 2003). Context, cultural differences, developmental changes, and the interrelation of positive and negative qualities are among the many things that confound attempts to establish clear distinctions. Examples are easy to find. Posttraumatic growth (discussed in Chapter 4) shows how significant positive lessons can result from negative experiences. We saw in Chapter 7 that "giving up" a personal aspiration, though widely stigmatized, can be a positive adaptation because it may prevent the futile pursuit of unattainable goals. Some traits may have desirable effects in one situation but undesirable

effects in another. Many individual characteristics necessary for success at work, for example, would likely reduce the quality of one's family life (e.g., competitiveness).

Developing clear guidelines for the positive/negative distinction is one important item on positive psychology's future agenda. In the meantime, we can describe four interrelated general standards used by well-being researchers to assess positive and negative qualities. First, following the hedonic conception of well-being, subjective well-being (SWB) researchers examine whether a particular individual characteristic enhances or diminishes a person's level of happiness. Given the three components of SWB, a positive quality may increase the experience of positive emotions, decrease negative emotions, or increase life satisfaction. Effects on SWB are the most common basis for defining a positive quality because SWB measures are the ones most frequently used in positive psychology research.

Second, the eudaimonic view of well-being provides a related, yet distinctive basis for evaluating positive qualities. Eudaimonic research and theory focus on emotional health, positive social relationships, finding meaning and purpose in life, and effective coping and adaptation. Positive qualities are those that enhance mental health, foster high-quality relations with others, and contribute to success in meeting life's many challenges. From this perspective, happiness is not a central or exclusive criterion for evaluating a trait as positive. Happiness *may* be enhanced by increased eudaimonic well-being (as discussed in Chapter 2); however, many qualities that enhance our health may not increase personal happiness. Having the courage to do the hard things in life, like telling your kids "no," confronting interpersonal conflicts, and breaking off bad relationships, are good for our own and others' emotional health, but may reduce our enjoyment of life, at least in the short term.

Third, many researchers have focused on the physical health advantages and disadvantages of various psychological traits. Physical health measures may include longevity, as in the Nun Study (see Chapter 1), level of risk for serious disease (e.g., heart disease), physical illness symptoms, speed of recovery from illness or medical treatment (e.g., surgery), levels of stress, and the effectiveness of an individual's health-maintenance practices.

In Chapter 10, we will review research related to a fourth criterion for defining a positive trait.

A large-scale investigation of virtuous behavior across time and culture has provided a taxonomy of traits from a moral point of view (Peterson & Seligman, 2004). Certain human qualities appear to be universally regarded as positive, not because they make people happy or healthy, but because they represent morally virtuous behavior and strength of character, as defined by religion and culture. Examples of traits defining people of good character include modesty, humility, kindness, forgiveness, bravery, and integrity. These qualities are positively valued because they reflect people's understanding of morality, good conduct, and good character. Character strengths may increase our life satisfaction and make life more meaningful and healthy. However, virtuous behavior is also positively regarded in its own right because of its connection to religious and secular mores.

Our review of positive traits in this chapter will focus on the first three criteria. We will examine differences in personality and address two questions. First, *what* traits are associated with differences in well-being? (More specifically, what constellation of personality traits and beliefs predicts a happy and emotionally and physically healthy person?) Second, and more important, *how* does a particular trait influence well-being? Individual characteristics describe differences among people, but they do not necessarily explain why these differences exist. Finding that optimists are happier than pessimists does not tell us *why* or *how* optimism influences well-being. Answers to the "why" and "how" questions require more detailed research investigating the thinking and actions of optimists compared to pessimists. Currently, we know more about *what* traits are related to well-being than we do about *how* they exert their influence. Fortunately, a growing body of recent research is directed at investigating the specific mechanisms through which traits affect well-being.

PERSONALITY, EMOTIONS, AND BIOLOGY

"Some men are just born three drinks behind" (saying from the old "Wild West" quoted by Meehl, 1975, p. 298). Paul Meehl is often credited with advancing the study of positive emotions through his compelling description of individual differences in people's ability to experience pleasure. He called this ability "hedonic capacity" and, more humorously,

"cerebral joy-juice" (Meehl, 1975, p. 299). Meehl proposed that hedonic capacity is a stable personality aspect that is largely genetic in origin. He also believed that hedonic capacity is strongly tied to the personality trait of extraversion. Being outgoing and sociable goes together with the experience of positive emotions. Finally, Meehl argued that a person's capacity for positive emotions was independent and distinct from a similar capacity for negative emotions. In other words, differences in people's hedonic capacity include all possible combinations of emotional experiences. A person might characteristically experience many positive emotions and many negative emotions, few of either, or more of one than the other.

Positive and Negative Affectivity

Research has supported Meehl's early observations concerning individual differences in emotional capacity. Research by Watson and his colleagues has shown that positive and negative affect are, in fact, two independent dimensions of people's long-term emotional experience (Watson, 2002; Watson & Clark, 1992; Watson & Walker, 1996). The PANAS scale, described in Chapter 2, was developed to provide a simple measure of emotional experience (Watson, Clark, & Tellegen, 1988). Respondents rate the extent to which they experience a number of positive (e.g., proud, excited) and negative feelings (e.g., distress, guilt). Separate scores are calculated for positive and negative emotions. The independence of positive and negative affect means that people can score high or low on either or both dimensions.

When used across short time intervals, the PANAS is sensitive to situational events that affect people's current positive and negative emotional states. Over longer time periods, PANAS scores reflect trait differences in people's characteristic emotional experience, referred to as **positive affectivity** and **negative affectivity.** People high in positive affectivity have frequent and intense experiences of pleasant, enjoyable moods and are generally cheerful, enthusiastic, and confident about their lives. People high in negative affectivity have more frequent emotional episodes involving feelings of anger, sadness, distress, guilt, and fear (Watson et al., 1988).

Support for positive and negative affectivity as enduring traits comes from studies showing long-term stability and cross-situational consistency. Positive and negative affectivity are very stable over periods ranging from a few weeks to 24 years (McCrae et al., 2000; Watson, 2002; Watson & Walker, 1996). Diener and Larsen (1984) found that an individual's emotional experiences were consistent across different activities. A person's self-reported mood was very similar whether he or she was socializing, working, recreating, or spending time alone. Our basic affective orientation appears to show itself wherever we go and whatever we do.

Positive affect is one of the strongest predictive components of happiness. Recall the three-part conception of SWB: frequent experience of positive emotions, relatively low-frequency negative emotions, and life satisfaction (see Chapter 2). Positive affectivity is built into the emotional component of SWB. Watson's research is perhaps most noteworthy for having identified the most central defining feature of happy people, namely positive affectivity. Happiness and positive affectivity go together, not so much because positive affect explains differences in happiness, but because they are essentially the same thing. Happy people seem best characterized as people who experience lots of positive emotions. Support for this conclusion comes from the prominence of positive affect in measures of happiness and the pattern of relationships to other variables. Many of the relationships between SWB and demographic variables (discussed in Chapters 5 and 6) are also found for positive affect when it is measured alone. Like SWB, high positive affectivity shows relatively small relationships to income, education, age, and gender, but is heavily influenced by, and strongly predictive of satisfying relationships (see Watson, 2002). Watson's research suggests that the bottom line of differences in people's levels of happiness boils down to differences in positive and negative affectivity.

Genetics and Happiness

Meehl's idea that people may be born "three drinks behind" or "three drinks ahead" (as cited by Watson, 2002, p. 116) is also supported by heritability studies. As we saw in Chapter 5, estimates of heritability are based on studies that compare monozygotic (identical) twins, who have 100% of their genes in common, to dizygotic (fraternal) twins, who share about 50% of their genes. Some studies also compare identical twins raised together to those who grew up in separate environments. Evidence of genetic influence is shown when the

similarity of identical twins significantly exceeds that of fraternal twins, and when identical twins show strong similarities despite being raised in separate environments. Research by Tellegen and his colleagues suggests that genetic factors account for 40% of the difference in long-term levels of positive affect, and 55% of the difference in negative affect (Tellegen et al., 1988).

A biological basis for people's characteristic emotional orientation receives further support from research showing that temperament differences emerge early in life. **Temperament** refers to a genetically-determined physiological disposition to respond to the environment in a stable and typical manner. Even in the first few weeks of life, infants show temperament differences in activity level, mood, responsiveness, and how readily they can be soothed and comforted by parents. Some infants are irritable, cranky, quick to become upset, and quick to cry in response to new situations and environmental changes. Others are calm, placid, and approach (rather than avoid) new things in the environment. Jerome Kagan has probably conducted the most well-known investigation of temperament differences. Kagan found that about 20% of infants fell into one of two extreme temperament types called **"reactive"** and **"non-reactive"** (Kagan, 1994; Kagan & Snidman, 2004). Highly reactive infants are easily upset by anything new in their environment. Whether it's a new babysitter, a loud noise, or group of new kids to play with, reactive children are likely to respond with more timidity, shyness, and fear than most kids. Non-reactive children are more laid back and comfortable with new situations and environmental changes. They are more outgoing, curious, and eager to explore the world and the people in it.

A biological basis for reactivity is suggested by differences in physiological arousal related to sympathetic nervous system activity. Increases in heart rate, brain activity, and the production of stress hormones have all been linked to reactive children's response to mildly stressful situations. Non-reactive children do not show this "uptight" response. Kagan also found that early childhood temperament was related to differences in personality and behavior years later. Reactive infants were more likely to become shy, anxious, and reserved adults, while non-reactive infants tended to become extraverted, easygoing, and talkative people with a ready smile. Many researchers believe that each individual's basic biological temperament establishes a foundation for the later development of more specific personality traits (McCrae et al., 2000; Rothbart, Ahadi, & Evans, 2000).

Personality and Happiness: The "Big Five"

Meehl's prediction about the relationship of positive affectivity to the personality trait of extraversion has been borne out by subsequent research. Studies also find a strong tie between negative affectivity and neuroticism. Extraversion and neuroticism are two factors in what is called the *Big Five Theory*, or **five-factor model** of personality. Before examining the connection of affectivity to personality, we will summarize the five-factor model. Over the last three decades, personality researchers have accumulated an impressive amount of evidence that five relatively independent factors describe the essential features of individual personality (John & Srivastava, 1999; McCrae & Allik, 2002). The five factors are very stable across a person's lifetime and have been validated in cultures around the world (McCrae & Costa, 1997; McCrae & Terracciano, 2005). Each of the five global traits (extraversion, neuroticism, openness to experience, agreeableness, and conscientiousness) is made up of more specific, subordinate traits. A commonly used questionnaire measure assesses six facets for each of the five global trait dimensions (Costa & McCrae, 1992; McCrae, Costa, & Martin, 2005).

Extraversion

Extraverted people are sociable, outgoing, and actively engaged with the world. More specific traits of extraversion include characteristics like personal warmth, gregariousness, assertiveness, excitement-seeking, and frequent positive emotions. *Introversion,* which is at the opposite end of this dimension and is indicated by a low score on the extraversion scale, describes people who are relatively detached from others, withdrawn, unassertive, contemplative, and reserved in their emotional expression.

Neuroticism

People high in *neuroticism* tend to be tense, anxious, moody, and more emotionally reactive to events than most people. They experience more frequent negative emotions like anger and depression,

and are more impulsive, self-conscious, and vulnerable. *Emotional stability* is the opposite of neuroticism and is characterized by calmness, emotional control, feelings of security, low reactivity, and relative freedom from persistent negative feelings.

Agreeableness

Agreeableness reflects a person's concern with getting along and cooperating with others, even if it means compromising their own interests. Specific traits related to agreeableness include being trusting, straightforward, helpful, compliant, modest, and tender-minded (in the sense of believing in the honesty and basic goodness of other people). *Antagonism* or disagreeableness is at the opposite end of this continuum and is characterized by suspicion and distrust of others, and a conniving, selfish, non-compliant, hard-hearted, and cynical stance toward others.

Conscientiousness

Conscientiousness refers to people's level of discipline, self-control, and organization. Highly conscientious people are organized, competent, self-disciplined, deliberative, persistent, and dutiful, and have strong strivings for achievement. At the opposite end of this continuum, *undirectedness* is characterized by less competence, lack of achievement orientation, disorganization, impulsivity, carelessness, and neglectfulness.

Openness to Experience

Openness to experience describes the difference between people who are imaginative and creative and those who are more conventional and down-to-earth. Openness to experience includes specific traits related to fantasy, preference for variety and novelty, aesthetics (appreciation of art and beauty), and independence. Conversely, *non-openness* is characterized by practical-mindedness, preference for routine over variety, preference for the straightforward over the complex, and greater conformity.

After examining descriptions of the five factors, you may wonder if that is all there is to your personality. Do these five factors adequately describe the many features of your personality? Two things are worth keeping in mind. First, when personality researchers measure a large number of traits within a population of people, they do indeed find that most traits are related to one of the Big Five. That is, no matter what they assess, the same underlying five-part structure emerges. Second, each dimension is made up of a number of more specific traits that help capture people's unique personalities. If you are curious about your own Big Five scores, you might want to look at one of several versions of the five-factor questionnaire currently on the Internet. If you do a Google search using the term "Big Five Personality test," you can take a self-test and see how your own personality would be described in terms of a Big Five profile.

Each of the Big Five personality traits has been found to be highly heritable. Adoption and twin studies show heritability estimates between 0.40 and 0.60 (Bouchard, 2004; Loehlin, 1992; Loehlin, McCrae, Costa, & John, 1998; Lykken & Tellegen, 1996; Tellegen et al., 1988; Yamagata et al., 2006). On average, about 50% of the variance in personality traits within a group of people are attributable to genetic differences. Together with studies finding a genetic basis for affectivity, these results point to the powerful role of heritability in determining people's overall and long-term levels of happiness and well-being.

TEASING OUT CAUSE AND EFFECT Consistent with Meehl's early predictions, positive affectivity is strongly related to extraversion; studies also show a consistent relationship between negative affectivity and neuroticism (DeNeve & Cooper, 1998; McCrae & Costa, 1991; Watson & Clark, 1992). The causal relation of positive affectivity to extraversion is most probably bidirectional (Watson & Clark, 1992). On the one hand, people who are cheerful and enthusiastic about life are likely to prefer social interactions over more solitary activities. Positive affect may increase desire for the company of others. On the other hand, relationships are one of the more significant sources of positive emotional experiences. Most of our good times are spent with others. Positive affectivity may be both a cause and an effect of enjoyable interactions with others. Neuroticism and negative affectivity may also have a bidirectional relationship. Neuroticism may predispose people to experience more frequent negative emotions and to overreact to life events, particularly those that lead to unpleasant emotions.

Another possible explanation for the relation of extraversion and neuroticism to affectivity involves overlapping concepts and measures. Negative affectivity and neuroticism may go together because they tap the same underlying dimension of negative mood. The high correlation between negative affectivity and neuroticism has suggested to some researchers that the two variables are very similar and may not actually be separate individual traits (Diener & Lucas, 1999; Diener, Suh, Lucas, & Smith, 1999; McCrae & Costa, 1991). Both statistical analyses and comparisons of questionnaire items used to assess mood and personality traits show that neuroticism and negative affectivity are very difficult to distinguish.

The same kind of overlap appears in the positive affectivity–extraversion relationship. That is, positive affectivity may be highly related to extraversion—not because one causes the other, but because they are essentially measures of the same thing—namely, positive emotion. For example, extraversion contains a positive emotion component in both its definition and its measurement. Perhaps we are really talking about only two, rather than four separate traits. Positive affectivity–extraversion may represent a dimension of positive emotionality, and negative affectivity–neuroticism may represent negative emotionality. This possibility complicates the assumption that the traits of extraversion and neuroticism cause, and therefore help explain individual differences in happiness.

The overlap of extraversion and neuroticism with affectivity suggests that the connection of these two personality traits with SWB is somewhat tautological. In other words, the positive correlation of extraversion and the negative correlation of neuroticism with SWB may not suggest causality, but may instead reflect the strong relationship of both variables to affectivity, with affectivity playing a central role in defining SWB. Whether extraversion and neuroticism make separate contributions to individual happiness beyond their connection to affectivity will have to be sorted out in future research.

Other traits among the Big Five show more modest relationships to SWB (DeNeve & Cooper, 1998; Diener & Lucas, 1999; McCrae & Costa, 1991; Watson & Clark, 1992). Researchers seem to agree that *openness to experience* is only weakly related to happiness. *Agreeableness*, reflecting a concern with getting along with others and the tendency to take a positive, optimistic view of human nature, shows a small positive correlation with positive affect. The agreeableness–positive affect connection may result from enhanced personal relationships that may follow naturally from concern with social harmony. A positive life outlook resulting from an optimistic view of others might also increase positive affect. *Conscientious* people who are disciplined, organized, and achievement-oriented tend to score higher on the life satisfaction component of SWB measures (DeNeve & Cooper, 1998). This may result from conscientiousness providing a basis for goal-directed activities and the self-control necessary for goal achievement. Increased life satisfaction may follow from the sense of accomplishment and purpose that comes from successful self-directed actions.

PERSONALITY AND EUDAIMONIC WELL-BEING
Positive psychologists working from the eudaimonic perspective have examined the relation of the Big Five to measures of psychological well-being (PWB), defined in terms of optimal functioning and success in coping with life's challenges. Schmutte and Ryff (1997) found a pattern of relationships between each of the Big Five personality traits and measures of PWB, suggesting that the influence of personality extends beyond its effects on happiness. Ryff's conception of PWB (reviewed in Chapter 2) describes six aspects of psychological functioning:

- *Self-Acceptance:* a positive evaluation of self and one's past
- *Environmental Mastery:* competence in managing one's life and environment
- *Positive Relations:* high quality connections to others
- *Purpose in Life:* strong sense of meaning and purpose in life
- *Personal Growth:* sense of continuing growth and development as an individual
- *Autonomy:* sense of self as directing and determining actions and choices

In Schmutte and Ryff's (1997) study, 215 midlife adults (ages 44–65 years) completed a Five Factor personality inventory and a self-report measure of the six dimensions of PWB. Results showed that neuroticism was inversely linked with each of the six PWB dimensions, while extraversion, agreeableness, and conscientiousness showed consistent positive correlations with PWB. Openness to experience showed weak positive connections to overall well-being. These findings are generally in line with those of SWB researchers. Neuroticism seems to

undercut happiness (SWB) and optimal psychological functioning (PWB), while extraversion, agreeableness, and conscientiousness appear to be foundations for happiness and health. Despite similarities to SWB findings in the overall pattern of results, there were also important differences.

Schmutte and Ryff's findings suggest that personality may contribute to well-being in multiple ways—not just by influencing positive affect, as suggested by SWB research. Within SWB studies, the influence of neuroticism and extraversion on happiness is primarily the result of the effects of these traits on the positive and negative affect components of SWB. Traits not directly related to affect (like conscientiousness or openness to experience) generally show smaller correlations with happiness. In contrast, within the PWB model, conscientiousness showed relatively strong correlations with self-acceptance, environmental mastery, and purpose in life—the three important elements of psychological health. The self-discipline, persistence, and achievement strivings that define conscientiousness made significant contributions to healthy functioning, even though they do not increase happiness (SWB). In a similar vein, openness to experience contributed to personal growth, despite its lack of relationship to happiness.

The major point of Schmutte and Ryff's study goes back to the distinction between hedonic (SWB) and eudaimonic (PWB) conceptions of well-being. The effect of personality on well-being depends, in part, on how well-being is defined. Personality is clearly related to both happiness and health; however, certain traits may enhance health more than happiness and *vice versa*. For example, conscientiousness has been shown to be a very strong predictor of good physical health practices and, consequently, longevity. In their review of the connections between conscientiousness and health, Roberts and his colleagues report that "... people tend to live longer if, as 8-year-olds, they were rated as more conscientious by parents and teachers. Moreover, the impact of conscientiousness has been shown to be equivalent to cardiovascular disease" (Roberts, Wilson, & Bogg, 2005, p. 156). Conscientious people take better care of themselves through diet and exercise, and they avoid risky behaviors such as smoking, excessive use of alcohol, and unsafe driving habits. Here again, the point is that, whether or not conscientious people are happier, most of us would agree that living a healthier, longer life is an important part of well-being. To get a complete picture of well-being, both health and happiness criteria should be examined.

Neurobiology and Approach/ Avoidance Motives

Affectivity, personality, and temperament may be considered foundations of well-being because they represent stable genetically based dispositions that influence multiple aspects of our lives. For example, a person high in positive affectivity experiences life very differently than someone high in negative affectivity, and this difference is likely to be present, in general, over the entire life course. Another foundational disposition that may underlie well-being has to do with differences in people's basic tendencies toward approach or avoidance.

In Chapter 8, we reviewed studies showing the different achievement outcomes and emotional consequences of pursuing positive goals compared to avoiding negative outcomes. People who strive toward approach goals are more likely to be successful, experience more positive emotions, and suffer fewer self-regulation difficulties along the way. In contrast, avoidance goals are associated with less achievement success, more negative emotions, and many self-regulation problems that undermine positive well-being outcomes. Questions concerning individual differences in approach/avoidance motives are raised when we ask, "Why do some people characteristically pursue approach goals, while others focus mostly on avoiding undesirable outcomes?" One answer (discussed in Chapter 8) was suggested by research related to Higgins' work on self-discrepancy theory (1987, 1996, 1998). Higgins found that different parenting styles were linked to children adopting either a prevention (avoidance) or a promotion (approach) focus toward personal goal strivings.

Like Higgins, many psychologists have come to regard approach and avoidance tendencies as building blocks for more complex behaviors. Recent reviews note that this increased interest in approach/avoidance issues arises from the possibility that many emotional experiences, motivations, personality dispositions, and self-regulated behaviors may boil down to approach or avoidance tendencies (e.g., Carver, Sutton, & Scheier, 2000; Carver & White, 1994; Elliot & Church, 1997; Gable, 2006). Formerly separate areas of research might be brought together because they share a common approach/avoidance explanation. In addition, advances in the field of neuropsychology suggest that people's basic approach/avoidance tendencies may have a biological basis (see Carver et al., 2000 for a review).

For example, Grey (1990) describes a **Behavioral Activation System (BAS)** and a **Behavioral Inhibition System (BIS).** The specific neural mechanisms that make up these two systems are still unclear. However, research with both animals and humans suggests that different neurotransmitter pathways and brain regions may be involved in the operation of the two systems. The BAS is responsive to environmental cues that signal opportunities for rewards, non-punishment, and escape. This incentive-sensitive system motivates approach behaviors that increase movement toward positive goals. On the other hand, the BIS is responsive to cues signaling punishment and non-reward. This threat-sensitive system inhibits goal-directed behaviors to avoid negative outcomes. The activation and inhibition systems are thought to operate independently of one another and to be related to differences in emotional experience produced by rewards and threats. The BAS is related to positive affect and such emotions as happiness, elation, and hope. The BIS may underlie negative affect and emotions such as fear, sadness, anxiety, and frustration. Although much more clarifying research needs to be done, researchers are excited by the possibility that the BAS and BIS model may serve as one biological foundation for understanding emotional and personality differences among people.

Do people differ in their fundamental approach/avoidance dispositions? If so, are differences in approach/avoidance orientation related to differences in emotional experiences, personality, and goal behaviors that, in turn, impact well-being? Carver and White (1994) created and validated a self-report scale of Behavioral Activation Sensitivity and Behavioral Inhibition Sensitivity that closely parallels Grey's BAS/BIS conception. The BAS sensitivity scale assesses an overall approach tendency involving a person's active interest in positive goals, strong response to rewards, and eagerness/quickness in pursuing reward opportunities. Items on this scale asked people to rate the extent of their agreement or disagreement with statements such as "When I get something I want, I feel excited and energized." "When I want something, I usually go all out to get it." "I'm always willing to try something new if I think it will be fun." (Carver & White, 1994, p. 323). The BIS scale evaluates a general avoidance tendency that reflects a person's over-response to, and ongoing worry about, bad outcomes. The scale includes statements such as, "If I think something unpleasant is going to happen I usually get pretty 'worked up.'" "I feel pretty worried or upset when I think or know somebody is angry at me." "I feel worried when I think I have done poorly at something" (Carver & White, p. 323).

Consistent with the idea of BAS/BIS sensitivity as a basis for emotional and personality differences, Carver and White, along with other researchers, have found moderate correlations among BAS sensitivity, positive affectivity and extraversion, and among BIS sensitivity, negative affectivity and neuroticism. Approach-motivated individuals appear to be "attracted," in terms of seeking out and being differentially sensitive to rewarding and positive emotional experiences. This may explain why they are high in positive affectivity. Because relationships are one of the most significant sources of enjoyment, it makes sense that an approach orientation would come along with extraversion. Avoidance-motivated individuals are probably not "attracted," in terms of seeking out unpleasant emotions, but their strong reaction and sensitivity to negative outcomes may make negative emotions more chronically salient in the present and in memories of the past. This greater sensitivity to negative than to positive features of life may contribute to the higher negative affectivity associated with an avoidance orientation. The neurotic tendency to ruminate about negative experiences may also express this selective focusing on negative events that have occurred in the past and that may occur in the future.

Clearly, a self-report measure of approach/ avoidance tendencies does not directly assess the neurophysiological processes that may underlie them. However, Carver and White's scale may measure the conscious manifestations of the BAS and BIS described by Grey. At the very least, thinking of approach/avoidance tendencies as foundations for a wide variety of traits and behaviors has provided a basis for new conceptual and empirical studies. In addition to the connections with emotionality, neuroticism and extraversion, dispositional differences in approach/avoidance motives have also been related to many factors, including the daily frequency of positive and negative emotions (Carver & White, 1994), social relationships (Elliot, Gable, & Mapes, 2006), achievement motivation (Elliot & Church, 1997), self-control and self-regulation (e.g., Carver & Scheier, 1998; Fishbach & Shah, 2006; Higgins, 1998),

therapist/client satisfaction (Elliot & Church, 2002), and happiness judgments (Gable, 2006; Updegraff, Gable, & Taylor, 2004). Together with the work of goal researchers (reviewed in Chapter 8), these findings suggest that biologically organized and genetically influenced differences in people's approach/ avoidance tendencies may serve as foundations for many important determinants of well-being.

One reason for the expanding research on approach/avoidance motivation is that it seems to circumvent some of the tautology of trait descriptions discussed earlier. Saying someone is happy because they are high in positive affectivity is somewhat like saying happy people are happy because they experience many happy emotions. Approach and avoidance motives, however, point to how and why motives may be related to well-being. Each motive provides a different basis for people's actions, life orientations, and interpretations of the world. Because these differences may underlie many behaviors, from social relationships to personal goals, approach/avoidance tendencies may make multiple contributions to well-being. Recent studies have begun to describe what approach-motivated people *do* that increases their personal well-being and what avoidance-motivated people *do* that reduces their well-being. At present, one thing seems clear: an approach motivational orientation toward life belongs on the list of positive traits.

Genetics and Change

The bottom-line conclusion of our discussion to this point is that genetically-influenced differences in personality, emotionality, temperament, and approach/avoidance orientation explain as much as half of the variation in people's long-term levels of happiness. Does this mean that each of us is essentially stuck for life with whatever happiness we inherit? Does each of us have a genetically-determined set-point level of happiness to which we consistently return? Are we condemned to a hedonic treadmill, with positive life events causing only temporary increases in happiness (see Chapter 5)? Some researchers have suggested as much. Lykken and Tellegen (1996) once remarked, "It may be that trying to be happier is as futile as trying to be taller and therefore is counterproductive." This possibility is based on the fact that long-term happiness is "determined by the great genetic lottery that occurs at conception" (p. 189).

However, a number of researchers have argued against this conclusion based on newer evidence suggesting the need to revise both the original version of the hedonic treadmill concept and the idea that genetic influence means a person's happiness set-point cannot be changed. For example, Diener and his colleagues have suggested several empirically-based revisions to the hedonic treadmill theory (Diener, Lucas, & Scollon, 2006). These authors note that even if people *do* have different genetically-established levels of happiness, these levels appear to be "set" pretty high. Study after study has found that most people (75% or so) report being very happy or quite happy most of the time. In the aftermath of life events that can push happiness up or down in the short term, people return to a positive level of happiness—not to neutrality, as would be suggested by the strong adaptation process described in the hedonic treadmill theory. Research reviewed by Diener and colleagues also shows that people have multiple set-points, rather than one overarching set-point. Well-being is made up of separable components (positive and negative affect, life satisfaction) relevant to different domains of life (e.g., work and family). Each of these components and life domains can increase or decrease independently. Life satisfaction may increase even though positive affect is decreasing. Happiness at work may be coupled with unhappiness at home. While there is stability in overall happiness, consistent with the set-point idea, people may have different set-points for different aspects of happiness and domains of life. The idea of a single baseline or set-point for happiness does not explain how different dimensions of well-being can move in different directions over time.

Newer studies provide some of the strongest evidence against the hedonic treadmill theory, and against the idea that long-term changes in happiness set-points are largely impossible. Several large-scale longitudinal studies have shown significant changes in people's baseline levels of happiness. In a 17-year longitudinal study, for example, Fujita and Diener (2005) found that 24% of their research participants had experienced significant changes in their baseline levels of happiness from the first 5 years of the study to the last 5 years. In particular, negative life events such as divorce, death of a spouse, and physical disabilities can produce long-term decreases in happiness. It is also true that there are individual differences in adaptation to life events. These differences may be

washed out in studies that look only at overall averages. For example, the study by Lucas and colleagues (2003) described in Chapter 5 found large differences in the effects of marriage. Marriage produced only short-term happiness gains for the study participants when viewed collectively. However, nearly half of the people in the study showed long-term gains in happiness and nearly half showed decreased happiness. As a general conclusion, it seems fair to say that happiness is clearly in our genes, but just as clearly, life events and personal choices can change our happiness set-point. For example, research reviewed in Chapters 7 and 8 suggests that making the "right" personal goal choices contributes in a major way to a happy/healthy life.

POSITIVE BELIEFS

The World Through Happy and Unhappy Eyes

Happiness itself may be regarded as a positive trait because of its long-term stability and connection to genetically-influenced dispositions like positive affectivity and extraversion (McCrae & Costa, 1991). Lyubomirsky and her colleagues have taken this happiness-as-a-trait approach and examined how chronically happy and unhappy people differ in the way they think about and interpret their lives. Her research supports the general view that ". . . happy and unhappy individuals appear to experience—indeed, to reside in—different subjective worlds" (Lyubomirsky, 2001, p. 244). In other words, happy and unhappy people have very different ways of looking at life that both reflect and sustain their characteristic emotional state.

Lyubomirsky developed a 4-item Subjective Happiness Scale to provide a simple and direct basis for distinguishing between people who consider themselves to be generally happy and those who regard themselves as typically unhappy (see Lyubomirsky & Lepper, 1999, and Chapter 2 of this text). Happy and unhappy people (as defined by high or low scores on the scale) are then presented with a variety of judgment tasks and their responses are compared. You can probably anticipate many of Lyubomirsky's findings if you think about what you are like when you are unhappy compared to when your life is going well. In a bad mood, we are more likely to be envious and jealous of what others have that we don't, to take some comfort—perhaps even delight—in the failings and misfortunes of others, and to dwell on the negative rather than the positive aspects of our lives. In contrast, happiness produces a more positive pattern. We appreciate what we have, are not so sensitive to the failings or accomplishments of others, and focus on the positive aspects of life.

These temporary effects of fleeting happy and unhappy moods capture many of the enduring differences between characteristically happy and unhappy people found in Lyubomirsky's studies (see Lyubomirsky, 2001, for a review). Feedback about performance relative to peers, for example, had a much greater effect on unhappy people than on happy people. Happy people were less sensitive to social comparison information, especially when it was negative (i.e., information that they had performed worse than their peers). In contrast, unhappy people were highly sensitive to comparisons with others and felt deflated by others' superior performance. Unhappy people felt good about their performance only when others performed more poorly than they did. And these effects were largely independent of their actual performance quality. Unhappy people felt happier when they received a poor performance evaluation, but knew peers did even worse, than they did when they received an excellent evaluation, but knew peers had done even better!

Research comparing how happy and unhappy people evaluate various life events has shown that happy people give more favorable interpretations, remember positive experiences more than negative ones, and find humor and opportunities for self-improvement in negative events. Conversely, unhappy people spend more time ruminating about negative events, missed opportunities, and how others are doing relative to themselves. Happy and unhappy people do, indeed, seem to live in separate worlds. Differences in perception, interpretation, and evaluation of life lead happy and unhappy individuals to construct different personal realities that have opposite emotional consequences.

Self-Esteem

Our discussion of self-esteem is focused on North American cultures. As we saw in Chapter 5, more collectivist cultures (like Japan) have very different self-conceptions that do not place such heavy emphasis on positive self-feelings. Although self-esteem is related to life satisfaction in many cultures (e.g., Diener & Diener, 1995), it seems clear that the need for a positive self-view is not as prominent within collectivist societies as it is in individualistic societies (e.g., Heine, Lehman, Markus, & Kitayama, 1999). Within the United States, self-esteem is one of the most heavily researched areas in psychology; and in popular U.S. culture, self-esteem has been the topic of countless self-help books and many programs aimed at solving a wide array of social problems.

Self-esteem refers to the evaluative component of self-concept (Baumeister, 1998; Coopersmith, 1967). It is the feeling of self-worth and value that results when the self judges itself. One of the more widely used measures of self-esteem asks people for straightforward ratings of how they feel about themselves (Rosenberg, 1965). Items that people with high self-esteem would endorse include: "I feel I have a number of good qualities." "I take a positive attitude toward myself." "I feel I am a person of worth, at least on an equal plane with others." People with low self-esteem would endorse items such as: "I wish I could have more respect for myself." "I feel I do not have much to be proud of." "I certainly feel useless at times." Whether we have a positive, uncertain, or negative view of ourselves, depends on the subjective judgment we make of our abilities, talents, relationships with others, and success in achieving important goals. People with high self-esteem have a favorable view of themselves as competent, likeable, attractive, and successful people. In the extreme case (e.g., depression), low self-esteem may reflect an opposite pattern in which people see themselves as incompetent, unlikeable failures. However, research findings suggest that more typically, low-self esteem is related to uncertain and conflicted views of the self that are overly sensitive to the ups and downs of life; feeling good one day and bad the next (Baumeister, Tice, & Hutton, 1989; Campbell, Chew, & Scratchley, 1991). Compared to those with high self-esteem, people with low self-esteem are less confident that they can achieve their personal goals (McFarlin & Blascovich, 1981).

Self-esteem is influenced by others and bears some relationship to our actual abilities and talents. We all feel good when we receive praise from people we care about, and a "straight-A" student certainly has a reason to feel academically competent. However, because self-esteem also reflects a person's own subjective perception of self, it may or may not match up with the views of others or with objectively defined qualities or accomplishments. A person may have an inflated view of self that is not supported by his or her actual abilities. On the other hand, a person may also dislike who he or she is, despite admiration from others or success and competence in various life endeavors.

Like many personality characteristics, self-esteem can be thought of as both a trait and a state. A recent analysis of 50 published studies and data from national samples of nearly 75,000 people found strong evidence for the stability of self-esteem from age 6 to age 83 (Trzesniewski, Donnellan, & Robins, 2003). On the other hand, many studies find that self-esteem fluctuates in response to feedback, such as acceptance or rejection by others (e.g., Heatherton & Polivy, 1991; Leary, Tambor, Terdal, & Downs, 1995). Evidence supporting both the trait and state views suggests that people have a relatively stable baseline level of self-esteem (trait self-esteem) to which they return after specific life events have temporarily pushed self-esteem up or down (state self-esteem).

SELF-ESTEEM AND HAPPINESS Self-esteem is consistently found to be a powerful predictor of happiness and life satisfaction. In a study of over 13,000 college students representing 31 different nations, Diener and Diener (1995) reported across-the-board correlations of 0.47 between self-esteem and life satisfaction. This correlation was even higher in individualistic cultures (e.g., $r = 0.56$ in the United States). Studies of adult populations show the same connection between self-esteem and happiness (see Baumeister, Campbell, Krueger, & Vohs, 2003, for a review). Self-esteem is also related to people's confidence and initiative in tackling new endeavors, whether this is striking up conversations with others, persevering at challenging tasks, speaking in front of groups, or resisting the influence of others (Baumeister et al., 2003; Baumeister, Campbell, Krueger, & Vohs, 2005). People with low self-esteem are not as happy, not as confident and adventuresome, and may give up rather than try harder when faced with a difficult challenge or initial failure at a task.

The Value of Self-Esteem. Many psychologists believe that the need for positive self-regard is one of the strongest human motives (e.g., Baumeister, 1998; Sheldon, Elliot, Kim, & Kasser, 2001; Taylor & Brown, 1988; Tesser, 1988). People go to great lengths to protect, enhance, and maintain a positive self-image. Research suggests that the vast majority of us are successful in these efforts (Baumeister, 1999; Diener & Diener, 1995; Myers, 1992). Most people score in the mid range on self-esteem measures; extremely low self-esteem scores are relatively uncommon. What motivates our need for self-esteem? What value does a positive self-view have for our health and happiness?

One answer, suggested by Myers (1992), is that life satisfaction may begin with self-satisfaction. A positive view of self may color our view of life in general. Can you be very positive about yourself and very negative about your life? Perhaps you can think of how this might occur, but self-evaluation and life evaluation seem intimately intertwined. General life satisfaction shows stronger links to self-esteem than it does to satisfaction with friends, family, income, or job. Even though correlational studies do not tell us about cause and effect, it is hard to imagine a happy and satisfying life without a strong measure of self-acceptance, self-respect, and positive self-regard.

High self-esteem may also have value as a buffer against stress and anxiety caused by life experiences that can threaten and deflate our self-image (Baumeister, 1992; Steele, 1988). Self-esteem may act as a coping resource that affirms the self when we confront failure, losses, criticism, and conflict with others. People with low or fragile self-esteem may experience debilitating stress and worry over such events. They may become discouraged and dejected by failure. People high in self-esteem are not so easily overwhelmed by negative events and are better able to endure and maintain a positive outlook. They have more "reserve" self-esteem, which helps them absorb blows to self-regard without caving in. The buffering effect is a major reason why high self-esteem is considered an important resource for mental and physical health. According to terror management theory, self-esteem may also buffer the anxiety caused by the ultimate threat to self—our own death (see Chapter 7). The theory argues that a culture provides its individual members with means of achieving a sense of value through social status and conditions of worth, in order to bring the fear of death to manageable proportions.

According to another prominent theory, self-esteem plays an important role in maintaining the social relationships that are so vital to our health and well-being. **Sociometer Theory** takes an evolutionary perspective, arguing that the purpose of self-esteem is to monitor social inclusion and exclusion (Leary & Baumeister, 2000; Leary et al., 1995). Human survival was likely very dependent on maintaining close relationships with others, both as protection from larger animals and for the safety of infants who could not fend for themselves during the early years of life. An internal monitoring system that is sensitive to social rejection and exclusion would signal the need for corrective action to repair the social relationships that are so important to survival.

Leary and his colleagues (1995) believe self-esteem is just such a system. A growling stomach and a parched mouth tell us when we need to eat and drink—two things that are obviously important to our survival. Decreases in self-esteem may tell us something equally important about our relationships. Using the analogy of a car's gas gauge that monitors fuel level, Leary and colleagues believe that self-esteem is a gauge of our social relationships. Like a gas gauge, self-esteem is important because of what it measures and what it causes us to do.

A gas gauge does not make your car more efficient or faster. It simply tells you when you need gas so you don't get stranded somewhere. Self-esteem has an analogous metering function. It lets you know when to mend relationships so you don't get stranded without your friends or family. Self-esteem functions as an internal, subjective monitor of social acceptance.

You can easily find support for one of the major tenets of sociometer theory within your own experience. Think about a time that you felt very good about yourself, and a time you felt very bad about yourself. Odds are that good self-feelings involved times when you received praise or recognition from others, moments of intimacy with friends or lovers, and shared activities. Our worst feelings often reflect social ridicule, rejection, failed romance, and moments when our actions made us feel embarrassed or ashamed in front of others. Leary and colleagues have found that self-esteem is highly sensitive to social inclusion and exclusion, and that being liked by others is linked to positive self-evaluation (Leary & Baumeister, 2000; Leary et al., 1995; Srivastava & Beer, 2005). Consistent with the idea of self-esteem as a sociometer of where we stand in our relationships, social acceptance increases self-esteem and rejection lowers self-esteem.

Self-esteem may also function as a sociometer of our personal traits. Traits that are associated with high self-esteem, such as competence, likeability, attractiveness, and morality, are the same traits that make a person appealing to others. Self-esteem also seems to "meter" the extent to which we possess qualities that contribute to social acceptance by others. People with high self-esteem may have an easier time and be more comfortable obtaining and maintaining social acceptance because they may come to find that they are generally likeable people. Consistent with this possibility, measures of social anxiety (concern with acceptance and rejection) show negative correlations with self-esteem (Leary & Kowalski, 1995). In other words, compared to people with low self-esteem, individuals with high self-esteem are not as worried about fitting in and being liked by others.

IS SELF-ESTEEM ALL YOU NEED? If you are happy with yourself, odds are high that you will be happy with your life. And compared to those with a poor self-image, people with a positive self-view are likely to enjoy more initiative, more persistence in the face of obstacles, more effective stress coping, and more positive social relationships. Given these benefits, is self-esteem all you need for a happy life? Is increasing people's self-esteem an antidote to unhappiness? For awhile, particularly within popular culture, the answer to these questions was thought to be yes. At one time, low self-esteem was considered a major psychological cause of individual problems, and programs to increase self-esteem were widely viewed as the cure.

Over the last 30 years, psychologists have generated an extensive research focused on sorting out the value, limitations, and complexities of self-esteem. This research has a counterpart in an equally large body of self-improvement literature within popular culture. One review identified over 15,000 research articles on self-esteem, and a multitude of self-help books focus on ways to feel better about your self (Baumeister et al., 2003). A brief history may be useful in sorting out the massive amount of self-esteem research and its connection to popular culture. Psychologists' understanding of self-esteem and its role in individual and social problems appears to have gone through three overlapping, yet discernable phases, starting in the 1970s and continuing to the present. This historical sketch is an oversimplified view and has more to do with different programs of research than the development of ideas over time. However, it will hopefully help organize some of the paradoxical and contradictory research findings concerning self-esteem and temper the many unfounded claims of the self-improvement literature.

Self-Esteem as a Significant Variable in Individual and Social Problems. In the first phase, many psychologists and practitioners (e.g., teachers, school administrators, and leaders of social agencies) had high hopes for the potential of self-esteem studies to both explain and help solve many pressing social problems (e.g., Dawes, 1994; Hewitt, 1998; Mecca, Smelsor, & Vasconcellos, 1989). Based largely on correlation studies, low self-esteem was believed to be a potentially significant and pervasive cause of many social problems, including poor academic achievement, bullying, aggression, attraction to gangs, teenage pregnancy, drug abuse, smoking, delinquency, eating disorders, depression, suicide, shyness, and loneliness. Among practitioners, feeling bad about oneself was likened to a nationwide viral epidemic and raising self-esteem was the obvious "social vaccine" (California Task Force to Promote Self-Esteem and Personal and Social Responsibility, 1990). California appropriated money and developed programs to enhance self-esteem. In schools, for example, helping students feel good about themselves was expected to pay big dividends in the form of improved academic achievement.

Self-Esteem as a Symptom—Not a Cause—of Behavior. In the second phase, enthusiasm for the self-esteem movement began to wane because many programs produced disappointing results. Efforts to raise self-esteem did not produce noticeable benefits and may have produced other problems such as the "social promotion" of students (passing students to the next grade level despite their failure to learn lower-grade skills). Psychologists also began to take a critical look at self-esteem research. Several reviews concluded that low self-esteem is not clearly related to individual problems and that the benefits of high self-esteem were much more limited than previously thought (Baumeister, 1992: Baumeister, 1998; Baumeister et al., 2003, 2005).

Reviewers encountered two major problems in sorting fact from fiction in self-esteem research.

First, most findings showing the benefits of self-esteem were based on correlational studies, making it difficult to determine cause and effect. Does a positive relationship between self-esteem and academic achievement mean high self-esteem causes better performance or does it mean that good students have higher self-esteem because they have something to feel good about? We can ask the same question for low self-esteem. Is low self-esteem the cause or the result of poor performance? Second, many benefits of a positive self-image were assessed by self-report measures. People high in self-esteem have many positive beliefs about themselves. They regard themselves as attractive, likeable, competent, and superior to others, but are they *actually so* when evaluated by objective standards?

In their review, Baumeister and his colleagues examined only those studies that included some objective/behavioral measure of outcomes and judgments. They found that high self-esteem was strongly related to happiness and life satisfaction, and to enhanced initiative in tackling new challenges and maintaining persistence in the face of obstacles. However, high self-esteem was largely unrelated to independently assessed school achievement, occupational success, likeability, attractiveness, or to teenage smoking, pregnancy, and drug use. Furthermore, people with certain types of high self-esteem such as narcissism (which involves inflated and highly defensive self-esteem) are more prone to violence. Such people are overly sensitive to anyone who challenges their high opinion of themselves and respond aggressively to anyone who threatens their inflated self-image. Low self-esteem did show significant connections to depressive symptoms and vulnerability to the negative effects of stress. The bottom line for Baumeister was that low self-esteem did not appear to underlie most social problems and the benefits of high self-esteem were not backed up by objective evidence.

Contingent Self-Esteem: It's Not the Level, but the Basis of Esteem That Matters. In the third phase, researchers have begun to develop more complex models in an attempt to clarify some of the controversies concerning the role of self-esteem in individual and social life. For example, Crocker and her colleagues, have argued that self-esteem researchers have paid too much attention to *levels* of self-esteem (high versus low), and too little attention to the *basis* of self-esteem (Crocker & Wolfe, 2001). People "hang" their self-esteem, so to speak, on different activities, competencies, and areas of life. One person may take pride in his intellectual abilities and another on being liked by others. How people respond to a life experience depends on its self-relevance. For example, getting a "C" in a college class may be a major blow to individuals with an academic competence-based sense of self-worth, but no big deal for someone whose self-image is contingent on social relationships and not on high academic achievement. Most researchers have relied on global measures of self-esteem that do not assess the specific and differing bases for people's evaluation of self-worth. They only tell us about a person's level of self-esteem. Crocker believes that thinking of self-worth only in terms of level is an oversimplified view that has led to misunderstandings concerning the role self-esteem plays in social problems.

"A **contingency of self-worth** is a domain or category of outcomes on which a person has staked his or her self-esteem, so that a person's view of his or her value or worth depends on perceived successes or failures or adherence to self-standards in that domain" (Crocker & Park, 2004, p. 594, bold face ours). Crocker and her colleagues developed a scale to measure seven sources of self-esteem (Crocker, Luthanen, Cooper, & Bouvrette, 2003). Each source describes a different contingent basis for feelings of self-worth. Samples of scale items are shown in Table 9.1. For some contingency dimensions, items related to both the absence and to the presence of a self-worth contingency are given (Crocker et al., 2003, p. 899). The list of contingencies of self-worth is meant to be representative and not exhaustive. You can easily think of additional sources of self-pride and worth (e.g., athletic ability, physical health, public service).

This "contingencies of self-worth" model is supported by studies showing that contingent domains of self are powerful guides for people's behavior (Crocker & Luthanen, 2003; Crocker & Wolfe, 2001; Park & Crocker, 2005). What people do to protect, maintain, and enhance their self-esteem depends on its source. People who take pride in

---

TABLE 9.1 Contingencies of self-worth—sample items

1. Approval of Others
"I don't care what other people think of me."
"I can't respect myself if others don't respect me."

2. Appearance
"My self-esteem does not depend on whether or not I feel attractive."
"When I think I look attractive, I feel good about myself."

3. Competition
"Doing better than others gives me a sense of self-respect."
"Knowing that I am better than others on a task raises my self-esteem."

4. Academic Competence
"My opinion about myself isn't tied to how well I do in school."
"Doing well in school gives me a sense of self-respect."

5. Family Support
"My self-worth is not influenced by the quality of my relationships with my family members."
"When my family members are proud of me, my sense of self-worth increases."

6. Virtue
"My self-respect would suffer if I did something that was unethical."
"I couldn't respect myself if I didn't live up to my moral code."

7. God's Love
"I feel worthwhile when I have God's love."
"My self-esteem would suffer if I didn't have God's love."

their appearance were found to spend more hours grooming, shopping, and partying. Those whose self-esteem was based on God's love, party less, but pray and go to church more. Academic competence as a basis of self-esteem was linked to success in getting into graduate school. More importantly for our historical sketch, the self-contingency model suggests that social problems (such as school failure, drug abuse, and violence) may be linked less to the level of global self-esteem and more to the source of self-esteem. Based on studies exploring levels of global esteem, Baumeister and colleagues concluded that low self-esteem is not a major cause of problems. However, Crocker and her colleagues suggest level of esteem may not be the critical factor. Contingencies of self-worth *may be* central to many individual and social problem behaviors.

One way in which contingencies of self-worth are implicated in social problems is through people's disengagement from the specific life domains in which they are continually frustrated in their attempts to achieve esteem-confirming results. Why should someone hang his or her self-worth on an area that never affirms it?

For example, Steele (1997) argues that the high college dropout rate among African Americans may result from disconnecting self-esteem from academic performance. This disengagement may occur because of frustrated efforts to succeed in an environment that may be perceived as non-supportive, or worse yet, that is perceived as assuming academic inferiority. A similar dilemma is suggested by studies finding that African American adolescents may feel they must choose between being popular with peers or doing well in school (Arroyo & Zigler, 1995; Steinberg, Dornbusch, & Brown, 1992). Peer support for high school performance appears weaker for African American students than for Caucasian or Asian students. On a day-to-day basis, maintaining solidarity with same-race peers may be more important than school achievement as a basis for self-esteem. If peer-based self-esteem is the primary contributor to a person's overall level of self-esteem, then studies using only a global self-esteem measure might easily conclude that self-esteem does not predict school performance. However, this would miss the critical point that Crocker and her colleagues want to make. Namely, that self-esteem, considered in terms of contingencies of self-worth, may be very relevant to the school achievement of some groups of students. Baumeister may be right, that raising

students' self-esteem may not increase school performance. However, finding ways to increase students' active engagement and identification with school might enhance academic achievement.

THE DARKER SIDE OF SELF-ESTEEM Crocker and her colleagues make an important distinction between global and contingent self-esteem. In terms of benefits, the basis of our self-esteem matters. Not all forms of positive self-image are beneficial. Crocker's recent studies examine how the pursuit of self-esteem as a desirable end may entail a potentially darker side that is self-defeating—and even harmful. Her studies affirm classical humanistic psychology ideas about the basis of self-worth.

Contingent versus Non-contingent Self-Esteem. Years ago Carl Rogers (1961) argued for the value of unconditional positive regard as a basis for parents' love of their children. Children who experienced love that was unconditional would grow up to believe in their own inherent value. Conditional positive regard, on the other hand, was considered damaging to the child because receiving love and approval are contingent on meeting parental standards and expectations. Conditional love creates a continual source of insecurity for a child, because love can be withdrawn whenever conditions of worth are not fulfilled. Rogers argued that people whose self-worth is contingent on meeting external standards are likely to have fragile, defensive, and unstable self-esteem and suffer more problems as a result. Recent theoretical and empirical studies support Rogers' early observations.

First, researchers have distinguished between people with contingent self-esteem, who feel pressure to meet external standards of worth, and people with non-contingent or "true" self-esteem that is grounded in unconditional self-acceptance and feelings of personal value (Deci & Ryan, 1995; Kernis, 2003a, 2003b). Supporting this distinction are studies showing that contingent self-esteem is linked to a number of negative emotions such as feelings of guilt, conflict, pressure, and anxiety, and problems such as fragile and unstable self-esteem, poor coping after failure, defensiveness, and risk for depression (see Baumeister et al., 2003, 2005; Crocker & Wolfe, 2001; Deci & Ryan, 1995; Kernis, 2003).

Pursuing Self-Esteem. Second, studies by Crocker and her colleagues have shown that the effects of pursuing self-esteem as a primary life goal are strikingly parallel to those associated with materialism (Crocker and Park, 2004; Crocker and Wolfe, 2001; Park & Crocker, 2005). Recall our discussion of materialism and its discontents in Chapter 7. Viewed from the perspective of self-determination theory, the trouble with materialistic aspirations is that they do not yield happiness, and may interfere with the fulfillment of basic needs that *are* the foundations of health and happiness (i.e., autonomy, competence, and belongingness). Crocker provides evidence and arguments to the effect that the pursuit of self-esteem as a primary life aspiration may also subvert satisfaction of these three important needs and, therefore, undermine well-being. Ironically, self-esteem can be undermined in the same process.

To understand the logic of Crocker's analysis, consider the following example in which the need for competence may be sacrificed in the service of pursuing self-esteem. A college student whose self-esteem is heavily invested in, and contingent upon, high academic performance may be very motivated to study hard and get good grades. However, if a positive academic self-image becomes the single most important goal, then actual competence and learning might be compromised by the need to protect and maintain this image. Both of your textbook authors have encountered students who are highly protective of their GPAs, to the detriment of obtaining the skills needed to fulfill graduate school aspirations. To maintain a high GPA necessary for graduate school admission, some students take easy classes, avoid useful (but harder) classes (like advanced statistics in psychology), and withdraw from classes at the first sign that their GPA might suffer. Instead of taking classes they need or might enjoy, they select classes that are likely to increase their GPA and flatter their academic self-image. In addition, poor performance and criticism may be taken as threats to self-esteem rather than as useful feedback to improve learning. The net result of these possibilities is that self-esteem may go up, but competence may be sacrificed in the process.

A similar logic links the pursuit of self-esteem to disruptions in the ability to fulfill needs for autonomy and belongingness. The well-being benefits derived from freely and autonomously chosen actions may be compromised by excessive concern with self-esteem. For example, a person whose self-esteem is contingent on the approval of others may make choices and take actions according to what will please others rather than themselves. Living up to others' expectations rather than one's own undermines autonomy, intrinsic motivation, and personally expressive actions. In a similar vein, seeking self-esteem may interfere with satisfying relationships and the need for belongingness if it leads to competing with friends and partners rather than developing intimacy and mutual regard. Satisfying relationships benefit more from self-less, rather than self-centered attitudes. Like materialism, seeking self-esteem for its own sake may decrease well-being by diverting attention away from more important needs.

As an addendum to the three decades of research on self-esteem, a recent article argues that the understanding of this popular concept may have come full circle (Swann, Chang-Schneider, & McClarty, 2007). Research began with a misplaced belief that low self-esteem predicted a wide variety of important personal behaviors from poor academic achievement to drug abuse and violence. The concept was then subjected to highly critical evaluations that led many researchers to conclude that self-esteem didn't predict much of anything related to important social or personal problems. Swann and his colleagues argue that recent work supports an understanding of self-esteem as a global aspect of self that is vitally important to people's lives. Such work makes efforts to improve self-esteem potentially valuable. As they note, the history of self-esteem research parallels other concepts, for which early enthusiasm was followed by criticism and disillusionment (e.g., the study of attitudes in social psychology). In these cases, too much specific predictive power was expected too soon. That is, enthusiasm for a concept leads researchers to assume that it predicts a wide variety of specific behaviors. When specific predictions are not born out, researchers assume the basic concept is problematic. However, as Swann and colleagues note, self-esteem is most appropriately conceived as a global aspect of self that would be expected to influence and predict global—not specific—behavioral outcomes. For example, depression is a global behavior describing a general condition that is strongly related to low self-esteem. Research reviewed by these authors suggests that, if self-esteem is considered a global rather than specific aspect of self, then self-esteem compares favorably with other well-established concepts in psychology.

For instance, self-esteem may be only weakly related to a specific behavior, such as alcohol use by teenagers. However, if behaviors were bundled into a global measure of healthy/unhealthy teen life styles (one that included things like drug use, depression, anxiety, tobacco use, poor school performance, and delinquency), then self-esteem *would* be a significant predictor variable, with low self-esteem linked to an unhealthier lifestyle and high self-esteem to a healthier lifestyle. From this view, self-esteem is an important foundation for health and happiness.

Personal Control

Chapter 7 provided an extended discussion of personal control in the regulation of goal-directed behavior. Here, we will only note that a sense of personal causation, meaning a feeling that you are the originator of action in your life, has long been regarded as a basic motive of the self (Baumeister, 1998; deCharms, 1968) and an important foundation of well-being (Argyle, 2001; Myers, 1992). Many prominent theories related to well-being, such as self-efficacy theory, self-determination theory, and control theory (reviewed in Chapter 7) place personal control at the center of healthy and adaptive functioning. The importance of a belief in personal control is also reinforced by theories of depression that regard loss of this belief as a significant contributor to emotional problems. Early work suggested that repeated experience of negative events may undercut confidence and produce a condition of "learned helplessness," in which people feel like helpless, hopeless victims of stressful life circumstances over which they have no control (Seligman, 1975). Later studies suggested that the critical factor was not so much the occurrence of negative events but people's beliefs about control (Seligman, 1990). Depressed individuals tend to believe that they have little control over their negative emotions or the situations that engender them. As described in Chapter 7, a sense of control and personal empowerment has been related to a variety of positive health and well-being outcomes.

Optimism

Everyday wisdom suggests that the fundamental difference between an optimist and a pessimist is captured in the answer to the question, "Is the glass half empty, or is it half full?" Looking at the exact same reality, a pessimist takes a more negative view, focusing on what is missing, while an optimist takes a positive view, seeing what is available. Psychologists have viewed optimism/pessimism primarily as an individual difference variable describing people's general positive or negative expectations about the future. People vary in their degree of optimism/pessimism and these differences are potentially important to a wide assortment of life activities and choices. We can be optimistic or not about finding the perfect gift for a significant other, getting the house clean before guests arrive, recovering from a heart attack, getting a job promotion, making financial gains from investments, or having good weather on a vacation.

Certainly, people's beliefs can be affected by the specifics of a situation. You can be pessimistic that your favorite political candidate will win because currently he or she is behind in the polls, but optimistic that you will get a house project completed before winter because you have hired extra help. However, research makes it clear that people do vary in their overall level of optimism/pessimism. Studies also show that positive and negative expectations about the future show a consistent pattern of relatedness to measures of well-being.

We will discuss the two major approaches to optimism in psychological research: optimism as an individual disposition or trait and optimism as an explanatory style describing how people characteristically interpret the causes of bad events in their lives. We will also consider other versions of optimism and pessimism and whether an optimistic attitude is always beneficial. Studies of defensive optimism, unrealistic optimism, and realistic optimism help clarify the advantages and disadvantages of different expectations about future events.

DISPOSITIONAL OPTIMISM Scheier and Carver (1992) define **dispositional optimism** as a global expectation that the future will bring a bounty of good things and a scarcity of bad things. Pessimism is an opposite expectation—that the future will have more bad than good outcomes. As a general expectation, applicable to many areas of life, optimists are confident that they can achieve their goals, while pessimists doubt their ability. In current research, dispositional optimism is measured by a revised version of the Life Orientation Test (LOT) (Scheier, Carver, & Bridges, 1994). Six items are rated on a 0 to 4 scale, where 0 = strongly disagree and 4 = strongly agree. In the list of items below, "R" indicates a reverse-scored item.

1. In uncertain times, I usually expect the best.
2. If something can go wrong for me, it will. (R)
3. I'm always optimistic about the future.
4. I hardly ever expect things to go my way. (R)
5. I rarely count on good things happening to me. (R)
6. Overall, I expect more good things to happen to me than bad.

Scheier and Carver view optimism in the context of self-regulated actions aimed at the achievement of personal goals (see Chapter 8). In their self-regulation model, expectations and confidence become important when people face challenges and obstacles to goal achievement. Faced with difficulties, optimists believe they can overcome them and therefore persevere in their efforts. Pessimists, on the other hand, have less confidence and positive expectations and are likely to become passive or give up their efforts.

As you might anticipate, optimism is related to other positive traits we have discussed in this chapter. Specifically, dispositional optimism as measured by the LOT shows moderate positive correlations with traits such as self-mastery and self-esteem, and negative associations with traits that detract from well-being, such as neuroticism, anxiety, and depression (Scheier, Carver, & Bridges, 2002; Scheier et al., 1994). These correlations suggest that optimism and pessimism share some degree of overlap with other positive and negative traits. For example, a person with high self-esteem is also likely to be optimistic. However, research by Scheier and his colleagues has shown that when the effects of other traits are statistically controlled, optimism remains a significant and independent predictor of positive outcomes. An optimistic attitude pays significant dividends in individual health and happiness, particularly when people face difficult life changes (see Carver & Scheier, 2002b; Scheier et al., 2002; Chang, 2002a).

Optimism and Well-Being

Dispositional optimism is perhaps best regarded as a personal resource that fosters resistance to distress. Researchers have studied people facing a variety of challenging life situations and found that optimism is consistently linked to lower levels of personal distress, and pessimism to higher levels of distress. Longitudinal studies that assess levels of distress at multiple points over time provide some of the clearest evidence for the benefits of optimism.

Coping with Distress and Life Transitions. A woman's first child represents a major life transition that sometimes leads to depressed feelings after childbirth. Several studies suggest that an optimistic attitude may offer resistance to postpartum depression (Carver & Gaines, 1987; Fontaine & Jones, 1997; Park, Moore, Turner, & Adler, 1997). Women in these studies completed the LOT at several times during pregnancy and in the several weeks after the births of their children. Optimistic women reported fewer depressive symptoms, both during pregnancy and during the postpartum period, compared to more pessimistic women. During pregnancy, optimism was associated with less anxiety and an ability to maintain a positive outlook (Park et al., 1997).

People recovering from coronary bypass surgery also benefit from an optimistic attitude (Fitzgerald, Tennen, Affleck, & Pransky, 1993; Scheier et al., 1989). Men undergoing bypass surgery were surveyed before, and at several times after their surgery. Compared to more pessimistic patients, optimists reported less presurgical distress, more confidence in and satisfaction with their medical care, more relief and happiness shortly after surgery, and greater post-surgery life satisfaction in the months following their operation. A similar pattern of findings has been reported for women coping with treatment for early stage breast cancer (Carver et al., 1993). Although the prognosis is generally good when caught early, breast cancer is obviously a serious, life-threatening disease that often evokes both fear and depression. Carver and his colleagues found that optimism helped offset the distress of dealing with breast cancer. LOT scores taken at the time of diagnosis predicted women's self-reported level of distress both before and after surgery (assessed at 1 week, and at 3, 6, and 12 months). Women who were optimistic at the time of diagnosis experienced less emotional upset before surgery, and were more resilient in the weeks and months following surgery.

The optimism that helps women cope with breast cancer also helps those who care for them. Family members who provide care for loved ones with serious long-term illnesses like cancer and Alzheimer's disease face an emotionally taxing and energy-draining task. An optimistic attitude is a valuable resource. Studies find that optimistic family caregivers experience lower levels of depression, better physical health, and less disruption of their daily schedules (Given et al., 1993; Hooker, Monahan, Shifren, & Hutchinson, 1992).

The transition from high school to college is a significant event in the lives of millions of college freshmen each year. Faculty members, counselors, administrators, and many parents know that some students adjust to the increased freedom and academic demands of college more successfully than others. What personal qualities might be the basis for effective adjustment to a new college environment? Aspinwall and Taylor (1992) examined three individual difference variables as potential predictors of successful adaptation: self-esteem, perceived control, and optimism. Each of these variables has been regarded as an individual resource that helps people cope with challenge and change. Aspinwall and Taylor enlisted 676 college freshmen early in the fall semester to complete measures of self-esteem, personal control and optimism (LOT). Three months later, at the start of the next semester, these same students completed four measures related to college adjustment, responding to items addressing their levels of stress, their happiness, and their general well-being. Results showed that, while each of the three individual dispositions was related to college adjustment, only optimism had a direct and independent positive effect. The benefits of self-esteem and personal control were more indirect and depended on their relation to active rather than avoidant coping with college stress. That is, high self-esteem and personal control improved adjustment only if students also actively sought solutions and help for adjustment problems. If they avoided rather than confronted their problems, the benefits of self-esteem and personal control were diminished. In contrast, optimism was directly related to measures of successful college adjustment and more effective, active coping.

Physical and Emotional Health. Compared to pessimists, many studies find that people with an optimistic attitude enjoy better mental and physical health (see Affleck, Tennen, & Apter, 2002; Carver & Scheier, 2002b; Peterson & Bosio, 2002; Scheier et al., 2002). Optimists are less likely than pessimists to suffer from depression. They experience less anxiety in adjusting to new life tasks such as medical school

and law school. And they take better care of themselves by not smoking or abusing drugs or alcohol, and by maintaining a healthy diet, exercising regularly, and following their doctors' advice in screening for and treating illness. Optimistic people suffering from chronic illnesses such as rheumatoid arthritis, asthma, and fibromyalgia maintain a more positive daily mood compared to less optimistic people coping with the same illnesses. Following bypass surgery, optimists reach behavioral milestones (such as sitting up in bed, walking, resuming an exercise routine, and returning to full-time work) more quickly than patients with less optimistic outlooks (Scheier et al., 1989).

Studies suggest that the cumulative effects of an optimistic attitude toward life may increase longevity. Recall the Nun Study from Chapter 1. On average, the more cheerful nuns lived a full 10 years longer than their least cheerful counterparts. A study of 839 Mayo Clinic patients tracked over a 30-year period found that optimism was correlated with a lower risk of death (Maruta, Colligan, Malinchoe, & Offord, 2000). A final example of research showing the relationship between positive thinking and longer life, focused on older adults' attitudes toward self and aging (Levy, Slade, Kunkel, & Kasl, 2002). Participants' attitudes were assessed for as long as 23 years before mortality data were collected. Those with positive attitudes (e.g., "I have as much pep as I did last year." "As I get older, things are better than I thought they would be.") lived an average of 7.5 years longer than people with more negative views (e.g., "As you get older, you are less useful.") (p. 263).

OPTIMISM AS EXPLANATORY STYLE Research supports the value of an optimistic outlook in coping with a variety of negative life events. One reason optimists do better involves how they explain why bad things happen. Certain types of explanations soften the blow of disappointments and protect our self-image and positive view of life. Other types contribute to a negative self-image and a more depressing view of life. Seligman and his colleagues have conceptualized optimism and pessimism in terms of **explanatory style,** defined as people's characteristic way of explaining negative events (Peterson, 2000; Reivich & Gillham, 2003; Seligman, 1990). Originally focused on the thinking patterns of depressed individuals (Abramson, Seligman, & Teasdale, 1978), studies of explanatory style evolved to describe the differences between optimistic and pessimistic interpretations of bad life events (Peterson & Villanova, 1988). The explanation that pessimists give for a particular setback or misfortune points to causes that are stable, global, and internal. *Stable* causes are those that are enduring and unlikely to change in the future. *Global* refers to general causes that affect almost everything about a person's life, and *internal* causes are those stemming from the traits and beliefs of the individual rather than external circumstances.

A pessimistic explanatory style is exemplified by a college student who fails a big math exam and says, "I'm just no good at math" or "I'm a bad test-taker." Each of these two explanations refers to stable causes (e.g., if you're not good at math today, odds are you won't be tomorrow, either); global causes (e.g., being a bad test-taker will affect performance in all classes); and internal causes (e.g., it's me; it's my fault—not the test or how much I studied). In contrast, an optimist sees disappointments as caused by more *unstable, specific,* and *external* causes. An optimist might offer the following explanations for a failed exam. "I failed the exam because the instructor didn't make clear what material would be covered." "The exam was ambiguous and unrelated to what we studied in class." "I had to work late and didn't have much time to study." These interpretations of failure point to unstable causes (e.g., next time the instructor may be more clear), specific causes (e.g., I had to work late), and external causes (e.g., it was the poor instructor, a bad test, or working late—not my lack of ability or laziness, etc.).

Explanatory style is frequently assessed by the Attributional Style Questionnaire (ASQ) (Peterson et al., 1982) or the Content Analysis of Verbatim Explanations (CAVE) (Peterson, Bettes, & Seligman, 1985). The ASQ provides brief descriptions of six negative and six positive events. People are asked to imagine that each event happened to them. Examples of positive events: "Your significant other (spouse, boyfriend, or girlfriend) has been treating you more lovingly." "You complete a project that is highly praised." Examples of negative events: "You meet a friend who acts hostilely toward you." "You can't get all the work done that others expect of you." People are then asked to describe the one major cause of each event, and then to rate each cause on the internal–external, stable–unstable, and global-specific dimensions. Was the cause something about you (internal) or about the situation

(external)? Was the cause a permanent aspect of life (stable) or temporary and likely to change (unstable)? Was the cause true of your life or personality generally (global) or limited to this one situation (specific)? Separate scores are calculated for positive and negative events.

For the CAVE measure, researchers code the various dimensions of explanatory style based on written documents. These might involve personal essays, autobiographies, therapy transcripts, personal letters, diaries, or interviews. Researchers identify naturally occurring explanations for bad events in these documents. Identified explanations are then rated by judges according to the ASQ scales (internality-externality, global-specific, stable-unstable). The CAVE measure allows researchers to assess the relationship of optimism/pessimism to life outcomes without conducting long-term longitudinal studies. For example, Peterson, Seligman, and Vaillant (1988) used the CAVE measure to evaluate interviews of Harvard students in the late 1930s and early 1940s (average age of 25 years). Optimism and pessimism scores were then related to data on physical health and morbidity, collected 35 years later in 1970. Optimistic young adults enjoyed better physical and mental health later in life, even after adjusting for differences in their physical health and mental health at age 25.

Studies have shown that people's explanatory style for negative events is a better predictor of behavior than their explanatory style for positive events. Research has also found that the internal-external dimension is less predictive than the stability and global dimensions (Abramson, Metalsky, & Alloy, 1989; Peterson, 1991). From the perspective of explanatory style, the difference between an optimist and a pessimist concerns whether bad events are seen as relatively permanent or only temporary features of life (stable or unstable), and whether they affect most aspects of one's life (global) or are limited to particular situations (specific). Optimism as an explanatory style, measured using the ASQ or CAVE, shows a pattern of relationships to positive outcomes similar to those shown in dispositional optimism research (Peterson & Park, 1998).

HOW OPTIMISM WORKS First, optimism is a source of motivation. It is much easier to initiate action when we believe our actions will lead to positive outcomes. This is particularly important when we face obstacles that may tax our persistence. In the face of disappointments, optimism energizes continued action, while pessimism may lead to giving up. The explanatory style of optimists offers one reason for these motivational benefits. By interpreting bad events as temporary and limited to specific situations, optimists protect themselves from strong negative emotional reactions that might undermine confidence and interfere with effective coping (Carver & Scheier, 2002b).

The connection of optimism to more effective coping is a second way in which optimism works. Optimists are better at dealing with stress (Aspinwall, Richter, & Hoffman, 2002; Ness & Segerstrom, 2006). They are more likely than pessimists to use active coping strategies aimed at confronting and solving problems. In their study of college students' adjustments to the stresses of college, Aspinwall and Taylor (1992) found that optimistic students set to work finding ways to deal directly with the challenges of attending class, preparing for exams, writing papers, and developing new relationships. Studying, preparing for tests, talking with other students, and planned use of time were among the active stress-reducing approaches used by optimistic students. More pessimistic students tended to avoid problems by pretending they did not exist, wishfully thinking that they would somehow go away, and reducing rather than increasing social interaction with fellow students.

A third advantage of optimism is flexibility in the use of different coping approaches. Based on their review of dispositional optimism and coping research, Ness and Segerstrom (2006) suggest that optimists distinguish between controllable and uncontrollable life stressors and adjust their coping strategies appropriately. Faced with less controllable threats, such as life-threatening illness, optimists disengage from what may be fruitless efforts, at least in the short term, to solve an unsolvable problem. Instead, they shift their coping orientation from active problem-solving to more emotion-focused coping based on acceptance of a reality that cannot be changed. Emotional coping involves finding ways to reduce and manage the emotional consequences of stressful events and conditions. This might involve engaging in enjoyable activities, sharing feelings with others, or looking past the stressful present situation to a more positive future. Knowing what you can and cannot change is a critical element of

effective coping captured in the well-known Serenity Prayer, made famous by Alcoholics Anonymous: "God grant me the serenity to accept the things I cannot change; courage to change the things I can; and wisdom to know the difference" (Rheinhold Niebuhr). Research suggests that optimists appear to know the difference (Aspinwall et al., 2002).

A summary of research studies comparing the coping strategies of optimists versus pessimists is shown in Table 9.2. These results are based on the LOT measure of dispositional optimism developed by Scheier and Carver (1992).

Fourth, to the extent that an optimistic attitude contributes to more frequent experiencing of positive affect, optimists may also reap the benefits described by Fredrickson's broaden-and-build theory of positive emotions (Chapter 3). Positive emotions contribute to more creative problem-solving, offset the effects of negative emotions, enhance resilience in the face of distress, and increase the likelihood of social support from others. Finally, an optimism–positive emotion connection would also include the beneficial effects of positive emotions on physical health (Chapter 3). It is clear that negative emotions suppress immune-system functioning. Recent studies strongly suggest that positive emotions may enhance the body's ability to fight disease. The health benefits of optimism and the

TABLE 9.2 Coping strategies of optimists and pessimists

Optimists	Pessimists
Information seeking	Suppression of thoughts
Active coping and planning	Giving up
Positive reframing	Self-distraction
Seeking benefit	Cognitive avoidance
Use of humor	Focus on distress
Acceptance	Overt denial

Source: Scheier, M. F., Carver, C. S., & Bridges, M. W. (2002). Optimism, pessimism, and psychological well-being. In E. C. Chang (Ed.), *Optimism and pessimism: Implications for theory, research and practice* (pp. 189–216). Washington, DC: American Psychological Association. Copyright American Psychological Association. Reprinted by permission.

health risks of pessimism may stem, in part, from physiological factors related to differences in the relative prevalence of positive and negative emotions.

VARIETIES OF OPTIMISM AND PESSIMISM

Hope Theory. Dispositional optimism focuses on positive *expectations* for the future that motivate goal-directed behavior. Optimism as explanatory style focuses on a sense of *agency* in describing how people stay on course in achieving their goals by explaining bad events (setbacks) in a way that preserves a positive attitude. Snyder's **hope theory** combines these two elements of expectation and agency in defining hope as willpower and "waypower" (Snyder, 1994, 1995). Agency is the willpower that provides the energy and determination to persist in the pursuit of personally important goals. What Snyder calls "pathways thinking" is the "waypower," which he explains as confidence that routes to desired goals can be identified and, when obstacles are encountered, alternative routes can be found. The Hope Scale contains items assessing both agency and pathways (Snyder, 1994; Snyder et al., 1991). Example items are given below. People rate the extent to which each item is true for them and a summary score describes a person's degree of hope.

1. I energetically pursue my goals. (agency)
2. My past experiences have prepared me well for the future. (agency)
3. I can think of many ways to get out of a jam. (pathways)
4. Even when others get discouraged, I know I can find a way to solve the problem. (pathways)

Hope shows substantial correlations with optimism. Hopeful people also tend to be optimistic (Snyder, 2000; Snyder, Rand, & Sigmon, 2002). However, hope adds the importance of flexible thinking, problem-solving ability, and self-motivation to an understanding of the coping benefits of optimism. Hopeful people, compared to those who are less hopeful, are more skilled in generating alternative means for achieving goals when they encounter roadblocks to their original plans. Hopeful people are better problem-solvers. They are also more likely to use positive "self-talk" (e.g., "I can do this") to maintain their motivation when faced with obstacles. Hopeful people focus on what needs to be done rather than ruminating about what went wrong. Hope shows patterns similar to optimism in its relationships to adjustment, achievement, and health.

"The Positive Power of Negative Thinking." In everyday life we encounter expressions describing a variety of expectations about the future. People say they are "cautiously optimistic," or that someone is "wildly unrealistic," "pursuing a pipedream" or "takes pride in their realistic assessment of the future." It is clear that optimism and pessimism are not the only options for thinking about and preparing for the future. For example, think of someone you know who fits the following description: The person is very anxious when thinking about his or her performance on an upcoming task, expecting the worst; the person gives detailed descriptions of all the things that will go wrong; and yet the person is usually very successful. Norem and her colleagues describe this sort of thinking and behavior as **defensive pessimism** (Norem & Cantor, 1986). The title of Norem's book *The Positive Power of Negative Thinking: Using Defensive Pessimism to Harness Anxiety and Perform at Your Peak* provides a succinct summary of research findings regarding this form of pessimism (Norem, 2001). Defensive pessimism is negative thinking that channels anxiety about potential failure into successful achievement.

Defensive pessimism is measured with a questionnaire that asks people to consider how they prepare for and think about different situations (e.g., academic and social). They are then asked to rate how much the kinds of statements given below describe themselves (Norem, 2002, p. 83). Defensive pessimists would endorse these sample questionnaire items:

> *"I go into these situations expecting the worst, even though I know I will probably be OK."*
>
> *"I often worry that, in these situations, I won't be able to carry through my intentions."*
>
> *"I often try to figure out how likely it is that I will do poorly in these situations."*
>
> *"I spend a lot of time planning when one of these situations is coming up."*

Defensive pessimism serves three positive functions. First, by setting low expectations (i.e., expecting the worst), this form of pessimism softens the blow of failure if it does occur. If you expect success, failure is disheartening. If you expect failure, success is a pleasant surprise. Second, by anticipating and reflecting on worst-case outcomes you can prepare in advance to prevent failure from occurring. Third, if you are anxious about how you will do in various performance situations, pouring over all the ways you may fail, and making preparations to avoid each potential source of failure "harnesses" and channels your anxiety into a productive purpose. By mentally rehearsing what you will do and how you will avoid potential pitfalls, you increase your confidence, reduce anxiety, and feel more in control of the situation—all of which helps maximize your chances of success. Research affirms each of these three functions of defensive pessimism (see Norem, 2001, 2002; Norem & Chang, 2002).

Defensive pessimists think quite differently about a future performance than do optimists. This is clearly shown in a study that asked college students to describe their thoughts and feelings about college exams (Norem & Canter, 1986). Table 9.3 shows the different responses of optimists versus defensive pessimists.

Defensive pessimists perform just as well as optimists, but use a very different strategy. Optimists set high expectations and avoid extensive thinking about future outcomes. They are confident that things will work out well. Defensive pessimists set low expectations, are anxious, and worry about failing, but prepare thoroughly to ensure success. In fact, defensive pessimists "need" to follow this strategy to be successful, as evidenced by the fact that their performance suffers in studies in which they are prevented from thinking and worrying about possible outcomes of an upcoming task.

Despite their performance success, defensive pessimists may pay an emotional price (see Norem, 2002, for a review). Related to their higher levels of performance anxiety and focus on the negatives (what may go wrong), defensive pessimists show

TABLE 9.3 Optimists' and defensive pessimists' thoughts about upcoming exams

Optimist Statements

1. I'm studying the material
2. Feel confident
3. Feel "a little" nervous
4. Feel relaxed/calm
5. I feel like I'm prepared
6. I would psych out the exam questions
7. Plan sleep/study schedule
8. I'm not nervous/worried

Defensive-Pessimism Statements

1. I anticipate doing poorly
2. Feel nervous
3. Feel anxious
4. I think about how unprepared I am in order to get myself to work harder
5. I study as much as possible
6. I think about the exam
7. I think about what will happen if I fail
8. I usually do better than expected

Source: Norem, J. K., & Cantor, N. (1986). Defensive pessimism: Harnessing anxiety as motivation. *Journal of Personality and Social Psychology, 51,* 1208–1217. Copyright American Psychological Association. Adapted with permission.

elevated scores on measures of trait anxiety and neuroticism. Their negative thinking about situations in which they may fail seems to spill over into self-evaluations. Defensive pessimism is correlated with lower self-esteem. Finally, even though there is no specific research to this point, Norem (2002) suggests that the negative thinking and anxiety of defensive pessimists may be annoying to others and result in interpersonal costs. People may get tired trying to be supportive in the face of the defensive pessimist's incessant worrying, especially when things generally turn out well.

From the perspective of positive psychology, defensive pessimism is something of an anomaly, given the widespread assumption that optimism leads to good outcomes and pessimism to bad. Here is a form of pessimism defined by negative expectations and negative emotions that produces positive results. Norem and Chang (2002) believe that defensive pessimism should serve as a reminder to positive psychologists that "As we study how people make positive progress in their lives, we need to take care not to let the power of any one pathway keep us from seeing the alternative routes individuals devise toward their goals" (p. 999).

Unrealistic Optimism. Another distinction among the varieties of optimism concerns the difference between realistic and unrealistic optimism. Not all forms of optimism are beneficial. When optimistic expectations become too far removed from reality, they may do more harm than good. For example, research by Weinstein has shown an unrealistically optimistic bias in people's assessments of their likelihood of experiencing negative life events such as cancer, heart attacks, romantic failure, serious accidents, alcoholism, and divorce (Weinstein, 1980, 1982, 1989; Weinstein & Klein, 1996). When asked to estimate the probability of these events happening to us, most of us seem to believe such things "always happen to the other guy," but not to us. We all think we are below average in risk for serious problems, which of course cannot be true. Bad things happen to somebody! Such optimism may be comforting, but may also inhibit preventative action. If it won't happen to me, why worry? Failure to get regular medical check-ups, continuing to smoke, and not using contraceptives to prevent unwanted pregnancy all reflect the potential dangers of an unrealistically optimistic attitude that discounts personal susceptibility.

Focus on Research and Theory: Unresolved Issues in the Study of Optimism

Studies of defensive pessimism and unrealistic optimism unsettle the simple conclusion that optimism is always good and pessimism is always bad. Other issues relating to the meaning and measurement of optimism also raise complications and temper an unqualified endorsement of the value of positive thinking. At first glance, you may think these issues may be of interest only to professionals. However, enthusiasm for the value of optimism has spawned attempts to teach optimistic thinking to children and the general public (see Norem & Chang, 2002, for a review and Seligman, 1990, for a specific example). Researchers have raised concerns about the complexities of optimism that are similar to those raised about the unqualified value of self-esteem, reviewed earlier in this chapter. Like self-esteem, many psychologists believe that the benefits, costs, measurement, and forms of optimism should be clarified before it is recommended as a way to improve people's lives.

Realism and Optimism

Research suggests that optimism needs to be realistic in order to have a positive effect on outcomes (Schneider, 2001). Unfortunately, researchers do not typically evaluate the information, resources, and judgments upon which an individual's positive expectations are based. Peterson and Chang (2003) note that researchers seem to assume either that optimism is realistically based or that only optimism—not realism—matters. These assumptions create two problems. First, studies of optimism should distinguish between realistic and unrealistic optimism because of the opposite effects involved. Knowing when optimism is warranted and when it is not, is useful information not only to researchers, but also to the general public, because it establishes boundary conditions for the effects of optimism. Peterson (2000) refers to studies of **John Henryism** to exemplify the importance of realistic optimism. The term John Henryism is taken from railroad folklore about a man (John Henry) who competed with a steam-powered spike driver and won, but died as a result. John Henryism refers to a personality trait defined by a belief that dreams and aspirations can be assured if you work hard enough and long enough. Strong optimism coupled with an absence of resources to control outcomes may be a significant source of ongoing stress that contributes to health problems. Research has shown that this trait is associated with high blood pressure and increased risk of heart attack among low socioeconomic status African Americans (James, Storgatz, Wing, & Ramsey, 1987). As Peterson notes, the influence of people's life circumstances needs to be taken into account in evaluating the value of optimism. Optimism matters, but only within the constraints of people's actual levels of control and resources.

Second, without knowing something about the reality of a person's situation, it is hard to determine the extent to which optimism contributed to the outcome, and how much situational variables may have influenced the outcome. Peterson and Chang (2003) give the example of a very wealthy person who is optimistic about getting his bills paid each month. In this case, it is the size of the bank account—not the optimism—that gets the job done. Knowing we have a "sure thing" may make us feel optimistic, but our beliefs are largely irrelevant to outcomes. If optimism is important to outcomes, then the effects of positive expectations should go beyond those caused by situational factors.

Are Optimism and Pessimism Opposite or Independent?

It is generally assumed that optimism and pessimism are at opposite ends of a single continuum—in other words, that people who are high in optimism are inherently low in pessimism and *vice versa*. In the early development of the LOT, inverse correlations were found between optimistic items and pessimistic items ($r = 0.64$) in a sample of college students (Scheier & Carver, 1985). However, subsequent research, particularly with older adults, has found much smaller correlations, suggesting that optimism and pessimism may be two independent constructs rather than a single bipolar one (see Carver & Scheier, 2003; Kubzansky, Kubzansky, & Maselko, 2004; Norem & Chang, 2002; Peterson & Chang, 2003). If there *are* two independent constructs involved, then the opposite of optimism would not be pessimism, but the lack of optimism. The opposite of pessimism would not be optimism, but an absence of pessimism. Studies using a single summary score to assess the degree of optimism may mask the separate and different effects of optimism and pessimism. In line with this possibility,

several studies that calculated separate optimism and pessimism scores have found pessimism to be the more significant predictor. That is, the absence of pessimism was more strongly related to positive outcomes than the presence of optimism (e.g., Robinson-Whelen, Kim, MacCallum, & Kiecolt-Glaser, 1997; Schulz, Bookwala, Knapp, Scheier, & Williamson, 1996).

Similar issues have been raised about the ASQ. This measure of optimism is based on how people explain good and bad life events. Explanatory style for good events is largely independent of explanatory style for bad events. The way we explain negative events is the best predictor of outcomes. A revised version of the ASQ now includes *only* negative events to assess optimistic versus pessimistic explanatory style (Peterson & Villanova, 1988). As several researchers have noted, defining optimism according to how people explain *negative* events seems a bit "curious," if not altogether "backwards" (Norem & Chang, 2002; Peterson, 2000; Snyder, 1995). Shouldn't optimism reflect how people think about the causes of positive events? And shouldn't people's explanations for good events predict positive outcomes and enhanced adjustment? The fact that this is not the case suggests that optimism as explanatory style tells us mostly about how people offset the effects of negative events by explaining them away in a manner that preserves self-esteem and a positive view of the future. Less is revealed about how people's thinking about positive events might promote health and happiness. Future research will need to continue to untangle and clarify the conceptual problems raised by these measurement issues.

Age and Culture

It has been said that "if you're not idealistic when you are young, you have no heart, and if you are not a bit cynical when you are old, you have no head" (original source unknown). Youthful optimism is tempered by the harshness and disappointments of life experience. Like most research in psychology, studies of optimism rely primarily on college students as participants. The possibility that optimism and pessimism may work differently in younger adults than in older adults is suggested by the studies mentioned above. Optimism and pessimism have shown a one-dimensional structure among college populations, but a more two-dimensional, independent structure among older adults (see Norem & Chang, 2002). In addition, studies suggest that the costs and benefits of optimism and pessimism may change with age. For example, a study of middle-aged cancer patients found that the presence of pessimism predicted earlier mortality. However, optimism did not predict increased longevity (Schulz et al., 1996). Another investigation found that optimistic thinking did not predict emotional well-being and physical health outcomes within a sample of older adult family caregivers (Robinson-Whelen et al., 1997). This stands in contrast to the countless studies showing positive benefits of optimism among young adults. Although there are too few studies on which to draw firm conclusions, it may well be that our thinking about optimism and pessimism becomes more complex and less black-and-white as we age. The benefits of optimism and the costs of pessimism may change across the life span.

Questions have also been raised regarding the cross-cultural validity of optimism research. As discussed in Chapter 6, positive thinking is highly valued and actively promoted in American culture. Parents, teachers, and media celebrities encourage a "can do" and "be all you can be" attitude. Asian cultures, on the other hand, emphasize modesty, humility, and a self-critical attitude that is focused on maintaining harmony in interpersonal relationships. Given the effects of culture on people's self-definition, researchers have examined whether culture also influences the value of optimism. Does optimism work in the same way in Asian cultures as it does in American culture? A growing literature suggests the answer is no (see Chang, 2002b; Peterson & Chang, 2003, for reviews).

For example, studies using the LOT have found that while Asian and European Americans *do not* differ in their level of overall optimism, they *do* differ in their degree of pessimism, with Asians being more pessimistic. Furthermore, while optimism predicts positive coping among Americans, it is pessimism that predicts the use of effective coping among Asians. Findings for Asians parallel those for defensive pessimists, as described earlier in this chapter. That is, the pessimism of Asian Americans may be the basis for anticipating future negative outcomes (the pessimism component), and taking steps to prevent their occurrence (the defensive component). Defensive pessimism would have positive value and might perpetuate itself because it works. Focusing

on the negative possibilities may motivate proactive behaviors (e.g., problem-solving) that reduce the likelihood of bad outcomes and increase the odds of good ones. The bottom line here is that the meaning, operation, and costs/benefits of optimism and pessimism appear to vary significantly between Western and Eastern cultures.

At a practical level within Western cultures, the conceptual and empirical complexities of optimism may be partially resolved by thinking of optimism and pessimism as involving a choice. In the conclusion of his book on *Learned Optimism*, Seligman (1990) recommends a "flexible optimism" that recognizes the costs and limitations of an across-the-board or habitual optimism. (His arguments would also seem to apply to people who are habitually pessimistic.) Seligman believes that, reminiscent of the Serenity Prayer, assessments of control over events and outcomes should inform our degree of optimism in a given situation. Realism, acceptance, and even pessimism may be more adaptive when we face things we cannot control and the potential costs are high. Research on goal disengagement supports the value of a flexible rather than a hard-and-fast optimism and the importance of realistic assessment. Recall from Chapter 8, that giving up unattainable goals is a healthy response that avoids the frustration and emotional drain that may result from striving for an outcome that cannot be achieved. Realistic assessments and pessimistic expectations prevent us from wasting time and energy. Following the Serenity Prayer, knowing the difference between things you can and cannot change, is one way to sort out the costs and benefits of optimism and pessimism.

Positive Illusions

The work of Shelly Taylor and her colleagues may provide a clarifying summary of our discussion of positive beliefs. While people differ in their degrees of happiness, self-esteem, and optimism, Taylor's work suggests that most people maintain a positive outlook even when facing stressful events (Taylor & Armor, 1996; Taylor & Brown, 1988; Taylor, Kemeney, Reed, Bower, & Gruenewald, 2000). Some amount of optimism may be built into human nature as a basic requirement of life that, if nothing else, gets you out of bed in the morning to face another day (Peterson, 2000). If our view of life is "too" close to reality, all the pain and suffering in the world (including our own) may become downright depressing.

Evidence suggests that most people share four **positive illusions.** First, people have a self-serving view of themselves as better than average compared to other people. We tend to think we are more competent and better liked than other people and describe ourselves primarily in positive terms. Second, people are "unrealistically" optimistic and see a rosy future for themselves in which many good things and few bad things will happen. Third, most of us exaggerate the amount of control we have over our lives. Fourth, people often show a self-serving bias in attributing their failures to external circumstances, rather than to personal factors such as lack of ability or effort. This bias helps maintain a positive self-image in the face of negative and potentially self-deflating events. These beliefs are considered illusions because they are not literally true. Not everyone can be better than average and have a rosy future, and there are limits to our control over life events. However, these beliefs are not so far-removed from reality that they constitute delusional or irrational thinking that would interfere with a healthy life. In fact, quite the opposite. Positive illusions are mild distortions in how we view life and ourselves that promote health, happiness, and coping with stress and trauma.

Rather than dramatic departures from reality, positive illusions are consistent, modest biases that put a positive spin on our view of the world. Feedback from the environment and especially other people keep us from going to extremes. Few of our friends and family members are likely to tolerate highly inflated expressions of our abilities or endorse pie-in-the-sky expectations about our futures. Positive illusions that are too extreme are likely to be brought back to reality, unless we stick our head in the sand and ignore the "reality checks" available to us.

A variety of studies suggest that in situations that challenge people's illusions (such as serious illness), they make active efforts to restore their positive views. Like optimism, positive illusions have been consistently associated with healthy psychological adjustment (Taylor, 1989; Taylor & Armor, 1996; Taylor, Lerner, Sherman, Sage, & McDowell, 2003). People's attempts to recapture a positive view of self (even if unrealistic), a sense of personal control, and an optimistic view of the future are adaptive mechanisms for dealing with stressful events. Furthermore, the absence of positive illusions has been linked to mild depression (Alloy & Abramson, 1979). **Depressive realism** (also known as the "sadder-but-wiser effect") refers to the surprising finding that *mildly* depressed individuals are actually more accurate (realistic) in their judgments of themselves and life than are non-depressed individuals. Negative distortions and intense pessimism are characteristic of severe depression, but among mildly depressed people, a more realistic view and the loss of positive illusions contribute to the depression. The differing beliefs of mildly depressed and non-depressed people are compared in Table 9.4.

Mildly depressed individuals do not exaggerate their competencies or their likeability, as non-depressed individuals do. Depressed people are more accurate in their assessment of how much control they have, and are less susceptible to the illusion of control that characterizes non-depressed people. Depressed people have a more realistic and accurate view of their futures because their expectations include a balance of good and bad things, rather

TABLE 9.4 Depressive realism versus positive illusions

Mildly Depressed: Depressive Realism	Non-Depressed: Positive Illusions
Accurate perception of self	Inflated perception of self
Realistic assessment of past and balance of positives and negatives predicted in future	Recall positive past and predict a rosy future
Realistic assessment of how much control they have in their life	Exaggerated sense of control
Accept responsibility for negative outcomes	Self-serving bias—failure attributed to circumstances beyond personal control

than the rosy "everything-will-be-good" optimism of non-depressed people. Depressed people are also likely to take personal responsibility for failure rather than following the self-serving bias. In summary, Taylor (1989, p. 214) concludes that ". . . on virtually every point on which normal people show enhanced self-regard, illusions of control, and unrealistic visions of the future, depressed people fail to show the same biases. 'Sadder but wiser' does indeed appear to apply to depression."

Taylor's work is a reminder that, while too much unrealistic optimism may have its costs, too much realism may also come with a price tag. Viewing ourselves as somewhat better than we really are, seeing the future as more positive than it probably will be, and believing that we have more control over our lives than we actually do, may be "unrealistic" and illusory. However, such views also invigorate action, sustain a positive view of our present and future, and allow us to cope and rebound in the face of life's inevitable disappointments, setbacks, and traumas. As Schneider (2001) has argued, the available information on which to assess the likelihood of a certain outcome is seldom so definitive that reality compels one—and only one—possibility. From getting a good job, to having a happy marriage, to surviving cancer, reality usually allows some wiggle room in what we may expect. That is, several outcomes may be equally reasonable possibilities. The value of choosing a positive view, within the limits of reality's wiggle room, may exemplify one of the central messages of research in positive psychology.

In this chapter, we have reviewed research and theory focused on traits regarded as positive because of their contributions to happiness, positive emotional experiences, life satisfaction, emotional well-being, effective coping, and physical health. Positive affectivity, extraversion, cheerful temperament, approach motivation, self-esteem, optimism, and positive illusions all contribute to a life lived above the neutral or zero-point for health and happiness. Consistent with a major theme of positive psychology, happiness is not just the absence of sadness; health is not just the absence of misery or illness; and a good life is not just the absence of a bad life. While positive traits do help us cope and offset the effects of negative events, they also contribute to happiness and positive mental and physical health—that is, life on the plus side of zero.

Chapter Summary Questions

1. What four criteria are used to define a trait as positive?
2. a. What did Paul Meehl mean when he said some people are just born "three drinks behind?"
   b. How has research on positive and negative affectivity supported Meehl's predictions?
3. What is the difference between reactive and non-reactive infants, according to Kagan's research?
4. What are the overlapping and complicating relationships among positive and negative affectivity, extraversion, neuroticism, and SWB?
5. How is the pattern of relationships of the Big Five personality traits to eudaimonic criteria of well-being different from that for SWB?
6. How may behavioral activation systems and behavioral inhibition systems underlie differences in people's tendency toward an approach or avoidance goal orientation?
7. What recent evidence and arguments suggest that people's happiness set-point can change, and that we are not condemned to a "hedonic treadmill?"
8. What differences led Lyubomirsky to conclude that happy and unhappy people live in separate worlds?
9. What is the value of self-esteem as a general life outlook and a coping resource?
10. How does sociometer theory explain the importance of self-esteem from an evolutionary perspective? What does self-esteem meter?
11. Based on research reviews, what were the major problems with the assumptions of the self-esteem movement in our culture in the 1980s? What was, and what was not, related to self-esteem?
12. What are contingencies of self-worth and how may they be related to social and individual problems, according to Crocker and her colleagues?
13. What is the potential "darker" side of pursuing self-esteem, as described by Carl Rogers and recent studies by Crocker and her colleagues?
14. What role do optimism and pessimism play in self-regulated actions, according to Scheier and Carver's model of dispositional optimism?

15. According to the explanatory style view of optimism developed by Seligman and his colleagues, what explanations for negative events characterize the difference between optimists versus pessimists?
16. How does optimism "work," and what positive functions does it serve?
17. What two problems are created when researchers fail to measure and evaluate the information and resources on which people base their optimistic expectations for the future?
18. Why is the measure of optimism within the explanatory style model a bit "curious?"
19. How do American and Asian cultures differ in the level, meaning, and benefits of optimism and pessimism?
20. a. What positive illusions do most people share?
    b. How do studies of "depressive realism" show the benefits of positive illusions?

Key Terms

traits *177*
positive affectivity *178*
negative affectivity *178*
temperament *179*
reactive and non-reactive temperaments *179*
five-factor model *180*

behavioral activation system *183*
behavioral inhibition system *183*
self-esteem *186*
sociometer theory *188*
contingency of self-worth *190*
dispositional optimism *193*
optimism as explanatory style *195*

hope theory *198*
defensive pessimism *198*
John Henryism *200*
positive illusions *203*
depressive realism *203*

Web Resources

Dispositional Optimism

www.psy.miami.edu/faculty/ccarver This is Charles Carver's web page. In addition to many references to his work on dispositional optimism, his site also includes free printable copies of the LOT-R measure of optimism and the measures of BIS and BAS.

Sonja Lyubomirsky

www.faculty.ucr.edu/~sonja/index.html This web site describes the research by Sonja Lyubomirsky on the differences between happy and unhappy people and her efforts to find ways to increase people's level of happiness.

Self-Esteem

www.discoveryhealth.queendom.com/self_esteem_abridged_access.html Several self-esteem tests are available that can be taken and scored on line. Address leads to one example.

Contingent Self-Esteem

www.rcgd.isr.umich.edu/crockerlab/projects.htm Web site for researcher Jennifer Crocker at the University of Michigan. In addition to descriptions of her research, links on the site take you to measures of contingent self-esteem that can be printed and scored.

Authentic Happiness

www.authentichappiness.sas.upenn.edu This is Martin Seligman's site at the University of Pennsylvania. Many positive psychology trait tests are available on this site. You must provide log in, create a password, and provide demographic information to take the tests and have them scored for you. A profile of scores on all tests is computed and can be accessed at any time.

The optimism test on this site is a version of the Attributional Style measure of optimism.

Defensive Pessimism

www.defensivepessimism.com This is Julie Norem's web site, describing her work on defensive pessimism and the power of negative thinking. A free online test of defensive pessimism is available on the site.

Suggested Readings

Baumeister, R. F., Campbell, J. D., Krueger, J. I., & Vohs, K. D. (2005). Exploding the self-esteem myth. *Scientific American, 292,* 84–91.

Carver, C. S., & White, T. L. (1994). Behavioral inhibition, behavioral activation, and affective responses to impending reward and punishment: The BIS/BAS scales. *Journal of Personality and Social Psychology, 67,* 319–333.

Chang, E. C. (Ed.). (2002). *Optimism and pessimism: Implications for theory, research and practice.* Washington, DC: American Psychological Association.

Crocker, J., & Park, L. E. (2004). The costly pursuit of self-esteem. *Psychological Bulletin, 130,* 392–414.

McCrae, R. R., & Costa, P. T., Jr. (1997). Personality trait structure as a human universal. *American Psychologist, 52,* 509–516.

Ness, L. S., & Segerstrom, S. C. (2006). Dispositional optimism and coping: A meta-analytic review. *Personality and Social Psychology Review, 10,* 25–251.

Norem, J. K. (2001). *The positive power of negative thinking: Using defensive pessimism to harness anxiety and perform at your peak.* New York: Basic Books.

Peterson, C. (2000). The future of optimism. *American Psychologist, 55,* 44–55.

Seligman, M. E. P. (1990). *Learned optimism.* New York: Pocket Books.

Seligman, M. E. P. (2002). *Authentic happiness: Using the new positive psychology to realize your potential for lasting fulfillment.* New York: Free Press.

Taylor, S. E. (1989). *Positive illusions: Creative Self-deceptions and the healthy mind.* New York: Basic Books.

Watson, D., Wiese, D., Vaidya, J., & Tellegen, A. (1999). The two general activation systems of affect: Structural findings, evolutionary considerations, and psychobiological evidence. *Journal of Personality and Social Psychology, 76,* 820–838.

10

Virtue and Strengths of Character

Think of someone you hold in high regard and look up to as a model for yourself and others. Perhaps a friend, relative, or a person from history or contemporary society comes to mind. Think about this individual's personal qualities and how you might describe the basis of your admiration to another person. Make a mental list of 4 or 5 qualities that make this person deserving of your respect. Now compare your list to the positive traits discussed in Chapter 9. How many of them overlap? Did your list include extraversion, cheerfulness, self-esteem, or optimism? What traits on your list are not in Chapter 9? Did you include any of the following qualities: integrity, courage, honesty, kindness, religious conviction, wisdom, fairness, or modesty? The point here, affirmed by how we think about people we respect, is that a description of positive human traits would be incomplete without including personal qualities judged as positive because they are "good" in moral and ethical terms. Clearly, we may admire people who are outgoing, upbeat, and positive about the future. But just as clearly, and perhaps at a deeper level, we also admire individuals who show strengths of character that reflect virtuous qualities like integrity, kindness, and compassion. In short, virtue and character strengths belong on a list of positive human traits.

The traits reviewed in Chapter 9 were evaluated as positive because of their benefits to individual well-being—specifically health, happiness, and emotional well-being. Virtuous behavior may also increase our life satisfaction and make life more meaningful and healthy. However, virtue is also considered a positive trait independent of any benefit or "pay-off" to the individual. Virtue is positively regarded in its own right because of its connection to religious and secular mores and its value to society. A consideration of virtue and character strengths provides an additional way to think about the meaning of "positive." In this chapter, we will first review a recent attempt to provide a comprehensive classification of character strengths and virtues. Then, we will focus on two foundational virtues (wisdom and religion) in more detail by examining how they contribute to well-being and a life well-lived.

DEVELOPING A CLASSIFICATION OF HUMAN VIRTUES

For a considerable time in psychology's history, virtue was not considered an appropriate construct for scientific investigation. The study of virtue was thought to be too easily tainted and biased by the moral beliefs of researchers and the prevailing cultural mores of the day (Tjeltveit, 2003). Many psychologists believed that science should provide only objective facts about *how* people act. Questions about how people *should* conduct themselves—that is, whether their actions were good, bad, moral, or immoral—were left for philosophers and theologians to decide. However, a renewed interest in character strengths has begun to emerge as more psychologists have come to realize that a complete account of human behavior needs to include the moral dimension of people's lives (Fowers & Tjeltveit, 2003). Recent events from the Enron scandal to the influence-peddling of lobbyist Jack Abramoff have reinforced the importance of ethical behavior. People's anger and outrage at these sorts of improprieties stem primarily from moral considerations. In short, people lead moral lives in the sense of evaluating themselves and others according to moral criteria.

Describing the features of a life well-lived is a central theme of positive psychology. Because the meaning of a good person and a good life are intimately connected to virtue, positive psychology has given virtue particular prominence. This is most apparent in a recent collaborative research project (the Values in Action Project, Peterson & Seligman, 2004) that had the lofty goal of developing a classification of character strengths and virtues that would parallel the *Diagnostic and Statistical Manual of Mental Disorders* (DSM), developed by the American Psychiatric Association (2000). The DSM provides a classification of mental disorders and an extensive "language" for describing human psychological weaknesses and pathologies. Authors of the **Values in Action Project** (VIA) hoped to create a comprehensive classification system similar to the DSM, but one that was focused on human strengths rather than weaknesses. They also hoped to provide a language describing positive human qualities that defined a healthy person living a good life. Put another way, the DSM describes aspects of life "below zero" (with "zero" representing the threshold dividing mental health from emotional illness). One goal of the VIA was to describe life "above zero" (i.e., to identify the traits that define emotional health and strength). This goal is consistent with positive psychology's emphasis on restoring balance to the field, in place of psychology's historic focus on problematic human behaviors.

Developing a classification of character strengths is a daunting task. Virtue and character are obviously complex topics. What, exactly, is a human virtue or character strength? Do people have a common understanding of traits that qualify as virtuous? Getting answers to these questions was one of the major purposes of the VIA. The VIA, coordinated by Christopher Peterson and Martin Seligman (2004), brought together a group of researchers who sought to describe those strengths of character that were most prominent across history and culture. Is there a common set of human qualities universally regarded as positive virtues? A list of possible "candidates" was generated by examining virtues and strengths described in a variety of philosophic, religious, and cultural traditions. This list included virtues described in major religions and philosophies (e.g., Confucianism, Buddhism, Hinduism, Judeo-Christianity, and ancient Greek philosophy), the works of famous historical figures (e.g., Benjamin Franklin), and in popular culture (e.g., Boy and Girl Scout Guides, Hallmark greeting cards, popular songs, *Saturday Evening Post* covers by Normal Rockwell).

From a long list of candidates, 24 character strengths were selected and organized around 6 virtues. The 6 virtues—wisdom, courage, humanity, justice, temperance, and transcendence—were selected because they appear to be universal across history and across societies. They represent moral virtues as defined by most religions and ethical philosophies. Peterson and Seligman regard these virtues as core defining features of good character. Each virtue is defined by a set of character strengths that represent the ingredients, expressions, and potential means of developing the virtue. For example, temperance as a virtue refers to people's strength in avoiding excesses. The ingredients and expressions of temperance would include self-control, gratitude toward others, humility, prudent decision-making, and the ability to forgive the transgressions of self and others. Developing this virtue would involve efforts to exert more self-control, become more humble and less self-aggrandizing, and more grateful and forgiving in relationships with others.

Character strengths were selected by applying a set of criteria to the list of strengths identified in the first phase of the project. A sample of the set of criteria used is shown in Table 10.1. To be included in the final classification, a character strength had to meet all or nearly all of these criteria.

Half of the strengths selected met the entire set of criteria. The other half did not. As Seligman and Peterson note, disagreements can arise about the inclusion of one or another of the strengths, the placement of a given strength under a particular virtue, and whether some other important strength was omitted. However, taken in total, this classification system "hangs together" as a reasonably coherent first effort at describing what may be universally regarded as human strengths and virtues. The final classification of strengths and virtues is described in Table 10.2. For a complete description of the selection criteria, previous classification models, and literature reviews detailing what is known about each character strength, see Peterson and Seligman's *Character Strengths and Virtues: A Handbook and Classification* (2004).

Wisdom and Knowledge

As a virtue, wisdom refers to a general intellectual strength involving the development and use of knowledge. Wisdom does not necessarily follow from a formal education or a high IQ score. Wisdom refers to a more practical intelligence and good judgment based on learning life's lessons—perhaps through hardships. A wise person puts things in the proper perspective and avoids the pitfalls of narrowly focused and self-interested understandings. Wisdom means being able to offer good counsel to others about how to live and how to understand and deal with life's challenges, uncertainties, and choices.

Courage

Courage is the emotional strength to overcome fear in the face of opposition and adversity. Courage is

---

TABLE 10.1 Criteria for selecting character strengths

Regarded as a valued moral quality in and of itself, whether or not it led to concrete benefits.

Contributes to personal fulfillment in the sense of enhancing personal expressiveness, meaningfulness, satisfaction, and happiness.

Constitutes a stable individual difference trait for which reliable measures had been previously developed.

Be distinctive and not overlap with other strengths.

Have an opposite that was clearly negative (e.g., the opposite of courage is cowardice).

Enhances rather than diminishes other people when expressed (i.e., the trait must evoke admiration or respect rather than envy, inferiority, or lowered self-evaluation).

Be the focus of institutional efforts (e.g., education, churches) to promote its development.

TABLE 10.2 Classification of virtues and character strengths

I. Wisdom and Knowledge—cognitive strengths that entail the acquisition and use of knowledge.
Defining Strengths
1. *Creativity*—thinking of novel and productive ways to do things
2. *Curiosity*—taking an interest in all ongoing experience
3. *Open-mindedness*—thinking things through and from all sides
4. *Love of learning*—mastering new skills, topics, and bodies of knowledge
5. *Perspective*—being able to provide wise counsel to others

II. Courage—emotional strengths that involve exercise of will in the face of opposition, external or internal.
Defining Strengths
6. *Authenticity*—speaking the truth and presenting yourself in a genuine way
7. *Bravery*—not shrinking from threat, challenge, difficulty, or pain
8. *Persistence*—finishing what one starts despite obstacles along the way
9. *Zest*—approaching life with excitement and energy

III. Humanity—interpersonal strengths that involve "tending and befriending" others.
Defining Strengths
10. *Kindness*—doing favors and good deeds for others
11. *Love*—valuing close relations with others
12. *Social intelligence*—being aware of the motives and feelings of self and others

IV. Justice—civic strengths that underlie healthy community life.
Defining Strengths
13. *Fairness*—treating all people the same according to notions of fairness and justice
14. *Leadership*—organizing group activities and seeing that they happen
15. *Teamwork*—working well as member of a group or team

V. Temperance—strengths that protect against excess.
Defining Strengths
16. *Forgiveness*—forgiving those who have done wrong
17. *Modesty*—letting one's accomplishments speak for themselves
18. *Prudence*—being careful about one's choices; not saying or doing things that might be later regretted
19. *Self-regulation*—regulating what one feels and does

VI. Transcendence—strengths that forge connections to the larger universe and providing meaning.
Defining Strengths
20. *Appreciation of beauty and excellence*—noticing and appreciating beauty, excellence, and/or skilled performance in all domains of life
21. *Gratitude*—being aware of and thankful for good things that happen
22. *Hope*—expecting the best and working to achieve it
23. *Humor*—liking to laugh and tease; bringing smiles to other people
24. *Religiousness/Spirituality*—having coherent beliefs about the higher purposes and meaning of life

Source: Seligman, M. E. P., Steen, T. A., Park, N., & Peterson, C. (2005). Positive psychology progress: Empirical validation of interventions. *American Psychologist, 60,* 410–421. Copyright American Psychological Association. Adapted and reprinted with permission.

exemplified in confronting and accepting one's own death; dealing with a debilitating illness or disease; honestly confronting one's own limitations, weaknesses, or bad habits; and standing up for one's convictions, despite the possibility of negative consequences (e.g., chastisement by others).

Humanity

Humanity refers to our capacity for sympathy, empathy, compassion, and love in our relationships with others. Humanity is the basis for nurturing and caring relationships focused on another's needs rather than one's own needs and interests. Humanity is expressed in our willingness to help others in need, to be kind, to be generous, and to respect the feelings and values of others.

Justice

Justice is an essential ingredient in healthy societies, communities, and relationships with others. This virtue is shown when people are fair minded and even-handed rather than being biased by self-interest. Justice also includes strengths that contribute to community well-being, such as working cooperatively with others and taking the initiative to develop and follow through on goals and projects.

Temperance

Temperance is the strength to control excesses and restrain impulses that may harm the self and others. It expresses the idea of "willpower" in the face of temptations. Temptations and the benefits of restraint might be focused on eating; drinking; smoking; expressing of anger, hatred, or arrogance toward others; or excessive self-promotion at the expense of others. Chapter 8 described some of the psychological processes involved in self-control and self-directed actions that are relevant to temperance. Temperance is a kind of ongoing self-awareness and self-discipline that affirms the "look before you leap" dictum of everyday wisdom. Temperance also involves the ability to let go and forgive the indiscretions and hurtful actions of others.

Transcendence

To transcend means to go beyond or rise above the ordinary and the everyday. Transcendent thinking lifts us out of the usual concrete preoccupations of daily life and out of an individualized sense of self by providing a broader view of the world and the universe. Transcendence puts things in perspective and keeps us from worrying about or striving for things that don't really matter. Religion and spirituality are the clearest examples of transcendence because they involve a belief in a higher power and a greater purpose for life. Whatever their various forms, transcendent beliefs connect the individual to a more encompassing understanding and a deeper meaning of life. The character strength of religiousness clearly fits the virtue of transcendence.

The other strengths listed under transcendence may not seem to fit so well. Peterson and Seligman (2004) believe that the common theme here is providing opportunities to appreciate and develop a bigger picture of the world that may provide a more enduring and satisfying understanding and purpose for life. "Appreciation of beauty is a strength that connects someone to excellence. Gratitude connects someone directly to goodness. Hope connects someone directly to the dreamed-of future" (Peterson & Seligman, 2004, p. 519). Humor, they admit, seems a bit of stretch as an expression of transcendence. However, as they point out, humor keeps us from taking our selves and our virtues too seriously. It reminds us to "lighten up." Laughter holds nothing sacred and can cut through everything from self-righteousness to passionate conflicts over important issues. On a daily basis, Jay Leno and David Letterman create humor out of pain and tragedy, from political scandals to the war in Iraq. Perhaps humor serves a protective function by connecting us directly to life's absurdities and getting us to laugh at them.

Measuring Strengths of Character

A major goal of the VIA project was the development of measures for each of the 24 strengths of character. Based on existing knowledge and assessment instruments for each of the strengths, a 240-item self-report questionnaire was created. Ten items were used to assess each character strength. For example, *forgiveness* is measured by items such as, "I always allow others to leave their mistakes in the past and make a fresh start." *Kindness* is measured by items like, "I'm never too busy to help a friend." Curiosity is measured through items such as, "I am never bored." Items like, "I always keep my promises" measure *integrity* (Peterson & Seligman, 2004, pp. 629–630). Respondents rate their degree of endorsement on a scale from 1 (very unlike me) to 5 (very much like me). Rating summaries produce a profile of an individual's relative standing on each of the 24 character strengths. The entire VIA inventory of strengths takes 30 to 40 minutes to complete. You can take the VIA inventory of strengths online at www.authentichappiness.sas.upenn.edu/. There are several questionnaires on this site. You want to select the VIA Signature Strengths Questionnaire, which gives you a character strength profile and identifies your top five strengths, called "signature" strengths. You will need to log on to the site, provide some basic information, and create a password to take the test and have your responses scored.

Although still a work in progress, the VIA Strengths Inventory has shown good internal consistency and test–retest reliability. Individual self-ratings have been validated against ratings by informed observers. A youth version of the VIA inventory has also been developed and tested (see Peterson & Seligman, 2004). The inventory has been taken by over 350,000 people of all ages and backgrounds, representing 50 countries and all 50 U.S. states (Peterson, 2006; Peterson & Seligman, 2004; Seligman, Steen, Park, & Peterson, 2005).

Analysis of character-strength profiles in relation to respondents' backgrounds revealed several interesting patterns. People from around the world show substantial agreement regarding the strengths rated as "most like me." The most commonly endorsed character strengths in 50 countries were fairness, kindness, authenticity, gratitude, and open-mindedness. The least frequently endorsed strengths were prudence, self-regulation, and modesty. The correlations of strength rankings across nations were typically in the +0.80 range. Despite widely different cultures, religions, and ethnic backgrounds, people seem to share a common understanding of character strengths and virtues. Within the United States, the same pattern of rankings was apparent with the exception of religiousness, which was stronger in the southern states.

Interestingly, there was less agreement in rankings between U.S. teenagers and U.S. adults than among adults from different countries. American adolescents rated hope, teamwork, and zest as "most like me," while American adults gave higher endorsements to authenticity, appreciation of beauty, leadership, and open-mindedness.

Character strengths related to relationships (love) and positive emotions (e.g., zest, hope, and gratitude) were more strongly related to measures of life satisfaction than were more intellectual-cognitive strengths (e.g., curiosity and love of learning). "Strengths of the heart," as Peterson and Seligman call them (experiences such as kindness, love, and gratitude), contribute the most to our individual happiness.

Profiles of character strength also fit with the matching hypothesis discussed in Chapter 7. People were asked to think about personal experiences involving their most rewarding and fulfilling jobs and hobbies, their "truest" love, and their best friends. The experiences they chose as the "most satisfying (they) had ever had" were those that matched their character strengths. For example, people strong in kindness enjoyed working as mentors for others. Those with curiosity as strength valued and enjoyed romantic partners who were adventuresome risk-takers.

Finally, factor analysis revealed a five-factor dimensional structure of the 24 character strengths that was similar (but not identical) to the original organization of strengths around the six virtues. The five factors were identified as strengths relating to *restraint* (e.g., humility, prudence, and mercy), *intelligence* (e.g., creativity and curiosity), *relationships* (e.g., love and kindness), *emotions* (e.g., bravery, hope, and self-regulation), and *religion* (e.g., spirituality and gratitude). Peterson and Seligman acknowledge the tentative nature of the organization of character strengths around the six core virtues. Subsequent research will undoubtedly refine the virtue categories and the strengths that define them. For example, a recent study examining the factor structure of 42 positive character traits, including those from the VIA project, found only a partial overlap with the VIA six-virtue model (Haslam, Bain, & Neal, 2004). Results suggested that categories of self-control, love, wisdom, drive, and vivacity may better capture how people think about and organize character strengths. Whatever the final organization, the VIA project has provided a useful starting point, by proposing a detailed list of character strengths and strong evidence for their universality across time and culture.

In the remainder of this chapter, we will review research and theory related to the virtues of wisdom and transcendence. Chapter 11 is focused on the virtue of love. Literature relevant to other strengths has been discussed in previous chapters as described below. Peterson and Seligman (2004) provide a comprehensive review of research and theory relating to each character strength.

Strength	Topic	Chapter
Curiosity	Five Factor Model (FFM) Openness to experience	Chapter 9
Love of Learning	Approach/avoidance goals Intrinsic/extrinsic motivation	Chapter 7
Persistence	Commitment	Chapter 7
	Persistence and self-esteem	Chapter 9
Integrity	Autonomy Self-determination theory	Chapters 2; 7
Prudence	FFM—conscientiousness	Chapter 9
Self-regulation	Self-control and regulation	Chapter 8
Hope	Optimism/hope	Chapter 9

WISDOM AS A FOUNDATIONAL STRENGTH AND VIRTUE

From the ancient Greeks to the present, wisdom and living a good life have been intimately connected. Despite cultural differences in the specifics (e.g., Yang, 2001), wisdom is most generally understood to mean a philosophic understanding of *what* matters in life and the practical knowledge of *how* to conduct a life that matters (Baltes & Freund, 2003b; Peterson & Seligman, 2004; Robinson, 1990). Theoretical wisdom and practical wisdom are thus wedded together and assumed to produce a happy and satisfying life. The happiness connected to wisdom has more to do with the eudaimonic than with the hedonic perspective (see Chapter 4). Wisdom involves identifying and pursuing the deeper and enduring purposes of life, beyond individual happiness. Wisdom is the ability to balance your needs and happiness with those of others (Sternberg, 1998). Wisdom serves the common rather than the purely individual good by finding a balance between the two. Many psychologists have come to regard wisdom as a foundation for a life well-lived and one of humans' most important strengths (e.g., Baltes & Freund, 2003a, 2003b; Baltes, Gluck, & Kunzman, 2002; Csikszentmihalyi & Rathunde, 1990; Sternberg, 1990, 1998a).

What Is Wisdom?

One way to explore the meaning of wisdom is to examine people's everyday understanding. Each of us has some implicit idea about wisdom, drawn from cultural characterizations that are embodied in exemplars of "wise" people. Think of famous people, past and present, who exemplify your understanding of a wise person. Who comes to mind? The top 15 answers given by college students are shown in Table 10.3. Interestingly, along with well-known wise people like Gandhi, Confucius, Jesus Christ, Martin Luther King, and Socrates, "wisdom nominees" also included Oprah Winfrey and Ann Landers (Paulus, Wehr, Harms, & Strasser, 2002).

This study also investigated whether people distinguish among wisdom, intelligence, creativity, and sheer fame by having different groups of participants make nominations for each of the specified characteristics. Table 10.3 shows that the nominations for each of the categories include a blend of historic and contemporary figures. Evidence of the differences people perceive among wise, intelligent, creative, and just famous people was shown by the low degree of overlap in the various nominee lists. Only one person, Oprah Winfrey, was on both the wisdom list and the intelligence list. There was no overlap between nominees for creativity and wisdom, a 27% overlap between creative and intelligent people, and a 7% overlap between wisdom and creativity. People do not use pure fame or notoriety as a basis for nominating wise, creative, or intelligent people. Sheer fame nominees never exceeded 20% of overlap with the other three categories.

To get at the specific factors that define folk wisdom, researchers have asked people to identify

TABLE 10.3 Nominations for intelligent, creative, wise, and famous people

Intelligent	Creative	Wise	Sheer Fame
1. Einstein	Da Vinci	Gandhi	Princess Diana
2. Bill Clinton	Picasso	Confucius	Elvis Presley
3. Da Vinci	Michelangelo	Jesus Christ	Michael Jordan
4. Prime Minister	Mozart	M. L. King	Muhammad Ali
5. Gates	Spielberg	Socrates	Michael Jackson
6. Shakespeare	Shakespeare	Mother Theresa	Bill Clinton
7. Hawking	Michael Jackson	Solomon	Madonna
8. Oprah	Beethoven	Buddha	Wayne Gretzky
9. Newton	Walt Disney	Pope	Bill Gates
10. Mozart	Robin Williams	Oprah Winfrey	John F. Kennedy
11. Edison	Salvador Dali	Winston Churchill	Nelson Mandela
12. Suzuki	Madonna	Dalai Lama	Marilyn Monroe
13. Madonna	Sigmund Freud	Ann Landers	Adolph Hitler
14. Gorbachev	Alexander Graham Bell	Nelson Mandela	George Bush, Sr.
15. Trudeau	Margaret Atwood	Queen Elizabeth	Jesus Christ

Source: Paulus, D. L., Wehr, P., Harms, P. D., & Strasser, D. H. (2002). Use of exemplars to reveal implicit types of intelligence. *Personality and Social Psychology Bulletin, 28*, 1051–1062. Copyright American Psychological Association. Reprinted by permission.

wise behaviors and have analyzed the characteristics of wisdom described in cultural, historical, and philosophical writings. For example, Sternberg (1985) asked a group of college professors and lay-persons to list characteristics they associated with wise people. Researchers then took the top 40 wisdom characteristics and asked college students to sort them into piles, according to "which behaviors [were] likely to be found together in a person." Based on students' sortings, Sternberg identified six groupings of attributes that characterize a wise person:

1. *Reasoning ability*: Uncommon ability to look at a problem and solve it through good logical reasoning ability, by applying knowledge to particular problems, by integrating information and theories in new ways, and by possessing a huge store of knowledge.
2. *Sagacity*: A keen understanding of human nature, thoughtfulness, fairness, good listening abilities, knowledge of self, and placing value on the advice and knowledge of others.
3. *Learning from ideas and the environment*: Places value on ideas, is perceptive, and learns from others' mistakes.
4. *Judgment*: Has good, sensible judgment at all times, takes a long-term rather than a short-term view, and thinks before acting and speaking.
5. *Expeditious use of information*: Learns and retains information from experience (both mistakes and successes), willingness to change one's mind based on new experience.
6. *Perspicacity*: Demonstrates perceptiveness, intuition, ability to see through things, read between the lines; and discern the truth and the right thing to do.

In his analysis of wisdom in philosophical writings, Baltes (1993) identified seven properties describing the nature of wisdom (taken from Baltes & Staudinger, 2000, Appendix A, p. 135).

1. "Wisdom addresses important and difficult questions and strategies about the conduct and meaning of life."

2. "Wisdom includes knowledge about the limits of knowledge and the uncertainties of the world."

3. "Wisdom represents a truly superior level of knowledge, judgment, and advice."

4. "Wisdom constitutes knowledge with extraordinary scope, depth, measure, and balance."

5. "Wisdom involves a perfect synergy of mind and character, that is, an orchestration of knowledge and virtues."

6. "Wisdom represents knowledge used for the good or well-being of oneself and that of others."

7. "Wisdom is easily recognized when manifested, although difficult to achieve and specify."

Wisdom, then, is not the same thing as technical knowledge, "book learning," fame, or intelligence as measured by an IQ test. Having lots of education, being a "smart" person, or being an expert in a given area (like computer technology or finance) does not by itself qualify a person as wise. Many people are clever, intelligent, or experts in their field, but far fewer are wise. Wisdom embodies a particular kind of knowledge, intelligence, and judgment focused on the conduct of a virtuous life. Wise people have learned life's most important lessons. The broad scope of their understanding includes the uncertainties of life—that is, knowing what cannot be definitively known. Two prominent theories attempt to capture wisdom's essential elements: Sternberg's balance theory and the work of Paul Baltes on wisdom as expertise in the conduct of life (often referred to as the Berlin wisdom model).

Theories of Wisdom

BALANCE THEORY Sternberg's balance theory describes the practical intelligence necessary to take wise action when confronting difficult and complex life situations (Sternberg, 1990, 1998a). Wisdom is based on tacit knowledge that is built up over time as people learn how to pursue and achieve valued goals successfully. Tacit knowledge is the action-oriented component of practical intelligence (i.e., knowing "how" rather than know "what"). Sternberg believes that knowledge of how to

live successfully is learned in the trenches of life experience—not through formal education or direct instruction from others. Tacit knowledge becomes the foundation for wisdom when it is used to achieve a common good rather than a self-interested good, and when it is focused on finding ways to balance the often conflicting interests and choices involved in real-life situations.

According to Sternberg's **balance theory,** wise people are skillful in balancing three interests and three possible courses of action in arriving at solutions to life problems. The three interests are (a) one's own interests and needs (intrapersonal); (b) the interests and needs of important others like a spouse, friend, or employer (interpersonal); and (c) those related to community, country, environment, or religion (extrapersonal). Balancing these multiple interests to achieve a common good requires consideration of three courses of action concerning whether and how much individuals need to (a) change themselves (adaptation); (b) change their environment, including others; or (c) select a new environment altogether.

Consider the following example of a life dilemma that confronts many "baby boomers," often referred to as the "sandwich generation" because they are "sandwiched" between the needs of their aging parents and their own children. Imagine yourself in this situation. You and your spouse both have successful, but demanding careers. You have two children, one child is in college and the other, a sophomore in high school, will be off to college in two years. Retirement is still a number of years off, in part because of the need to pay your children's college expenses. Your aging parents are becoming increasingly frail. They have several significant health issues and cannot live by themselves much longer. Your parents want to maintain their independence and do not want to move into an assisted living facility or nursing home. What would be a wise course of action here?

To meet Sternberg's criteria for wisdom, you must find ways to balance your own interests and those of your family with the increasing need for support required by your parents' deteriorating situation. You must consider and find answers to questions like the following: How much should your own family have to sacrifice, and how much should your parents have to sacrifice? How can you balance all the interests in this case? In terms of specific actions, the question becomes, whose environment and life must change the most? Yours? Your family's? Your parents'? Should you adjust your life to your parents' needs and move closer to your parents? Should they move in with you, or nearby? Should you try to place them in an assisted living facility? These are obviously hard choices! It's not easy to know what balance of interests and actions constitute a wise solution. Wisdom does not lead to a perfect balance of interests and actions, in the sense that everyone will be happy and won't have to accommodate change or make sacrifices. Instead, Sternberg's idea is that wisdom means applying tacit knowledge to find the best possible solution that balances both multiple interests and possible actions involving adaptation and change. A balance of interests defines a common good, and balanced actions serving a common good define wisdom.

WISDOM AS EXPERT KNOWLEDGE IN THE CONDUCT OF LIFE Baltes and his colleagues at the Max Planck Institute in Berlin, Germany, have developed a set of specific criteria for defining and measuring wisdom that provides the basis for an ongoing program of empirical studies. In their Berlin wisdom model, **wisdom** is defined **as expert knowledge** concerning the "fundamental pragmatics of life" (Baltes, 1997; Baltes & Smith, 1990, Baltes & Staudinger, 2000). The phrase, "fundamental pragmatics of life" refers to "... knowledge and judgment about the essence of the human condition and the ways and means of planning, managing, and understanding a good life" (Baltes & Staudinger, 2000, p. 124). Wisdom is assessed according to the following five criteria.

1. *Factual knowledge*: Extensive knowledge of the pragmatics of life. Knowing the "whats" of the human condition and human nature (e.g., differences among people, social relationships, society, social norms, etc).
2. *Procedural knowledge*: Knowing "how." Strategies and approaches for solving life's problems, achieving goals, dealing with conflict, etc.
3. *Lifespan contextualism*: Knowledge of different life settings and social environments (e.g., work, education, family, leisure, and friends), and how these roles and settings change over time, both for individuals and for society.
4. *Relativism of values*: Awareness of individual and cultural differences in values and life priorities. Wise people are committed to the common

good, so this does not mean "anything goes." Relativism means consideration and sensitivity to value differences among people from different backgrounds.
5. *Awareness and management of uncertainty*: Recognizing the limits of knowledge. The future cannot be fully known ahead of time. An understanding of how to cope effectively with the uncertainty of knowledge about the world.

Because wisdom is defined by superior knowledge in the conduct of life, few people are expected to meet all five of the wisdom criteria. Measures of wisdom indicate people's *degree* of wisdom-related knowledge. Wisdom is assessed by presenting research participants with challenging, hypothetical life situations and dilemmas, and asking them to describe aloud what should be considered and what should be done in response to each dilemma. Participant responses are tape-recorded and evaluated by a panel of trained judges, who assess the degree of correspondence between participants' responses and the five wisdom criteria. The life dilemmas include situations like the following two examples (from Baltes & Staudinger, 2000, p. 126):

1. "Someone receives a phone call from a good friend who says that he or she cannot go on like this and has decided to commit suicide. What might one/the person take into consideration and do in such a situation?"
2. "In reflecting over their lives, people sometimes realize that they have not achieved what they had once planned to achieve. What should they do and consider?"

Judges' evaluations of respondents' answers show substantial inter-judge agreement; test–retest reliability is also high. Sample excerpts from low-rated and high-rated responses are given below (Baltes & Staudinger, 2000, Appendix B, p. 136) for the following life dilemma:

"A 15-year old girl wants to get married right away. What should one/she consider and do?"

Example of a Response Judges Rated as Low-Wisdom:

"A 15-year old girl wants to get married? No, no way, marrying at age 15 would be

utterly wrong. One has to tell the girl that marriage is not possible. [After further probing] It would be irresponsible to support such an idea. No, this is just crazy."

Example of a Response Judges Rated as High-Wisdom:

"Well, on the surface, this seems like an easy problem. On average, marriage for a 15-year old girl is not a good thing. But there are situations where the average case does not fit. Perhaps in this instance, special life circumstances are involved, such that the girl has a terminal illness. Or the girl has just lost her parents. And also, this girl may live in another culture or historical period. Perhaps she was raised with a value system different from ours. In addition, one also has to think about adequate ways of talking with the girl and to consider her emotional state."

Using the life dilemmas measure, Baltes and his colleagues have provided some interesting answers to wisdom-related questions (see Baltes & Staudinger, 2000; Baltes et al., 2002; Kramer, 2000; Kunzmann & Baltes, 2003, for research summaries).

Does Wisdom Increase with Age? Conventional wisdom about wisdom suggests that we become wiser as we age and accumulate more life experiences. Studies provide only partial support for this belief. Wisdom has been found to increase dramatically during adolescence and young adulthood; it then appears to remain relatively stable until age 75, when it begins to decline. Getting older, by itself, does not enhance wisdom. However, examination of the top 20% of wise people showed that a higher proportion of the "very wise" were middle-aged (Baltes & Staudinger, 2000).

Are "Experts" Wiser than Non-Experts? Clinical psychologists have extensive experience in helping people review, plan, and manage their lives. They also might be expected to develop an understanding of the dilemmas of life through their clinical training and work as psychotherapists. Are they wiser than comparably educated individuals whose careers are not focused on life dilemmas? Several studies (see Baltes & Staudinger, 2000) found that clinical psychologists

did show higher wisdom scores than a control group of non-psychologist professionals—a finding that pleased the second author of your text, who is a practicing clinical psychologist. However, several considerations may qualify this finding (sorry, Marie!). First, clinical psychologists *did* score significantly higher than members of the control group on the wisdom measure, but their scores did not approach the top end of the scale. (Specifically, the scale ran from 1 to 7, with 7 reflecting a high level of wisdom. Clinical psychologists scored an average of 3.8, just above the scale's midpoint.) Second, it is entirely possible that individuals with a propensity toward wisdom self-select into clinical psychology careers. In line with this possibility, professional specialization accounted for more variation in wisdom scores than did intelligence and personality factors. Third, Baltes wondered whether the superior performance of clinical psychologists might reflect a professional bias imbedded in the measure of wisdom. That is, since the test-maker and the test-takers are both psychologists, do clinical psychologists have an edge over non-psychologists because they think more like the test developers than other respondents? To find out, researchers compared the performance of clinical psychologists to a sample of individuals nominated as wise by an independent panel of non-psychologists. Wisdom nominees were found to perform just as well as the clinical psychologists, suggesting that the measure of wisdom is not biased against non-psychologists.

Are Wise People Happier? Given the connection of wisdom to a good life, one might think the answer would be yes. However, wisdom is connected to deeper meanings and dilemmas of life that go beyond the simple pursuit of happiness. Wisdom is not guided by the "pleasure principle" (Kunzmann & Baltes, 2003). It is possible that wisdom might even reduce personal happiness. If breadth of factual knowledge and complex understandings lead to greater awareness of pain and suffering in the world and the uncertainties of life, perhaps wisdom comes with an emotional price tag. Perhaps ignorance really is bliss. Another possibility is that wise people may excel at coming to terms with the emotional ups and downs of life. Their expertise in living a good life may include more peace of mind and less extreme mood swings.

To evaluate these questions, Kunzmann and Baltes (2003) examined the relationship of wisdom to affective experience in a sample including young adults (15–20 years), middle-aged adults (30–40 years), and older adults (60–70 years). Higher wisdom scores were associated with *less* frequent experiencing of negative affects (such as anger, sadness, fear, disappointment, shame, and indifference), *less* frequent experiencing of pleasure-oriented, positive affects (such as happiness, cheerfulness, amusement, exuberance, and pride), but *more* frequent experiencing of feelings related to affective involvement with the environment (such as feelings of interest, alertness, inspiration, attentiveness, and active engagement). Kunzmann and Baltes argue that these results support the connection of wisdom to emotional regulation. Wise people, perhaps because of their "big picture view" and skill in self-control, are less reactive to life events, whether positive or negative. In addition, wise people are not oriented toward pursuing pleasure or avoiding pain. Instead, they are energized by emotions that enhance active involvement and learning. Wise people are motivated to explore and understand the complexities and paradoxes of life. It makes sense that wisdom would be associated with more frequent experience of emotions that motivate and result from active engagement with the world (e.g., inspiration, interest, and attentiveness).

Wisdom in Action: The (SOC) Model of Effective Life Management

Baltes and his colleagues have recently begun to describe a wisdom-based framework for identifying the essential features of a good life (Baltes & Freund, 2003a, 2003b; Baltes & Staudinger, 2000; Freund & Baltes, 2002; Kramer, 2000; Kunzmann, 2004). Wisdom, as defined in Baltes and colleagues' earlier work, involved an understanding of both the deeper purposes and meanings of a good life (what) and an understanding of the means by which a good life could be achieved (how). The Berlin wisdom model was initially directed more at knowledge-related wisdom than at wisdom-related action. Recent work has shifted to include a more specific model of action that describes how *theoretical* wisdom about *what* matters in life may direct *practical* wisdom concerning *how* to live a life that matters. Practical wisdom is described by their SOC Model of Effective Life Management (SOC refers to "select, optimize, and compensate"). The model describes the role of wisdom in effective life management and optimal human functioning (see Figure 10.1).

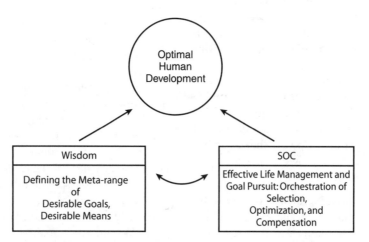

FIGURE 10.1 **The SOC Model of Effective Life Management**
Source: Baltes, P. B., & Freund, A. M. (2003b). The intermarriage of wisdom and selective optimization with compensation: Two meta-heuristics guiding the conduct of life. In C. L. M. Keyes & J. Haidt (Eds.), *Flourishing: Positive psychology and the life well-lived* (pp. 249–273). Washington, DC: American Psychological Association. Copyright American Psychological Association. Reprinted by permission.

The SOC model does not specify details concerning management of a successful life. The specifics are dependent on each individual's needs, values, personality, resources, stage of life, and environmental context. The SOC specifies three general strategies, applicable across the life span, for how to achieve personally important goals. In many ways, the selection, optimization, and compensation model describes an approach to life planning that serves to organize the major research findings concerning personal goals and the self-regulation processes necessary to achieve them (discussed in Chapters 7 and 8). Baltes and his colleagues make the connection between goal research and SOC explicit in their recent work (e.g., Baltes & Freund, 2003a, 2003b).

SELECTION *Selection* is the first step in life planning and is an integral part of personal development and well-being. Choosing appropriate goals among a variety of options contributes to a purposeful, meaningful, and organized life. While the definition of "appropriate" depends on a person's resources and life circumstances, goal research provides some guidance in distinguishing between goals that enhance and goals that detract from well-being. Approach goals that are personally expressive, related to intrinsic needs, and freely chosen are likely to inspire strong commitment, successful achievement, and increased well-being and life satisfaction.

OPTIMIZATION Optimization refers to all the choices and actions that lead to successful goal achievement. Optimization overlaps with many of the processes described in Chapter 8. Goal achievement involves self-regulation, monitoring of progress, belief in personal control and competence, and ability to delay short-term gratification in the service of pursuing long-term goals. The optimization element also includes the importance of repeated practice and effort in developing skills necessary for goal attainment.

COMPENSATION Compensation refers to developing alternative means for achieving and maintaining goals when previously effective means are blocked. Compensation strategies might involve finding new means and resources, activating unused resources, or relying on others for help and support. A student who loses a lucrative summer job that pays half of her yearly college expenses might take out a student loan, dip further into her savings, or ask her parents for more financial help to compensate for the drop in financial resources.

In an empirical test of the SOC model, Freund and Baltes (2002) developed a self-report questionnaire to assess people's endorsement of SOC. Well-being, personality, and cognitive style were also assessed. Study participants ranged in age from 14 to 89 years. Items measuring *selection* focused on the clarity, importance, and prioritizing of personal goals, and on the degree of goal commitment. *Optimization* items asked about expenditure of effort, goal planning, and modeling one's behavior after the strategies used by successful others. *Compensation* was measured by statements concerning efforts to find other means of goal achievement, renewed effort and commitment, and seeking help from others when initial paths to goal achievement were blocked.

Two of the study's noteworthy findings related SOC to age and well-being. Consistent with the pattern of findings from wisdom research, endorsement of SOC strategies increased with age from young to middle age and then showed a decrease in late adulthood. Middle age appears to be the peak period of refined skill in using SOC behaviors for effective life management. Each component of the SOC model was significantly related to Ryff's six-part measure of psychological well-being (see Chapter 2). This measure is based on the eudaimonic conception of well-being, and evaluates a person's degree of self-acceptance, personal growth, sense of purpose, environmental mastery, autonomy, and positive relationship with others. Freund and Baltes also found a strong positive relationship between SOC strategies and higher levels of positive emotions. The SOC model appears to be an informative framework for thinking about the determinants of well-being across the life span (see Baltes & Freund, 2003b, for a review of other SOC confirming studies). The SOC model specifies the general skills necessary to achieve personal goals and compensate for setbacks, and recognizes the importance of goals in relation to well-being. The SOC model both draws from and affirms the major findings of goal research described in Chapters 7 and 8.

You may have noticed that the SOC model does not specify *what goals* a person should choose to pursue. Rather, it focuses only on means. As Baltes and Freund note, "Criminals and Mafia bosses . . . can be masters of SOC" (2003a, p. 30). In other words, the model does not address questions about what goals are good or virtuous, or what means for goal achievement are acceptable and desirable from an ethical or a moral point of view. Baltes and his colleagues argue that it is the role of wisdom to determine what goals and what means are the most important and morally desirable. "Wisdom provides a selector concerning which goals and means are of fundamental significance in the life course and, in addition, are ethically and morally desirable" (Baltes & Freund, 2003a, p. 34). In other words, because of the breadth and depth of their understanding of life and virtue, wise people would be expected to devote themselves to personally meaningful goals that contribute both to their own good and to the common good.

In summary, a good life, from the perspective of wisdom in action, may be described as infusing effective life management strategies with the knowledge and virtue of wisdom. In the words of Baltes and Freund (2003a, p. 33), ". . . we propose that wisdom, the knowledge of the fundamental pragmatics of life, be viewed as a desirable end state of human development that can be lived and implemented through selective optimization with compensation."

Focus on Theory: Wisdom or Self-Control as Master Virtues?

It is easy to think of wisdom as a master virtue. The development of wisdom would seem to include a concomitant development of other virtuous behaviors such as compassion, kindness, humility, fairness, and prudence. In fact, we think of wise people as wise, largely because they embody multiple virtues. It is somewhat harder to think of a single other virtue that has this foundational quality. However, Baumeister and Exline (1999) argue that self-control might also be a candidate for master virtue status. They describe self-control as the "moral muscle" behind many virtuous behaviors. Their thesis is built on a number of interrelated and empirically-grounded arguments (see Chapter 8 for a review of self-control research).

Baumeister and Exline are among an increasing number of psychologists who believe that explorations of morality and virtue have been neglected by psychologists. Virtue and morality are highly important personal qualities that may be more defining of

an individual's identity than the traits studied by personality psychologists. For example, they note that people regard moral traits such as honesty, trustworthiness, and fidelity, as among the most desirable qualities for a potential spouse.

One important function of morality and virtue is to facilitate the development and maintenance of harmonious relationships, which are critically important to the well-being of individuals and society. Major research reviews conclude that the need to belong is one of the most fundamental human motives, the fulfillment of which is a foundation for well-being (e.g., Baumeister & Leary, 1995). A major impediment to relationship harmony occurs when people pursue self-interested needs at the expense of their relationships. This might involve relations between individuals, or between individuals and the broader society. The crucial role of morality within cultures, and virtue within individuals, is to control selfish interests for the sake of the greater common good. Much of what we regard as virtuous behavior and much of what we know about successful relationships involves putting needs of others ahead of your own. Restraining self-interest means exerting self-control. Baumeister and Exline believe that self-control is the psychological foundation for most virtues and that the opposite of virtue, namely sin and vice, result from failed self-control.

As Baumeister and Exline note, self-control failure seems clearly involved in the Seven Deadly Sins described in Christian theology: gluttony, sloth, greed, lust, envy, anger, and pride. Each of these sins and vices exemplifies one or another form of failed control: gluttony by self-indulgence and excessive pursuit of pleasure; sloth or laziness by failed initiative and self-motivation; greed, lust, and envy by selfish and exploitive dealings with others centered on gratifying only individual needs; anger by lack of emotional restraint and impulse control; and pride by self-aggrandizement at the expense of others.

The relation of sin to failed self-control finds a counterpart in the connection between virtue and the exertion of self-control. For example, prudence refers to reasoned action guided by consideration of long-term implications rather than immediate needs or opportunities. Delay of gratification and staying on course with a long-term goal in mind are central features of self-control and self-regulation. Similarly, justice requires control of self-interest in upholding standards of conduct aimed at the common good.

The virtue of temperance (which refers to exercising emotional restraint and avoiding excesses) also clearly requires self-control.

In addition to its links with specific virtues, self-control and self-regulation also help explain how virtue may guide behavior. Recall from Chapter 8 that self-regulation involves monitoring and changing behavior in relationship to a standard. Applied to personal goals this means establishing a goal, monitoring progress, and altering actions and the self over time to achieve a goal. Baumeister and Exline argue that virtue's role in behavior fits this same general pattern. Most of us aspire to be morally responsible people. Each of us has moral standards that can be used to monitor our ongoing behavior. If we maintain some level of self-awareness, we know the extent to which our actions are consistent or inconsistent with our standards. Feelings of guilt are clear signals of inconsistency. Self-control is required in order to conform to our own standards, rather than giving in to temptations or momentary emotional impulses. It is this self-control that keeps behavior in line with moral standards that Baumeister and Exline believe is the "moral muscle" underlying virtue; thus, virtue is dependent on self-control. "Vice signifies failure of self-control, whereas virtue involves the consistent, disciplined exercise of self control. Self-control can fairly be regarded as the master virtue" (Baumeister & Exline, 1999, p. 1189).

TRANSCENDENCE: RELIGION AND SPIRITUALITY

The Search for Meaning

Viktor Frankl (1976/1959) was an early psychiatrist who argued that finding meaning in life was essential for survival. Frankl's argument was based on his experiences as a prisoner in multiple Nazi death camps during World War II. His observations convinced him that surviving the horrors of the camps depended, in large part, upon people's ability to make sense of their experience; that is, their ability to find some sustaining meaning and hopeful vision for the future. The fact that many in the death camps *did* find such meaning was testimony to humans' ability to find meaningfulness, even in the face of immense suffering. Following Frankl's lead, many psychologists have come to regard the pursuit of meaning as a central feature of human life (e.g., Baumeister, 1991). Humans are "meaning makers" in the sense of seeking and creating an understanding of the specific and broader purposes of life (Bruner, 1990).

The importance of meaning may reflect a connection to basic human needs. In his book, *Meanings of Life*, Roy Baumeister (1991) describes four needs that underlie the pursuit of meaning: purpose, value, self-efficacy, and self-worth. These four needs help explain the basis for people's motivation to find meaning in life, but they do not specify the specific sources of need satisfaction. The sources of need satisfaction (and thus, of meaning) are, to some extent, interchangeable. Baumeister gives the example of career women who leave work to have children. If raising children becomes a significant source of personal meaning, the desire to return to their careers may fade. The life meaning involved in a career has been replaced or interchanged with that of raising children. This interchangeability also applies to religion, although Baumeister acknowledges that most religious people would find ridiculous or offensive the idea that their religion is interchangeable with another. Baumeister's point is that, at a conceptual level, all religions seem to serve similar psychological purposes, despite beliefs in the unique positive qualities of "my" religion expressed by adherents.

The need for **purpose** refers to a desire for direction in life. Organizing life around the pursuit of personally significant goals and ideal end states are major ways people fulfill their need for purpose (see Chapter 7). Working on, making progress toward, and achieving important goals and ideals are important sources of meaning. A second need is for **value.** The need for value is fulfilled by finding justifications for actions that affirm the positive value of one's life. People want to believe their actions are "right" or "good" as judged by a system of values. Values and codes of conduct provide standards for judging right, wrong, moral and immoral acts and provide guideposts for evaluating specific actions and the overall quality of life.

A third need is for a sense of **self-efficacy.** People need to feel that they have control over the things that happen to them so that life does not seem chaotic, capricious, and beyond their control. Meeting challenges and accomplishing goals are two major ways that people develop feelings of self-efficacy. Control may take the form of changing the environment to meet individual needs and goals, or changing the self in order to adapt to the environment when the environment cannot be changed (see Rothbaum, Weisz, & Snyder, 1982, and the introduction to Chapter 8 in this textbook). An important form of control, particularly relevant to religion and spirituality, is **interpretive control.** As Baumeister notes, being able to understand why things occur is an important source of meaning. Even if we cannot change the outcome, finding meaningful interpretations for life events contributes to a sense of control and provides a basis for adaptation to life's challenges. For example, accepting the reality of death may be easier for people who believe life and death are part of God's plan and that heaven awaits them after they die.

Self-worth is the fourth basis for meaning. Self-worth reflects people's need for positive self-evaluation and self-esteem (see Chapter 9). Unlike values, which are tied primarily to morality, a sense of self-worth may be based on a variety of non-moral qualities and activities. Talents, accomplishments, recognition and admiration from others, and favorable social comparisons (i.e., doing better than others) may all contribute to a sense of self-worth.

The four needs provide a way of thinking about the psychological foundations of a meaningful life and the role religion plays in addressing what Emmons (1999a) called people's "ultimate concerns"—the highest-order meanings of human existence. From Baumeister's perspective, life is likely to be experienced as meaningful when people have a strong sense of purpose, clear values for making moral judgments, beliefs in their own self-efficacy/control, and a positive sense of self-worth. In contrast, a less meaningful or meaningless life results from the loss of sustaining purpose, confusion about values, loss of perceived control, and feelings of low self-worth. Meaning and meaningfulness exist at different levels, from the relatively concrete and here-and-now actions of daily life to the abstract and enduring (eternal) meanings of human existence. Religion and spirituality offer satisfaction of each the four needs at the highest level of meaning. As Baumeister notes, religion defines the purpose of life, provides a code of moral values, offers interpretive control by explaining the meaning and origins of life, and provides a basis for self-worth within a religious framework (e.g., affirmation by fellow believers, God's love of the faithful).

As mentioned above, Baumeister regards religions as being, to some extent, interchangeable in their ability to satisfy the four needs for meaning. Despite differences in beliefs, doctrines, and practices, major world religions and spiritual traditions appear to share a common set of core features, and seem to serve a common set of human needs. Anthropologist Joseph Campbell has probably done more than anyone to promote an understanding of the universal aspects of religion for a broad cultural audience. In his best selling books, *The Power of Myth* (1988) and *Myths to Live By* (1993), and his widely watched and praised PBS series on the Power of Myth with Bill Moyers, Campbell has described the universal questions of existence addressed by Eastern and Western religions, and the power of religion's answers to guide and transform people's lives.

Religion provides answers to fundamental questions concerning human existence. How did life and the universe begin? What happens after you die? What is the purpose of life on earth? What moral values should guide human actions? Certainly religion is not the only basis for addressing these questions. Science, nature, and humanitarian philosophies may also provide answers. It is also true that some percentage of people are simply not interested in, or do not believe that there are answers to, life's ultimate mysteries. Yet, survey research suggests that the vast majority of Americans address these questions from a spiritual or religious perspective (see Gallup & Lindsay, 1999, for reviews and Chapter 6 in Spilka, Hood, Hunsberger, & Gorsuch, 2003). In national surveys over the last 50 years, between 90 and 95% of Americans said they believed in God or a higher power and nearly 90% say they pray. Nearly 70% are members of a church or synagogue and 40% report regular attendance. Polls also show that 60% of Americans said religion was very important in their lives and another 26 to 30% report that religion is fairly important. Religious affiliations in the United States are dominated by the Protestant and Roman Catholic faiths. Summarizing data from the U.S. Census Bureau, Spilka and his colleagues (2003) report that in 1999, the breakdown of religious affiliations was as follows: 55% of Americans identified themselves as Protestants; 28% as Roman Catholics; 2% as Jewish; 6% as "other"; and 8% reported no religious affiliation. Interestingly, the percentage of people in the United States who believe in God is higher than in most European countries (see Table 10.4). All these

TABLE 10.4 Percentages of people in various countries who believe in God and have had religious experiences

Country	Belief in God (%)	Religious experience (%)
United States	95	41
Czech Republic	6	11
Denmark	57	15
France	52	24
Great Britain	69	16
Hungary	65	17
Ireland	95	13
Italy	86	31
Netherlands	57	22
Northern Ireland	92	26
Norway	59	16
Poland	94	16
Russia	52	13
Spain	82	19
Sweden	54	12

Source: Spilka, B., Hood, R. W., Jr., Hunsberger, B., & Gorsuch, R. (2003). *The psychology of religion: An empirical approach.* New York: Guilford Press. Copyright The Guilford Press. Reprinted by permission.

statistics speak to the importance of religion in American individual and cultural life.

Religion and Spirituality: The Diversity of Views

Defining religion and spirituality are formidable tasks. At the operational level, researchers often bypass definitional complexities by relying on global self-report measures (see Tsang & McCullough, 2003, for a review of measurement issues). People might be asked to rate their degree of religiousness, report on their frequency of church attendance, or indicate their denominational affiliation. Despite the fact that these global measures are often found to bear significant relationships to health and well-being, they do not tell us much about what it means to be religious, nor do they distinguish spirituality from other concerns in life. For example, a person might go to church primarily because it's a congenial social activity and not because of religious commitments or concern with spirituality.

Empirical studies affirm the diversity of views among social scientists, clergy, and lay-persons concerning what it means to be religious (e.g., Zinnbauer et al., 1997). For example, Pargament and his colleagues (Pargament, Tarakeshwar, Ellison, & Wulff, 2001) asked college students and clergy members to rate the degree of religiousness for 100 profiles of hypothetical people. Each profile represented a different combination of 10 cues, such as church attendance, frequency of prayer and meditation, feeling God's presence, monetary donations to a church, knowledge of church doctrines, personal benefits from religious beliefs (comfort, support, and meaning), and altruistic acts of giving. Every individual in the study showed a relatively consistent reliance on certain cues in making her or his judgments. However, there was little consensus among or between students and clergy on exactly which cues indicate a "religious person." Among students, personal benefits were used by a narrow 55% majority and among clergy, 86% relied on church attendance as an important cue in rating a persons' degree of religiousness. With these two exceptions, religiousness meant very different things to different individual participants.

Researchers have struggled to develop definitions that are specific enough to capture what is unique and distinctive about religion and spirituality, but broad enough to apply to all or most religions. Given the diversity of views, it is clear that no single definition of religion and spirituality will be satisfactory to all scholars or individual religious practitioners. This state of affairs is succinctly captured in a frequently cited quote by Yinger (1967): "any definition of religion is likely to be satisfactory only to its author" (p. 18). However, empirical and conceptual work in the psychology of religion has expanded dramatically over the last decade. Prominent researchers in the field have begun to find some common ground in the variety of definitions offered by individual researchers and theorists (e.g., Emmons, 1999a, 1999b; Hill & Pargament, 2003, Hill et al., 2000; Pargament, 1997; Zinnbauer, Pargament, & Scott, 1999; Zinnbauer et al., 1997).

At the center of recent conceptualizations is the relationship between religion and spirituality. Within psychology, since the classic work of William James (1985) (*The Varieties of Religious Experience*), religion has been regarded as having both an institutional meaning and an individual meaning. As an institution, religion is an organized set of beliefs, practices, doctrines, and places of worship (e.g., churches or synagogues) associated with the different world religions and their denominations. The individual meaning of religion concerns the personal side of faith, defined by a person's unique relationship, experiences, and activities with the object of her or his faith (e.g., God, a religious doctrine, a revelation, God's love, and Ultimate Truth).

In recent times, the complementary and overlapping relationship between the individual and institutional aspects of religion has been defined as more dichotomous, particularly in American culture (Hill et al., 2000; Zinnbauer et al., 1999). You have probably heard someone say that he or she is "spiritual, but not religious." Spirituality has, more and more, come to define the subjective, individual aspects of religious experience, while religion refers to the fixed doctrines and practices of organized religions. The separation of religion and spirituality was particularly prominent within American culture

during the 1960s. The "counter-culture" that emerged from the youthful days of the baby-boomer generation was highly critical of established institutions, including religion. Religion became associated with dogma, authoritarianism, blind faith, and conformity. Many baby boomers left established religions in apparent agreement with humanistic psychologists, like Abraham Maslow (1968), who argued that spiritual concerns could be pursed outside of traditional religions. Many of the "New Age" philosophies that developed during this period appealed to baby boomers' spiritual needs and desire for growth without formal ties to traditional religions. Many psychologists believe that the separation of spirituality and religion within popular culture has led to an unfortunate polarization (e.g., Hill & Pargament, 2003; Hill et al., 2000; Zinnbauer et al., 1999). Individual spirituality is regarded as "good" and institutional religion as "bad," from the perspective of a person's individual character and development. Some psychologists have even regarded religion as an impediment to spiritual understanding (see Hill et al., 2000; Zinnbauer et al., 1999, for reviews).

The need to explore the interrelationship of spirituality and religion is suggested by empirical studies showing that most people, at least within the United States, consider themselves both religious *and* spiritual. This was clearly shown in a study by Zinnbauer and colleagues (1997). The 346 participants in the study represented a variety of religious backgrounds and ranged in age from 15 to 84, with a mean age of 40. One measure in the study asked participants to choose one of four statements that best defined their religiousness and spirituality (Zinnbauer et al., 1997). The choices were: "I am spiritual and religious; I am spiritual but not religious; I am religious but not spiritual; I am neither spiritual nor religious" (p. 553). A strong majority of the participants (74%) endorsed the religious *and* spiritual statement; 19% described themselves as spiritual but not religious; 4% as religious but not spiritual; and 3% as neither spiritual nor religious. Participants were also asked about the relationship between religiousness and spirituality. Only a small percentage (6.7%) indicated that religiousness and spirituality were completely different, with no overlap in meaning, or endorsed a belief that they were the same concept and overlapped completely (2.6%). Overall, this study suggests two major conclusions. First, most people do distinguish between religiousness and spirituality. Second, a majority of people identify themselves as both religious and spiritual.

Zinnbauer and his colleagues also investigated differences between the 74% of people who identified themselves as spiritual and religious (SR group) and the 19% of people who considered themselves spiritual but not religious (SnR group). Interestingly, the SnR group fit the general profile of baby boomers. Compared to the SR group, they grew up with parents who attended church less frequently, were more educated and individualistic, were less likely to hold orthodox or traditional Christian beliefs, were more likely to be agnostic and hold non-traditional "New Age" beliefs, and were somewhat more likely to have a negative conception of religiousness as reflecting a need to feel superior to others, or as something people pursue for extrinsic reasons (such as social image and status). The SR group was associated with church attendance, frequency of prayer, and orthodox religious beliefs. These results are generally in line with a recent study that found that the personality and social attitude profiles of "spiritual-but-not-religious" people were very different than those who held more traditional religious beliefs (Saucier & Skrzypinska, 2006). Taken in total, these findings suggest both differences and commonalities in people's understanding of religion and spirituality. The most recent work in the psychology of religion acknowledges the many differences, but focuses on what religion and spirituality seem to have in common for the majority of people.

Defining Religion and Spirituality

Recent conceptualizations attempt to tie together rather than separate the meaning of religion and spirituality (see Hill & Pargament, 2003; Hill et al., 2000; Pargament, 1997, 1999; Zinnbauer et al., 1999). Pargament's (1997) work, summarized in his insightful book, *The Psychology of Religion and Coping*, appears particularly influential in recent definitions of religion and spirituality. Pargament's analysis begins with a seemingly straightforward question: What makes religion special? What is the essential quality that distinguishes religion from other domains and concerns of life? Based on his review and synthesis of previous work, Pargament concluded that it is the unique substance and function of religion that makes it special. Substantively, the defining essence of religion is the sacred. The

sacred refers to things set apart from ordinary life because of their connection to God, the holy, the divine; to transcendent forces, Ultimate Truths and Ultimate Reality. The sacred evokes a sense of awe, respect, reverence, and veneration. It encompasses the beliefs, practices, and feelings relating to a higher being and ultimate truth of existence.

In addition to its sacred substance, religion is also distinguished by its distinctive function in people's lives. Religion is not just a set of beliefs and practices; it also involves how these beliefs are *used* to answer life's most profound questions and cope with life's most difficult challenges. Religion addresses existential questions concerning the meaning of life and its inevitable pain, tragedies, suffering, injustices, and the finality of death. People's religious beliefs exert powerful influence on the ways in which they cope with these fundamental problems of existence and find significance and meaning in life.

Pargament attempts to combine substance and function in his definition of religion and spirituality. He defines **religion** as "a search for significance in ways related to the sacred" (1997, p. 32), and **spirituality** as a "search for the sacred" (1997, p. 39). "Search" incorporates a functional view of religion and spirituality as a means to address life's most important questions. "Sacred" identifies the special substance of this search that distinguishes religion and spirituality from other life domains. In this conception, religion is the broader concept because it includes both sacred and secular purposes (Pargament, 1999; Pargament & Mahoney, 2002). The "search for significance" in a religious context (i.e., ways related to the sacred) overlaps with secular routes and means. Religion serves a variety of purposes, not all of which are sacred in nature. For example, many people find caring, supportive relationships through their churches. They could also find such relationships in private clubs or community organizations. Church relationships are "related" to the sacred but not necessarily sacred themselves. "Significance" is meant to include the many individual variations in the meaning of this term, including those related to the four needs for meaning described earlier. Through religion, people might seek peace of mind, a sense of worth, self-control, intimacy, caring relationships, life direction, or personal growth. Again, these forms of significance may or may not be regarded as sacred.

The unique and distinctive function of religion is defined by spirituality. The "sacred" connects the search for significance to the special understandings associated with a religious perspective. People are spiritual to the extent ". . . that they are trying to find, know, experience, or relate to what they perceive as sacred" (Pargament & Mahoney, 2002, p. 648). The immaterial world of the sacred stands in general contrast to the profane world of material objects and forces. However, profane objects may become sacred if they are imbued with sacred meaning. Pargament calls this transformation of meaning **sanctification,** which is described as "the perception of an object as having spiritual significance and character" (Pargament & Mahoney, 2002, p. 649). Almost any ordinary object can take on sacred symbolic meaning. Food in the form of a wafer is a scared sacrament in many religious ceremonies. Water used in baptism is regarded as Holy water when blessed by a priest. Many Americans consider the American flag to be a sacred symbol deserving reverence. Respect for the flag is embodied in laws that punish its destruction and desecration.

When secular objects are imbued with sacred meanings or when secular ends are pursued though sacred means, people are likely to be more respectful, protective, and caring. For example, a satisfying marriage is a goal for many people, whether or not they are religious. However, married couples who think of their marriage in religious or sacred terms have transformed their relationship into one with sacred significance. Interestingly, one study found that couples who thought of their marriage as sacred reported greater marital satisfaction, more constructive problem-solving, less conflict, and greater commitment to the marriage, compared to couples who ascribed a lower degree of sacredness to their marriages (Mahoney et al., 1999).

In Pargament's conception, religion is not limited to organized religions, and spirituality is not limited to belief in God. There are multiple pathways in the search for the sacred. As Pargament and Mahoney put it ". . . the sacred can be found on earth as well as in heaven" (2002, p. 649). The search for the sacred would include such things as mediation; the transcendent beliefs that are part of the Alcoholics Anonymous Twelve-Step program; Native American Indians' reverent and spiritual view of animals and the environment; Scientology; and a variety of other personal searches focused on the sacred. Spiritual practices devoted to the sacred are similarly diverse. Among those mentioned by Pargament and Mahoney (2002) are praying, engaging in traditional

religious practices, reading the Bible, and watching religious television programs, listening to music, appreciating art, and engaging in social actions and educational opportunities that are directed toward sacred goals.

Pargament (1999) does not regard religion and spirituality as universally good. His definitions allow for the many uses and abuses of sacred means and ends, from the tyranny and oppression of faith-based governments to the schemes of some religious groups that con people out of their money through false promises and devious means. The value of spirituality and religion clearly depend on their particular form and use. Like any other complex system of beliefs and practices, people can use them for both constructive and destructive purposes, and can experience both negative and positive outcomes (see Exline, 2002).

Religion/Spirituality and Well-Being

Given the diversity of religions and forms of spirituality, it would be somewhat surprising to find a general relationship between religion/spirituality and well-being. This is particularly true considering that most studies employ global measures of self-reported religiousness, such as frequency of church attendance and religious affiliation. These global assessments do not get at the specific aspects of people's religious orientation, depth of commitment, or the function of religion/spirituality in their lives. However, a number of major reviews by prominent researchers have concluded that religion does have a small, but consistent positive relationship to measures of health and well-being. On average, religious people are found to be happier and more satisfied with life (Argyle, 2001; Diener & Clifton, 2002; Diener, Suh, Lucas, & Smith, 1999; Myers, 2000a, 2000b; Peterson & Seligman, 2004). Studies that measure degrees of religious involvement, such as "closeness to God," "spiritual strivings", or "spiritual commitment," generally find that higher levels of religious commitment are related to higher levels of life satisfaction (Argyle, 2001; Emmons, 1999b; Myers, 2000a). The positive connection of religion and happiness is somewhat stronger among the elderly. Interestingly, for children and adolescents, religious involvement is associated with less delinquency, less alcohol and drug abuse, and a lower incidence of early sexual activity.

In their *Handbook of Religion and Health*, Koenig, McCullough, and Larson (2001) provide an extensive review of the relationship between religious involvement and health outcomes. Mental health outcomes included the presence or absence of depression, suicide, anxiety disorders, alcohol and drug abuse, delinquency, and marital instability. Physical health outcomes included longevity and the presence or absence of heart disease, hypertension, and cancer. Overall, the preponderance of evidence supported positive benefits of religious involvement. The most consistent results are found for physical health. Results for mental health have been somewhat mixed, and some studies have found isolated negative effects. However, the mental health evidence is generally positive, leading Koenig and colleagues (2001) to conclude that ". . . for the vast majority of people, the apparent benefits of devout religious belief and practices probably outweigh the risks" (p. 228) (see also Worthington, Kurusu, McCullough, & Sandage, 1996).

Four major variables are typically used to assess religiousness/spirituality in research (George, Ellison, & Larson, 2002). These are: church attendance and participation in religious activities (prayer and study groups), affiliation with a major religion and/or denomination (e.g., Protestant, Lutheran, Methodist, etc.), private religious practices such as prayer, meditation, and Bible reading, and the use of religion to cope with stressful and challenging life events. In their review, George and her colleagues (2002) note that of these four variables, attendance at religious services shows the strongest positive correlations with physical and mental health and with longevity. People who attend church on a regular basis (once a week or more) have been found to enjoy better overall health, recover more quickly from sickness, and live longer than less frequent church attendees. Studies that track the course of illness over time find that religious coping is the most powerful predictor. That is, people who rely on their religious beliefs as a means of coping with illness recover more quickly, and are more likely to survive their illness, and to recover from major medical procedures (e.g., coronary bypass surgery).

To be convincing, the religion–health connection needs to remain after other health prediction variables are factored out or controlled (George et al., 2002; Koenig & Cohen, 2002; McCullough & Laurenceau, 2005; Powell, Shahabi, & Thoresen, 2003). Potential competing variables would include, age, sex, race, marital status, smoking, obesity, existing medical conditions, social class, level of education, and stress from social circumstances (such as poverty). Recent studies have found that a sizable effect of religiousness still remains after the effects of these variables have been statistically controlled. For example, a well-designed longitudinal study found a 23% lower death rate among people who attended church once a week or more (Strawbridge, Cohen, Shema, & Kaplan, 1997). This study examined the health histories of over 5,000 adult community members for nearly three decades (28 years). The lower rate of mortality among frequent church attendees remained after the usual predictors of survival (assessed at the beginning of the study) were factored out. A number of other large-scale longitudinal studies also affirm that the connection between frequent church attendance and a longer and healthier life remains, even after other health and longevity predictors are controlled (see Koenig & Cohen, 2002; Koenig et al., 2001, for recent reviews).

What might explain the health benefits of religion? Researchers have suggested a number of possible mechanisms and pathways. The literature evaluating the potential mediators of religion and health is in an early stage of development. The factors discussed here must be viewed as potential, rather than well-established, empirically validated explanations. In their review, George and colleagues (2002) focused on improved health practices, increased social support, availability of psychosocial resources, and an enhanced sense of meaning in life as major mediating factors helping to explain the religion–health relationship. Each of these will be explored further in the sections that follow.

HEALTH PRACTICES Some religions include clear prescriptions for good health. For example, the Mormon religion explicitly prohibits smoking, drinking, and sex outside of marriage. Many other religions promote a sacred view of the body as "temple of the soul." This belief may encourage care and concern about maintaining good physical and mental well-being by giving personal health a special and sacred significance. Support for the role of religion in good health-care practices comes from studies showing that, on average, regular church attendees smoke less and are less likely to abuse alcohol and other drugs.

SOCIAL SUPPORT The caring and supportive relationships that develop through church membership may be one of the most significant sources of health benefits. Religion and church attendance can provide a stable and long-term basis for strong support from others who share the same spiritual commitment. Religious support might provide a number of benefits, such as practical help in time of need, an enduring source of comfort, and a buffer against the effects of stress in times of crisis. Hill and Pargament (2003) note that social support might be enhanced by its religious basis. We may take special comfort in knowing that people are praying for us, or from a belief that God is working through others on our behalf.

PSYCHOSOCIAL RESOURCES AND MEANING
Religious/spiritual beliefs can provide a basis for a transcendent sense of personal worth, efficacy, mastery, and purpose in life. People with strong spiritual strivings report higher levels of satisfaction, a greater sense of purpose in life, and higher levels of well-being (e.g., Emmons, Cheung, & Tehrani, 1998). Studies have linked religious affiliation to optimism and hope (Koenig & Cohen, 2002). Positive emotions such as joy are frequently associated with attendance at church and other religious activities (Argyle, 2001). Taken together, and in light of Fredrickson's broaden-and-build theory of positive emotions (Chapter 3) and the role of positive attitudes in coping and health (Chapter 9), these findings suggest that religious beliefs may provide an important source of personal strength that promotes health and enhances people's coping resources. In addition, as we noted earlier, religion/spirituality offers a unique and special source of meaning concerning the ultimate questions of human existence. A sacred understanding of life and death may be a particularly powerful source of strength and meaning when confronting a life-threatening event or illness.

Religious Orientation

Religious involvement generally seems to have positive benefits. However, this conclusion requires several qualifications. First, the study of religion has been largely limited to North American samples that are dominated by Protestants and Catholics and their various denominations. There are few empirical studies of Middle Eastern (e.g., Muslim, Hindu) or Far Eastern religions (e.g., Shintoism, Buddhism). Further, people of Jewish faith in the United States have

received little research attention. Whether current findings apply to all, most, or only some religious traditions is still an open question. Secondly, the "average" benefits of religion are not the whole story. A balanced presentation must also point out the potential misuses of religion and the possibilities for negative outcomes (see Exline, 2002). Throughout history and the contemporary world, all manner of mayhem and atrocities have been committed in the name of religion and with "God on our side." Scholars may never sort out the paradoxes of religion. For psychologists, Peterson (2006) probably summed up the prevalent sentiment when he commented that distinguishing between "good" and "bad" religion is ". . . dangerous territory into which I care not to enter" (p. 291). However, at the individual level, psychologists have encountered puzzling and contradictory effects of religion in their empirical studies. In an attempt to account for these varied outcomes, researchers have focused on differences in people's orientation toward their religion.

INTRINSIC AND EXTRINSIC RELIGIOUS ORIENTATION
Gordon Allport was an early psychologist who investigated the puzzling relationships between religion and prejudicial attitudes. In his classic book, *The Nature of Prejudice*, Allport concluded that "The role of religion is paradoxical. It makes prejudice and it unmakes prejudice. While the creeds of the great religions are universalistic, all stressing brotherhood, the practice of these creeds is frequently divisive and brutal" (1958, p. 413). That is, most religions preach tolerance and compassion toward others, but these teachings do not necessarily affect the prejudices of religious followers. The empirical basis for this paradox involves attitude surveys showing that churchgoers tend to be *more* prejudiced against various groups (e.g., African Americans, Jews) than people who *do not* attend church. Major reviews of attitude studies affirm the positive correlation between church attendance and prejudiced attitudes (e.g., Batson, Schoenrade, & Ventis, 1993; Wulf, 1997). Allport noted that if religion itself was the cause of prejudice, then the most religious people should be the most prejudiced (Allport & Ross, 1967). However, he pointed out that available studies did not support this conclusion. Many studies suggested that people who attended church frequently were less prejudiced than infrequent attendees. If we take frequency of church attendance as a

measure of religious commitment and exposure to religious influence, then the most religious appear to be the least prejudiced among those with religious affiliations. Since Allport's original work, this latter point has become a source of controversy among researchers (see Chapter 14 in Spilka et al., 2003).

To unravel the religion–prejudice relationship, Allport distinguished between an intrinsic and extrinsic religious orientation. This distinction has to do with the differing means, ends, and functions of people's individual religious beliefs and practices. The extrinsic orientation describes people who "use" their religion for non-religious purposes, such as to engage in a congenial social activity or to maintain a favorable social status in the community. The intrinsic orientation describes those who "live" their religion and embrace its fundamental teachings. Allport and Ross (1967) developed a scale to measure these two orientations and reported that, as a group, extrinsically oriented people were significantly more prejudiced than people with an intrinsic orientation. In the concluding discussion of their study, Allport and Ross (1967) summarized the intrinsic–extrinsic difference and how it explains the apparent paradox of religion and prejudice, as quoted below.

Extrinsic Religious Orientation.

". . . A person with an extrinsic religious orientation is using his religious views to provide security, comfort, status, or social support for himself—religion is not a value in its own right, it serves other needs, and is a purely utilitarian formation. Now prejudice too is a 'useful' formation; it too provides security, comfort, status, and social support. A life dependent on the supports of extrinsic religion is likely to be dependent on the supports of prejudice, hence our positive correlations between the extrinsic orientation and intolerance" (Allport & Ross, 1967, p. 441).

Intrinsic Religious Orientation.

Continuing to quote Allport and Ross, "Contrariwise, the intrinsic religious orientation is not an instrumental device. It is not a mere mode of conformity, nor a crutch, nor a tranquilizer, nor a bid for

status. All needs are subordinated to an overarching religious commitment. In internalizing the total creed of his religion the individual necessarily internalizes its values of humility, compassion, and love of neighbor. In such a life (where religion is an intrinsic and dominant value) there is no place for rejection, contempt or condescension toward one's fellow man" (Allport & Ross, 1967, p. 441).

Originally focused on prejudice, the intrinsic–extrinsic orientation measure has become one of the most frequently used assessments of religiousness. Several revised versions of the original scale have been developed (e.g., Gorsuch & McPherson, 1989; Hoge, 1972). Research suggests that people's religious orientation is an important variable in the relationship between religion and well-being, particularly regarding mental health (see Batson et al., 1993; Worthington et al., 1996, for examples). Whether religiousness enhances or has no effect on mental health and other well-being variables (such as quality of family life, drug abuse, and self-esteem) seems to depend in part on the intrinsic–extrinsic orientation. A higher intrinsic orientation is generally associated with positive outcomes. For example, a recent study found a positive association between intrinsic religiousness and life satisfaction, but no association between extrinsic religiousness and satisfaction (Salsman, Brown, Brechting, & Carlson, 2005). Higher degrees of optimism and social support among intrinsically religious people partially accounted for the enhanced life satisfaction. People with an intrinsic religious orientation were more optimistic in outlook and enjoyed greater social support from others, compared to people with a more extrinsic orientation.

Quest Religious Orientation.
Though widely accepted, Allport's original conception and measure of intrinsic–extrinsic religious orientations is not without its critics (see Pargament, 1997, for a detailed review; Spilka et al., 2003, Chapter 14). Regarding religion and prejudice, subsequent researchers noted that an intrinsic orientation is only related to decreased prejudice if a person's religious beliefs and community condemn prejudice toward certain groups (e.g., gays and

lesbians). If prejudice is not prohibited, or if prejudice is given religious sanction, the intrinsic orientation is associated with increased, rather than decreased prejudice (e.g., Herek, 1987). Batson and his colleagues have addressed this issue by developing a third dimension of religious orientation they call "quest religious orientation" (Batson et al., 1993), and they constructed a 12-item scale to measure this orientation. A **quest religious orientation** refers to a complex, flexible, and tentative view of religion and spirituality. More emphasis is placed on the search for religious truths than on obtaining or accepting clear-cut answers. People with a quest orientation appreciate and are willing to confront and struggle to understand the complexities of religion and the world. They are skeptical and doubtful about simple or "final" answers to life's biggest questions. A strong quest religious orientation has consistently been associated with lower levels of prejudice and a high degree of sensitivity to the needs of others that promotes helping those in need (Batson et al., 1993). Other studies suggest that people who have both a flexible orientation toward their religion (high quest orientation) and strong religious commitment (high intrinsic orientation) have better physical health and adjustment to negative life events (McIntosh & Spilka, 1990).

Attachment Theory and Relationship to God

People's relationship to God, the divine, the spiritual, and the transcendent is highly personal. This relationship may take a variety of forms such as feeling "God's presence and love," the "wrath of God or of nature," a sense of awe and wonder, reverence and respect, security and comfort, inspiration, fear, guilt, and anxiety. Kirkpatrick (1992) noted these different images of God and the divine are quite similar to different images people have of their parents. Within developmental psychology, **attachment theory** has described the nature of the attachment between parent and child as an important index of a healthy family and a foundation for later development. Kirkpatrick proposed that it might be informative to view God as an attachment figure. He did not mean to reduce God to the "father figure" described in the Freudian conceptualization of religion. Religion offers a unique and sacred foundation for life, well beyond the protection and comfort suggested by a Freudian view of God as a symbolic, benevolent father. But, like a secure and loving attachment to parents, a secure relationship with God may also function as a foundation for exploring life and its many challenges. Pargament described it this way: "Armed with the knowledge that protection can always be found in God's loving arms, the religious individual may feel greater confidence venturing out in the world, searching for other forms of significance" (Pargament, 1997, p. 355).

An attachment perspective suggests that a person's relationship with the divine might show some correspondence with parental attachment. A secure relationship with parents might set the stage for a secure, positive relationship with God. In a similar vein, insecure and conflicted relationships with parents might lead to either a compensating *secure* attachment to God or to a relationship to the divine that is also *insecure and conflicted*. Studies support a significant connection between childhood parental attachments and adult religious attachments (e.g., Birgegard & Granqvist, 2004; Granqvist, 2002; Kirkpatrick & Shaver, 1990). Studies also show that people's self-identified attachment style is related to measures of well-being. Kirkpatrick and Shaver asked a sample of community adults to select which of three attachment styles best described their own relationship to God. The three styles were described as quoted below (with labels removed for study participants).

Secure Attachment. "God is generally warm and responsive to me. He always seems to know when to be supportive and protective of me, and when to let me make my own mistakes. My relationship with God is always comfortable, and I am very happy and satisfied with it" (Kirkpatrick & Shaver, 1992, p. 270).

Avoidant Attachment. "God is generally impersonal, distant, and often seems to have little or no interest in my personal affairs and problems. I frequently have the feeling that He doesn't care very much about me, or that He might not like me" (Kirkpatrick & Shaver, 1992, p. 270).

Anxious/Ambivalent Attachment. "God seems to be inconsistent in His reactions to me. He sometimes seems warm and responsive to my needs, but sometimes not. I'm sure that He loves me and cares about me, but sometimes He seems to show it in ways I don't really understand" (Kirkpatrick & Shaver, 1992, p. 270).

Compared to people with a secure religious attachment, the two insecure attachment styles (avoidant and anxious/ambivalent) showed lower self-reported life satisfaction and physical health, and higher levels of anxiety, feelings of loneliness, and depression. The attachment-based measure of religiousness was also found to be a better predictor of well-being and mental health than several measures of religiousness commonly used in research.

Styles of Religious Coping

Our beginning discussion of religion and spirituality noted the importance of finding meaning in life, particularly when confronting challenges such as serious illness and death. An old adage has it that there are "no atheists in foxholes," meaning that almost everyone becomes religious and hopes that God will save them when confronting his or her own death. While there probably *are some* atheists in foxholes, the saying captures the importance of spirituality and religion in times of crisis. Because religion addresses life's essential meaning, religious beliefs provide a potentially powerful means of coping with life's existential struggles. Like other aspects of people's religious beliefs and orientations, people differ in the particular style of their religious coping. And just as certain religious orientations are more beneficial than others, styles of coping differ in producing positive or negative outcomes. Kenneth Pargament (1997) has probably done more than any other psychologist to describe and evaluate the various ways in which people use their religious beliefs as coping resources. He notes that religious coping is clearly tied to the depth of people's religious commitment. When religion is a significant part of people's overall orientation toward life, religion becomes an important means of coping.

In their initial work, Pargament and his colleagues identified three distinct styles of religious coping and problem-solving (Pargament, 1997; Pargament et al., 1988). The independence of each style, the internal coherence of the styles, and scales to measure each style were validated in an adult sample of Presbyterian and Lutheran church members.

Definitions and sample scale items are given below (from Pargament, 1997, pp. 180–182).

Self-Directing Style. In this approach, people rely on themselves rather than God to solve their problems. People maintain their church affiliation, but score low on measures of religiousness. "When thinking about a difficulty, I try to come up with possible solutions without God's help." "After I've gone through a rough time, I try to make sense of it without relying on God." The self-directing style was associated with a heightened sense of personal control in life, higher self-esteem, and a religious quest orientation.

Deferring Style. The deferring style refers to people who put their problems and responsibility for solutions in God's hands. "Rather than trying to come up with the right solution to a problem myself, I let God decide how to deal with it." "When a troublesome issue arises, I leave it up to God to decide what it means to me." This coping style was connected to more religious orthodoxy (deference to the authority of church & religion) and an extrinsic religious orientation. Of the three styles, this deferring approach was related to the lowest levels of personal competence, self-esteem, and effective problem-solving. The strong reliance on an external source of coping may contribute to feelings of helplessness and passivity.

Collaborative Style. In this style, God and the individual are active partners in the problem-solving process. "When it comes to deciding how to solve a problem, God and I work together as partners." "When I have a problem, I talk to God about it and together we decide what it means." A collaborative style was associated with a strong intrinsic religious orientation and commitment to religious beliefs and practice. The collaborative approach to problem-solving showed positive correlations with personal control, competency, and self-esteem.

Pargament and his colleagues have subsequently developed a more comprehensive measure of religious coping that captures the diverse ways in which people use religion in times of stress and challenge (Pargament, 1997; Pargament, Smith, Koenig, & Perez, 1998; Pargament et al., 2001). In the development and validation of an expanded religious coping scale (RCOPE), Pargament and colleagues (1998, 2001) found that coping styles could be classified as positive or negative based on their relationship to well-being outcomes. **Positive coping strategies** reflected a secure relationship with

God and a belief that deeper meanings can be found in life (including tragedies) and in spiritual connections with others. Positive coping methods included benevolent religious appraisals (e.g., redefining a stressful situation as beneficial for spiritual growth), collaborative religious coping, seeking spiritual support through God's love and care, seeking help from clergy or fellow church members, and spiritual purification (asking God's forgiveness and blessing). **Negative religious coping** reflected a less secure relationship with God and a more uncertain and threatening view of the world. Negative coping methods included negative and punitive religious appraisals (e.g., tragic events as God's punishment for sin or the work of the devil), reappraisals of God's powers (doubt about God's ability to help), spiritual discontent (confusion and dissatisfaction with God), interpersonal religious discontent (dissatisfaction with clergy or church), and deferring religious coping (passively waiting for God's solution to the problem).

The influences of positive and negative religious coping on well-being outcomes have been examined in diverse samples: community members dealing with the Oklahoma City bombing; college students dealing with life stresses (such as the death of loved one or a failed romance); people hospitalized for medical illness; older individuals coping with serous illness; and members of the clergy (Pargament et al., 1988, 1998, 2001). Despite the diversity of the crises in which participants were involved, results showed a consistent pattern of good outcomes related to positive coping styles and neutral to poor outcomes for negative coping styles. The majority of participants reported using positive religious coping methods. Positive religious coping was generally related to higher levels of well-being, more religious growth, less distress, and better mental health. Negative religious coping was correlated with lower levels of well-being and more emotional distress and depression.

One of Pargament and his colleagues' studies (2001) compared clergy members, church elders, and rank-and-file church members affiliated with the Presbyterian Church. Interestingly, the impact of positive and negative coping was strongest for the clergy members. They enjoyed the greatest benefits of positive coping, but *also* suffered more deleterious effects of negative coping. The overwhelming majority of clergy members relied primarily on positive coping methods. However, they also tended to

use more negative coping than the other two groups in the study. The relationship between negative coping and depression was particularly strong among clergy members, compared to church elders and church members. Why would this be the case? Pargament and colleagues (2001) suggest that negative coping may reflect a kind of religious struggle, in which crises may challenge aspects of an individual's religious beliefs. Clergy members' personal and professional identities as "men and women of God" are inextricably tied to their religious convictions. Doubt about these convictions might be expected to cause more turmoil for clergy members than for people whose commitments are not so deep and whose lives and identities are not so invested in religion. For the clergy members, ". . . those who encounter spiritual struggles in times of difficulty (e.g., feeling that God has abandoned them, anger at God, religious doubts) may find the coping process particularly devastating. Religious professionals and leaders might well experience such painful struggles to be fundamentally incompatible with their training and career and thus, threatening to core aspects of their personal identity" (Pargament et al., 2001, p. 510).

"Explaining Religion versus Explaining Religion Away"

The heading of this section is taken from Pargament's insightful article titled, "Is Religion Nothing But . . . .? Explaining Religion versus Explaining Religion Away" (Pargament, 2002). The point of the title is to ask whether there is anything special or unique about religion and spirituality that cannot be accounted for by psychological, social, and biological explanations. For example, if we remove the effects of social support, finding meaning and purpose in life, increased self-esteem and competence, and the benefits of positive attitude on immune-system functioning from the health benefits of religion, is there anything left over that results from spirituality alone? The answer to this question is perhaps one dividing line between spiritual and non-spiritual people, or between those who believe religion is "nothing but" and those who believe religion is a unique dimension of human life.

Psychologists' answer to this question has important implications for how religion is studied. If the effects of religion are entirely mediated by other factors, such as social support, then only these other factors need to be studied. However, if the sacred dimension of life makes an independent contribution, psychologists will need to give religion more serious and thoughtful attention. As we noted, studies that control for known health-enhancing and health-detracting factors have found that the benefits of religion and spirituality are reduced, but not eliminated. Such findings are suggestive of the distinctive effects of spirituality. At this point is probably best to conclude, with Pargament, that the "jury is still out" on this question.

RELIGION AND VIRTUE

The Values in Action Project (Peterson & Seligman, 2004) discussed earlier in this chapter drew heavily on the moral principles embodied in the major religions of the world. While one can certainly be virtuous without being religious, religion has provided an important foundation for thinking about morality, virtue, and the difference between "right" and "wrong" conduct in human affairs. Empirical investigations of the relationship between religion and virtue are in the beginning stages of development. Survey researchers do find that religion is related to more traditionally conservative moral attitudes toward contemporary issues. Spilka and colleagues (2003) review studies showing that, on average, the more religious people are, the more likely they are to oppose pornography, divorce as a solution to marital unhappiness, homosexuality and AIDS education, premarital sex, feminism, and rap music. Religious people are also more likely to approve of more severe sentences for criminal offenders, support censorship of sexual and violent programming in the mass media, and to be more politically conservative. Obviously, the problem with these "on average" findings is that many religious *individuals* hold quite liberal political and moral outlooks. Based on their religious beliefs, many people *oppose* the death penalty, seek *more* compassion for criminal offenders, and *support* sex education and AIDS education. In their research review, Peterson and Seligman (2004) cite studies supporting a number of positive associations between religion and virtuous behaviors such as healthy relationships, forgiveness, kindness, compassion, altruism, and volunteering in community service activities. However, they also note that the general relationship between religious beliefs and virtue is complicated by individual diversity in the religion–morality connection and how

individual researchers measure religiousness. As we saw in our earlier discussion, the effects of religion and spirituality depend heavily on the particular, individualized form of people's religious beliefs and their level of religious commitment.

That said, research has begun to explore the connection between virtue and religion and to examine how virtue functions in individual and social life, whether or not it has a religious basis. Forgiveness and gratitude are among the most heavily researched virtues in recent research. Both figure prominently in world religions as essential components of a religious life. Seeking God's forgiveness for sin and giving thanks for God's love, grace, and blessing are common elements of many religious traditions and teachings.

Forgiveness

Most researchers see the value of forgiveness in terms of its potential ability to offset the debilitating effects of the anger and hostility associated with a desire to avenge the hurtful act of another (Fincham & Kashdan, 2004; McCullough, Pargament, & Thoresen, 2000; McCullough & Witvliet, 2002; Worthington, 1998). Being insulted, betrayed, taken advantage of, or wronged by others are inevitable, painful aspects of the human experience. The anger and resentment created by interpersonal transgressions can destroy relationships and suspend us in obsessive rumination over the offense. For example, considerable research suggests that bad marriages are typified by needs to "get even," leading to an endless cycle of reciprocating negative comments and actions (Gottman, 1994, 1998; Reis & Gable, 2003). Forgiveness has the potential to repair relationships and undo the negative emotions related to revenge and resentment.

Although there is no consensual definition of forgiveness, several reviews point to core features shared among the major conceptualizations (Fincham & Kashdan, 2004; McCullough et al., 2000; McCullough & Witvliet, 2002; Peterson & Seligman, 2004). Fincham and Kashdan argue that "at the center of various approaches to forgiveness is the idea of a freely chosen motivational transformation in which the desire to seek revenge and to avoid contact with the transgressor is lessened, a process sometimes described as an 'altruistic gift' " (p. 618). Most researchers also agree that forgiveness is distinct from related concepts such as excusing (concluding that the hurt was not the transgressor's fault or intention), condoning (reframing the act as not really being an offense), denial (not confronting the offense), and forgetting (allowing memory of the offense to fade) (Enright & Coyle, 1998). Reconciliation is also viewed as different than forgiveness because it involves a mutual effort to restore a relationship by both the offender and the offended (McCullough & Witvliet, 2002).

Researchers disagree about whether forgiveness requires positive feelings and actions toward the transgressor (e.g., increased kindness, compassion, making contact), or whether the absence of negative responses is sufficient (e.g., decreased revenge, hostility, and avoidance). Research suggests that the positive and negative responses may be independent dimensions of forgiveness that lead to different outcomes, and that these outcomes may be related to stages of forgiveness. For example, Enright and his colleagues (1998) view forgiveness as a developmental process involving stages or degrees of forgiveness that can be evaluated according to their degree of genuineness. An act of forgiveness may be heartfelt or disingenuous. Genuine forgiveness requires compassion, benevolence, and love for the offender, together with a relinquishment of the right to revenge, resentment, and indifference.

A final definitional complication concerns the difference between laypersons' and psychologists' understandings of forgiveness. While laypersons' understanding of forgiveness overlaps considerably with psychologists' conceptions, there are also important differences (Kantz, 2000; Kearns & Fincham, 2004). Recall that psychologists express the opinion that forgiving someone does *not* mean the same thing as simply excusing, condoning, denying, forgetting, or reconciling the hurt. Kearns and Fincham (2004) found that, contrary to psychologists' definitions, 28% of laypeople believed forgetting about the offense *was* an important attribute of forgiveness and 28% thought reconciliation *was* a significant potential outcome of forgiveness.

The burgeoning research literature presents a complicated picture of the outcomes of forgiveness. This is partly because researchers define and measure forgiveness in different ways (Thompson & Snyder, 2003). Some reviews suggest that forgiveness generally leads to small, but consistent positive outcomes in health and well-being (e.g., McCullough & Witvliet, 2002), while others argue that such conclusions are premature (e.g., Fincham & Kashdan, 2004). All researchers recognize the tentative nature of

conclusions in this new area of research and the need to understand the many factors mediating the effects of forgiveness. For example, the *reasons why* people forgive are important to the *effects* of forgiveness. In one study, people who forgave out of a sense of obligation rather than love showed no decrease in anger and related physiological responses such as blood pressure (Huang & Enright, 2000). Here, we will review studies that exemplify the potential of forgiveness to reduce the deleterious effects of hostility caused by a personal offense.

Anger and hostility are strongly implicated in cardiovascular disease (Friedman & Rosenman, 1974). Evidence that forgiveness might be an antidote for the negative effects of hostility is shown in a recent study by Witvliet, Ludwig, and Vander Laan (2001). In this study, a variety of physiological measures were taken as college undergraduates imagined forgiving and unforgiving responses to a real-life offense. In the forgiveness imagination exercise, students were asked to empathize with the humanity of the offender and grant forgiveness. In the unforgiveness condition, they mentally rehearsed the hurt of the offense and nursed their grudge against the offender. Students in the unforgiveness condition showed significantly more cardiovascular reactions (heart rate & blood pressure increases), exhibited more sympathetic nervous system arousal (skin conductance), and reported more negative emotions (e.g., anger, sadness) than students in the forgiveness imagination condition. In contrast, the forgiveness imagination exercise produced lower physiological reactivity, more positive emotions, and greater feelings of control. Although only a short-term study, these results affirm the potential health benefits of forgiveness.

Forgiveness seems particularly important as a possible repair mechanism for the inevitable conflict that occurs in relationships. As we have noted many times, caring relations with others are one of the more significant factors in our health and happiness. Studies support the contribution of forgiveness to marital quality and the connection between forgiveness and other relationship factors, such as higher overall relationship satisfaction, greater empathy for one's partner, stronger commitment to the relationship, and less rumination about past offenses and about whether the offending partner apologized (Fincham & Beach, 2004; Fincham, Beach, & Davila, 2004; Finkel, Rusbult, Kumashiro, & Hannon, 2002; McCullough & Worthington, 1997;

McCullough et al., 2000; Paleari, Regalia, & Fincham, 2005). Forgiveness seems to both *express* and *enhance* close, caring, and healthy relationships. Let's explore this reciprocal influence a bit further: Forgiveness as an *expression* of marital quality has been demonstrated in studies showing specific variables that predict people will forgive one another. Specifically, strong commitment to the relationship, high levels of satisfaction and closeness, high levels of emotional empathy for the offending partner, and low levels of rumination about the offense by the offended partner are all variables that predict that a person will forgive a loved one for a serious transgression. On the flip side, the positive *effects* of forgiveness are shown in the form of enhanced marital quality, increased likelihood of future forgiveness, and the observation that forgiveness contributes to the restoration of closeness after a transgression occurs (e.g., McCullough et al., 1998; Paleari et al., 2005).

Gratitude

Like forgiveness, gratitude is deeply embedded in most religious traditions, but defies easy definition. Gratitude is widely regarded as a virtue and ingratitude as a vice (Bono, Emmons, & McCullough, 2004). Studies show that feelings of gratitude are among the more commonly experienced positive emotions, making us feel happy, contended, and joyful (Bono et al., 2004; Emmons & McCullough, 2004). Expressions of gratitude can range from a polite and obligatory "thank you" in everyday life to an appreciation and thankfulness for life itself. A prominent feature of gratefulness is an appreciation for the enhanced well-being that derives from another source (e.g., a person, God, or nature). Feelings and expressions of gratitude would seem particularly strong when the benefit received was freely given and when the benefactor incurred some cost and sacrifice (Emmons & Shelton, 2002).

McCullough, Kilpatrick, Emmons, and Larson (2001) provided one of the first conceptualizations of gratitude. These researchers define gratitude as *moral affect* because both the origins and consequences of gratitude are oriented toward the well-being of another person. That is, gratitude arises from virtue and concern with doing the right thing. It is also a prosocial act that sustains and reinforces the practice of virtue because of the positive consequences for both the benefactor and the beneficiary. Gratitude is distinct from other moral emotions, like shame and guilt, because these emotions mean we have fallen short of our moral standards and committed some transgression against another. In contrast, gratitude derives from being the recipient of helpful acts from another.

McCullough and his colleagues believe gratitude serves three moral or social functions: Gratitude can function as a moral barometer, a moral motive, and a moral reinforcer. As a *moral barometer*, gratitude signals a change in one's social relationships, as both the recipient (the person who received the kind act) and the benefactor (the person who offered the kind act) acknowledge their roles in each other's well-being. Positive feelings are the barometer or index of this change. As a *moral motive*, gratitude may serve to energize gratefulness among recipients of kind acts, in a reciprocating, "treat-kindness-with-kindness" mindset. Recipients of a particular kind act may also start thinking of *other* kind things done for them by *other* people, which may motivate them to express gratitude to *those* benefactors. As a *moral reinforcer*, gratitude may fuel the benefactor's desire to continue helping others in the future. In other words, receiving heartfelt thanks from someone creates positive emotions, and thereby serves as powerful reinforcement, leading to increased likelihood of future helpful acts. An evaluation of empirical evidence relevant to the three functions of gratitude found moderate support for gratitude as a moral barometer, weak support for the moral motive function, and very strong support for gratitude as a moral reinforcer (Bono et al., 2004; Emmons & McCullough, 2004; McCullough et al., 2001).

Focus on Research: Increasing Well-Being by Counting Your Blessings

Since gratitude is associated with positive feelings, could well-being be enhanced by asking people to think about and keep track of their blessings? This was the question examined by Emmons and McCullough (2003) in three separate studies. In their first study, college students were assigned to one of three conditions.

In the *grateful condition*, students were given the following instructions: "There are many things in our lives, both large and small, that we might be grateful about. Think back over the last week and write down on the lines below up to five things in your life that you are grateful or thankful for" (Emmons & McCullough, 2003, p. 379). In this condition, students mentioned such things as the helpfulness of friends, having great parents, and thankfulness to God for his help in their life.

In the *hassles condition*, the following instructions were given: "Hassles are irritants—things that annoy or bother you. They occur in various domains of life, including relationships, work, school, housing, finances, health, and so forth. Think back over today and, on the lines below, list up to five hassles that occurred in your life" (Emmons & McCullough, 2003, p. 379). Hassles mentioned by the student participants included things like dwindling finances for school, a messy kitchen that no one would clean, poor test performance in a college class, and lack of appreciation from friends.

Instructions for the *events condition* were as follows: "What were some of the events or circumstances that affected you in the past week? Think back over the past week and write down on the lines below five events that had an impact on you" (Emmons & McCullough, 2003, p. 379). Events mentioned included attending a festival, learning a new skill, taking a trip and cleaning up one's place of residence.

Students also completed well-being measures that included ratings of mood, overall well-being, physical health symptoms, and the experience of 30 different positive and negative emotions. Students in each condition (*grateful, hassles,* or *events*) completed all measures once each week over a period of 10 weeks. In a second study, students were again assigned to either a *grateful* condition or a *hassles* condition, but a *downward comparison* condition was substituted for the *events* condition. For downward comparisons, participants were asked to think of ways in which they were better off than others. In this second study, students recorded their responses daily, over a 2-week period.

Compared to students in the *hassles* and *events* conditions, students in the *grateful* condition appeared to reap a number of well-being benefits. They reported being more grateful; said they felt better about life in general; experienced more positive emotions; reported fewer negative emotions; and were more optimistic about the future. In the 10-week study, students also reported fewer health problems and increases in both the amount and quality of sleep experienced. Perhaps because of its short duration, health benefits were not found in the 2-week daily diary study.

In a third study, adult participants with neuromuscular diseases were recruited through a university neuromuscular disease clinic.

Participants kept daily diaries for 21 days and were assigned to either a *grateful* condition (as in previous studies) or a "*no-manipulation*" condition in which *only* the well-being measures were completed. Reports from spouses or significant others were also gathered to help validate the self-reports of participants. Results showed that, compared to the *no-manipulation* group, participants assigned to the *grateful* condition reported higher overall subjective well-being, more optimistic views of the future, more frequent positive emotions, a reduction in negative emotions, more sleep, sleep of improved quality, and a stronger sense of connection to others. These changes were corroborated by the reports of others who saw improved well-being among participants in the *grateful* condition, as compared to participants in the *no-manipulation* condition.

In their conclusion, Emmons and McCullough suggest that, because grateful expressions increase positive emotions, gratitude might be an important contributor to the upward spiral of well-being described in Fredrickson's broaden-and-build theory of positive emotions (see Chapter 2). That is, gratitude has the potential to promote positive emotions, repair relationships, and offset the toxic effects of revengeful hostility. These effects are consistent with Fredrickson's idea that positive emotions build psychological and social resources for healthy and adaptive functioning.

We began this chapter by describing the monumental effort to develop a classification system of human virtues and strengths of character (the "Values in Action" Project). The purpose of this effort was to provide a language for describing the "good," in human behavior and what goes *right* in people's lives, in order to balance psychology's long-standing focus on the "bad" and what goes *wrong. The Diagnostic and Statistical Manual of Mental Disorders* catalogues the many mental and emotional problems that plague human beings. Mental health professionals have developed a variety of therapies to treat mental disorders. In many ways, the VIA project is an analogous effort, but one that is focused on well-being and happiness. The VIA project aims to delineate the positive behaviors that underlie well-being and happiness. In this regard, practicing forgiveness and gratitude are examples of interventions analogous to psychotherapy, but intended to promote a life on the *positive* side of zero, rather than to treat illness.

Chapter Summary Questions

1. Why have psychologists tended to avoid the study of morality and virtue?
2. How did the Values in Action Project researchers develop and select their list of 6 virtues and 24 character strengths?
3. What is the difference between wisdom and "book learning," intelligence, technical knowledge, or being "smart?" What does it mean to be wise?
4. What three interests are wise people skillful at balancing, according to Sternberg's balance theory?
5. What do Baltes and his colleagues mean when they describe wisdom as expert knowledge of the "fundamental pragmatics of life?"
6. How does wisdom relate to happiness, according to research by Baltes and his colleagues? Are wise people happier?
7. What role does wisdom play in the SOC model of effective life management, according to Baltes and his colleagues?
8. What are the arguments supporting self-control as a master virtue? How is failed self-control evident in the "Seven Deadly Sins," according to Baumeister and Exline?
9. How may religion fulfill the four needs (described by Baumeister) that underlie a meaningful life (purpose, value, self-efficacy, and self-worth)?
10. What does it mean when someone describes themselves as "spiritual, but not religious?" What has research shown about the percentage of people who make and identify with this distinction?
11. How does Pargament define religion and spirituality? What is the defining feature of each; and why is religion considered the broader concept?
12. What general conclusions are drawn from research investigating the relationship between religion and well-being? Of the four measures used to measure religiousness, which is the strongest predictor of well-being?
13. How may the relationship between health and religion be explained (3 factors)?
14. According to the classic work of Gordon Allport, how does the distinction between intrinsic and extrinsic religious orientation help solve the religious-prejudice puzzle?
15. How may an attachment to God serve a function similar to attachment to parents?
16. a. What is the difference between positive and negative coping styles, according to Pargament and his colleagues?
    b. What "religious struggle" might cause clergy members to use more negative coping styles than rank-and-file church members, according to Pargament and his colleagues?
17. What is the difference between "explaining religion versus explaining religion away," according to Pargament?
18. Why do researchers believe forgiveness may release people from the damaging effects of negative emotions like anger and revenge and also help repair and enhance relationships? What does preliminary research suggest about these possibilities?
19. a. How may gratitude function as a moral barometer, a moral motive, and a moral reinforcer, according to McCullough and his colleagues?
    b. What positive outcomes were associated with gratitude among college students and adults suffering from neuromuscular diseases in the recent study by Emmons and McCullough?

Key Terms

values in action project *208*
wisdom *209*
courage *209*
humanity *211*
justice *211*
temperance *211*
transcendence *211*
balance theory *215*
wisdom as expert
    knowledge *216*

SOC Model: selection,
    optimization, and
    compensation *218*
purpose *221*
value *221*
self-efficacy *221*
interpretive control *222*
self-worth *222*
religion (Pargament) *225*
spirituality (Pargament) *225*

sanctification *226*
intrinsic versus extrinsic religious
    orientation *228*
quest religious orientation *230*
attachment theory *230*
positive coping styles *231*
negative coping styles *232*
forgiveness *233*
gratitude *235*

Web Resources

Values in Action Project

www.viastrengths.org/index.aspx?ContentID=1 This is the web site for the Values in Action Project. Follow the links to VIA Measurement Instruments and you can register (free) to take a long or brief version of the character strength inventories. You do have to provide demographic information that is used along with your responses in an online study of character strengths.

Authentic Happiness

www.authentichappiness.sas.upenn.edu This is Martin Seligman's site at the University of Pennsylvania. The same VIA Project measures of character strengths are available on this site. There is also a measure of forgiveness. You must log in, create a password, and provide demographic information to take the tests and have them scored for you. A profile of scores on all tests is computed and can be accessed at anytime.

Psychology of Religion

virtualreligion.net/vri/psych.html This site provides a large number of links to research and researchers in the psychology of religion, from classic works by William James to recent studies.

www.apa.org/about/division/div36.html This is the web site for Division 36, Psychology of Religion of the American Psychological Association. Contains information about conferences and current research.

www.bgsu.edu/organizations/cfdr/about/facultymembers/pargament.html This web site is by Kenneth Pargament (Bowling Green University), one of the top researchers in the psychology of religion. It provides listing of his past and recent research.

Gratitude and Forgiveness

www.psy.miami.edu/faculty/mmccullough/index.html This site for Michael McCullough provides access to research articles on gratitude and forgiveness, a gratitude questionnaire, and links to Robert Emmons and other researchers in this area.

Suggested Readings

Baumeister, R. F. (1991). *Meanings of life*. New York: Guilford.

Baumeister, R. F., & Exline, J. J. (1999). Virtue, personality, and social relations: Self-control as a moral muscle. *Journal of Personality, 67*, 1165–1194.

Baltes, P. B. (1997). On the incomplete architecture of human ontogeny: Selection, optimization, and compensation as foundations of developmental theory. *American Psychologist, 52*, 366–380.

Emmons, R. A. (1999). *The psychology of ultimate concerns: Motivation and spirituality in personality*. New York: Guilford Press.

Hill, P. C., & Pargament, K. I. (2003). Advances in the conceptualization and measurement of religion and spirituality. *American Psychologist, 58*, 64–74.

Koenig, H. G., & Cohen, H. J. (Eds.). (2002). *The link between religion and health: Psychoneuroimmunology and the faith factor*. New York: Oxford University Press.

Koenig, H. G., McCullough, M. E., & Larson, D. B. (2001). *Handbook of religion and health*. New York: Oxford University Press.

Linley, P. A., & Joseph, S. (Eds.). (2004). *Positive psychology in practice*. Hoboken, NJ: John Wiley & Sons.

McCullough, M. E. (Ed.). (1999). *Forgiveness: Theory, research and practice*. New York: Guilford Publications.

Pargament, K. I. (1997). *The psychology of religion and coping: Theory, research and practice*. New York: Guilford Publications.

Paulus, D. L., Wehr, P., Harms, P. D., & Strasser, D. H. (2002). Use of exemplars to reveal implicit types of intelligence. *Personality and Social Psychology Bulletin, 28*, 1051–1062.

Peterson, C., & Seligman, M. E. P. (2004). *Character strengths and virtues: A handbook of classification*. Washington, DC: American Psychological Association/ New York: Oxford University Press.

Spilka, B., Hood, R. W., Jr., Hunsberger, B., & Gorsuch, R. (2003). *The psychology of religion: An empirical approach*. New York: Guilford Press.

11

Close Relationships and Well-Being

As humans, we are fundamentally social beings whose connections to others are vital to our health and happiness. As we have noted in many places throughout this book, the evidence connecting well-being to relationships is overwhelming (see Chapters 3 and 5). David Myers referred to the contribution of relationships to health and happiness as a "deep truth" (1992, p. 154). The "truth" of the well-being/relationship connection appears to be universal. Of the many factors that contribute to well-being, only social relationships consistently predict happiness across widely differing cultures (Diener & Diener, 1995).

Relationships are responsible for our greatest joys and our most painful sorrows. Our physical and emotional well-being is enhanced as much by supporting and caring connections with others as it is jeopardized by social isolation and bad relationships. For physical health and longevity, the magnitude of these effects rival those of well-established health risks such as smoking, obesity, diet, and lack of exercise (see Chapter 3). The quality of our relationships has equally powerful effects on mental health and happiness. Healthy people have strong, supportive connections to others and happy people have rich social lives, satisfying friendships, and happy marriages (see Chapters 3 and 5).

The importance of positive relationships is widely recognized by psychologists and non-psychologists alike. People typically list close relationships as one of their most important life goals and a primary source of meaning in life (Emmons, 1999b). In one study, 73% of college students said they would sacrifice another important life goal (e.g., good education, career) before they would give up a satisfying romantic relationship (Hammersla & Frease-McMahan, 1990). In answer to the "deathbed test" most people point to relationships as a major factor that contributes to a satisfying and meaningful life (Reis & Gable, 2003; Sears, 1977). A full appreciation of the value of close relationships is one of life's more important lessons, often learned in the face of life-threatening events (see Chapter 4 on Posttraumatic Growth).

We have also discussed the multiple ways that relationships contribute to well-being. Relationships provide an important coping resource through social support, fulfill needs for intimacy and sharing of life's burdens through self-disclosure, and represent an ongoing source of enjoyment and positive emotions through interactions with others. Many psychologists believe these positive effects are built on a biological foundation reflecting our evolutionary heritage. Humans are not particularly imposing figures compared to the other animals they confronted in pre-historic times, and human infants remain relatively defenseless for many years. Evolution may have selected for a genetically-organized bonding process. Going it alone likely meant the end of a person's genetic lineage. In short, humans probably would not have survived if they did not have a built-in biological motive to form cooperative bonds with others and nurturing connections with their own offspring. As we noted in Chapter 5, the evolutionary basis of human connections, together with the extensive literature showing the importance of human bonds, led Baumeister and Leary (1995) to conclude that belongingness is a fundamental human need which they described as, "a pervasive drive to form and maintain at least a minimum quantity of lasting, positive, and significant interpersonal relationships" (p. 497). Food and water are essential supplies for a healthy life. Similarly, caring relationships with others also appear to be essential to well-being.

Recent studies have begun to explore some of the biological underpinnings of our need for belonging. For example, **oxytocin** is a pituitary hormone that has physiological effects that counter the flight-or-fight stress response. That is, this hormone reduces fearfulness and the physiological arousal associated with stress by producing relaxation and calmness (Carter, 1998; Taylor, Klein, Lewis, et al., 2000; Uvnas-Moberg, 1998). Oxytocin is sometimes referred to as the "cuddle hormone" because close physical contacts such as touching, hugging, and kissing stimulate its release (Hazan, Campa, & Gur-Yaish, 2006). Oxytocin is responsible for the release of milk in nursing mothers. The calm emotional state and feelings of safety produced by the hormone are thought to contribute to infant–maternal bonds. For both men and women, oxytocin levels are at their highest during sexual orgasm (Uvnas-Moberg, 1997). These findings suggest that our desire for intimate connections with others and the comfort these connections provide are at least partially mediated by biological responses. Obviously, there's more to a hug than just biology, but that hug might not feel quite as good if it *weren't* for biology.

The connection of satisfying relationships to well-being is clear. What is not so clear is how people develop and maintain good relationships. In this chapter, we will explore what psychologists have learned about close, intimate relationships that addresses the following sorts of questions: What is the difference between close relationships and more casual acquaintances? How does an intimate connection develop between two people? What does it mean to be someone's friend? To be in love? What characterizes good and bad relationships? Given the widely shared belief in the importance of close relationships, why do half of all marriages end in divorce? Why is it so difficult to sustain a satisfying long-term marriage? Can "happy" couples tell us something about the ingredients of a successful marriage?

DEFINING CLOSE RELATIONSHIPS

Characteristics

We encounter many people each day as we shop, talk on the phone, keep appointments, visit, work, go to school, go to church, and relax with family members, friends, or spouses at the end of the day. While all the relationships involved in these encounters are potentially significant, researchers have spent most of their time studying our closest relationships—specifically friendship, romantic love, and marriage. Our best friends, lovers, and spouses are the most important people in our lives and have the most impact on our overall well-being across the life span.

Close relationships can be distinguished from more casual acquaintances in a number of ways, but the degree of intimacy seems most central to the distinction. In everyday language, intimacy often implies a sexual and romantic relationship. We may be more likely to describe a good friend as a best friend or a close friend, rather than an intimate friend. However, relationship researchers use the term "intimacy" to capture mutual understanding, depth of connection, and degree of involvement, whether or not the relationship is sexual. The term "intimacy" can apply both to friends and to lovers. It is in this sense that our closest relationships, sexual or not, are the most intimate ones. Although some researchers believe that close relationships and intimate relationships are distinct and independent types (see Berscheid & Reis, 1998), we will use the term "intimate" to describe our closest relationships.

Based on an extensive review of the literature, Miller, Perlman, and Brehm (2007) suggest that both lay-persons and psychologists seem to agree on six core characteristics that set intimate relationships apart from more casual relationships: knowledge, trust, caring, interdependence, mutuality, and commitment (see also Berscheid & Reis, 1998; Harvey & Weber, 2002).

Brief descriptions of these six characteristics are given in Table 11.1.

KNOWLEDGE Our closest friends and intimate partners know more about us than anyone else. They have extensive knowledge of our personal history, deepest feelings, strengths, and faults. Intimate knowledge in close relations develops through the mutual self-disclosure of personal information and feelings. **Self-disclosure** means revealing intimate details of the self to others (Derlega, Metts, Petronio, & Margulis, 1993). These details have to do with our "true self" and the actual state of affairs in our lives, which is likely different than the public self presented to less intimate others in everyday interactions. That is, we share things with intimate others that we typically keep private when we are in the company of strangers or casual acquaintances. Sharing of personal information, in turn, provides the basis for developing a deeper connection than is typical in casual associations. To have someone accept, like or love you, when they know you as you know yourself, is powerful affirmation of the essence and totality of self. This is one reason why rejection by a good friend or romantic partner may be so painful. The relatively complete self-knowledge shared with another may make rejection by that person feel profound. In contrast, the rejection of someone who has minimal and partial knowledge of us is likely to be less upsetting,

---

TABLE 11.1 Characteristics of intimate relationships

Knowledge—mutual understanding based on reciprocal self-disclosure.

Trust—assumption of no harm will be done by the other. Keeping confidences.

Caring—genuine concern for the other and ongoing monitoring and maintenance of relationship

Interdependence—intertwining of lives and mutual influence.

Mutuality—sense of "we-ness" and overlapping of lives.

Commitment—intention to stay in the relationship through its ups and downs.

because only the more superficial aspects of the self are invested.

Research suggests that self-disclosure both signifies and enhances mutual liking and affection. A major review by Collins and Miller (1994) found strong empirical support for three disclosure-liking effects. (1) We disclose to people we like. (2) We like people who disclose intimate self-information more than those whose disclosures are less intimate. (3) We like people to whom we have disclosed. Research has also identified a strong tendency for disclosure to beget disclosure, an effect called **disclosure reciprocity** (Derlega et al., 1993; Miller, 1990; Reis & Shaver, 1988). People tend to both reciprocate a disclosure and match its level of intimacy. The process often begins with non-intimate information and then moves on to more intimate factual and emotional disclosures over time. If initial conversations are rewarding, then over time both the breadth (diversity of topics) and the depth (personal significance and sensitivity) of topics that are discussed increases (Altman & Taylor, 1973). This movement of communication from small talk to the exchange of more sensitive personal information is considered central to the development of relationships. Reciprocal self-disclosure captures the process of how we get to know someone. The knowledge that results from disclosure describes what it means to know and be known by someone.

The power of self-disclosure to produce feelings of closeness is dramatically shown by a study that manipulated the intimacy of two conversation partners (Aron, Melinat, Aron, Vallone, & Bator, 1997). Participants began their exchange as complete strangers. They were first instructed to talk for 15 minutes about personal topics that were relatively low in intimacy such as, "When did you last sing to yourself?" During the second 15-minute interval, topic intimacy increased to include things like, "What is your most treasured memory?" During the final 15 minutes, conversation partners were instructed to talk about very personal topics invoked by questions such as, "When did you last cry in front of another person? By yourself?" "Complete this sentence: 'I wish I had someone with whom I could share . . .' " Compared to a group of non-disclosing participants who engaged in 45 minutes of small talk (e.g., "What's is your favorite holiday?"), participants in the disclosure condition reported feeling very close to their conversational partners by the conclusion of the experience. The researchers compared closeness ratings for the group that engaged in self-disclosure and the group that made small-talk. Surprisingly, the experimental subjects reported feeling closer to their experimental partners, than one-third of the small-talk subjects reported feeling to the person with whom they shared the closest *real-life* relationship! This is strong evidence for the importance of self-disclosure to the development of intimacy.

Reciprocal disclosure is most evident at the beginning of relationships and less so once relationships are well established (Altman, 1973; Derlega, Wilson, & Chaikin, 1976). In a new friendship, we are likely to feel an obligation to reciprocate when a person opens up to us with personal information. In a budding romance, the disclosure may be quite rapid and emotionally arousing, which may add to the passion we feel. Telling a romantic partner your deepest secrets and your innermost feelings is exciting, especially when it is reciprocated. One of the ironies of romance is that the better we know our partners, the less we may experience the excitement of disclosure. Baumeister and Bratslavsky (1999) argue that passion and deepening intimacy are strongly linked. They believe one reason passion fades in long-term marriages is that spouses already know most everything about each other.

In well-established relationships, intimacy is sustained more by *responsiveness* than by reciprocity (Reis & Patrick, 1996). That is, in our interactions with best friends, family members, and marital partners, it is less important to reciprocate and more important to respond in a supporting, caring, and affectionate manner (Laurenceau, Barrett, & Pietromonaco, 1998). If you tell your spouse all your angry feelings about your boss after a bad day at work, you aren't looking for reciprocation. You don't really want to hear about her or his bad day at that moment. What you want is a sounding board, a sympathetic ear, and expressions of care and empathy for your feelings.

TRUST   Mutual trust is another vital ingredient of intimate and close relationships. To trust someone means that you expect they will do you no harm. Chief among the harms we are concerned about is the breaking of confidences. When we open up to other people we make ourselves vulnerable. It is a bit like taking your clothes off and feeling self-conscious about the less than perfect shape of your body. In a network of friends or co-workers, sensitive information can have damaging consequences if someone tells others how you "really" feel about someone—your boss, for example. Violation of trust is damaging to relationships and will likely lead the betrayed person to be less open and more guarded in revealing personally sensitive information in the future (Jones, Crouch, & Scott, 1997). Trust is an essential ingredient in close relationships, partly because it is a necessary precondition for self-disclosure. We don't disclose to people we don't trust.

CARING Caring means concern for and attention to the feelings of others. We feel more affection and appreciation for our close partners than for most people. When we ask a casual acquaintance, "how are you doing?" we most often expect and receive an obligatory and cliché response: "Fine," "Hanging in there," "Not bad," and so forth. Neither person expects a deep revelation about personal feelings. At one level, in those passing greetings, we aren't actually asking for information about how the person is *really* doing. We're just following polite social rules for greeting and acknowledging people as we encounter them. In our intimate relationships, the same question carries different expectations. We expect and want a more detailed and genuine response, especially if things are not going well. And the other person is expected to be more honest in describing how they *really* feel, and not to pass off the question with a stock answer used in low-intimacy exchanges. Caring also involves all the little things we do to express our appreciation and valuing of a relationship: providing support in times of need; recognizing special occasions like birthdays, holidays, and anniversaries; inviting people for dinner and other shared activities; and keeping in touch with a phone call or an invitation to get together over coffee or lunch. All these things reflect the simple fact that more intimate relationships take high priority in our lives. We have more invested, so we take care to maintain the quality of our close relationships.

INTERDEPENDENCE The lives of people in intimate relationships are deeply intertwined. The mutual influence of each person on the actions, feelings, and thinking of the other is, for some researchers, a defining characteristic of close relationships (Berscheid & Reis, 1998). We typically care more

and give greater weight to the advice and judgments our family members, friends, and spouses than we do to people we know less well. This is particularly true regarding self-relevant personal issues and actions. We may consult an expert when our computer malfunctions, but we are likely to seek the support and advice of spouses and friends in times of personal challenge, such as interpersonal conflicts at work or caring for aging parents. Our feelings and actions are also intertwined. The emotional ups and downs of our intimate partners affect our own emotional states and actions. Intimate partners share in each other's emotional experiences. Compared to casual relationships, the mutual influences characterizing close relationships are more frequent and involve more areas of our lives. And they are long-term. For example, most parents find that they never stop being parents, in terms of showing concern, giving advice, and offering help and support to their children. Children would likely agree that the influence of parents does not end when they leave their parents' home and begin their own lives.

MUTUALITY Mutuality is another distinctive feature of our closest relationships. Mutuality refers to feelings of overlap between two lives—that is, the extent to which people feel like separate individuals or more like a couple. These feelings are revealed in the language we use to describe our connection to others. Plural pronouns (we and us) have been found to both express and contribute to close relationships (e.g., Fitzsimons & Kay, 2004). People use "we" to signify closeness. In a developing relationship, shifting from singular pronouns (e.g., "she and I") to plural ("we" or "us") contributes to feelings of closeness and mutuality.

Another way of capturing mutuality and feelings of closeness is to ask people to pick among pairs of circles that overlap to varying degrees (see Figure 11.1). Called the Inclusion of Other in the Self Scale, this measure has been found effective in assessing interpersonal closeness (Aron, Aron, & Smollan, 1992). Sample items from this scale are shown in Figure 11.1. People simply pick the circle pair that best describes a relationship partner specified by the researcher (e.g., closest relationship, best friend, spouse, etc.). The pictorial representation of mutuality seems to be a direct and meaningful way for people to express their feelings of closeness for another person.

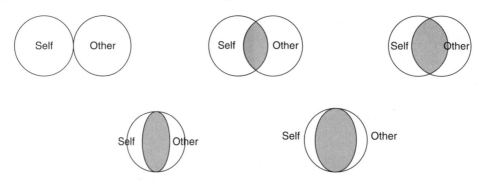

FIGURE 11.1   Sample Items—Inclusion of Other in the Self Scale

COMMITMENT Commitment is a final component of intimate relationships. Commitment is a desire or intention to continue a relationship into the future. Research suggests that people associate commitment with loyalty, faithfulness, living up to your word, hard work, and giving your best effort (Fehr, 1988, 1996). In short, commitment means persevering "through thick and thin." This can be contrasted with the lack of commitment shown by a "fair weather friend," who is there when things are going well, but not when a supportive friend is needed most. Successful friendships and marriages require some amount of work. This means spending time and energy maintaining closeness and working through the inevitable conflicts and problems that arise in long-term relationships. Close relationships also require some degree of personal sacrifice and compromise of individual self-interests for the good of the relationship. Mutual commitment helps ensure that relationship partners will do the work and make the sacrifices and compromises necessary to sustain an intimate connection.

Our most satisfying relationships will likely involve all six characteristics: knowledge, trust, caring, interdependence, mutuality, and commitment (Miller et al., 2007). Both research and everyday personal experience suggest that these characteristics do, indeed, capture the essential elements of what it means to be a close friend or intimate partner. If we view these six features as ideal standards, then degree of intimacy and closeness might be evaluated according to the relative prominence of each characteristic. Fehr (1996) argues that the difference between a friend, a good friend, and a best friend is largely a matter of degree. With our best friends, we know more, trust more, care more, are more deeply committed, and so forth.

It is important to recognize the diversity of relationships. That is, close relationships are a bit too complex to be captured by six ideal characteristics. Deep affection and caring can exist without passing the six-feature test. For example, the movie *Grumpy Old Men* portrayed two elderly men (played by Walter Matthau and Jack Lemmon) who competed for a woman's affection, constantly criticized and insulted each other, and spent considerable time planning and carrying out acts of revenge that stopped just short of mayhem. Yet their relationship was utterly endearing, caring, affectionate and, despite its peculiar nature, loving. Fitting this long-term friendship to the six characteristics would be a challenge! In a similar vein, marriages come in all shapes and sizes, reflecting the unique needs and personalities of spouses. A marriage may "work" despite a lack of fit to the ideal. Both of your textbook authors, for instance, know of a successful marriage based on high independence rather than interdependence. That is, a couple that takes pride in not exerting much influence on each other in terms of careers, vacation travel, mutual friends, or even shared activities at home. This may not seem to many of us like a recipe for a satisfying relationship, but they are both very happy with their marriage and wouldn't have it any other way.

It is worth keeping in mind that none of these characteristics, in and of itself, guarantees an intimate relationship. Self-disclosure, for instance, does not guarantee intimacy or deep affection. Sometimes when you really get to know a person, you find that you really dislike them! Perhaps this has happened with a relative or a co-worker with whom you've had frequent and long-term contact. In a similar vein, commitment might not signify a desire to work on or enhance a relationship. A married couple in an unhappy marriage might make a mutual commitment to stay together because they believe it is best for their kids. In short, relationships are complex. The six features of intimate relationships should be considered general guidelines rather than hard-and-fast criteria.

Exchange and Communal Relationships

In addition to the six characteristics that *define* intimate relationships, such relationships also differ in how we think about and evaluate them. According to Clark and Mills, relationships come in two basic forms, exchange relationships and communal relationships (Clark, 1984; Clark & Mills, 1979, 1993). The two forms are related to different patterns of thinking, evaluating and behaving in a relationship, and to different levels of intimacy and closeness. Clark and Mills provide evidence showing that, as intimacy increases, people's relationships shift from an exchange form to a communal form.

Exchange relationships are typically more formal, less personal, and in the beginning stages of development. They are built on fairness and mutual reciprocity. That is, in an exchange relationship each party is expected to return favors in a mutual fashion. I do something nice for you and you return the favor. Exchange relationships are evaluated by keeping mental track of what we have done for others in comparison to what they have done for us. We may feel satisfied if our exchange ratio is fairly equal; conversely, resentment may build if we feel we are putting ourselves out, but getting nothing back. A sense of indebtedness might result from believing we are "falling behind" in doing nice things for another person.

Communal relationships are more typical with our closer friends, romantic partners, and family members. In these relationships, the tit-for-tat reciprocation of exchange relationships would probably feel a bit funny and might even be damaging. What would you think if your best friend reciprocated every one of your favors, like an accountant who keeps track of assets and liabilities on a ledger sheet? Clark and Mills (1979, 1993) found that while tit-for-tat reciprocation of favors increased liking among low-intimacy and formal relationships, the same favor reciprocation decreased liking among friends and in more intimate relationships. With our long-term friends, family members, and spouses we are in it for the long haul. We tend to pay more attention to keeping track of others' *needs*, rather than logging all the specific things we have done for them and they have done for us. We are highly responsive to others' emotional states and respond appropriately. In communal relationships, we share an ongoing mutual concern focused on the overall quality of a relationship and the needs and welfare of the other. We do not expect to be repaid for each positive act.

The distinction between exchange and communal relationships is not hard-and-fast. All relationships probably involve some kind of exchange and a close relationship does not necessarily mean that each person takes a communal view (Clark & Mills, 1993; Mills & Clark, 2001). Some married couples undoubtedly *do* focus on what they put in versus what they get out of their marriage, although this probably signifies a less healthy and less mature relationship. And, thinking about costs and benefits seems entirely appropriate when close relationships become hurtful, conflicted, or dominated by one person's self-centered needs.

ON THE LIGHTER SIDE

Love and friendship are built on the same foundation. Knowledge, trust, caring, interdependence, mutuality, and commitment are the basic building blocks of all close relationships. As these basic ingredients develop, our thinking shifts from an exchange perspective to a more communal perspective. One reason relationships are so strongly connected to health and happiness is that they represent a sort of safety net to catch us when life knocks us off balance. The depth of knowledge, care, concern, and trust that characterize close relationships provide confidence that we don't have to go it alone. Support from friends, family members, and intimate partners in times of trouble has been consistently documented as one of our strongest coping resources (Berscheid & Reis, 1998; Ryff & Singer, 2000; Salovey, Rothman, Detweiler, & Steward, 2000; Salovey, Rothman, & Rodin, 1998; Taylor et al., 2000). However, relationships also enhance our well-being when things are going well. Most of the "good times" we have in life involve shared activities and fun with our families and friends. These good times translate into more frequent positive emotional experiences that, in turn, allow us to reap the benefits of positive emotions shown in research and described by

Fredrickson's broaden-and-build theory of positive emotions (Chapter 3).

Teasing and Humor

Aside from sex, which is arguably more intense, but far less frequent (at least when you're older), laughter is one of our most commonly experienced sources of positive emotion. From childhood to old age, laughter is a universal experience and it's almost always social (Lefcourt, 2002). We may, on occasion, laugh when we're alone, but we have the most fun with others. We both enjoy and seek out people who make us laugh. Large-scale surveys find that a sense of humor is one of the most valued qualities that people seek in choosing opposite- and same-sex friends, dating partners, and marriage partners (Sprecher & Regan, 2002). Certainly, humor can be used for negative purposes, such as the humiliating teasing of a schoolyard bully. However, in satisfying relationships, humor is typically prosocial and serves positive functions (Keltner, Young, Heerey, & Oemig, 1998). Teasing, playful banter, exchanging jokes, and contagious laughter are typical features of close relationships and one of the primary reasons we enjoy them. Even serious occasions are often marked by humor. For example, it is not uncommon for people to tell humorous stories about the deceased at a funeral reception, especially if the person was elderly and lived a long, full life. Humor is a positive coping strategy in the face of loss (Bonanno & Keltner, 1997). Humor helps lighten up serious situations by replacing negative emotions with more positive ones. Humor is widely regarded as an effective way to release stress-related tension, deal with sensitive issues, and help confront and resolve interpersonal conflicts (Argyle, 2001; Lefcourt, 2002; Martin, 2007). Laughter helps put both the mind and body at ease.

Humor is important in forming and maintaining social bonds. We like and feel closer to people who make us laugh (e.g., Fraley & Aron, 2004), including teachers and professors. Studies show that students believe a sense of humor is one of the most desirable teacher characteristics that contributes to more classroom enjoyment, engagement, and learning (see Chapter 11 in Martin, 2007). Research also consistently finds that humor contributes to satisfying long-term relationships (see Martin, 2007, for a review). The more married individuals value their partner's sense of humor, the more satisfied they

tend to be with their marriages. In short, high levels of reciprocated humor are one mark of a happy marriage. In fact, humor may well be a key ingredient for a successful long-term marriage, in part because it outlasts the pleasures of sex. When couples who had been married for over 50 years were asked why their marriage had lasted so long, "laughing together frequently" was one of the top reasons (Lauer, Lauer, & Kerr, 1990). They didn't say, "fantastic sex!" As the frequency and importance of sexual pleasure decline with age, humor may become a more significant source of enjoyment. In our later years of life, we may not want, or be able, to have sex on a regular basis, but there is no indication that we lose our ability to enjoy laughter, or our affection for people with whom we laugh.

One of the more prominent humor-related features of close and developing relationships is playful prosocial teasing. Flirtatious teasing is common in dating couples (Keltner et al., 1998) and playful teasing is regarded by people across different cultures as a basic "rule of friendship" (Argyle & Henderson, 1984, 1985). In a large-scale survey of four different cultures, Argyle and Henderson found that teasing and joking were expected features of friendships. This is true despite the fact that teasing is something of a paradox. As Keltner and his colleagues have noted, "Teasing criticizes, yet it compliments, attacks yet makes people closer, humiliates yet expresses affection" (Keltner et al., 1998, p. 1231). Despite its surface negativity, teasing says, "I like you well enough to tease you" and "I enjoy our good-natured fun together." It signifies closeness, trust, caring, and mutual understanding. In contrast, teasing a casual acquaintance risks misinterpretation, because a good tease and a stinging put-down are just a step apart. Interestingly, the absence of teasing and taking teasing literally are probably signs that a relationship is in trouble. If our best friend stopped teasing us, or took offense at our own well-intentioned teasing, we would clearly take notice and wonder what was wrong. And it goes without saying that if teasing turns aggressive or hurtful, this is also damaging to relationships (Keltner, Capps, Kring, Young, & Heerey, 2001).

Focus on Research: Sharing What Goes Right in Life

Because caring relations increase our experience of positive emotions, they enhance our well-being on an ongoing basis. Consistent with the **direct effects**

hypothesis of social support, close relationships contribute to health and happiness even when we are not facing stressful life events (see Chapter 3). The basic idea here is that positive emotions have beneficial effects that are both independent of, and beyond those of negative emotions. That is, in addition to offsetting the ill-effects of negative affect, positive emotions independently enhance the quality of our lives. In line with the direct effects hypothesis, Shelly Gable and her colleagues have recently shown that it is just as important to receive supportive responses to our positive life experiences, as it is to receive support when we're having trouble (Gable, Reis, Impett, & Asher, 2004). When people share or celebrate a positive life event with others, they derive additional benefits beyond the effect of the event itself. Drawing from earlier work, Gable and colleagues refer to this process as **capitalization** (i.e., capitalizing on a positive event to receive additional benefits). The benefits of capitalization may occur because sharing a positive event with others causes us to relive its emotional effects. A partner's enthusiastic response, indicating genuine pleasure at our good fortune, also enhances our positive feelings. In four separate studies, Gable and her colleagues examined the individual and interpersonal well-being benefits of sharing positive events.

In the first study, participants kept a daily diary in which they recorded their positive and negative emotions and their life satisfaction over an average period of 5 days. For each day, participants also recorded their most important positive event and whether they had shared that event with someone else. Results showed that on 70% of the days, people *had* shared their most positive event. Analysis of daily positive affect and daily life satisfaction ratings revealed that well-being was enhanced on "sharing" compared to "non-sharing" days.

In the second and third studies, dating and married couples were recruited to examine whether a partner's perceived responsiveness to positive sharing enhanced the quality of relationships. Various measures of relationship quality were completed independently by each partner (e.g., commitment, satisfaction, trust, and intimacy). An important feature of these studies was the development and use of a newly developed Perceived Responses to Capitalization Attempts scale. This scale measured the degree and nature of a partner's responsiveness to a positive event by asking people to answer the

following question: "*Please take a moment to consider how your partner responds when you tell him or her about something **good** that has happened to you*" (Gable et al., 2004, p. 233, emphasis in original). Examples of positive events were given, such as a promotion at work, a positive conversation with a family member, winning a prize or doing well at school. Each participant rated his or her partner's response using rating items describing four types of reactions to sharing a positive event: (1) *active-constructive* (e.g., "I sometimes get the sense that my partner is even more happy and excited than I am"); (2) *passive-constructive* (e.g., "My partner tries not to make a big deal out of it, but is happy for me"); (3) *active-destructive* (e.g., "He/she points out the potential downside of the good event"); (4) and *passive-destructive* (e.g., "My partner doesn't pay much attention to me") (Gable et al., 2004, p. 233). Both studies found that only active-constructive responses to the sharing of positive life events were related to enhanced relationship quality. The three other response types were associated with decreased relationship quality, making it clear that capitalization is dependent on an active, enthusiastic, and supporting reaction from one's partner. In a final 10-day diary study, Gable and her colleagues examined the individual benefits of capitalization. Would sharing a positive event and receiving an active-constructive response also increase the subjective well-being (SWB) of the person who shared? Answer: yes. On days when people told others about a positive event, both life satisfaction and positive affect increased. The more people they told, the more their well-being increased, especially if the responses received were supportive and enthusiastic. Altogether, these four studies provide strong support for the value of capitalizing on the good things that happen to us by sharing them with others. They also suggest another basis for the connection between relationships and well-being. The well-being enhancing effects of positive emotions can be relived and extended through our connections with caring others.

FRIENDSHIP AND ROMANTIC LOVE

Liking and loving, friendship and romance overlap considerably (Rubin, 1973). We love our good friends and like our romantic partners. When people were asked to write about their romantic relationships, the dominant theme was friendship—nearly half the participants said their romantic partner was also their closest friend (Hendrick & Hendrick, 1993). Though we use "love" to describe many of our closest relations, "in love" seems to have a more specific meaning related to sexual desire and attraction. Meyers and Berscheid (1997) had people sort their relationships into categories of *love, in love*, and *sexual attraction/desire* by naming people who fit into each. The *love* category was the largest, followed by *sexual attraction/desire*. The *in love* classification contained the fewest names and showed overlap with names in the *sexual attraction* category. In short, being in love means romantic love, involving strong sexual desire and attraction. This is where friendship and love part company. Telling a romantic partner "let's just be friends" or "I love you, but I'm not in love with you" usually signals the end of a romance because sexual attraction and desire are weak or absent. Romantic love includes fascination, passion, infatuation, sexual desire, and a more total absorption in the relationship. We seldom use the language of romance to describe our good friends, which are most often of the same sex (opposite sex for homosexual individuals). Our friendships are less *emotionally intense* partly because they do not typically involve sexual intimacy.

In addition to *emotional intensity*, friendship and romantic love are also distinguished by differences in the *clarity of rules* governing the relationship, the *complexity of feelings*, and the *expectations* concerning the emotional consequences of the relationship.

Clarity of Rules

A seminal study by Argyle and Henderson (1984) suggests some universality in people's understanding of what it means to be someone's friend. These researchers presented participants from different cultures (England, Italy, Hong Kong, and Japan) with a large set of rules for friendship and asked them which ones they endorsed. Interestingly, a number of these rules, described in Table 11.2 were widely endorsed across cultures.

You can think of these rules as a kind of test, apparently widely shared, that people use to evaluate their friendships. Friendship involves a set of obligations and rules defining what friends are supposed to do. If you fulfill these obligations and live by the rules, you pass the test for friendship, and if you don't, you fail. Argyle and Henderson found that

TABLE 11.2 Rules of friendship
Being supportive
Volunteer help in time of need
Show emotional support
Stand up for the other person in their absence
Being a trustworthy confidant
Respect the friend's privacy
Trust and confide in the other
Keep confidences
Don't criticize each other in public
Disclose personal feelings or problems to a friend
Being a source of enjoyment and humor
Strive to make him/her happy while in each other's company
Engage in joking or teasing with a friend
Share news of success with the other
Being tolerant and accepting
Don't be jealous or critical of each other's relationships
Be tolerant of each other's friends
Ask for personal advice
Don't nag

people did, in fact, think of past failed friendships in terms of their friends or themselves failing to follow one or more of these rules.

Do these rules also apply to romantic involvements? Is there a set of rules governing love? Certainly, between Oprah Winfrey and Dr. Phil and the self-help section of your local bookstore, there is no shortage of advice for developing and maintaining marriage and romance. And relationship researchers have described general guidelines for maintaining healthy relationships (e.g., Gottman & Silver, 1999; Harvey & Omarzu, 1997, 1999). However, we are unaware of empirical studies describing reasonably clear and shared rules that people possess for romantic love like those for friendship (although see Baxter, 1986). Consistent with the idea that "all's fair in love and war," the complexity and emotionally volatile nature of romance and passion would seem to preclude clear rules. In fact, given the importance of spontaneity, passion, and exclusivity, some might argue that if you are following rules, you probably aren't in love. Compared to friendship, love seems more varied in its particular form of expression and individual meaning, as we shall see in our discussion of the varieties of love.

Complexity of Feelings

Romantic love involves more complex feelings, more stringent demands, and higher expectations than friendship. The complexity of love is reflected in researchers' inability to define it and in the dominance of love-related themes in music, movies, and popular culture. Harvey and Weber (2002) note that prominent relationship researcher Ellen Berscheid probably had it right when she commented (in Sternberg & Barnes, 1988, p. 362) that ". . . love is a huge and motley collection of many different behavioral events whose only commonalities are that they take place in a relationship with another person . . . ." As for music, movies, and pop culture, no aspect of love's many-faceted mystery and no detail of celebrities' love-life intrigues are left unexplored. Love for hire, love for money, love for power, love for life, fatal attractions, tragedies of love, love conquering all, losing all for love, hate turned to love, love turned to hate, etc . . ., — all "in the name of love." Our fascination with love does not have a counterpart in friendship. How many songs and movies explore the "mysteries" of friendship?

Further, we do not demand the same level of loyalty, faithfulness, and exclusivity of our friends that we do of our romantic partners (Miller et al., 2007). Being someone's good friend does not preclude you or your friend from being good friends with someone else. Hearing that a good friend went out for dinner and a movie with another friend is not a cause for alarm. Among romantic and marital partners it is obviously a different story. Finding out that your spouse went out on a dinner-movie "date" would probably be upsetting or at least require explanation. Suspicions of infidelity are raised if one party in a romantically-involved couple pursues an opposite-sex friendship without his or her partner present. In a similar vein, showing strong interest in, or talking and joking with another person is not typically an affront to a good friend. But, if the same behaviors are interpreted as flirtation, they may well get you in trouble with your romantic partner.

Expectations

A final difference between friendship and love concerns emotional expectations. A number of social observers have noted that we demand a good deal more emotional fulfillment from marriages and romantic relationships today than in the past, and certainly more than we expect from our friendships (e.g., Myers, 2000b; Phillips, 1988). Historically, marriages were built more on practical matters having to do with finances, family connections, and raising children. Romantic love was important, but it was not the exclusive or most significant foundation for marriage. Today, large-scale surveys indicate that being in love is the primary basis for getting married and that maintaining love is an important requirement for staying married (Simpson, Campbell, & Berscheid, 1986). More so today than in the past, we expect marriage to fulfill our deepest emotional needs, to be exciting, and to make us happy. Marriage is expected to be personally fulfilling, lifelong, and romantically and sexually satisfying. As many researchers have noted, this is a tall order, perhaps destined for disappointment. The point here is that we do not hold our friends responsible for our personal fulfillment and happiness. Certainly our friends contribute to our enjoyment of life, but personal fulfillment and life satisfaction are our responsibility—not theirs. Friends give us room to maneuver through life on our own terms, pursuing our own unique talents and interests. In contrast, a strong mutual expectation of emotional fulfillment in a marriage intertwines each person's happiness with the other's. Given the many contributors to happiness, from genetics to life choices, expecting a marriage to make you happy may be expecting too much, and assuming responsibility for another's happiness may be too great a burden.

VARIETIES OF LOVE

Passionate versus Companionate Love

Love comes in many shapes and sizes. One of the most basic distinctions is between passionate or romantic love and companionate love (Berscheid & Walster, 1978; Hatfield, 1988; Walster & Walster, 1978). This distinction parallels our discussion of the overlapping, yet different meanings of love and friendship. **Passionate or romantic love** typically involves strong sexual attraction, infatuation, total absorption, exclusivity (nobody but you), and emotions that run the full gamut from ecstasy to anguish. Specific components of passionate love include, preoccupation with our lover, idealization of his or her personal attributes, physiological arousal when in the person's company, desire for physical closeness, and a strong need for reciprocity (to be loved in return) (Hatfield & Sprecher, 1986). As you might guess, passionate love describes romance in its early stages. Your first author has been married for 40 years, and guarantees that his wife does not idealize him, is not particularly aroused in his presence (other than humor or irritation), and is certainly not preoccupied or infatuated with their relationship.

Companionate love, on the other hand, built on a special kind of loving friendship, would describe your first author's marriage. Some years ago, my wife and I gave each other identical Hallmark cards for our anniversary. The cards celebrated deep and abiding friendship and not romantic or passionate love. We had both started feeling a bit awkward about the passionate, "can't wait to get in bed," "you make my life complete," and "without you I'm nothing" sayings, in what we came to regard as "syrupy" anniversary cards. We love each other dearly, but it is not the hot fire of passion, but the warm glow of affection and appreciation that come from having spent four decades in the trenches of life together that make our marriage satisfying. This slower-developing **companionate love** is less emotional, calmer, and more serene than passionate love. It reflects the fact that your spouse has become your best friend and soul mate in your journey through life. After decades of marriage, who else knows you as well? Who else have you shared so much of your life with? If nothing else, the sheer amount of years together is not replaceable. For me, at 60 years old, I will never have another 40-year marriage. I know I'm not living to 100! It should be noted that, despite the similarities between companionate love and close friendships, there is a difference. A warm hug from your wife is different than a heartfelt hug from a good same-sexed friend. Both feel good, but you can't get sex out of the equation. Even older couples still "do it," even if not as frequently as when they were first married!

Triangular Theory of Love

The varieties of love are captured in Sternberg's three-part theory of love's essential ingredients (Sternberg, 1986, 1987). In Sternberg's model, intimacy, passion, and commitment each represent one side of a triangle describing the love shared by two people. **Intimacy** refers to mutual understanding, warm affection, and mutual concern for the other's welfare. **Passion** means strong emotion, excitement, and physiological arousal, often tied to sexual desire and attraction. **Commitment** is the conscious decision to stay in a relationship for the long haul. It includes a sense of devotion to the relationship and a willingness to work on maintaining it. By putting together different combinations of the three ingredients, Sternberg's model describes several varieties of love and the specific components of romantic and companionate love discussed above.

ROMANTIC LOVE (INTIMACY + PASSION) High intimacy and passion describe romantic love in Sternberg's model. It may seem strange not to include commitment, but Sternberg argues that commitment is not a defining feature of romantic love. A summer romance, for example, may involve intimate mutual disclosure and strong passion, but no commitment to continue the relationship at summer's end.

COMPANIONATE LOVE (INTIMACY + COMMITMENT) As we have noted, companionate love is a slow-developing love built on high intimacy and strong commitment. When youthful passions fade in a marriage, companionate love, based on deep, affectionate friendship provides a solid foundation for a lasting and successful relationship.

FATUOUS LOVE (PASSION + COMMITMENT) AND INFATUATED LOVE (PASSION ONLY) Both of these types might be regarded as forms of immature, blind or unreasonable love built on passion. Fatuous love combines high passion and commitment with an absence of intimacy. This would describe people who hardly know each other, but are caught up in a whirlwind passionate romance. Their commitment is based on passion and sustained solely by passion. Because passion is likely to fade with time, fatuous love relationships are unlikely to last. The same can be said for infatuated love, based only on passion, without intimacy or commitment. This might describe a teen romance in which sexual passion is taken for love, or a one-night sexual affair between people who barely know each other, and have no intentions of developing a relationship. Infatuated love may also describe the sense of awe, adoration, and sex-related feelings that some people have for their favorite Hollywood movie or music celebrity.

EMPTY LOVE (COMMITMENT ONLY) No passion, no intimacy, just a commitment to stay together. Appropriately called empty love, this would describe an emotionally "dead" relationship that both members find some reason to continue. Reasons might include things such as convenience, financial benefits, keeping up appearances, or a sense of obligation or duty.

CONSUMMATE LOVE (INTIMACY + PASSION + COMMITMENT) Consummate or complete love is marked by high intimacy, passion, and commitment. It is a form of love that many people desire, but Sternberg is doubtful that it can be sustained. As in romantic love, the passionate component typically decreases over time. Yet as Hacker (1979) points out, most of us know a couple that seems to epitomize this type of love: "We all know couples who have been married twenty or thirty years and still seem passionately attached to each other. A few look as if they just came away from bed, or can't wait to get back there. We see them at restaurant tables for two, chattering together—and not about the children. Or they prefer to stay home by themselves, perhaps each engrossed in a book, so long as they are across from each other" (p. 27).

Sternberg's three-component model of love has received good empirical support. People's understanding of love's primary features and the differences among various types of relationships appear to fit well with the intimacy/passion/commitment conception (Aron & Westbay, 1996; Sternberg, 1998b). For example, an ideal lover was rated high on all three components; friendship was rated high on intimacy and commitment, but low on passion; and a sibling relationship scored high on commitment, but low on intimacy and passion. Other taxonomies have also been developed and found empirically useful in capturing the richness of love and love styles (e.g., Hendrick & Hendrick, 1993, 2003; Lee, 1988). Of love's many varieties, romantic and companionate love, involving varying degrees and combinations of romance/passion and friendship, seem the most basic and widely applicable way to think about differences in our closest relationships.

Cultural Context of Love, Marriage, and Divorce

In the remainder of this chapter, we will concentrate on one of our most important intimate relationships, namely marriage. Marriage and well-being are strongly connected. A successful marriage is one of the more powerful contributors to enhanced individual health and happiness (see Chapter 5). Unhappy marriages have an equally strong connection to unhappiness and diminished health. As David Myers remarked, ". . . a bad marriage is worse than no marriage at all" (1992, p. 158). Since most people marry, the level of well-being within society as a whole would also seem to be influenced by the overall quality and state of individual marriages. U.S. Census Bureau statistics show that about 90% of us will eventually marry at some time during our lives (Goldstein & Kenney, 2001; Noller & Feeney, 2006). U.S. census data for 2002 showed that 60% of men and 57% of women were currently married at the time they completed the survey. Statistics also tell us something about the state of marriage today compared to the past. Most of the news is not good. Despite its potential for contributing to lasting happiness, the ratio of successful to failed marriages is not high. Major reviews of census data, national attitude surveys, and longitudinal studies of married couples paint a rather dismal picture of the current state of marriage compared to the past (e.g., Berscheid & Reis, 1998; Bryant, Bolland, Burton, Hurt, & Bryant, 2006; Goldstein & Kenney, 2001; Miller et al., 2007; Myers, 2000b; Popenoe & Whitehead, 2004).

Starting in the mid-1960s through the 1970s, dramatic changes occurred in marriage and these have been sustained to the present. Most of us are familiar with the most significant change: marriages no longer last. The divorce rate can be computed in several ways, but the basic conclusion remains the same. In today's America, some 50% of all new marriages will end in divorce or separation (Myers, 2000b; Popenoe & Whitehead, 2004). Other Western societies, such as Netherlands, Sweden, Canada, and England, have also seen increases in divorce, but U.S. divorce rates are nearly double those of other developed countries. Divorce rates have always been higher within the first 5 to 7 years of marriage, consistent with the conventional wisdom about the "7-year itch." However, today many longer-term marriages also fail (i.e., 10 years and up). There appears to be no "safe" point beyond which all marriages last, although after 15 years, the divorce rate does drop substantially. And while most people will eventually remarry after divorce, second and third marriages fail at higher rates than first-time marriages.

Other statistics seem to signal a retreat from marriage (data from reviews by Bryant et al., 2006; Miller et al., 2007; Myers, 2000b; Noller, 2006). Compared to the 1950s and 1960s, people are marrying later (in their early 20s then, versus later 20s now), with more than 33% of people now remaining single into their middle 30s. A retreat from marriage is also suggested by the facts that more people are choosing to remain single; the remarriage rate after divorce has declined, particularly among women; and the cohabitation rate has increased. The percentage of people who live together before marriage has increased dramatically. Nearly a third of American households are made up of unmarried men and women living together. An estimated 50% of college students live with a romantic partner without being married. Does cohabitation increase the success of a future marriage? The idea that a "trial" marriage may help couples know if they are "right" for each other is undercut by the fact that couples who cohabitate before marriage have higher divorce rates than non-cohabitating couples, unless they cohabitate after getting engaged to be married. It appears that cohabitation before marriage attracts people with less commitment to marriage and less willingness to work at dealing with the inevitable conflicts that long-term relationships entail. Cohabitation may also make marriage seem less desirable and easier to dissolve if it is considered dissatisfying. Is cohabitation an alternative form of a stable marriage? Apparently not. Noller (2006) cites evidence that cohabitating couples part ways at rates of 50% within 2 years and 90% by five.

Why Don't Marriages Last?

Cultural changes are clearly implicated in our country's high divorce rate. If the divorce rate were 1% instead of 50%, then a failed marriage would suggest individualized causes of divorce. We could ask the few divorced couples, "Why didn't your marriage make it when almost everyone else's does?" And we could study what is unique and different about divorcing couples. However, a 50% divorce rate suggests two things. First, there must be commonalities in the reasons for divorce. There are about 1 million divorces per year in this country. Can there be 1 million different reasons for failed marriages? Second, the high prevalence of divorce suggests it is successful marriages, not failed ones that are becoming unique. That is, it seems increasingly appropriate to ask happy,

long-term married couples, "How has your marriage made it when so many others don't?"

INCREASED FREEDOM AND DECREASED CONSTRAINTS A number of researchers have noted the interplay between internal and external factors in people's decisions to stay or leave a relationship (e.g., Kelley, 1979; Kelley & Thibaut, 1978; Levinger, 1976; Levinger & Levinger, 2003; Myers, 2000b). Both Levinger (1976) and Rusbult (1983), for example, have developed models focusing on how commitment to marriage is affected by a couple's level of satisfaction, by the costs and barriers related to leaving the relationship, available alternatives, and the extent of accumulated personal investment in the marriage. If you consider the cultural/historical changes relevant to these factors over the last 40 years or so, one explanation for the rise in divorce seems clear. It is simply easier today than in the past to get out of an unhappy marriage and with fewer costs. In short, more freedom and fewer constraints means more divorce.

In the past, unhappy married couples considering a divorce faced a number of barriers to dissolving their relationship (see Bryant et al., 2006; Harvey & Weber, 2002; Miller et al., 2007; Myers, 2000b, for reviews). First, before the women's movement and two-career families, many stay-at-home women were dependent on their husbands for their financial livelihood. Divorce often meant a dramatic drop in income, a relatively bleak future in providing for their children, and the prospect of entering the workforce with few job skills and little or no experience. Second, divorce at one time carried a significant cultural stigma for both men and women. Prominent politicians, for example, needed to keep their marital difficulties private so as to preserve a good family image because divorce could be very damaging to a political career. Third, the importance of staying together "for the sake of the kids" was a common belief. Sacrificing one's own happiness for the well-being of one's children was a stronger expectation in the past. Fourth, beliefs about the sanctity of marriage—that it should be preserved at all cost—were reflected in social norms and in the laws governing divorce. For example, a woman seeking advice about marriage difficulties from a friend, parent, counselor, or minister was more likely told to "kiss and make-up" (that is, to find ways to make the marriage work), rather than consider a divorce. The legal system also upheld the importance of marriage by permitting a divorce only when relatively serious offenses or prolonged conflict could be shown. In the past, even if they weren't particularly happy, married couples could find a number of reasons for maintaining a commitment to their marriage. This may have led some couples to work out their difficulties and develop satisfying marriages. For others, it may have meant being trapped in an emotionally empty or conflict-ridden relationship.

The direction of cultural change since the 1960s has been toward a reduction in the barriers to, and costs of, divorce. Marriages between two people with professional careers are now quite common. Each spouse can make it on her or his own if the marriage ends. Within the United States, women's increasing participation in the workforce is strongly correlated with the rise in divorce rates. And, a woman who brings in significantly more money than her husband has a higher risk of future divorce than a woman whose income is equal to, or less than, her husband's (Miller et al., 2007). Increased financial independence allows greater freedom to leave an unhappy marriage. Spouses who *do* divorce are less likely to face social disapproval. Divorce, in large measure because it is so common, is not stigmatized as strongly as in the past. Politicians, corporate executives, and other prominent people no longer cover up their failed marriages and seem to suffer few, if any, consequences. Surveys show that staying together for the sake of the kids is also less of a barrier to divorce today. Thornton (1989) found that by 1985 only 20% of women in his survey believed that unhappily married couples should stay together because they had children. A common belief today seems to be that a stable and conflict-free single-parent family is a better environment for kids than a two-parent family with emotional problems.

Finally, the courts and conventional wisdom have also accommodated the changing cultural context of marriage. Many states now have no-fault divorce laws that grant divorces because of "irreconcilable differences," which would seem to include everything from boredom and unhappiness to, "I think I can do better with someone else." Because divorce is commonly accepted, the advice and help couples in troubled marriages receive from others is likely to be more accepting of divorce as well. In summary, compared to the past, more people today seem to believe that divorce is a reasonable and viable solution to marital problems. The increased freedom to dissolve a marriage, like the constraints that held marriages together in the past, may be a dual-edged sword that cuts both ways. On one hand, freedom means the possibility of a better life, rather than being trapped in an unhappy marriage. On the other hand, increased freedom may make ending a marriage *too* easy an option. That is, rather than making a commitment to do the hard work that might resolve marital difficulties, people may view divorce as the simplest and easiest solution.

GETTING MARRIED AND STAYING MARRIED: IS LOVE THE ANSWER? More so today than in the past, marriage is not a prerequisite for having sex, for having children, or for a woman's financial well-being. Sex outside marriage is widely accepted (Myers, 2000b); a third of children are born out of wedlock (Miller et al., 2007); and many women enjoy financial independence. A man's ability to provide for his family is less important to women when they can provide for themselves. In addition, people used to believe that a pre-marital pregnancy meant the couple "had to get married." If they didn't, we had the image of the "shotgun" wedding, in which the bride's father compelled the groom to take responsibility for the child and to maintain the social respectability of his daughter. Today, marriage is more of a choice—freer of the constraints, social norms, and practical necessities of the past. Survey research suggests marriage is a choice that is increasingly and more exclusively based on love.

Think about the following question: If a person had all the other qualities you desired, would you marry this person if you were *not* in love? When American college students were surveyed in 1967, 35% of men and 76% of women said yes to this question (Simpson et al., 1986). Men evidently had more romantic notions for the basis for marriage, whereas women were more practical-minded. For women, desirable qualities trumped love. However, nearly three decades later, "no" was the overwhelming answer to the same question by both men and women (86% of men and 91% of women said no) (Allgeier & Wiederman, 1991, cited in Hatfield & Rapson, 2006). In current American culture, being in love appears to be the major reason to get married. The ability of love to prevail over differences in people's social status, religion, backgrounds, and life circumstances is a prominent theme in romantic movies. Think of the classic love story in the movie

Pretty Woman. Why would a rich, powerful attorney marry a prostitute? Answer: He fell in love.

Is the importance of romantic love a peculiar feature of Western individualistic cultures? For a time, historical investigations suggested that romantic love was a Western cultural invention that was not prominent in non-Western societies. More collectivist cultures—especially those in which parents arranged marriages—were thought to emphasize more practical considerations, such as endowments, social status, and religious compatibility. However, more extensive and detailed recent work by anthropologists has shown that passionate romantic love appears to be nearly universal in cultures around the world, with few exceptions (Jankowiak, 1995). Culture shapes its prominence and particular expressive form, but passionate love is not unique to Western individualistic societies.

Large-scale survey studies affirm the universality of passion and romance as bases for marriage. In his monumental study of mate selection, Buss (1994) asked over 10,000 people from 37 different countries to rate 18 characteristics according to their desirability in choosing a mate. Participants varied widely in their levels of affluence, language, religion, ethnic/racial background, and political beliefs. Despite these differences, the number-one desirable trait, chosen by men and women across all the countries, was love/mutual attraction. After love, cultures did vary in the particular qualities viewed as desirable. For example, among Chinese, Indonesians, Iranians, and Israelis, chastity was important. For French, Norwegian, and Swedish individuals, this was not an important trait and some even considered it a disadvantage.

Cross-cultural studies that ask, "If a person had all the other qualities you desired, would you marry him/her if you were not in love?" also find strong support for the love–marriage connection (e.g., Levine, Sato, Hashimoto, & Verma, 1995; Sprecher et al., 1994). Among diverse cultures around the globe, few people endorse a loveless marriage. Based on their review of cultural differences and historical changes in passionate love, Hatfield and Rapson concluded that the differences between Western and Eastern cultures appear to be "fast disappearing." ". . . Young people in a variety of traditional cultures are increasingly adopting 'Western' patterns—placing a high value on 'falling in love,' pressing for gender equality in love and sex, and insisting on marrying for love (as opposed to agreeing to arranged marriages)" (2006, p. 240).

Passion and romance have much do with why people marry. What do they have to do with why people divorce? If you recall our discussion of the difference between friendship and romantic love, you can probably anticipate the answer. First, many social observers believe that the increased emphasis on passion/romance is linked to the increased emotional expectations for marriage (Miller et al., 2007; Myers, 2000b; Phillips, 1988). As practical reasons for marriage have faded, expectations of personal satisfaction and fulfillment seem to have taken their place. A marriage today seems to depend more and more on the "sweetness of its contents" (Berscheid & Campbell, 1981). Why should you stay married if you're marriage is not happy, satisfying, exciting, and sexually/emotionally fulfilling? In the past, answers might have included children, finances, and social respectability. Today, the answer seems to be that if you're not happy and fulfilled there is something wrong with your marriage. The concern here is that these expectations are simply too high and set people up for disappointment when the realities of marriage start to sink in. Disillusionment may then lead to divorce. Clearly, saying that people expect too much of marriage is a judgment call related to the scope and degree of expectations. A good marriage certainly is a significant source of personal happiness and no one expects or wants an unhappy marriage. But the exact point at which expectations become unreasonable is difficult to pinpoint.

However, a second problem with the romantic love–marriage connection helps clarify the issue of reasonable versus unreasonable expectations. Here, the evidence is fairly clear. One significant difficulty with passionate romance is that it does not last. Marrying for romance is one thing, but staying married only if passionate romance continues is quite another. Evaluating a marriage primarily on the strength of romantic and passionate emotions seems a recipe for disillusionment and divorce. Longitudinal studies consistently find a decline in men and women's ratings of satisfaction with their marriages, ratings of overall marriage quality, and the frequency of expressions of positive affection (Bradbury, 1998; Karney & Bradbury, 1995; Kurdek, 1999). As you can see in Figure 11.2 based on Kurdek's (1991) data, the decline in marital satisfaction is steepest in the first few years of marriage, then levels off to remain somewhat stable, and then shows another drop at 8 to 10 years. Studies of long-term marriages (20 years and more) do show more

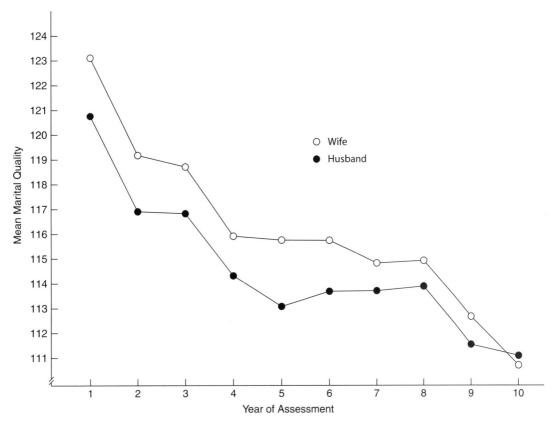

FIGURE 11.2 **Decline in Marital Satisfaction for Husbands and Wives Over 10 Years**
Source: Kurdek, L. A. (1999). The nature and predictors of the trajectory of change in marital quality for husbands and wives over the first 10 years of marriage. *Developmental Psychology, 35*, 1283–1296. Copyright American Psychological Association. Reprinted by permission.

stable levels of satisfaction and there is some debate about whether there is an upswing in satisfaction in very long-term marriages (Berscheid & Reis, 1998). These data do not mean that couples typically go from newlywed bliss to misery. The declines are relative to where most marriages start. The number of couples describing their marriages as "very happy" is high at the beginning, but much lower as the length of marriage increases. At one time, the decline in marriage satisfaction was thought to be associated with having children and assuming the challenges associated with parenthood. However, more recent research shows similar declines occurring among couples without children (Berscheid & Reis, 1998).

Research by Huston and his colleagues provides an instructive example of how these changes are related to divorce (Huston, Caughlin, Houts, Smith, & George, 2001; Huston, Niehuis, & Smith, 2001). This study is also known as the PAIR Project, which stands for The Process of Adaptation in Intimate Relationships. This is an ongoing longitudinal study of 168 couples that were married in 1981. Results for the first 13 years showed that 35% of the couples had divorced, another 20% were unhappy with their marriages, and only 45% were considered happily married. Even the happily married couples were less affectionate and less satisfied than they had been at the beginning of their marriages. PAIR Project researchers found strong support for a disillusionment model of marital satisfaction and divorce. The couples at greatest risk for divorce were those who experienced the steepest declines in marital satisfaction and feelings of love and romance. Ironically, couples that divorced after 7 years *began* their marriages with *higher* levels of both affection and romance. "As newlyweds, the couples who divorced after 7 or more years were almost giddily affectionate, displaying about one-third more affection than spouses who were later happily married. However, consistent with the disillusionment model, the intensity of their romance dissipated over the 1st year of marriage, reflected in a dramatic drop in how affectionate they were with each other and declines in their views of each other's responsiveness" (Huston et al., 2001, p. 249).

REALISM OR IDEALISM? Most couples seem to go through a period of disillusionment, as the realities of marriage sink in and the idealization of one's partner and one's relationship begin to fade. Does this mean that the happy couples are those who began their marriages with more realistic views and avoided disillusionment? Or might it be that happy couples began with the same illusions, but found ways to maintain them? The research literature does not provide a definitive answer to these questions. The value of *both* realism *and* idealization are supported. Studies by Murray and her colleagues suggest that some degree of idealization contributes to a couple's happiness and satisfaction (Murray, Holmes, & Griffin, 1996a, 1996b). Couples who had the most positive views of each other's personal qualities were not only happier, but were less likely to break up. Murray and her colleagues believe that the tendency to view our partners more positively than they see *themselves* means that we overlook or put a positive spin on our partners' shortcomings. This is the view that mothers often have of their children. They see the best in their kids and downplay or ignore faults. To the extent that this idealization is mutual, it is easy to see how each person's self-esteem and satisfaction with a relationship would be enhanced.

Self-verification theory posits that people desire evaluations that affirm or verify their own self-views (Swann, 1983, 1987). Specifically, people want positive feedback about positive qualities and negative evaluations of their less desirable qualities. We each want verification of our own self-view. As Swann (1990) put it, people want to be "known"— not necessarily "adored." Relationships are enhanced when your partner affirms your own self-view because this means that she or he knows you as you know yourself. The authenticity of your partner's understanding of "who you really are" creates strong feelings of intimacy.

The opposing nature of idealistic and realistic appraisals may be more apparent than real: (a) because the effect of each may depend on the length and developmental stage of a relationship, and (b) because both probably co-exist in healthy

relationships. Research suggests that idealized and positive views of the partner contribute to satisfaction and feelings of intimacy in short-term dating relationships and at the beginning of marriage. However, as relationships mature, more accurate information becomes important and contributes more to satisfaction and intimacy (Campbell, Lackenbauer, & Muise, 2006; Swann, De La Ronde, & Hixon, 1994). Too much idealization may actually get a longer-term relationship in trouble. It is important to know with some degree of accuracy your partner's strengths and weaknesses. Imagine if excessive drinking were given a positive spin or if you glossed over your partner's lack of financial planning and checkbook balancing ability. Probably both realism and a degree of positive idealization co-exist in healthy longer-term relationships. Realism about specific traits and abilities would seem to contribute both to feelings of intimacy and to more effective assignment of relationship roles and responsibilities according to each partner's strengths and weaknesses.

On the other hand, some idealization is undoubtedly important in making people feel an overall sense of positive regard and acceptance. That is, we need to feel that, despite the reality of our imperfections, we are loved, appreciated, and positively viewed. A recent longitudinal study of married couples by Neff and Karney (2005) affirmed the dual importance of accuracy and global adoration. Feelings of mutual and global adoration ("you're the greatest") were widely shared among newlyweds. However, the *benefits* of this adoration depended on whether it reflected an *accurate* understanding of partners' specific traits. Adoration alone was not enough. Neff and Karney concluded that "Global adoration lacking in specific accuracy not only leaves spouses vulnerable to disappointment as their partners' faults surface over the course of the relationship but also may lead partners to doubt the credibility of their spouses' love" (2005, p. 495).

SATISFACTION AND CONFLICT As if the picture were not gloomy enough already, studies suggest that married couples today experience more conflict and somewhat less marital satisfaction than in the past. Family life appears more complicated and hectic today, in part because both husbands and wives typically work and have less time to spend together (Amato & Previti, 2003; Rogers & Amato, 2000). Managing family concerns, from childcare and paying bills, to getting older kids to their many after-school activities, may take a toll on a marriage.

National surveys show some drop (5% or so) in the percentage of married couples describing their marriage as very happy today compared to the 1970s (Glenn, 1991; Glenn & Weaver, 1988). The cause of this decline is unclear. Does it reflect an actual decline in marital happiness, perhaps due to the increase in conflict? Or might it be the exaggerated expectations of marital happiness that are disappointed by the realities of marriage, or some combination of both? Whatever the case, it is worth remembering two facts: (1) married people are still consistently found to be significantly happier than never-married singles; and (2) there is a strong tendency for very happy people to report that their marriages are also happy and satisfying (Myers, 2000a). The question is, "What are the ingredients of a happy marriage?" Some of the answers are suggested by studies of what people bring to a marriage.

WHAT PEOPLE BRING TO ROMANTIC RELATIONSHIPS

Experts seem to agree that cultural changes have made happy long-term marriages somewhat more difficult to achieve today than in the past. The success or failure of marriage also depends on the particular mix of the two spouses' characteristics. People bring a diversity of personality traits and beliefs to their romantic relationships (Fitness, 2006; Vangelisti, 2006). Some people are better suited to intimate relationships than others. For example, the emotional instability and negative emotionality of people high in the personality trait of neuroticism make satisfying relationships difficult for them to achieve, and we know that drug abuse, alcoholism, and physical abuse are frequent causes of divorce (see Miller et al., 2007). Some amount of failure undoubtedly also occurs because the wrong people got married. As they try to build a life together, a married couple's differences may cause too much conflict, making love difficult to sustain. One of the more important things people bring to a marriage is their particular style of relating to intimate partners.

Attachment Style

Think for a minute about your first close and intimate relationship. When did you: first learn about trusting someone and having your emotional needs attended to and cared for; first reveal your deeper feelings, fears, and needs; first feel that no one else could replace this person in your life; first display lots of mutual affection, like hugging, kissing, and holding; first know that this relationship was for life? For most of us, our first "love" experiences were with parents—often our moms. Nearly all of us develop an intense attachment bond with our primary caretakers—most frequently our biological parents. **Attachment theory** raises the intriguing possibility that some of our most basic, and perhaps unconscious, emotional responses to intimacy are shaped by the kind of relationship we had with our parents. If this seems a bit far-fetched, consider this: Think of a romantic involvement in which you got to know your partner extremely well, including all his or her little quirks and peculiarities. Then, think of the first time you met your partner's family. Did you have any "aha" experiences such as, "*Now* I see why you avoid emotionally charged issues in our relationship. Your whole family does!" Or, "No wonder you say whatever is on your mind, even if it's negative and critical. Your family is like the show *Brothers and Sisters* on TV—absolute honesty in expressing feelings, no matter who it might offend!" How early relationships might affect later ones begins with studies of infants and young children.

Infant Attachments

Psychiatrist John Bowlby was one of the first to describe different types of attachment between children and their parents. During World War II, many British parents sent their children to the country where they would be safer from Germany's nightly bombings of London. Bowlby observed that children's reactions to separation from their parents were quite varied and seemed to reflect different kinds of parent–child bonds or attachments (see Bowlby, 1988, for a current review). Ainsworth and her colleagues developed a more formal assessment of attachment styles using what became known as the "strange situation test" (Ainsworth, Blehar, Waters, & Wall, 1978). Paralleling Bowlby's earlier work, these researchers found three distinct attachment patterns between infants and mothers (or any caretaker to whom an infant is attached). The strange situation test involves observing an infant, its mother, and an adult stranger in an unfamiliar room with toys available. The mother and stranger move in and out of the room according to a set sequence.

Infants are sometimes with their mothers only, sometimes with the stranger only, and sometimes alone. A majority of infants tested in this situation show a *secure attachment style*. In this style, the infant explores the room and the toys confidently when its mother is present, becomes mildly upset and explores less when it is left by the mother (either alone or with the stranger), shows pleasure and reassurance when the mother returns, and then resumes exploring the room. Home observations show that mothers of securely attached infants responded warmly and promptly to their infants' desires for contact comfort.

A minority of infants show an *avoidant attachment style*. Here, infants do not show any visible distress when separated from their mothers and, most tellingly, they actively avoid contact with their mothers when the mothers re-enter the room. At home, mothers of avoidant infants are consistently negative, rejecting, critical and often neglectful, in the form of failing to provide comfort when their infants are upset.

An even smaller minority of infants showed an *anxious-ambivalent attachment style*, in which the infant does not explore much, even when its mother is present, becomes very upset when she leaves, and both seeks *and* simultaneously resists her comfort when she returns. Mothers of this style are found to be unpredictable in their responses to their infants' desires for comfort, sometimes showing a positive response and sometimes responding in a rejecting or controlling manner.

The nature of childhood attachment has been shown to predict behavior in later relationships (e.g., Ainsworth, 1989; Schneider, Atkinson, & Tardiff, 2001). As you might expect, securely attached infants generally go on to have healthier relations with others. For example, longitudinal studies find that compared to insecure children, securely attached children tend to be more socially skilled and competent and are more likely to have close families, friendships, and longer-term romantic relations (e.g., Carlson, Sroufe, & Egeland, 2004). Other studies find that attachment styles may be transferred from one relationship to the next, building upon early attachment histories (Brumbaugh & Fraley, 2006) and that a couple's personal attachment styles are predictive of how they perceive, feel about, and relate to each other after the birth of their first child (Wilson, Rholes, Simpson, & Tran, 2007). In this latter study, anxious and avoidant styles were related to

less supportive partner responses and more jealousy of the infant.

Researchers do not believe that early childhood experiences represent adulthood destiny (see Hazan et al., 2006). Despite evidence of moderate levels of stability in attachment style over the first 19 years of life (Fraley, 2002), people's orientation toward relationships can be altered and changed by life experiences. Divorce, death of a spouse or parent, new relationship experiences, and new partners can all influence our basic attachment style. In addition, studies that do show stability may be confounded with genetically-determined temperament. Some infants are constitutionally "laid back" or "high strung," making the infant's temperament—not treatment by parents—primarily responsible for the nature of the parent–child relationship.

It also needs to be noted that the meaning and value of different attachment styles may be unique to Western individualistic societies like the United States. For example, Japanese parents *appear* to foster insecure attachment and "needy" children when evaluated by Western attachment criteria (Rothbaum, Weisz, Pott, Miyake, & Morelli, 2000). Japanese parents appear indulgent, permissive, and overly protective to Western eyes. They do not seem to foster the secure base necessary for independence and self-confidence that defines secure attachment. However, these judgments likely reflect Western standards and biases. The Japanese and all other cultures have their own criteria for relationships and they raise their children accordingly. They nurture healthy children who are well-adapted *to their culture*. Rothbaum and his colleagues point out that attachment theory and measurement, in its current Westernized form, simply does not fit other, non-Westernized cultures.

Despite these qualifications, the possibility remains that that our childhood experiences, at least in the West, may be significant. For example, a person whose own childhood was marked by an absence of warmth and love might be strongly motivated to find an intense and all-absorbing romantic love relationship as a teen or adult. And it makes sense that a person who experienced harsh criticism and rejection when she sought the love of her parents may be "gun shy" when it comes to developing intimate adult relationships. Finally, if you experienced a healthy, warm, and loving relationship with your parents, wouldn't this inform your ideas about desirable and undesirable relationships in the future, perhaps even influencing the qualities you look for in a spouse? Setting aside all the possible Freudian dynamics, why wouldn't a young girl or boy think of marrying someone like Dad or Mom if they loved, respected, and admired their parents and experienced an enjoyable childhood because their parents were good parents who were happily married?

With both the possibilities and qualifications in mind, researchers have found attachment styles to be extremely useful in capturing adults' cognitive and emotional orientation toward romantic and other close relationships (Cassidy & Shaver, 1999). Measures of adult attachment styles have a good deal of face validity in the sense that we can often "see" ourselves or someone we know as typifying one, or some combination of the different attachment styles.

Adult Attachment Styles

Which of the following would best describe how you think about close relationships? (from Hazan & Shaver, 1987):

A. I am somewhat uncomfortable being close to others; I find it difficult to trust them completely, difficult to allow myself to depend on them. I am nervous when anyone gets too close, and often, others want to be more intimate that I feel comfortable being.

B. I find it relatively easy to get close to others and am comfortable depending on them and having them depend on me. I don't worry about being abandoned or about someone getting too close to me.

C. I find others are reluctant to get as close as I would like. I often worry that my partner doesn't really love me or won't want to stay with me. I want to get very close to my partner, and this sometimes scares people away.

Shaver and his colleagues found that this simple one-item test was sufficient for people to reliably classify themselves according to their attachment style (A is avoidant, B is secure, and C is anxious-ambivalent) (Bartholomew & Shaver, 1998; Hazan & Shaver, 1987).

Over time, both the conceptualization and measurement of adult attachment styles have been refined. The current view is that attachment styles are continuous rather than discrete categories and reflect two underlying dimensions: *anxiety* and *avoidance* (Bartholomew & Horowitz, 1991; Brennan, Clark, & Shaver, 1998; Fraley & Waller, 1998; Hazan et al., 2006). The *anxiety* dimension describes a fear of abandonment and rejection and is assumed to express low self-esteem and a negative view of self. A lack of self-confidence and a belief in one's inadequacy causes anxiety in close relationships, perhaps because a person feels that her faults will be discovered or that he is not the kind of person that anyone would love. Conversely, people with a positive self-view are low in anxiety, do not fear abandonment, and are comfortable and confident in their intimate relationships.

The *avoidance* dimension describes the degree of trust and comfort (or lack thereof) in becoming intimate with others. High intimacy-avoidance presumably stems from viewing others with a mistrustful and suspicious eye or dismissing intimate relationships altogether as unnecessary because of a strong belief in one's own self-reliance (i.e., "I don't need intimate relationships"). Conversely, people low in avoidance are more trusting of others, enjoy intimacy, and do not worry that they will be mistreated. Because people can be high or low on the *anxiety* and/or the *avoidance* dimension, four different attachment styles can be described. These styles are overlapping, but for purposes of clarity they are described below as four distinct styles. Included in these descriptions are results from the multitude of studies that have examined the connection between individual differences in attachment style and characteristics of people's close and romantic relationships (see Bartholomew, 1990; Collins & Feeney, 2000; Feeney, 1999; Hazan et al., 2006, for reviews). Figure 11.3 shows the four styles defined by the two dimensions of avoidance and anxiety.

Secure attachment describes people with positive self-images who are low on both relationship anxiety and avoidance. These people are confident in themselves and the ability of their relationships to satisfy their needs. Compared to other attachment styles, the intimate and romantic relationships of people with a secure attachment style are characterized by greater trust and closeness, more positive than negative emotions, lower levels of jealousy, higher levels of marital satisfaction and adjustment, and more sensitive and supportive responses to the needs of one's

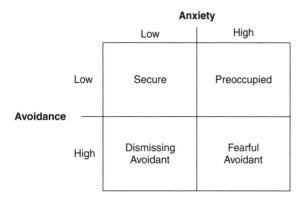

FIGURE 11.3 Four Attachment Styles Defined by Level of Anxiety and Avoidance

partner. Securely attached people are comfortable seeking support from others in times of distress. Surveys suggest that about 60% of people fit this attachment style (Mickelson, Kessler, & Shaver, 1997). Overall, secure attachment is associated with longer, stronger, and more satisfying intimate relations.

The **preoccupied attachment** style describes people who are low on avoidance because they want and enjoy intimacy, but are high in anxiety as a result of their low self-esteem. This style was referred to as anxious/ambivalent in previous classifications. The preoccupied style reflects a need for the approval and affection of others to prop up one's own lack of self-esteem. Such people might be described as "needy," "clingy," or even "greedy" in their need for intimacy and acceptance. While they may appear to be sensitive, caring, and supporting, these behaviors stem more from their own self-centered needs than from genuine concern for their partner. Their fear of abandonment may cause them to be highly controlling of their partners, to experience wide mood swings, and to experience intense jealousy concerning their romantic involvements. Although an extreme example, one can't help but think about the neurotic lover portrayed by Glenn Close in the movie *Fatal Attraction* as exemplifying the worst features of preoccupied attachment.

People with a **fearful avoidant attachment** style are high in avoidance and high in anxiety. A fear of rejection keeps people with this style from getting close to others, and their low opinion of themselves seems to be the major reason. If you don't like or love yourself you may assume others won't love you either. A fear of being unlovable and, therefore, likely to be rejected when people get

to know you well is strong motivation to avoid intimacy. People with this style view others as untrustworthy and likely to let them down. They feel that relying on others is too risky and are more pessimistic about lasting love. As you might expect, fearful attachment is associated with a variety of interpersonal difficulties including less willingness to provide comfort and support to others and being perceived by others as emotionally distant and even hostile.

Dismissing avoidant attachment combines high avoidance with low anxiety. This style describes people who are confident, self-reliant, and take pride in their independence. They view others as essentially irrelevant. That is, whether people like them or not is not a major concern, because they believe they can make it on their own. Intimate involvements with others are thought to be fraught with problems and not worth the trouble. The relationships of people with this style are marked by lower enjoyment, less commitment, and less intimacy compared to those with secure and preoccupied styles. If you recall our earlier discussion of the universal need for human attachments, you may wonder if people who dismiss the importance of relationships are exceptions to this general rule. A recent study titled, "No man is an island: The need to belong and dismissing avoidant attachment style," suggests that the answer is no (Carvallo & Gabriel, 2006). In this study, people with a dismissive orientation were found to experience more positive feelings in response to feedback that others liked and accepted them than people with a low dismissive view. Perhaps because dismissive types typically receive less affirmation from others, they are more affected when they do. Contrary to their claims, dismissive individuals *do* seem to care about how people think of them. Carvallo and Gabriel conclude that ". . . people with a dismissive attachment style also have a fundamental need to feel connected to others but because they have buried it under denial and a hard shell of indifference, it can only be glimpsed by giving them a taste of what all people need and desire most: inclusion and acceptance from others" (2006, p. 707).

Overall, secure attachment is a strong foundation for healthy and satisfying relationships, particularly if this style is shared between romantic partners. In their review of studies, Miller and his colleagues (2007) provide a long list of positive outcomes associated with this style. Compared to the other styles, secure people are more supportive of their partners, particularly in times of distress. They are more disclosing of intimate life details and have more satisfying social lives with their friends and lovers. Secure people also enjoy higher levels of emotional well-being and lower levels of emotional distress. Securely attached people seem to recapitulate the health of their relationships with their parents, which built a strong foundation for the rich and satisfying relationships that contribute so much to a happy life.

Research suggests that the majority (60%) of us fit, moreso than less, into the secure attachment style. However, it is important to remember that the four types are meant to be continuous—not discrete—categories. So, despite the virtues of secure attachment, most of us are probably a combination of attachment orientations defined by our degree of anxiety and avoidance. The more problematic styles are in the minority, although we can probably think of someone who fits the preoccupied, fearful avoidant, or dismissive style. The point here is to resist believing that, just because you are not overly confident in yourself or that you are somewhat cautious in opening up to others, this means you fit one of the negative styles and will have relationship problems, or that this fully explains the problems you have. The distance between high self-esteem and low self-esteem and between caution and avoidance is large. Even if we are not "pure" secure attachment types, we can still have satisfying relationships.

Conflict and Communication Skills

Attachment styles describe important features of people's global orientation toward intimate relationships. More specific behaviors and ways of thinking that enhance or damage relationships have also been studied extensively. A great deal of research has focused on how relationship partners deal with conflict and interpret negative behaviors. This is because some amount of conflict is inevitable in our intimate relations. Married couples may confront differences in their expectations and desires regarding managing finances, spending habits, frequency of sex, displays of affection, raising kids, dealing with in-laws, and keeping the house clean. Studies make clear that the success of a marriage depends heavily on open communication about disagreements and the ability to resolve them.

Focus on Research: The Power of the "Bad"

A curious implication of relationship research is that once a relationship is well established, its success seems to depend more on the *absence of conflict* (the bad) than it does on the *presence of affection* (the good) (Reis & Gable, 2003). A couple's satisfaction with their marriage is tied significantly more strongly to the level of conflict than it is to the level of positive behaviors. A well-known daily diary study found that nearly two-thirds of couples' marital satisfaction was related to the occurrence (or lack) of negative behaviors and conflict, and much less so to the occurrence (or lack) of positive behaviors (Wills, Weiss, & Patterson, 1974). In our intimate relationships, the bad seems much stronger than the good. A single negative act appears capable of "undoing" countless acts of affection and kindness.

The most extensive studies of marital conflict have been conducted by John Gottman and his colleagues (Gottman, 1994, 1998, 1999; Gottman & Krokoff, 1989; Gottman & Levenson, 1992). Among his many studies were intensive observations of married couples in his "love lab." This was an apartment set up to video-tape verbal, nonverbal, and physiological responses of couples as they talked about topics posed by Gottman. Some topics concerned sources of conflict and how they viewed each other's strengths and weaknesses, but the main point was to get couples to talk and to analyze their style of communication. Both the husbands' and wives' verbal and nonverbal behaviors were carefully recorded. Observations captured both subtle nonverbal behaviors (like a faint frown or raised eyebrows), and more obvious behaviors (such as smiling, one spouse interrupting the other, and expressions of anger, resentment, affection, and support).

Gottman and his colleagues consistently found that negative communication patterns were more predictive of marital satisfaction level and overall relationship quality than were displays of affection and kindness. Patterns of negative interaction were summarized as the "Four Horsemen of the Apocalypse" because of their destructive effects on relationships. The "Four Horsemen" are:

1. *Criticism*: A high percentage of negative as compared to positive comments, remarks, and nonverbal communications.
2. *Defensiveness*: Taking comments and criticism personally and responding to the feelings they created, rather than to the behavior they describe. This included rehearsing defensive thoughts such as "I'm not going to take it any more," or "Next time he/she says that, I am going to say . . . "
3. *Stonewalling*: Punishing a partner with the "silent treatment" by clamming up, refusing to respond and holding in anger, resentment, hurt feelings, and the real reasons for refusing to talk.
4. *Contempt*: Showing scorn, anger, and rejection through verbal and nonverbal means (e.g., rolling of eyes) and generally condemning the actions, motives, or personality of the other.

All marriages involve some amount of mutual criticism and hurtful things said in the heat of argument. Gottman's research found that it was *not* simply the presence of negative behaviors that distinguished happy/stable couples from those headed for divorce. Instead, what mattered was the *ratio* of positive to negative behaviors and the *degree of reciprocation* of negative behaviors ("negative affect reciprocity"). Somewhat amazingly, in counting up the positives and negatives in "love lab" observations, a ratio of 5 positive interactions to 1 negative interaction was found to be the dividing line between successful and unsuccessful relationships. That is, in healthy relationships, likely to last, there were five times more positive than negative interactions. Troubled relationships had very low ratios, meaning that negatives and positives were about equal, or that negatives out numbered positives. The 5-to-1 ratio supports the general principle that "bad is stronger than good." Evidently, the harm done by one bad thing needs to be offset by five good things for marriages to be satisfying. The 5-to-1 ratio suggests a fairly obvious approach to improving the quality of a relationship—namely, find ways to reward your partner! Gottman and Levenson (1992) argue that frequent and simple acts of kindness, concern, care, and affection can shift the ratio into the positive range. This makes conflict less likely and easier to resolve when it occurs.

Negative affect reciprocity may be one reason unhappy couples have a low positive-to-negative ratio. This term describes a tit-for-tat exchange of negative expressions, both verbal and nonverbal, that Gottman and his colleagues found contributes to the downward spiral of a relationship. If you think about your own relationships, you know that it's hard not to retaliate against a critical or hurtful comment made by an intimate partner. One partner's negative critical comment invites reciprocation from the other, which invites further retaliation, which may then escalate into a heated argument. As Gottman notes, anger, conflict, and disagreements can all be opportunities for deepening mutual understanding and increasing future satisfaction. Successful couples find ways to turn disagreements into growth in their relationship, and ways to repair the damage of conflict. However, distressed couples seem stuck in this negative affect reciprocity pattern and are unable or unwilling to respond in more constructive ways.

Demand/withdraw can be added to the list of negative interaction patterns described by Gottman's research. This pattern reflects what seems to be a fairly typical gender difference in response to conflict (Grossman & Wood, 1993). Women, who are often more attuned to and concerned about the ongoing quality of close relationships, make more demands to resolve problems and to improve a marriage than men (Christensen & Heavey, 1993). Relationship problems raised by one partner are sensitive issues because they directly or indirectly imply criticism of the other partner. In raising these issues, women are generally more emotionally expressive and report more intense emotions than men (Grossman & Wood, 1993). Men seem generally less sensitive to relationship problems and less comfortable talking about them. These differences may produce a pattern of interactions in which the woman makes demands to talk about a concern and the man withdraws or becomes defensive and refuses to confront the issue (Eldridge & Christensen, 2002). This frustrates the wife, who then makes more demands, which may lead to more strident withdrawal on her husband's part, like stomping off and slamming the door on the way out. This interaction pattern would likely frustrate both husband and wife and decrease the odds that problems will be resolved.

Attributions

In addition to negative communication patterns, people's characteristic style of explaining their partner's transgressions and faults also has much to do with relationship satisfaction (Bradbury & Fincham, 1990). If your partner forgets to do a favor you requested, or misses an important occasion like your birthday or anniversary, how do you explain it? Does it mean they really don't care about you, or do you give them the benefit of the doubt and assume there must have been a good reason? As you probably guessed, satisfied couples assume the best and unhappy couples assume the worst. **Relationship-enhancing attributions** are explanations for a partner's faults and transgressions that "excuse" the behavior because it is seen as determined by situations, rather than as a reflection of an enduring trait or lack of concern for the other partner. "Having a bad day" or "just being forgetful because of preoccupation with other things," puts a positive spin on otherwise negative and potentially hurtful actions. Enhancing attributions also work on the positive side. Positive behaviors are seen as stemming from a partner's desirable qualities and from their care and concern for the relationship. When good things happen, they are attributed to the person—not the situation. "He or she is so thoughtful and loving, look what I got for our anniversary." In contrast, unhappy couples show a **distress-maintaining** pattern of attributions. Negative behaviors, hurtful comments, and forgetting special occasions are attributed to permanent characteristics of the individual. "This just shows that you don't really care, and nothing is going to change because that's just the way you are!" It is little wonder that longitudinal studies have linked distress-maintaining attributions to low marital satisfaction throughout the course of a marriage (Fincham, Harold, & Gano-Phillips, 2000; Karney & Bradbury, 2000).

Implicit Theories and Expectations

People come into relationships with different implicit or informal theories about how relationships are supposed to work. These general ideas may shape the more specific ways people respond to, and evaluate, intimate relations. Knee and his colleagues have identified two distinct implicit theories, defined either by a belief in **romantic destiny** or by a belief in **relationship growth** (Knee, 1998). The basic premise of the romantic destiny theory is that two people are either compatible or they are not. If a marriage runs into difficulty, this signals a lack of compatibility—namely, an assumption that "we aren't right for each other." The growth theory,

on the other hand, assumes relationships are challenging and will grow and develop over time. As Knee and his colleagues described it, people following the growth theory ". . . are primarily interested in developing the relationship, and believe that relationships grow, not *despite* obstacles, but rather *because* of them" (Knee, Patrick, & Lonsbary, 2003, p. 41). Sample items from their Implicit Theory of Relationship Scale make the distinction between the two theories very clear. People who hold to the romantic destiny theory endorse items such as, "A successful relationship is mostly a matter of finding a compatible partner right from the start," and "Early troubles in a relationship signify a poor match between partners." Growth theory advocates would agree with items like the following: "Challenges and obstacles in a relationship can make love even stronger," and "It takes a lot of time and effort to cultivate a good relationship" (Knee et al., 2003, p. 41).

Research by Knee and his colleagues suggests that these general beliefs influence many aspects of a relationship—perhaps most importantly, the decision to stay or leave (Knee, Nanayakkar, Vietor, & Neighbors, 2002; Knee, Patrick, Vietor, Nanayakkar, & Neighbors, 2002; Knee, Patrick, Vietor, & Neighbors, 2004). A strong belief in romantic destiny leads to an interpretation of conflict as a sign of incompatibility over which couples can exert little control (i.e., "We're either right for each other or we're not"). Attributions for problems are likely to focus on individual traits (such as personality incompatibility) rather than circumstances. This makes relationship problems seem more stable and enduring and thus, unfixable. As marriages progress, a romantic destiny view may cause that typical drop in marital satisfaction (described earlier) to be seen as a sure sign of a bad choice. In fact, research shows that people with strong destiny beliefs are more likely to end a relationship if they are not satisfied with how it goes at the beginning (Knee, 1998).

The work-it-out perspective of the relationship growth theory is clearly a more hopeful and, many would say, more realistic approach to marriage, unless of course there really is one "right" person for each of us, and our job is to find that person for a marriage made in heaven. A belief in relationship growth provides a more positive and accepting perspective on the inevitable conflicts and disappointments married couples confront. From a growth perspective, conflict is a natural part of all relationships and does not mean that someone has to be at fault or that partners are incompatible. Instead, problems are seen as temporary and situational and, thus, solvable and likely to pass. Therefore, effort and commitment can make the difference between failure and success.

FOOD FOR THOUGHT: THE CONTOURS OF A HAPPY MARRIAGE

Two lessons of positive psychology that you have hopefully learned by now are: (1) The absence of the "bad" does not mean the presence of the "good." (2) Positive and negative emotional experiences are independent of one another. Applied to marriage, this means that, while the negative relationship behaviors we just reviewed make a marriage bad, their absence does not necessarily make a marriage good. It also means that good relationship behaviors are not simply the opposite of destructive behaviors. As Reis and Gable put it, "Relating well is not the same thing as not relating badly" (2003, p. 152). What takes a marriage above zero? Beyond just the absence of the bad to some level of enjoyment, contentment, and happiness? Studies of long-term and happily married couples provide some clues.

What Can Happy Couples Tell Us?

In a seminal study by Lauer and Lauer, 351 couples (married 15 years or more) were asked to select from a list of 39 statements those that best explained why their marriages had lasted (Lauer & Lauer, 1985; Lauer et al., 1990). Husbands and wives responded separately. The overwhelming majority of couples (300) described their marriages as happy ones. And men and women showed an amazing degree of agreement as to *why* their marriages were happy and successful. The most frequently endorsed reasons for a happy and enduring marriage can be grouped into two general categories: friendship and commitment.

FRIENDSHIP Deep and abiding friendship was the top reason couples gave for their lasting marriages. Both husbands and wives agreed, "My spouse is my best friend." Other statements clarified what they meant. "I like my spouse as a person." "My spouse has grown more interesting." "I confide in my spouse." In response to the more open-ended questions on the survey, one woman commented that she would want her husband as a friend even

if they weren't married—that's how much she liked him. A man married over 30 years said it had almost been like being married to "a series of different women" because he had watched his wife grow and change over time (Lauer & Lauer, 1985, p. 24). He found his wife more interesting now than when they first married. Others shared that they thought liking was as important as loving in a marriage. These positive views of marriage partners were reflected in the enjoyment of shared activities. "We laugh together." Men endorsed, "We share outside hobbies and interests" and women, "We have a stimulating exchange of ideas." Shared activities that are fun, exciting, and arousing may be very important in offsetting the boredom that can set in, in long-term marriages. This possibility received experimental support from a study that found an increase in global marital satisfaction after couples completed a novel and physiologically arousing activity (Aron, Norman, Aron, McKenna, & Heyman, 2000). In this study, married couples traversed an obstacle course while holding a cylindrical pillow between their bodies or heads. No hands, legs, or teeth were allowed to keep the pillow from falling to the ground. Couples found this activity, reminiscent of sack races at summer camp, to be fun and exciting. Evidently, the positive emotion they experienced generalized to their relationship, resulting in a more favorable evaluation. One ingredient in a successful marriage seems to be the ability to find exciting and fun things to do together.

Husbands and wives in happy marriages also share similar views on many of the potentially contentious issues within a marriage. "We agree on aims and goals." "We agree on a philosophy of life." "We agree on how and how often to show affection." "We agree about our sex life." Interestingly, fewer than 10% of these couples believed that enjoyable sex kept their marriages together. Most couples were happy with their sex lives, but others, even if they weren't, or had stopped having sex altogether, were still happy with their marriages (Lauer, et al., 1990). Evidently, if you have an enjoyable intimate friend as a spouse, sex is not critical to the success of your marriage, at least after you have been married for 15 years or more.

COMMITMENT Happy couples recognized the importance of strong commitment to making their marriages work and agreed with the statement, "Marriage is a long-term commitment." The basis of their commitment was also suggested by other responses (e.g., "Marriage is sacred." "An enduring marriage is important to social stability." "I want the relationship to succeed."). Consistent with Knee's work on the growth theory of relationships, successful couples believed that all marriages run into troubles and that you just have to "take it" until you can find ways to work it out. Agreement that "We discuss things calmly" suggests that happy couples take a positive approach to resolving conflicts.

These results affirm our earlier discussion of the differences between friendship and passionate romance. The deep friendship, intense liking, respect, comfort, and enjoyment expressed by the happy couples in the Lauer's study stand in contrast to marriages based on the more tenuous and fickle nature of passionate romance. The stable solidarity of friendship makes passion look like a shaky basis for a stable marriage. Many relationship researchers would agree that companionate love built on friendship is more enduring than romantic love built on passion. Contemplating the future of marriage, Hendrick and Hendrick (2002) see hopeful signs that companionate love and passionate love are being brought into better balance in young people's thinking about intimate relationships. They point to studies showing that college students frequently name their romantic partners as their closest friends. Hendrick and Hendrick conclude that "If one could also be good friends, perhaps even best friends with one's passionate lover, then perhaps the relationship could survive the turbulent comings and goings of passion" (2002, p. 473). Couples in the Lauer and Lauer study provided strong affirmation of this possibility.

Humor and Compatibility

One final morsel of food-for-thought: Earlier in this chapter, we discussed the importance of teasing, humor, and laughter to all our close relationships. Social support, intimacy, and concern are all significant, but for sheer pleasure and enjoyment you can't beat having fun with people you care about. It's no accident, then, that happy couples say they laugh together and that a sense of humor is high on the list of desirable qualities people seek in a potential mate. We know that frequency of sex declines even in good marriages, although

Hendrick and Hendrick (2002) argue that "sexual expression" might show up as declining far less if researchers included hugs, kisses, and other physical displays of affection as part of sexual behavior. Humor, however, apparently does not decline. Why else would 50-years-married couples say laughing together is what made their marriages last (Lauer et al., 1990)? Humor is undoubtedly one major reason happy couples enjoy each other's company. Given the benefits of positive emotions described throughout this book, it's no wonder successful couples enjoy enhanced health and happiness. In addition, as we mentioned earlier in this chapter, humor can detoxify conflict and relieve stress in a relationship.

The value of humor may go beyond its role in making a couple's life together more enjoyable. Husbands and wives who share a similar sense of humor may also share something deeper—namely a match of personalities and emotional orientations. The idea that what a person honestly finds funny might be a window into his or her personality is widely shared among humor theorists and researchers (see Martin, 2007). The logic of the argument is that laughter is an emotional reaction that most people cannot fake (accomplished actors may be an exception). An obligatory and forced laugh is easily distinguished from the real thing. Because it is less subject to conscious control, a genuine laugh is thought to an honest expression of how a person really feels. This, in turn, is assumed to reflect significant and genuinely expressed aspects of personality. Both research and everyday interactions affirm this possibility. Studies show that humor and personality are connected and tend to reflect traits that are prominent in our personalities (see Martin, 2007, Chapter 7, for review). For example, aggressive people prefer harsh and aggressive jokes; conservatives prefer "safe" jokes such as puns; and people who are intelligent risk-takers with a high tolerance for ambiguity and openness to new experiences enjoy more bizarre and highly imaginative humor. In our own experience, most of us have been in the company of people who laugh heartily at a joke that we find personally offensive. This can be an immediate source of alienation. We may think, "If you find that funny, you're not my kind of person." Shared humor can create an opposite feeling: "That's my favorite kind of joke, so you're my kind of person."

The idea that humor is a window to thoughts and feelings that lie beneath the surface of conscious awareness is exemplified in an engaging book by Leon Rappoport titled, *Punchlines: The Case for Racial, Ethnic and Gender Humor* (2005). Rappoport argues that racial, ethnic, and gender-based forms of humor are typically viewed as insulting and prejudicial, which they certainly can be. However, at a deeper level such humor serves the important function of expressing those forbidden thoughts and feelings that are buried deep beneath the veneer of polite society and, more recently, the culture of political correctness. Comedians who make fun of their own race, ethnicity, or gender open the door to honest consideration of stereotypes and hostilities by reducing the anxieties, tensions, and guilt experienced by people who hold them. Laughing releases the tension created by consciously denied, but honestly felt emotions and beliefs, and brings them out in the open. Because humor detoxifies stereotypes and prejudices by holding them up for public ridicule, Rappoport argues that the net effect is to reduce—not increase—their potency.

Rappoport believes that humor may serve a similar function in marriage (L. Rappoport, personal communication, April 20, 2007). Because people differ in what they find funny, humor reflects something important about a person's personality. Most intriguing is the idea that humor represents accurate information about a person because genuine laughter is spontaneous and cannot be produced on demand. Much of what people reveal to others is disingenuous, not necessarily because of manipulative intentions, but because people are being polite, want to make a good impression, or are following their expectations about how to act in a particular kind of relationship. Compared to the similarities revealed in people's consciously controlled actions, responses to humor may represent honest and deeper similarities between two people.

Studies support the value of similarity as an essential foundation for successful close relationships (Noller & Feeney, 2006). Opposites may be interesting, but they don't seem to attract, as conventional wisdom suggests. Significant differences, not similarities, cause spouses the most trouble. However, knowing if you are similar to someone at a deeper level is difficult to determine. How many couples wonder after a year of marriage why their spouse seems so different from when they were dating or first married? A shared sense of humor may increase the odds that when the distorting effects of self-conscious impression management fade, some basic compatibility will remain.

While there is not a large literature examining the relationship value of a shared sense humor, what there *is* provides some support (see Martin, 2007, Chapter 5). Similarity in humor is affirmed as a basis for initial attraction. We like people who share our sense of what's funny, in part because we assume we also share other beliefs and qualities. Married couples do tend to share a similar sense of humor. However, higher ratings of humor similarity do not reliably predict marital *satisfaction*. Part of the problem here may have to do with the limitations of self-report assessments of shared humor. Because humor in real life is spontaneous, self-report questionnaires may not be the best way to measure it, because they are far-removed from the moments of actual humor that occur in the context of everyday life. To this point, Gottman's "love lab" observational studies do show that happy couples' interactions are characterized by a good deal of humor and reciprocated laughter. Humor, marital harmony, and effective relational problem-solving were found to go together. Perhaps we need a "humor lab" to specifically assess couples' shared and non-shared humorous reactions to situations, issues, and problems that typically occur in a marriage.

Though the empirical jury is still out, a shared sense of humor is an intriguing way to think about an index of basic compatibility between intimate partners. Similarity in humor may be important in knowing whether someone is "right" for you, and in sustaining a mutually enjoyable and enduring future relationship. Our guess would be that successful couples have humor in common, whether or not they realized this at the beginning of their relationships. As research shows, we are attracted to people who laugh at the same things we do.

So there you have it. Friendship, humor, and commitment. Three essential ingredients in the complex recipe for a successful marriage. Looking for a romantic partner? Find yourself a best buddy/best friend who laughs at all the same things you do and you should find it easier to make and sustain a long-term commitment!

Chapter Summary Questions

1. a. What evolutionary arguments support the conclusions that belongingness is a fundamental need?

   b. How does oxytocin figure into biological foundations for relationships with others?

2. How does disclosure reciprocity help build close relationships?

3. How do trust and caring contribute to close relationships?

4. What does it mean to say that close relationships are characterized by high levels of interdependence and mutuality?

5. Why is commitment important to close relations with others?

6. How do the descriptions of exchange and communal relationships describe the differences between casual acquaintances and close relationships?

7. What does research suggest about the role of teasing and humor in developing close relationships, and in successful long-term marriages?

8. How does capitalization enhance individual and relationship well-being, according to the research by Gable and her colleagues?

9. How do clarity of rules, complexity of feelings, and differing expectations explain the differences between friendship and romantic love?

10. What are love's three essential ingredients, according to Sternberg's triangular theory of love?

11. Why doesn't cohabitation increase the success of a future marriage?

12. What evidence supports the importance of increased freedom and decreased restraints as explanations for our culture's 50% divorce rate?

13. Is romantic love as a basis for marriage unique to American culture?

14. a. How might the increasing importance of love as a basis for marriage contribute to high divorce rates?

    b. How does research by Huston and his colleagues support a disillusionment model of divorce?

15. How does the research by Neff and Karney show the importance of both realism and idealism in marital satisfaction?

16. What arguments support a connection between infant–parent relationships and adult romantic relationships, according to attachment theory?

17. How may the different adult attachment styles reflect two underlying dimensions of anxiety and avoidance?

18. In his "love lab" studies, what critical ratio did Gottman find made the difference between good and bad marriages?

19. What qualities characterize long-term happily married couples, according to the Lauers' study?

20. What arguments and evidence suggest that a shared sense of humor may be an important measure of compatibility between romantic partners and may contribute to a satisfying marriage?

Key Terms

oxytocin *240*
self-disclosure *241*
disclosure reciprocity *242*
exchange versus communal relationships *245*
direct effects hypothesis *246*
capitalization *247*
passionate love *249*
companionate love *250*
triangular theory of love *250*

intimacy *250*
passion *250*
commitment *250*
self-verification theory *256*
attachment theory *257*
secure attachment *259*
preoccupied attachment *260*
fearful avoidant attachment *260*
dismissing avoidant attachment *260*
negative affect reciprocity *262*

demand/withdraw *262*
relationship-enhancing attributions *263*
distress-maintaining attributions *263*
romantic destiny *263*
relationship growth *263*

Web Resources

Relationship Research—Gottman

www.gottman.com/research/about This is the Gottman Institute site for the study of relationships. Links to an abundance of useful information, research articles, John Gottman's love lab studies, and other relevant sites and articles.

Love and Intimate Relationships

www2.hawaii.edu/~elaineh This site by Elaine Hatfield offers many research references as well as commonly used measures of passionate and companionate love.

Triangular Theory of Love

psychcentral.com/lib/2007/sternbergs-triangular-theory-of-love-scales This site for PsychCentral is run by mental health professionals. It has a variety of useful information. The address above is for Sternberg's triangular theory of love and a questionnaire that measures each of the three basic dimensions of love.

Attachment Theory

psychology.ucdavis.edu/labs/Shaver/measures.htm This site is for the Attachment Lab of Phillip Shaver and R. Chris Farley. In addition to listing recent publications, many links to the labs and research of other attachment theorists are listed.

Suggested Readings

Baumeister, R., & Leary, M. R. (1995). The need to belong: Desire for interpersonal attachments as a fundamental human motivation. *Psychological Bulletin, 117,* 497–529.

Gable, S. L., Reis, H. T., Impett, E. A., & Asher, E. R. (2004). What do you do when things go right? The intrapersonal and interpersonal benefits of sharing positive events. *Journal of Personality and Social Psychology, 87,* 228–245.

Gottman, J. M. (1994). *What predicts divorce? The relationship between marital processes and marital outcomes.* Hillsdale, NJ: Erlbaum.

Keltner, D., Capps, L., Kring, A. M., Young, R. C., & Heerey, E. A. (2001). Just teasing: A conceptual analysis and empirical review. *Psychological Bulletin, 127,* 229–248.

Meyers, S. A., & Berscheid, E. (1997). The language of love: The difference a preposition makes. *Personality and Social Psychology Bulleting, 23,* 347–362.

Miller, R. S., Perlman, D., & Brehm, S. (2007). *Intimate relationships* (4th ed.). New York: McGraw Hill.

Noller, P., & Feeney, J. A. (Eds.). (2006). *Close relationships: Functions, forms and processes.* New York: Psychology Press.

Ryff, C. D., & Singer, B. (2000). Interpersonal flourishing: A positive health agenda for the new millennium. *Personality and Social Psychology Review, 4,* 30–44.

Simpson, J. A., & Rholes, W. S. (Eds.). (1998) *Attachment theory and close relationships.* New York: Guildford Press.

Sternberg, R. J. (1998b). *Cupid's arrow: The course of love through time.* New York: Cambridge University Press.

12

Life Above Zero

POSITIVE PSYCHOLOGY REVISITED

The title of this chapter may seem strange for a book about positive psychology. But we want to emphasize a central theme, bordering on a mantra, of this newly emerging area. The theme is this: happiness and health are far more than the absence of unhappiness or illness. If you are not depressed, not unhappy, not bored, not stressed, not confronting major challenges or failures, and not arguing with your family or significant other, this by itself only signifies that you are not *unhappy* and are not dealing with emotional difficulties. It does not mean that you enjoy health and happiness. The absence of negatives without the presence of positives may be thought of as defining a "life at zero"—a kind of neutral zone where not much is wrong, but not much is right either, in terms of interest, purpose, and joy in life. Traditional psychology has told us much about "life below zero," from the damaging effects of stress, bad marriages, and dysfunctional families to genetic influences in mental illness. However, this only tells us what goes *wrong* to produce misery—not what goes *right* to produce health.

Positive psychology is all about what needs to go right to bring our lives "above zero."

When positive functioning is measured directly, rather than inferred from the absence of illness, the picture of health and happiness becomes dramatically different. This is clearly shown in the groundbreaking conceptual and empirical work of Corey Keyes that extends Carol Ryff's work on the foundations of psychological health (Keyes, 2003, 2005; Ryff, 1989; Ryff & Keyes, 1995). In his model of mental health, Keyes describes a *continuum* running from complete mental illness to complete mental health. Based on a eudaimonic model of psychosocial well-being (see Chapter 2), criteria for positive health and optimal functioning were added to traditional symptoms defining mental illness.

Based on both health and illness criteria, **mental illness** was defined as a high degree of mental illness symptoms and a low degree of mental *health* indicators. Complete mental health (**"flourishing"**) was defined as the absence of mental illness symptoms and the prominence of mental health symptoms (rather than just the absence of illness symptoms as implied in traditional mental illness models). Most interesting are degrees of health and illness lying between these two extremes. **Moderate mental health** involves some degree of positive functioning and a low degree of mental illness symptoms. **Languishing,** which fits the idea of life near zero, was defined as a low degree of mental illness together with a low degree of positive mental health. Keyes (2003) describes languishing as a state of incomplete mental health, because while there are few signs of illness, there are also few signs of health.

Keyes tested his "complete state model of health" in a sample of 3,032 adults, ages 25 to 74 (MIDUS—Midlife in the Untied States Survey; see Keyes, 2003, 2005). Participants were interviewed over the telephone and they also completed a self-report questionnaire assessing symptoms of mental health and mental illness. Keyes found that a majority of his adult sample fit the criteria for moderate mental health (about 60%), but less than one-fifth would be regarded as showing complete mental health or flourishing (about 17%). Interestingly, the percentage of adults characterized as languishing was about the same as the percentage regarded as flourishing. Extrapolations from this sample to the general population suggest that a substantial percentage of Americans age 25 to 74 are languishing in life (Keyes, 2003, estimated 18.6 million). Such people may lead lives of quiet desperation and distress, but currently "fly beneath the radar" of the conventional criteria used to define mental illness. Keyes regards this group as being at-risk for future mental health problems. This is one reason Keyes believes that the promotion of positive health may be just as important as the treatment of mental illness. And this is why it is important to develop models of life on the positive side of zero (Keyes, 2007). People in states of languishing may benefit as much (or more) from learning how to live a positive life as from traditional mental health services focused on remediation of distress.

INTERCONNECTION OF THE "GOOD" AND THE "BAD"

Positive psychology's focus on optimal functioning, flourishing, and happiness should not be taken to mean that positive psychology is only about good experiences, desirable personal qualities, or some idyllic life in which everything is wonderful (Ryff & Singer, 1998). Instead, as noted in the beginning chapter of this book, the goal is to promote balance in psychology's understanding of human behavior by focusing on the long-neglected *good* things in life—namely, positive health and happiness. That is, positive psychology complements, rather than replaces, time-honored understandings of how positive and negative life events and emotions are interconnected.

Psychologists have known for some time about human resilience and the fact that positive outcomes can grow out of negative experiences. No life is without turmoil, disappointments, conflicts, and setbacks and its share of tragedies. That many valuable lessons can be learned in the trenches of life's hardships is shown by posttraumatic growth (PTG) research, and the fact that many people adopt healthier lifestyles after suffering a heart attack or stroke. Facing and overcoming challenge is an important impetus for personal growth and development. Positive psychologists did not "discover" resilience or PTG, or the strong motivations for health and happiness that can emerge from tragedy and life-threatening events. These were topics in developmental and health psychology before the currently emerging field of positive psychology incorporated them under its umbrella. In a similar vein, studies showing that positive emotions stemming from humor, love, and the caring support of friends and family members can help offset the effects of stressful experiences have been standard fare in health psychology for some time. Finally, the fact that a positive outlook is typically preferable to a negative one is not exactly recent news. Before positive psychology came along, a variety of positive traits, such as optimism, hardiness, and self-esteem were connected to good outcomes and effective coping.

In our opinion, what seems genuinely "new" is that positive psychology has taken these and other ideas that have been largely peripheral to mainstream psychology, and is focusing squarely on them as central constructs. In particular, we think positive psychology's unique contributions are that it clarifies the relative independence of the "good" and "bad" and develops empirically-based, positive criteria to define health and happiness. It is easy to assume (as psychologists historically have) that mental health requires and begins with an absence of mental illness, that happiness requires an absence of distress and depression, and that happy marriages have less conflict and animosity than unhappy ones. However, positive psychologists have helped develop some new perspectives on these assumptions. First, as already mentioned, the absence of the bad does not necessarily mean the presence of the good. As we saw in Chapter 11, for example, good relating and bad relating in a marriage are not simple opposites. Second, positive psychology has highlighted the importance of positive emotional states to health and happiness beyond their ability to offset the bad. As described in Chapter 3, positive emotions have many potential beneficial effects, including enhancing our immune system's ability to fight disease, improving and indexing our mental and emotional health, promoting individual success, and contributing to satisfaction in a marriage. These benefits go beyond the ability of positive emotions to reduce the ill-effects of negative emotions. Positive emotions are good for us all the time, whether or not we are distressed. Life above zero means that the good things contribute to a satisfying and meaningful life, and go beyond simply compensating for the bad.

Third, and perhaps most importantly, before positive psychology came along, traditional psychology had few voices and even fewer empirical studies describing what it meant to be healthy and happy. Certainly, humanistic psychology (i.e., Maslow and Rogers) and other visionary thinkers (e.g., Jahoda, 1958; World Health Organization, 1948) noted the importance of positive functioning and the need to develop criteria for positive mental health. In many ways, positive psychology can be viewed as an attempt to bring these earlier ideas to more systematic and empirical fruition. What's new is the sheer volume of research and the number of psychologists who are devoting their lives to the study of positive human functioning. Positive psychology has moved "live above zero" from the periphery to center-stage.

CONTOURS OF A POSITIVE LIFE: MEANING AND MEANS

Meaning

No positive psychologist is presumptuous enough to think that she or he has definitive answers to the meaning or the means of a positive life. Countless writers from the ancient Greeks to present-day philosophers, religious scholars, sociocultural observers, and self-help gurus have described the contours of a good life. What can positive psychology add to this commentary? For one, positive psychologists are producing a rich empirical literature that helps sort out the complex factors that do and do not contribute to well-being. Research relating to positive emotions, life circumstances and stages, money and happiness, materialism, personal goals, positive traits, strengths of character, transcendent purposes, and close relationships, provides a comparative picture of the kinds of life choices, personal strengths, and life involvements that increase well-being and those that produce only temporary increases, or that actually reduce our health and happiness.

In addition to specific research findings, positive psychologists have also developed models and theories, and have identified patterns of findings that offer different ways of thinking about the basic contours of a good life. These include the subjective well-being (SWB) conception of happiness, eudaimonic models of positive health and optimal func-tioning, the classification system of virtues and character strengths, the wisdom-based select-optimize-compensate (SOC) model of a good life, and the research and theory evaluating personal goals according to their impact on well-being. These areas of work offer distinctive, yet overlapping perspectives on the criteria for judging a good life.

Sociocultural research reminds us that the meaning of a good life is shaped by culture and context. People's fundamental assumptions about self, values, relationships, life tasks, and purposes are powerfully influenced by culture, history, and social circumstances. As we saw in Chapter 6, the particular defining features of happiness and health are quite different in Western cultures as compared to East-Asian societies. In a similar vein, sociocultural change influences what is considered "true" and "good." The dramatic changes in women's roles and in our culture's views of homosexuality over the last 40 years are easy examples. Social conditions are also important. Poverty and the availability of resources such as quality education and health may also influence the meaning of a good life. However, acknowledging the role of culture, history, and social conditions does not preclude a shared understanding of the essential ingredients of a good, healthy, happy life. While the particulars of an individual's life reflect multiple cultural and social influences, Seligman and Csikszentmihalyi (2001, p. 90) argue that people share a common humanity in the form of goals and needs that "cut across social and cultural divides." They believe that "just as physical health, adequate nutrition, and freedom from harm and exploitation are universally valued, so must psychologists ultimately aim to understand the positive states, traits and institutions that all cultures value" (Seligman & Csikszentmihalyi, 2001, p. 90). Addressing the issue of universality versus cultural relativity will likely be a major part of positive psychology's future research agenda.

In addition to culture, the meaning of a good life also needs to be placed within the context of lifespan development. A good life is not a fixed or static state. It is a striving toward optimal functioning, involving a continual process of growth and change. This point is especially emphasized in eudaimonic models of well-being that note the changing pattern of adaptations, competencies, self-conceptions, and social relationships that characterize healthy people at different points in the life cycle. Like arguments about cultural influence, developmental researchers point to the unique tasks, skills, and personal qualities that define health at different stages of development. A happy and healthy life at age 15 is obviously different than a happy-healthy life at 80. However, just as shared goals and psychological needs may create a common humanity that transcends cultural differences, a similar set of goals and needs may transcend differences in age-related tasks and challenges. Consider the six dimensions of psychological well-being described by Ryff (1989): environmental mastery, purpose in life, self-acceptance, personal growth, autonomy, and positive relationships (see Chapter 2). How would each of these positive health characteristics be expressed by teenagers and by elderly individuals? Hopefully, the point here is clear. Despite differences in their particular form of expression and the developmental tasks involved, both teens and elderly individuals can be evaluated according to common health criteria of mastery, purpose, growth, and so forth. Arguments about a common humanity support the possibility of universality in the meaning of a good life. Core defining features of psychological health allow for the same possibility of universality in describing a good life at every age and stage of life.

With considerations of culture and development in mind, we can go back to Seligman's three-part analysis of happiness (described in Chapter 1) as a shorthand summary of a good life. Seligman combines the major elements of hedonic and eudaimonic perspectives in his description of a pleasant life, an engaged life, and a meaningful life (Seligman, 2002a; Seligman, Rashid, & Parks, 2006).

A PLEASANT LIFE A pleasant life takes note of the importance of positive emotions and experiences for happiness and health. Consistent with the subjective well-being conception of happiness, an abundance of positive emotions and few negative emotions, combined with overall life satisfaction, defines the pleasant side of happiness. As we have seen throughout this book, positive emotions (and the traits, relationships, and life commitments that promote and sustain them) have consistently been shown to enhance both health and happiness. Following Fredrickson's theory (Chapter 3), positive emotions broaden our life perspective and help build physical, psychological, and social well-being resources. Therefore, activities, choices, and self-changes that cultivate positive emotions tend to improve our quality of life. "Flow" and "savoring" (highlighted in Chapter 3) are two examples of experiences that increase positive emotions. Chapter 11 described the well-being benefits of sharing positive life experiences with others and the value of humor in relationships. The bottom line here is that the things we do for fun, based on their intrinsic enjoyment value, should be regarded as important contributors to well-being above and beyond their value in reducing negative emotions such as stress, anxiety, and depression.

AN ENGAGED LIFE An engaged life is characterized by active involvement in need-fulfilling and personally expressive life pursuits such as work, family, and leisure. Life involvements that use an individual's special talents or "signature strengths" are especially likely to be personally meaningful and gratifying (Seligman, 2002b). Engagement provides a sense of competence and purpose that gives direction to life and contributes to personal growth (Ryff & Singer, 1998). The kinds of engagement that are likely to be most satisfying and health-promoting are suggested by eudaimonic theories of well-being and by research on personal goals. From the perspective of self-determination theory (SDT), for example, activities that promote and express autonomy, personal competence, and positive relations with others contribute most to our well-being. Goal research affirms SDT by showing the importance of pursuing goals that are freely chosen, intrinsically enjoyable, and that match and express psychological needs. Goals reflecting personal values and aspects of people's unique personal identities also enhance well-being. Distinguishing between the "right" goals and commitments and the "wrong" ones would seem to be a foundation for choosing activities that fit Seligman's idea of engagement.

Selecting the right goals requires a measure of self-awareness and understanding. Self-awareness brings an understanding of which life goals will be the best fit with one's own unique needs, interests, and talents. Such an understanding is a buffer against living a life imposed by the wishes of others or being seduced by the "money buys happiness" message of our materialistic culture. Hopefully, this book has increased your personal awareness of some of the differences between life choices that do increase well-being and happiness, and those that do not. Of course, the resources to support one's personal choices are also important (e.g., social support, determination, and finances). Poverty undermines well-being for many reasons, but one major reason is that the lack of resources constrains personally expressive choices.

A MEANINGFUL LIFE Engagement and meaning are very much related, if for no other reason than it is hard to maintain engagement in activities that are not personally meaningful. Seligman believes that a meaningful life takes us beyond our own life interests by connecting us to something bigger than ourselves. As action identification theory posits (Vallacher & Wegner, 1987, Chapter 8), any activity can be viewed at different levels of generality and meaning, depending on the person and the context. A glass of wine, for example, may be just a drink with friends, a way to relax at the end of the day, a symbol of romance at a dinner with someone you love, or a sacred sacrament in a religious ceremony. Like many positive psychologists, Seligman regards higher-order, transcendent meanings as more deeply satisfying, enduring, and significant to people's sense of a life well-lived. These larger life meanings include religion, spirituality, human virtues, serving others, sharing life's accumulated wisdom with others, volunteering in one's community, and contributing time and effort to worthy causes (Chapter 10). Finding purpose in life, both large and small, is an essential ingredient in psychological health (Ryff & Keyes, 1995). The importance of meaning reflects the fact that humans are meaning-makers in the sense of seeking the broad, deep, and enduring purposes of life. At its most basic level, life is a "search for meaning" (Frankl, 1976/1959). In short, a meaningful life is an important foundation for personal satisfaction and health. The opposite is also true. A life regarded as meaningless is likely to be accompanied by profound unhappiness and emotional distress (Baumeister, 1991).

Means

Describing the meaning of a good life is difficult, but specifying the means—the "how to" of a good life—is an even more vexing problem. Human behavior is obviously complex and we are creatures of habit. This makes change difficult, if not downright threatening. As if that weren't enough, Lyubomirsky, Sheldon, and Schkade (2005) remind us of three other reasons to be pessimistic about people's ability to increase their long-term levels of happiness. First, there is substantial research on genetically-determined levels of happiness, summarized by the idea of an individual set-point for happiness. As described in Chapter 9, some people are just born "three drinks ahead," and others "three drinks behind" and there isn't much that can be done about it. Each of us may have a characteristic and relatively fixed level of happiness to which we return after life events have temporarily pushed us above or below our usual baseline level.

Secondly, personality researchers have shown that several basic traits which are powerfully related to well-being are very stable over time. For example, neuroticism and extraversion (two of the "Big Five" personality traits) are not only strongly related to one's personal level of happiness, but are also quite stable across the entire life span. Since the Big Five are known to be quite heritable, they may contribute to our set-point level of happiness and our basic outlook on life (Chapter 9). Finally, human biology helps ensure that no emotion is made to last and that people quickly adapt to emotionally-charged events. The idea of the hedonic treadmill (Chapter 6), while not written in stone, means that happiness founded on the continuous pursuit of pleasurable events may be a pipe-dream built on transient effects. Like on an actual treadmill, you walk and walk, but you don't get anywhere. Only short-term increases in happiness are possible according to the treadmill theory.

However, Lyubomirsky and colleagues see reason for optimism. Genetics and biology are not necessarily destiny. According to their estimates, 50% of a person's baseline level of happiness is determined by genetic factors and another 10% is determined by life circumstances. This still leaves 40% for the effects of what they call intentional activity (see Figure 12.1). Intentional activity means activities we consciously choose, and that require sustained effort. In line with this 40% "room-for-change," early studies by Fordyce (1977, 1983) suggest that people's well-being can be enhanced through awareness and effort. Fordyce developed "14 happiness fundamentals" that characterized happy people, as profiled by research, and suggested that the average person could reasonably be expected to emulate these characteristics. The logic of his program was simple. If you become more like a happy person, your happiness should increase. Fordyce tested his happiness enhancement program among adult community college students who enrolled in his psychology courses. He provided an overview of happiness studies and gave specific instruction on tactics to increase the 14 fundamentals listed below (Fordyce, 1983, p. 484).

1. Become more active.
2. Spend more time socializing with others.

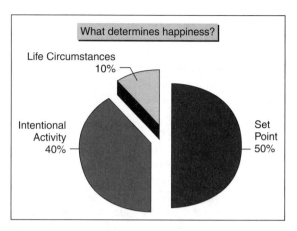

FIGURE 12.1 Three Primary Factors Influencing People's Level of Happiness
Source: Sheldon, K. M., & Lyubomirsky, S. (2004). Achieving sustainable new happiness: Prospects, practices, and prescriptions. In P. A. Linley & S. Joseph (Eds.), *Positive psychology in practice* (pp. 127–145). New York: John Wiley & Sons. Copyright by John Wiley & sons. Reprinted by permission.

3. Be productive at meaningful work.
4. Become more organized and better at planning.
5. Reduce your amount of worrying.
6. Lower expectations and aspirations.
7. Learn to be more positive and optimistic.
8. Become more present-oriented.
9. Develop a healthier personality.
10. Develop a more outgoing and social personality.
11. Be yourself.
12. Reduce negative feelings and problems.
13. Recognize close relationships as critical to happiness.
14. Make happiness an important life priority.

In addition to a general discussion of happiness research, Fordyce presented his students with detailed information about each of the 14 fundamentals, including research findings and theories relevant to why they were important and how they contributed to happiness. Fordyce also gave specific suggestions concerning ways to implement the happiness fundamentals. These included such strategies as scheduling enjoyable activities into one's daily routine, learning about goal-setting and priority-setting strategies, and keeping a record of daily worries and evaluating them according to their importance and factual basis.

Across multiple studies varying in length from several weeks to over a year, Fordyce found consistent evidence that his program enhanced individual happiness compared to control groups. Across seven studies, 81% of the participants reported that their levels of happiness had increased and 38% reported that they were "much happier." These results, as Fordyce acknowledges, need to be viewed with caution. First, the results do not tell us about the comparative importance of the 14 fundamentals. Are all 14 equally important to enhancing happiness? Only a few? Does their importance vary from person to person? Second, because Fordyce himself administered the program it is difficult to disentangle his personality and manner of presentation from the results. That is, how much of the increased happiness was due to the content of the program and how much to the motivational ability and enthusiasm of the presenter?

INTENTIONAL ACTIVITIES AND SELF-CONCORDANT GOALS Lyubomirsky and colleagues (2005) have recently studied a more focused approach to enhancing well-being based on goal research. They argue that longer-term increases in happiness may be possible when people (1) pursue goals that match or fit with personal characteristics, (2) that are autonomously chosen, and (3) for which implementation plans have been laid out, so that working on them becomes relatively automatic and conserves limited self-control resources.

A good deal of research supporting this view was reviewed in Chapters 7 and 8. Much of this literature is also reviewed in the article by Lyubomirsky and colleagues. For example, studies with college students have shown that adopting self-concordant goals at the beginning of a semester can lead to higher rates of goal achievement and higher levels of well-being at semester's end (e.g., Sheldon, Kasser, Smith, & Share, 2002). Year-long studies suggest that some students may enjoy an upward spiral of well-being based on their initial success in pursuing self-concordant goals (e.g., Sheldon & Houser-Marko, 2001). However, the sustainability of well-being gains was dependent on continued success. Many students lost their initial gains because of poor subsequent progress toward their personal goals. Based on her intervention research, Lyubomirsky has found that increasing one's happiness is hard work (Lyubomirsky, as interviewed by Krakovsky, 2007, *Scientific American*). People who stopped following intervention exercises after a study's completion often lost their gains in happiness.

DEVELOPING AND EXPRESSING VIRTUE Numerous other interventions have also been shown to increase well-being, but face the same nagging problem of sustainability. Studies of the positive well-being effects of virtuous behavior have found that people who are asked to perform acts of kindness (Lyubomirsky et al., 2005), forgiveness (McCullough & Worthington, 1997), and gratitude (Emmons & McCullough, 2003) enjoy increased levels of well-being. (The details of several of these studies are reviewed at the end of Chapter 10.)

Of the many virtues, wisdom has received the most research attention as a foundation for a good life. Wisdom involves self-understanding and knowing what is important in life. As described in the SOC Model (select-optimize-compensate), developed by Baltes and his colleagues, a good life is based on integrating wisdom, goal selection, and goal pursuit (Chapter 10). Wisdom facilitates the *selection* of life's more important goals. Even writing about personal goals may help people clarify, prioritize, and become more aware of what is important to them. In line with this possibility, King (2001) found that people who wrote about goals related to their "best possible future self" showed increased well-being that was maintained over a period of 5 months. In addition to its role in selecting goals worth pursuing, wisdom helps *optimize* choices regarding the *means* by which to achieve those goals. Much of optimization has to do with issues of self-regulation (as discussed in Chapter 8). Finally, the pursuit of important and challenging goals typically runs into roadblocks along the way. Wise people find ways to *compensate* for the loss of previously effective means by developing viable alternatives. For example, with advancing age, people must find ways to compensate for their declining physical vitality and mobility in order to continue satisfying lives.

USING POSITIVE PSYCHOLOGY TO TREAT DEPRESSION Seligman and his colleagues (Seligman et al., 2006) have packaged these and other interventions in an approach to treating depression they refer to as **positive psychotherapy (PPT).** The PPT approach was based on Seligman and Peterson's work regarding virtue and character strengths, and seeks to develop signature strengths and enhance well-being by encouraging the individual to engage in virtuous behaviors (Chapter 10). Mildly and moderately depressed participants shared in discussions and presentations focused on positive aspects of life and how to reframe negative experiences. Participants were also given specific homework activities that included identifying and cultivating their unique signature strengths, writing letters of forgiveness to someone who had transgressed against them, expressing gratitude to helpful others who were never thanked, cultivating positive and more optimistic attitudes by seeing opportunities rather than loss when things go wrong, savoring pleasurable and meaningful moments in life, and giving time to help others in ways that express their signature character strengths. Results of several PPT intervention studies showed significant reductions in depressive symptoms over periods of 6 months to 1 year, compared to placebo controls. Many people described the experience as "life-changing." Seligman and his colleagues regard these encouraging findings as preliminary because the PPT strategy was tested only in small groups.

INCREASING PSYCHOLOGICAL WELL-BEING Ruini and Fava (2004) have recently provided a review of their work on Well-Being Therapy (WBT), based on Ryff's (1989) eudaimonic model of psychological well-being. The purpose of WBT is to move people from impaired to improved functioning, as defined by the six attributes of health described by Ryff. Ruini and Fava found Ryff's model easily adaptable to clinical population. Patients typically show impairments in one or more of the six area of functioning and Ryff's model provides helpful defining elements of the treatment outcome goals of psychotherapy. Their modification of Ryff's model to fit a clinical population is shown in Table 12.1.

Well-Being Therapy is in its initial phase of development. It is meant to be a helpful counterpart to, rather than a substitute for well-established psychotherapies. Ruini, Fava, and their colleagues developed an 8-week program of WBT sessions that each lasted 30 to 50 minutes. WBT relies heavily on self-observation, with patients recording their thoughts and feelings in a diary. The overall goal of WBT is to get patients to see how their own thoughts and feelings short-circuit the basis of healthy well-being in their everyday life. In the first session, patients are asked to record episodes of healthy well-being and specify the situation in which these episodes occurred. Intermediate sessions are used to identify thoughts and feelings that disrupted episodes of well-being. That is, what causes well-being to be interrupted? Often, irrational and stress-inducing thoughts return patients to their ongoing levels of distress. Information gathered in earlier sessions is used in later sessions to assess specific impairments (based on a modification of Ryff's six-dimensional model of health). Individual patient reports and diaries are discussed in relation to the modified model (see Table 12.1) when relevant and helpful. Although they consider their results very preliminary, Ruini and Fava report encouraging signs that WBT may prove to be a useful intervention for counteracting distress by increasing psychological well-being.

"MINDING" CLOSE RELATIONSHIPS The quality of our friendships, marriages, and families has much to do with the quality of our lives. Healthy and happy people have satisfying relationships—a point supported by countless studies (Chapter 11). This fact means that efforts to maintain and enhance the quality of our close relationships are likely to enhance our own and others' well-being. Relationship researchers have developed a number of models describing what people do to maintain and repair their most significant relationships (see Harvey & Weber, 2002; Miller, Perlman, & Brehm, 2007; Noller & Feeney, 2006). "Minding the close relationship" is one of the more comprehensive theories that provide general guidelines for how to maintain and enhance close relationships (Harvey & Omarzu, 1997, 1999; Harvey, Pauwels, & Zickmund, 2002). Harvey and Omarzu (1997, 1999) describe "minding" as a set of five interrelated thinking and behavior patterns (to be described momentarily) that contribute to stable and satisfying relationships when practiced over time by both partners in a relationship. Each of the five "minding" components enhances feelings of closeness. Minding a relationship is like looking after a garden. It is not something you do once in while, when you feel like it, or only if the weeds are taking over. A good garden requires a steady, frequent, and watchful eye and a good deal of effort across time.

Knowing and Being Known

Knowing and being known is largely a matter of reciprocal self-disclosure motivated by shared desire to learn about each other's thoughts, feelings,

TABLE 12.1 Modification of Ryff's six dimensions of psychological well-being

Dimensions	Impaired Level	Optimal Level
Environmental mastery	The subject has or feels difficulties in managing everyday affairs; feels unable to change or improve surrounding context; is unaware of surrounding opportunities; lacks a sense of control over the external world.	The subject has a sense of mastery and competence in managing the environment; controls external activities; makes effective use of surrounding opportunities; is able to create or choose contexts suitable to personal needs and values.
Personal growth	The subject has a sense of personal stagnation; lacks a sense of improvement or expansion over time; feels bored and uninterested with life; feels unable to develop new attitudes or behaviors.	The subject has a feeling of continued development; sees self as growing and expanding; is open to new experiences; has a sense of realizing own potential; sees improvement in self and behavior over time.
Purpose in life	The subject lacks a sense of meaning in life; has few goals or aims, lacks a sense of direction, does not see purpose in past life; has no outlooks or beliefs that give life meaning.	The subject has goals in life and a sense of directedness; feels there is meaning to present and past life; holds beliefs that give life purpose; has aims and objectives for living.
Autonomy	The subject is overconcerned with the expectations and evaluation of others; relies on judgment of others to make important decisions; conforms to social pressures to think or act in certain ways.	The subject is self-determining and independent; able to resist social pressures; regulates behavior from within; evaluates self by personal standards.
Self-acceptance	The subject feels dissatisfied with self; is disappointed with what has occurred in past life; is troubled about certain personal qualities; wishes to be different from what he or she is.	The subject has a positive attitude toward the self; accepts his or her good and bad qualities; feels positive about his or her past life.
Positive relations with others	The subject has few close, trusting relationships with others; finds it difficult to be open and is isolated and frustrated in interpersonal relationships; is not willing to make compromises to sustain important ties with others.	The subject has warm and trusting relationships with others; is concerned about the welfare of others; is capable of strong empathy, affection, and intimacy; understands the give and take policy of human relationships.

Source: Ruini, C., & Fava, G. A. (2004). Clinical applications of well-being therapy. In P. A. Linley & S. Joseph (Eds.), *Positive psychology in practice* (pp. 371–387). New York: John Wiley & Sons. Copyright John Wiley and Sons. Reprinted by permission.

and personal histories. Harvey and Omarzu emphasize the importance of partners actively seeking honest and open self-expression from each other, rather than just expressing their own feelings without encouraging the other to do the same. In well-minded relationships an ongoing atmosphere of openness is created, in which both partners are comfortable talking about difficult issues, hopes, and fears. This openness creates trust that reduces defensiveness, and caring that reduces perceptions of insensitivity or lack of concern. Over time,

extensive reciprocal personal knowledge can lead to highly individualized partner behaviors and communication. For example, long-term married couples may intuit from nonverbal cues what their spouses are thinking and feeling. In a group situation, couples may smile at each other over an inside joke that only they understand. These idiosyncratic behaviors may come to be expressed in all facets of a couple's relationship. These special communications maintain and enhance closeness because they reflect each person's unique personality, quirks, hang-ups, strengths, and weaknesses. Because people and life circumstances change over time, knowing and being known is a never-ending process of discovering how each partner responds and adapts to the journey through life. The specific behaviors that facilitate disclosure are listed below (Harvey & Omarzu, 1997, p. 235):

> Questioning one's partner about feelings/behavior
>
> Utilizing effective listener responses
>
> Accurate reflection of a partner's disclosure
>
> Accurate, detailed knowledge of the partner's preferences/opinions

Attribution

Attribution concerns the pattern of explanations typically given for a partner's behavior. In Chapter 11, we discussed the differences between relationship-enhancing explanations and those that reflect a desire to blame and punish a partner's transgressions. Successful relationships are built on giving one's partner the benefit of the doubt and avoiding quick (and perhaps mistaken) explanations. Generally, this means viewing positive behaviors as reflecting positive, internal traits (e.g., care and sensitivity) and negative behaviors as occurring due to external circumstances (e.g., a bad day at work). However, in well-minded relationships, this general pattern will be tempered by accurate understanding of a partner's personality, to achieve a balance of internal and external explanations and thus avoid a one-sided or distorted understanding of a partner's behavior. That is, explanations will fit the self-understanding of one's partner. Closeness is fostered by authenticity and accuracy in each partner's understanding of the other—not by consistently relying on either sugar-coated or negative explanations. Specific behaviors facilitating enhancing attributions include:

> Making generally positive attributions regarding the partner's behavior
>
> Attributing negative relationship events to external factors
>
> Making attributions for the partner that match the partner's self-attributions

Although it is not listed as one of the five basic components of minding, authenticity is an important, related ingredient of successful relationships. *Authenticity* means being truthful with yourself and others (Harter, 2002). Our everyday experience with authenticity is perhaps best understood as a feeling of "naturalness" in our relation with another person. That is, we are who we are—no phoniness, no covering up our true feelings, and no attempt to create a good impression or to please another by insincere flattery. If we follow the age-old saying "to thine own self be true" (Shakespeare, *Hamlet*) and a relationship still works, this captures the meaning of an authentic connection in which people don't have to compromise who they are for the sake of preserving their connection to another person. Based on her research, Harter (2002) argues that in successful relationships, people balance autonomy and connectedness in a relationship style she calls *mutuality*. This means that people are not self-focused (so that one's own needs take precedence over the other's), or other-focused (so that one's own needs are sacrificed to the needs of the other). In relationships characterized by mutuality, people show high levels of authentic self-behaviors while at the same time accepting and validating their partner. They do not "lose" their sense of self in a relationship. Instead, they balance needs for independence with the equally important need for connectedness. Mutuality may also be enhanced by the acceptance and respect that characterize well-minded relationships.

Acceptance and Respect

The opposites of acceptance and respect are criticism, dismissing defensiveness, and contempt. Here, Harvey and Omarzu rely on Gottman's love lab research (reviewed in Chapter 11) that details the difference between healthy marriages and unhealthy ones. In healthy relationships people listen respectfully, embrace all of their partner's qualities (good and bad), accept rather than dismiss their partner's feelings, and find ways to compromise and work out differences. Unhealthy marriages show an essentially opposite pattern. In well-minded relationships, partners are aware of the dangers of getting locked into long periods of negative interaction. Acceptance and respect are principles that provide a foundation for perceiving one's partner and the basic requirements of all interactions—even those involving conflict and sensitive issues. Over time, acceptance and respect foster closeness by promoting the development of strong feelings of mutual trust, sincerity, and caring. Some of the behaviors that contribute to acceptance and respect are described below:

Pride in the other person's abilities

Expressed feelings of trust and commitment

Behaviors that acknowledge the other person's preferences/concerns

Behaviors/verbal expressions that acknowledge self-disclosures

Reciprocity

Reciprocity refers to the need for both partners to participate in minding their relationship. Reciprocity means that both partners invest relatively equal levels of effort in learning about each other, making adjustments and attributions based on this knowledge, and exchanging mutual acceptance and respect. Women may be better at minding intimate relationships than men. However, Harvey and his colleagues argue that "minding does not insist that men become aware of relationships in the same ways as are women, but it does insist that partners in an individual relationship strive for equal awareness of each other and each other's needs" (Harvey et al., 2002, p. 429). Specific behaviors related to reciprocity are listed below:

Perception that the partner's effort in the relationship matches one's own effort

Ability to identify the partner's contribution to the relationship

Recognition of the other person's support and effort

Perception of synergy (a feeling of being stronger together than separately)

Continuity

Continuity reflects the fact that successful relationships take time and that minding is an ongoing process that is essential to the continued health of a relationship. That is, minding needs to become a permanent feature of a relationship and it takes time to have its positive effects. Although empirical studies of minding close relationships are just beginning, Harvey and his colleagues believe that partners who build a personal life history together based on a well-minded relationship are likely to enjoy the following benefits:

A sense of "we-ness," or togetherness permeates the relationship

Agreement in charting the ups and downs of the relationship over time

An optimistic view of the future of the relationship

Feelings of influence in the relationship

Hope for the future in general

MINDFULNESS AND WELL-BEING

In addition to the evolving list of well-being enhancement strategies described above, a quite different approach has grown out of the meeting of Eastern philosophy and Western psychology. Eastern meditative practices, like those of Buddhist traditions have a long past in their own right, but only a short history in psychology. However, this has begun to change as Buddhist philosophy, particularly the concept and practice of mindfulness, has made its way into Western empirical psychology, perhaps most notably beginning with the work of Ellen Langer (Langer, 1989, 2002; Langer & Moldoveanu, 2000). Historically, mainstream psychology has viewed mindfulness and meditation as falling under the umbrella of "states of consciousness"—a popular topic in the 1970s and 1980s. A number of texts and anthologies on the topic emerged during this period (e.g., Ornstein, 1973; Wallace & Fisher, 1983). A chapter on human consciousness has become fairly standard in general psychology textbooks ever since.

Mindfulness is a slippery concept that will be defined more fully in a subsequent discussion. For now, think of mindfulness as a present-centered attention focused on the "here and now" of our experience. That is, seeing clearly what is actually going on in our lives when our perception is uncluttered by wishes, desires, and needs. Mindfulness meditation is a means of increasing the clarity of perception by observing and learning about the self. Meditation is aimed at increasing the accuracy of our self-understanding and providing a basis for self-improvement and enhanced quality of life.

Mindfulness meditation has been most extensively investigated as a therapeutic practice for people dealing with a variety of mental and physical disorders, particularly those caused by high levels of stress. Although some have criticized this research for its lack of rigor (e.g., Bishop, 2002), others argue that over the last 30 years a substantial research literature has established the value of mindfulness meditation in improving the lives of people coping with diverse problems (e.g., Shapiro, Schwartz, & Santerre, 2002; Walsh & Shapiro, 2006). Such problems include psychosomatic and cardiovascular disorders, asthma, hypertension, chronic pain, cancer, panic attacks, anxiety, phobias, and eating disorders. The most well-known clinical intervention program based on mindfulness was developed by Jon Kabat-Zinn, founder of the Center for Mindfulness in Medicine, Health Care and Society (CFM) at the University of Massachusetts Medical School. The CFM website provides many informative resources. In his well-known book *Full Catastrophe Living: Using the Wisdom of Your Body and Mind to Face Stress, Pain, and Illness* (1990), Kabat-Zinn gives a detailed description of his mindfulness training program.

However, it is only recently that psychologists have begun to define and measure mindfulness and assess its effects on well-being in non-clinical settings and populations (Brown & Ryan, 2003, 2004; Wallace, 2005, 2006; Wallace & Shapiro, 2006; Walsh & Shapiro, 2006). The bottom-line assumption of this work is that mindfulness may be an important vehicle for self-change and improved well-being.

What is Mindfulness?

MINDFULNESS AS AN ANTIDOTE FOR MINDLESSNESS
More than one author has commented that it is easier to describe the absence of mindfulness than its presence. The opposite of mindfulness is mindlessness, captured by phrases such as "the lights are on, but nobody is home" and "going through the motions, but my heart's not in it." Mindlessness, here, does not mean being crazy or reckless, although not paying attention to what is in front of you can certainly get you into trouble. **Mindlessness** refers to a state of consciousness marked by little awareness of what is going on in the present moment. It is a state "governed by rule and routine" (Langer, 2002, p. 214) rather than by what is happening "right now." All of us are familiar with mindless states. We may read a book or talk with another person, but our minds are absorbed in our own thoughts, emotions, worries, concerns, and anxieties about the future, or ruminations about the past.

The review of self-regulation research in Chapter 8 points to another potentially significant source of mindless behavior. In a typical day many

of our behaviors are habitual and automatic, requiring little, if any, conscious attention (like driving a car). Bargh and Chartrand (1999) describe the implications of this fact of life as the "unbearable automaticity of being." They believe the value of automatic, unconsciously controlled behavior is great, but it is "unbearable" because it contradicts both psychologists' and lay-persons' belief in conscious, volitional control through self-directed actions. Bargh and Chartrand argue that the benefits of automaticity include releasing us from the burden of continual effortful control and providing a non-conscious and "truer" expression of our preferences than is revealed in the consciously stated reasons people give for their behavior. Despite its value, automaticity is negatively regarded because it contradicts people's view that they "know" why they do things.

Proponents of mindfulness acknowledge the efficiency of well-learned, automatic behaviors and their value in conserving conscious self-control resources. However, they point out that people can easily become victims of their own unconscious habits and knee-jerk emotional reactions. Ask any smoker who wants to quit or any dieter who wants to stop overeating. An undesirable habit that is automatically triggered by many external and internal cues, like a morning cup of coffee, an after-dinner drink, stress, or boredom, is difficult to break. From the perspective of mindfulness, awareness of when and why you smoke or overeat is necessary to control the habit.

At a more general level, Brown and Ryan (2003) note that the potential value of mindfulness for improving well-being is suggested by substantial research on the importance of attention in the self-regulation of behavior (see Chapter 8). Successful goal pursuit requires some degree of continuous attention (mindfulness) so that goal progress is monitored, necessary adjustments made, and efforts remain focused on, rather than distracted from, goal achievement. In addition, mindfulness may contribute to more self-determined and autonomous actions. As we saw in Chapter 7, personal goals that are freely chosen are likely to be personally expressive and therefore more satisfying than goals imposed by circumstances or by others.

Autonomy means making a choice when multiple alternatives are on the table. Automatic behaviors which, by definition, are "unthinking" (i.e., mindless) may limit our understanding of options and, therefore, may also limit freely-chosen, intentional action. In some ways, automatic behaviors operate like the genetic happiness set-point because they represent potential barriers to change. This may be a significant issue when automatic behaviors are not personally expressive or desirable (e.g., bad habits or a short temper). In such cases, self-change would first seem to require conscious recognition that past behaviors have been controlled by factors of which one was largely unaware. This recognition would then need to be followed by ongoing attention and efforts to exert conscious control over the behavior. A mindful state focused on the here-and-now opens the possibility that we can consciously override automatic behaviors that might occur if we lapse into a state of mindlessness. (For a review of supporting evidence, see Brown & Ryan, 2004; also see a recent study by Chatzisarantis & Hagger, 2007.) Mindfulness is a potential avenue to greater autonomy because it expands our awareness of choices by disengaging us from reflexive thought patterns and habitual/automatic responses. And, when more options are on the table, we are more likely to make freely-chosen, personally expressive decisions that enhance our well-being.

MINDFULNESS AS PRESENT-CENTERED AWARENESS AND ATTENTION Weston (1999) describes consciousness as the interrelation of awareness and attention. *Awareness* describes all the things that are presently on our minds. Awareness involves continual monitoring of the internal and external environment. At any given moment, we may be conscious of our immediate circumstances and activities (external) and a rich array of associated thoughts, feelings, and experiences (internal). *Attention* focuses our conscious awareness on a more limited set of experiences. Take vision as an example. We may be conscious of events occurring in both our peripheral vision (awareness) and at the focal point of our visual field (attention). We can be aware of things without responding to them or having them as the center of our attention. Awareness and attention are intimately connected such that ". . . attention continually pulls 'figures' out of the 'ground' of awareness, holding them focally for varying lengths of time" (Brown & Ryan, 2003, p. 822).

As Brown and Ryan (2003) note, a central feature of mindfulness is an open and receptive, present-centered attention and awareness that is pre-reflexive and non-judgmental. **Mindfulness** means focusing on the here-and-now, rather than ruminating about the past, or entertaining anxieties and wishful thinking about the future. This means living *in* the present—*not for* the present. Mindfulness does not mean living for the moment without regard for the future. In this respect, mindfulness is similar to the present-centered awareness and activity-focused attention described by Csikszentmihalyi as "flow experience" (Csikszentmihalyi, 1990; Chapter 3). Secondly, while mindfulness may be a vehicle for self-analysis, it is oriented toward simply observing, rather than evaluating the self. In this regard, increasing mindfulness is analogous to increasing the sensitivity of a radar system that is not programmed to look for anything in particular. More objects are "seen," but what is seen is not constrained or biased by attention to some objects and not others. A radar operator can decide what is and what is not worth paying attention to. But the main advantage is the ability to "see" more of what is actually out there. It is this "seeing more" that makes mindfulness a potential antidote for the blunted awareness stemming from hectic lives, defensiveness in self-examination of faults, and unexamined cultural assumptions about how we should live. Instead of relying on habitual reactions and ways of thinking that fit current reality into pre-established boxes, mindfulness provides an opening for understanding "the way things *are*" before we judge, analyze, and evaluate.

This may seem like some idealized state of omnipotent knowing, but all of us have had times of great clarity and epiphany when we finally see what is really going on and what is really important. For many people such epiphanies result from dramatic events that force a rethinking of assumptions about the self and life. Death, loss, and tragedy, as we saw in Chapter 4, lead many people to see themselves and life more clearly. Before considering mindfulness meditation as a gentler and more gradual approach to many of these same ends, we will review some recent studies related to posttraumatic growth (PTG) and the changes in life values that may result from confrontations with death.

Focus on Research: Getting to Life's Bottom Line

Recall (from Chapter 4) the naturalistic studies showing that many people confronting life-threatening events report positive life benefits from such experiences (see Tedeschi, Park, & Calhoun, 1998, for a review). These events can include divorce, sexual assault, bone marrow transplants, cancer, heart attacks, HIV infection, house fires, and loss of a loved one. Researchers have also studied the aftermath of near-death experiences among people who were close to dying or who had been declared clinically dead. The pattern of positive growth that sometimes emerges following such crises involves a general shift from extrinsic values toward more intrinsic life values. People become less concerned about materialistic issues such as money, possessions, appearances, getting ahead and social status, and more focused on personal relationships, compassion for others, and transcendent meanings and purposes in life. Wealth and success often seem shallow and meaningless after a tragedy or a close brush with death. Many people also report increased feelings of autonomy, self-reliance, resilience, and a greater appreciation and zest for life. In short, confronting tragedy seems to shake up people's priorities so that the most important things in life—the bottom lines, so to speak—become much clearer. As you may have noticed, many of these new priorities and self-perceptions are in line with the life orientations of happy and healthy people identified by positive psychology research.

When posttraumatic growth (PTG) is discussed in your first author's positive psychology class, students reliably raise two questions. First, how long do the positive changes following tragedy last? Are they long-term, or is it back to life as usual fairly quickly? Secondly, students ask whether these changes can be achieved without confronting actual tragedy or threats to life and limb. Does it take tragedy to shake us out of our take-life-for-granted complacency and make us more mindful of what is important in life? Can we experience PTG vicariously, through imaginative thinking (e.g., of our own death)? Or does it require the real thing? Several recent studies suggest that the PTG changes may be relatively long-term and that PTG *can* be engendered through imagined experiences.

The two studies to be reviewed focused on an apparent contradiction between PTG (Chapter 4) research and terror management theory (Chapter 7). PTG research documents the change in life values that result from actual life-threatening events that bring people into acute awareness of their own mortality. Terror management theory and the work of Earnest Becker (*The Denial of Death*) argue that death awareness causes an opposite, defensive reaction driven by the need to reduce the anxiety associated with thinking about one's own inevitable mortality. Rather than changing life priorities, terror management theory predicts that death awareness causes us to reaffirm our beliefs and our sense of self-worth, and to seek feelings of security in material possessions and the accumulation of wealth. Put another way, PTG research supports the role of death awareness in producing shifts toward more intrinsic values and toward an acceptance of death. Terror management theory predicts that awareness of death reinforces extrinsic and materialistic values in an attempt to deny the reality of death.

Attempts to reconcile these contradictory predictions have focused on the very different death awareness experiences studied by PTG researchers, as compared to terror management researchers. Terror management researchers use a manipulation called **mortality salience** to create awareness of death. This might involve brief exposure to death-related scenes (e.g., a funeral home) and words. A common procedure involves simply asking people to write down their thoughts, feelings, and emotions when thinking about their own death. In contrast, PTG researchers study people who have actually experienced tragic and life-threatening events that cannot be duplicated in laboratory studies. As researches have noted, PTG is more concrete, more emotionally absorbing, and takes place over a much longer period of time, allowing a person to review his or her life through the lens of having nearly lost it (Cozzolino, Staples, Meyers, & Samboceti, 2004; Lykins, Segerstrom, Averill, Evans, & Kemeny, 2007). Studies by Cozzolino and colleagues (2004) and Lykins and associates (2007) have evaluated the importance of the severity of mortality threats, the duration of such threats, and the importance of life review in differentiating between PTG effects (i.e., shifts toward intrinsic values) and those predicted by terror management theory (i.e., affirmation of extrinsic values).

Lykins and her colleagues (2007) examined life value changes among California residents who experienced a major earthquake in 1994, and among college students who vicariously experienced, through media coverage, the 9/11 attacks on the World Trade Center in New York. Compared to appropriate control groups, people who directly or vicariously confronted events that were powerful reminders of their own mortality reported significant shifts away from extrinsic goals (related to money, appearances, and social status), and toward more intrinsic goals (involving cultivating close relationships, giving to others, and engaging in personal growth). Consistent with predictions, both the intensity of the perceived threat to life and the duration of the threat were related to the degree of shift in values. In the earthquake study, those who were most acutely aware that they could have died showed the strongest shift toward intrinsic values. In the 9/11 investigation, shifts toward more intrinsic values were most evident several months after the attack. Lykken and her colleagues argue that time factors and threat intensity are important in PTG and help distinguish PTG effects from those predicted by terror management theory. That is, defensive responses to death occur when exposure to threat is low-intensity and short-term. PTG requires a significant perception of threat to survival and takes time to develop, as people think about the event and reevaluate their life priorities. People's initial response to life-threatening events may be defensive. However, over time, continuing mortality awareness may contribute to positive psychological growth.

Cozzolino and his colleagues (2004) created a vicarious **death reflection** manipulation that paralleled the essential features of near-death experiences. The positive growth effects of near-death experiences are thought to result from life review processes and from taking the perspective of others. Life review and perspective-taking are based on reports of people who have had near-death experiences. Such individuals say they intensely relived their lives and their interactions with significant others. Reliving life through one's own eyes and through the eyes of others is thought to be responsible for the changes in life priorities and self-conceptions associated with near-death experiences.

Participants in the death reflection condition were asked to read and imagine the following event actually happening to them (Cozzolino et al., 2004, p. 290, Appendix A):

> Imagine that you are visiting a friend who lives on the 20th floor of an old, downtown apartment building. It's the middle of the night when you are suddenly awakened from a deep sleep by the sound of screams and the choking smell of smoke. You reach over to the nightstand and turn on the light. You are shocked to find the room filling fast with thick clouds of smoke. You run to the door and reach for the handle. You pull back in pain as the intense heat of the knob scalds you violently. Grabbing a blanket off the bed and using it as protection, you manage to turn the handle and open the door. Almost immediately, a huge wave of flame and smoke pours into the room, knocking you back and literally off your feet. There is no way to leave the room. It is getting very hard to breathe and the heat from the flames is almost unbearable. Panicked, you scramble to the only window in the room and try to open it. As you struggle, you realize that the old window is virtually painted shut around all the edges. It doesn't budge. Your eyes are barely open now, filled with tears from the smoke. You try calling for help but the air to form the words is not here. You drop to the floor hoping to escape the rising smoke, but it is too late. The room is filled top to bottom with thick fumes and nearly entirely in flames. With your heart pounding, it suddenly hits you, as time seems to stand still, that you are literally moments away from dying. The inevitable unknown that was always waiting for you has finally arrived. Out of breath and weak, you shut your eyes and wait for the end.

After reading this death scenario, participants were asked to answer the following questions (Cozzolino et al., 2004, p. 281):

> *1. Please describe in detail the thoughts and emotions you felt while imagining the scenario.*
>
> *2. If you did experience this event, how do you think you would handle the final moments?*
>
> *3. Again imagining it did happen to you, describe the life you led up to that point.*
>
> *4. How do you feel your family would react if it did happen to you?*

Questions 3 and 4 were meant to parallel the life review and perspective-taking described by individuals who have actually survived near-death experiences. Participants in the control conditions read and imagined more positive scenarios and were asked to write about their thoughts and feelings about the scenario in response to questions paralleling those of the death reflection condition.

In an additional study, PTG and terror management predictions were evaluated by comparing the effects of death reflection to those of mortality salience. In this "mortality salience" condition (following terror management research methodology), participants were simply asked to describe their thoughts and feelings regarding their own death.

The death reflection manipulation (imagining dying in a fire) was found to produce significant emotional and value changes in comparison to control and mortality salience conditions. Content analysis of participants' responses in the *death reflection* condition revealed a significant degree of life reflection that focused on regrets and thoughts about important people in their lives. Consistent with findings from near-death studies, the experience of imagining oneself dying in a fire appeared to prompt life review and taking the perspective of others. In addition, the death reflection caused people with a high extrinsic value orientation to become more intrinsically oriented as assessed by a behavioral measure of greediness (they were less likely to take more than their fair share of lottery tickets). As evidence for the power of the vicarious experience of death, consider the two quotes below (Cozzolino et al., 2004, p. 289):

> "I realize now that our time here is relatively short and it makes me want to live life to the fullest. It seems like such a waste of precious time to become caught up in materialistic modes of thinking."

> "I wondered if I had done all that I could to make my life meaningful. I thought of expressing to my family that I loved them. I wondered if there were people whose feelings I've hurt and I was sorry for that."

The first quote is from a man who had an actual near-death experience resulting from a river rafting accident. The second quote is from a research participant in the *death reflection* condition.

Lykins, Cozzolino, and their colleagues acknowledge the preliminary nature of their conclusions. Yet they offer suggestive answers to the two questions raised by students in the first author's positive psychology class. Do the effects of PTG last? Lykins and colleagues argue that the answer is likely, yes. As they note, "As intrinsic goal shifts appear to lead to the building of important resources (i.e., close relationships, feelings of competence), it is difficult to imagine that these effects would be transient. Thus, long-term changes in goal values appear possible as a link between confrontations with death and PTG" (Lykins et al., 2007, p. 1097).

Can PTG effects occur without confronting an actual life-threatening experience? Results of both studies reviewed here would suggest that the answer to this question is a qualified yes. Three conditions appear to increase the odds that reflecting on one's own mortality will increase awareness of life's bottom lines (i.e., what is most important). First, death reflection needs to occur over some period of time rather than being a quick consideration that will most likely produce defensive reactions. Second, thinking about mortality needs to prompt a life review in which death is incorporated into life and accepted, rather than denied. Third, it seems important that death reflection include consideration of how friends and family would respond to one's own death. One important bottom line of life involves our important, but often taken-for-granted connection to those who love us.

The connection between death awareness and our next topic—mindfulness—is made explicit in the concluding section of Cozzolino and colleagues' article. In considering the deeper existential-philosophic meanings of death awareness, Cozzolino and his colleagues (2004, p. 289) note that ". . . individuals can take one of two routes to existing in the world; one in which they are forgetful of being and one in which they are mindful of being." The first route means forgetfulness of the fact of death and leads people to immerse themselves in the everyday materialistic world. However, ". . . . people who are mindful of being are more apt to become intimately aware of their own existence and feel responsible for—and capable of—changing their lives. It is these persons who embrace their potential and become aware of their ability to transcend their limits" (Cozzolino et al., 2004, p. 289). The most significant limit to be transcended is our anxiety about the reality of death. Mindfulness and acceptance of death reduce the deleterious effects of fear and denial of death, thereby allowing people to live fuller and richer lives.

Mindfulness Meditation

Within Eastern philosophy (e.g., Buddhism, Taoism), mindfulness practice in the form of meditation and *zazen* (sitting) has a long tradition as one vehicle for enhancing clarity and well-being. An excellent introduction to Zen meditation and practice can be found in Shunryu Suzuki's book, *Zen Mind, Beginner's Mind* (1986). For an exploration of one man's journey through a year of "sitting and running," see Leo DiPorta's *Zen Running* (1977). An informative discussion of Buddhism and the psychology of well-being are provided by recent articles in *American Psychologist* by Walsh and Shapiro (2006) and by Wallace and Shapiro (2006). McIntosh (1997) provides an excellent review of the relationships between Zen Buddhism and social psychology. For the general reader, Kabat-Zinn's (1994), *Wherever You Go There You Are: Mindfulness Meditation in Everyday Life*, offers a highly accessible understanding of the purpose, value, and specific techniques of mindfulness practice. We will rely heavily on Kabat-Zinn's work in our review of mindfulness meditation. According to Walsh and Shapiro (2006), despite the diversity of Eastern meditative traditions, they share a common focus on attention and awareness (i.e., mindfulness): "The term *meditation* refers to a family of self-regulation practices that focus on training attention and awareness in order to bring mental processes under greater voluntary control and thereby foster general mental well-being and development and/or specific capacities such as calm, clarity and concentration" (p. 228, emphasis in original).

It is important to point out that even though mindfulness meditation training is an integral part of Eastern philosophies and religions, it is not in itself a religion, particularly as translated into Western psychology and culture. As Speca and his colleagues put it, ". . . Derived from what were originally and primarily religious or spiritual practices, meditation has been adapted for secular purposes" (Speca, Carlson, Goodey, & Angen, 2000). It does not require you to believe in anything—except perhaps yourself. In its secular form, mindfulness is a means of self-change through self-discovery, but its purpose is not to convert people to a particular set of doctrines. People

from a variety of religious traditions practice mindfulness. Kabat-Zinn (1990) points out that mindfulness is not a mystical or spiritual activity and it is not ". . . the 'answer' to all life's problems. Rather it is that all life's problems can be seen more clearly through a clear mind" (p. 26). Mindfulness meditation is actually quite practical and, at one level, even simple. It is not an all-encompassing activity that requires major changes in your everyday life routine. It is more like taking a walk every day, setting aside time to pray if you are religious, or taking time to step out of the hectic pace of life.

The basic idea of **mindfulness meditation** begins with an awareness that most of our waking consciousness is dominated by a steady stream of unexamined thoughts and feelings. The constant mental chatter of one thought after another consumes our mental energies and may distract us from what is actually taking place in the moment. Even though we live in the present, our minds frequently drift off to the past, or to anxieties about the future. Mentally removed from the here-and-now, people often imbue their thoughts with a sense of reality that they don't deserve—or perhaps more correctly, they fail to separate their thoughts from what is truly happening in the present. In its more extreme forms, this confusion of thoughts with reality is the basis for many kinds of pathology and many irrational fears, in which people's internal beliefs distort their perceptions in ways that are personally distressing. To a less extreme degree, living in our thoughts rather than in the present is a common part of everyday experience. Kabat-Zinn (1990) gives the example of someone whose attention is captured by a particularly beautiful sunset. Instead of savoring the moment, enjoying and taking in the fading sun and all its brilliant colors, the person describes his/her feelings to a companion and begins to think about similar sunsets observed in the past. Now, instead of experiencing the sunset as an unmediated sensory event, the person experiences the sunset through the filter of his/her thoughts and verbal descriptions. The actual sunset is lost in the person's thoughts *about* it. In line with this example, Langer (2002) argues that mindfulness involves an understanding that "events do not come with evaluations; we impose them on our experiences, and in so doing create our experience of the event" (p. 219). The point of mindfulness is to see the world before we judge, evaluate, and stuff it into preconceived categories and boxes.

The sunset experience described by Kabat-Zinn can be contrasted with the experience of an accomplished photographer or landscape artist who "sees" keenly what is actually there and finds ways to capture it. Famous nature photographers like Ansel Adams (1985) have the ability able to capture the subtleties and nuances of light, shadow, reflections, and human feelings that put the snapshots of the untrained eye to shame. Seasoned photographers may spend days waiting for the right combination of conditions, and may spend hours positioning themselves to get the right perspective and "feel" for a scene before shooting a photograph. In a similar vein, an informed sports fan sees more of what is going on during a game as a result of extensive knowledge and past observations. When the first author of your textbook was in graduate school, he remarked to a faculty member who was a devoted baseball fan that, while baseball was relaxing to watch, it was kind of boring. The professor's response was, "That's because you are utterly ignorant of the game!" He went on to explain the nuances of in-field and out-field adjustments for each batter's typical pattern of hitting, the way catchers call pitches to offset a batter's strengths, and how pitch sequencing can create a batter's expectations of the next pitch (which can be used to make the batter swing at a pitch outside the strike zone). After he finished, I did indeed feel like an ignorant fan! I had no idea so much was going on during a baseball game.

The point of these examples is twofold. First, mindfulness is not foreign to people's experience. We have all had experiences of living in the moment and probably each of us has an area of expertise or knowledge that makes us more attentive and aware than others in observing some aspect of life. Secondly, at one level, the purpose of mindfulness meditation is to extend the context of limited mindful experiences, like the ones described above, to develop a generalized ability to see life more clearly, in all its moment-to-moment richness and subtlety. Mindfulness as a personal quality is first cultivated gradually in the limited context of meditation, and then begins to transfer to other aspects of life. This is analogous to the common experience of immersing yourself in an intensive study and observation of a particular activity and finding that you can't help thinking of other life domains in new ways as a result of what you have learned. For example, your first author knows lifelong fly fishermen who began their trout fishing careers with only the enjoyment of the sport and the desire to catch fish. Over time, however, with increasing experience and knowledge, trout fishing mushroomed into an understanding of insect entomology, trout ecosystems, damage to the environment, and the necessity of protecting the environment. In addition, as partially captured in the film *A River Runs Through It*, flying fishing teaches discipline, patience, attention to detail and mindful awareness of changing environmental conditions, and the complexities of trout behavior. Skills and attitudes learned on the trout stream have a way of spilling over to all areas of life.

ATTRIBUTES OF MINDFUL AWARENESS Becoming more mindful through meditation involves setting aside a piece of time (perhaps 15 to 45 minutes a day), and a place to quiet the mind down and gain some insight into how thoughts control our experience. Although there are many forms of mindfulness practice, sitting and following your breath is perhaps the most common. Kabat-Zinn (1994) provides one of the more straightforward descriptions of mindfulness practice for a Western audience. You might sit on a cushion or pillow with legs crossed in front and hands on your knees, or in a straight-backed chair. You should be comfortable and a bit relaxed, but the head, back, and neck should align vertically so that you are alert to good posture. Then you focus your attention on your breathing, following your breath in and out without trying to control or change it, but just experiencing its ebb and flow. When your attention wanders away to something else, just note the occurrence and bring your attention back to your breathing. Beginning meditators often discover how difficult this seemingly simple task can be. The mind wells up an endless stream of distracting thoughts—discomfort, boredom, fantasies, memories from the past, plans for the future, thinking about your spouse, boss, work, vacation, what you need to do after this, and so forth. Our thoughts seem to have a life of their own, coming in an endless stream that is difficult to shut off, even for a few brief moments. As Kabat-Zinn (1990) tells his beginning meditation practitioners, whatever your mind brings to your attention, just acknowledge it and let it go. Don't judge or evaluate, just accept and return to your breath. The idea is to watch your thoughts rather than trying to suppress them.

As Shapiro and her colleagues argue "All meditation techniques are founded on the cultivation of attention. Attention by itself, however, is not enough" (Shapiro et al., 2002, p. 639). Kabat-Zinn (1990) describes seven interrelated attitudes that are important in understanding the purpose of mindful meditation. The purpose of mindfulness is to cultivate these seven qualities. By practicing them in small doses they begin to carry over into everyday life, increasing a person's general level of mindfulness.

1. Non-Judging

The basic idea of non-judging is to recognize that we continually evaluate things in our lives as "good" or "bad" when, in fact, most things, events, and people we encounter are not inherently so. Langer (2002) has pointed out that "things out there are not self-evidently good or bad," and that "the prevalence of value judgments in our lives reveals nothing about the world, but much about our minds" (p. 218). It is the lack of awareness of this fact that represents one important difference between mindlessness and mindful awareness. The point of mindfulness practice is not to stop our constant evaluation of the world, but to be aware that we are doing it. That is, it would be counterproductive to "judge the judging and make matters even more complicated for yourself" (Kabat-Zinn, 1990, p. 34). The value of non-judgment is that we see the world more clearly by recognizing that much of what we like and dislike is not literally true of the world. This does not mean that we should try to give up our preferences or take a completely neutral stance toward the world. That would be foolish and impossible. Rather, nonjudging makes us aware that our immediate responses are likely to be limited by our preferences. Langer's (1989) work has been devoted to showing that a significant benefit of mindfulness is opening people up to novel ways of thinking and dealing with life's problems. This opening-up occurs when we become aware that we frequently put the world into our little, preferential boxes. To use the popular catch phrase, mindfulness allows us to "think outside the box" of our own established patterns of thinking.

2. Patience

Patience means allowing events to unfold in their own time rather than always pushing, wishing, or working to make things happen according to our present desires. Kabat-Zinn gives the example of a child who opens a butterfly's cocoon hoping to help it emerge earlier. Of course, this is not good for the butterfly that is not yet fully formed or ready to emerge. Patience extends to oneself, others, and the present moment. Its value lies in making us more open to what is going on right now, in the present moment, and encouraging us to take comfort in the idea that things will develop in their own time—rushing ahead usually causes difficulties.

3. Beginner's Mind

Beginner's mind means an open mind that "is willing to see everything for the first time" (Kabat-Zinn, 1990, p. 35). A drawback of knowledge and familiarity is that we may begin to take things and activities for granted because we have seen them, done them, and think we understand them. What we "know" may deaden our sensitivity to seeing old things in new ways, or to appreciating how things change. This may happen with people, places, activities, and aspects of our environment. Perhaps you have passed an object such as a tree, building, or particular landscape every day without really looking; then one day you've noticed something unusual or interesting about it. This would be an example of seeing something very familiar as if for the first time. The value of an open beginner's mind is to see the world in its present richness and not just through our past experiences and understandings. Beginner's mind is an antidote for boredom and our seemingly insatiable need to see and do "new" things. Newness is always here. We just need to become aware of it.

4. Trust

Trust is captured in Shakespeare's familiar dictum, "To thine own self be true." Trust means taking responsibility for being yourself; some psychologists describe this as authenticity (Harter, 2002). Imitating others, trying to be someone other than who you are, and relying too much on others' ideas would all indicate a lack of trust in self. Trust is important because even if you make mistakes in the course of following your own intuitions and feelings, at least they are *your* mistakes. Learning about the self requires, first of all, that we try to *be* ourselves.

5. Non-striving

Non-striving is a slippery concept because it is often taken to mean a lack of desire and purpose, as if the goal of meditation is to eliminate desires, or to see them as trivial, or as roadblocks to some "higher" state of awareness. Kabat-Zinn focuses non-striving on the practice of mindful meditation. By this, he only means that people should take up mindfulness meditation without preconceived ideas regarding what will or should happen. Striving to achieve a particular result of meditation sets us up to make ongoing comparisons of what is happening against what we want or expect to happen. This distorts and forecloses the processes of discovering what actually *does* happen. Not to expect and not to strive creates a more receptive attitude to what mindfulness means for each individual.

6. Acceptance

Acceptance means being yourself rather than denying who you are, wishing you were different, or feeling bad because you aren't the person you would like to be. Acceptance does not mean passive resignation or losing the desire to change aspects of your self and your life. It means letting go of some of the tension caused by the constant comparison of who you are now and who you would like to be. Perhaps having some compassion for yourself is another way to put it. The value of acceptance is that "you are much more likely to know what to do and have an inner conviction to act when you have a clearer picture of what is actually happening than when your vision is clouded by your mind's self-serving judgments and desires or its fear and prejudices" (Kabat-Zinn, 1990, p. 39). In other words, acceptance is a basis for action—not an impediment.

7. Letting Go

Like non-striving and acceptance, letting go can easily be misinterpreted as giving up on, or renouncing life goals. In mindfulness meditation, "letting go" refers to practicing non-attachment to prominent thoughts and feelings. In meditation, people find that certain thoughts, feelings, and experiences occur more frequently or with greater emotional intensity. That is, there are certain things that "the mind seems to want to hold on to" (Kabat-Zinn, 1990, p. 39). People may hold onto some thoughts because they are pleasant or try to avoid others because they are upsetting. In meditation practice, such thoughts are simply noted and then let go, as attention returns to the breath. Letting go within meditation may set the stage for acceptance and more detached

consideration of why certain thoughts, fantasies, or experiences have such prominence in our mental life. It is useful to ask ourselves why we are so obsessed with a particular thought or past experience. This, in turn, may be a valuable source of self-insight.

Overall, mindfulness practice is a way to observe the processes of your own mind from a perspective akin to that of an outside, non-judgmental observer. This is quite a different experience than our usual state of conscious awareness, in which we often get caught up in our thoughts, feelings, and actions without much awareness of these mental preoccupations. Kabat-Zinn argues that the most dramatic effect of mindfulness meditation among his practitioners is the realization that *they* are not their thoughts. "It is remarkable how liberating it feels to be able to see that your thoughts are just thoughts and that they are not 'you' or 'reality' " (Kabat-Zinn, 1990, p. 69). This realization allows people to consciously choose how they respond or do not respond to their thoughts about themselves and the world they live in. Mindfulness helps us distinguish between reality and illusion—that is, between the world as experienced through our self-generated thoughts, and the world as it *is*. If you are considering trying mindfulness meditation, it is important to have help from experienced practitioners. Most large cities have Zen and other meditation centers and the Internet can be very helpful. For example, Kabat-Zinn's web site offers numerous instructional tapes and print resources.

Mindfulness and Positive Psychology Research

A recent review (Shapiro et al., 2002) notes that considerable research has been devoted to examining the well-being benefits of mindfulness meditation of the sort described by Kabat-Zinn (see also Walsh & Shapiro, 2006). Despite concerns about the scientific rigor and datedness of early studies, Shapiro and her colleagues believe they represent a hopeful beginning that supports the value of mindfulness in improving positive health and well-being. In addition to emotional and physical health benefits (such as relaxation and more effective coping with illness, stress, and pain), studies have also connected mindfulness meditation to increased self-actualization; a positive sense of control; emotional maturity and autonomy; and heightened alertness, concentration, and attention. More directly related to the goals of positive psychology, Shapiro and her colleagues note studies showing that even brief mindfulness meditation training (1 to 6 weeks) was found to be associated with increased self-esteem, happiness, daily positive affect, and personality growth, as assessed by the Big Five personality factors. Specifically, researchers have found increases in extraversion, agreeableness, openness to experience, emotional stability, self-esteem, happiness, and daily positive affect. Mindfulness has also been related to enhanced interpersonal behaviors such as empathy and trust, and to greater receptivity to spiritual concerns and experiences. These researchers concluded that "meditation appears to enhance physiological, psychological and transpersonal well-being. Specific enhancements observed include physiological rest and increased happiness, acceptance, sense of coherence, stress hardiness, empathy and self-regulation. Thus meditation may help human beings identify and actualize their potentials" (Shapiro et al., 2002, p. 638). However, they also note the need for more systematic and well-controlled explorations of the mechanisms linking mindfulness to enhanced well-being.

Recent studies by Brown and Ryan (2003, 2004) may exemplify the kind of research needed in order to address the limitations of previous studies. As noted in our previous discussion of mindfulness as an antidote to mindlessness, Brown and Ryan approach mindfulness from the perspective of self-determination theory, specifically the ability of mindfulness to facilitate autonomous and self-regulated actions. Using well-established measures, these researchers have defined mindfulness clearly, operationalized and validated its measurement and shown, in well-controlled studies, a relationship between mindfulness and improved well-being. Mindfulness is defined as "an open or receptive awareness of and attention to what is taking place in the present moment" (Brown & Ryan, 2004, p. 116).

Brown and Ryan have taken an individual differences approach to mindfulness on the assumption that people vary in their characteristic levels of "present-centered" awareness. That is, some people are more mindful than others, whether or not they have had any kind of mindfulness

training. In a series of studies, these researchers developed and validated a Mindful Attention Awareness Scale (MAAS). Perhaps because examples of mindlessness are more common and easier to discern than mindfulness, Brown and Ryan (2003) found that statistically, the best way to measure mindfulness was indirectly. In other words, they measure mindfulness in terms of the absence of mindless behaviors. This may seem problematic, but validating studies strongly suggest that the scale does indeed measure the presence mindfulness. Respondents rate the frequency of their experiences with instances of mindlessness on a 1–6 scale (where 1 = almost always and 6 = almost never). Sample items from the 15-item MAAS scale are given below (Brown & Ryan, 2003, p. 826):

- "I could be experiencing some emotion and not be conscious of it until some time later."
- "I find it difficult to stay focused on what's happening in the present."
- "I tend not to notice feelings of physical tension or discomfort until they really grab my attention."
- "It seems I am 'running on automatic' without much awareness of what I'm doing."
- "I rush through activities without really being attentive to them."
- "I get so focused on the goal I want to achieve that I lose touch with what I am doing right now to get there."
- "I find myself listening to someone with one ear, doing something else at the same time."
- "I find myself preoccupied with the future or the past."
- "I snack without being aware that I'm eating."

Evaluated in diverse samples, the MAAS has shown good test-retest reliability and meaningful patterns of positive and negative correlations with measures of other, related experiences, such as self-consciousness, self-monitoring, rumination-reflection, absorption, and openness to experience. The MAAS shows a strong positive relationship to other scales dealing with attention, clarity of experience, and active life engagement. In line with the present-centered nature of mindfulness, the MAAS was weakly or negatively related to measures of rumination (rehashing events and experiences) and self-consciousness. Mindfulness is significantly related to measures of both subjective and eudaimonic well-being, and negatively correlated with negative affectivity.

Consistent with the predicted relationship between mindfulness and autonomy as described by self-determination theory (SDT), the MAAS was positively related to measures of autonomy, competence, and relatedness. In addition, an alternative form of the MAAS with items written in the mindfulness direction (i.e., endorsement indicates the *presence* of mindfulness) correlated highly with the MAAS scale ($r = 0.7$). Overall, these results suggest that people high in mindfulness are more aware of both their inner experiences and their overt behavior, and are more likely to report fulfillment of their basic psychological needs as specified by SDT. Perhaps as a consequence, they enjoy a higher level of well-being than those who score low in mindfulness.

Further validating studies showed that (1) students actively practicing Zen mindfulness training scored significantly higher on the MAAS scale than a matched community sample; (2) people high in mindfulness showed greater concordance between their consciously controlled, explicit emotional reactions and their implicit, intuitive, and unconscious reactions; (3) day-to-day state increases in mindfulness were related to increased autonomy and lower levels of negative affect; and (4) mindfulness training reduced levels of mood disturbance and stress among people dealing with prostate and breast cancer. Brown and Ryan (2003) conclude that ". . . mindfulness is a reliably and validly measured characteristic that has a significant role to play in a variety of aspects of mental health. Further research into this attribute may open up significant new avenues for well-being enhancement" (p. 844).

In its most general form, mindfulness might be considered a foundation for the many well-being enhancement interventions that are built on increased self-understanding. What many interventions may share is their ability to cultivate a mindful awareness that leads people to become more self-aware, more focused on the present, more conscious of the conditions of their lives, and how consciously-chosen actions might improve well-being. For example, when people are asked to practice gratitude, forgive others, write about meaningful goals, or engage in intentional activities that are personally expressive, they presumably "discover" something important about themselves and what makes them happy and healthy. Mindfulness may cultivate a kind of consciousness that is more receptive to these "discoveries."

Mindfulness and Psychotherapy

Why does increased mindfulness improve well-being? Walsh and Shapiro (2006) argue that a major reason may be the "refined awareness" that meditation practices share with many forms of psychotherapies. As they note, the idea that heightened awareness is, in itself, a healing and health-promoting quality is central to both Eastern meditative traditions and Western psychotherapies. Observing the self clearly and setting aside the blinders of habit and reflexive emotional responses are considered foundations for healthy functioning in both the East and the West.

As a practicing psychotherapist, your second author sees firsthand the close connection between mindfulness and psychotherapy. When life presents hardships, troubling situations, or traumatic experiences, it's easy to get caught up in our distressing emotions, or in the anxiety of struggling to cope. We often resort to "defense mechanisms," which are very adaptive in the short haul because they allow us to continue functioning through crises and highly emotional circumstances. But over the long haul, defense mechanisms, if used rigidly and in excess, can rob us of the opportunity to cope with hardships in a straightforward manner that will promote healing. We end up expending so much energy to hold our defenses in place that little energy remains available for more direct coping.

In essence, psychotherapy is a form of mindfulness coaching. A client may enter treatment deeply immersed in a troubling situation and struggling to hold his or her life together. When people are in such situations, they have a strong tendency to cope defensively, avoiding their feelings at all cost. They fear that if they allow themselves to really feel their emotions fully, they will become overwhelmed and incapacitated. They experience their own powerful emotion as "the enemy," which needs to be vanquished. The skillful psychotherapist provides reassurance that the client can dare to feel his or her emotions without fear of losing control.

Clients are often surprisingly unaware of their own feelings until they try to communicate them to the psychotherapist. Sometimes, just hearing themselves speak aloud about strong emotions leads to heightened mindfulness. Other times, defenses are so thick that the therapist needs to assist the client in truly hearing himself. This can often be accomplished using the most basic and time-honored of all therapeutic skills—simple reflection. It is the psychotherapist's craft to be keenly attentive to both the spoken and unspoken aspects of human communication, and to reflect these back as accurately as possible, as if holding up a mirror so the client can become self-aware. Countless times, I listen as a client describes deeply emotional material in a tone that suggests an almost complete absence of emotion. A gentle, well-placed reflection often allows the client to get in touch with the emotion that has been walled off. Tears often flow at moments like this, and such moments can be profoundly challenging and painful; but it is precisely these difficult moments that often turn out to be the pivot points in therapy, because once the true emotions are acknowledged, the energy the client has been deploying to hold emotions at bay becomes available for the work of healing. What has occurred, in essence, is that the psychotherapist has invited the client to enter a state of mindfulness—a state in which strong emotion is acknowledged, accepted, and embraced. Once there, the therapist provides encouragement for the client to "stay with the feeling" rather than recoiling into a defensive stance. Clients often emerge from these periods of intense mindfulness with calm expressions of surprise that they did not become incapacitated by the emotion, that they weathered it quite well, and that they feel a sense of relief and wholeness that was absent before, while they were working so hard to suppress their emotions.

Frederick Perls developed a therapeutic approach known as Gestalt psychotherapy (Perls, 1969). This approach is based upon the idea that psychological problems arise when we split off parts of ourselves, refusing to acknowledge personality characteristics and emotions that we deem unsavory or distressing. The goal of Gestalt therapy is to heighten the client's awareness of emotions and personality aspects that have been disowned—to restore wholeness. This is simply another specialized language for describing a specific type of increased mindfulness.

A final example of the connection between mindfulness and psychotherapy is Aaron Beck's classic work on the cognitive underpinnings of depression and his development of cognitive therapy as an effective treatment (Beck, 1967; Beck, Rush, Shaw, & Emery, 1979). Beck found that many depressed patients were locked into a particular, negative way of interpreting their experiences that fed their depressed emotional state. Research has shown that depressed people tend to believe they are responsible for the bad things that happen to them. They see the worst in every situation and feel they have little control over the occurrence of unpleasant experiences (Abramson, Metalsky, & Alloy, 1989; Alloy & Abramson, 1979; Seligman, 1975). Cognitive therapy helps patients to see how their interpretations of an experience (rather than the experience itself) contribute to their depression. In some cases, this involves giving specific homework assignments in which people note their immediate reactions to emotional events during the day, along with their underlying thought patterns. Then, they are encouraged to think of alternative explanations that are less toxic and self-defeating.

A telltale sign of emotional problems is when little things become big things. A depressed person, anticipating a call from a significant other, may believe that not getting the call means the person does not care about him. For example, the person may think, "one more case of failed relationship." Or, "when people get to know me they don't like what they see." The point of cognitive therapy is to become aware of these irrational, depressing explanations and to think of more rational ones, like "maybe she had to work late," or "maybe she is waiting for me to call her." Becoming more aware through cognitive therapy is quite similar to becoming more mindful through meditation. Both lead to new insights regarding the ways our thoughts can determine our "reality." These insights may result from a process called **disidentification,** which is described in meditative practice, but which also seems to apply to cognitive and other therapies (Walsh & Shapiro, 2006). Disidentification means observing oneself closely and stopping the process of identifying with one's thoughts rather than with reality. As we disidentify with our thoughts, they lose their power to control our reactions, thereby allowing us to see more clearly the difference between what *is* actually happening and our *interpretations* of what is happening.

In short, many psychotherapy approaches have the goal of heightening, clarifying, and increasing the accuracy of the client's self-awareness, to enable the client to see self and situation clearly. Then, from this new position of clear self-understanding, self-acceptance, and acknowledgment and "owning" of one's full emotional experience, healing and growth begin to occur quite naturally and spontaneously.

Eastern meditative practices are meant to go beyond the specific problems that are the focus of Western psychotherapy. They are meant to be an approach to improving the well-being of life as a whole (Wallace & Shapiro, 2006; Walsh & Shapiro, 2006). The processes by which mindfulness improves health and happiness seems to have much in common with the kinds of mechanisms exemplified in cognitive therapeutic approaches to depression. Despite its Eastern origins and unfamiliarity in the West, mindfulness may not be as "mysterious" or "foreign" to Western understandings as it may initially appear.

EAST–WEST AND POSITIVE PSYCHOLOGY

As Eastern philosophic and Buddhist meditative traditions were translated and imported into Western culture and psychology, much of their original purpose and context were stripped away. "As a result, in the vast majority of meditation studies, the focus has been on the content of meditation as a generic, replicable technique that is independent of the religious and philosophical *context* within which it was embedded historically" (Shapiro et al., 2002, p. 39, emphasis in original). Buddhism, in all its complex forms, offers both an image of a good life and suggestions about how to achieve it. The meaning of happiness and a balanced life, and their ability to promote mental health are extensively described in Buddhist writings. The Dalai Lama commented that "the purpose of our life is to seek happiness" (the Dalai Lama in Dalai Lama & Cutler, 1998, p. 15, as quoted in Wallace & Shapiro, 2006, p. 691).

Positive psychology has recently moved from describing and defining the meaning of a good life to exploring ways to achieve it. Eastern philosophy offers a comprehensive picture of both the "what" and the "how" of a good life. Several authors have suggested that Eastern ideas of health and happiness, along with approaches to achieving them,

may represent a fruitful research agenda for the future in positive psychology (McIntosh, 1997; Shapiro et al., 2002; Wallace & Shapiro, 2006). Some advocates of the mindfulness approach to well-being suggest that positive psychology lacks depth and takes a piecemeal and indirect approach to improving well-being. As one critic remarked, "if the walls of your house are in decay it doesn't make much sense to put new vinyl siding on it just to make it look good" (L. Rappoport, personal communication, June 14, 2007). It makes more sense to examine and fix the basic structure first. Mindfulness may be one way to examine and alter the basic structure of self so that improvements and changes are built on a solid foundation that is more likely to last. Mindfulness appears to cultivate many of the personal qualities associated with a fully functioning person, as described by classic humanistic psychology and by recent work in positive psychology. More than one author has suggested that mindfulness in both its Western and Eastern forms may provide an overarching perspective for thinking about the meaning of well-being and ways to achieve it (e.g., Brown & Ryan, 2003, 2004; Demick, 2000; Kabat-Zinn, 1990, 1994; McIntosh, 1997; Wallace & Shapiro, 2006; Walsh & Shapiro, 2006).

However, it is also undoubtedly true that there are many routes to well-being. If, as Buddhist philosophy suggests, the Buddha is indeed everywhere (which is to say that opportunities for enlightened awareness are all around us), then well-practiced, specific, and targeted changes may open up a larger awareness to improved well-being. Like a naturalist whose eyes are opened to a larger view of life by observing nature, intensive practice in one domain of life may spread to others.

One seductively appealing aspect of mindfulness as an approach to well-being is that it begins with a simple prescription that we are all capable of following—one that may be particularly important in cultural life today, when so much information is available to us and so many people and activities compete for our attention, time, and energies. We can easily lose ourselves in the hectic and frantic pace of life and be pushed along by external pressures, rather than consciously following our idea of a good life. Mindfulness reminds us to slow down a bit and to be more aware of what is going on in our minds and in the world around us. Above all, mindfulness reminds us to pay attention!

Chapter Summary Questions

1. In contrast to traditional psychology, what is the meaning of happiness and health when described as "life above zero?"
2. How did Cory Keyes create a continuum of mental health and overcome the limitations of defining health as the absence of illness?
3. According to your textbook authors, what is genuinely new about positive psychology?
4. What are the three elements of a "good life," according to Seligman? Briefly describe each element.
5. According to Lyubomirsky and colleagues, what are the major barriers to increasing people's level of happiness?
6. a. How might intentional activities and self-concordant goals help increase long-term happiness?
   b. What are the limitations and qualifications concerning the possibility of an "upward spiral of well-being?"
7. What are the major elements of positive psychotherapy and how successful is this approach in treating depression, according to studies by Seligman and his colleagues?
8. What is Well-Being Therapy, and how is it based on a modification of Ryff's six-dimensional model of psychological well-being?
9. a. What behaviors and ways of thinking are involved in "minding" close relationships?

   b. Why is authenticity important to successful "minding?"
10. What characterizes mindlessness and how does automaticity contribute to this mental state?
11. How may mindful awareness be analogous to increasing the sensitivity of a radar system so that more is "seen" in an unbiased and non-judgmental manner?
12. a. What is the difference between PTG effects and the effects of mortality salience as related to terror management theory?
    b. What conditions seem to be necessary in order for vicarious experiences of death to have effects similar to those shown in PTG?
13. a. What is the purpose of mindfulness meditation?
    b. What are the seven major attributes of mindfulness meditation, according to Kabat-Zinn?
14. How is mindfulness defined by the Mindful Attention Awareness Scale developed by Brown and Ryan?
15. From the perspective of self-determination theory, why does mindfulness increase well-being?
16. What do mindfulness training and psychotherapy therapy have in common?
17. How might Eastern philosophical traditions enhance positive psychology's ideas about the meaning and the means of a good life?

Key Terms

mental illness *270*
flourishing *270*
moderate mental health *270*
languishing *270*
pleasant life *272*
engaged life *273*
meaningful life *273*

positive psychotherapy (PPT) *275*
mindlessness *280*
mindfulness *281*
mortality salience *282*
death reflection *283*
mindfulness meditation *285*
non-judging *287*

patience *287*
beginner's mind *287*
trust *287*
non-striving *287*
acceptance *288*
letting go *288*
disidentification *291*

Web Resources

Values in Action Project

www.viastrengths.org/index.aspx?ContentID=1 Web site for the Values in Action Project. Follow the links to VIA Measurement Instruments and you can register (free) to take a long or brief version of the character strength inventories. This will give you a profile of your "signature" character strengths. You do have to provide demographic information that is used along with your responses in an online study of character strengths.

Authentic Happiness

www.authentichappiness.sas.upenn.edu This is Martin Seligman's site at the University of Pennsylvania. The same VIA Project measures of character strengths are available on this site. You can also get a complete testing profile to assess your overall happiness and character strengths. You must log in, create a password, and provide demographic information to take the tests and have them scored for you. A profile of scores on all tests is computed and can be accessed at anytime.

Mindfulness

A number of informative sites are found with mindfulness as the search term. Many of these are related to Eastern meditative practices. Those tied to Western academic psychology are listed below *www.umassmed.edu/cfm/index.aspx*

This is the site for the Center for Mindfulness in Medicine Health Care and Society (CFM) at the University of Massachusetts Medical School. This is an extensive and highly informative site for understanding mindfulness and health-enhancing benefits. *www.umassmed.edu/behavmed/faculty/kabat-zinn.cfm*

This is Kabat-Zinn's site, also at the University of Massachussetts Medical School. Contains information about Kabat-Zinn's groundbreaking studies and therapeutic uses of mindfulness meditation.

Suggested Readings

Brown, W. K., & Ryan, R. M. (2003). The benefits of being present: Mindfulness and its role in psychological well-being. *Journal of Personality and Social Psychology, 84*, 822–848.

Harvey, J. H., & Omarzu, J. (1999). *Minding the close relationship: A theory of relationship enhancement.* New York: Cambridge University Press.

Kabat-Zinn, J. (1990). *Full catastrophe living: Using the wisdom of your body and mind to face stress, pain and illness.* New York, Delacourt.

Kabat-Zinn, J. (1994). *Wherever you go there you are: Mindfulness meditation in everyday life.* New York: Hyperion.

Keyes, C. L. M. (2005). Mental illness and/or mental health? Investigating the axioms of the complete state of mental health. *Journal of Counseling and Clinical Psychology, 73*, 539–548.

Keyes, C. L. M. (2007). Promoting and protecting mental health and flourishing: A complementary strategy for improving national mental health. *American Psychologist, 62*, 95–108.

Langer, E. J. (1989). *Mindfulness.* Reading, MA: Addison-Wesley.

Lyubomirsky, S., Sheldon, K. M., & Schkade, D. (2005). Pursuing happiness: The architecture of sustainable change. *Review of General Psychology, 9*, 111–131.

Ryff, C. D., & Singer, B. (1998). The contours of positive human health. *Psychological Inquiry, 9*, 1–28.

Seligman, M. E. P., Rashid, T., & Parks, A. C. (2006). Positive psychotherapy. *American Psychologist, 61*, 774–788.

Seligman, M. E. P., Steen, T. A., Park, N., & Peterson, C. (2005). Positive psychology progress: Empirical validation of interventions. *American Psychologist, 60*, 410–421.

Wallace, B. A., & Shapiro, S. L. (2006). Mental balance and well-being: Building bridges between Buddhism and Western psychology. *American Psychologist, 61*, 690–701.

Walsh, R., & Shapiro, S. L. (2006). The meeting of meditative disciplines and Western psychology. *American Psychologist, 61*, 227–239.

REFERENCES

Abramson, L. Y., Metalsky, G. I., & Alloy, L. B. (1989). Hopelessness depression: A theory-based subtype of depression. *Psychological Review, 96*, 358–372.

Abramson, L. Y., Seligman, M. E. P., & Teasdale, J. D. (1978). Learned Helplessness in humans: Critique and reformulation. *Journal of Abnormal Psychology, 87*, 49–74.

Adams, A. (1985). *Ansel Adams: An autobiography.* Boston: Little, Brown.

Affleck, G., & Tennen, H. (1996). Construing benefits from adversity: Adaptational significance and dispositional underpinnings. *Journal of Personality, 64*, 899–902.

Affleck, G., Tennen, H., & Apter, A. (2002). Optimism, pessimism, and daily life with chronic illness. In E. C. Chang (Ed.), *Optimism & pessimism: Implications for theory, research, and practice* (pp. 147–168). Washington, DC: American Psychological Association.

Ainsworth, M. D. S. (1989). Attachments beyond infancy. *American Psychologist, 44*, 709–716.

Ainsworth, M. D. S., Blehar, M. C., Waters, E., & Wall, S. (1978). *Patterns of attachment: A psychological study of the strange situation.* Hillsdale, NJ: Lawrence Erlbaum.

Allgeier, E. R., & Wiederman, M. W. (1991). Love and mate selection in the 1990s. *Free Inquiry, 11*, 25–27.

Alloy, L. B., & Abramson, L. Y. (1979). Judgment of contingency in depressed and nondepressed students: Sadder but wiser? *Journal of Experimental Psychology: General, 108*, 441–485.

Allport, G. W. (1937). *Personality: A psychological interpretation.* New York: Holt.

Allport, G. W. (1958). *The nature of prejudice* (abridged). Garden City, NY: Anchor Books.

Allport, G. W., & Ross, J. M. (1967). Personal religious orientation and prejudice. *Journal of Personality and Social Psychology, 5*, 432–443.

Altman, I. (1973). Reciprocity of interpersonal exchange. *Journal for the Theory of Social Behavior, 3*, 249–261.

Altman, I., & Taylor, D. A. (1973). *Social penetration: The development of interpersonal relationships.* New York: Holt Rinehart & Winston.

Amato, P. R., & Previti, D. (2003). People's reasons for divorcing: Gender, social class, the life course, and adjustment. *Journal of Family Issues, 24*, 602–624.

American Psychiatric Association (2000). *Diagnostic and statistical manual of mental disorders* (4th ed., Text Rev.). Washington, DC: Author.

Ames, E. W. (1997). *The development of Romanian orphanage children adopted to Canada* (Final report to the National Welfare Grants Program: Human Resources Development Canada). Burnaby, British Columbia, Canada: Simon Fraser University.

Andrews, F. M., & Robinson, J. P. (1992). Measures of subjective well-being. In J. P. Robinson, P. R. Shaver, & L. S. Wrightsman (Eds.), *Measures of personality and social psychological attitudes* (pp. 61–114). San Diego, CA: Academic Press.

Andrews, F. M., & Withey, S. B. (1976). *Social indicators of well-being: Americans' perception of life quality.* New York: Plenum Press.

Antonucci, T., & Jackson, J. (1983). Physical health and self-esteem. *Family and Community Health, 6*, 1–9.

Archer, J. (2005). Are women or men the more aggressive sex? In S. Fein, G. R. Goethals, & M. J. Sanderstrom (Eds.), *Gender and aggression: Interdisciplinary perspectives.* Mahwah, NJ: Lawrence Erlbaum.

Archer, J., & Coyne, S. M. (2005). An integrated review of indirect, relational, and social aggression. *Personality and Social Psychology Review, 9*, 212–230.

Arendt, H. (1963). *Eichman in Jerusalem: A report on the banality of evil.* New York: Viking Press.

Argyle, M. (1999). Causes and correlates of happiness. In D. Kahneman, E. Diener, & F. Strack (Eds.), *Well-being: The foundations of hedonic psychology* (pp. 353–373). New York: Russell Sage Foundation.

Argyle, M. (2001). *The psychology of happiness* (2nd ed.). Great Britain: Routledge.

Argyle, M., & Henderson, M. (1984). The rules of friendship. *Journal of Social and Personal Relationships, 1*, 211–237.

Argyle, M., & Henderson, M. (1985). *The anatomy of relationships.* London: Penguin Books.

Aron, A., Aron, E. N., & Smollan, D. (1992). Inclusion of Other in the Self Scale and the structure of interpersonal closeness. *Journal of Personality and Social Psychology, 63*, 596–612.

Aron, A., Melinat, E., Aron, E. N., Vallone, R. D., & Bator, R. (1997). The experimental generation of interpersonal closeness: A procedure and some preliminary findings. *Personality and Social Psychology Bulletin, 23*, 363–377.

Aron, A., Norman, C. C., Aron, E. N., McKenna, C., & Heyman, R. E. (2000). Couples' shared participation in novel and arousing activities and experienced relationship quality. *Journal of Personality and Social Psychology, 78*, 273–284.

Aron, A., & Westbay, L. (1996). Dimensions of the prototype of love. *Journal of Personality and Social Psychology, 70*, 535–551.

Arroyo, C. G., & Zigler, E. (1995). Racial identity, academic achievement, and the psychological well-being of economically disadvantaged adolescents. *Journal of Personality and Social Psychology, 69*, 903–914.

Aspinwall, L. G. (1998). Rethinking the role of positive affect in self-regulation. *Motivation and Emotion, 22*, 1–32.

Aspinwall, L. G., Richter, L., & Hoffman-III, R. R. (2002). Understanding how optimism works: An examination of optimists' adaptive moderation of belief and behavior. In E. C. Chang (Ed.), *Optimism & pessimism: Implications for theory, research, and practice* (pp. 217–238). Washington, DC: American Psychological Association.

Aspinwall, L. G., & Staudinger, U. M. (Eds.). (2003). *A psychology of human strengths: Fundamental questions and future directions for a positive psychology.* Washington, DC: American Psychological Association.

Aspinwall, L. G., & Taylor, S. E. (1992). Modeling cognitive adaptation: A longitudinal investigation of the impact of individual differences and coping on college adjustment and performance. *Journal of Personality and Social Psychology, 63*, 989–1003.

Aspinwall, L. G., & Taylor, S. E. (1997). A stitch in time: Self-regulation and proactive coping. *Psychological Bulletin, 99*, 229–246.

Austin, J. T., & Vancouver, J. B. (1996). Goal constructs in psychology: Structure, process, and content. *Psychological Bulletin, 120*, 338–375.

Baltes, P. B. (1993). The aging mind: Potential and limits. *Gerontologist, 33*, 580–594.

Baltes, P. B. (1997). On the incomplete architecture of human ontogeny: Selection, optimization, and compensation as foundation of developmental theory. *American Psychologist, 52*, 366–380.

Baltes, P. B., & Baltes, M. M. (Eds.). (1990). *Successful aging: Perspectives from the behavioral sciences.* New York: Cambridge University Press.

Baltes, P. B., & Freund, A. M. (2003a). Human strengths as the orchestration of wisdom and selective optimization with compensation. In L. G. Aspinwall & U. M. Staudinger (Eds.), *A psychology of human strengths: Fundamental questions and future directions for a positive psychology* (pp. 23–35). Washington, DC: American Psychological Association.

Baltes, P. B., & Freund, A. M. (2003b). The intermarriage of wisdom and selective optimization with compensation: Two meta-heuristics guiding the conduct of life. In C. L. M. Keyes & J. Haidt (Eds.), *Flourishing: Positive psychology and the life well-lived* (pp. 249–273). Washington, DC: American Psychological Association.

Baltes, P. B., Gluck, J., & Kunzman, U. (2002). Wisdom: Its structure and function in regulating successful life span development. In C. R. Snyder & S. J. Lopez (Eds.), *Handbook of positive psychology* (pp. 327–346). New York: Oxford University Press.

Baltes, P. B., & Smith, J. (1990). The psychology of wisdom and its ontogenesis. In R. J. Sternberg (Ed.), *Wisdom: Its nature, origins and development* (pp. 8–120). New York: Cambridge University Press.

Baltes, P. B., & Staudinger, U. M. (2000). Wisdom: A meta-heuristic (pragmatic) to orchestrate mind and virtue towards excellence. *American Psychologist, 55*, 122–136.

Bandura, A. (1977). Self-efficacy: Toward a unifying theory of behavioral change. *Psychological Review, 84*, 191–215.

Bandura, A. (1997). *Self-efficacy: The exercise of control.* New York: W.H. Freeman.

Bandura, A. (1999). A sociocognitive analysis of substance abuse: An agentic perspective. *Psychological Science, 10*, 214–218.

Bargh, J. A. (1996). Principles of automaticity. In E. T. Higgins & A. Kruglanski (Eds.), *Social psychology: Handbook of basic principles* (pp. 169–183). New York: Guilford Press.

Bargh, J. A., & Chartrand, T. L. (1999). The unbearable automaticity of being. *American Psychologist, 54*, 462–479.

Barrett, L. M. (2006). Solving the emotion paradox: Categorization and the experience of emotions. *Personality and Social Psychology Review, 10*, 20–46.

Bartholomew, K. (1990). Avoidance of intimacy: An attachment perspective. *Journal of Personal and Social Relationships, 7*, 147–178.

Bartholomew, K., & Horowitz, L. M. (1991). Attachment styles among young adults: A test of a four-category model. *Journal of Personality and Social Psychology, 61*, 226–244.

Bartholomew, K., & Shaver, P. R. (1998). Measures of attachment: Do they converge? In J. A. Simpson & W. S. Rholes (Eds.), *Attachment theory and close relationships* (pp. 25–45). New York: Guildford Press.

Batson, C. D., Schoenrade, P., & Ventis, W. L. (1993). *Religion and the individual: A social-psychological perspective.* New York: Oxford University Press.

Baumeister, R. F. (1990). Suicide as escape from self. *Psychological Review, 97*, 90–113.

Baumeister, R. F. (1991). *Meanings of life.* New York: Guilford Press.

Baumeister, R. F. (1992). *Self-esteem: The puzzle of low self-regard.* New York: Plenum Press.

Baumeister, R. F. (1998). The self. In D. T. Gilbert, S. T. Fiske, & G. Lindzey (Eds.), *The handbook of social psychology* (4th ed., Vol. 1, pp. 680–740). New York: McGraw-Hill.

Baumeister, R. F. (Ed.). (1999). *The self in social psychology.* Philadelphia, PA: Psychology Press.

Baumeister, R. F., & Bratslavsky, E. (1999). Passion, intimacy and time: Passionate love as a function of change in intimacy. *Personality and Social Psychology Review, 3*, 49–67.

Baumeister, R. F., Bratslavsky, E., Finkenauer, C., & Vohs, K. D. (2001). The bad is stronger than the good. *Review of General Psychology, 5*, 323–370.

Baumeister, R. F., Bratslavsky, E., Muraven, M., & Tice, D. M. (1998). Ego-depletion: Is the active self a limited resource? *Journal of Personality and Social Psychology, 74*, 1252–1265.

Baumeister, R. F., Campbell, J. D., Krueger, J. I., & Vohs, K. D. (2003). Does high self-esteem cause better performance, interpersonal success, happiness, or healthier lifestyles? *Psychological Science in the Public Interest, 4*, 1–44.

Baumeister, R. F., Campbell, J. D., Krueger, J. I., & Vohs, K. D. (2005). Exploding the self-esteem myth. *Scientific American, 292*, 84–91.

Baumeister, R. F., & Exline, J. J. (1999). Virtue, personality, and social relations: Self-control as a moral muscle. *Journal of Personality, 67*, 1165–1194.

Baumeister, R. F., Heatherton, T. F., & Tice, D. M. (1994). *Losing control: How and why people fail at self-regulation.* San Diego, CA: Academic Press.

Baumeister, R., & Leary, M. R. (1995). The need to belong: Desire for interpersonal attachments as a fundamental human motivation. *Psychological Bulletin, 117*, 497–529.

Baumeister, R. F., Tice, D. M., & Hutton, D. G. (1989). Self-presentational motivations and personality differences in self-esteem. *Journal of Personality and Social Psychology, 57*, 547–579.

Baumeister, R., & Vohs, K. D. (2002). The pursuit of meaningfulness in life. In C. R. Snyder & S. J. Lopez (Eds.), *Handbook of positive psychology* (pp. 608–617). New York: Oxford University Press.

Baumgardner, S. R. (1989). *College and jobs: Conversations with recent graduates.* New York: Human Sciences Press.

Baumgardner, S. R. (2001). Multiplicity at work: Reinventing the self in the new economy. Paper presented at meeting of the International Society for Theoretical Psychology, Calgary, Alberta.

Baxter, L. A. (1986). Gender differences on the heterosexual relationship rules embedded in break-up accounts. *Journal of Social and Personal Relationships, 3*, 289–306.

Beck, A. T. (1967). *Cognitive therapy and the emotional disorders.* New York: Meridian.

Beck, A. T., Rush, A. J., Shaw, B. F., & Emery, G. (1979). *Cognitive therapy of depression.* New York: Guilford Press.

Becker, E. (1973). *The denial of death.* New York: Free Press.

Berkman, L. F., & Syme, S. L. (1979). Social networks, host resistance, and mortality. *American Journal of Epidemiology, 109*, 186–204.

Berscheid, E. (2003). The human's greatest strength: Other humans. In L. G. Aspinwall & U. M. Staudinger (Eds.), *A psychology of human strengths: Fundamental questions and future directions for a positive psychology* (pp. 37–48). Washington, DC: American Psychological Association.

Berscheid, E., & Campbell, B. (1981). The changing longevity of heterosexual close relationships: A commentary and forecast. In M. J. Lerner & S. C. Lerner (Eds.), *The justice motive in social behavior* (pp. 31–60). New York: Academic Press.

Berscheid, E., & Reis, H. T. (1998). Attraction and close relationships. In D. T. Gilbert, S. T. Fiske, & G. Lindzey (Eds.), *The handbook of social psychology* (4th ed., Vol. 2, pp. 193–281). New York: McGraw-Hill.

Berscheid, E., & Walster, E. (1978). *Interpersonal attraction* (2nd ed.). Reading, MA: Addison-Wesley.

Betancourt, H., & Lopez, S. R. (1993). The study of culture, ethnicity, and race in American psychology. *American Psychologist, 48*, 629–637.

Bettencourt, B. A., & Miller, N. (1996). Sex differences in aggression as a function of provocation: A meta-analysis. *Psychological Bulletin, 119*, 442–447.

Birgegard, A., & Granqvist, P. (2004). The correspondence between attachment to parents and God: Three experiments using subliminal separation cues. *Personality and Social Psychology Bulletin, 30*, 1122–1135.

Bishop, S. R. (2002). What do we really know about mindfulness-based stress reduction? *Psychosomatic Medicine, 64*, 71–84.

Biswas-Diener, R., & Diener, E. (2001). Making less of a bad situation: Satisfaction in the slums of Calcutta. *Social Indicators Research, 55*, 329–352.

Blatt, S. J. (1995). The destructiveness of perfectionism: Implications for the treatment of depression. *American Psychologist, 50*, 1003–1020.

Block, J. H., & Block, J. (1980). The role of ego-control and ego-resiliency in the organization of behavior. In W. A. Collins (Ed.), *Development of cognition, affect and social relations: The Minnesota Symposium on Child Development* (Vol. 13, pp. 39–101). Hillsdale, NJ: Lawrence Erlbaum.

Bogart, L. M., & Helgeson, V. S. (2000). Social comparisons among women with breast cancer: A longitudinal investigation. *Journal of Applied Social Psychology, 30*, 547–575.

Boldero, J., & Francis, J. (2002). Goals, standards, and the self: Reference values serving different functions. *Personality and Social Psychology Review, 6*, 232–241.

Bonanno, G. A. (2004). Loss, trauma and human resilience: Have we underestimated the human capacity to thrive after extremely aversive events? *American Psychologist, 59*, 20–28.

Bonanno, G. A., & Keltner, D. (1997). Facial expressions of emotion and the course of conjugal bereavement. *Journal of Abnormal Psychology, 106*, 126–137.

Bond, M. H., & Cheung, T. (1983). College students' spontaneous self-concept: The effect of culture among respondents in Hong Kong, Japan and the United States. *Journal of Cross-Cultural Psychology, 14*, 153–171.

Bono, G., Emmons, R. A., & McCullough, M. E. (2004). Gratitude in practice and the practice of gratitude.

In P. A. Linley & S. Joseph (Eds.), *Positive psychology in practice* (pp. 464–481). Hoboken, NJ: John Wiley & Sons.

Borges, M. A., & Dutton, L. J. (1976). Attitudes toward aging. *The Gerontologist, 16,* 220–224.

Bouchard, T. J. (2004). Genetic influence on human psychological traits: A survey. *Current Directions in Psychological Science, 13,* 148–151.

Bowlby, J. (1988). *A secure base: Parent-child attachment and healthy development.* London, UK: Basic Books.

Bradburn, N. M. (1969). *The structure of psychological well-being.* Chicago: Aldine.

Bradbury, T. N. (Ed.). (1998). *The developmental course of marital dysfunction.* Cambridge, England: Cambridge University Press.

Bradbury, T. N., & Fincham, F. D. (1990). Attributions in marriage: Review and critique. *Psychological Bulletin, 107,* 3–33.

Brandstatter, V., Lengfelder, A., & Gollwitzer, P. M. (2001). Implementation intentions and efficient action initiation. *Journal of Personality and Social Psychology, 81,* 946–960.

Brennan, K. A., Clark, C. L., & Shaver, P. R. (1998). Self-report measures of adult attachment: An integrative overview. In J. A. Simpson & W. S. Rholes (Eds.), *Attachment theory and close relationships* (pp. 46–76). New York: Guilford Press.

Brickman, P. (1987). *Commitment, conflict and caring.* Englewood Cliffs, NJ: Prentice-Hall.

Brickman, P., & Campbell, D. (1971). Hedonic relativism and planning the good society. In M. H. Appley (Ed.), *Adaptation-level theory: A symposium* (pp. 287–302). New York: Academic Press.

Brickman, P. D., Coates, D., & Janoff-Bulman, R. (1978). Lottery winners and accident victims: Is happiness relative? *Journal of Personality and Social Psychology, 36,* 917–927.

Brief, A. P., Butcher, A. H., George, J. M., & Link, K. E. (1993). Integrating bottom-up and top-down theories of subjective well-being: The case of health. *Journal of Personality and Social Psychology, 64,* 646–653.

Brody, L. R., & Hall, J. A. (1993). Gender and emotion. In M. Lewis & J. M. Haviland (Eds.), *Handbook of emotions* (pp. 447–460). New York: Guilford Press.

Brown, K. W., & Ryan, R. M. (2003). The benefits of being present: Mindfulness and its role in psychological well-being. *Journal of Personality and Social Psychology, 84,* 822–848.

Brown, K. W., & Ryan, R. M. (2004). Fostering healthy self-regulation from within and without: A self-determination theory perspective. In P. A. Linley & S. Joseph (Eds.), *Positive psychology in practice* (pp. 105–124). New York: John Wiley & Sons.

Brumbaugh, C. C., & Fraley, R. C. (2006). Transference and attachment: How do attachment patterns get carried forward from one relationship to the next? *Personality and Social Psychology Bulletin, 32,* 552–560.

Bruner, J. (1990). Culture and human development: A new look. *Human Development, 33,* 344–355.

Brunstein, J. C. (1993). Personal goals and subjective well-being: A longitudinal study. *Journal of Personality and Social Psychology, 65,* 1061–1070.

Brunstein, J. C., Schultheiss, O. C., & Grassman, R. (1998). Personal goals and emotional well-being: The moderating role of motive dispositions. *Journal of Personality and Social Psychology, 75,* 494–508.

Bryant, C. M., Bolland, J. M., Burton, L. M., Hurt, T., & Bryant, B. M. (2006). The changing social context of relationships. In P. Noller & J. A. Feeney (Eds.), *Close relationships: Functions, forms and processes* (pp. 25–47). New York: Psychology Press.

Bryant, F. B., & Verhoff, J. (1982). The structure of psychological well-being: A sociohistorical analysis. *Journal of Personality and Social Psychology, 43,* 653–673.

Bryant, F. B., & Verhoff, J. (2007). *Savoring: A new model of positive experience.* Mahwah, NJ: Lawrence Erlbaum.

Buckner, J. C., Mezzacappa, E., & Beardslee, W. R. (2003). Characteristics of resilient youths living in poverty: The role of self-regulatory processes. *Development and Psychopathology, 15,* 139–162.

Buss, D. M. (1994). *The evolution of desire.* New York: Basic Books.

Cacioppo, J. T., Berntson, G. G., Larsen, J. T., Poehlmann, K. M., & Ito, T. A. (2000). The psychophysiology of emotions. In M. Lewis & J. M. Haviland-Jones (Eds.), *Handbook of emotions* (2nd ed., pp. 173–191). New York: Guilford Press.

California Task Force to Promote Self-Esteem and Personal and Social Responsibility (1990). *Toward a state of self-esteem.* Sacramento, CA: California State Department of Education.

Campbell, A., Converse, P. E., & Rodgers, W. L. (1976). *The quality of American life.* New York: Russell Sage Foundation.

Campbell, J. (1988). *The power of myth.* New York: Doubleday.

Campbell, J. (1993). *Myths to live by.* New York: Viking Penguin.

Campbell, J. D., Chew, B., & Scratchley, L. S. (1991). Cognitive and emotional reactions to daily events: The effects of self-esteem and self-complexity. *Journal of Personality, 59,* 473–493.

Campbell, L., Lackenbauer, S. D., & Muise, A. (2006). When is being known or adored by romantic partners beneficial? Self-perceptions, relationship length, and responses to partner's verifying and enhancing appraisal. *Personality and Social Psychology Bulletin, 32,* 1283–1294.

Cantor, N. (1990). From thought to behavior: "Having" and "doing" in the study of personality and cognition. *American Psychologist, 45,* 735–750.

Cantor, N., & Sanderson, C. A. (1999). Life task participation and well-being: The importance of taking part in daily life. In D. Kahneman, E. Diener, & N. Schwarz (Eds.), *Well-being: The foundations of hedonic psychology* (pp. 230–243). New York: Russell Sage Foundation.

Cantor, N., & Zirkel, S. (1990). Personality, cognition, and purposive behavior. In L. A. Pervin (Ed.), *Handbook of personality: Theory and research* (pp. 135–164). New York: Guilford Press.

Carlson, E. A., Sroufe, L. A., & Egeland, B. (2004). The construction of experience: A longitudinal study of representation and behavior. *Child Development, 75*, 66–83.

Carstensen, L. L. (1992). Social and emotional patterns in adulthood: Support for socioemotional selectivity theory. *Psychology and Aging, 7*, 331–338.

Carstensen, L. L. (1998). A life-span approach to motivation. In J. Heckhausen & C. S. Dweck (Eds.), *Motivation and self-regulation across the life span* (pp. 341–364). New York: Cambridge University Press.

Carstensen, L. L., & Charles, S. T. (2003). Human aging: Why is even the good news taken as bad? In L. G. Aspinwall & U. M. Staudinger (Eds.), *A psychology of human strengths: Fundamental questions and future directions for a positive psychology* (pp. 75–86). Washington, DC: American Psychological Association.

Carstensen, L. L., & Freund, A. (1994). The resilience of the aging self. *Developmental Review, 14*, 81–92.

Carstensen, L. L., Graff, J., Levenson, R. W., & Gottman, J. M. (1996). Affect in intimate relationships: A developmental course of marriage. In C. Magai & S. H. McFadden (Eds.), *Handbook of emotion, adult development, and aging* (pp. 227–247). New York: Academic Press.

Carstensen, L. L., Gross, J. J., & Fung, H. (1998). The social context of emotional experience. In K. W. Schaie & M. P. Lawton (Eds.), *Annual Review of Gerontology and Geriatrics: Vol. 17. Focus on emotion and development* (pp. 325–352). New York: Springer.

Carstensen, L. L., Isaacowitz, D. M., & Charles, S. T. (1999). Taking time seriously: A theory of socioemotional selectivity. *American Psychologist, 54*, 165–181.

Carstensen, L. L., Pasupathi, P., Mayr, U., & Nesselroade, J. R. (2000). Emotional experience in everyday life across the adult life span. *Journal of Personality and Social Psychology, 79*, 644–655.

Carter, C. S. (1998). Neuroendocrine perspectives on social attachment and love. *Psychoneuroendocrinology, 23*, 779–818.

Carvallo, M., & Gabriel, S. (2006). No man is an island: The need to belong and dismissing avoidant attachment style. *Personality and Social Psychology Bulletin, 32*, 697–709.

Carver, C. S. (2005). Impulse and constraint: Perspectives from personality psychology, convergence with theory in other areas, and potential integration. *Personality and Social Psychology Review, 9*, 312–333.

Carver, C. S., & Baird, E. (1998). The American dream revisited: Is it what you want or why you want it that matters? *Psychological Science, 9*, 289–292.

Carver, C. S., & Gaines, J. G. (1987). Optimism, pessimism and postpartum depression. *Cognitive Therapy and Research, 11*, 449–462.

Carver, C. S., Pozo, C., Harris, S. D., Noriega, V., Scheier, M. F., Robinson, D. S., Ketcham, A. S., Moffat, F. L., & Clark, K. C. (1993). How coping mediates the effects of optimism on distress: A study of women with early stage breast cancer. *Journal of Personality and Social Psychology, 65*, 375–390.

Carver, C. S., & Scheier, M. F. (1982). Control theory: A useful conceptual framework for personality-social, clinical, and health psychology. *Psychological Bulletin, 42*, 111–135.

Carver, C. S., & Scheier, M. F. (1998). *On the self-regulation of behavior.* New York: Cambridge University Press.

Carver, C. S., & Scheier, M. (2002a). Optimism. In S. J. Lopez & C. R. Snyder (Eds.), *Positive psychological assessment: A handbook of models and measures* (pp. 75–90). Washington, DC: American Psychological Association.

Carver, C. S., & Scheier, M. F. (2002b). Optimism, pessimism and self-regulation. In E. C. Chang (Ed.), *Optimism & pessimism: Implications for theory, research, and practice* (pp. 31–51). Washington, DC: American Psychological Association.

Carver, C. S., & Scheier, M. F. (2002c). Control processes and self-organization as complementary principles underlying behavior. *Personality and Social Psychology Review, 6*, 304–315.

Carver, C. S., & Scheier, M. F. (2003). Three human strengths. In L. G. Aspinwall & U. M. Staudinger (Eds.), *A psychology of human strengths: Fundamental questions and future directions for a positive psychology* (pp. 87–102). Washington, DC: American Psychological Association.

Carver, C. S., Sutton, S. K., & Scheier, M. F. (2000). Action, emotion and personality: Emerging conceptual integration. *Personality and Social Psychology Bulletin, 26*, 741–751.

Carver, C. S., & White, T. L. (1994). Behavioral inhibition, behavioral activation, and affective responses to impending reward and punishment: The BIS/BAS scales. *Journal of Personality and Social Psychology, 67*, 319–333.

Cassidy, J., & Shaver, P. R. (Eds.). (1999). *Handbook of attachment: Theory, research and clinical applications.* New York: Guilford Press.

Center for Family Development (2004). Romanian orphanages and children. Retrieved January 10, 2004, at http://www.center4familydevelop.com/helpromanian.htm.

Chang, E. C. (Ed.). (2002a). *Optimism and pessimism: Implications for theory, research and practice*. Washington, DC: American Psychological Association.

Chang, E. C. (2002b). Cultural influences on optimism and pessimism: Differences in Western and Eastern construals of the self. In E. C. Chang (Ed.), *Optimism and pessimism: Implications for theory, research and practice* (pp. 257–280). Washington, DC: American Psychological Association.

Charles, S. T., Reynolds, C. A., & Gatz, M. (2001). Age-related differences and change in positive and negative affect over 23 years. *Journal of Personality and Social Psychology, 80,* 136–151.

Chatzisarantis, N. L. D., & Hagger, M. S. (2007). Mindfulness and the intention-behavior relationship within the theory of planned behavior. *Personality and Social Psychology Bulletin, 33,* 663–676.

Christensen, A., & Heavey, C. L. (1993). Gender differences in marital conflict: The demand/withdraw interaction pattern. In S. Oskamp & M. Costanzo (Eds.), *Gender issues in contemporary society* (pp. 113–141). Newbury Park, CA: Sage Publications.

Cicchetti, D., & Garmezy, N. (Eds.). (1993). Milestones in the development of resilience (Special Issue). *Development and Psychopathology, 5,* 497–574.

Clark, A. E., & Oswald, A. J. (1996). Satisfaction and comparison income. *Journal of Public Economics, 61,* 359–381.

Clark, M. S. (1984). Record keeping in two types of relationships. *Journal of Personality and Social Psychology, 47,* 549–577.

Clark, M. S., & Mills, J. (1979). Interpersonal attraction in exchange and communal relationships. *Journal of Personality and Social Psychology, 37,* 12–24.

Clark, M. S., & Mills, J. (1993). The difference between communal and exchange relationships: What it is and is not. *Personality and Social Psychology Bulletin, 15,* 684–691.

Cohen, S. (2002). Psychosocial stress, social networks, and susceptibility to infection. In H. G. Koenig & H. J. Cohen (Eds.), *The link between religion and health: Psychoneuroimmunology and the faith factor* (pp. 101–123). New York: Oxford University Press.

Cohen, S., Doyle, W. J., Skoner, D. P., Fireman, P., Gwaltney, J. M., & Newsom, J. T. (1995). State and trait negative affect as predictors of objective and subjective symptoms of respiratory virus infections. *Journal of Personality and Social Psychology, 68,* 159–169.

Cohen, S., & Rodriguez, M. S. (1995). Pathways linking affective disturbance and physical disorders. *Health Psychology, 14,* 374–380.

Cohen, S., Underwood, L. G., & Gottlieb, B. H. (Eds.). (2000). *Social support measurement and intervention: A guide for health and social scientists*. New York: Oxford University Press.

Collins, N. L., & Feeney, B. C. (2000). A safe haven: An attachment theory perspective on support-seeking and caregiving in adult romantic relationships. *Journal of Personality and Social Psychology, 58,* 644–663.

Collins, N. L., & Miller, L. C. (1994). Self-disclosure and liking: A meta-analytic review. *Psychological Bulletin, 116,* 457–475.

Compton, W. C., Smith, M. L., Cornish, K. A., & Qualls, D. L. (1996). Factor structure of mental health measures. *Journal of Personality and Social Psychology, 71,* 406–413.

Coopersmith, S. (1967). *The antecedents of self-esteem*. San Francisco: Freeman.

Costa, P. T., & McCrae, R. R. (1988). Personality in adulthood: A six year longitudinal study of self-reports and spouse ratings on the NEO Personality Inventory. *Journal of Personality and Social Psychology, 54,* 853–863.

Costa, P. T., Jr., & McCrae, R. R. (1992). *The NEO-PI-R Professional Manual*. Odessa, FL: Psychological Assessment Resources.

Costa, P. T., McCrae, R. R., & Zonderman, A. B. (1987). Environmental and dispositional influences on well-being: Longitudinal follow-up of an American national sample. *British Journal of Psychology, 78,* 299–306.

Costa, P. T., Zonderman, A. B., McCrae, R. R., Cornoni-Huntley, J., Locke, B. Z., & Barbano, H. E. (1987). Longitudinal analyses of psychological well-being in a national sample: Stability of mean levels. *Journal of Gerontology, 42,* 50–55.

Cousins, N. (1979). *Anatomy of an illness*. New York: Norton.

Cousins, S. D. (1989). Culture and self-perception in Japan and the United States. *Journal of Personality and Social Psychology, 56,* 124–131.

Covert, M. D., & Reeder, G. D. (1990). Negativity effects in impression formation: The role of unit information and schematic expectancies. *Journal of Experimental Social Psychology, 26,* 49–62.

Cozzolino, P. J., Staples, D. A., Meyers, L. S., & Samboceti, J. (2004). Greed, death and values: From terror management to transcendence management theory. *Personality and Social Psychology Bulletin, 30,* 278–292.

Crocker, J., & Luthanen, R. K. (2003). Level of self-esteem and contingencies of self-worth: Unique effects on academic, social, and financial problems in college students. *Personality and Social Psychology Bulletin, 29,* 701–712.

Crocker, J., Luthanen, R. K., Cooper, M. L., & Bouvrette, A. (2003). Contingencies of self-worth in college students: Theory and measurement. *Journal of Personality and Social Psychology, 5,* 894–908.

Crocker, J., Major, B., & Steele, C. (1998). Social stigma. In D. T. Gilbert, S. T. Fiske, & G. Lindzey (Eds.), *The handbook of social psychology* (4th ed., Vol. 2, pp. 504–553). New York: McGraw-Hill.

Crocker, J., & Park, L. E. (2004). The costly pursuit of self-esteem. *Psychological Bulletin, 130,* 392–414.

Crocker, J., & Wolfe, C. T. (2001). Contingencies of self-worth. *Psychological Review, 108,* 593–623.

Cross-National Collaborative Group (1992). The changing rate of major depression: Cross-national comparisons. *Journal of the American Medical Association, 268,* 3098–3195.

Csikszentmihalyi, M. (1990). *Flow: The psychology of optimal experience.* New York: HarperCollins.

Csikszentmihalyi, M. (1997). *Finding flow.* New York: Basic Books.

Csikszentmihalyi, M. (1999). If we are so rich, why aren't we happy? *American Psychologist, 54,* 821–827.

Csikszentmihalyi, M., & Larsen, R. (1984). *Being adolescent: Conflict and growth in the teenage years.* New York: Basic Books.

Csikszentmihalyi, M., & Rathunde, K. (1990). The psychology of wisdom: An evolutionary interpretation. In R. J. Sternberg (Ed.), *Wisdom: Its nature, origins, and development* (pp. 25–51). New York: Cambridge University Press.

Csikszentmihalyi, M., & Schneider, B. (2000). *Becoming adult: How teenagers prepare for the world of work.* New York: Basic Books.

Cushman, P. (1990). Why the self is empty: Toward a historically situated psychology. *American Psychologist, 45,* 599–611.

Dalai Lama, & Cutler, H. C. (1998). *The art of happiness: A handbook for living.* New York: Riverhead Books.

Danner, D., Snowdon, D., & Friesen, W. (2001). Positive emotions in early life and longevity: Findings from the nun study. *Journal of Personality and Social Psychology, 80,* 804–813.

Davis, C. G., Nolen-Hoeksema, S., & Larson, J. (1998). Making sense of loss and benefiting from the experience: Two construals of meaning. *Journal of Personality and Social Psychology, 75,* 561–574.

Dawes, R. M. (1994). *House of cards: Psychology and psychotherapy built on myth.* New York: Free Press.

deCharms, R. (1968). *The internal affective determinants of behavior.* New York: Academic Press.

Deci, E. L., & Ryan, R. M. (1991). A motivational approach to self: Integration in personality. In R. Dienstbier (Ed.), *Nebraska symposium on motivation: Vol. 38. Perspectives on motivation* (pp. 237–288). Lincoln: University of Nebraska Press.

Deci, E. L., & Ryan, R. M. (1995). Human autonomy: The basis for true self-esteem. In M. H. Kernis (Ed.), *Efficacy, agency, and self-esteem* (pp. 31–49). New York: Plenum Press.

Deci, E. L., & Ryan, R. M. (2000). The "what" and the "why" of goal pursuits: Human needs and the self-determination of behavior. *Psychological Inquiry, 11,* 227–268.

Demick, J. (2000). Toward a mindful psychological science: Theory and application. *Journal of Social Issues, 56,* 141–159.

DeNeve, K. M. (1999). Happy as an extraverted clam? The role of personality for subjective well-being. *Current Directions in Psychological Science, 8,* 141–144.

DeNeve, K. M., & Cooper, H. (1998). The happy personality: A meta-analysis of 137 personality traits and subjective well-being. *Psychological Bulletin, 124,* 197–229.

Derlega, V. J., Metts, S., Petronio, S., & Margulis, S. T. (1993). *Self-disclosure.* Newbury Park: CA: Sage Publications.

Derlega, V. J., Wilson, M., & Chaikin, A. J. (1976). Friendship disclosure reciprocity. *Journal of Personality and Social Psychology, 34,* 578–587.

Diener, E. (1984). Subjective well-being. *Psychological Bulletin, 95,* 542–575.

Diener, E. (1993). Assessing subjective well-being: Progress and opportunities. *Social Indicators Research, 31,* 103–157.

Diener, E. (1995). A value-based index for measuring national quality of life. *Social Indicators Research, 36,* 107–127.

Diener, E. (2000). Subjective well-being: The science of happiness and a proposal for a national index. *American Psychologist, 55,* 34–43.

Diener, E., & Biswas-Diener, R. (2002). Will money increase subjective well-being? A literature review and guide to needed research. *Social Indicators Research, 57,* 119–169.

Diener, E., & Clifton, D. (2002). Life satisfaction and religiosity in broad probability samples. *Psychological Inquiry, 13,* 206–209.

Diener, E., & Diener, C. (1996). Most people are happy. *Psychological Science, 7,* 181–185.

Diener, E., & Diener, M. (1995). Cross-cultural correlates of life satisfaction and self-esteem. *Journal of Personality and Social Psychology, 68,* 653–663.

Diener, E., Diener, M., & Diener, C. (1995). Factors predicting the subjective well-being of nations. *Journal of Personality and Social Psychology, 69,* 851–864.

Diener, E., & Emmons, R. A. (1984). The independence of positive and negative affect. *Journal of Personality and Social Psychology, 47,* 1105–1117.

Diener, E., Emmons, R. A., Larsen, R. J., & Griffen, S. (1985). The satisfaction with life scale. *Journal of Personality Assessment, 49,* 71–75.

Diener, E., & Fujita, F. (1995). Resources, personal strivings, and subjective well-being: A nomothetic and idiographic approach. *Journal of Personality and Social Psychology, 68,* 926–935.

Diener, E., Horwitz, J., & Emmons, R. A. (1985). Happiness of the very wealthy. *Social Indicators Research, 16,* 263–274.

Diener, E., & Larsen, R. J. (1984). Temporal stability and cross-situational consistency of affective, behavioral, and cognitive responses. *Journal of Personality and Social Psychology, 47*, 580–592.

Diener, E., & Lucas, R. E. (1999). Personality and subjective well-being. In D. Kahneman, D. Diener, & N. Schwarz (Eds.), *Well-being: The foundations of hedonic psychology* (pp. 213–229). New York: Russell Sage Foundation.

Diener, E., & Lucas, R. E. (2000). Subjective emotional well-being. In M. Lewis & J. M. Haviland (Eds.), *Handbook of Emotions* (2nd ed., pp. 325–337). New York: Guilford Press.

Diener, E., Lucas, R. E., & Oishi, S. (2002). Subjective well-being: The science of happiness and life satisfaction. In C. R. Snyder & S. J. Lopez (Eds.), *Handbook of positive psychology* (pp. 63–73). New York: Oxford University Press.

Diener, E., Lucas, R. E., & Scollon, C. N. (2006). Beyond the hedonic treadmill: Revising the adaptation theory of well-being. *American Psychologist, 61*, 305–314.

Diener, E., Nickerson, C., Lucas, R. E., & Sandvik, E. (2002). Dispositional affect and job outcomes. *Social Indicators Research, 59*, 229–259.

Diener, E., & Oishi, S. (2000). Money and happiness: Income and subjective well-being across nations. In E. Diener & E. M. Suh (Eds.), *Culture and subjective well-being* (pp. 185–218). Cambridge, MA: MIT Press.

Diener, E., & Oishi, S. (2005). Target article: The nonobvious social psychology of happiness. *Psychological Inquiry, 16*, 162–167.

Diener, E., Oishi, S., & Lucas, R. E. (2003). Personality, culture, and subjective well-being: Emotional and cognitive evaluations of life. *Annual Review of Psychology, 54*, 403–425.

Diener, E., Sandvik, E., & Larsen, R. J. (1985). Age and sex effects for emotional intensity. *Developmental Psychology, 21*, 542–546.

Diener, E., Sandvik, E., & Pavot, W. (1991). Happiness is the frequency, not the intensity, of positive versus negative affect. In F. Strack, M. Argyle, & N. Schwarz (Eds.), *Subjective well-being: An interdisciplinary perspective* (pp. 119–139). New York: Pergamon.

Diener, E., Sandvik, E., Seidlitz, L., & Diener, M. (1993). The relationship between income and subjective well-being: Relative or absolute? *Social Indicators Research, 28*, 195–223.

Diener, E., Sapyta, J. J., & Suh, E. (1998). Subjective well-being is essential to well-being. *Psychological Inquiry, 9*, 33–37.

Diener, E., Scollon, C. N., & Lucas, R. E. (2004). The evolving concept of subjective well-being: The multifaceted nature of happiness. In P. T. Costa & I. C. Siegler (Eds.), *Advances in cell aging and gerontology* (Vol. 15, pp. 187–220). Amsterdam: Elsevier.

Diener, E., & Seligman, M. (2004). Beyond money: Toward an economy of well-being. *Psychology in the Public Interest, 5*, 1–31.

Diener, E., & Suh, E. M. (1997). Measuring quality of life: Economic, social and subjective indicators. *Social Indicators Research, 40*, 189–216.

Diener, E., & Suh, E. M. (1998). Subjective well-being and age: An international analysis. In K. W. Schaie & M. P. Lawton (Eds.), *Annual review of gerontology and geriatrics: Vol. 17. Focus on emotion and adult development* (pp. 304–324). New York: Springer.

Diener, E., & Suh, E. M. (Eds.). (2000a). *Culture and subjective well-being.* Cambridge: MIT Press.

Diener, E., & Suh, E. M. (Eds.). (2000b). Measuring subjective well-being to compare the quality of life of cultures. In E. Diener & E. M. Suh (Eds.), *Culture and subjective well-being* (pp. 3–12). Cambridge, MA: MIT Press.

Diener, E., Suh, E. M., Lucas, R. E., & Smith, H. L. (1999). Subjective well-being: Three decades of progress. *Psychological Bulletin, 125*, 276–302.

Diener, E., Suh, E. M., Smith, H. L., & Shao, L. (1995). National differences in subjective well-being: Why do they occur? *Social Indicators Research, 34*, 7–32.

Dienstbier, R. A., & Pytlik Zillig, L. M. (2002). Toughness. In C. R. Snyder & S. J. Lopez (Eds.), *Handbook of positive psychology* (pp. 515–527). New York: Oxford University Press.

Dillon, K. M., Minchoff, B., & Baker, K. H. (1985). Positive emotional states and enhancement of the immune system. *International Journal of Psychiatry in Medicine, 15*, 13–17.

DiPorta, L. (1977). *Zen running.* New York: Everest House.

Dunn, E. W., Wilson, T. D., & Gilbert, D. T. (2003). Location, location, location: The misperception of satisfaction in housing lotteries. *Personality and Social Psychology Bulletin, 29*, 1421–1432.

Eagly, A. H., & Steffen, V. J. (1986). Gender and aggressive behavior: A meta-analytic review of the social psychological literature. *Psychological Bulletin, 100*, 309–330.

Easterbrook, G. (2003). *The progress paradox: How life gets better while people feel worse.* New York: Random House.

Egeland, J., & Hostetter, A. (1983). Amish study, I: Affective disorders among the Amish. *American Journal of Psychiatry, 140*, 56–61.

Egloff, B., Tausch, A., Kohlmann, C. W., & Krohne, H. W. (1995). Relationships between time of day, day of the week, and positive mood: Exploring the role of the mood measure. *Motivation and Emotion, 19*, 99–110.

Eid, M., & Diener, E. (1999). Intraindividual variability in affect: Reliability, validity, and personality correlates. *Journal of Personality and Social Psychology, 76*, 662–676.

Ekman, P., & Friesen, W. (1976). Measuring facial movement. *Journal of Environmental Psychology and Nonverbal Behavior, 1,* 56–75.

Ekman, P., & Friesen, W. (1978). *Facial action coding system: A technique for the measurement of facial movement.* Palo Alto, CA: Consulting Psychologists Press.

Eldridge, K. A., & Christensen, A. (2002). Demand-withdraw communication during couple conflict: A review and analysis. In P. Noller & J. A. Feeney (Eds.), *Understanding marriage: Developments in the study of couple interaction* (pp. 289–322). Cambridge, UK: Cambridge University Press.

Elliot, A. J., & Church, M. A. (1997). A hierarchical model of approach and avoidance achievement motivation. *Journal of Personality and Social Psychology, 72,* 218–232.

Elliot, A. J., & Church, M. A. (2002). Client-articulated avoidance goals in the therapy context. *Journal of Counseling Psychology, 49,* 243–254.

Elliot, A. J., Gable, S. L., & Mapes, R. R. (2006). Approach and avoidance motivation in the social domain. *Personality and Social Psychology Bulletin, 32,* 376–391.

Elliot, A. J., & Sheldon, K. M. (1997). Avoidance achievement motivation: A personal goal analysis. *Journal of Personality and Social Psychology, 73,* 171–185.

Elliot, A. J., & Sheldon, K. M. (1998). Avoidance personal goals and the personality-illness relationship. *Journal of Personality and Social Psychology, 75,* 1282–1299.

Elliot, A. J., Sheldon, K., & Church, M. A. (1997). Avoidance personal goals and subjective well-being. *Personality and Social Psychology Bulletin, 23,* 915–927.

Emmons, R. A. (1986). Personal strivings: An approach to personality and subjective well-being. *Journal of Personality and Social Psychology, 51,* 1058–1068.

Emmons, R. A. (1992). Abstract versus concrete goals: Personal striving level, physical illness, and psychological well-being. *Journal of Personality and Social Psychology, 62,* 292–300.

Emmons, R. A. (1996). Striving and feeling: Personal goals and subjective well-being. In P. M. Gollwitzer & J. A. Bargh (Eds.), *The psychology of action: Linking cognition and motivation of behavior* (pp. 313–337). New York: Guilford Press.

Emmons, R. A. (1999a). Religion in the psychology of personality: An introduction. *Journal of Personality, 67,* 873–888.

Emmons, R. A. (1999b). *The psychology of ultimate concerns: Motivation and spirituality in personality.* New York: Guilford Press.

Emmons, R. A. (2003). Personal goals, life meaning, and virtue: Wellsprings of positive life. In C. L. M. Keyes & J. Haidt (Eds.), *Flourishing: Positive psychology and the life well-lived* (pp. 105–128). Washington, DC: American Psychological Association.

Emmons, R. A., Cheung, C., & Tehrani, K. (1998). Assessing spirituality through personal goals: Implications for research on religion and subjective well-being. *Social Indicators Research, 45,* 391–422.

Emmons, R. A., & Kaiser, H. (1996). Goal orientation and emotional well-being: Linking goals and affect through the self. In A. Tesser & L. Martin (Eds.), *Striving and feeling: Interactions among goals, affect, and self-regulation* (pp. 79–98). New York: Plenum Press.

Emmons, R. A., & King, L. A. (1988). Conflict among personal strivings: Immediate and long-term implications for psychological and physical well-being. *Journal of Personality and Social Psychology, 54,* 1040–1048.

Emmons, R. A., & McCullough, M. E. (2003). Counting blessings versus burdens: An experimental investigation of gratitude and subjective well-being in daily life. *Journal of Personality and Social Psychology, 84,* 377–389.

Emmons, R. A., & McCullough, M. E. (2004). *The psychology of gratitude.* New York: Oxford University Press.

Emmons, R. A., & Shelton, C. M. (2002). Gratitude in the science of positive psychology. In C. R. Snyder & S. J. Lopez (Eds.), *Handbook of positive psychology* (pp. 459–471). New York: Oxford University Press.

Enright, R. D., & Coyle, C. T. (1998). Researching the process model of forgiveness within psychological interventions. In E. L. Worthington, Jr. (Ed.), *Dimensions of forgiveness: Psychological research and theological perspectives* (pp. 139–161). Philadelphia: Templeton Foundation Press.

Esterling, B. A., L'Abate, L., Murray, E. J., & Pennebaker, J. W. (1999). Empirical foundations for writing in prevention and psychotherapy: Mental and physical health outcomes. *Clinical Psychology Review, 19,* 79–96.

Estrada, C. A., Isen, A. M., & Young, M. J. (1997). Positive affect facilitates integration of information and decreases anchoring in reasoning among physicians. *Organizational Behavior and Human Decision Processes, 72,* 117–135.

Exline, J. J. (2002). Stumbling blocks on the religious road: Fractured relationships, nagging voices, and the inner struggle to believe. *Psychological Inquiry, 13,* 182–189.

Fabes, R. A., & Martin, C. J. (1991). Gender and age stereotypes of emotionality. *Personality and Social Psychology Bulletin, 17,* 532–540.

Feeney, J. A. (1999). Adult romantic attachment and couples relationships. In J. Cassidy & P. R. Shaver (Eds.), *Handbook of attachment: Theory, research, and clinical implications* (pp. 267–299). New York: Guilford Press.

Fehr, B. (1988). Prototype analysis of the concepts of love and commitment. *Journal of Personality and Social Psychology, 55,* 557–579.

Fehr, B. (1996). *Friendship processes.* Thousand Oaks, CA: Sage Publications.

Feingold, A. (1994). Gender differences in personality: A meta-analysis. *Psychological Bulletin, 116*, 429–456.

Feldman Barrett, L., Robin, L., Pietromonaco, P. R., & Eyssell, K. M. (1998). Are women the "more emotional" sex? Evidence from emotional experiences in social context. *Cognition and Emotion, 12*, 555–578.

Fincham, F. D., & Beach, S. R. (2004). Forgiveness in marriage: Implications for psychological aggression and constructive communication. *Personal Relationships, 9*, 239–251.

Fincham, F. D., Beach, S. R., & Davila, J. (2004). Forgiveness and conflict resolution in marriage. *Journal of Family Psychology, 18*, 72–81.

Fincham, F. D., Harold, G. T., & Gano-Phillips, S. (2000). The longitudinal association between attributions and marital satisfaction: Direction of effects and role of efficacy expectations. *Journal of Family Psychology, 14*, 267–285.

Fincham, F. D., & Kashdan, T. D. (2004). Facilitating forgiveness: Developing group and community interventions. In P. A. Linley & S. Joseph (Eds.), *Positive psychology in practice* (pp. 617–637). Hoboken, NJ: John Wiley & Sons.

Fineburg, A. C. (2004). Introducing positive psychology to the introductory psychology student. In P. A. Linley & S. Joseph (Eds.), *Positive psychology in practice* (pp. 197–209). New York: John Wiley & Sons.

Finkel, E. J., Rusbult, C. E., Kumashiro, M., & Hannon, P. A. (2002). Dealing with betrayal in close relationships: Does commitment promote forgiveness? *Journal of Personality and Social Psychology, 82*, 956–974.

Fishbach, A., & Shah, J. Y. (2006). Self-control in action: Implicit dispositions toward goals and away from temptations. *Journal of Personality and Social Psychology, 90*, 820–832.

Fiske, A. P., Kitayama, S., Markus, H. R., & Nisbett, R. E. (1998). The cultural matrix of social psychology. In D. T. Gilbert, S. T. Fiske, & G. Lindzey (Eds.), *The handbook of social psychology* (4th ed., Vol. 2, pp. 915–981). New York: McGraw-Hill.

Fiske, A. P., & Taylor, S. F. (1991). *Social cognition*. New York: McGraw-Hill.

Fitness, J. (2006). Emotion and cognition in close relationships. In P. Noller & J. A. Feeney (Eds.), *Close relationships: Functions, forms and processes* (pp. 285–303). New York: Psychology Press.

Fitzgerald, T. E., Tennen, H., Affleck, G., & Pransky, G. (1993). The relative importance of dispositional optimism and control appraisals in quality of life after coronary artery bypass surgery. *Journal of Behavioral Medicine, 16*, 25–43.

Fitzsimons, G. M., & Kay, A. C. (2004). Language and interpersonal cognition: Causal effects of variations in pronoun usage on perception of closeness. *Personality and Social Psychology Bulletin, 30*, 547–557.

Folkman, S., & Tedlie Moskowitz, J. (2000). Positive affect and the other side of coping. *American Psychologist, 55*, 647–654.

Fontaine, K. R., & Jones, L. C. (1997). Self-esteem, optimism, and postpartum depression. *Journal of Clinical Psychology, 53*, 59–63.

Fordyce, M. (1977). Development of a program to increase personal happiness. *Journal of Counseling Psychology, 24*, 511–520.

Fordyce, M. (1983). A program to increase happiness: Further studies. *Journal of Counseling Psychology, 30*, 483–498.

Fowers, B. J., & Tjeltveit, A. C. (2003). Virtue obscured and retrieved: Character, community and practices in behavioral science. *The American Behavioral Scientist, 47*, 387–394.

Fraley, R. C. (2002). Attachment stability from infancy to adulthood: Meta-analysis and dynamic modeling of developmental mechanisms. *Personality and Social Psychology Review, 6*, 123–151.

Fraley, B., & Aron, A. (2004). The effect of shared humorous experiences on closeness in initial encounters. *Personal Relationships, 11*, 61–78.

Fraley, R. C., & Waller, N. G. (1998). Adult attachment patterns: A test of the typological model. In J. A. Simpson & W. S. Rholes (Eds.), *Attachment theory and close relationships* (pp. 77–144). New York: Guilford Press.

Frankl, V. E. (1976). *Man's search for meaning: An introduction to Logotherapy* (3rd ed.). New York: Pocket. (Original work published in 1959.)

Frederick, S., & Lowenstein, G. (1999). Hedonic adaptation. In D. Kahneman, D. Diener, & N. Schwarz (Eds.), *Well-being: The foundations of hedonic psychology* (pp. 302–329). New York: Russell Sage Foundation.

Fredrickson, B. L. (2001). The role of positive emotions in positive psychology: The broaden-and-build theory of positive emotions. *American Psychologist, 56*, 218–226.

Fredrickson, B. L. (2002). Positive emotions. In C. R. Snyder & S. J. Lopez (Eds.), *Handbook of positive psychology* (pp. 120–134). New York: Oxford University Press.

Fredrickson, B. L., & Kahneman, D. (1993). Duration neglect in retrospective evaluations of affective episodes. *Journal of Personality and Social Psychology, 65*, 45–55.

Fredrickson, B. L., & Losada, M. F. (2005). Positive affect and the complex dynamic of human flourishing. *American Psychologist, 60*, 678–686.

Freedman, J. L. (1978). *Happy people*. San Diego: Harcourt Brace Jovanovich.

Freud, S. (1961). *Civilization and its discontents*. New York: W.W. Norton.

Freund, A., & Baltes, P. B. (2002). Life-management strategies of selection, optimization, and compensation: Measurement by self-report and construct validity.

Journal of Personality and Social Psychology, 82, 642–662.

Friedman, H. S., & Booth-Kewley, S. (1987). The "disease-prone personality:" A meta-analytic view of the construct. *American Psychologist, 42*, 539–555.

Friedman, M., & Rosenman, R. H. (1974). *Type A behavior and your heart.* New York: Knopf.

Frijda, N. C. (1999). Emotions and hedonic experience. In D. Kahneman, D. Diener, & N. Schwarz, (Eds.), *Well-being: The foundations of hedonic psychology* (pp. 190–210). New York: Russell Sage Foundation.

Frodi, A., Macaulay, J., & Thomas, P. R. (1977). Are women always less aggressive than men? A review of the experimental literature. *Psychological Bulletin, 84*, 634–660.

Frontline (2002). The lost children of Rockdale County. Retrieved September, 2004, at http://www.pbs.org/wgbh/pages/frontline/shows/georgu/etc/script.html.

Fujita, F., & Diener, E. (2005). Life satisfaction set point: Stability and change. *Journal of Personality and Social Psychology, 88*, 158–164.

Fujita, F., Diener, E., & Sandvik, E. (1991). Gender differences in negative affect and well-being: The case for emotional intensity. *Journal of Personality and Social Psychology, 61*, 427–434.

Fujita, K., Trope, Y., Liberman, N., & Levin-Sagi, M. (2006). Construal levels and self-control. *Journal of Personality and Social Psychology, 90*, 351–367.

Gable, S. L. (2006). Approach and avoidance social motives and goals. *Journal of Personality, 74*, 175–222.

Gable, S. L., & Haidt, J. (2005). What (and why) is positive psychology? *Review of General Psychology, 9*, 103–110.

Gable, S. L., Reis, H. T., Impett, E. A., & Asher, E. R. (2004). What do you do when things go right? The intrapersonal and interpersonal benefits of sharing positive events. *Journal of Personality and Social Psychology, 87*, 228–245.

Gabriel, S., & Gardner, W. L. (1999). Are there "his" and "hers" types of interdependence? The implications of gender differences in collective versus relational interdependence for affect, behavior and cognition. *Journal of Personality and Social Psychology, 77*, 642–655.

Gailliot, M. T., Baumeister, R. F., DeWall, N. C., Maner, J. K., Plant, E. A., Tice, D. M., et al. (2007). Self-control relies on glucose as a limited energy source: Willpower is more than a metaphor. *Journal of Personality and Social Psychology, 92*, 325–336.

Gallup, G., Jr., & Lindsay, D. M. (1999). *Surveying the religious landscape: Trends in U.S. beliefs.* Harrisburg, PA: Morehouse.

Garmezy, N. (1991). Resiliency and vulnerability of adverse developmental outcomes associated with poverty. *American Behavioral Scientist, 34*, 416–430.

Geen, R. G., (1998). Aggression and antisocial behavior. In D. T. Gilbert, S. T. Fiske, & G. Lindzey (Eds.), *The handbook of social psychology* (4th ed., Vol. 2, pp. 317–356). New York: McGraw-Hill.

George, L. L., Ellison, C. G., & Larson, D. B. (2002). Explaining the relationship between religious involvement and health. *Psychological Inquiry, 13*, 190–200.

Gilbert, D. T. (1998). Ordinary personology. In D. T. Gilbert, S. T. Fiske, & G. Lindzey (Eds.), *The handbook of social psychology* (4th ed., Vol. 2, pp. 89–150). New York: McGraw-Hill.

Gilbert, D. T., Driver-Linn, E., & Wilson, T. D. (2002). The trouble with Vronsky: Impact bias in the forecasting of future affective states. In P. Salovey & L. Feldman-Barrett (Eds.), *The wisdom of feeling* (pp. 144–146). New York: Guilford Press.

Gilbert, D. T., Morewedge, C. L., Risen, J. L., & Wilson, T. D. (2004). Looking forward to looking backward: The misdirection of regret. *Psychological Science, 15*, 346–350.

Gilbert, D. T., Pinel, E. C., Wilson, T. D., Blumberg, S. J., & Wheatley, T. (1998). Immune neglect: A source of durability bias in affective forecasting. *Journal of Personality and Social Psychology, 75*, 617–638.

Gilligan, C., Lyons, N. P., & Hammer, T. J. (Eds.). (1999). *Making connections: The relational worlds of adolescent girls at Emma Willard School.* Cambridge, MA: Harvard University Press.

Given, C. W., Stommel, M., Given, B., Osuch, L., Kurtz, M. E., & Kurtz, J. C. (1993). The influence of cancer patients' symptoms and functional states on patients' depression and family caregivers' reactions and depression. *Health Psychology, 12*, 277–285.

Glenn, N. D. (1991). The recent trend in marital success in the United States. *Journal of Marriage and the Family, 53*, 261–270.

Glenn, N. D. (1996). Values, attitudes and the state of American marriage. In D. Popenoe, J. B. Elshtain, & D. Blankenhorn (Eds.), *Promises to keep: Decline and renewal of marriage in America* (pp. 15–33). Lanham, MD: Rowan and Littlefield.

Glenn, N. D., & Weaver, C. N. (1988). The changing relationship of marital status to reported happiness. *Journal of Marriage and Family Relations, 50*, 317–324.

Goldstein, J. R., & Kenney, C. (2001). Marriage delayed or marriage forgone? New cohort forecasts of first marriage for U.S. women. *American Sociological Review, 66*, 506–519.

Goleman, D. (1995). *Emotional intelligence.* New York: Bantam Books.

Goleman, D. (1998). *Working with emotional intelligence.* New York: Bantam Books.

Gollwitzer, P. M. (1999). Implementation intentions: Strong effects of simple plans. *American Psychologist, 54*, 493–503.

Gollwitzer, P. M., & Brandstatter, V. (1997). Implementation intentions and effective goal pursuit. *Journal of Personality and Social Psychology, 73*, 186–199.

Gorsuch, R. L., & McPherson, S. E. (1989). Intrinsic/Extrinsic measurement: I/E-revised and single-item scales. *Journal for the Scientific Study of Religion, 42*, 43–55.

Gottfredson, M. R., & Hirschi, T. (1990). *A general theory of crime.* Stanford, CA: Stanford University Press.

Gottman, J. M. (1994). *What predicts divorce? The relationship between marital processes and marital outcomes.* Hillsdale, NJ: Lawrence Erlbaum.

Gottman, J. M. (1998). Psychology and the study of marital processes. *Annual Review of Psychology, 49*, 169–197.

Gottman, J. M. (1999). *The marriage clinic: A scientific-based marital therapy.* New York: W.W. Norton.

Gottman, J. M., & Krokoff, L. J. (1989). Marital interaction and satisfaction: A longitudinal view. *Journal of Counseling and Clinical Psychology, 57*, 47–52.

Gottman, J. M., & Levenson, R. W. (1992). Marital processes predictive of later dissolution: Behavior, physiology, and health. *Journal of Personality and Social Psychology, 78*, 1135–1149.

Gottman, J. M., & Silver, N. (1999). *The seven principles for making marriage work.* New York: Crown.

Gove, W. R., Hughes, M., & Style, C. B. (1983). Does marriage have positive effects on the psychological well-being of the individual? *Journal of Health and Social Behavior, 24*, 122–131.

Gramzow, R. H., Sedikides, C., Panter, A. T., & Insko, C. A. (2000). Aspects of self-regulation and self-structure as predictors of perceived emotional distress. *Personality and Social Psychology Bulletin, 26*, 188–205.

Granqvist, P. (2002). Attachment and religiosity in adolescence: Cross-sectional and longitudinal evaluations. *Personality and Social Psychology Bulletin, 28*, 260–270.

Gray-Little, B., & Hafdahl, A. R. (2000). Factors influencing racial comparisons of self-esteem: A quantitative review. *Psychological Bulletin, 126*, 26–54.

Greeley, A. (1991). *Faithful attraction.* New York: Tor Books.

Greenberg, J. L., Solomon, S., & Pyszczynski, T. (1999). Terror management theory of self-esteem and cultural worldviews: Empirical assessments and conceptual refinements. In M. P. Zanna (Ed.), *Advances in experimental social psychology* (Vol. 29, pp. 61–139). Orlando, FL: Academic Press.

Grey, J. A. (1990). Brain systems that mediate both emotion and cognition. *Cognition and Emotion, 4*, 269–288.

Gross, J. J., Carstenson, L. L., Pasupathi, M., Tsai, J., Skorpen, C. G., & Hsu, A. Y. C. (1997). Emotion and aging: Experience, expression and control. *Psychology and Aging, 12*, 590–599.

Grossman, M., & Wood, W. (1993). Sex differences in intensity of emotional experience: A social role interpretation. *Journal of Personality and Social Psychology, 65*, 1010–1022.

Grouzet, F. M. E., Kasser, T., Ahuvia, A., Dols, J. M. F., Kim, Y., Lau, S., et al. (2005). The structure of goal contents across 15 cultures. *Journal of Personality and Social Psychology, 89*, 800–816.

Hacker, A. (1979). *Divorce à la mode. The New York Review of Books,* May 3, pp. 23–27.

Halberstadt, A. G., & Saitta, M. B. (1987). Gender, nonverbal behavior and perceived dominance: A test of the theory. *Journal of Personality and Social Psychology, 54*, 257–272.

Hall, J. A. (1984). *Nonverbal sex differences: Communication accuracy and expressive style.* Baltimore: John Hopkins University Press.

Hammersla, J. F., & Frease-McMahan, L. (1990). University students' priorities versus life goals: Life goals versus relationships. *Sex Roles, 23*, 1–14.

Harackiewicz, J. M., & Sansone, C. (1991). Goals and intrinsic motivation: You can get there from here. In M. L. Maehr & P. R. Pintrich (Eds.), *Advances in motivation and achievement* (Vol. 7, pp. 21–49). Greenwich, CT: JAI Press.

Haring, M. J., Stock, W. A., & Okun, M. A. (1984). A research synthesis of gender and social class correlates of subjective well-being. *Human Relations, 37*, 645–657.

Haring-Hidore, M., Stock, W. A., Okun, M. A., & Witter, R. A. (1985). Marital status and subjective well-being: A research synthesis. *Journal of Marriage and the Family, 47*, 947–953.

Harker, L., & Keltner, D. (2001). Expressions of positive emotion in women's college yearbook pictures and their relationship to personality and life outcomes across adulthood. *Journal of Personality and Social Psychology, 80*, 112–124.

Harlow, R. E., & Cantor, N. (1996). Still participating after all these years: A study of life task participation in later life. *Journal of Personality and Social Psychology, 71*, 1235–1249.

Harter, S. (2002). Authenticity. In C. R. Snyder & S. J. Lopez (Eds.), *Handbook of positive psychology* (pp. 382–394). New York: Oxford University Press.

Harvey, J. H., & Omarzu, J. (1997). Minding the close relationship. *Personality and Social Psychology Review, 1*, 224–240.

Harvey, J. H., & Omarzu, J. (1999). *Minding the close relationship: A theory of relationship enhancement.* New York: Cambridge University Press.

Harvey, J. H. Pauwels, B. G., & Zickmund, S. (2002). Relationship connection: The role of minding in the enhancement of closeness. In C. R. Snyder & S. J. Lopez (Eds.), *Handbook of positive psychology* (pp. 423–433). New York: Oxford University Press.

Harvey, J. H., & Weber, A. L. (2002). *Odyssey of the heart: Close relationships in the 21st century* (2nd ed.). Mahwa, NJ: Lawrence Erlbaum.

Haslam, N., Bain, P., & Neal, D. (2004). The implicit structure of positive characteristics. *Personality and Social Psychology Bulletin, 30,* 529–541.

Hatfield, E. (1988). Passionate and companionate love. In R. J. Sternberg & M. L. Barnes (Eds.), *The psychology of love* (pp. 191–217). New Haven, CT: Yale University Press.

Hatfield, E., & Rapson, R. L. (2006). Passionate love, sexual desire, mate selection: Cross-cultural and historical perspectives. In P. Noller & J. A. Feeney (Eds.), *Close relationships: Functions, forms and processes* (pp. 227–243). New York: Psychology Press.

Hatfield, E., & Sprecher, S. (1986). Measuring passionate love in intimate relations. *Journal of Adolescence, 9,* 383–410.

Hazan, C., Campa, M., & Gur-Yaish, N. (2006). Attachment across the life-span. In P. Noller & J. A. Feeney (Eds.), *Close relationships: Functions, forms and processes* (pp. 189–209). New York: Psychology Press.

Hazan, C., & Shaver, P. R. (1987). Romantic love conceptualized as an attachment process. *Journal of Personality and Social Psychology, 52,* 511–524.

Headey, B., & Wearing, A. (1989). Personality, life events, and subjective well-being. Toward a dynamic equilibrium model. *Journal of Personality and Social Psychology, 57,* 731–739.

Headey, B., & Wearing, A. (1991). Subjective well-being: A stocks and flows framework. In F. Strack, M. Argyle, & N. Schwarz (Eds.), *Subjective well-being: An interdisciplinary perspective.* Oxford: Pergamon Press.

Headey, B., & Wearing, A. (1992). *Understanding happiness: A theory of subjective life satisfaction.* Melbourne, Australia: Longman Cheshire.

Heatherton, T. F., & Polivy, J. (1991). Development and validation of a scale for measuring state self-esteem. *Journal of Personality and Social Psychology, 60,* 895–910.

Heine, S. J., Lehman, D. R., Markus, H. R., & Kitayama, S. (1999). Is there a universal need for positive regard? *Psychological Review, 106,* 766–794.

Heine, S. J., Takata, T., & Lehman, D. R. (2000). Beyond self-presentation: Evidence for self-criticism among Japanese. *Personality and Social Psychology Bulletin, 26,* 71–78.

Helson, H. (1964). *Adaptation-level theory.* New York: Harper & Row.

Hendrick, S. S., & Hendrick, C. (1993). Lovers as friends. *Journal of Social and Personal Relationships, 10,* 459–466.

Hendrick, S. S., & Hendrick, C. (2002). Love. In C. R. Snyder & S. J. Lopez (Eds.), *Handbook of positive psychology* (pp. 472–484). New York: Oxford University Press.

Hendrick, S. S., & Hendrick, C. (2003). Romantic love: Measuring Cupid's arrow. In S. J. Lopez & C. R. Snyder (Eds.), *Positive psychology assessment: A handbook of models and measures.* Washington, DC: American Psychological Association.

Herbert, T. B., & Cohen, S. (1993). Depression and immunity: A meta-analytic review. *Psychological Bulletin, 113,* 472–486.

Herek, G. M. (1987). Religious orientation and prejudice: A comparison of racial and sexual attitudes. *Personality and Social Psychology Bulletin, 13,* 34–44.

Hermans, H. J. M., & Kempen, H. J. G. (1998). Moving cultures: The perilous problems of cultural dichotomies in a globalizing society. *American Psychologist, 53,* 111–120.

Hetherington, E. M., Bridges, M., & Insabella, G. M. (1998). What matters? What does not? Five perspectives on the association between marital transitions and children's adjustment. *American Psychologist, 53,* 167–184.

Hewitt, J. P. (1998). *The myth of self-esteem: Finding happiness and solving problems in America.* New York: St. Martin's Press.

Higgins, E. T. (1987). Self-discrepancy: A theory relating self and affect. *Psychological Review, 94,* 319–340.

Higgins, E. T. (1996). The "self digest:" Self-knowledge serving self-regulation functions. *Journal of Personality and Social Psychology, 71,* 1062–1083.

Higgins, E. T. (1997). Beyond pleasure and pain. *American Psychologist, 52,* 1280–1300.

Higgins, E. T. (1998). Promotion and prevention: Regulatory focus as a motivational principle. In M. Zanna (Ed.), *Advances in experimental social psychology* (Vol. 30, pp. 1–46). San Diego, CA: Academic Press.

Hill, P. C., & Pargament, K. I. (2003). Advances in the conceptualization and measurement of religion and spirituality. *American Psychologist, 58,* 64–74.

Hill, P. C., Pargament, K. I., Hood, R. W., Jr., McCullough, M. E., Swyers, J. P., Larson, D. B., et al. (2000). Conceptualizing religion and spirituality: Points of commonality, points of departure. *Journal for the Theory of Social Behavior, 30,* 51–77.

Hobfoll, S. E. F. (1989). Conservation of resources: A new attempt at conceptualizing stress. *American Psychologist, 44,* 513–524.

Hobfoll, S., & Lieberman, J. (1987). Personality and social resources in immediate and continued stress resistance among women. *Journal of Personality and Social Psychology, 52,* 18–26.

Hoge, D. R. (1972). A validated intrinsic motivation scale. *Journal for the Scientific Study of Religion, 11,* 369–376.

Hong, Y. Y., Morris, M. W., Chiu, C. Y., & Benet-Martinez, V. (2000). Multicultural minds: A dynamic constructivist approach to culture and cognition. *American Psychologist, 55,* 709–720.

Hooker, K., Monahan, D., Shifren, K., & Hutchinson, C. (1992). Mental and physical health of spouse caregivers: The role of personality. *Psychology and Aging, 7,* 367–375.

Horwitz, A. V., White, H. R., & Howell-White, S. (1996a). Becoming married and mental health: A longitudinal study of a cohort of young adults. *Journal of Marriage and the Family, 58*, 895–907.

Horwitz, A. V., White, H. R., & Howell-White, S. (1996b). The use of multiple outcomes in stress research: A case study of gender differences in responses to marital dissolution. *Journal of Health and Social Behavior, 37*, 278–291.

House, J. S., Landis, K. R., & Umberson, D. (1988). Social relationships and health. *Science, 241*, 540–545.

Huang, S. T., & Enright, R. D. (2000). Forgiveness and anger-related emotions in Taiwan: Implications for therapy. *Psychotherapy, 37*, 71–79.

Huston, T. L., Caughlin, J. P., Houts, R. M., Smith, S. E., & George, L. J. (2001). The connubial crucible: Newlywed years as predictors of marital delight, distress and divorce. *Journal of Personality and Social Psychology, 80*, 237–252.

Huston, T. L., Niehuis, S., & Smith, S. E. (2001). The early marital roots of conjugal distress and divorce. *Current Directions in Psychological Science, 10*, 116–119.

Inglehart, R. (1990). *Cultural shift in advanced industrial society*. Princeton, NJ: Princeton University Press.

Inglehart, R. (1997). *Modernization and postmodernization: Cultural, economic and political change in society*. Princeton, NJ: Princeton University Press.

Inglehart, R., & Klingemann, H. D. (2000). Genes, culture, democracy and happiness. In E. Diener & E. M. Suh (Eds.), *Culture and subjective well-being* (pp. 165–184). Cambridge, MA: MIT Press.

Isen, A. M. (2002). A role for neuropsychology in understanding the facilitating influence of positive affect on social behavior and cognitive processes. In C. R. Snyder & S. J. Lopez (Eds.), *Handbook of positive psychology* (pp. 528–540). New York: Oxford University Press.

Isen, A. M. (2003). Positive affect as a source of human strength. In L. G. Aspinwall & U. M. Staudinger (Eds.), *A psychology of human strengths: Fundamental questions and future directions for positive psychology*. Washington, DC: American Psychological Association.

Jahoda, M. (1958). *Current conceptions of positive mental health*. New York: Basic Books.

James, S. A., Storgatz, D. S., Wing, S. B., & Ramsey, D. L. (1987). Socioeconomic status, John Henryism, and hypertension in blacks and whites. *American Journal of Epidemiology, 126*, 664–673.

James, W. (1985). *The varieties of religious experience*. Cambridge, MA: Harvard University Press. (Original work published in 1902.)

Jankowiak, W. (Ed.). (1995). *Romantic passion: A universal experience?* New York, NY: Columbia University Press.

Janoff-Bulman, R. (1992). *Shattered assumptions: Towards a new psychology of trauma*. New York: Free Press.

Janoff-Bulman, R., & Frieze, I. R. (1983). A theoretical perspective for understanding reactions to victimization. *Journal of Social Issues, 39*, 1–18.

John, O. P., & Srivastava, S. (1999). The Big Five trait taxonomy: History, measurement, and theoretical perspectives. In L. A. Pervin & O. P. John (Eds.), *Handbook of personality: Theory and research* (Vol. 2, pp. 102–138). New York: Guilford Press.

Johnson, D. R., & Wu, J. (2002). An empirical test of crisis, social selection, and role explanations of the relationship between marital disruption and psychological distress: A pooled time-series analysis of four-wave panel data. *Journal of Marriage and the Family, 64*, 211–224.

Jones, W. H., Crouch, L. L., & Scott, S. (1997). Trust and betrayal: The psychology of trust violations. In R. Hogan, J. Johnson, & S. R. Briggs (Eds.), *Handbook of personality psychology* (pp. 466–482). New York: Academic Press.

Kabat-Zinn, J. (1990). *Full catastrophe living: Using the wisdom of your body and mind to face stress, pain and illness*. New York: Delacourt.

Kabat-Zinn, J. (1994). *Wherever you go, there you are: Mindfulness meditation in everyday life*. New York: Hyperion.

Kagan, J. (1994). *Galen's prophecy: Temperament in human nature*. New York: Basic Books.

Kagan, J., & Snidman, N. (2004). *The long shadow of temperament*. Cambridge, MA: Belknap Press.

Kahneman, D. (1999). Objective happiness. In D. Kahneman, E. Diener, & N. Schwarz (Eds.), *Well-being: The foundations of hedonic psychology* (pp. 3–25). New York: Russell Sage Foundation.

Kahneman, D., Diener, E., & Schwarz, N. (Eds.). (1999). *Well-being: The foundations of hedonic psychology*. New York: Russell Sage Foundation.

Kahneman, D., Fredrickson, B. L., Schreiber, C. A., & Redelmeir, D. A. (1993). When more pain is preferred to less: Adding a better ending. *Psychological Science, 4*, 401–405.

Kahneman, D., Krueger, A. B., Schkade, D. A., Schwarz, N., & Stone, A. A. (2004). A survey method for characterizing daily life experience: The day reconstruction method. *Science, 306*, 1776–1780.

Kantz, J. E. (2000). How do people conceptualize and use forgiveness? The Forgiveness Attitudes Questionnaire. *Counseling and Values, 44*, 174–186.

Kaprio, J., Koskenvuo, M., & Rita, H. (1987). Mortality after bereavement: A prospective study of 95,647 widowed persons. *American Journal of Public Health, 77*, 283–287.

Karney, B. R., & Bradbury, T. N. (1995). The longitudinal course of marital quality and stability: A review of theory, methods and research. *Psychological Bulletin, 118*, 3–34.

Karney, B. R., & Bradbury, T. N. (2000). Attributions in marriage: Trait or state? A growth curve analysis. *Journal of Personality and Social Psychology, 78,* 295–309.

Karolyi, P. (1999). A goal systems-self-regulatory perspective on personality, psychopathology, and change. *Review of General Psychology, 3,* 264–291.

Kasser, T. (2002). *The high price of materialism.* Cambridge: MIT Press.

Kasser, T. (2004). The good life or the goods life? Positive psychology and personal well-being in the culture of consumption. In P. A. Linley & S. Joseph (Eds.), *Positive psychology in practice.* Hoboken, NJ: John Wiley & Sons.

Kasser, T., & Kanner, A. D. (Eds.). (2004). *Psychology and consumer culture: The struggle for a good life in a materialistic world.* Washington, DC: American Psychological Association.

Kasser, T., & Ryan, R. M. (1993). A dark side of the American dream: Correlates of financial success as a central life aspiration. *Journal of Personality and Social Psychology, 65,* 410–422.

Kasser, T., & Ryan, R. M. (1996). Further examining the American dream: Differential correlates of intrinsic and extrinsic goals. *Personality and Social Psychology Bulletin, 22,* 280–287.

Kasser, T., Ryan, R. M., Couchman, C. E., & Sheldon, K. M. (2004). In T. Kasser & A. D. Kanner (Eds.), *Psychology and consumer culture: The struggle for a good life in a materialistic world* (pp. 11–28). Washington, DC: American Psychological Association.

Kasser, R., & Sheldon, K. M. (2000). Of wealth and death: Materialism, mortality salience, and consumption behavior. *Psychological Science, 11,* 352–355.

Kearns, J. N., & Fincham, F. D. (2004). A prototype analysis of forgiveness. *Personality and Social Psychology Bulletin, 30,* 838–855.

Kelley, H. H. (1979). *Personal relationships: Their structure and processes.* Hillsdale, NJ: Lawrence Erlbaum.

Kelley, H. H., & Thibaut, J. W. (1978*). Interpersonal relationships: A theory of interdependence.* New York: John Wiley & Sons.

Keltner, D., Capps, L., Kring, A. M., Young, R. C., & Heerey, E. A. (2001). Just teasing: A conceptual analysis and empirical review. *Psychological Bulletin, 127,* 229–248.

Keltner, D., Young, R. C., Heerey, E. A., & Oemig, C. (1998). Teasing in hierarchical and intimate relations. *Journal of Personality and Social Psychology, 75,* 1231–1247.

Kernis, M. H. (2003a). High self-esteem: A differentiated perspective. In E. C. Chang & L. J. Sanna (Eds.), *Virtue, vice and personality: The complexity of behavior.* Washington, DC: American Psychological Association.

Kernis, M. H. (2003b). Toward a conceptualization of optimal self-esteem. *Psychological Inquiry, 14,* 1–26.

Kessler, R. C., & Frank, R. G. (1997). The impact of psychiatric disorders on work loss days. *Psychological Medicine, 27,* 861–873.

Kessler, R. C., McGonagle, K. A., Zhao, S., Nelson, C. B., Hughes, M., Eshleman, S., et al. (1994). Lifetime and 12 month prevalence of DSM-III-R psychiatric disorders in the United States. *Archives of General Psychiatry, 51,* 8–19.

Keyes, C. L. M. (1998). Social well-being. *Social Psychology Quarterly, 61,* 121–140.

Keyes, C. L. M. (2002). The mental health continuum: From languishing to flourishing in life. *Journal of Health and Social Behavior, 43,* 207–222.

Keyes, C. L. M. (2003). Complete mental health: An agenda for the 21st century. In C. L. M. Keyes & J. Haidt (Eds.), *Flourishing: Positive psychology and the life well-lived* (pp. 293–312). Washington, DC: American Psychological Association.

Keyes, C. L. M. (2005). Mental illness and/or mental health? Investigating the axioms of the complete state of mental health. *Journal of Consulting and Clinical Psychology, 73,* 539–548.

Keyes, C. L. M. (2007). Promoting and protecting mental health and flourishing: A complementary strategy for improving national mental health. *American Psychologist, 62,* 95–108.

Keyes, C. L. M., & Haidt, J. (Eds.). (2003). *Flourishing: Positive psychology and the life well-lived.* Washington, DC: American Psychological Association.

Keyes, C. L. M., & Lopez, S. J. (2002). Toward a science of mental health: Positive directions in diagnosis and intervention. In C. R. Snyder & S. J. Lopez (Eds.), *Handbook of positive psychology* (pp. 45–59). New York: Oxford University Press.

Keyes, C. L. M., & Magyar-Moe, J. L. (2003). The measurement and utility of adult subjective well-being. In S. J. Lopez & C. R. Snyder (Eds.), *Positive psychological assessment: A handbook of models and measures* (pp. 411–425). Washington, DC: American Psychological Association.

Keyes, C. L. M., & Ryff, C. D. (2000). Subjective change and mental health: A self concept theory. *Social Psychology Quarterly, 63,* 264–279.

Keyes, C. L. M., Shmotkin, D., & Ryff, C. D. (2002). Optimizing well-being: The empirical encounter of two traditions. *Journal of Personality and Social Psychology, 82,* 1007–1022.

Kiecolt-Glaser, J. K., & Glaser, R. (1987). Psychosocial moderators of immune function. *Annals of Behavioral Medicine, 9,* 16–20.

King, L. A. (2001). The health benefits of writing about life goals. *Personality and Social Psychology Bulletin, 27,* 798–807.

King, L. A., & Emmons, R. A. (1991). Psychological, physical, and interpersonal correlates of emotional expressiveness, conflict, and control. *European Journal of Personality, 5,* 131–150.

King, L. A., Hicks, J. A., Krull, J. L., & Del Gaiso, A. K. (2006). Positive affect and the experience of meaning in life. *Journal of Personality and Social Psychology, 90,* 179–196.

King, L. A., & Napa, C. K. (1998). What makes a life good? *Journal of Personality and Social Psychology, 75,* 156–165.

Kirkpatrick, L. A. (1992). An attachment-theoretical approach to the psychology of religion. *International Journal for the Psychology of Religion, 2,* 3–28.

Kirkpatrick, L. A., & Shaver, P. R. (1990). Attachment theory and religion: Childhood attachments, religious beliefs and conversions. *Journal for the Scientific Study of Religion, 29,* 315–334.

Kirkpatrick, L. A., & Shaver, P. R. (1992). An attachment-theoretical approach to romantic love and religious belief. *Personality and Social Psychology Bulletin, 18,* 266–275.

Kitayama, S., & Markus, H. R. (2000). The pursuit of happiness and the realization of sympathy: Cultural patterns of self, social relations, and well-being. In E. Diener & E. M. Suh (Eds.), *Culture and subjective well-being* (pp. 113–162). Cambridge, MA: MIT Press.

Kitayama, S., Markus, H. R., & Kurokawa, M. (2000). Culture, emotion, and well-being: Good feelings in Japan and the United States. *Cognition and Emotion, 14,* 93–124.

Klinger, E. (1977). *Meaning and void: Inner experience and the incentives in people's lives.* Minneapolis, MN: University of Minnesota Press.

Klinger, E. (1998). The search for meaning in evolutionary perspective and its clinical applications. In P. T. P. Wong & P. S. Fry (Eds.), *The human quest for meaning* (pp. 27–50). Mahway, NJ: Erlbaum.

Knee, C. R. (1998). Implicit theories of relationships: Assessment and prediction of romantic relationship initiation, coping, and longevity. *Journal of Personality and Social Psychology, 74,* 360–370.

Knee, C. R., Nanayakkar, A., Vietor, N. A., & Neighbors, C. (2002). Implicit theories of relationships: Who cares if romantic partners are less than ideal? *Personality and Social Psychology Bulletin, 27,* 808–819.

Knee, C. R., Patrick, H., & Lonsbary, C. (2003). Implicit theories of relationships: Orientations towards evaluation & cultivation. *Personality and Social Psychology Review, 7,* 41–55.

Knee, C. R., Patrick, H., Vietor, N. A., Nanayakkar, A., & Neighbors, C. (2002). Self-determination as growth motivation in romantic relationships. *Personality and Social Psychology Bulletin, 28,* 609–619.

Knee, C. R., Patrick, H., Vietor, N. A., & Neighbors, C. (2004). Implicit theories of relationships: Moderators of the link between conflict and commitment. *Personality and Social Psychology Bulletin, 30,* 617–628.

Kobasa, S. C., Maddi, S. R., & Kahn, S. (1982). Hardiness and health: A prospective study. *Journal of Personality and Social Psychology, 42,* 168–177.

Koenig, H. G., & Cohen, H. J. (Eds.). (2002). *The link between religion and health: Psychoneuroimmunology and the faith factor.* New York: Oxford University Press.

Koenig, H. G., McCullough, M. E., & Larson, D. B. (2001). *Handbook of religion and health.* New York: Oxford University Press.

Krakovsky, M. (2000). The science of lasting happiness. *Scientific American, 296,* 36–38.

Kramer, D. A. (2000). Wisdom as a classical source of human strength: Conceptualization and empirical inquiry. *Journal of Social and Clinical Psychology, 19,* 83–101.

Kubzansky, L. D., Kubzansky, P. E., & Maselko, J. (2004). Optimism and pessimism in the context of health: Bipolar opposites or separate constructs? *Personality and Social Psychology Bulletin, 30,* 943–956.

Kubzansky, L. D., Sparrow, D., Vokonas, P., & Kwachi, I. (2001). Is the glass half empty or half full? A prospective study of optimism and coronary heart disease in the Normative Aging Study. *Psychosomatic Medicine, 63,* 910–916.

Kunzmann, U. (2004). Approaches to a good life: The emotional-motivational side to wisdom. In P. A. Linley & S. Joseph (Eds.), *Positive psychology in practice* (pp. 504–517). Hoboken, NJ: John Wiley & Sons.

Kunzmann, U., & Baltes, P. B. (2003). Wisdom-related knowledge: Affective, motivational, and interpersonal correlates. *Personality and Social Psychology Bulletin, 29,* 1104–1119.

Kunzmann, U., Little, T. D., & Smith, J. (2000). Is age-related stability of subjective well-being a paradox? Cross-sectional and longitudinal evidence from the Berlin Aging Study. *Psychology of Aging, 15,* 511–526.

Kunzmann, U., Stange, A., & Jordan, J. (2005). Positive affectivity and lifestyle in adulthood: Do you do what you feel? *Personality and Social Psychology Bulletin, 31,* 574–588.

Kurdek, L. A. (1991). The relations between reported well-being and divorce history, availability of a proximate adult, and gender. *Journal of Marriage and Family Relations, 53,* 71–78.

Kurdek, L. A. (1999). The nature and predictors of the trajectory of change in marital quality for husbands and wives over the first 10 years of marriage. *Developmental Psychology, 35,* 1283–1296.

Langer, E. J. (1989). *Mindfulness.* Reading, MA: Addison-Wesley.

Langer, E. J. (2002). Well-being: Mindfulness versus positive psychology. In C. R. Snyder & S. J. Lopez (Eds.), *Handbook of positive psychology* (pp. 214–230). New York: Oxford University Press.

Langer, E. J., & Moldoveanu, M. (2000). The construct of mindfulness. *Journal of Social Issues, 56*, 1–9.

Larsen, R. J., & Fredrickson, B. L. (1999). Measurement issues in emotion research. In D. Kahneman, E. Diener, & N. Schwarz (Eds.), *Well-being: The foundations of hedonic psychology.* New York: Russell Sage Foundation.

Larsen, J. T., Hemenover, S. H., Norris, C. J., & Cacioppo, J. T. (2003). Turning adversity to advantage: On the coactivation of positive and negative emotions. In L. G. Aspinwall & U. M. Staudinger (Eds.), *A psychology of human strengths: Fundamental questions and future directions for a positive psychology* (pp. 211–225). Washington, DC: American Psychological Association.

Larsen, R. J., & Kasimatis, M. (1990). Individual differences in entrainment of mood to the weekly calendar. *Journal of Personality and Social Psychology, 58*, 164–171.

Lauer, R. H., & Lauer, R. (1985, June). Marriages made to last. *Psychology Today*, pp. 22–26.

Lauer, R. H., Lauer, R., & Kerr, S. T. (1990). The long-term marriage: Perceptions of stability and satisfaction. *International Journal of Aging and Human Development, 31*, 189–195.

Laurenceau, J. P., Barrett, L. F., & Pietromonaco, P. R. (1998). Intimacy as an interpersonal process: The importance of self-disclosure, partner disclosure, and perceived partner responsiveness in interpersonal exchanges. *Journal of Personality and Social Psychology, 74*, 1238–1251.

Lawton, M. P. (2001). Emotion in later life. *Current Directions in Psychological Science, 10*, 120–123.

Lawton, M. P., Kleban, M. H., & Dean, J. (1993). Affect and age: Cross-sectional comparisons of structure and prevalence. *Psychology and Aging, 7*, 172–184.

Layard, R. (2005). *Happiness: Lessons from a new science.* New York: Penguin Press.

Lazarus, R. S. (2000). Toward better research on stress and coping. *American Psychologist, 55*, 665–673.

Lazarus, R. S., & Folkman, S. (1984). *Stress, appraisal and coping.* New York: Springer.

Leary, M. R., & Baumeister, R. F. (2000). The nature and function of self-esteem: Sociometer theory. In M. P. Zanna (Ed.), *Advances in Experimental Social Psychology* (Vol. 32, pp. 1–62). San Diego, CA: Academic Press.

Leary, M. R., & Kowalski, R. (1995). *Social anxiety.* New York: Guilford Press.

Leary, M. R., Tambor, E. S., Terdal, S. K., & Downs, D. L. (1995). Self-esteem as an interpersonal monitor: The sociometer hypothesis. *Journal of Personality and Social Psychology, 68*, 518–530.

Lee, G. R., Seccombe, K., & Shehan, C. L. (1991). Marital status and personal happiness: An analysis of trend data. *Journal of Marriage and the Family, 53*, 839–844.

Lee, J. A. (1988). Love styles. In R. J. Sternberg & M. L. Barnes (Eds.), *The psychology of love.* New Haven: Yale University Press.

Lefcourt, H. M. (2002). Humor. In C. R. Snyder & S. J. Lopez (Eds.), *Handbook of positive psychology* (pp. 619–631). New York: Oxford University Press.

Lefcourt, H. M., Davidson, K., & Kueneman, K. (1990). Humor and immune system functioning. *Humor—International Journal of Humor Research, 3*, 305–321.

LeFrance, M., Hecht, M. A., & Paluck, E. L. (2003). The contingent smile: A meta-analysis of sex differences in smiling. *Psychological Bulletin, 129*, 305–334.

Lengfelder, A., & Gollwitzer, P. M. (2001). Reflective and reflexive action control in patients with frontal lobe lesions. *Neuropsychology, 15*, 80–100.

Lent, R. W. (2004). Toward a unifying theoretical and practical perspective on well-being and psychosocial adjustment. *Journal of Counseling Psychology, 51*, 482–509.

Lerner, M. J. (1980). *The belief in a just world.* New York: Plenum Press.

Levenson, R. W., Carstensen, L. L., & Gottman, J. M. (1993). Long-term marriage: Age, gender and satisfaction. *Psychology and Aging, 8*, 301–313.

Levenson, R. W., Carstensen, L. L., & Gottman, J. M. (1994). Influence of age and gender on affect, physiology, and their interactions: A study of long-term marriages. *Journal of Personality and Social Psychology, 67*, 56–68.

Levin, D. E., & Linn, S. (2004). The commercialization of childhood. In T. Kasser & A. D. Kanner (Eds.), *Psychology and consumer culture: The struggle for a good life in a materialistic world* (pp. 213–232). Washington, DC: American Psychological Association.

Levine, R., Sato, S., Hashimoto, T., & Verma, J. (1995). Love and marriage in eleven cultures. *Journal of Cross-Cultural Psychology, 26*, 554–571.

Levinger, G. (1976). A social psychological perspective on marital dissolution. *Journal of Social Issues, 32*, 21–47.

Levinger, G., & Levinger, A. (2003). Winds of time and place: How context has affected a 50-year marriage. *Personal Relationships, 10*, 285–306.

Levinson, D. J. (1978). *The seasons of a man's life.* New York: Ballantine.

Levy, B. R., Slade, M. D., Kunkel, S. R., & Kasl, S. V. (2002). Longevity increased by positive self-perceptions of aging. *Journal of Personality and Social Psychology, 83*, 261–270.

Linley, P. A., & Joseph, S. (2004). *Positive psychology in practice.* Hoboken, NJ: John Wiley & Sons.

Little, B. R. (1989). Personal projects analysis: Trivial pursuits, magnificent obsessions, and the search for coherence, In D. Buss & N. Cantor (Eds.), *Personality psychology: Recent trends and emerging directions* (pp. 15–31). New York: Springer-Verlag.

Little, B. R. (1993). Personal projects and the distributed self: Aspects of conative psychology. In J. Suls (Ed.), *Psychological perspectives on the self* (Vol. 4, pp. 157–181). Hillsdale, NJ: Lawrence Erlbaum.

Little, B. R., Salmela-Aro, K., & Phillips, S. D. (2007). *Personal project pursuit: Goal action and human flourishing.* Mahway, NJ: Lawrence Erlbaum.

Locke, E. A., & Latham, G. P. (1990). *A theory of goal setting and task performance.* Englewood Cliffs, NJ: Prentice-Hall.

Locke, E. A., & Latham, G. P. (2002). Building a practically useful theory of goal setting and task motivation: A 35 year odyssey. *American Psychologist, 57,* 705–717.

Loehlin, J. C. (1992). *Genes and environment in personality development.* Newbury Park, CA: Sage Publications.

Loehlin, J. C., McCrae, R. R., Costa, P. T., Jr., & John, O. P. (1998). Heritability of common and measure specific components of the Big Five personality factors. *Journal of Research in Personality, 32,* 431–453.

Lopez, S. J., & Snyder, C. R. (Eds.). (2003). *Positive psychological assessment: A handbook of models and measures.* Washington, DC: American Psychological Association.

Lucas, R. E., Clark, A. E., Georgellis, Y., & Diener, E. (2003). Reexamining adaptation and the set point model of happiness: Reactions to changes in marital status. *Journal of Personality and Social Psychology, 84,* 527–539.

Lucas, R. E., Clark, A. E., Georgellis, Y., & Diener, E. (2004). Unemployment alters the set point for life satisfaction. *Psychological Science, 15,* 8–13.

Lucas, R. E., Diener, E., & Larsen, R. J. (2003). Measuring positive emotions. In S. J. Lopez & C. R. Snyder (Eds.), *Positive psychological assessment: A handbook of models and measures* (pp. 201–218). Washington, DC: American Psychological Association.

Lucas, R. E., Diener, E., & Suh, E. (1996). Discriminant validity of well-being measures. *Journal of Personality and Social Psychology, 71,* 616–628.

Lucas, R. E., & Gohm, C. L. (2000). Age and sex differences in subjective well-being across cultures. In E. Diener & E. M. Suh (Eds.), *Culture and subjective well-being* (pp. 291–317). Cambridge MA: MIT Press.

Luthar, S. S. (1999). *Poverty and children's adjustment.* Thousand Oaks, CA: Sage Publications.

Luthar, S. S. (2003). The culture of affluence: Psychological costs of material wealth. *Child Development, 74,* 1581–1593.

Luthar, S. S., & D'Advanzo, K. (1999). Contextual factors in substance abuse: A study of suburban and inner city adolescents. *Development and Psychopathology, 11,* 845–867.

Luthar, S. S., & Zigler, E. (1991). Vulnerability and competence: A review of research on resilience in childhood. *Journal of American Orthopsychiatry, 61,* 6–22.

Lykins, L. B. E., Segerstrom, S. C., Averill, A. J., Evans, D. R., & Kemeny, M. E. (2007). Goal shifts following reminders of mortality: Reconciling posttraumatic growth and terror management theory. *Personality and Social Psychology Bulletin, 33,* 1088–1099.

Lykken, D. (1999). *Happiness: The nature and nurture of joy and contentment.* New York: St. Martin Press.

Lykken, D., & Tellegen, A. (1996). Happiness is a stochastic phenomenon. *Psychological Science, 7,* 186–189.

Lyubomirsky, S. (2001). Why are some people happier than others? The role of cognitive and motivational processes in well-being. *American Psychologist, 56,* 239–249.

Lyubomirsky, S., King, L., & Diener, E. (2005). The benefits of frequent positive affect. *Psychological Bulletin, 131,* 803–855.

Lyubomirsky, S., & Lepper, S. H. (1999). A measure of subjective happiness: Preliminary reliability and construct validation. *Social Indicators Research, 46,* 137–155.

Lyubomirsky, S., Sheldon, K. M., & Schkade, D. (2005). Pursuing happiness: The architecture of sustainable change. *Review of General Psychology, 9,* 111–131.

Maddux, J. E. (1995). *Self-efficacy, adaptation, and adjustment: Theory, research, and application.* New York: Pearson.

Maddux, J. E. (2002). Self-efficacy: The power of believing you can. In C. R. Snyder & S. J. Lopez (Eds.), *Handbook of positive psychology* (pp. 277–287). New York: Oxford University Press.

Mahoney, A., Pargament, K. I., Jewell, T., Swank, A. B., Scott, E., Emery, E., & Rye, M. (1999). Marriage and the spiritual realm: The role of proximal and distal religious constructs in marital functioning. *Journal of Family Psychology, 13,* 321–338.

Maier, S. F., Watkins, L. R., & Fleshner, M. (1994). The interface between behavior, brain, and immunity. *American Psychologist, 49,* 1004–1017.

Manstead, A. S. R. (1992). Gender differences in emotion. In A. Gale & M. W. Eyesenck (Eds.), *Handbook of individual differences: Biological perspectives* (pp. 355–387). New York: John Wiley & Sons.

Markus, H. R., & Kitayama, S. (1991). Culture and the self: Implications for cognition, emotion and motivation. *Psychological Review, 98,* 224–253.

Markus, H., & Nurius, P. S. (1986). Possible selves. *American Psychologist, 41,* 954–969.

Markus, H., & Wurf, E. (1987). The dynamic self-concept: A social psychological perspective. *Annual Review of Psychology, 38,* 299–337.

Martin, R. A. (2007). *The psychology of humor: An integrative approach.* Burlington, MA: Elsevier Academic Press.

Maruta, T., Colligan, R. C., Malinchoe, M., & Offord, K. P. (2000). Optimism versus pessimism: Survival rate among medical patients over a 30-year period. *Mayo Clinic Proceedings, 75,* 140–143.

Maslow, A. (1943). A theory of human motivation. *Psychological Review, 50,* 370–396.

Maslow, A. H. (1954). *Motivation and personality.* New York: Harper & Row.

Maslow, A. H. (1968). *Toward a psychology of being* (2nd ed.). Princeton, NJ: Van Nostrand.

Mastekaasa, A. (1992). Marriage and psychological well-being: Some evidence on selection into marriage. *Journal of Marriage and Family, 54,* 901–911.

Mastekaasa, A. (1993). Marital status and psychological well-being: A changing relationship? *Social Indicators Research, 29,* 249–276.

Masten, A. S. (2001). Ordinary magic: Resilience processes in development. *American Psychologist, 56,* 227–238.

Masten, A. S., Best, K., & Garmezy, N. (1990). Resilience and development: Contributions from the study of children who overcame adversity. *Development and Psychopathology, 2,* 425–444.

Masten, A. S., & Coatsworth, J. D. (1998). The development of competence in favorable and unfavorable environments: Lessons from research on successful children. *American Psychologist, 53,* 205–220.

Masten, A. S., & Reed, M. J. (2002). Resilience in development. In C. R. Snyder & S. J. Lopez (Eds.), *Handbook of positive psychology* (pp. 74–88). New York: Oxford University Press.

Matsumoto, D. (1997). *Culture and modern life.* Pacific Grove, CA: Brooks/Cole.

McAdams, D. P. (1995). What do we know when we know a person? *Journal of Personality, 63,* 365–396.

McAdams, D. P. (1996). Personality, modernity and the storied self: A contemporary framework for studying persons. *Psychological Inquiry, 7,* 295–321.

McCrae, R. R., & Allik, J. (Eds.). (2002). *The Five Factor model of personality across cultures.* New York: Klewer Academic/Plenum Press.

McCrae, R. R., & Costa, P. T., Jr. (1990). *Personality in adulthood.* New York: Guilford Press.

McCrae, R. R., & Costa, P. T., Jr. (1991). Adding *Liebe und Arbeit*: The full Five-Factor model and well-being. *Personality and Social Psychology Bulletin, 17,* 227–232.

McCrae, R. R., & Costa, P. T., Jr. (1997). Personality trait structure as a human universal. *American Psychologist, 52,* 509–516.

McCrae, R. R., Costa, P. T., Jr., & Martin, T. A. (2005). The NEO-PI-3: A more readable revised NEO personality inventory. *Journal of Personality Assessment, 84,* 261–270.

McCrae, R. R., Costa, P. T., Jr., Ostendorf, F., Angleitner, A., Hrebickova, M., Avia, M. D., et al. (2000). Nature over nurture: Temperament, personality, and life span development. *Journal of Personality and Social Psychology, 78,* 173–186.

McCrae, R. R., & Terracciano, A. (2005). Universal features of personality traits from the observer's perspective: Data from 50 cultures. *Journal of Personality and Social Psychology, 88,* 547–561.

McCullough, M. E. (Ed.). (1999). *Forgiveness: Theory, research and practice.* New York: Guilford Press.

McCullough, M. E., Kilpatrick, S., Emmons, R. A., & Larson, D. (2001). Gratitude as moral affect. *Psychological Bulletin, 127,* 249–266.

McCullough, M. E., & Laurenceau, J. P. (2005). Religiousness and the trajectory of self-rated health across adulthood. *Personality and Social Psychology Bulletin, 31,* 560–573.

McCullough, M. E., Pargament, K. I., & Thoresen, C. E. (Eds.). (2000). *Forgiveness: Theory, research and practice.* New York: Guilford Press.

McCullough, M. E., Rachal, K. C., Sandage, S. J., Worthington, E. L., Jr., Brown, S. W., & Hight, T. L. (1998). Interpersonal forgiving in close relationships: II. Theoretical elaboration and measurement. *Journal of Personality and Social Psychology, 75,* 1586–1603.

McCullough, M. E, & Witvliet, C. V. (2002). The psychology of forgiveness. In C. R. Snyder & S. J. Lopez (Eds.), *Handbook of positive psychology* (pp. 446–458). New York: Oxford University Press.

McCullough, M. E., & Worthington, E. L., Jr. (1997). Interpersonal forgiving in close relationships. *Journal of Personality and Social Psychology, 73,* 321–336.

McFarlin, D. B., & Blascovich, J. (1981). Effects of self-esteem and performance feedback on future affective preferences and cognitive expectations. *Journal of Personality and Social Psychology, 40,* 521–531.

McGregor, I., & Little, P. (1998). Personal projects, happiness and meaning: On doing well and being yourself. *Journal of Personality and Social Psychology, 74,* 494–512.

McIntosh, D. N., & Spilka, B. (1990). Religion and physical health: The role of personal faith and control. In M. L. Lynn & D. O. Moberg (Eds.), *Research in the social scientific study of religion* (Vol. 2, pp. 167–194). Greenwich, CT: JAI Press.

McIntosh, W. D. (1997). East meets West: Parallels between Zen Buddhism and social psychology. *International Journal for the Psychology of Religion, 7,* 37–52.

McLoyd, V. C. (1998). Socioeconomic disadvantage and child development. *American Psychologist, 53,* 185–204.

Mecca, A. M., Smelsor, N. J., & Vasconcellos, J. (1989). *The social importance of self-esteem.* Berkeley: University of California Press.

Meehl, P. E. (1975). Hedonic capacity: Some conjectures. *Bulletin of the Menninger Clinic, 39,* 295–307.

Metcalfe, J., & Mischel, W. (1999). A hot/cool system analysis of delay of gratification: Dynamics of willpower. *Psychological Review, 106*, 3–19.

Meyers, S. A., & Berscheid, E. (1997). The language of love: The difference a preposition makes. *Personality and Social Psychology Bulletin, 23*, 347–362.

Michalos, A. C. (1991). *Life satisfaction and happiness: Global report on student well-being: Vol. 1.* New York: Springer-Verlag.

Mickelson, K. D., Kessler, R. C., & Shaver, P. R. (1997). Adult attachment in a national representative sample. *Journal of Personality and Social Psychology, 73*, 1092–1106.

Milgram, S. (1974). *Obedience to authority.* New York: Harper & Row.

Miller, L. C. (1990). Intimacy and liking: Mutual influence and the role of unique relationships. *Journal of Personality and Social Psychology, 59*, 50–60.

Miller, L. C., & Read, S. J. (1987). Why am I telling you this? Self-disclosure in a goal-based model of personality. In V. J. Derlega & J. Berg (Eds.), *Self-disclosure: Theory, research, and therapy.* New York: Plenum Press.

Miller, R. S., Perlman, D., & Brehm, S. (2007). *Intimate relationships* (4th ed.). New York: McGraw-Hill.

Miller, W. R., & Thoresen, C. E. (2003). Spirituality, religion and health: An emerging research field. *American Psychologist, 58*, 24–35.

Mills, J., & Clark, M. S. (2001). Viewing close romantic relationships as communal relationships: Implications for maintenance and enhancement. In J. H. Harvey & A. Wenzel (Eds.), *Close romantic relationships: Maintenance and enhancement* (pp. 13–25). Mahwah, NJ: Lawrence Erlbaum.

Mischel, W. (1974). Processes in delay of gratification. In Berkowitz (Ed.), *Advances in experimental psychology* (Vol. 7, pp. 249–292). New York: Academic Press.

Mischel, W., Ebbesen, E. B., & Zeiss, A. (1972). Cognitive and attentional mechanisms in the delay of gratification. *Journal of Personality and Social Psychology, 28*, 172–179.

Mischel, W., & Mendoza-Denton, R. (2003). Harnessing willpower and socioemotional intelligence to enhance human agency and potential. In L. G. Aspinwall & U. M. Staudinger (Eds.), *A psychology of human strengths: Fundamental questions and future directions for a positive psychology* (pp. 245–256). Washington, DC: American Psychological Association.

Moller, A. C., Deci, E. L., & Ryan, R. M. (2006). Choice and ego-depletion: The moderating role of autonomy. *Personality and Social Psychology Bulletin, 32*, 1024–1036.

Mroczek, D. K., & Almeida, D. M. (2004). The effects of daily stress, age, and personality on daily negative affect. *Journal of Personality, 72*, 354–378.

Mroczek, D. K., & Avron, S., III (2005). Change in life satisfaction during adulthood: Findings from the Veterans Affairs Normative Aging Study. *Journal of Personality and Social Psychology, 88*, 189–202.

Mroczek, D. K., & Kolarz, C. M. (1998). The effect of age on positive and negative affect: A developmental perspective on happiness. *Journal of Personality and Social Psychology, 75*, 1333–1349.

Muraven, M., & Baumeister, R. F. (2000). Self-regulation and depletion of limited resources: Does self-control resemble a muscle? *Psychological Bulletin, 126*, 247–259.

Muraven, M., & Slessareva, E. (2003). Mechanisms of self-control failure: Motivation and limited resources. *Personality and Social Psychology Bulletin, 29*, 894–906.

Murray, A. L., Holmes, J. G., & Griffin, D. W. (1996a). The benefits of positive illusions: Idealization and the construction of satisfaction in close relationships. *Journal of Personality and Social Psychology, 70*, 79–98.

Murray, A. L., Holmes, J. G., & Griffin, D. W. (1996b). The self-fulfilling nature of positive illusions in romantic relationships: Love is not blind, but prescient. *Journal of Personality and Social Psychology, 71*, 155–180.

Myers, D. G. (1992). *The pursuit of happiness.* New York: Avon Books.

Myers, D. G. (1999). Close relationships and quality of life. In D. Kahneman, E. Diener, & N. Schwarz (Eds.), *Well-being: The foundations of hedonic psychology* (pp. 374–391). New York: Russell Sage Foundation.

Myers, D. G. (2000a). The funds, friends, and faith of happy people. *American Psychologist, 55*, 56–67.

Myers, D. G. (2000b). *The American paradox: Spiritual hunger in an age of plenty.* New Haven: Yale University Press.

Myers, D. G., & Diener, E. (1995). Who is happy? *Psychological Science, 6*, 10–19.

Nakamura, J., & Csikszentmihalyi, M. (2002). The concept of flow. In C. R. Snyder & S. J. Lopez (Eds.), *Handbook of positive psychology* (pp. 89–105). New York: Oxford University Press.

Nakamura, J., & Csikszentmihalyi, M. (2003). The construction of meaning through vital engagement. In C. L. M. Keyes & J. Haidt (Eds.), *Flourishing: Positive psychology and the life well-lived* (pp. 83–104). Washington, DC: American Psychological Association.

Neff, L. A., & Karney, B. R. (2005). To know you is to love you: The implications of global adoration and specific accuracy for marital relationships. *Journal of Personality and Social Psychology, 88*, 480–497.

Ness, L. S., & Segerstrom, S. C. (2006). Dispositional optimism and coping: A meta-analytic review. *Personality and Social Psychology Review, 10*, 235–251.

Nolen-Hoeksema, S. (1995). Epidemiology and theories of sex differences in depression. In M. Seeman (Ed.),

Gender and psychopathology (pp. 63–87). Washington, DC: American Psychiatric Association Press.

Nolen-Hoeksema, S., & Davis, C. G. (2002). Positive responses to loss: Perceiving benefits and growth. In C. R. Snyder & S. J. Lopez (Eds.), *Handbook of positive psychology* (pp. 598–607). New York: Oxford University Press.

Nolen-Hoeksema, S., & Rusting, C. L. (1999). Gender differences in well-being. In D. Kahneman, E. Diener, & N. Schwarz (Eds.), *Well-being: The foundations of hedonic psychology* (pp. 330–350). New York: Russell Sage Foundation.

Noller, P. (2006). Marital relationships. In P. Noller & J. A. Feeney (Eds.), *Close relationships: Functions, forms and processes* (pp. 67–88). New York: Psychology Press.

Noller, P., & Feeney, J. A. (Eds.). (2006). *Close relationships: Functions, forms and processes*. New York: Psychology Press.

Norem, J. K. (2001). *The positive power of negative thinking: Using defensive pessimism to harness anxiety and perform at your peak*. New York: Basic Books.

Norem, J. K. (2002). Defensive pessimism, optimism and pessimism. In E. C. Chang (Ed.), *Optimism & pessimism: Implications for theory, research, and practice* (pp. 77–100). Washington, DC: American Psychological Association.

Norem, J. K., & Cantor, N. (1986). Defensive pessimism: Harnessing anxiety as motivation. *Journal of Personality and Social Psychology, 51*, 1208–1217.

Norem, J. K., & Chang, E. C. (2002). The positive psychology of negative thinking. *Journal of Clinical Psychology, 58*, 993–1001.

Oishi, S. (2000). Goals as cornerstones of subjective well-being: Linking individuals and cultures. In E. Diener & E. M. Suh (Eds.), *Culture and subjective well-being* (pp. 87–112). Cambridge, MA: MIT Press.

Oishi, S., & Diener, E. (2001). Goals, culture, and subjective well-being. *Personality and Social Psychology Bulletin, 27*, 1674–1682.

Oishi, S., Diener, E., Lucas, R. E., & Suh, E. M. (1999). Cross-cultural variations in predictors of life satisfaction: Perspectives from needs and values. *Personality and Social Psychology Bulletin, 25*, 980–990.

Oishi, S., Diener, E., Suh, E., & Lucas, R. E. (1999). Value as moderator in subjective well-being. *Journal of Personality, 67*, 157–184.

Okun, M. A., Stock, W. A., Haring, M. J., & Witter, R. A. (1984). The social activity/subjective relationship: A quantitative synthesis. *Research on Aging, 6*, 45–65.

Ornstein, R. E. (1973). *The nature of human consciousness*. San Francisco, CA: W.H. Freeman.

Oyserman, D., Coon, H. M., & Kemmelmeier, M. (2002). Rethinking individualism and collectivism: Evaluation of theoretical assumptions and meta-analysis. *Psychological Bulletin, 128*, 3–72.

Paleari, E. G., Regalia, C., & Fincham, F. (2005). Marital quality, forgiveness, empathy, and rumination: A longitudinal study. *Personality and Social Psychology Bulletin, 31*, 368–378.

Palys, T. S., & Little, B. R. (1983). Perceived life satisfaction and the organization of personal project systems. *Journal of Personality and Social Psychology, 44*, 1221–1230.

Pargament, K. I. (1997). *The psychology of religion and coping: Theory, research and practice*. New York: Guilford Press.

Pargament, K. I. (1999). The psychology of religion *and* spirituality? Yes and no. *International Journal for the Psychology of Religion, 9*, 3–16.

Pargament, K. I. (2002). The bitter and the sweet: An evaluation of the costs and benefits of religiousness. *Psychological Inquiry, 13*, 168–181.

Pargament, K. I., Kennell, J., Hathaway, W., Grevengoed, N., Newman, J., & Jones, W. (1988). Religion and the problem-solving process: Three styles of coping. *Journal for the Scientific Study of Religion, 27*, 90–104.

Pargament, K. I., & Mahoney, A. (2002). Spirituality: Discovering and conserving the sacred. In C. R. Snyder & S. J. Lopez (Eds.), *Handbook of positive psychology* (pp. 646–659). New York: Oxford University Press.

Pargament, K. I., Smith, B. W., Koenig, H. G., & Perez, L. (1998). Patterns of positive and negative religious coping with major life events. *Journal for the Scientific Study of Religion, 37*, 710–724.

Pargament, K. I., Tarakeshwar, N., Ellison, C. G., & Wulff, K. W. (2001). Religious coping among the religious: The relationship between religious coping and well-being in a national sample of Presbyterian clergy, elders and members. *Journal for the Scientific Study of Religion, 40*, 496–513.

Park, C. L. (1998). Implications of posttraumatic growth for individuals. In R. G. Tedeschi, C. L. Park, & L. G. Calhoun (Eds.), *Posttraumatic growth: Positive changes in the aftermath of crisis* (pp. 153–178). Mahwah, NJ: Lawrence Erlbaum.

Park, L. E., & Crocker, J. (2005). Interpersonal consequences of seeking self-esteem. *Personality and Social Psychology Bulletin, 31*, 1587–1598.

Park, C. L., Moore, P. J., Turner, R. A., & Adler, N. E. (1997). The roles of constructive thinking and optimism in psychological and behavioral adjustment during pregnancy. *Journal of Personality and Social Psychology, 73*, 584–592.

Paterson, M. (2006). *Consumption and everyday life*. London/New York: Routledge.

Paulus, D. L., Wehr, P., Harms, P. D., & Strasser, D. H. (2002). Use of exemplars to reveal implicit types of intelligence. *Personality and Social Psychology Bulletin, 28*, 1051–1062.

Pavot, W., & Diener, E. (1993). Review of the Satisfaction with Life Scale. *Psychological Assessment, 5,* 164–172.

Peele, S. (1989). *The diseasing of America.* New York: Houghton Mifflin.

Pennebaker, J. W. (1993). Putting stress into words: Health, linguistic, and therapeutic implications. *Behavioral Research and Therapy, 31,* 539–548.

Pennebaker, J. W., & Beall, S. K. (1986). Confronting a traumatic event: Toward an understanding of inhibition and disease. *Journal of Abnormal Psychology, 95,* 275–281.

Pennebaker, J. W., Colder, M., & Sharp, L. K. (1990). Accelerating the coping process. *Journal of Personality and Social Psychology, 58,* 528–537.

Pennebaker, J. W., Kiecolt-Glaser, J. K., & Glaser, R. (1988). Disclosure of traumas and immune function: Health implications for psychotherapy. *Journal of Consulting and Clinical Psychology, 56,* 239–245.

Pennebaker, J. W., & O'Heeron, R. C. (1984). Confiding in others and illness rate among spouses of suicide and accidental death victims. *Journal of Abnormal Psychology, 93,* 473–476.

Perloff, L. S. (1983). Perceptions of invulnerability to victimization. *Journal of Social Issues, 39,* 41–62.

Perls, F. S. (1969). *Gestalt Therapy Verbatim.* Lafayette, CA: Real People Press.

Peterson, C. (1991). Meaning and measurement of explanatory style. *Psychological Inquiry, 2,* 1–10.

Peterson, C. (2000). The future of optimism. *American Psychologist, 55,* 44–55.

Peterson, C. (2006). *A primer in positive psychology.* New York: Oxford University Press.

Peterson, C., Bettes, B. A., & Seligman, M. E. P. (1985). Depressive symptoms and unprompted causal attributions: Content analysis. *Behavior Research and Therapy, 23,* 379–382.

Peterson, C., & Bosio, L. M. (1991). *Health and optimism.* New York: Free Press.

Petersen, C., & Bosio, L. M. (2002). Optimism and physical well-being. In E. C. Chang (Ed.), *Optimism & pessimism: Implications for theory, research, and practice* (pp. 127–145). Washington, DC: American Psychological Association.

Peterson, C., & Chang, E. C. (2003). Optimism and flourishing. In C. L. M. Keyes & J. Haidt (Eds.), *Flourishing: Positive psychology and the life well-lived* (pp. 55–75). Washington, DC: American Psychological Association.

Peterson, C., & Park, C. (1998). Learned helplessness and explanatory style. In D. F. Bourne, V. B. Van Hasselt, & M. Hersen (Eds.), *Advanced personality* (pp. 287–310). New York: Plenum Press.

Peterson, C., Semmel, A., von Baeyer, C., Abramson, L. Y., Metalsky, G. I., & Seligman, M. E. P. (1982). The Attributional Style Questionnaire. *Cognitive Therapy and Research, 6,* 287–299.

Peterson, C., & Seligman, M. E. P. (2004). *Character strengths and virtues: A handbook of classification.* Washington, DC: American Psychological Association/ New York: Oxford University Press.

Peterson, C., Seligman, M. E. P., & Vaillant, G. E. (1988). Pessimistic explanatory style is a risk factor for physical illness: A 35-year longitudinal study. *Journal of Personality and Social Psychology, 55,* 23–27.

Peterson, C., & Villanova, P. (1988). An Expanded Attributional Style Questionnaire. *Journal of Abnormal Psychology, 97,* 87–89.

Phillips, R. (1988). *Putting asunder: A history of divorce in Western society.* Cambridge: Cambridge University Press.

Pinquart, M. (2001). Age differences in perceived positive affect, negative affect, and affect balance in middle and old age. *Journal of Happiness Studies, 2,* 375–405.

Pittman, T. S. (1998). Motivation. In D. T. Gilbert, S. T. Fiske, & G. Lindzey (Eds.), *The handbook of social psychology* (4th ed., Vol. 1, pp. 549–590). New York: McGraw-Hill.

Popenoe, D., & Whitehead, B. (2004). *The state of our unions.* Piscataway, NJ: The National Marriage Project.

Powell, L. H., Shahabi, L., & Thoresen, C. E. (2003). Religion and spirituality: Linkages to physical health. *American Psychologist, 58,* 36–52.

Power, M. J. (2003). Quality of life. In C. R. Snyder & S. J. Lopez (Eds.), *Handbook of positive psychology* (pp. 427–441). New York: Oxford University Press.

Pratto, F., & John, O. P. (1991). Automatic vigilance: The attention-grabbing power of negative social information. *Journal of Personality and Social Psychology, 61,* 380–391.

Pressman, S. D., & Cohen, S. (2005). Does positive affect influence health? *Psychological Bulletin, 131,* 925–971.

Putnam, R. D. (2000). *Bowling alone: The collapse and revival of American community.* New York: Simon & Schuster.

Rabin, B. S. (2002). Understanding how stress affects the physical body. In H. G. Koenig & H. J. Cohen (Eds.), *The link between religion and health: Psychoneuroimmunology and the faith factor* (pp. 43–68). New York: Oxford University Press.

Rappoport, L. (2005). *Punchlines: The case for racial, ethnic and gender humor.* Westport, CT: Praeger.

Ray, O. (2004). How the mind hurts and heals the body. *American Psychologist, 59,* 29–40.

Read, S. J., & Miller, L. C. (1998). On the dynamic construction of meaning: An interactive activation and competition model of social perception. In S. J. Read & L. C. Miller (Eds.), *Connectionist models of social reasoning and behavior.* Mahwah, NJ: Lawrence Erlbaum.

Read, S. J., & Miller, L. C. (2002). Virtual personalities: A neural network model of personality. *Personality and Social Psychology Review, 6,* 357–369.

Redelmeir, D., & Kahneman, D. (1996). Patients' memories of painful medical treatments: Real-time and retrospective evaluations of two minimally invasive procedures. *Pain, 116,* 3–8.

Regier, D. A., Boyd, H. J., Burke, J. D., Rae, D. S., Myers, J. K., Kramer, M., et al. (1988). One month prevalence of mental disorders in the United States. *Archives of General Psychiatry, 45,* 977–986.

Reis, H. T., & Gable, S. L. (2003). Toward a positive psychology of relationships. In C. L. M. Keyes & J. Haidt (Eds.), *Flourishing: Positive psychology and the life well-lived* (pp. 129–159). Washington, DC: American Psychological Association.

Reis, H. T., & Patrick, B. C. (1996). Attachment and intimacy: Component processes. In E. T. Higgins & A. Kruglanski (Eds.), *Social psychology: Handbook of basic principles* (pp. 523–563). New York: Guilford Press.

Reis, H. T., & Shaver, P. (1988). Intimacy as an interpersonal process. In S. Duck (Ed.), *Handbook of personal relationships: Theory, relationships and interventions* (pp. 367–389). London: John Wiley & Sons.

Reis, H. T., Sheldon, K. M., Gable, S. L., Roscoe, J., & Ryan, R. M. (2000). Daily well-being: The role of autonomy, competence, and relatedness. *Personality and Social Psychology Bulletin, 26,* 419–435.

Reivich, K., & Gillham, J. (2003). Learned optimism: The measurement of explanatory style. In S. J. Lopez & C. R. Snyder (Eds.), *Positive psychological assessment: A handbook of models and measures* (pp. 57–74). Washington, DC: American Psychological Association.

Reivich, K., & Shatte, A. (2002). *The resilience factor.* New York: Broadway Books.

Rhee, E., Uleman, J., Lee, H., & Roman, R. (1995). Spontaneous self-descriptions and ethnic identities in individualistic and collectivist cultures. *Journal of Personality and Social Psychology, 69,* 142–152.

Rhodes, S. R. (1983). Age-related differences in work attitudes and behavior: A review and conceptual analysis. *Psychological Bulletin, 93,* 328–367.

Riediger, M., & Freund, A. M. (2004). Interference and facilitation among differential associations with subjective well-being and persistent goal pursuit. *Personality and Social Psychology Bulletin, 30,* 1511–1523.

Roberts, B. W., & DelVecchio, W. F. (2000). The rank-order consistency of personality traits from childhood to old age: A quantitative review of longitudinal studies. *Psychological Bulletin, 126,* 3–25.

Roberts, B. W., Wilson, K. E., & Bogg, T. (2005). Conscientiousness and health across the life course. *Review of General Psychology, 9,* 156–168.

Robinson, D. N. (1990). Wisdom through the ages. In R. J. Sternberg (Ed.), *Wisdom: Its nature, origins, and development* (pp. 13–24). New York: Cambridge University Press.

Robinson, M. D., & Clore, G. L. (2002). Belief and feeling: Evidence for an accessibility model of emotional self-report. *Psychological Bulletin, 128,* 934–960.

Robinson, M. D., & Johnson, J. T. (1997). Is it emotion or is it stress? Gender stereotypes and the perception of subjective experience. *Sex Roles, 36,* 235–258.

Robinson, M. D., Johnson, J. T., & Shields, S. A. (1998). The gender heuristic and the database: Factors affecting the perception of gender-related differences in the experience and display of emotions. *Basic and Applied Social Psychology, 20,* 206–219.

Robinson-Whelen, S., Kim, C., MacCallum, R. C., & Kiecolt-Glaser, J. K. (1997). Distinguishing optimism from pessimism in older adults: Is it more important to be optimistic or not to be pessimistic? *Journal of Personality and Social Psychology, 73*(6), 1345–1353.

Rogers, C. R. (1961). *On becoming a person.* Boston: Houghton Mifflin.

Rogers, S. J., & Amato, P. R. (2000). Have changes in gender relations affected marital quality? *Social Forces, 79,* 731–753.

Rohan, M. J. (2000). A rose by any name? The value construct. *Personality and Social Psychology Review, 4,* 255–277.

Rokeach, M. (1973). *The nature of human values.* San Francisco: Jossey-Bass.

Rosenberg, M. (1965). *Society and the adolescent self-image.* Princeton, NJ: Princeton University Press.

Rothbart, M. K., Ahadi, S. A., & Evans, D. E. (2000). Temperament and personality: Origins and outcomes. *Journal of Personality Social Psychology, 78,* 122–135.

Rothbaum, F., Weisz, J., Pott, M., Miyake, K., & Morelli, G. (2000). Attachment and culture: Security in the United States and Japan. *American Psychologist, 55,* 1093–1104.

Rothbaum, F., Weisz, J. R., & Snyder, S. S. (1982). Changing the world and changing the self: A two process model of perceived control. *Journal of Personality and Social Psychology, 42,* 5–37.

Rowe, J. W., & Kahn, R. L. (1987). Human aging: Usual and successful. *Science, 237,* 143–149.

Rowe, J. W., & Kahn, R. L. (1998). *Successful aging.* New York: Pantheon.

Rozin, P., & Royzman, E. B. (2001). Negativity bias, negativity dominance, and contagion. *Personality and Social Psychology Review, 5,* 296–320.

Rubin, Z. (1973). *Liking and loving.* New York: Holt Rinehart & Winston.

Ruini, C., & Fava, G. A. (2004). Clinical applications of well-being therapy. In P. A. Linley & S. Joseph (Eds.), *Positive Psychology in practice* (pp. 371–387). New York: John Wiley & Sons.

Rusbult, C. E. (1983). A longitudinal test of the investment model: The development (and deterioration) of satisfaction and commitment in heterosexual involvements. *Journal of Personality and Social Psychology, 45*, 101–117.

Rutter, M. (1985). Resilience in the face of adversity: Protective factors and resistance to psychiatric disorder. *British Journal of Psychiatry, 147*, 598–611.

Rutter, M., & The English and Romanian Adoptees (ERA) Study Team (1998). Developmental catch-up and deficit, following adoption after severe global early privation. *Journal of Child Psychology and Psychiatry, 39*, 465–476.

Ryan, R. M. (2002). Foreword to Kasser, T. *The high price of materialism* (pp. ix–xiii). Cambridge, MA: MIT Press.

Ryan, R. M., & Deci, E. L. (2000). Self-determination theory and the facilitation of intrinsic motivation, social development, and well-being. *American Psychologist, 55*, 68–78.

Ryan, R. M., & Deci, E. L. (2001). On happiness and human potentials: A review of research on hedonic and eudaimonic well-being. *Annual Review of Psychology, 52*, 141–166.

Rybash, J. M., Roodin, P. A., & Hoyer, H. J. (1995). *Adult development and aging* (3rd ed.). Dubuque, IA: Brown & Benchmark.

Ryff, C. D. (1989). Happiness is everything, or is it? Explorations on the meaning of psychological well-being. *Journal of Personality and Social Psychology, 57*, 1069–1081.

Ryff, C. D., & Keyes, C. L. M. (1995). The structure of psychological well-being revisited. *Journal of Personality and Social Psychology, 57*, 1069–1081.

Ryff, C. D., & Singer, B. (1998). The contours of positive human health. *Psychological Inquiry, 9*, 1–28.

Ryff, C. D., & Singer, B. (2000). Interpersonal flourishing: A positive health agenda for the new millennium. *Personality and Social Psychology Review, 4*, 30–44.

Ryff, C. D., & Singer, B. (2002). From social structure to biology: Integrative science in the pursuit of human health and well-being. In C. R. Snyder & S. J. Lopez (Eds.), *Handbook of Positive Psychology* (pp. 541–555). New York: Oxford University Press.

Ryff, C. D., & Singer, B. (2003a). Flourishing under fire: Resilience as a prototype of challenged thriving. In C. L. M. Keyes & J. Haidt (Eds.), *Flourishing: Positive psychology and the life well-lived* (pp. 15–36). Washington, DC: American Psychological Association.

Ryff, C. D., & Singer, B. (2003b). Ironies of the human condition: Well-being and health on the way to mortality. In L. G. Aspinwall & U. M. Staudinger (Eds.), *A psychology of human strengths: Fundamental questions and future directions for a positive psychology* (pp. 271–288). Washington, DC: American Psychological Association.

Sagiv, L., & Schwartz, S. H. (1995). Value priorities and readiness for out-group social contact. *Journal of Personality and Social Psychology, 69*, 437–448.

Salovey, P., Mayer, J. D., & Caruso, D. (2002). The positive psychology of emotional intelligence. In C. R. Snyder & S. J. Lopez (Eds.), *Handbook of Positive Psychology* (pp. 159–171). New York: Oxford University Press.

Salovey, P., Rothman, A. J., Detweiler, J. B., & Steward, W. T. (2000). Emotional states and health. *American Psychologist, 55*, 110–121.

Salovey, P., Rothman, A. J., & Rodin, J. (1998). Health behavior. In D. T. Gilbert, S. T. Fiske, & G. Lindzey (Eds.), *The handbook of social psychology* (4th ed., Vol. 2, pp. 633–683). New York: McGraw-Hill.

Salsman, J. M., Brown, T. L., Brechting, E. H., & Carlson, C. R. (2005). The link between religion and spirituality and psychological adjustment: The mediating role of optimism and social support. *Personality and Social Psychology Bulletin, 31*, 522–535.

Sanderson, C. A., & Cantor, N. (1995). Social dating goals in late adolescence: Implications for safer sexual activity. *Journal of Personality and Social Psychology, 68*, 1121–1134.

Sandvik, E., Diener, E., & Seidlitz, L. (1993). Subjective well-being: The convergence and stability of self-report and non-self-report measures. *Journal of Personality, 61*, 317–342.

Saucier, G., & Skrzypinska, K. (2006). Spiritual but not religious? Evidence for two independent dispositions. *Journal of Personality, 74*, 1257–1292.

Scheier, M. F., & Carver, C. S. (1985). Optimism, coping and health: Assessment and implications of generalized expectancy on health. *Health Psychology, 4*, 219–247.

Scheier, M. F., & Carver, C. S. (1992). Effects of optimism on psychological and physical well-being: Theoretical overview and empirical update. *Cognitive Therapy and Research, 16*, 201–228.

Scheier, M. F., Carver, C. S., & Bridges, M. W. (1994). Distinguishing optimism from neuroticism (and trait anxiety, self-mastery, and self-esteem): A reevaluation of the Life Orientation Test. *Journal of Personality and Social Psychology, 67*, 1063–1078.

Scheier, M. F., Carver, C. S., & Bridges, M. W. (2002). Optimism, pessimism, and psychological well-being. In E. C. Chang (Ed.), *Optimism and pessimism: Implications for theory, research and practice* (pp. 189–216). Washington, DC: American Psychological Association.

Scheier, M. F., Matthews, K. A., Owens, J. F., Magovern, G. J., Lefebvre, R. C., Abbott, R. A., et al. (1989). Dispositional optimism and recovery from coronary artery bypass surgery: The beneficial effects on physical and psychological well-being. *Journal of Personality and Social Psychology, 57*, 1024–1040.

Schimmack, U., & Diener, E. (1997). Affect intensity: Separating intensity and frequency in repeatedly measured affect. *Journal of Personality and Social Psychology, 73*, 1313–1329.

Schkade, D. A., & Kahneman, D. (1998). Does living in California make people happy? A focusing illusion in judgments of life satisfaction. *Psychological Science, 9*, 340–346.

Schlenker, B. R., Pontari, B. A., & Christopher, A. N. (2001). Excuses and character: Personal and social implications of excuses. *Personality and Social Psychology Review, 5*, 15–32.

Schmutte, P. S., & Ryff, C. D. (1997). Personality and well-being: Reexamining methods and meanings. *Journal of Personality and Social Psychology, 73*, 549–559.

Schneider, B. H., Atkinson, L., & Tardiff, C. (2001). Child-parent attachment and children's peer relations: A quantitative review. *Developmental Psychology, 37*, 86–100.

Schneider, S. (2001). In search of realistic optimism: Meaning, knowledge, and warm fuzziness. *American Psychologist, 56*, 259–263.

Schulz, R., Bookwala, J., Knapp, J. E., Scheier, M., & Williamson, G. M. (1996). Pessimism, age, and cancer mortality. *Psychology and Aging, 11*, 304–309.

Schwartz, B. (2004). *The paradox of choice: Why more is less.* New York: Ecco Press.

Schwartz, B., & Ward, A. (2004). Doing better but feeling worse: The paradox of choice. In P. A. Linley & S. Joseph (Eds.), *Positive psychology in practice* (pp. 86–104). New York: John Wiley & Sons.

Schwartz, S. H. (1992). Universals in the content and structure of values: Theoretical advances and empirical tests in 20 countries. In M. P. Zanna (Ed.), *Advances in experimental social psychology* (Vol. 24, pp. 1–65). San Diego: Academic Press.

Schwartz, S. H. (1994). Are there universal aspects in the content and structure of values? *Journal of Social Issues, 50*, 19–45.

Schwartz, S. H., & Bilsky, W. (1987). Toward a universal psychological structure of human values. *Journal of Personality and Social Psychology, 53*, 550–562.

Schwartz, S. H., & Bilsky, W. (1990). Toward a theory of the universal content and structure of values: Extensions and cross-cultural replications. *Journal of Personality and Social Psychology, 58*, 878–891.

Schwartz, S. H., & Sagiv, L. (1995). Identifying cultural specifics in the content and structure of values. *Journal of Cross-Cultural Psychology, 26*, 92–116.

Schwarz, N. (1990). Feelings as information: Informational and motivational functions of affective states. In E. T. Higgins & R. M. Sorrentino (Eds.), *Handbook of motivation and cognition* (Vol. 2, pp. 527–561). New York: Guilford Press.

Schwarz, N., & Strack, F. (1999). Reports of subjective well-being: Judgmental processes and their methodological implications. In D. Kahneman, E. Diener, & N. Schwarz (Eds.), *Well-being: The foundations of hedonic psychology* (pp. 61–84). New York: Russell Sage Foundation.

Sears, R. R. (1977). Sources of life satisfaction of the Terman gifted men. *American Psychologist, 32*, 119–128.

Seeman, T. E., Dubin, L. F., & Seeman, M. (2003). Religiosity/spirituality and health: A critical review of the evidence for biological pathways. *American Psychologist, 58*, 53–63.

Segall, M. H., Lonner, W. J., & Berry, J. W. (1998). Cross-cultural psychology as a scholarly discipline: On the flowering of culture in behavioral research. *American Psychologist, 53*, 1101–1110.

Segerstrom, S. C., Taylor, S. E., Kemeny, M. E., & Fahey, J. L. (1998). Optimism is associated with mood, coping and immune change in response to stress. *Journal of Personality and Social Psychology, 74*, 1646–1655.

Seidlitz, L., Wyer, R. S., & Diener, E. (1997). Cognitive correlates of subjective well-being: The processing of valenced life events by happy and unhappy persons. *Journal of Research in Personality, 31*, 240–256.

Seligman, M. E. P. (1975). *Helplessness: On depression, development, and death.* San Francisco: Freeman.

Seligman, M. E. P. (1990). *Learned optimism.* New York: Pocket Books.

Seligman, M. E. P. (1998, April). Positive social science. *APA Monitor, 29*(4), 2, 5.

Seligman, M. E. P. (2002a). *Authentic happiness: Using the new positive psychology to realize your potential for lasting fulfillment.* New York: Free Press.

Seligman, M. E. P. (2002b). Positive psychology, positive prevention, and positive therapy. In C. R. Snyder & S. J. Lopez (Eds.), *Handbook of positive psychology* (pp. 515–527). New York: Oxford University Press.

Seligman, M. E. P. (2003). Foreword: The past and future of positive psychology. In C. L. M. Keyes & J. Haidt (Eds.), *Flourishing: Positive psychology and the life well-lived* (pp. xi–xx). Washington, DC: American Psychological Association.

Seligman, M. E. P., & Csikszentmihalyi, M. (2000). Positive psychology: An Introduction. *American Psychologist, 55*, 5–14.

Seligman, M. E. P., & Csikszentmihalyi, M. (2001). Reply to comments. *American Psychologist, 56*, 89–90.

Seligman, M. E. P., Rashid, T., & Parks, A. C. (2006). Positive psychotherapy. *American Psychologist, 61*, 774–788.

Seligman, M. E. P., Steen, T. A., Park, N., & Peterson, C. (2005). Positive psychology progress: Empirical validation of interventions. *American Psychologist, 60*, 410–421.

Shapiro, D. H., Schwartz, C. E., & Astin, J. A. (1996). Controlling ourselves, controlling our world: Psychology's role in understanding positive and negative consequences of seeking and gaining control. *American Psychologist, 51*, 1213–1230.

Shapiro, S. L., Schwartz, G. E. R., & Santerre, C. (2002). Meditation and positive psychology. In C. R. Snyder

& S. J. Lopez (Eds.), *Handbook of positive psychology* (pp. 632–645). New York: Oxford University Press.

Sheldon, K. M., & Elliot, A. J. (1998). Not all personal goals are personal: Comparing autonomous and controlled reasons as predictors of effort and attainment. *Personality and Social Psychology Bulletin, 24,* 546–557.

Sheldon, K. M., & Elliot, A. J. (1999). Goal striving, need satisfaction, and longitudinal well-being: The self-concordance model. *Journal of Personality and Social Psychology, 76,* 482–497.

Sheldon, K. M., Elliot, A. J., Kim, Y., & Kasser, T. (2001). What is satisfying about satisfying events? Testing 10 candidate psychological needs. *Journal of Personality and Social Psychology, 80,* 325–339.

Sheldon, K. M., & Houser-Marko, L. (2001). Self-concordance, goal attainment, and the pursuit of happiness: Can there be an upward spiral? *Journal of Personality and Social Psychology, 80,* 152–165.

Sheldon, K. M., & Kasser, T. (1995). Coherence and congruence: Two aspects of personality integration. *Journal of Personality and Social Psychology, 68,* 531–543.

Sheldon, K. M., Kasser, T., Smith, K., & Share, T. (2002). Personal goals and psychological growth: Testing an intervention to enhance goal-attainment and personality integration. *Journal of Personality, 70,* 5–31.

Sheldon, K. M., & King, L. (2001). Why positive psychology is necessary. *American Psychologist, 56,* 216–217.

Sheldon, K. M., & Lyubomirsky, S. (2004). Achieving sustainable new happiness: Prospects, practices, and prescriptions. In P. A. Linley & S. Joseph (Eds.), *Positive psychology in practice* (pp. 127–145). New York: John Wiley & Sons.

Sheldon, K. M., Ryan, R. M., Deci, E. L., & Kasser, T. (2004). The independent effects of goal contents and motives on well-being: It's both what you pursue and why you pursue it. *Personality and Social Psychology Bulletin, 30,* 475–486.

Sheldon, K. M., Ryan, R. M., Rawsthorne, L. J., & Ilardi, B. (1997). Trait self and true self: Cross-role variation in the Big-Five personality traits and its relations with psychological authenticity and subjective well-being. *Journal of Personality and Social Psychology, 73,* 1380–1393.

Shweder, R. A., & Bourne, E. J. (1984). Does the concept of the person vary cross-culturally? In R. A. Shweder & R. A. LeVine (Eds.), *Culture theory: Essays on mind, self and emotion* (pp. 158–199). New York: Cambridge University Press.

Silver, R. L. (1982). *Coping with an undesirable life event: A study of early reactions to physical disability.* Unpublished doctoral dissertation, Northwestern University, Evanston, IL.

Simonton, D. K., & Baumeister, R. F. (2005). Positive psychology at the summit. *Review of General Psychology, 9,* 99–102.

Simpson, J. A., Campbell, B., & Berscheid, E. (1986). The association between romantic love and marriage: Kephart (1967) twice revisited. *Personality and Social Psychology Bulletin, 12,* 363–372.

Smith, E. R., & DeCoster, J. (2000). Dual processes models in social and cognitive psychology: Conceptual integration and links to memory systems. *Personality and Social Psychology Review, 4,* 108–131.

Snyder, C. R. (1994). *The psychology of hope: You can get there from here.* New York: Free Press.

Snyder, C. R. (1995). Conceptualizing, measuring, and nurturing hope. *Journal of Counseling and Development, 73,* 355–360.

Snyder, C. R. (Ed.). (2000). *Handbook of hope: Theory, measures, and applications.* San Diego, CA: Academic Press.

Snyder, C. R., Harris, C., Anderson, J. R., Holleran, S. A., Irving, L. M., Sigmon S. T., et al. (1991). The will and the ways: Development and validation of an individual difference measure of hope. *Journal of Personality and Social Psychology, 60,* 570–585.

Snyder, C. R., & Higgins, R. L. (1988). Excuses: Their effective role in the negotiation of reality. *Psychological Bulletin, 104,* 23–35.

Snyder, C. R., & Lopez, S. J. (Eds.). (2002). *Handbook of positive psychology.* New York: Oxford University Press.

Snyder, C. R., Rand, K. L., & Sigmon, D. R. (2002). Hope theory: A member of the positive psychology family. In C. R. Snyder & S. J. Lopez (Eds.), *Handbook of positive psychology* (pp. 257–276). New York: Oxford University Press.

Solberg, E. G., Diener, E., & Robinson, M. D. (2004). Why are materialists less satisfied? In T. Kasser & A. D. Kanner (Eds.), *Psychology and consumer culture: The struggle for a good life in a materialistic world* (pp. 29–48). Washington, DC: American Psychological Association.

Solomon, S., Greenberg, J. L., & Pyszczynski, T. A. (1991). A terror management theory of social behavior: The psychological functions of self-esteem and cultural worldviews. In M. P. Zanna (Ed.), *Advances in experimental social psychology* (Vol. 24, pp. 91–159). Orlando, FL: Academic Press.

Solomon, S., Greenberg, J. L., & Pyszczynski, T. A. (2004). Lethal consumption: Death-denying materialism. In T. Kasser & A. D. Kanner (Eds.), *Psychology and consumer culture: The struggle for a good life in a materialistic world* (pp. 127–146). Washington, DC: American Psychological Association.

Somerfield, M. S., & McCrae, R. R. (2000). Stress and coping research: Methodological challenges, theoretical advances, and clinical applications. *American Psychologist, 55,* 620–625.

Speca, M., Carlson, L. E., Goodey, E., & Angen, M. (2000). A randomized wait-list controlled clinical trail: The effect of mindfulness meditation-based stress reduction programs on mood and symptoms of stress in cancer outpatients. *Psychosomatic Medicine, 62*, 613–622.

Spiegel, D., & Fawzy, I. F. (2002). Psychosocial interventions and prognosis in cancer. In H. G. Koenig & H. J. Cohen (Eds.), *The link between religion and health: Psychoneuroimmunology and the faith factor* (pp. 84–100). New York: Oxford University Press.

Spilka, B., Hood, R. W., Jr., Hunsberger, B., & Gorsuch, R. (2003). *The psychology of religion: An empirical approach*. New York: Guilford Press.

Sprecher, S., Aron, A., Hatfield, E., Cortese, A., Potapova, E., & Levitskaya, A. (1994). Love: American style, Russian style, and Japanese style. *Personal Relationships, 1*, 349–369.

Sprecher, S., & Regan, P. C. (2002). Liking some things (in some people) more than others: Partner preferences in romantic relationships and friendships. *Journal of Social and Personal Relationships, 19*, 463–481.

Srivastava, A., Locke, E. A., & Bartol, K. M. (2001). Money and subjective well-being: It's not the money, it's the motives. *Journal of Personality and Social Psychology, 80*, 959–971.

Srivastava, S., & Beer, J. S. (2005). How self-evaluations relate to being liked by others: Integrating sociometer and attachment perspectives. *Journal of Personality and Social Psychology, 89*, 966–977.

Stacey, C. A., & Gatz, M. (1991). Cross-sectional age differences and longitudinal change on the Bradburn Affect Balance Scale. *Journal of Gerontology: Psychological Sciences, 46*, 76–78.

Steele, C. M. (1988). The psychology of self-affirmation: Sustaining the integrity of the self. In L. Berkowitz (Ed.), *Advances in experimental social psychology: Vol. 21*. Orlando, FL: Academic Press.

Steele, C. M. (1997). A threat in the air: How stereotypes shape intellectual identity and performance. *American Psychologist, 52*, 613–629.

Steinberg, L., Dornbusch, S. M., & Brown, B. B. (1992). Ethnic differences in adolescent achievement: An ecological perspective. *American Psychologist, 47*, 723–729.

Sternberg, R. (1985). Implicit theories of intelligence, creativity, and wisdom. *Journal of Personality and social Psychology, 49*, 607–627.

Sternberg, R. J. (1986). A triangular theory of love. *Psychological Review, 93*, 119–135.

Sternberg, R. J. (1987). *The triangle of love: Intimacy, passion, commitment*. New York: Basic Books.

Sternberg, R. (Ed.). (1990). *Wisdom: Its nature, origins, and development*. New York: Cambridge University Press.

Sternberg, R. (1998a). A balance theory of wisdom. *Review of General Psychology, 2*, 347–365.

Sternberg, R. J. (1998b). *Cupid's arrow: The course of love through time*. New York: Cambridge University Press.

Sternberg, R. J., & Barnes, M. L. (Eds.). (1988). *The psychology of love*. New Haven: Yale University Press.

Stone, A. A., Neale, J. M., Cox, D. S., Napoli, A., Valdimarsdottir, H., & Kennedy-Moore, E. (1994). Daily events are associated with a secretory immune response to an oral antigen in men. *Health Psychology, 13*, 440–446.

Stone, A. A., Shiffman, S. S., & DeVries, M. W. (1999). Ecological momentary assessment. In D. Kahneman, E. Diener, & N. Schwarz (Eds.), *Well-being: The foundations of hedonic psychology* (pp. 26–39). New York: Russell Sage Foundation.

Storey, J. (1999). *Cultural consumption and everyday life*. New York: Oxford University Press.

Strack, F., & Deutsch, R. (2004). Reflective and impulsive determinants of social behavior. *Personality and Social Psychology Review, 8*, 220–247.

Strawbridge, W. J., Cohen, R. D., Shema, S. J., & Kaplan, G. A. (1997). Frequent attendance at religious services and mortality over 28 years. *American Journal of Public Health, 87*, 957–961.

Stroebe, M. S., & Stroebe, W. (1993). The mortality of bereavement: A review. In M. S. Stroebe, W. Stroebe, & R. O. Hansson (Eds.), *Handbook of bereavement: Theory, research and intervention* (pp. 175–195). Cambridge: Cambridge University Press.

Stroebe, M. S., & Stroebe, W. (1996). The social psychology of social support. In E. Higgins & A. Kruglanski (Eds.), *Social psychology: Handbook of basic principles* (pp. 597–621). New York: Guilford Press.

Suh, E. (2000). Self, the hyphen between culture and subjective well-being. In E. Diener & E. M. Suh (Eds.), *Culture and subjective well-being* (pp. 63–86). Cambridge, MA: MIT Press.

Suh, E., Diener, E., & Fujita, F. (1996). Events and subjective well-being: Only recent events matter. *Journal of Personality and Social Psychology, 70*, 1091–1102.

Suh, E., Diener, E., Oishi, S., & Triandis, H. C. (1998). The shifting basis of life satisfaction judgments across cultures: Emotion versus norms. *Journal of Personality and Social Psychology, 74*, 482–493.

Swann, W. B., Jr. (1983). Self-verification: Bringing social reality into harmony with the self. In J. Suls & A. G. Greenwald (Eds.), *Social psychological perspectives on the self* (Vol. 2, pp. 33–66). Hillsdale, NJ: Lawrence Erlbaum.

Swann, W. B., Jr. (1987). Identity negotiation: Where two roads meet. *Journal of Personality and Social Psychology, 53*, 1038–1051.

Swann, W. B., Jr. (1990). To be adored or to be known: The interplay of self-enhancement and self-verification. In R. M. Sorrentino & E. T. Higgins (Eds.), *Foundations of social behavior* (Vol. 2, pp. 408–448). New York: Guilford Press.

Swann, W. B., Jr., Chang-Schneider, C., & McClarty, L. K. (2007). Do people's self-views matter? Self-concept and self-esteem in everyday life. *American Psychologist, 62*, 84–94.

Swann, W. B., Jr., De La Ronde, C., & Hixon, J. G. (1994). Authenticity and positive strivings in marriage and courtship. *Journal of Personality and Social Psychology, 66*, 857–869.

Swindle, R., Heller, K., Pescosolido, B., & Kikuzawa, S. (2000). Responses to nervous breakdowns in Americans over a 40-year period: Mental health policy implications. *American Psychologist, 55*, 740–749.

Tajfel, H. (1982). Social psychology of intergroup relations. *Annual Review of Psychology, 33*, 1–39.

Tamres, L. K., Janicki, D., & Helgeson, V. C. (2002). Sex differences in coping behavior: A meta-analytic review and an examination of relative coping. *Personality and Social Psychology Review, 6*, 2–30.

Taylor, S. E. (1989). *Positive illusions: Creative self-deception and the healthy mind.* New York: Basic Books.

Taylor, S. E. (1999). *Health psychology* (4th ed.). Boston: McGraw-Hill.

Taylor, S. E., & Armor, D. A. (1996). Positive illusions and coping with adversity. *Journal of Personality, 64*, 873–898.

Taylor, S. E., & Brown, J. D. (1988). Illusions and well-being: A social psychological perspective on mental health. *Psychological Bulletin, 103*, 193–210.

Taylor, S. E., Dickerson, S. S., & Cousino Klein, L. (2002). Toward a biology of social support. In C. R. Snyder & S. J. Lopez (Eds.), *Handbook of positive psychology* (pp. 556–569). New York: Oxford University Press.

Taylor, S. E., Kemeny, M. E., Reed, G. M., Bower, J. E., & Gruenewald, T. L. (2000). Psychological resources, positive illusions and health. *American Psychologist, 55*, 99–109.

Taylor, S. E., Klein, L. A., Lewis, B. P, Gruenewald, T. L., Gurung, R. A. R., & Updegraff, J. A. (2000). Biobehavioral responses to stress in females: Tend-and-befriend, not fight-or-flight. *Psychological Review, 107*, 411–429.

Taylor, S. E., Lerner, J. S., Sherman, D. K., Sage, R. M., & McDowell, N. K. (2003). Are self-enhancing cognitions associated with healthy or unhealthy biological profiles? *Journal of Personality and Social Psychology, 85*, 605–615.

Taylor, S. E., Repetti, R. L., & Seeman, T. (1997). Health psychology: What is an unhealthy environment and how does it get under our skin? *Annual Review of Psychology, 48*, 411–447.

Taylor, S. E., & Sherman, D. K. (2004). Positive psychology and health psychology: A fruitful liaison. In P. A. Linley & S. Joseph (Eds.), *Positive psychology in practice* (pp. 305–319). New York: John Wiley & Sons.

Tedeschi, R. G., & Calhoun, L. G. (Eds.). (1995). *Trauma and transformation: Growing in the aftermath of suffering.* Thousand Oaks, CA: Sage Publications.

Tedeschi, R. G., Park, C. L., & Calhoun, L. G. (Eds.). (1998). *Posttraumatic growth: Positive changes in the aftermath of crisis.* Mahwah, NJ: Lawrence Erlbaum.

Tellegen, A., Lykken, D., Bouchard, T. J., Wilcox, K. J., Segal, N. J., & Rich, S. (1988). Personality similarity in twins reared apart and together. *Journal of Personality and Social Psychology, 54*, 1031–1039.

Tennen, H., & Affleck, G. (2002). Benefit-finding and benefit-reminding. In C. R. Snyder & S. J. Lopez (Eds.), *Handbook of positive psychology* (pp. 584–597). New York: Oxford University Press.

Terman, L. M. (1939). The gifted student and his academic environment. *School and Society, 49*, 65–73.

Terman, L. M., Buttenwieser, P., Ferguson, L. W., Johnson, W. B., & Wilson, D. P. (1938). *Psychological factors in marital happiness.* New York: McGraw-Hill.

Terracciano, A., Costa, P. T., Jr., & McCrae, R. R. (2006). Personality plasticity after age 30. *Personality and Social Psychology Bulletin, 32*, 999–1009.

Tesser, A. (1988). Toward a self-evaluation maintenance model of social behavior. In L. Berkowitz (Ed.), *Advances in experimental social psychology* (Vol. 21, pp. 181–227). San Diego, CA: Academic Press.

Thomas, D., & Diener, E. (1990). Memory accuracy in the recall of emotions. *Journal of Personality and Social Psychology, 59*, 291–297.

Thompson, L. Y., & Snyder, C. R. (2003). Measuring forgiveness. In S. J. Lopez & C. R. Snyder (Eds.), *Positive psychological assessment: A handbook of models and measures* (pp. 301–341). Washington, DC: American Psychological Association.

Thornton, A. (1989). Changing attitudes toward family issues in the United States. *Journal of Marriage and the Family, 51*, 873–893.

Tice, D. M., & Baumeister, R. F. (1997). Longitudinal study of procrastination, performance, stress and health: The costs and benefits of dawdling. *Psychological Science, 8*, 454–458.

Tjeltveit, A. C. (2003). Implicit virtues, divergent goods, multiple communities: Explicitly addressing virtues in the behavioral sciences. *The American Behavioral Scientist, 47*, 395–414.

Trafimow, D., Triandis, H. C., & Gotto, S. G. (1991). Some tests of the distinction between private self and collective self. *Journal of Personality and Social Psychology, 60*, 649–655.

Triandis, H. C. (1989). Self and social behavior in different cultural contexts. *Psychological Review, 96*, 269–289.

Triandis, H. C. (2000). Cultural syndromes and subjective well-being. In E. Diener & E. M. Suh (Eds.), *Culture and subjective well-being* (pp. 13–36). Cambridge, MA: MIT Press.

Trope, Y., & Pomerantz, E. M. (1998). Resolving conflicts among self-evaluation motives: Positive experiences as a resource for overcoming defensiveness. *Motivation and Emotion, 22*, 53–72.

Trzesniewski, K. H., Donnellan, M. B., & Robins, R. W. (2003). Stability of self-esteem across the life span. *Journal of Personality and Social Psychology, 84*, 205–220.

Tsang, J. A., & McCullough, M. E. (2003). Measuring religious constructs: A hierarchical approach to construct organization and scale selection. In S. J. Lopez & C. R. Snyder (Eds.), *Positive psychological assessment: A handbook of models and measures* (pp. 345–360). Washington, DC: American Psychological Association.

Tyler, T. R., & Smith, H. J. (1998). Social justice and social movements. In D. T. Gilbert, S. T. Fiske, & G. Lindzey (Eds.), *The handbook of social psychology* (4th ed., Vol. 2, pp. 595–629). New York: McGraw-Hill.

Twenge, J. M., & Crocker, J. (2002). Race and self-esteem: Meta-analysis comparing Whites, Blacks, Hispanics, Asians and American Indians, *Psychological Bulletin, 128*, 371–408.

Uchino, B. N., Cacioppo, J. T., & Kiecolt-Glaser, J. K. (1996). The relationship between social support and physiological responses: A review with emphasis on underlying mechanisms and implications for health. *Psychological Bulletin, 119*, 488–531.

Updegraff, J. A., Gable, S. L., & Taylor, S. E. (2004). What makes experiences satisfying? The interaction of approach-avoidance motivations and emotions in well-being. *Journal of Personality and Social Psychology, 86*, 496–504.

U.S. Bureau of Census (1999). *Poverty in the United States: 1998* (Current Population Reports, Series P60–207). Washington, DC: U.S. Government Printing Office.

Uvnas-Moberg, K. (1997). Physiological and endocrine effects of social contact. In I. Lederhendler & S. Carter (Eds.), *The integrative neurobiology of affiliation* (pp. 146–163). New York: New York Academy of Sciences.

Uvnas-Moberg, K. (1998). Oxytocin may mediate the benefits of positive social interaction and emotions. *Psychoneuroendocrinology, 23*, 819–835.

Vaillant, G. E. (1997). *Adaptation to life*. Boston: Little Brown.

Vaillant, G. E. (2000). Adaptive mental mechanisms: Their role in positive psychology. *American Psychologist, 55*, 89–98.

Vallacher, R. R., & Wegner, D. M. (1987). What do people think they're doing? Action identification and human behavior. *Psychological Review, 94*, 3–15.

Van Boven, L. (2005). Experientialism, materialism, and the pursuit of happiness. *Review of General Psychology, 9*, 132–142.

Van Boven, L., & Gilovich, T. (2003). To do or to have? That is the question. *Journal of Personality and Social Psychology, 85*, 1193–1202.

Vandello, J. A., & Cohen, D. (1999). Patterns of individualism and collectivism in the United States. *Journal of Personality and Social Psychology, 77*, 279–292.

Vangelisti, A. L. (2006). Relationship dissolution: Antecedents, processes and consequences. In P. Noller & J. A. Feeney (Eds.), *Close relationships: Functions, forms and processes* (pp. 353–374). New York: Psychology Press.

Vaux, A., & Meddin, J. (1987). Positive and negative life changes and positive and negative affect among the rural elderly. *Journal of Community Psychology, 15*, 447–458.

Veenhoven, R. (1988). The utility of happiness. *Social Indicators Research, 20*, 333–353.

Veenhoven, R. (1995). The cross-national pattern of happiness. Test of predictions implied in three theories of happiness. *Social Indicators Research, 34*, 33–68.

Veenhoven, R. (2000). Freedom and happiness: A comparative study in forty-four nations in the early 1990s. In E. Diener & E. M. Suh (Eds.), *Culture and subjective well-being* (pp. 165–184). Cambridge, MA: MIT Press.

Veroff, J., Douvan, E., & Kulka, R. A. (1981). *Mental health in America: Patterns of help-seeking from 1957–1976*. New York: Basic Books.

Visintainer, M., & Seligman, M. (1983). The hope factor. *American Health, 2*, 58–61.

Vohs, K. D., Mead, N. L., & Goode, M. R. (2006). The psychological consequences of money. *Science, 314*, 1154–1156.

Waite, L. J., & Gallagher, M. (2000). *The case for marriage*. New York: Broadway Books.

Wallace, B. A. (2005). *Genuine happiness; Meditation as the path to fulfillment*. Hoboken, NJ: John Wiley & Sons.

Wallace, B. A. (2006). *The attention revolution: Unlocking the power of the focused mind*. Hoboken, NJ: John Wiley & Sons.

Wallace, B. A., & Fisher, L. E. (1983). *Consciousness and behavior*. Newton, MA: Allyn & Bacon.

Wallace, B. A., & Shapiro, S. L. (2006). Mental balance and well-being: Building bridges between Buddhism and Western psychology. *American Psychologist, 61*(7), 690–701.

Walsh, R., & Shapiro, S. L. (2006). The meeting of meditative disciplines and Western psychology. *American Psychologist, 61*(3), 227–239.

Walster, E., & Walster, G. W. (1978). *A new look at love*. Reading, MA: Addison-Wesley.

Warr, P. (1992). Age and occupational well-being. *Psychology and Aging, 7*, 37–45.

Waterman, A. S. (1990). Personal expressiveness: Philosophical and psychological foundations. *Journal of Mind and Behavior, 11*, 47–74.

Waterman, A. S. (1993). Two conceptions of happiness: Contrast of personal expressiveness (eudaimonia) and hedonic enjoyment. *Journal of Personality and Social Psychology, 64*, 678–691.

Waterman, A. S., Schwartz, S. H., Goldbacher, E., Green, H., Miller, C., & Philip, S. (2003). Predicting the subjective experience of intrinsic motivation: The roles of self-determination, the balance of challenge and skills, and self-realization of values. *Personality and Social Psychology Bulletin, 11*, 1447–1458.

Watson, D. (2002). Positive affectivity: The disposition to experience pleasurable emotional states. In C. R. Snyder & S. J. Lopez (Eds.), *Handbook of positive psychology* (pp. 106–119). New York: Oxford University Press.

Watson, D., & Clark, L. A. (1991). Self versus peer ratings of specific emotional traits: Evidence of convergent and discriminant validity. *Journal of Personality and Social Psychology, 60*, 927–940.

Watson, D., & Clark, L. A. (1992). On traits and temperament: General and specific factors of emotional experience and their relation to the Five Factor model. *Journal of Personality, 60*, 441–476.

Watson, D., Clark, L. A., & Tellegen, A. (1988). Development and validation of brief measures of positive and negative affect: The PANAS scales. *Journal of Personality and Social Psychology, 54*, 1063–1070.

Watson, D., & Tellegen, A. (1985). Toward a consensual structure of mood. *Psychological Bulletin, 98*, 219–235.

Watson, D., & Walker, L. M. (1996). The long-term stability and predictive validity of trait measures of affect. *Journal of Personality and Social Psychology, 70*, 567–577.

Watson, D., Wiese, D., Vaidya, J., & Tellegen, A. (1999). The two general activation systems of affect: Structural findings, evolutionary considerations, and psychobiological evidence. *Journal of Personality and Social Psychology, 76*, 820–838.

Wegner, D. M. (1989). *White bears and other unwanted thoughts.* New York: Vintage.

Wegner, D. M. (1994). Ironic processes of mental control. *Psychological Review, 101*, 34–52.

Wegner, D. M. (1997). When the antidote is the poison. *Psychological Science, 8*, 148–153.

Wegner, D. M., Ansfield, M., & Pilloff, D. (1998). The putt and the pendulum: Ironic effects of mental control of action. *Psychological Science, 9*, 196–199.

Wegner, D. M., & Bargh, J. A. (1998). Control and automaticity in social life. In D. T. Gilbert, S. T. Fiske, & G. Lindzey (Eds.), *The handbook of social psychology* (4th ed., Vol. 1, pp. 446–496). New York: McGraw-Hill.

Wegner, D. M., Schneider, D., Carter, S. R., & White, T. L. (1987). Paradoxical effects of thought suppression. *Journal of Personality and Social Psychology, 53*, 5–13.

Wegner, D. M., Shortt, J. W., Blake, A. W., & Paige, M. S. (1990). The suppression of exciting thoughts. *Journal of Personality and Social Psychology, 58*, 409–418.

Weinstein, N. D. (1980). Unrealistic optimism about future life events. *Journal of Personality and Social Psychology, 39*, 806–820.

Weinstein, N. D. (1982). Unrealistic optimism about susceptibility to health problems. *Journal of Behavioral Medicine, 5*, 441–460.

Weinstein, N. D. (1989). Optimistic biases about personal risks. *Science, 246*, 1232–1233.

Weinstein, N. D., & Klein, W. M. (1996). Unrealistic optimism: Present and future. *Journal of Social and Clinical Psychology, 15*, 1–8.

Wenzlaff, R. M., Wegner, D. M., & Roper, D. W. (1988). Depression and mental control: The resurgence of unwanted negative thoughts. *Journal of Personality and Social Psychology, 55*, 882–892.

Werner, E. E., & Smith, R. S. (1982). *Vulnerable but invincible: A study of resilient children.* New York: McGraw-Hill.

Werner, E. E., & Smith, R. S. (1992). *Overcoming the odds: High-risk children from birth to adulthood.* Ithaca, NY: Cornell University Press.

Weston, D. (1999). *Psychology: Mind, brain, and culture* (2nd ed.). New York: John Wiley & Sons.

Wethington, E., Cooper, H., & Holmes, C. S. (1997). Turning points in midlife. In I. H. Gotlib & B. Wethington (Eds.), *Stress and adversity over the life course: Trajectories and turning points* (pp. 215–231). Cambridge, England: Cambridge University Press.

Wheeler, L., & Miyake, K. (1992). Social comparison in everyday life. *Journal of Personality and Social Psychology, 62*, 760–773.

Wicklund, R. A., & Gollwitzer, P. M. (1982). *Symbolic self-completion.* Hillsdale, NJ: Lawrence Erlbaum.

Williamson, G. M. (2002). Aging well: Outlook for the 21st century. In C. R. Snyder & S. J. Lopez (Eds.), *Handbook of positive psychology* (pp. 676–686). New York: Oxford University Press.

Wills, T. A. Weiss, R. L., & Patterson, G. R. (1974). A behavioral analysis of the determinants of marital satisfaction. *Journal of Consulting and Clinical Psychology, 42*, 802–811.

Wilson, C. L., Rholes, W. S., Simpson, J. A., & Tran, S. (2007). Labor, delivery, and early parenthood: An attachment perspective. *Personality and Social Psychology Bulletin, 33*, 505–518.

Wilson, T. D., & Gilbert, D. T. (2003). Affective forecasting. *Advances in Experimental Social Psychology, 35*, 345–411.

Wilson, T. D., Meyers, J., & Gilbert, D. T. (2001). Lessons from the past: Do people learn from experiences that emotional reactions are short-lived? *Personality and Social Psychology Bulletin, 27*, 1648–1661.

Wilson, W. (1967). Correlates of avowed happiness. *Psychological Bulletin, 67*, 294–306.

Winter, L., Lawton, M. P., Casten, R. J., & Sando, R. L. (1999). The relationship between external events and affect states in older people. *International Journal of Human Development and Aging, 50*, 1–12.

Winter, D. G., John, O. P., Stewart, A. J., Klohnen, E. C., & Duncan, L. E. (1998). Traits and motives: Toward an integration of two traditions in personality research. *Psychological Review, 105*, 230–250.

Witness (2004). The journey home: A Romanian adoption. Canadian Broadcasting Corporation. Retrieved October 14, 2004, at http://www/tv.cbc.ca/witness/rom/romhis.htm.

Witvliet, C. V. O., Ludwig, T., & Vander Laan, K. (2001). Granting forgiveness or harboring grudges: Implications for emotion, physiology and health. *Psychological Science, 121*, 117–123.

Wolfe, R. N., & Johnson, S. D. (1995). Personality as a predictor of college performance. *Educational and Psychological Measurement, 55*, 177–185.

Woods, W., Rhodes, N., & Whelan, M. (1989). Sex differences in positive well-being: A consideration of emotional style and marital status. *Psychological Bulletin, 106*, 249–264.

World Bank (1992). *World Development Report 1992.* New York: Oxford University Press.

World Health Organization (1948). World Health Organization constitution. In *Basic documents.* Geneva: Author.

World Value Survey Study Group (1994). *World Values Survey, 1981–1984 and 1990–1993.* ICPSR. Ann Arbor, MI: Institute for Social Research.

Worthington, E. L., Jr. (1998). *Dimensions of forgiveness: Psychological research and theological perspectives* (pp. 139–161). Philadelphia: Templeton Foundation Press.

Worthington, E. L., Jr., Kurusu, T. A., McCullough, M. E., & Sandage, S. J. (1996). Empirical research on religion and psychotherapeutic processes and outcomes: A 10-year review and research prospectus. *Psychological Bulletin, 119*, 448–487.

Wrosch, C., Scheier, M. F., Miller, G. E., Schulz, R., & Carver, C. S. (2003). Adaptive self-regulation of unattainable goals: Goal disengagement, goal reengagement, and subjective well-being. *Personality and Social Psychology Bulletin, 29*, 1494–1508.

Wulf, D. M. (1997). *Psychology of religion: Classic and contemporary views* (2nd ed.). New York: John Wiley & Sons.

Yamagata, S., Suzuki, A., Ando, J., Ono, Y., Kijima, N., Yoshimura, K., et al. (2006). Is the genetic structure of human personality universal? A cross-cultural twin study from North America, Europe and Asia. *Journal of Personality and Social Psychology, 90*, 987–998.

Yang, S. (2001). Conceptions of wisdom among Taiwanese Chinese. *Journal of Cross-Cultural Psychology, 32*, 662–680.

Yik, M. S. M., Bond, M. H., & Paulhaus, D. L. (1998). Do Chinese self-enhance or self-efface? It's a matter of domain. *Personality and Social Psychology Bulletin, 24*, 399–406.

Yinger, J. M. (1967). Pluralism, religion, and secularism. *Journal for the Scientific Study of Religion, 6*, 17–28.

Zajonc, R. B. (1998). Emotions. In D. T. Gilbert, S. T. Fiske, & G. Lindzey (Eds.), *The handbook of social psychology* (4th ed., Vol. 1, pp. 591–632). New York: McGraw-Hill.

Zautra, A. J., Potter, P. T., & Reich, J. W. (1997). The independence of affects is context-dependent: An integrative model of the relationship of positive and negative affect. In K. W. Schaie & M. P. Lawton (Eds.), *Annual review of gerontology and geriatrics* (Vol. 17, pp. 75–103). New York: Springer.

Zinnbauer, B. J., Pargament, K. I., Cole, B., Rye, M., Butter, E. M., Belavich, T. G., et al. (1997). Religion and spirituality: Unfuzzying the fuzzy. *Journal for the Scientific Study of Religion, 36*, 549–564.

Zinnbauer, B. J., Pargament, K. I., & Scott, A. B. (1999). *Journal of Personality, 67*, 889–919.

Zirkel, S., & Cantor, N. (1990). Personal construal of life tasks: Those who struggle for independence. *Journal of Personality and Social Psychology, 58*, 172–185.

AUTHOR INDEX

SUBJECT INDEX